Decisive Battles of World War II:

THE GERMAN VIEW

Edited by
H. A. Jacobsen and J. Rohwer

INTRODUCTION BY CYRIL FALLS

TRANSLATED FROM THE GERMAN

BY EDWARD FITZGERALD

G. P. Putnam's Sons   New York

Contents

Contents

Illustrations

(between pp. 192 & 193 and pp. 224 & 225)

INTRODUCTION

There is surely no precedent for what happened to Germany after her defeat in the Second World War. Not only was there a rigid political division between East and West, but even from West Germany a great mass of the most important military documents was removed to the United States; a smaller share went to Britain. A considerable number must have been lost or destroyed at the last moment, though we do not know how many. These handicaps have now been surmounted. So far as I know, the victorious states have never before opened their archives so freely to German historians, while their own histories have been pouring out in great quantity. There have been admirable records of phases or campaigns produced in the Federal Republic already, but nothing on this scale. Though the standard of the writing naturally varies, it is consistently high: the best writers are brilliant and the rest highly competent.

I make no excuse for warning the reader who likes easy reading that he should be prepared to brace himself on facing this symposium. The average German military historian does not let you off lightly. To take an example, when senior commanders are struggling to get Hitler's orders altered or modified, as is very often the case, every message that passed is quoted. This method in the long run heightens the interest. It shows how heavily the generals were handicapped, especially as there were one or two – Busch is an outstanding example – who abandoned their personal convictions because they never shook off the belief that the Führer could not be wrong. It was a tragedy for the German cause that he brought off with outstanding success his venture in Norway, of which his admirals had been so scared.

In the phase to be examined first, beginning with the wonderfully successful invasion of France, Belgium and Holland, and ending at Dunkirk, there can be no doubt that Hitler's hesitation at the final stage enabled the Allies to re-embark an unexpectedly large number of troops. On May 17th, 1940, Halder noted that 'The Führer is excessively nervous'. Dr Jacobsen rightly derides the suggestion that he was offering Britain a 'golden bridge' for her army when on the night of May 22nd he ordered the armoured forces to be halted; but he goes on to say that he was hoping she would submit to a peace treaty. The facts are that he had too readily accepted the argument of Göring that the Luftwaffe could do the job and that the tanks could be rested for the coming Battle of France. The tank crews were indeed weary. But if you do *not* open a golden bridge when in a position to do so, you obviously must take into account the possibility of the enemy's making a stout final stand. On this occasion French troops who had done none too well so far fought with great courage and tenacity in defence while embarkation was being carried on in face of incredible difficulties and in the most unfavourable circumstances that it is possible to conceive.

Among the points made by Dr Klee on this extraordinary and unique battle, one is well known to students but may be worth repeating for a wider public: that the aim of the Luftwaffe was to wear out the British fighters before committing its own bombers and that it finally found this impossible without attacking London, which was of such importance from many points of view that the British War Cabinet had to take the risk of fighters being worn down in its defence. The writer gives the losses of the Luftwaffe as 2,784 aircraft in three months. Later Britain had an easier time of it because the Luftwaffe's main striking power had to be transferred to Russia.

Dr Gundelach's narrative covers what seems to me, small as was the scale, the most brilliant of all the German feats of arms – the capture of Crete. A handicap which the defence faced, but which hampered the attack to a far greater extent, was the difficulty of movement, the roads being few and mostly bad. He does not discuss the question, much debated in this country, of whether preparations for defence could have been better. The picture from the German side, in air and infantry alike, is that of improvisation after initial set-backs.

The invasion of Russia and the Battle of Moscow has one feature in common with the article on Stalingrad and that on the 'Collapse of Army Group Centre in 1944': the paucity of information about Russian dispositions below Army level. General Hofmann brings out Hitler's obstinacy, but a far more adverse factor this time was the country. It seems almost incredible that the German armies should have done as well as they did. They fought under terrible handicaps: exposure to intense cold without winter clothing; tanks and internal combustion vehicles unsuited to the mud which succeeded the frost; no sleighs. The Russians, on the other hand, were used to very low temperatures; their tanks operated better in mud, and their vehicles were little affected by it. The verdict of the narrator on Hitler's final 'hold-on' order in front of Moscow differs from that widely held in the West. He declares that it was not necessary or justified by results. He should know better than the Western interpreters, but I leave the problem open.

A distinguished soldier, General Warlimont, deals with the Mediterranean in 1942. We learn that after Rommel's defeat at Alamein Hitler remained blind to the threat of an Allied landing in French North Africa, but that his junior partner, Mussolini, was on this occasion wiser. There was also a complete difference of opinion between the two dictators over the value of Malta, the Italian urging that it was of vital importance and must be taken, the German shying off the project. It may well be that Hitler thought it would fail. It would assuredly have been costly, since the island was by now well prepared for defence in the air as well as on the ground, but we cannot honestly conclude that it would have ended in defeat. This chapter gives a relatively short account of the Battle of Alamein and then describes only the opening of the campaign in French North Africa. It is a highly complex story, marking the turn of the tide, just as Stalingrad marked it on the Russian Front.

I take a particular interest in the chapter on Stalingrad by Herr Walter Görlitz because I had the honour of writing a preface to a shortened English version of his excellent book, *The German General Staff*.* Many writers have argued that too much emphasis has been put on Hitler's errors and demands for the impossible. Such distortion may occasionally occur, but in this case the criticism appears to me to be justified up to the hilt. He must have known how greatly the Russian armies had improved in leadership, training, and equipment since the last major battles, but he nevertheless set his forces the biggest tasks yet, the capture of Stalingrad, the long-delayed attack on Leningrad, and the seizure of the invaluable Caucasian oil wells and plant. On top of all this, he chose as army commander for the main part of the job a man peculiarly unsuited to it.

The psychological study of senior officers carrying a heavy burden is always interesting, perhaps most of all when they fail. Paulus was by character, inclination and training a Chief of Staff, and a first-rate one. When he served a good commander of resolute mind his weakness of will – I use the phrase relatively – did not matter, but it must have been noted by the closest observers. Manstein, who made a very fine effort to relieve him and to whom all jobs came alike, thought that when plans which might have saved his 6th Army from annihilation were turned down time after time by Hitler he should have acted without talking. For the second time Hitler was let down by Göring, who promised that the Luftwaffe would keep the Army supplied, and this time the narrator describes his offer as not only irresponsible but also dishonest. It was, in fact, a reckless gamble on the unlikely, if not the impossible, in an attempt to raise the declining prestige of the Luftwaffe.

The whole story is nauseating. By glorifying the heroism of the 6th Army with every trick that propaganda could muster, Hitler and his henchmen hoped to obscure the fact that it had been sacrificed to an unsound plan and rash ambition. Herr Görlitz, looking much farther forward, tells us that the aftermath has affected the attitude of many Germans today. The Luftwaffe made very heavy sacrifices in a hopeless task, but it did an invaluable service in flying out over forty thousand wounded. At this time Hitler had a strong Chief of Staff in General Kurt Zeitzler, who pleaded with him day after day to permit a withdrawal – which need not have been very deep – and at times thought he was convincing him; but he never did.

The account of what we call 'The Battle of the Atlantic' bears, in Herr Jürgan Rohwer's chapter, the title of 'The U-Boat War Against the Allied Supply Lines'. No section of the book will be found of greater interest to our readers. In the first place, we know that Britain would have starved if the battle had been lost; but there is another reason. It is always fascinating to watch a genius in his trade at work, even if his object was starvation. I am sure Dönitz

* Pub. Hollis and Carter, 1953.

was one. He must also have been a tireless worker. I cannot attempt to describe his constant changes of plan, sometimes on a big scale, sometimes apparently slight, but always aiming to win a point in the long struggle between attack and defence – a defence which was itself constantly changing its tactics and was very intelligently conducted. The writer describes our first great handicap when the Luftwaffe forced Allied freighters to come in and go out round the northern coast of Ireland. I must add that my Irish fellow-countrymen contributed greatly to this handicap by closing Cobh (earlier known as Queenstown); a good deal of shipping could have been brought in by the southern route had we been allowed to continue its use.

Convoy triumphed in the end, and it is remarkable that it should have done so about the time when the number of U-boats was at its maximum. In one long-drawn-out struggle six were sunk, and the period May 7th to 24th, 1943, is described as 'the collapse of the U-boat offensive'. It was after this that Dönitz virtually abandoned it in the Atlantic. Yet hc had come very close to winning, and this combat of brains and courage on both sides may be considered the closest shave of all.

One point made by Admiral Ruge in his study of the Invasion of Normandy is that Hitler had wasted German strength in committing an excessive number of troops to the defence of the Channel Islands. He thinks that we might have secured a bridgehead in France in 1942, at a time when the garrison was weak. I doubt it, and doubt still more that it could have been held. I have never seen any German comment – and there is none here – on why the Bay of the Seine was selected for the landing rather than the narrows. It was because it was vital to choose a place from which it would be as easy as possible to debouch quickly, and the region of Calais did not meet this requirement. The hasty preparations made by Rommel were in many respects typical of his brilliance in improvisation, but he made a serious mistake in holding his armoured divisions too far forward. The unlucky Geyr von Schweppenburg saw matters more clearly in this respect.

Herr Gackenholz in 'The Collapse of Army Group Centre in 1944' has an old story to tell, summed up in Hitler's familiar phrase: 'not a yard of ground to be yielded'. As in the case of Stalingrad, he got warning after warning of what would happen if he insisted on this strategy. Yet even Hitler sometimes listened to advice when it came from a first-class subordinate. When Model succeeded Busch he got a fairly free hand, but too late to do more than save as much as possible from the wreck. One figure given here is staggering: when the strength of the partisans in the neighbourhood of the Army Group reached its greatest height, it was estimated at 240,000. Just imagine what happened to the communications, railways above all! The Germans lost 350,000 in this series of battles.

Most interesting of all in some ways is the story of the Ardennes, the last German offensive. I have met and much admire the author, General von Manteuffel, who commanded one of the armies engaged. Model again appears on the scene, this time with a brilliant alternative to Hitler's plan, known as the 'modified' or 'small' solution. Here it seems to me not altogether easy to say whether he or Hitler was correct. When a situation such as that in which the Germans then found themselves has been reached (and theirs could hardly have been graver) it may be a case of all or nothing: a limited victory is not worth while and nothing short of a miraculous triumph meets the case. On the other hand Model's scheme, if successful, could have been expanded, though hardly up to the full scale of Hitler's.

General von Manteuffel, writing in the third person, is extremely modest. The *beau rôle* had been allotted to Sepp Dietrich's 6th SS Army, but it was in fact taken over by Manteuffel's 5th Panzer Army. The narrator naturally tells us that his command got its nose in front and kept it there, but he does not enlarge upon the errors of his next-door neighbour. Dietrich was a thruster and favoured by Hitler for that reason (as well as because he commanded the SS troops) but he was no strategist, hardly even a tactician. He was lost as soon as the defence began to rally and it became difficult to decide how its reserves were moving. The writer pays tribute to the part played by Montgomery in his command of American forces and the disposition of his own. They were not called upon, but they could have delivered a smashing flank attack had it been necessary.

The Germans were lucky at the start in that bad weather kept the American and British aircraft grounded, but as soon as it improved the issue was quickly decided. Many of us have deplored the demand for unconditional surrender, which may have prolonged the war, but even its strongest critics cannot be certain that without it Hitler would have been any less extravagant in his scheme in the Ardennes. The importance of the famous and heroic American stand at Bastogne is thoroughly examined and given the credit that is its due.

The might-have-been is always fascinating and not always as fruitless a study as it is said to be. Hindsight suggests that the most vital error on Germany's part was the invasion of Russia. Russia, except under Suvorov in Italy, has never accomplished great things outside her frontiers except against out-of-date Turkish armies; and Suvorov's victories were made relatively easy by the absence of Napoleon, the presence of Austrian allies with good staff officers, and the weakness of the French; but Hitler knew all about the fate of 'Swedish Charles' and of Napoleon, and really did better than either because he managed to extricate a greater proportion of his troops. It is even possible that he might have brought off victory inside Russia had he not been Hitler – but he was.

I will not comment further on the other great issues of the Second World War, nearly all of which are tackled here. This is not a work for those who like all problems reduced to pap – it is an essential study for the intelligent reader who wants to understand fully these crucial episodes of the Second World War.

CYRIL FALLS

PREFACE TO THE ENGLISH EDITION

The present English edition of *Decisive Battles of World War Two* differs from the original German edition in one important respect. In considering their German readers, whose outlook is, of course, greatly influenced by Continental considerations, the editors felt that it was particularly desirable to show the interrelations between the war in Europe and the war overseas. And in order to show more clearly to what extent non-European events—for example the war in the Pacific—influenced Allied strategy in the European theatre of war as well, and to make it clear that the prosecution of the war against Japan depended on the state of the war in Europe, two decisive battles of the war in the Pacific were also included in the book: the air-sea battle at Midway in 1942, dealt with by Jürgen Rohwer, and the Battle of Leyte in 1944, described by Bern Anderson.

These two contributions—the first by one of the editors of this book (a naval historian who has made a special study of the war in the Pacific), and the second by an American admiral who commanded a cruiser in the battle of Leyte and afterwards studied it as contributor to an American naval history of the war— were intended to make the German reader better acquainted with the nature of naval warfare, with its struggle for command of the sea and the air and its amphibious operations, against the background of both Japanese and Allied strategic planning. The problems of naval warfare are quite naturally much more familiar to an Anglo-American audience, and as there are, in any case, already numerous excellent descriptions of both these battles available in English, it was thought unnecessary to include these two contributions in the English edition.

This has, however, resulted in a certain shift of emphasis in the book's intention: whereas the German edition set out to present these various battles to the German reader as components of a world war, this English edition sets out to provide an Anglo-American audience with the current results of German research into the most important battles in the European arena of war, thus presenting its readers with, so to speak, the German view of these battles.

This shift of emphasis has also involved another change in the English edition by comparison with the original German one: it seemed desirable to the editors that a German audience should be given a description of the invasion of Normandy from the Allied viewpoint, from the angle of those who were taking the initiative. The contribution in the original German edition was therefore written by Albert Norman, who in 1944 was in charge of the war diary of General Bradley's Army Group, and who as a war historian has made a special study of Operation 'Neptune'. Thus the German reader was able to see this decisive battle in Western Europe through unfamiliar eyes, and from the angle of the attacker. On the other hand, it now seems desirable to provide an Anglo-American audience, used to seeing the invasion as from England, with a description of the battle from the angle of the defence. Friedrich Ruge, who was naval adviser to Field-Marshal Rommel in 1943–44, was therefore asked to deal with the battle of Normandy.

The maps for the English edition were redrawn by Johannes Schüren from sketches made by J. Rohwer.

Arbeitskreis für Wehrforschung

FRIEDRICH RUGE
Vice-Admiral retd. (President)

Dr HANS-ADOLF JACOBSEN   Dr JÜRGEN ROHWER

Bonn-Stuttgart, May 1963.

EDITORS' INTRODUCTION

The investigation of the Second World War is unquestionably one of the most urgent tasks of contemporary history. The Western Allies have already published various studies, both official and semi-official, detailed and general, on the basis of their own records and those they captured from their enemies. And, after a long period of silence, the Soviet Government has now published four volumes of a comprehensive *History of the Great Fatherland War*. Germany will be in a position to do that sort of thing only after the victorious powers of 1945 have returned to the Federal Republic those documents which have been retained by them, a matter which will inevitably take time.

But apart from such official or semi-official histories, the German Military Research Committee, formed in 1954, has instituted a scientific investigation of this fateful chapter of Germany's history. A number of books have already been published about particularly important phases and problems of the Second World War, and articles have appeared in periodicals such as the 'Wehrwissenschaftliche Rundschau' (Military Review) and 'Marine-Rundschau' (Naval Review). During the course of the preparatory work it seen again and again that, fortunately, the number and extent of the sources still available in Germany, though often scattered and little known, were considerably greater than had at first been supposed. A great deal of this material has since been collected, examined and made available in close co-operation with the various institutes, archives, libraries and individual scholars at home and abroad who occupy themselves with military history and current affairs.

Despite all the difficulties still existing, this wider use of sources has made it possible to carry our research beyond the stage previously reached by Assmann, Görlitz and Tippelskirch—to mention only the most prominent military writers—and provide a new general survey of the years 1939–45, more in accordance with the present extent of investigations. Any comprehensive history of the Second World War would require attention to many different problems and aspects; the following articles deal exclusively with military affairs, and with the most important phases on the various European fronts. It must therefore be regarded as no more than a contribution to the history of the Second World War, but as such it certainly does give some indication of the scope of the work the Committee proposes to undertake.

It is hardly necessary to point out in any detail that the results of the Second World War, which still profoundly influence our time, were not brought about by military operations alone. Since the First World War their scope and methods have fundamentally changed, and in the Second World War the belligerent peoples were mobilized to a degree never before known, and at the same time they were in consequence more deeply affected by the fortunes of war. And to crown it all, the ideologies of the twentieth century aroused hardly governable passions, and led to the profession of reckless and often ridiculous war aims which were quite impossible to attain with the existing military means. In such circumstances, therefore, individual battles were less and less able to achieve the real and ultimate decision, since their place was more and more taken by ideological and technical or economic factors. Nevertheless such battles were still culminating points which changed the course of events and introduced new phases of the conflict.

In choosing the operations to be dealt with here, the publishers were guided by the degree of their influence on the course of the war, and thus, to some extent at least, on its outcome. At the same time, it was seen that to consider purely Continental strategy in the European theatre would have been to present a one-sided and incomplete picture. More than ever before this was a war which developed into a simultaneous and often interlocking conflict on land, at sea, and in the air; at the same time, the Pacific theatre was of much greater importance in the general prosecution of the war than is generally realized here or in the Soviet Union.

The authors bear the responsibility for their individual contributions, which are based on an analysis of the source material so far available at home and abroad. In addition to a description of the course of the battle in its most important aspects, the authors have attached importance to the previous intentions of the leaders on both sides, and they have also sought to set the particular battle into its proper place in the general picture of the war as a whole. The reason for leaving out this or that 'decisive battle' (for example the so-called 'Air Battle of the Reich, 1942–44') is primarily because there is insufficient source material to allow it to be treated satisfactorily.

The editors have to thank the following institutions for friendly assistance: Bibliothek für Zeitgeschichte, Stuttgart; Bundesarchiv–Militärarchiv, Coblenz; Institut für Zeitgeschichte, Munich; Militärgeschichtliches Forschungsamt, Freiburg; Osteuropa-Institut, Munich; Staatliches Archivlager, Göttingen, Abt., Zeitgeschichte; Staatsarchiv Nuremberg; Studiengruppe Luftwaffe attached to the Führungsakademie of the Bundeswehr, Hamburg-Blankenese; Deutsches Kultur-Institut, Tokyo; Deutsch-Japanische Gesellschaft, Tokyo; Division of Naval History, Navy Department, Washington; Historical Section, Foreign Documents Branch, Admiralty, London; Imperial War Museum, London; Ufficio Storico della Marina Militare, Rome; Service Historique de l'Armée et de la Marine, Paris; and the War History Departments of the Dutch and Belgian General Staffs.

The editors similarly thank the following individuals for valuable assistance and generous advice: Dr Jack Bauer, Washington; H. C. Beaumont, London; Captain (German Navy) Theodor Freiherr von Bechtolsheim, Stuttgart; Lieutenant-Colonel Brusten, Brussels; Professor Charles Burdick, Santa Clara,

California; Captain (French Navy) S. Caroff, Paris; General Cossé-Brissac, Paris; Admiral A. Cocchia, Rome; Squadron Doctor Hervé Cras (Jacques Mordal), Paris; General (Air) Paul Deichmann, Hamburg-Blankensee; Grand Admiral Karl Dönitz, Aumühle; Rear-Admiral Ernest N. Eller, Washington; Rear-Admiral Siegfried Engel, Buxtehude; Admiral Guiseppe Fioravanzo, Rome; Rear-Admiral Eberhard Godt, Kiel; Colonel D. J. F. A. Goutard, Paris; Colonel Friedrich Greffrath, Hamburg-Blankenese; Colonel van Ham, The Hague; Colonel Takushiro Hattori, Tokyo; Commander Günter Hessler, Bochum; Dr Andreas Hillgruber, Marburg; Dr Anton Hoch, Munich; Commander P. K. Kemp, London; Rear-Admiral Hideo Koyima, Tokyo; Colonel Dr Hans Meier-Welcker, Freiburg; Captain Hans-Georg Model, Hamburg; Rear-Admiral Samuel E. Morison, Boston; Dr Erich Murawski, Coblenz; Dr Helmut Neubauer, Munich; Captain (Japanese Navy) Toshikazu Ohmae, Tokyo; Dr Roger Pineau, Washington; Dr Hans Pohle, Hamburg; Wilhelm Röhl, Tokyo; Commander M. G. Saunders, London; Lieutenant-General Arthur Schmidt, Hamburg; Dr Schnelbögl, Nuremberg; Dr Hans-Günther Seraphim, Göttingen; General (Air) Kurt Student, Rinkerode near Münster; Dr Georg Tessin, Coblenz; Jean Vanwelkenhuyzen, Soignies; and Dr Thilo Vogelsang, Munich.

ANTON FREIHERR VON BECHTOLSHEIM
Former President of the Arbeitskreis für Wehrforschung

Dr HANS-ADOLF JACOBSEN   Dr JÜRGEN ROHWER

Bonn-Stuttgart, July 1960

For the English edition the publishers are indebted to Mr Peter Lickfold for his invaluable and expert assistance in checking the military terminology.

Chronicle I

Events leading to the Second World War

November 11, 1918: End of the First World War.

June 28, 1919: Signing of the Versailles Treaty.

October 28, 1922: Mussolini's march on Rome. Victory of Fascism.

January 21, 1924: Death of Lenin. Stalin, General Secretary of the Communist Party of the Soviet Union, becomes his successor.

1929–1932: World economic crisis.

January 30, 1933: Hitler becomes Reich Chancellor of a 'National Government' composed of National Socialists and German Nationalists.

February 28, 1933: Emergency Decree 'in Defence of People and Nation'. Abolition of fundamental civil rights. Bill for establishment of concentration camps.

March 24, 1933: Enabling Bill passed.

July 14, 1933: Law against founding of new political parties. Beginning of totalitarian State.

October 14, 1933: Germany leaves League of Nations.

January 26, 1934: German-Polish Pact of Friendship and Non-aggression.

June 30 to July 2, 1934: SA leaders eliminated as a power factor; so-called 'Röhm revolt'.

July 26, 1934: Failure of National-Socialist *Putsch* in Vienna. Murder of Chancellor Dollfuss.

August 2, 1934: Death of Reichs President von Hindenburg. Hitler becomes 'Führer and Reichs Chancellor'. Reichswehr takes the oath to Hitler.

January 13, 1935: 91 per cent of the Saar voters in favour of reunion with Germany.

March 16, 1935: Reintroduction of compulsory general military service in Germany. Open rearmament begins.

April 11, 1935: Stresa Conference. Britain, France and Italy condemn any unilateral abrogation of treaties.

May 2, 1935: Franco-Soviet 'Mutual Assistance' Pact.

June 18, 1935: Anglo-German Naval Agreement.

October 3, 1935: Italy invades Abyssinia.

March 7, 1936: Hitler abrogates the Locarno Pact. German troops reoccupy the Rhineland.

July 18, 1936: Beginning of the Spanish Civil War.

October 25, 1936: Berlin-Rome Axis founded.

November 25, 1936: Conclusion of Anti-Comintern Pact between Germany and Japan.

July 7, 1937: Peking 'incident'. Beginning of the Sino-Japanese 'conflict'.

November 5, 1937: Hitler informs his Army commanders: 'There is only one way to solve the German problem, and that is by force.'

February 4, 1938: Reorganization of the Wehrmacht. Hitler now 'Supreme Commander'. Generals Blomberg and Fritsch dismissed.

March 12, 1938: German Army enters Austria. 'Greater Germany'.

May 30, 1938: Hitler's decision to destroy Czechoslovakia.

August 27, 1938: Chief of German General Staff, General Beck, resigns in protest against Hitler's policy.

September 29, 1938: Munich Agreement. Cession of the Sudetenland to Germany.

October 1, 1938: German troops enter the Sudetenland.

October 20, 1938: Hitler gives orders to destroy 'Rump of Czechoslovakia'.

November 9, 1938: Organized destruction of Jewish shops and synagogues throughout Germany.

March, 1939: Beginning of Franco-British negotiations in Moscow.

March 15–16, 1939: Establishment of Reichs Protectorate over Bohemia and Moravia. Entry of German troops in defiance of Munich Agreement; a decisive step to war.

March 21, 1939: German offer to Poland to settle frontier dispute.

March 23, 1939: German troops enter Memel area.

March 26, 1939: German offer to Poland rejected.

March 31, 1939: Franco-British guarantee to Poland announced.

April 3, 1939: Directive of Wehrmacht High Command (OKW) for an attack on Poland.

April 7, 1939: Italy occupies Albania.

April 28, 1939: Hitler abrogates 1935 Anglo-German Naval Agreement and 1934 German-Polish Non-aggression Pact.

May 20, 1939: German-Soviet negotiations begin in Moscow.

May 22, 1939: Italo-German military alliance – 'Pact of Steel'.

August 23, 1939: Signing of German-Soviet Non-Aggression Pact (secret codicil).

August 25, 1939: Anglo-Polish 'Mutual Assistance' Pact. Hitler postpones attack on Poland, which had been fixed for August 26th.

August 31, 1939: 12.40 hours. Hitler gives final order for attack on Poland.

September 1, 1939: German attack on Poland launched at 04.45 hours.

Chronicle II

September 1939
to
April 1940

	Politics		Conduct of the War
Neutrals	Axis Powers and their Allies		Axis Powers and their Allies
			August 19, 1939: Two pocket-battleships a eighteen U-boats sail to the Atlantic.
			September 1, 1939: Germany attacks Poland.
			September 3, 1939: Army Group C (von Le with 33 divisions defends Western Fr against 110 Allied divisions. Beginning German attacks on merchant shipping. *U. 30* sinks passenger ship *Athenia* believi her to be an auxiliary cruiser. U-boats l first magnetic mines along English coast.
			September 8, 1939: German forces reach Warsa
			September 12, 1939: Battle of Kutno (Bzura).
			September 17, 1939: Two Russian Army grou enter east Poland. *U. 29* sinks British aircr carrier *Courageous*.
			September 24, 1939: Battle for Warsaw.
September 28, 1939: Russia signs 'Mutual Assistance' Pact with Estonia.	September 28, 1939: German-Soviet Friendship Treaty.		September 28, 1939: Warsaw capitulates.
October 5, 1939: Same with Latvia.	October 6, 1939: Hitler announces 'peace offer' in the Reichstag.		October 6, 1939: Surrender of last Polish troo October 9, 1939: 'Führer Directive No. 6' for mo aggressive waging of war in the West.
October 10, 1939: Same with Lithuania.			October 10, 1939: Grand Admiral Raeder repo to Hitler on the strategic importance Norway.
October 11, 1939: Beginning of Russo-Finnish negotiations.			October 14, 1939: *U. 47* penetrates Scapa Flo defences and sinks battleship *Royal Oak*.
October 18, 1939: Three Scandinavian kings meet in Stockholm.	October 26, 1939: Establishment of *'Gouvernement-Générale'* in Poland. East Poland annexed by Russia.		October 16, 1939: First German air attack o British warships off the English coast. Fi minelaying operation by German destroye
			October 31, 1939: Manstein's first operation draft for a Western offensive.
November 7, 1939: Belgian-Dutch offer of mediation to the belligerent powers.	November 8, 1939: Attempt on Hitler's life in the Bürgerbräukeller in Munich.		
	November 9, 1939: 'Venlo incident'. Two members of the British Intelligence Service kidnapped on Dutch territory and taken into Germany.		
November 13, 1939: King Carol of Rumania offers to mediate.			November 12, 1939: Hitler fixes date for Weste offensive.
			November 21, 1939: German Fleet sails out engage British 'Northern patrol' to the sou of Iceland.
			November 30, 1939: Beginning of Russo-Finni winter campaign.
December 14, 1939: League of Nations brands Russia as an aggressor nation, and expels her from the League.			December 13, 1939: Naval engagement at t mouth of the River Plate.
			December 17, 1939: Pocket-battleship *Admir Graf Spee* scuttles herself off Montevideo.
			January 10, 1940: Two Luftwaffe officers carryir secret papers make forced landing ne Mechelen.
	February 11, 1940: Russo-German trade agreement.		January 27, 1940: Preparations for 'Weser Exercise Germany's secret plan to occupy Norway an Denmark.
			February 18, 1940: Operation 'Nordmark', con bined operations of the German fleet, U-boa and the Luftwaffe against Britain-Norwa communications, fails.
			February 24, 1940: German deployment plan i West completed.
	March 10, 1940: Ribbentrop arrives in Rome.		March 1, 1940: Directive 'Weser exercise' issue End of first phase of Battle of the Atlanti 750,000 GRT sunk.
March 12, 1940: Russo-Finnish Peace Treaty signed.	March 18, 1940: Hitler and Mussolini meet at the Brenner Pass. Mussolini agrees to enter war on Germany's side.		
	April 2, 1940: Hitler orders 'Weser Exercise' for April 9th.		April 9, 1940: 'Weser Exercise' begins; Germa troops occupy Norway and Denmark.
	May 9, 1940: Hitler gives definitive order for Western offensve.		May 10, 1940: Offensive launched in the West.

Dunkirk 1940

BY HANS-ADOLF JACOBSEN

THE PREPARATION

Hitler explains his Decision for a Western Offensive

On November 23rd, 1939, the generals of the Wehrmacht (Armed Forces) assembled in the Reichs Chancellery at Hitler's orders. He proposed to give them an insight into the ideas which, in view of the approaching events, were uppermost in his mind, and to inform them of his political decisions.

They, the representatives of the Wehrmacht, he began, should always bear in mind that the rebuilding of the Wehrmacht would have been unthinkable without the previous rise of the National Socialist Party. From the beginning of his political career in 1919, he personally had had to contend with incredible obstacles, and to wrestle over difficult decisions in his own mind. Only his unshakeable belief in Germany had sustained him. Never for one moment had he hesitated to make 'brutal decisions' if they were necessary to further his aims. In 1933, when everything in the country was in ruins, he had set about reorganizing, consolidating and strengthening Germany. At the same time he had begun to free Germany from her international chains, and restore her influence in the world. Despite many sceptical voices he had succeeded. His policy of annexation had also been carried through successfully, though the number of doubters had always been greater than the number of those who believed in him. Hitler now admitted frankly that he had been determined to destroy Czechoslovakia from the beginning. However, he had, he pointed out, been compelled to go forward by stages. As far as his ultimate aim of settling accounts with the Western Powers was concerned, the only thing which had not been clear in his mind from the start was whether to turn against the East or the West first. To those who constantly objected that his plans would mean struggle and nothing but struggle, he replied that for him struggle was, in fact, the destiny of all nations. Incidentally, he reminded them, the problem of Germany's *Lebensraum* was still unsettled. It was their business to bring her territory into line with the size of her population, and not vice versa. All creation had to fight for its *Lebensraum* as a matter of obligation. The alternative was to surrender its rights without a struggle.

However, there were still other reasons why the struggle in the west was unavoidable. Since the founding of the German Reich, the antagonism between France and England on the one hand and Germany on the other had steadily

29

intensified; the Western Powers had always tried to prevent the consolidation
of the Reich. By the end of the nineteenth century Moltke had already realized
quite clearly that sooner or later there would be a showdown, and for this
reason he had, for a while, been in favour of preventive war. Because
Bismarck's successors lacked resolution, the Reich had let the most favourable
opportunity slip. When the showdown finally came in the shape of the First
World War, the Reich had found itself facing the disaster of a war on two
fronts. Today, for the first time in sixty-seven years, *Germany need not fight on
more than one front*. But no one could foresee how long this favourable
situation would last, and therefore the time to act was there and then. In any
case, he certainly had not built up the Wehrmacht for no purpose.

Turning to the general political situation after the successful campaign
against Poland, Hitler pointed out that at the moment France and Great
Britain were standing practically inactive behind their own fortified lines.
But how long could Germany tolerate such a situation?

A general review of the position showed that Russia was certainly weakened,
and need not be rated very highly as a military factor. Further, she was bound
to Germany by a treaty—though, of course, they must remember that such
agreements were kept for just so long as they remained useful, and no longer.
Should it ever become necessary, Germany must be in a position to thwart the
far-reaching political designs of Russia in the Baltic, in the Balkans and on the
Persian Gulf. In Italy, the only favourable factor as far as Germany was
concerned was the personality of Mussolini himself. The Duce was anxious
to pursue imperial aims, but he had to reckon with opposition in his own
country, and only a German success in the west could carry him into the war on
Germany's side. It could not be denied that the sudden death of the leading
statesman in either of these two countries would tip the scales against Germany.
He, Hitler, was irreplaceable. Germany must therefore not let this opportunity
slip. No one could tell whether the present line-up of forces in eastern, southeastern and northern Europe would continue to be so favourable to Germany.
So far the Americans had adopted a neutral attitude. The present moment was
favourable for an offensive—in six months' time it might be too late. He was,
therefore, determined to end the war as quickly as possible by crushing the
enemy. Hitler then exclaimed: 'Anyone who disagrees lacks all sense of
responsibility.' At the moment Germany clearly held the upper hand militarily,
he went on. Germany had a greater number of regular divisions, her Luftwaffe,
tanks, anti-aircraft and other artillery were better than those of the enemy,
and above all, the fighting quality of her troops was better than that of the
Allies.

He had been deeply mortified to hear it said that the German Army had not
fought as well as had been expected in Poland. He was certainly not in favour
of uncritical enthusiasm, but the fact remained that the German Army was the
best in the world. There was also no reason to suggest any lack of aggressive-
ness, or any defects in its training. Further, the German Army of 1939 was

better equipped than that of 1914 had been. 'And I must pay the present commanders of the Wehrmacht the compliment of saying that the German Army is better led today than it was in 1914.' He then roundly condemned any suggestion that things were not altogether what they ought to be in the German Army. 'Everything now depends on its commanders. I can do anything I like with the German soldier, provided he is well led.' Let them take the small Navy as an example. In the very first months of the war it had succeeded in sweeping the North Sea clear of the British. The Navy and its Commander-in-Chief* (Grand Admiral Raeder) therefore deserved special recognition. At the same time, the feats of the Luftwaffe and the Army in Poland must not be overlooked.

They enjoyed military superiority at the moment, and they were backed by the strongest war industry in the world; everything now depended on making good use of it. A revolution in present-day Germany was simply out of the question.

A particular source of anxiety for him was the increasing activity of the British; within the space of six or eight months they had succeeded in increasing their strength in France very considerably.

Further, the Ruhr—Germany's Achilles heel—would be in grave danger as soon as the Allies occupied Holland and Belgium. All thoughts of compromise were to be dismissed. It was a question of victory or defeat. In the last resort the decisive question was: who was going to dominate Europe?

Britain could be forced to her knees by the U-boat and the mine. But before this could be done, Germany would have to capture better bases from which to operate. Belgium and Holland must therefore be occupied as quickly as possible. Without considering the cost to himself he had come to a heroic, unalterable decision: to attack France and Britain at the first favourable moment, and crush them both. It was a decision comparable only to that of Frederick the Great before the Second and Third Silesian Wars. In such a context the question of violating Dutch and Belgian neutrality was quite irrelevant. Once Germany was victorious no one would ask any questions. 'Without an offensive in the west we cannot win the war.' Therefore Germany's leadership must give the German people an example of fanatical determination. 'If commanders-in-chief were to suffer nervous breakdowns, as some of them did in 1914, how much could you ask of the ordinary infantryman?' Everything must be done to imbue the men with a determined aggressive spirit. He would therefore take strong action against anyone who tried to undermine this spirit, and he would unhesitatingly destroy anyone who opposed him.

Hitler ended his speech with a call for unflagging determination. 'If we emerge from this struggle as victors – and we shall be the victors! – then this day and age will enter into the history of our people. As for me, I shall stand or fall in this struggle. I should not survive the defeat of my people. No surrender abroad! No revolution at home!'[1]

*Commander-in-Chief of the Navy = *Oberbefehlshaber der Kriegsmarine* (abbreviated *Ob. d. M.*).

During this speech Hitler made it quite clear that he was absolutely deter-mined to win the war which had broken out with the Western Powers on September 3rd. He had called the generals of the Wehrmacht together on this occasion because he was bothered by the lack of fervour some military leaders had shown.[2] During the course of the campaign against Poland he had deter-mined to stage a final showdown with the Western Powers, but when he had made this decision known to the Commanders-in-Chief of the three services he had soon realized that they were sceptical about his plans. For one thing, they felt that there were still insufficient forces and material on hand for such an undertaking, and for another, they were still hoping for some sort of political agreement between the belligerent powers. However, at the end of September 1939, Hitler forced OKH (*Oberkommando des Heeres* = Army High Command) to abandon its defensive strategy in the west and to make preparations for an offensive.

Those at the head of OKH in Zossen (OKH HQ) at first resisted the idea, but when Hitler insisted they hurriedly drew up a preliminary plan of opera-tions which all too clearly betrayed its provisional nature – in fact it may have to be regarded as a tactical manœuvre on the part of OKH against Hitler.[3] The 'peace offer' announced by the latter in the Reichstag on October 6th was made merely to justify himself in the eyes of the German people, a fact he frankly admitted to the Italian Ambassador after the offensive in the west.[4] Brauchitsch, the Commander-in-Chief of the Army (*Oberfehlshaber des Heeres*, abbreviated to *Ob.d.H.*), and Halder, Chief of General Staff (Army) (*Chef des Generalstabes des Heeres*, abbreviated to *Chef Genst.d.H.*), both had good reason to doubt the possibility of forcing a decision on the Western Front in the autumn of 1939. Both these officers made it very clear to Hitler that the German Army was neither adequately trained nor sufficiently equipped to carry out such a difficult task at that time. Naturally, the two men based their judgement on the experiences of the First World War, and thus – unlike Hitler – they put a high estimate on the fighting qualities of the Allies, and particularly of the French. Also, the Commanders of the Army Groups concentrated in the west since October regarded the prospects of a winter offensive as distinctly unfavourable. They all feared the sort of frontal deadlock that had taken place in the First World War. But Hitler continued to press for an offensive, and his generals failed to form a solid front to thwart his plans.[5]

General Ritter von Leeb, C.-in-C. of Army Group C at the time, was particularly sceptical, and drew up a number of memoranda insisting that it would be impossible to force Britain and France to sue for peace by under-taking such a military offensive. In October he wrote a personal letter to Brauchitsch, declaring bluntly: 'The fate of the whole German people may depend on you in a few days', and pointing out that they deeply desired peace, and had no enthusiasm for the war. The German people were hoping that the Führer would now adopt a policy of peace, and they instinctively felt that it would be impossible to crush Britain and France. If the Führer would end the present impasse on more or less acceptable terms, no one would interpret this as a sign of weakness or surrender, but merely as a sober acknowledgement of the existing relation of forces. If the Führer did this he would certainly be hailed as a real Prince of Peace, not only by the whole German people but also by people throughout the world.[6]

But by the middle of October 1939, Hitler had announced his 'irrevocable decision' to launch an offensive in the west. He temporarily fixed November 12th as the date for the offensive. On November 5th, the day on which the preliminary order setting the preparations for the offensive in motion had to be given, Brauchitsch tried to persuade Hitler at least to postpone the offensive. What he had to say did not influence Hitler. Indeed, Hitler regarded his observations as a criticism of his work as the leader of the National Socialist Party, and he ordered that the offensive should take place as arranged. However, bad weather, unsatisfactory operational planning, and, of course, the manifest disapproval of many high officers, caused the repeated postponement of the operation (during the winter of 1939–40 it was postponed on no less than twenty-nine occasions). And so, finally, Hitler ordered his generals to gather in the Reichs Chancellery on November 23rd, 1939. He was anxious to stamp out the smouldering crisis amongst his high officers, and was determined to do everything possible to change their views, to dispose of certain critical elements once and for all, and to refute their arguments against an offensive in the west. What he said on this occasion left no doubt whatever that he had, without consulting even his closest military advisers, taken one of the most fateful decisions of the whole war: to turn what was variously called by the Germans '*Sitzkrieg*', or 'sit-down war', by the French the '*drôle de guerre*', and by the British 'the phoney war', into an actual Second World War.[7]

On the same day, Hitler summoned Brauchitsch and Halder at 18.00 hours, and upbraided them for their hesitant attitude towards the offensive he had ordered. The Chief of General Staff made this laconic note in his diary: 'Commander-in-Chief of the Army and myself – spirit of Zossen (crisis day).' Brauchitsch now offered his resignation in view of the intolerable situation in the Supreme Command of the Wehrmacht, but Hitler told him that he must do his duty like everybody else, and continue as Commander-in-Chief of the Army. General von Bock, C.-in-C., Army Group B, noted in his diary: 'There has been a very serious clash between the Führer and Brauchitsch, but the latter is still C.-in-C., so apparently he is now willing to take responsibility for the intended operations.'[8]

The Plan of Operations

OKH put forward its first deployment plan on October 19th, a few weeks after Hitler had ordered Brauchitsch to prepare plans for a western offensive. As both sides had built strong defensive lines, the Maginot Line and the West Wall, along the southern sector of the front, a frontal attempt at a break-through had little chance of success. OKH, acting at Hitler's instructions, made the following operational proposals: unlike the famous Schlieffen Plan, which had a strong right wing from Metz to Wesel, there was now to be only a stronger north wing (Army Group B), extending from Prüm to Wesel; this was to attack only in a westerly direction, with its flank protected by the operations of the southern wing (Army Group A). The main weight of the attack was to lie to the north of Liège, and its general direction towards the Channel coast in Belgium; its goal was to be an enveloping movement on Ghent, separating the British from the French if possible, and, in addition, securing air and sea bases for the war against the British Isles.

At that time, military circles in Berlin did not suppose that this preliminary operation could possibly meet with more than an initial success. Fundamentally speaking the plan lacked any far-reaching strategic conception, since, assuming that its first operational objective (the coast) was attained, the question of how the war would be continued in order to obtain a decision against Britain and France was left completely open. In addition, the plan also lacked organizational depth and made no provision for adequate reserves.[9]

This deployment plan – which was given the code-name 'Gelb', or 'Yellow' – provoked lively discussions. In a series of discussions between representatives of OKW* and the Army Groups Commands, it became even more obvious that opinions were deeply divided. One point that aroused particular controversy was whether the proposal to concentrate the armoured and mechanized divisions with Army Group B really held out any hope of success.

Hitler, who was kept closely informed by OKW as to the progress of the operational preparations, also occupied himself closely with this major question, and on October 25th he ordered both Brauchitsch and Halder to report on the operation. After this meeting, he summoned the commanders of the Army group and the armies which were to form the spearhead of the offensive. General von Bock and General von Reichenau, C.-in-C., 6th Army, both took the opportunity to remind Hitler of the prevailing bad weather, and both suggested that in any case to wait a little longer would give the Army a chance to improve its training; after which the proposed operations could be carried out in the spring. But these arguments made very little impression on Hitler, who was afraid that any postponement of the offensive would give the enemy a chance to increase his strength.

During the course of the discussion, Hitler suddenly turned to Brauchitsch and asked whether it would not be possible to deliver the main attack to the south of the Meuse only – perhaps with a subsidiary operation against Liège – and, going through the Ardennes, drive westward and then to the northwest, in order to envelop the Belgian fortress from the south, and so cut off and destroy everything the enemy threw in there. This was unquestionably a daring proposal, and well worthy of discussion. Hitler himself immediately expressed

*Wehrmacht High Command = *Oberkommando der Wehrmacht* (abbreviated and referred to throughout as OKW).

his own doubts about it, demanding (with justification): 'Can I get through there?' He then instructed OKH to examine the proposal again, and to let him know the result of its deliberations.[10] This was the first reference to the possibility of an enveloping movement, which at that time was rejected both by General Jodl, Chief of the Wehrmacht Operational Staff* and OKH, particularly because there was as yet no clear picture of the enemy's intentions. The Intelligence Department (Foreign Armies in the West) had so far been unable to form any general idea of enemy intentions. But only if it could be assumed with some confidence that in the event of a German offensive the Allied forces would automatically advance into Belgium, would any serious discussion of such an operational proposal be justified. On the other hand, if the enemy remained in his positions on the Franco-Belgian northwest frontier then the proposed offensive wedge would drive straight into his deployment. Hitler's proposal of October 25th was therefore turned down, and in consequence he now restlessly cast around for new proposals, always guided by his pet obsession in favour of placing the main weight of the offensive to the south of Liège. At the beginning of November,[11] he ordered an armoured force (consisting of two Panzer divisions and a two-thirds mechanized division) to be deployed in the sector manned by Army Group A opposite Sedan.

It is certainly to his credit that – without knowing it at the time – he directed German operational planning to one of the weakest points in the French fortified lines; a circumstance which was to be of decisive importance for the development of the western offensive when it came. However, his subsequent order, on November 20th, to send in further units to support this armoured force was a sheer dissipation of strength and no more than a half-measure, since he personally reserved the right to commit it and proposed to make such commitment depend on which front sector won the biggest preliminary successes.[12] He was not prepared to stake everything on one card; and up to February 1940 the 'three-pronged operational plan' remained in favour. In contrast with his approach to foreign policy, Hitler hesitated to take the daring step of seeking a military decision and putting the main weight of the operations from the beginning between Dinant and Sedan in a westerly direction. This is a clear indication that in those days he was still dependent on the experts, the General Staff and his own military advisers.[13] It was only during the subsequent weeks that, for tactical reasons and because of what happened on January 10th, 1940 (the forced landing near Mechelen of two Luftwaffe officers who had lost their way; they were carrying important plans which fell into enemy hands), he came round more and more to the view that it would perhaps be better to concentrate the greater part of the armoured and mechanized units in the direction of Sedan, since the enemy would certainly not expect the main weight of the German attack to fall there.[14]

In the meantime the then Chief of Staff of Army Group A, Lieutenant-General von Manstein, had carefully studied the first deployment plan drawn

Wehrmachtführungsamt.

up by OKH, and like so many other high Wehrmacht officers he found the proposed operations very unsatisfactory. His own conclusion was that in view of the uncompromising attitude of the enemy, Hitler's proposal to seek a military decision by an offensive was well worthy of consideraton. The situation as he saw it called for a plan of operations to crush the enemy and end the war in Germany's favour. Towards the end of October, therefore, he drew up a memorandum which he presented to OKH together with a detailed proposal for the conduct of the war in the west. Between that date and January 1940, Manstein presented no less than six memoranda![15] His first culminated in the demand that the proposed offensive must seek to force a decision on land. This was to take place in two stages. In the first, Germany would deploy her forces with their main weight to the south of Namur, in order to break through on the Somme and cut off and destroy all forces sent into Belgium by the enemy. An essential condition for this operation was that its south flank should be protected offensively. In the second stage, the German forces would swing southwards and complete their victory by an enveloping movement. Manstein assumed that the enemy would be expecting a repetition of the Schlieffen Plan, and that he would therefore concentrate strong forces as far eastward as possible to meet the expected German drive there, while at the same time seeking to roll up the whole German front by a counter-attack against the south flank of the offensive. His proposal was therefore that from the beginning the main weight of the offensive should lie with Army Group A, whose forces should carry out the operations (known as the Manstein Plan) as follows: one army would attack with infantry divisions in a general westerly direction between Dinant and Fumay. Its objective, in co-operation with the armoured and mechanized units of Army Group B, would be to cut off and destroy enemy forces advancing into Belgium. Simultaneously another army would drive across the Meuse, and then wheel in a southwesterly direction on both sides of Sedan to break up the confidently expected enemy offensive deployment there, and thus prepare the way for the final decision. For Manstein, two mobile corps represented a minimum if the preliminary success he desired against the advancing enemy forces in south Belgium were to be obtained. In accordance with Moltke's precept that no operational plan should extend beyond the first clash with the main enemy forces, Manstein proposed that the further use of the mobile units should depend on the reaction of the enemy. Once the danger of an enemy flanking offensive had been countered, all available forces could swing northward to help in the destruction of the enemy troops encircled there. But Manstein's plan provided that the main body of the armoured divisions should be with Army Group B! A third army was to set up a defensive front, on the Meuse at Carignan and on the Moselle at Mettlach.

OKH did somewhat hesitantly discuss Manstein's succession of proposals, but there was no real exchange of views, and this was probably largely due to the personal and professional differences between Manstein, Brauchitsch and

Halder. The proposals of Army Group A for the conduct of the war in the west were dealt with internally, and they were not presented to Hitler, as Manstein had wished. It was only the 'Mechelen Affair' in January and two *Kriegspiele* (map manœuvres) at Army Group A in February that persuaded OKH to shift its ground a little, particularly as by this time a much better picture of the enemy's intentions had been obtained. All signs now indicated that in the event of a German offensive the Allied northwest wing (mechanized forces) would automatically advance into Belgium.[16]

At last Hitler did get to hear of Manstein's memoranda, but not through the usual channels. At the end of January 1940, his chief military adjutant, Colonel Schmundt, visited Army Group A HQ, where he learned from the senior general staff officer that Manstein had at some time previously submitted a proposal to OKH for an offensive in the west, and on his return to Berlin Schmundt seems to have reported the matter to Hitler. In fact, it was probably at his insistence that in the middle of February, Hitler summoned Manstein – who had in the meantime been promoted to the command of a corps, perhaps as a consolation for the dismissal of his plans – to Berlin. In the course of this interview Manstein explained his proposals in detail, and Hitler was at once favourably impressed because, of course, he had himself expressed somewhat similar ideas the previous October. In the meantime OKH had on its own finally come round to accept the grand design, and the ultimate decision was taken on February 18th, at a meeting between Hitler, Brauchitsch and Halder. OKH has at least the credit of casting the German deployment in a form that was of decisive importance for the success of the campaign.

The new deployment plan of February 24th, 1940, was thus based on the brilliant operational proposals of Manstein and Hitler's own ideas: it culminated ultimately in the tactical commitment of the German forces by OKH, and it went into modern military history under the name of '*Sichelschnitt*' (scythe-cut) Plan. Germany's victory in the west in 1940 was largely based on this.[17]

The strategic aim of the offensive was the rapid occupation of Holland, in order to deprive Britain of the use of Dutch territory. Simultaneously, an offensive across Belgium and Luxembourg was to destroy as many French and British troops as possible and thus prepare the way for the final destruction of Allied military strength. At a conference of commanders-in-chief held on March 13th, Brauchitsch stressed that the primary task of the western army was to destroy the British forces after they had been cut off from their French allies.

Contrary to the first proposals in 1939, the main weight of the attack was now to lie with the south wing of the advancing armies. The basic idea of the operation was to destroy the enemy line between Liège and Sedan by exposing the south flank. For this purpose Army Group A (General von Rundstedt) was to use powerful mechanized and armoured units – operating independently for the first time. Moving from the south, his forces were to cut off everything the enemy threw into Belgium, and then destroy them in co-operation with Army Group B (von Bock), which would advance to the north of Liège. The task of Army Group B would be to occupy Holland as quickly as possible, with airborne and paratroop support, and to engage as many enemy forces as possible in Belgium and keep them pinned down. By launching vigorous attacks, this army was to deceive the enemy for as long as possible concerning the main thrust of the offensive, and to prevent his forces from attacking the inner flank of the enveloping wing. In fact the whole success of the daring plan of operations depended on this. In the meantime Army Group C, manning the West Wall and the Rhine front, was to pin down the enemy forces there by feints.[18]

The Allied Plans

Hitler's policy in the pre-war years, 1933–39, gradually convinced Britain and France that in any future war they would once again have to fight side by side, and soon after the German reoccupation of the Rhineland in 1936 the two general staffs began to exchange technical information. So far, however, the official British policy of 'appeasement' forbade any closer military contact. This final obstacle was removed by the German march into Czechoslovakia in March 1939, and the Western Powers at last recognized the necessity of offering vigorous joint resistance to what they now regarded as Hitler's boundless political ambitions. The first joint general-staff discussions began on March 29th, 1939, in Paris. During these discussions the possibility of war in north-west Europe was considered. The representatives of France made it clear that their primary aim would be to defend their own territory. Should it come to war, Germany would have to be held in check by an economic blockade until such time as the Allied forces were prepared and equipped to launch an offensive. Both general staffs were well aware that this could not possibly be the case before the end of 1940. They also realized that with superior forces on land and in the air, and vulnerable only at sea, the enemy would unquestionably seize the initiative. From the beginning, therefore, all the Allied plans were directed to countering the expected German offensive.

During these joint discussions it soon became clear that in the first months of a war, the French Army would have to bear the main burden of the defence. Britain feared that she would be able to send no more than two divisions to France. Other forces would be sent as quickly as possible, even armoured divisions, but these additional forces could hardly be ready for action before the spring of 1940.

A few days after the Anglo-French declarations of war on Germany, on September 3rd, 1939, the British began to despatch their first troops to northern France. By September 17th, the greater part of their expeditionary force was in France in pursuance of the so-called W-4 Plan. By the end of September, about 160,000 British soldiers were on French soil. By the end of

April 1940, the total strength of the British Army in France had been increased to ten divisions (half regular and half Territorial) with about 400,000 men.

During joint pre-war operational planning the French General Staff had first adopted 'Plan E'. The aim of this was to defend French territory along the northwest Franco-Belgian frontier. Only the First, Second and Third Armies on the French left wing were to oppose the enemy advance into Belgian territory, and even then with limited objectives only. The First Army was given the task of providing the defence between the North Sea and a general line St Quentin–Trelon. The plan was to occupy the middle Schelde – known in French as the Escaut, hence 'Plan E'. However, after the Allied guarantee to Poland at the end of March 1939, this plan was abandoned, and in a discussion between General Gamelin, Supreme Commander of the Allied forces, and the Polish War Minister, General Krasbrzysa, in April 1939, it was agreed that in the event of a German attack on Poland the majority of the French divisions available should be used in a relief offensive against the West Wall between the Rhine and the Moselle. On July 24th, 1939, General Gamelin signed orders to the effect that on the outbreak of war systematic operations were to begin to seal off the German defensive system between Hardt and the Moselle. However, because only very inadequate forces were available, 'and there was an even more serious lack of shells',* the French High Command had limited objectives in mind. In the circumstances a successful break-through of the West Wall seemed out of the question. But at least the French hoped that their operations would force the Germans to withdraw many divisions from the east to meet their threat.

What actually happened was very different from what had been planned. On September 7th French troops did advance, but before long the operations came to a standstill before the dominating heights of the West Wall, and soon afterwards the French High Command withdrew its forces to their starting-point. There was no question at any time of any real relief for the Poles in the east; though, of course, it must be pointed out that the German campaign against Poland came to a victorious end much sooner than the Allied High Command had expected. However, everything suggests that France was neither willing nor able to launch a serious offensive against Germany in order to secure a decision. In the last resort, of course, her armaments, and those of her British allies, were in any case quite inadequate for the purpose. Both Britain and France had encouraged Poland to resist Germany's demands, and they had both promised her military assistance in case of need. But when the war actually broke out, neither of them was in a position to implement these promises and help its eastern ally effectively. Instead they both looked on almost passively while their ally was militarily annihilated in a matter of days.[19]

The complete victory of the German armies in Poland forced the Western Allies – from about the middle of September 1939 – to revise their whole operational planning and give it a different aim. As they now obviously had to

*Statement by the Chief of the French Military Mission to the Editors.

expect a German offensive in the west, everything depended on their being able to defeat it with the means available to them at the time. It was also reasonable to assume that in launching such an offensive Germany would once again violate Belgian neutrality, and very likely Dutch neutrality as well. It was therefore highly desirable that these two countries be persuaded to work in military conjunctio.. with the Allies at once. But despite several requests – finally couched almost in the form of an ultimatum – both Holland and Belgium refused to veer from their publicly declared policy of independence and neutrality. Neither country was prepared to accept military co-operation with the Allies until German troops had actually marched into its territory. The Belgians believed that if they were invaded, they could hold the modern defence system they had built up in the east of the country along the Meuse and the Albert Canal long enough to give the Allies time to come to their assistance. In view of these facts, Hitler's claim that he had been forced to wage a preventive war in the west was merely one of his usual propaganda lies. [20]

The Allied Supreme Commander, General Gamelin, was the man ultimately responsible for Allied operational planning. Still obsessed by the ideas of the First World War, he assumed that in all probability the Germans would once again attack through north and central Belgium with a powerful right wing, in order at the very least to occupy Belgium and French territory between the Channel coast and Hirson. It would appear that the Allied war leaders gave no serious consideration to the steps to be taken should the Germans not do what was expected of them, but instead break through the French position on the Meuse and envelop the Allied forces already in Belgium.

This fateful omission was all the more extraordinary because at the end of the 'twenties and the beginning of the 'thirties British military writers (for example, Captain Liddell Hart) had already drawn attention to the possibility of a German attack through the Ardennes. The French High Command seems to have dismissed this possibility by exaggerating the difficulties of attacking with strong forces in the Ardennes. [21] Three defence variants were now discussed in the Allied High Command. One was that the main Allied forces should take up their position behind the Schelde, and dig themselves in there for a protracted defence. At the same time, units could be detached to reinforce the Belgian Army along the Ghent Canal. It was also regarded as practicable to push forward mobile forces (French and British divisions) as far as the Albert Canal, to reinforce the Belgian defensive positions there and to prevent the enemy from driving any farther into Belgian territory. And, finally, the defence of a central position, extending from Antwerp over Wavre–Namur to the Meuse near Givet, was considered. The second possibility depended largely on the attitude of the Belgians themselves. If they were wise enough to call on the Allies for assistance before the Germans actually attacked, then there was no doubt that this plan held out some prospects of success. However, in view of the unbending attitude of the Belgian Government, the Allied war leaders could only really contemplate the other two variants.

When, in October 1939, the signs of an imminent German offensive became more pronounced, and the Belgian military chiefs began to regroup their forces, the French General Staff returned to 'Plan E'. On October 24th, 1939, General Georges, Commander-in-Chief on the northeast front, issued the appropriate orders (No. 7) to the armies under his command. By occupying the central Schelde area the Allies hoped to secure certain advantages: with Allied reinforcement the Belgians would be able to hold the Germans within Belgian territory; the German forces would be denied access to the Belgian Channel ports; the British air defences could be extended in depth; and finally, French reserves in northern France could be adequately protected. An additional factor in favour of this plan was that it could be carried into execution within twenty-four hours. The main disadvantage was that the Allied forces would have to hold a very long front, and this gave rise to considerable anxiety.[22]

This first defensive plan was sharply criticized in the French High Command. For one thing it involved the abandonment, without a fight, of large stretches of Belgian territory, and this must inevitably have very grave effects on the morale of the Belgians. Also, it would prove very difficult to stave off the offensive of the powerful German right wing. In the following weeks these considerations led to the drafting of a second plan, known generally as the 'Dyle Plan', but to the Belgians as the 'KW Partition', because it ran from Koningshooikt (southeast of Antwerp) to Wavre (southeast of Brussels). The aim of this plan was to reinforce the Belgian defence on the Dyle to the east of Brussels, in the hope of holding the prepared positions there. In a supplement to this plan arrangements were also made to reinforce the Dutch Army to the south of 'Fortress Holland' with divisions from the French Seventh Army on the Allied left wing.

This 'Dyle Plan' was worked out in full detail during the winter of 1939–40, and in March 1940 the final orders were given. It was still the intention of the Allies to wheel First Army Group – beginning at Mezières on the Meuse – to the right in a general northeasterly direction, in order to counter the enemy attack on the line Namur–Wavre–Louvain and near Antwerp (Dyle Line). The greater part of the Belgian forces – as arranged subsequently with their commanders – was to defend the sector from the north of Louvain to the Dutch frontier. The Allies reckoned that the forward Belgian covering troops, which included cavalry units, would at least be able to hold up the German advance on the Albert Canal and the Meuse (by blowing up bridges, establishing road blocks, and so on) long enough for the Allied troops to get into position on the Dyle Line, and so give them a chance of accepting the decisive battle as far eastward as possible. The task of the French Seventh (mechanized) Army was to reinforce the Belgians in the Antwerp–Turnhout area, and – on receiving specific instructions – to move forward into Holland in order to strengthen the defence of the islands in south Holland and reinforce 'Fortress Holland'. In view of the great material and numerical superiority of the enemy, the Belgians would be compelled to withdraw their troops step by step from their advanced positions back to prepared defensive positions protected by tank obstacles and inundated areas, where the Allied troops could join them to meet the German offensive. The Belgian defence system as a whole was based in the north on fortified positions around Antwerp and on the so-called '*Reduit National*'; it then ran along the Albert Canal as far as Maastricht and Liège, where the focal point of the defence was the modern fortress of Eben-Emael. From Liège the defensive line ran along the Meuse in a southwesterly direction as far as Namur. The main Belgian forces were concentrated behind this line to repulse the German attack. Another force was situated in south Belgium to hold up the German attack there as long as possible, with instructions to retire behind the Meuse line near Namur when enemy pressure became too great.

Holland's defensive plan was based on an echelon of defensive positions of increasing strength from east to west. While minor frontier and coastal forces held the Ijssel–Meuse line as far as Maasbracht, the main Dutch forces were in position behind the so-called 'Peel–Raam' Line, and behind the Grebbe Line, which lay a little farther to the north. The third defensive line consisted of 'Fortress Holland', which was protected to the south by numerous river estuaries, and occupied by strong frontier battalions and an Army corps. Whereas the withdrawal into their '*Réduit National*' for protracted defence was to be only as a last resort for the Belgians, 'Fortress Holland' was the decisive basis from which the Dutch hoped to hold up the German attack for as long as it took the Allies to bring up adequate forces to assist them. Particular reliance was placed on the inundations to be carried out to the south of the 'Fortress', and it was hoped that they would seriously hamper enemy movements.[23]

THE GERMAN OFFENSIVE

The Break-through to the Channel Ports

The German offensive was launched at what was regarded as the most favourable moment for Germany. It began in the early hours of May 10th, 1940, with heavy air attacks on neutral and enemy airfields, traffic junctions, military installations, administrative centres and industrial targets. By this time the Wehrmacht had not only succeeded in fully training and equipping units with armoured vehicles and MT,[24] but had also completed its operational preparations for the offensive, which was to include airborne and other surprise undertakings on Dutch and Belgian territory. The offensive – launched by five armies from the North Sea to the Moselle – could now be said to have very good prospects of success.

There was no formal declaration of war; German troops just invaded Holland, Belgium and Luxembourg with the objective of destroying the military strength of the Allies. From the beginning the necessary operations were conducted with great vigour and *élan*, and with a good many factors in their favour.

First of all, the new mobilization procedure, adopted in January 1940, was highly successful; and the German troops benefited from complete surprise. The majority of the front-line divisions were ready for action within twenty-four hours; at the same time the operational use of the armoured forces was closely co-ordinated with the tactical operations of the Luftwaffe, which provided close support on the battlefield. Intensified security regulations and the adroit use of camouflage concealed the advance of the armoured forces, and thus left the enemy in doubt as to the main thrust of the offensive. The fact that the Luftwaffe established its air superiority in the first few days of the campaign, and went on to win command of the air, made far easier the operations of the land forces, and in particular those of the mobile units on Army Group A's sector of the front. The splendid fighting spirit of the troops, who had been brilliantly trained for their task during the winter 1939–40, was a factor of outstanding importance. Nevertheless, in view of the forces available to them, including their armoured units, the Allies – given a centralized and determined leadership and a high morale on the part of their troops – should have been in a position to counter the offensive.

The objective assigned to the 18th Army (Küchler) on the north wing of the offensive was to defeat the Dutch forces and occupy Holland as rapidly as possible, in order to eliminate the flanking threat from the north and to prevent Allied troops from using the country as a base of operations. In the early hours of May 10th, parachutists were dropped and airborne troops landed near Moerdijk, Rotterdam and The Hague in support of this operation; their orders were to capture the most important bridges over the Meuse and the Waal intact and hold them until the arrival of mobile units by land. Though the attack on The Hague failed, the parachutists did succeed in capturing the bridges at Moerdijk and Rotterdam intact and in holding them against all enemy attacks until the arrival of the 9th Panzer Division. The most difficult task of the German land forces at this stage of the operations was to relieve these airborne and parachute troops in time. The C.-in-C. of Army Group B and the commander of the 18th Army therefore drove forward the 9th Panzer Division, which had been chosen for this purpose, with all possible speed. It was expected that the Allies would rush troops across Belgium into 'Fortress Holland' to reinforce the Dutch, and, in fact, German air reconnaissance reported the first troop movements along the Antwerp–Roosendaal road in the morning of May 11th. These troops were units of the French 7th Army, and their advance was halted by fierce air attacks carried out by Putzier's Luftwaffe squadrons. Subsequently they were driven back altogether by the south wing of the 18th Army. In the meantime the 18th Army had succeeded in making the decisive break-through along the Peel Line, so that the 9th Panzer Division could drive forward swiftly as planned. In point of fact it met with little or no resistance, and its forward elements made contact with the airborne troops and parachutists at the Moerdijk bridge in the afternoon of May 12th. By that same evening, the rapid advance of the 18th Army to Best and Merle, had cut off the Dutch Army in 'Fortress Holland'. So far, however, all efforts to break through the strongly fortified Grebbe Line had been unsuccessful.

On May 13th a concentric attack from the south and east was launched against 'Fortress Holland'. By 18.00 hours German army units passed through Doordrecht and penetrated into the south of Rotterdam, which was already held by airborne troops. However all attempts, even with intensive support from the Luftwaffe, failed to make any impression on the Grebbe Line. It was only in the early hours of May 14th that it was discovered that the enemy had withdrawn under cover of night and of thick early morning mist, leaving only a very skilfully led rearguard still holding its positions. In the afternoon stronger German forces moved up and compelled Utrecht to·surrender.

In the meantime, a tragic misfortune had occurred at Rotterdam. Amidst the confusion of conflicting situation reports – including news of British landings in 'Fortress Holland', which subsequently proved to be false – the Commander of the 18th Army ordered an ultimatum to be delivered to Rotterdam, which was the decisive gateway to 'Fortress Holland', adding that if the town did not surrender it would be destroyed. Despite the fact that negotiations began in the morning on May 14th it proved impossible, owing to poor communications, to cancel the Luftwaffe attack on the town which had been fixed for 15.00 hours in support of the land operations. As a result something like 60 per cent of the bombers that set out on this mission actually dropped their bombs on the old part of the town, which was almost completely destroyed.[25]

In view of the hopeless operational situation, and the bombing and capitulation of Rotterdam, and realizing that no adequate assistance was to be expected from the Allies, General Winkelmann, the Commander-in-Chief of the Dutch forces in the field, broadcast an offer to cease all military operations. That was at 20.30 hours, and by 11.45 hours on May 15th Dutch and German representatives had signed the capitulation instrument. Five days of hard fighting[26] had proved sufficient to conclude the campaign against Holland.

In the meantime, the operations of the 6th Army in central Belgium and the operations of Army Group A to the south of the Meuse front Liège–Namur had also been successful.

The rapid advance of the 6th Army depended primarily on whether the various river and canal obstacles could be overcome in time to send forward the mobile units. Despite the successful operations of many special commandos and airborne units, the Dutch and Belgians did succeed in blowing up a number of bridges, but this did not materially hold up the advance of the German forces. The decisive operation in this respect was the swift capture of the modern Belgian fortress of Eben-Emael by units of the 7th Air Division and an infantry regiment.

The first improvised bridge was thrown over the Meuse at Maastricht on

May 11th, to enable the XVI Panzer Corps, under the command of General Hoepner, to attack the flank of the enemy near Gembloux, get ahead of the French troops hurrying towards their Dyle Line positions, and cut off the retreat of the Belgian troops withdrawing from Liège. This attack was also intended to fool the enemy into believing that it represented the main weight of the offensive. On May 12th came the first clash with advanced elements of the French 2nd and 3rd Mechanized Divisions, whose task it was to give the French forces sufficient time to establish themselves in the Dyle Line. Repeated attacks by VIII Air Corps were necessary to support the German Panzer corps, because the enemy was offering bitter resistance, particularly in the Hannut–Perwez sector. In the meantime infantry divisions of the 6th Army had already reached the Moll–Diest–Saint Trond Line.

On May 13th, OKH summed up the situation as follows: continuous troop movements by rail and road were taking place in the direction of Brussels and Antwerp from the Lille–Maubeuge area and the northeast of Paris. This suggested that the British Expeditionary Force and the French 1st Army were moving forward into Belgium, flanked by the 7th Army which had been operating on the northwest wing of the Allied forces since May 10th. In all, these enemy forces amounted to between 40 and 45 divisions, of which 21 divisions were opposite Army Group B. The Battle for Belgium was thus approaching its height. The enemy had walked into the trap; he had, as had been hoped, completed the swing forward of his northwesterly wing, pivoting on its hinge (at or about Mezières), and thus provided the most important preliminary condition for the success of Germany's daring 'scythe-cut' plan.[27] However, up to May 15th all attempts of the 6th Army to break into the Dyle Line had been unsuccessful. The resistance offered by the enemy compelled General von Reichenau, who was in command of this operation, to call off the attack until May 17th, by which time all the available units had been concentrated.

The very first days of the German offensive compelled the Allied commanders to take a number of very grave decisions. Most of their calculations had turned out to be wrong; and, in particular, their forces had not been given sufficient time to get into position along the Dyle Line. The German armoured drive had not been held up near Gembloux. The Belgians had abandoned their forward positions much more quickly than had been expected, and the weight of the German attack had thrown them back to the Dyle Line. General Georges, Commander-in-Chief of the Allied northwest front, was already considering withdrawing his troops, but at the last moment he decided that the German advance must be stemmed at all costs. At this time, the Allied High Command had not yet recognized where the real weight of the German offensive lay. It was not until May 15th, when German mobile units of Army Group A forced the river passage at Sedan and Dinant and moved rapidly in the direction of the Somme estuary,[28] that it realized the deadly danger that was beginning to develop to the west of the Meuse Line.

The operations of Army Group A, on which the success of the campaign as a whole depended, went forward almost completely according to plan. By May 13th the armoured units of the 4th Army and of von Kleist's group, succeeded in establishing bridgeheads over the Meuse, both at Houx and Sedan, without meeting any serious resistance. This surprising and unexpected success provoked General von Bock to remark: 'The French seem to have taken leave of their senses, otherwise they would have prevented that at all costs.'[29] Germany's generals found it impossible to understand why the enemy had not rapidly occupied the Namur–Sedan line in force. And they were astonished to discover that the enemy's fieldworks were extremely sketchy.

The truth was that the Allied military leaders failed to recognize the full significance of the dangerous threat represented by this massed armoured and mechanized drive. Further, the troops they despatched to the Meuse sector (French 2nd and 9th Armies) consisted chiefly of divisions of the A and B series, which did not have the best equipment, and which had many officers from the reserves. In consequence, the Meuse was not defended with sufficient vigour and energy. The French did not succeed in destroying the German bridgeheads, or even in sealing them off. At the same time, the air attacks flown in support of the Allied ground troops were not as effective as had been hoped, and heavy air losses were suffered because the bombers were sent in without adequate fighter protection. In addition, the closely co-ordinated tank and air attacks launched by the advancing Germans greatly demoralized large numbers of Allied troops. An armoured division brought up to launch a counter-attack on the 9th Army sector was prepared too slowly, sent into action unskilfully and, in consequence, was lost uselessly within a matter of hours.[30]

On the same day, after overcoming one or two local difficulties, the advance units of Army Group A continued their advance. General von Rundstedt continually impressed his commanders with the importance of pushing as rapidly as possible westward towards the Channel coast. On May 14th, OKW issued a new directive reinforcing this objective: operational aims remained almost unchanged, but instructions were now issued that Army Group A's drive should be reinforced as quickly as possible with all available mobile units.

The more the German break-through on the Meuse front was extended, and the farther the armoured units drove on towards the Channel coast, the more endangered the ever-lengthening southern flank appeared to Army Group A HQ. Rundstedt feared that the Allies would launch a counter-attack into his flank, and his HQ therefore worked constantly to ensure the uninterrupted movement of infantry divisions behind the front of the 16th Army from Sedan. On May 15th, Rundstedt even contemplated temporarily halting the mechanized forces on the Oise. He was most anxious that the enemy should not obtain any successes, even of a local nature, on the Aisne and in the Laon area.[31]

On May 16th the threat of encirclement which hung over 1st Army Group, the British Expeditionary Force, and the Belgian Army in central Belgium became more and more obvious to Allied Supreme Command. The main forces of its 9th and 2nd Armies had been badly mauled, and General Billotte therefore decided to abandon the Dyle Line and withdraw his troops to the Schelde front. This movement was to proceed in three stages over the Senne and over the Dendre Line. But almost all the measures taken by the Allied leaders throughout these days betrayed signs of hesitancy and uncertainty. The French High Command was not in a position to concentrate any strategic reserves and use them for a vigorous counter-attack. On May 16th, Winston Churchill, who had become British Prime Minister a few days previously, arrived in Paris, where to his dismay he discovered that the French no longer had any worthwhile reserves capable of countering the successful German break-through on the Meuse. The confidence of the British in their French allies suffered a severe shock. Even at this early stage Churchill began to entertain the possibility that France might be knocked right out of the struggle, and it put him in a very serious dilemma. On the one hand he was under a moral obligation to provide his hard-pressed ally with all available assistance as quickly as possible; but on the other hand he did not want to weaken Britain's own powers of resistance and undermine the defence of the British Isles.[32]

Halder, the Chief of the German General Staff, was able to note exultantly in his diary: 'The break-through is developing in positively classical fashion. The whole front is moving forward rapidly west of the Meuse. Enemy tank attacks are being broken up. Our infantry are performing outstanding feats of marching.' All possible armoured and mechanized forces now had to be rushed up to support the advancing spearhead. Apparently the French were bringing up reserves from the Dijon and Belfort areas on the left wing of the spearhead, but those which had come from the Charleroi area to attack the German right wing had already been heavily repulsed. However, so far the enemy had not used his main reserves, and it remained to be seen where he would do so. In all, if he were prepared to accept decisive battle, he would probably be able to muster some thirty divisions for use against the break-through. 'We can bring up further reserves from Army Group C's sector and use them if necessary to strengthen our left wing. The general picture of the situation and the present relation of forces is altogether favourable.'[33]

When the enemy began to withdraw his forces in full as a result of the dangerous armoured break-through on the Meuse, General Hoepner – in agreement with von Bock and von Reichenau – pressed after them in the Wavre area on May 16th. He attacked in a southwesterly direction with his two armoured divisions, and drove forward as far as Tilly. At first the northern wing of the 6th Army followed somewhat hesitantly, because in the early hours British counter-attacks on both sides of Louvain had temporarily forced the Army corps operating there on the defensive. By the evening of May 16th, the 6th Army's centre and south flank had reached the Nivelle Line. The British now beat a fighting retreat towards Brussels before the northern flank corps, but they still held their Dyle positions on both sides of Louvain. In the north, the 6th Army reached Antwerp's front line at Broechem and Koningshooikt. The intentions of the enemy still remained obscure. The Commander-in-Chief of Army Group B (von Bock) noted in his diary: 'Everyone is trying to guess at the enemy's intentions. Perhaps opposite me he will try to hold Antwerp, the *Réduit National* around Ghent and Bruges, and the Dendre Line. But the latest air reconnaissance reports make even this seem doubtful.'[34]

HQ Army Group A now turned its attention increasingly to the endangered south flank, but the tension was already less. The foremost infantry divisions, which were advancing behind the 16th Army, reached the Sedan area on the evening of May 16th, while the armoured units of von Kleist's Group secured the area between La Fère and Rethel. Rundstedt decided to allow strong forward elements of von Kleist's Group to push on to the Cambrai–St Quentin sector in order to keep the important crossings of the Somme and Schelde Canal open for May 18th. However, the main forces of von Kleist's Group were to concentrate on the Oise, whilst the infantry of the 12th Army followed up in support. The situation report on May 16th showed that on the whole there was little cause for anxiety now. However, OKW, and in particular Hitler himself, were not too confident about the course of the operations. At a situation conference which took place in OKW at midday on May 17th, Hitler stressed the great danger from the south, and ordered that infantry divisions should be despatched as quickly as possible to protect the south flank, because he felt that mobile units alone would not be sufficient to drive through to the northwest. General Halder comments on this in his notes: 'A very disagreeable day! The Führer is excessively nervous. He mistrusts his own success; he's afraid to take risks; he'd really like us to stop now. His excuse is anxiety about our left flank. What Keitel said in his instructions to Army Group A, and during his own visit to Army Group HQ, has produced only confusion and doubt.' On May 17th, Hitler visited Army Group A HQ for the first time, in order to obtain a general picture of the situation in person. On his visit, General von Rundstedt pointed out that the south flank was very sensitive, and then explained the measures which had already been taken to reinforce it, and those which were still to be put in operation. Hitler fully accepted Rundstedt's situation report, and approved the measures taken. In his own comments Hitler particularly stressed the importance of the south flank not only operationally, but also politically and psychologically. Under no circumstances must there be any set-back anywhere at the moment, since this would greatly hearten the enemy not only militarily but politically. For the time being it was more important to strengthen the defence on the Aisne and in the Laon area as quickly as possible, and afterwards on the Somme, than it was to drive forward rapidly to the Channel coast.[35]

On May 18th, Hitler also revealed an 'incomprehensible anxiety with regard to the south flank'. As the Chief of Staff noted, he raved and bellowed and alleged that 'they were well on the way to spoiling the whole operation and even risking the danger of a defeat'. However, in Charleville, the Chief of

Wehrmacht High Command, General Keitel, was able to placate him with the assurance that OKH and Army Group had between them taken all necessary measures to protect the south flank, and that in part they had already been carried out. Further, a discussion at Army Group HQ once again showed complete agreement between Rundstedt's judgement of the situation and that of OKW, so that when Keitel returned to the Führer's Headquarters he was able to phone back to Army Group and tell them that Hitler now felt easier in his mind about the south flank, and was quite satisfied with the measures Army Group had taken. The mobile units which had been restrained up to then were now given full freedom of movement again, and ordered to destroy the enemy forces to the north of the Somme and in Belgium.[36]

Rundstedt now decided to place the mobile units under command of the 4th Army for a decisive drive to the northwest. They consisted of the newly-formed Hoth Group (3rd, 4th, 5th and 7th Panzer Divisions, the 20th Mechanized Infantry Division, the SS Totenkopf Division, the 11th 'Mobile' Brigade), and the von Kleist Group (with 6th, 8th, 1st and 10th Panzer Divisions, and later the 2nd, 13th and 29th Mechanized Infantry Divisions). By May 20th, Army Group B reached the area to the northeast of Ghent, and its forward units reached the Schelde, but the outstanding event of the day was that the spearhead of the armoured forces reached the sea. At 21.00 hours advanced elements of the 2nd Panzer Division entered Abbeville. By midnight the 8th Panzer Division had reached the neighbourhood of Montreuil-sur-mer.

General Jodl, Chief of the Wehrmacht Operations Staff, noted in his diary that the Führer was beside himself with joy, and talking 'in tones of the highest praise concerning the German Army and its leadership'. He was, it appeared, already thinking about the Peace Treaty. Its main provision was to be: 'The return to Germany of all territories stolen from the German people during the past 400 years.' He was determined to conduct the first negotiations in Compiègne, as in 1918. As for the British, they could have peace 'at any time they wanted, provided they gave back Germany's colonies'. Jodl's entry for May 20th closed with the words: 'There was a special note in OKW's log concerning the moving words of the Führer on receiving news of the taking of Abbeville.'

By this time Air Fleets 2 and 3 had carried out the greater part of the task set them, flying both day and night missions. First of all, they had broken up the enemy's ground organization and crushed the resistance of his frontier fortifications. Secondly, they had given close support to the operations of the army. By May 14th, they had succeeded in winning air superiority, and then a few days later, the undisputed command of the air itself. After the successful break-through on the Meuse, Air Fleet 2 protected the northern flank of the advance towards the Channel coast, at the same time bombing enemy shipping. In the meantime, Air Fleet 3 protected the south flank, particularly by attacking enemy concentrations and the movements of his reserves. In addition, it practically drove the French Air Force out of the sky.[37]

The Crisis at Arras

On May 21st, certain very obvious difficulties arose in the 4th Army's sector;
particularly in the Maubeuge area, in Mormal Wood, and, above all, near
Arras. In the morning XVI Corps (Hoth Group) was to the south of Arras,
which was still occupied by strong French and British forces. The Corps was
to press forward, either towards Pernes (northwest) or towards Béthune
(north). For this purpose certain crossings of the river Scarpe had to be seized.
Any further advance to the north had been left to the 4th Army.

At 14.45 hours, the Corps Commander ordered his divisions to cross the
Scarpe at Acq and Aubigny-Savy. The 7th and the SS Totenkopf Divisions
were to drive past Arras to the south and west, and were then to turn northwards. In the meantime, however, the 3rd and 5th Panzer Divisions were not
in a position to attack to the east of the town simultaneously, as had been
planned. Thus the right wing of the 7th Panzer Division was left completely
exposed to the strong enemy forces in the town. Advanced units of the 7th
Panzer Division (Major-General Rommel) had passed to the east of Beaumont
in a northerly direction, when at 15.00 hours the main body of the division
was unexpectedly attacked in the flank and forced on the defensive by a strong
British armoured force coming from the Tilloy Road–Arras–Beaumetz area.
Other British tanks, advancing from Achicourt in a southwesterly direction,
ploughed through an infantry regiment of the division and attacked the SS
Totenkopf Division to the west of Wailly. The situation soon became critical,
and the advance of XVI Corps was halted. Before the 11th Infantry Brigade,
which had just been brought up, could reach the threatened area, British tanks
again broke through near Hanin-Broiry (to the southeast of Arras) and attacked
the moving columns and the Divisional Staff of the SS Totenkopf Division.
An armoured regiment of the 7th Panzer Division which had already reached
the Scarpe to the southwest of Acq, now had to be withdrawn. However,
repeated Stuka attacks launched from 18.30 to 20.30 hours brought noticeable
relief, and the enemy was compelled to retire on Arras again. By late evening,
the situation was more or less restored. At the same time, the 5th Panzer
Division had had to repulse strong British attacks from Arras.[38]

Rommel's battle report (7th Panzer Division) reads: 'Between 15.30 and
19.00 hours heavy fighting took place against hundreds of enemy tanks and
following infantry. Our anti-tank gun (PAK) is not effective against the heavy
British tanks, even at close range. The enemy broke through the defensive line
formed by our PAK, the guns were put out of action or overrun, and most of
their crews killed.'[39]

In the afternoon the Commander of the 4th Army made the following
report to OKH: on the right wing the situation near Maubeuge was resolving
itself. The enemy had obviously received orders to stand, and was fighting
obstinately. Mopping-up operations were making good progress in Mormal
Forest; enemy forces there were being destroyed. The 3rd and 4th Panzer

Divisions were still in action, but they had received instructions to be west of Arras early in the morning. All armoured divisions in the area would be concentrated between Arras and the sea on the next day. Montreuil was already in German hands. It was proposed to send XIII Corps into the Valenciennes–Denain–Bouchin area next day. II Army Corps was to the southwest of Cambrai. The same evening, 4th Army had informed Army Group HQ that the enemy break-through near Arras had been sealed off, and that the northern part of Mormal Forest had been cleared of the enemy. There was nothing new to report from the south front. The bridgeheads were being held. No orders had yet been issued to implement the instructions for an advance beyond the Arras–St Pol–Hesdin–Étaples line. It was first necessary to build up a powerful armoured spearhead to clear up the situation around Arras. The report concluded by admitting that this was 'the first day on which the enemy had met with any real success'.[40]

This counter-blow on the part of the Allied forces, which was rather more energetic than anything that had gone before, must be seen within the general framework of the operational plans of the Anglo-French leadership. On May 19th, the Allied Supreme Commander, General Gamelin, issued a personal and secret order, No. 12, for a concentric offensive drive to cut the rearward communication of the German armoured divisions. The task of 1st Army Group, cut off in the north, was to open up the way to the Somme. But what actually took place was a number of disconnected and ineffective single operations, because in these critical days the chief weakness of Allied war leadership was lack of co-ordination. General Franklin, Commander of the British 5th Division, was under the impression that his task was to lend support to the Arras garrison to the south and cut the German lines of communication by blocking the roads to the south of Arras. He was not informed that French divisions were also to take part in this drive southwards, nor that the counter-attack launched by him was to be the opening of a large-scale southern offensive. The result was that although the operations were carried out vigorously by the British troops, they lacked the necessary depth and weight.[41]

The news that a critical situation had arisen at Arras undoubtedly had certain psychological effects on the Germans. In the early hours of May 22nd, Hitler made Colonel Schmundt telephone Army Group A to inquire how its operations were developing. Colonel Blumentritt, Senior Operations Officer, was able to inform him that, although the enemy forces which had broken through on May 21st had succeeded in pushing back the 7th Panzer Division in one or two places, on the whole the situation had now been restored. Hitler then ordered that all available mobile troops be committed on both sides of Arras and in the westward area to the sea, while the infantry divisions were to be committed to the east of the town in order to clear the position between Maubeuge and Valenciennes. All other infantry divisions of the 12th, 2nd and 16th Armies were to be sent westward.

On May 22nd, General Keitel flew to Army Group A in order to speed up the execution of this order, and to stress again its special importance. But he was particularly anxious to form his own view of the situation at the front. In his discussion with the Army-Group Chief of Staff, he again stressed Hitler's demand that the mechanized divisions on the Somme front should be replaced as quickly as possible by infantry divisions, and that the armoured divisions of von Kleist's Group should be relieved of the role of protecting the flank and defensive operations between Amiens and Abbeville, and sent forward. In Hitler's view only mechanized forces were fast enough to drive the spearhead northward with the necessary speed. These forces must therefore be relieved of rearward flank-covering duties. Their task would be to reinforce and relieve the forward armoured units. To make this possible, the infantry divisions, at the least their advance elements, were to be sent westward in forced marches. These instructions were undoubtedly in accordance with the views of the Army Group, which immediately issued the necessary orders. Back in Führer HQ, General Keitel telephoned the Staff in Charleville on the same day to say that Hitler was in complete agreement with the measures taken by Rundstedt, adding that the Führer had particular confidence in the commander of Army Group A.[42]

On May 22nd, a local break-through by enemy forces near Cambrai was halted by infantry and air attacks, and then the offensive as a whole in the sector of the 4th Army went forward according to plan. That evening, OKH was able to inform Army Group HQ that the army was successfully proceeding with the encirclement of strong enemy forces. All infantry divisions were still moving westward. The armoured groups under Hoth and von Kleist were attacking in the direction of Calais, and their forward element had already reached the area between Boulogne and St Omer. The sector Lécluse–Feuchy had been sealed off. Such enemy attacks as were still proceeding could hardly be regarded as a systematic attempt to break through to the south with large forces. No enemy activity had been observed on the Somme front.

In the meantime, on the northern wing of the German attack Army Group B had succeeded, against bitter British resistance, in crossing the Schelde on a front of almost four miles. The 6th Army now held a bridgehead on the line Peteghem–Gyselbrechtteghem Road–Kerkhoven–Avelghem. At the same time, the 18th Army had moved into an attacking position on the de Gande Canal. The day had passed there without any noteworthy fighting.

Meanwhile, Air Fleets 2 and 3 had attacked enemy troop concentrations in the Roubaix–St Pol–Béthune–Cambrai–Arras area, and shipping in the harbours from Zeebrugge to Boulogne. To the east of Arras, they had also attacked railway stations such as Vitry le François, Fér, Champenoise-Nogent and Troyes, and bombed the permanent way in the neighbourhood of Arras. But for the first time VIII Air Corps was compelled to admit that its Stukas had suffered heavy losses from the unexpected appearance of numerous British fighter planes. Many RAF planes until now held back for the defence of the United Kingdom had obviously been flown from their bases in southeast England, and taken part in the air war on the Continent. With this, the situation in the air suddenly grew critical.[43]

The Decision to Halt the German Armoured Forces

The operations in Flanders having proceeded according to plan and almost without difficulty, and the two temporary set-backs near Arras and Cambrai having been satisfactorily overcome, OKH issued a directive in the night of May 22nd–23rd, setting out the guiding principles for the conduct of future operations. The ring around the encircled enemy was to be drawn closer, and at the same time the crossings on the Lower Somme were to be kept open. Army Group B received orders to push its left wing forward into the neighbourhood of Seclin, then to turn northward in order to roll up the French frontier fortifications from the south, and to hurl back the enemy to the south and east of Lille. For the rest, Army Group B was to hold the enemy by attacking along the whole front, while at the same time using its forces as sparingly as possible and offering any surplus strength as quickly as possible to OKH for use elsewhere. The political leadership did not want the big Flemish towns to be destroyed, and military operations were therefore to spare them as far as possible.

Army Group A was instructed that once it had reached the line Béthune–St Omer–Calais, it should wheel its mobile forces against the Armentières–Ypres–Ostend line, at the same time using its infantry divisions to seize the Lens–St Omer plateau as quickly as possible, and then send them after the mobile forces in a northeasterly direction. In the south, the crossings of the Lower Somme were to be kept open, and the bridgeheads were to be enlarged when adequate forces arrived. To the east of Amiens, the defence of the Somme crossings was to be moved to the line Amiens–Nyon as soon as adequate forces became available for the purpose. This OKH directive indicated quite clearly that the 'scythe-cut' idea was to be retained and, further, that OKH was convinced that the first phases of the offensive would be speedily and successfully concluded.[44]

But on May 23rd, Army Group B on the north wing found that it was able to move forward only slowly. Some of its units were sent along the Menin Road towards the French fortified line to the east of Roubaix and Lille. To the north of Ghent, also, enemy positions were holding firm, and only unimportant bridgeheads were secured. The fighting on this sector of the front showed that no further important progress could be expected either on the north or the south wing. Only in the centre did it prove possible to gain an advantage, and von Bock therefore decided to shift the focal point of his operations to his inner wings. It is possible that he was also thinking of carrying out a pincers movement and closing the trap to the south of Ostend–Dunkirk, thus cutting off the British retreat. However, in accordance with the directive of OKH, he now used his left wing as well, in support of the 4th Army, by attacking to the southeast of Lille.[45]

At the same time General von Kleist informed the Commander of the 4th Army by telephone that his (von Kleist's) group had suffered heavy losses in equipment: his forces were expected to safeguard the Somme front and establish strong bridgeheads; in addition, he was to take Boulogne and Calais and secure the territory in between; finally, he was to turn eastward and deploy on a thirty-five mile front for a vigorous attack in the Ypres–Dunkirk direction. Kleist pointed out that in the fourteen days of the campaign his divisions had suffered such losses in equipment that up to 50 per cent of his tanks had been put out of action. His group was therefore not in a position to attack a strong enemy unless reinforced. Kleist also communicated his misgivings on this score to OKH through his liaison officer. However, the Chief of General Staff, Halder, expressed the opinion that the crisis would be resolved within forty-eight hours. The men must be called upon for a supreme effort.[46]

In a telephone conversation with General von Rundstedt in the late afternoon, General von Kluge, GOC 4th Army, summed up the situation: fighting was still going on to the south of Calais; progress had been made to the south of St Omer; the Loretto heights were almost entirely in German hands, and he had succeeded in establishing a bridgehead to the east of Arras. A decision was necessary by the next day, May 24th, as to whether they should go north or east of Arras. In his view the men, too, would welcome it if they could close up a little more. Therefore he proposed that the situation on the Arras sector should be finally cleared up, that the mechanized units on the left wing should be allowed to close up, and that, if possible, the 2nd Mechanized Infantry Division on the Somme should be relieved. General Rundstedt agreed, and ordered that the right wing and the centre of the 4th Army should be sent forward for the rest to close up.[47]

Evidence from the period indicates that the subordinate commanders found these instructions rather puzzling, and that some of them were even opposed to them. Both General Guderian and General Reinhardt, the commanding officers of the two Panzer Corps, felt that the obvious thing to do was to go forward rapidly and remain in close contact with the enemy.

On May 23rd, OKH came to another far-reaching decision. The final phase of the great encirclement battle of the 'scythe-cut' plan, the total destruction of the enemy, now seemed at hand. The high strategic objective of the offensive now made firm leadership more than ever necessary, particularly as the mobile left wing of Army Group A (4th Army) was soon to make contact with the left wing of Army Group B. It was essential that all the resulting problems of organization should be settled well in advance. Did Brauchitsch, the C.-in-C. of Army High Command, not feel altogether up to the task? Was it a certain dissatisfaction with the less dynamic Rundstedt, together perhaps with sympathy for the more temperamental Bock, which caused his surprising decision to place the 4th Army under Army Group B? General Halder noted in his diary: 'The expressed determination of the C.-in-C. to entrust Army Group B with the last act of the encirclement battle will cause considerable difficulties, owing to the personality of Army Group B's commander and his staff. . . . C.-in-C.'s insistence on this solution strikes me as an evasion of responsibility. He keeps on saying that he must either restore harmony between the two forces advancing on the cauldron from different sides himself, or put them both under von Bock. The former alternative, which strikes me as the more natural and the more manly, fills him with misgiving. He seems to be only too anxious to shift the responsibility. But in doing this, of course, he is also surrendering the honour of success.' By midnight the new order from OKH, which the Chief of the General Staff deliberately omitted to initial in the usual way, in order to place his contrary opinion on record, had arrived at the HQs of Army Groups A and B. From 20.00 hours, May 24th, 1940, onwards, Army Group B was to take over the tactical command of the 4th Army with all units north of the line Huy–Dinant–Philippeville—Avesnes–Le Cateau–Bapaume–Albert–Amiens. This, it was pointed out, was in accordance with the instructions of May 22nd.[48]

While von Rundstedt, the Commander of Army Group A, naturally did not consider the new order 'a particularly fortunate one at the given moment', and did not fail to let his views be known to the Operations Branch of the General Staff, von Bock, the Commander of Army Group B, equally naturally welcomed it, and he wrote: 'At last the responsibility for fighting this battle to an end is placed in one hand. It's a pity it wasn't done earlier. It would have saved a great deal of time.'

Meanwhile, the Operations Staff of OKW had already begun preparations for the second phase of the campaign ('Red'), on May 20th. But Hitler's impulsive joy when the taking of Abbeville was reported seemed to have given way to a more sober view of the situation. After all, the enemy had demonstrated at Arras what he was still capable of if he decided to act with vigour. Incidentally, when Grand Admiral Raeder, C.-in-C. Navy, reported to him on May 21st, Hitler informed him that it would be as well to count on a long war. He would see to it that once the campaign in France had been successfully concluded, armament priority was given to the building of U-boats and Ju-88 aircraft. General Keitel, judging no doubt on the basis of his First World War experiences, and probably Jodl as well, reinforced Hitler in the opinion that the terrain in Flanders was not really suited to large-scale armoured operations. In the meantime, Field-Marshal Göring, as C.-in-C. Luftwaffe, sought to make his influence felt by protracting the course of operations for his own ends.

Göring had his mobile HQ on the railway in the neighbourhood of Polch (Eifel). Apparently he felt that 'his' Luftwaffe was not being given a big enough share in the coming great victory; which was, after all, 'to settle the fate of the German nation for the next thousand years'. And then, of course, there was his almost pathological hatred of the traditional and conservative Army. In any case, on May 23rd, he rang up the Führer at his HQ in Münstereifel, and sought to persuade him that this was the moment for the Luftwaffe to perform its supreme task – namely, the destruction of the British Army in northern France. After this, the Army would only have to 'occupy the territory'. He lent cogency to his demand by saying that the final destruction of the enemy should be left to the 'National Socialist' Luftwaffe. If this were not so he, Hitler, the Führer, would lose prestige to the Army generals. With this argument Göring probably succeeded in touching him on his most sensitive spot! It is therefore not difficult to understand Hitler's enthusiasm for the idea. OKW was not so pleased, and Jodl observed sceptically, referring to Göring: 'He's shooting his mouth off again!'[49]

On the morning of May 24th, Halder recorded with satisfaction: 'The situation continues to develop favourably, even though the progress of our infantry units in the direction of Arras is taking time. But as, for the moment at least, there is no danger south of the Somme, I do not regard this as disturbing. We needn't rate the enemy's powers of resistance very high, except for local fighting. Things will take their own time; we must be patient and let them develop. Von Kleist's Group reports enemy air superiority for the first time.' General Halder now got his deputy, General Mieth, to inquire of the 4th Army what measures OKH could take to speed up the encirclement of the enemy in the Flanders trap. In his own view: 'When the heights (to the north of Arras) are once firmly in our hands, we should consider a further armoured drive across the Estaires–Cassel Line, in order to link up with the spearhead driven over the Lys in the direction of Roulers by the 6th Army.'[50]

At 11.30, Hitler arrived at Army Group A HQ in Charleville, where he listened to a report of the fighting and heard the intentions of Army Group Command. Rundstedt suggested that the infantry should attack to the east of Arras, while the mobile units stood on a line Lens–Béthune–Aire–St Omer–Gravelines, in order to catch the enemy withdrawing before Army Group B. Obviously he was impelled to make this suggestion by the fear that von Kleist's weak armoured group would be overrun by the retreating British troops. Hitler was delighted to find that both what Rundstedt had done and what he proposed to do were in accordance with his own ideas, and he therefore expressed complete agreement with the Army Group Commander. He stressed his agreement once more, and went on to say that it was particularly necessary to husband the armour for the coming operations. Incidentally, too, the activity of the Luftwaffe would be hampered if the ring were drawn too closely around Dunkirk.

But, as Rundstedt was to surrender control of the 4th Army on this very day, it may well appear doubtful whether on this occasion he was expressing his own views or those he knew to be the Führer's. But one way or the other, the fact remains that Hitler and Rundstedt were in agreement in their judgement of the situation; as they had, in fact, repeatedly been in agreement during the preceding days.

During the course of the further conversation Hitler learned to his great surprise that from 20.00 hours on May 24th, the 4th Army, together with all mobile units, was to be placed under the command of Army Group B. Neither he nor OKW knew anything about this OKH order. Later on Hitler told Jodl that he regarded it as both militarily and psychologically wrong. At the same time, he was highly indignant that Brauchitsch and Halder had carried out what seemed to him such a radical reorganization of command responsibilities without informing him. Their action probably revived his doubts of their personal devotion to him; he immediately cancelled their orders.

So on May 24th there was a crisis of leadership. The real causes were probably, first, that Hitler agreed with Rundstedt's judgement of the situation; and, secondly, Göring's optimistic promise the previous day of what the Luftwaffe could do. The situation provided a welcome occasion for instructions issued by telephone at 12.31: 'At the Führer's orders the attack to the east of Arras with VIII and II Corps, in co-operation with the left wing of Army Group B, is to be continued towards the northwest. On the other hand, forces advancing to the northwest of Arras are not to go beyond the general line Lens–Béthune–Aire–St Omer–Gravelines (Canal Line). On the west wing, all mobile units are to close up and let the enemy throw himself against the above-mentioned favourable defensive line.' Thus Hitler sanctioned what Rundstedt proposed, and at the same time demonstrated that he was now ruthlessly determined to force through his own ideas, and to impose his own military leadership. He was anxious to show on the battlefield itself that his position as Supreme Commander of the Wehrmacht was no mere formality.[51]

Taken aback by this new Führer order, OKH was compelled to make new arrangements. Late in the afternoon, Hitler himself had personally drawn C.-in-C. Army's attention to his order. Both Brauchitsch and Halder were highly indignant at this direct interference in the operational conduct of the war, but what could they do? On the evening of May 24th, Brauchitsch was neither able nor willing to make a new decision.

Not so the Chief of the General Staff. The unexpected Führer order hit him particularly hard, because, in the last resort, he was responsible for the conduct of operations, and he felt that Hitler's interference endangered the successful conclusion of the first phase of operations, endangered the great concept of 'a battle of annihilation with reversed front'. He asked himself whether it would be possible to countermand Hitler's standstill order by supplementary instructions, and at the same time carry Brauchitsch and Army Group A with him. Halder and his closest military collaborator, Colonel von Greiffenberg, probably regarded this as their only chance of getting their own operational intentions carried out despite Hitler. That same night, therefore, they issued a wireless order to Army Groups A and B: 'Further to OKH's instructions of May 24th, *the continuation of the attack* up to the line Dunkirk–Cassel–Estaires–Armentières–Ypres–Ostend *is permissible.* Accordingly the space reserved for Luftwaffe operations is correspondingly reduced.'[52]

Army Group B welcomed this directive, because it hoped that it would at least give the 4th Army an opportunity of pushing forward to Dunkirk harbour, to put a stop to the shipping operations still going on there. No doubt, too, it very much regretted that the final act of encircling the enemy had not been placed under its control after all.

Thus OKH had not definitely issued instructions that the attack on Dunkirk was to be continued. It probably felt that in the given delicate situation it could not go that far, but at least it had given permission for such operations. In any case, the directive did give Army Group A a chance of recovering its freedom of action in the spirit of OKH, provided – and this point has been stressed repeatedly by all representatives of the Army Group since the war – that the Army Group was not in agreement with Hitler's decision. However, when the new order arrived in Charleville at 0.45 on May 25th, the Senior Operations Officer immediately reported to General von Rundstedt and Lieutenant-General von Sodenstern, and they unanimously decided that *the order should not be passed on to the 4th Army, because Hitler had left to the Army Group itself the way in which operations were to be conducted*. Rundstedt regarded it as urgently necessary that the mechanized group should first be concentrated, before there could be any question of its pushing on. He further underlined his view by pointing out that there would hardly be time to make those new arrangements with the Luftwaffe which would be necessary if the Canal Line were to be crossed. Assuming that Rundstedt's observations on the morning of May 24th represented his own opinion, because the 4th Army was in any case to be placed under the control of Army Group B, his intentions now became clear: supported by Hitler's authority, he ignored an order from his own direct superiors, because he had come to a different view of the situation from that of OKH. To say that his attitude was unusual is putting it mildly; it was probably unique in modern German military history. It seems likely that it can only be understood by reference to the entry in the War Diary of the same day: 'The battle in northern France is approaching its conclusion. There is no further possibility of any crisis – except perhaps of a purely local nature. On the whole, therefore, the task of Army Group A can be regarded as having been fulfilled.'

Rundstedt – like many others – was obviously convinced that sooner or later the Flanders cauldron would be mopped up, and by Army Group B. For the rest, he regarded the difficulties of the second phase of the campaign, to which he was now paying increasing attention, as very considerable. It therefore seemed to him more advisable to husband the armoured forces for use later. Here – as in the operational planning of the winter of 1939–40 – the extent to which the thoughts and feelings of Germany's generals were still rooted in the ideas and experiences of the First World War when judging the enemy and his intentions was made very clear.[53]

It has often been suggested since that with his order to halt Hitler was deliberately offering Britain 'a golden bridge', and that he knowingly allowed a great part of the British Army to escape in the belief that such a 'noble' gesture would make it easier for him later to come to a peaceful arrangement with the British. Such a suggestion should be banished to the realm of post-war fantasy. First of all, both the German Army and the Luftwaffe had clear and definite instructions to destroy the enemy in the Flanders cauldron,[54] and this was made unmistakably clear in Führer Directive No. 13, signed by Hitler on the evening of May 24th, 1940.

Further, such a suggestion hardly fits Hitler's general political ideas. It has been quite rightly pointed out on various sides that on September 1st, 1939, Germany had no very clearly developed war plans; this was to have far-reaching consequences. Nevertheless, Hitler did have certain quite definite ideas of how Britain would have to be defeated in the event of war. One thing was quite clear to him: if war did break out, Germany would have no possibility of settling it 'on the cheap'. Hitler was well aware that, on the contrary, it would be a life-and-death struggle, in which there would be no going back. He was under no illusions about his enemy; he knew that the British were proud, courageous, tough, obstinate and – what mattered a very great deal – capable of great improvisation. He had said as much to his closest collaborators more than once. He also knew that they had a genius for 'bending every new event to their purpose'. He never doubted Britain's very real strength, and he knew that it was based on a powerful navy and an efficient air force. However, he was convinced that this great power had an Achilles heel – supply. Cut off its sources of supply and it would have to surrender. Thus, if the German Army won better operational bases for the German Navy and the Luftwaffe in Holland, Belgium and France, it would prepare the way for the ultimate defeat of Britain. Thus from the first, Hitler believed that the only way to break Britain's resistance was by blockade, and this belief was reflected in supplementary Directive No. 9 of OKW, laying down new directives for the conduct of the war against the enemy's economy. A commentary provided by Germany's Naval Operations Staff stated that Germany's war objective was very clearly and definitely the defeat of the main enemy, Britain. The way to secure this victory was first to break France, her sword on the mainland of Europe, and then to starve out the British Isles and undermine her economic strength. Britain could be defeated only by the 'biggest economic war of all times'.

From the profusion of evidence now available it is beyond dispute today that up to May 10th, 1940, Hitler had two possible ways of making Britain sue for peace: by destroying the military strength of his enemies on the Continent (it was to this possibility that he attached most importance in May and June 1940), or by launching a determined war against Britain's economy. The possibility of an invasion of Britain was not seriously discussed until after the defeat of France.[55]

On the morning of May 25th, Brauchitsch tried once more to persuade Hitler to allow the armour to go forward, but Hitler refused to change his mind. He pointed out that he had left the decisions to Army Group A, whose command also was against letting the armour advance, feeling that it should be kept fully ready for action in the subsequent campaign southward. Commenting on this remarkable interview, Halder noted in his diary: 'the day begins with another disagreeable clash between Brauchitsch and the Führer concerning the further conduct of the encirclement battle. My plan was for Army Group A to launch a heavy frontal attack on the enemy, who is systematically withdrawing before it; driving into the rear of a defeated enemy in this way it could obtain the decision. The mobile units are the weapon for this. But now our political leadership feels that the final decisive battle must be fought not in Flanders, but in northern France. But in order to camouflage this political objective, we are told that the terrain in Flanders, with its many waterways, is not suitable for armoured operations. And so the armour must halt when it reaches the St Omer–Béthune line. I wanted to make Army Group A the hammer, and Army Group B the anvil; but now the situation is to be reversed, B is to be the hammer and A the anvil. But as B is faced with an organized front, this must necessarily be very costly and take a long time. Another thing, the Luftwaffe, on which so much hope is now being placed, is completely dependent on the weather. Because of these differences of opinion, a tug of war has developed which is more wearing to the nerves than the whole organization of the campaign itself.'[56]

Once the left, that is the inner-encircling, wing of the German attack had received orders from above to go over to the defensive, the success of the operations against the Flanders cauldron depended on whether Army Group B's divisions on the north wing, and the right wing of 4th Army, could first surround and destroy the enemy to the south of Bruges by a concentric pincer movement, and then push forward to the east of Arras. Finally, it still remained doubtful whether the Luftwaffe could effectively use its full strength against the encircled enemy within the cauldron.

In fact, on neither the north nor the south wing of the attacking Army Group B did the operations go forward as planned; only in the centre of the front did the advancing German forces manage by the evening to cross the Roulers–Menin Road and send advance parties into Geluwe. The result of the fighting now persuaded Army Group HQ to shift the main weight of the attack to the inner wing of the 6th and 18th Armies.

But the attempts of the right wing of 4th Army to cut off the enemy in the Valenciennes–Pallue–Douai–Carvin–Lille pocket were not particularly successful. The German forces to the southwest of Valenciennes met vigorous resistance, and were able to advance only slowly. In fact, parts of the French 1st Army even began to counter-attack here.

In its evening situation report, 4th Army HQ had to admit that owing to obstinate enemy resistance the right wing of the German forces had got no farther than a line from the west of Bouchain, along the canal east of La Bassée, to Fierrière, southwest of St Venant. Von Kleist's group was halted with its advanced posts at the bridgeheads to the east of the canal sector, La Fierrière–Gravelines. The enemy facing VIII Army Corps offered obstinate resistance from fortified field positions, and was supported by strong artillery fire. Only opposite II Corps was he slowly falling back, but even then fighting all the way. There was very little enemy activity to report opposite the Hoth and von Kleist groups.

Air reconnaissance reported enemy movements from the Courtrai–Lille area towards the north. The enemy obviously had no intention of trying to break out of the trap westwards. 4th Army also had the impression that no important counter-operations were being planned on the south front.

May 25th was the day the Luftwaffe was to be used much more intensively than before against the Flanders cauldron, in order to break the last resistance of the enemy and prevent his escape to the British Isles. All available Luftwaffe forces attacked the ports of Zeebrugge, Blankenberge, Ostend, Nieuport and Dunkirk in successive waves, obtaining direct hits on the port installations and doing a great deal of damage.[57]

In the meantime, the rapid developments compelled the new French Commander-in-Chief, General Weygand, to postpone the offensive which had been planned for May 23rd–27th, in an attempt to re-establish contact between the now-separated Allied forces in the north and the south. It seemed, in any case, very doubtful whether this offensive would succeed, in view of the lack of co-ordination and the confused conditions within the cauldron. On May 24th, the new Commander of Army Group I, General Blanchard (General Billotte, the previous commander, had met with a fatal accident), met General Lord Gort, Commander-in-Chief of the British Expeditionary Force, to discuss the details of the proposed offensive; but the very next day the situation on the Belgian front became so menacing that the plan had to be abandoned altogether. The German break-through at Courtrai forced Lord Gort to take the two divisions he had been holding in reserve, and use them in an attack southward into the breach between the Belgian and British positions, in the hope of saving the line. By May 26th, the situation had become so desperate that Churchill was compelled to agree to Lord Gort's proposal to start evacuating British troops at once, since it was obviously impossible to hold the defensive positions around Dunkirk much longer as they were threatened from all sides. The first precautionary measures for evacuating individual units had been taken as early as May 19th, and preparations for mass evacuation were now speeded up. At 18.57 hours on May 26th, the Admiralty ordered the launching of Operation 'Dynamo', and by the following day it was in full swing and both the British and French forces in the cauldron were being evacuated with all available means. The evacuation was completed on June 4th, when 350,000 men of the Allied forces had been saved to fight another day. Step by step, the Allied troops had fallen back to the coast, fighting a rearguard action all the way, keeping their covering lines intact to the east, south and west and withdrawing steadily into the Dunkirk sector. And they held the perimeter all the way, until the great majority had been taken off – though all material and equipment had to be sacrificed.[58]

The Order for the Armour to Move Again

On the morning of May 26th, Halder observed with resignation: 'Our armoured and mechanized forces are standing motionless on the heights of Béthune and St Omer as though they were rooted to the ground. On orders from above, they are not allowed to attack. At this rate, it can take weeks to clear up the cauldron, and that will be very damaging to our prestige and hamper our future plans.' During the morning, Halder recorded that Brauchitsch was very definitely on edge, which was, as he pointed out, not surprising, because Army Group B was attacking a front which was being cautiously and systematically withdrawn and was therefore capable of vigorous resistance, whereas Army Group A was marking time at a spot from which the rear of the enemy could be attacked with great effect. Obviously in the meantime Rundstedt himself had had misgivings, and he had gone forward to the Hoth and von Kleist groups to discover what the situation was, and to reconsider whether the mobile units should go forward again.[59]

At the same time, Army Group HQ was also beginning to have second thoughts. Wireless monitoring indicated powerful enemy concentrations to the south of the Somme; and there were constant messages between them and the enemy forces fighting in the neighbourhood of Lille, Douai and St Armand. There were also reports from Calais and other Channel ports concerning landing attempts. The suggestion was that the enemy was probably about to make a final attempt to re-establish contact between the north and south groups of his separated forces, probably by concentric attacks.

Though Army Group HQ did not regard the situation as at all serious, it seemed nevertheless highly advisable to bring the fighting in northern France to a victorious end as quickly as possible, in order to obtain full freedom of action for the subsequent southward drive. For the first time, therefore, Army Group A thought that the given situation called for the commitment of the mobile units again – along the line Béthune–St Omer–Gravelines. There is every reason to suppose that Hitler was immediately informed of this judgement. Colonel Schmundt, Hitler's chief adjutant, and Lieutenant-Colonel von Tresckow, on the Operations Staff of Army Group A, relatives and personal friends, constantly kept in touch with each other by telephone, thus short-circuiting the usual official channels. What could have been simpler than to bring about a new order from the Supreme Commander of the Wehrmacht via this unofficial channel? On May 26th, the War Diary of Army Group A contains the following significant entry: 'These discussions finally led to the Führer's giving permission for von Kleist's group to move eastward.' Hitler's decision was probably reinforced by the report that, as things were, the German attack was not making any material progress, either on the north wing of Army Group B, which was facing an organized and intact enemy line, or on the right wing of the 4th Army to the east of Arras. And there was a further report that in the meantime six large transports loaded with evacuated troops had left Dunkirk.

At 13.30 hours General Brauchitsch was called by Hitler. An hour later he returned to OKH in high spirits: the Führer had at last, though with certain reservations, given orders for an advance on Dunkirk in order to end the evacuation of enemy forces from there. OKW had already passed on these instructions to HQ Army Group A by telephone.[60]

Thus at 15.30, OKH was able to send out the order that the armoured forces were to go into action again, and Army Group A received orders to push its armour close enough to Dunkirk to bombard roads and railway points, and thus prevent enemy transports from taking off troops even under cover of darkness. At the same time, it was to make use of every opportunity to drive eastward to encircle the port. Infantry forces were also to advance to the south of the town, so that the road Bailleul–Cassel–Bergues could be kept under effective artillery bombardment. From two to three armoured divisions, supported by the necessary mechanized units, were to attack between Bailleul and Armentières, in order to make contact with Army Group B moving up from the east towards Ypres. A further two armoured divisions were to advance from the area to the south of La Bassée, via Seclin, and towards Tournai. This attacking force was to cut off the enemy still holding out to the south of Lille, and to establish contact with Army Group B to the west of Tournai. Army Group B was to continue its advance in accordance with its general offensive plans.[61]

At last the die was cast. However, a further sixteen hours were to pass before the mobile units were ready to move forward and attack Dunkirk and the heights around Cassel. Some of these units were resting, others were engaged in repair and maintenance work, or in reorganization; new orders had to be drafted and new objectives drawn up before they were ready to move off.

On the whole, too, the German attacks on May 26th were not very effective. On the right wing of the 4th Army, parts of VIII Corps had penetrated into Bouchain, and had extended the bridgeheads on both sides of the town. On Army Group B's sector, the 18th Army and the wing corps of 6th Army were not making as much progress as had been hoped. Their attacks petered out, and enemy resistance remained strong. However, at the least the general line Denterghem–Meulebeke–Iseghem was reached. IV Corps was the only force to make any real progress, and by evening it managed to reach the Yser Canal between Zillebeke and Comines, and get half way to the Dadizeele–Paschendaele area. Following this, the Commander of the 6th Army, General von Reichenau, decided to seal off the north and east front of the Lille fortress area, take the British in a pincer movement on both sides of Kemmel up to Raismes Wood, and at the same time defeat the enemy at Roulers with his right wing. In this way he sought to split the Belgian Army, make contact with von Kleist's group which was pushing forward to Kemmel, and at the same time close the pocket as quickly as possible to the north of Lille. He transferred the weight of his attack completely to XI and IV Corps.[62]

The Capture of Dunkirk

In the early hours of May 27th, the German units from Gravelines to Carvin (Army Group A) at last went forward to the attack, moving in a northeasterly direction. Halder recorded in his diary: 'By midday they were making only slow progress in the Douai pocket, but moving forward more quickly around Béthune. Progress between Bailleul and the coast seemed faster.' The 6th Army was also obviously gaining ground in the direction of Ypres. Enemy resistance was gradually collapsing, but it was a slow process. It should not be forgotten that there were four enemy armies encircled in the cauldron, and that they had no alternative but to stand and fight while their munitions and supplies lasted, though obviously this could not be for long.

Certainly, the course of the fighting on May 27th made it abundantly clear that the British intended to dispute every foot of ground for as long as they could. Everything depended on whether they could keep their east and west flanks intact long enough to allow the mass of their forces to withdraw along the route Lille–Armentières–Bailleul–Bergues into the Channel ports, to be taken off.

In its evening situation report, the 4th Army reported to Army Group A that von Kleist's group, which had reached a line Merville–Eecke–Cassel–Westledringhem–Bollezeele–Gravelines, was in contact with a superior enemy force which was utilizing old German fieldworks and offering obstinate resistance supported by artillery on the hills to the east of Hazebrouk and Cassel. Incidentally, the nature of the terrain did hamper the full use of armour.

For this day the war diaries of the attacking corps, and in particular those of the Panzer corps, all record that the enforced two-day idleness of the armoured divisions was exercising a very unfavourable influence on operations. In their attempts to cross the La Bassée Canal, now obstinately defended by the enemy, the attacking troops were suffering heavy losses. In the meantime, the enemy was engaged in embarking his troops and carrying them back to Britain. Later in the afternoon, 4th Army Command asked Army Group A to send in Air Fleet 2 against Ostend and the other Channel ports, in order to prevent the enemy from continuing his evacuation. In reply Colonel Blumentritt, Army Group Senior Operations Officer, passed on the information that Field-Marshal Göring had ordered the Luftwaffe to attack Dunkirk and prevent any further evacuation.

General Brennecke, Chief of Staff of the 4th Army, described the scene in the Channel ports still occupied by the enemy as follows: 'Large ships are being made fast to the quayside, planks are laid across and men swarm aboard.

All material and equipment is being abandoned.' He dryly suggested to the Senior Operations Officer of Army Group A that it would be a good thing if a subsequent meeting with these men, rested and once more fully equipped, could be avoided. A few hours later General Brennecke again reported that the enemy evacuation was still proceeding apace, and once more suggested that everything possible should be done to prevent or at least hamper it: with flat-trajectory fire, for example. Shortly after midnight, the Commander of the 4th Army informed General von Kleist that the artillery to bombard Dunkirk would arrive at 22.00 hours. It was to be speeded up as far as possible. In the meantime, the enemy had launched one or two counter-attacks on the Somme front, in order to relieve the pressure on Operation 'Dynamo', which was now in full swing.[63]

On May 27th, Army Group B did succeed in breaking through the enemy defences to the south of Thielt, thereby destroying the cohesion of the Belgian troops fighting there. This was the last straw for the Belgians, and it led to the capitulation of the Belgian Army (signed May 28th, at 10.00). However, the German attack from the west and the east was still making only very slow progress. The Dunkirk pocket was only gradually being reduced, and not enough to prevent the enemy from continuing to evacuate his troops, an operation which he was now supporting with all his strength on land, at sea, and in the air. In fact it was not until 09.40 on June 4th, that X Corps of 18th Army was able to report the capture of the bitterly disputed Channel port, after nine days of hard fighting. Both General von Bock and General Halder noted in their diaries: 'The town and the coast are in our hands!' – only to add, with some regret: 'British and French troops gone.'[64]

The obvious question is, why were the German forces unable to attain this objective more quickly? The following considerations may help to provide an answer. First of all, there is the indisputable fact that the Allies extracted every possible advantage from the valuable respite given to them when the German armour was halted. In those precious hours they consolidated their defensive positions, in the west and, in particular, the east. On the Channel front, the respite given was sufficient to allow them to reorganize their forces and establish an effective defensive line. Incidentally, the British were well aware that their position was much more critical on the east front, because they had to reckon at any moment with the collapse of the Belgian Army. It was certainly a cardinal decision on the part of Lord Gort, when he took the two divisions (the 5th and the 50th) which he had been holding in reserve, and committed them to the south of Ypres in support of his front line where it made contact with the Belgians. By so doing, he made it possible to withdraw most of the Allied units through a narrow corridor to the port of Dunkirk. Further, it must be stressed that the Allied troops fought magnificently, and worthily upheld the traditions that had so impressed the Germans in the First World War. Another factor which must not be overlooked in this connection was the courageous defence of Boulogne and Calais. This was by no means useless, since it delayed the attack of XIX Corps on Dunkirk for a number of crucial hours.[65]

But in the last resort, these were not the decisive factors; a number of German mistakes were made, and they contributed to the final result. The first mistake was to regard the Flanders cauldron as a subordinate front, and to shift the centre of attention too soon. In fact its strategic importance was not recognized until too late, and this was largely because it was not clear until almost the last moment how many enemy troops were actually in the cauldron. German estimates at the time were in the neighbourhood of only 100,000 men! From May 27th onwards, the attention of the higher Staffs was more and more directed to the next operational planning tasks, and so there was less time for Dunkirk.

Above all, the principle Rundstedt underlined after the war (with reference to Dunkirk): 'bring one operation to a close before you start thinking of the next', was insufficiently regarded. As a result, the battle in Flanders was not pursued with sufficient vigour and determination.

Again, it would have been more practical to put the 4th Army under the command of Army Group B, after the break-through to the Channel coast. This is what Brauchitsch wanted and Hitler prevented. In that case, Army Group A, whose attention had been turned more to the south from the start, and whose 71 divisions were obviously being over-strained, could then have held the Somme line (offensively or defensively). If all the forces operating against the Flanders cauldron had been put under General von Bock's command, the town and port of Dunkirk would have been captured sooner and more easily. If this had been done, certain defects of organization caused by the two Army groups coming together in such a confined space, could have been avoided. Again, it was certainly an error to move troops in gradually from the south (around Lille) instead of first sealing off the ring in the north – in the immediate neighbourhood of Dunkirk – by a reinforced outer enveloping wing (von Kleist's armoured group). It may be, too, that the German troops had lost some of their original *élan*. After uninterrupted heavy fighting and forced marches, they were beginning to feel the need for a rest. Their attention was drawn too soon to the next big tasks awaiting them, with the result that to some extent the Dunkirk operations were carried through half-heartedly, and the units concerned did not commit their full resources to the battle. This was true in particular of XVI and XIX Corps. Before the battle had reached its height the mobile units were already being relieved. Finally, the leaders of the Wehrmacht overestimated the ability and effectiveness of the Luftwaffe[66]. The limits of its powers became apparent for the first time and the legend of its 'invincibility' was destroyed.

The mistakes made by Germany's military leaders – certainly not the famous 'halt' order alone – as we have roughly sketched them here, together with the fight put up by the Allied troops, are the real reasons why the tactical objective of Operation 'Yellow' was not attained. The majority of the British Expeditionary Force was able to get back safe and sound, if without its equipment, to its home bases in the British Isles; and instead of winning a battle of annihilation, the German Army had to content itself with 'just an ordinary victory'.

Nevertheless, to assume from this that Great Britain would have been ready to conclude peace in the event of a 'total' German victory in the field, and that therefore in missing this victory Germany let slip her great historical chance, and dropped the palm of victory when it was practically in her hands, is going too far. It is in fact quite certain that even if the German Army had won a battle of annihilation in Flanders, the Churchill Government would still have fought on with all its strength. We must, therefore, not over-dramatize the battle of Dunkirk or exaggerate its influence on the further course of the war.[67]

The Outlook

The German divisions were regrouped as quickly as possible, and by June 5th they were ready to embark on Operation 'Red', of which the objective was to destroy 'all the Allied forces remaining in France'. This operation was planned to take place in three successive stages. The attack was to move forward in a southeasterly direction on both sides of Rheims, between Paris and the Argonne; destroy the French army in the Paris–Belfort–Metz area; and bring about the collapse of the Maginot Line positions by combined frontal and out-flanking attacks.

In the first stage of the forthcoming Battle of France, the decimated and already largely demoralized enemy was to be thrown back to the south and southwest by swift and concentric offensive blows, and then hurled against his own defensive line in the east. On June 14th, the day that Paris was occupied, without a struggle, Army Group C under General von Leeb, which had so far been held back on the south wing of the German advance, joined in the fighting. In a very short space of time, its 1st and 7th Armies broke into a fortified line which had been regarded as impregnable. On June 10th, Italy, encouraged by the military successes of her Axis partner, entered the war on Germany's side and launched an Alpine offensive. It proved a failure.

However, owing to the German attack, France's position rapidly deteriorated and within a few days was clearly hopeless. The Pétain Government, which had been formed on June 17th, had no alternative but to surrender, and the capitulation was signed on June 22nd, 1940, in the Forest of Compiègne. In an unexampled and breath-taking campaign, Germany had decisively defeated a gallant enemy who had withstood all her efforts in the First World War.[68]

Hitler was now master of the greater part of western and central Europe. Not unnaturally, the self-confidence of the German people soared in this great hour of triumph. The underlying danger was that reasonable and sober estimates of the military possibilities were scarce – and this was not merely true of Hitler. Above all, the leadership of the Reich did not succeed in extracting any real political advantage from this great military victory. All too quickly the great error became clear: Britain was not defeated and she had no intention of surrendering. On the contrary, she seemed more than ever determined to carry on the struggle to the bitter end and with all the resources she could muster.

As Hitler was unwilling to bring the struggle to an end by political means, he looked around for ways to satisfy his far-reaching ambitions by force of arms. The time for important, even fateful, decisions was rapidly approaching. For Germany's military leadership Dunkirk was the first great turning-point in the Second World War. Hitler was confident that with this battle he had demonstrated his 'military invincibility' to the world. Had not the victory been won, to some extent at least, in accordance with his own ideas? The campaign also confirmed his belief in his own military genius, while National Socialist propaganda went to reckless lengths to develop a single instance into a myth of invincibility. This was the original source of Hitler's military *hubris*, the psychological factor which as time went on was to exercise a more and more deleterious effect on Germany's conduct of the war. Further, it was during the Dunkirk campaign that Hitler first forced OKH to accept his own military views, by short-circuiting it at a critical juncture of the fighting and transferring a decision of far-reaching importance to a subordinate command whose views happened to coincide with his own. In the last resort this was an important step towards the confusion which later so confounded Germany's military leadership. What now developed was a gradual inner dissolution of the chain of command; the actual military instrument of leadership (OKH) was undermined, overruled, and finally abolished altogether – with terrible consequences for the German people.

Chronicle III

May 1940

to

December 1940

Politics		Conduct of the War
Neutrals	Axis Powers and their Allies	Axis Powers and their Allies
		May 10, 1940: German Western offensive. May 14, 1940: Luftwaffe attacks Rotterdam. May 20, 1940: German tanks break through to Channel coast.
June 12, 1940: Spain declares her intention of remaining non-belligerent. June 14–28, 1940: Soviet forces march into Lithuania, Latvia, Estonia, Bessarabia and North Bukovina.		June 4, 1940: Fall of Dunkirk. June 4 to 10, 1940: Operation 'Juno', with Germ Navy, against possible British evacuation northern Norway. June 5 to 24, 1940: Battle of France. June 22, 1940: Signing of Franco-German arm tice agreement. June 1940 to March 1941: Second Phase of th Battle of the Atlantic. Pocket battleships cruisers, auxiliary cruisers and U-boats in th North Atlantic and other world oceans.
	July 10, 1940: Italy declares war. July 19, 1940: Hitler's Reichstag speech, with its 'peace offer'. July 21, 1940: Hitler orders preparations for an attack on the Soviet Union.	July 10, 1940: Air attacks on British Chan convoys begin. July 16, 1940: Führer Directive No. 16 ('Sea Lio August 1, 1940: Führer Directive No. 17. August 5 to 19, 1940: Italians conquer Brit Somaliland. August 13, 1940: Beginning of the Battle of Brita August 17, 1940: Establishment of Germ 'operational area' around Britain, in wh all ships to be sunk without warning.
September 4, 1940: General Antonescu declared Head of State in Rumania. September 6, 1940: King Carol of Rumania abdicates in favour of his son Michael.	August 30, 1940: Second Vienna Arbitration Decision. September 27, 1940: Conclusion of a Three-Power Pact between Germany, Italy and Japan. October 23, 1940: Hitler meets Franco at Hendaye. October 24, 1940: Hitler meets Pétain in France.	September 13, 1940: Italian offensive agai Egypt begins. September 21 to 22, 1940: First successful operati of five U-boats against British conv 77,000 GRT sunk. October 12, 1940: Postponement of Operation 'S Lion' until 1941. October 17 to 20, 1940: Eight U-boats si 153,000 GRT in two convoys. October 28, 1940: Italians invade Greece. End of October 1940 to end of March 1941: Fo German warships sink 266,000 GRT in Atlantic.
December 7, 1940: Franco refuses German request for permission to send troops through Spain to attack Gibraltar. December 12, 1940: Hungarian-Yugoslav Pact of Friendship.	November 12 to 13, 1940: Soviet Foreign Minister Molotov visits Berlin. November 20, 1940: Hungary joins Three-Power Pact. November 23, 1940: Rumania joins Three-Power Pact. November 24, 1940: Slovakia joins Three-Power Pact. December 5, 1940: Marshal Badoglio resigns as Chief of the Italian General Staff. General Cavallero his successor.	November 12, 1940: Führer Directive No. 18. November 14 to 15, 1940: Luftwaffe attack Coventry. November 29, December 3 and 7, 1940: Sand-ta planning in German Army High Commar campaign against Russia. December 13, 1940: Führer Directive No. ('Marita'). December 18, 1940: Führer Directive No. ('Barbarossa').

Conduct of the War	Politics	
The Western Allies	The Western Allies	Neutrals

The Western Allies	The Western Allies	Neutrals
May 1 to 2, 1940: British forces evacuate Namsos and Andalsnes. May 10, 1940: British land in Iceland. May 15 to 16, 1940: Ninety-three RAF aircraft attack industrial targets in the Ruhr. May 26, 1940: Operation 'Dynamo' begins. June 3, 1940: Evacuation of Narvik begins.	May 15, 1940: Dutch sign capitulation. May 19, 1940: General Weygand appointed Supreme Commander of all Allied forces in France. May 28, 1940: Belgians sign capitulation.	
June 9, 1940: End of Norwegian resistance. June 11 to 12, 1940: First RAF raid on Turin.	June 10, 1940: Surrender of Norwegian fighting forces. June 16, 1940: Churchill's offer of Anglo-French political union rejected by France. June 17, 1940: Marshal Pétain asks for an armistice.	
July 3, 1940: Destruction of French fleet in Oran by British Task Force 'H'. July 9, 1940: First engagement between Italian fleet and British Mediterranean Fleet, near Punta Stilo in the Ionian Sea.	July 22, 1940: British Foreign Minister, Lord Halifax, rejects Hitler's 'peace offer'.	July 19, 1940: President Roosevelt signs the Two-Ocean Navy Expansion Act. August 8, 1940: US aircraft production reaches 900 a month.
August 25 to 26, 1940: First RAF raid on Berlin. September 6, 1940: 'Invasion alarm' in Britain. September 15, 1940: Fifty-six German planes shot down in Battle of Britain. September 23 to 25, 1940: Dakar bombarded by British naval forces. Landing abandoned in face of French resistance.	September 3, 1940: Anglo-American agreement. Britain cedes bases in the West Indies and islands to the east of the North American Continent in exchange for fifty US destroyers.	October 8, 1940: First RAF squadron exclusively of American volunteers is formed.
October 29, 1940: British troops land in Crete. November 11 to 12, 1940: British carrier-borne aircraft attack Italian Fleet in Taranto. November 27, 1940: Indecisive battle fought off Cape Teulada (Sardinia) between Italian Fleet and British Task Force 'H'. December 9, 1940: Beginning of Wavell's counter-offensive in Egypt. December 22, 1940: RAF Fighter Command resumes fighter sweeps over France.		November 4, 1940: Operational Plan 'Dog' in the event of America's entry into the war (Admiral Stark). November 5, 1940: Roosevelt becomes President of the United States for the third time in succession. November 10, 1940: Direct flights of US aircraft from Newfoundland to Northern Ireland begin. December 20, 1940: Formation of National Defense Committee to speed up US war production.

The Battle of Britain[1]

BY KARL KLEE

After the fall of France, Germany was at the height of her military power. There was no further armed enemy on the European mainland. However, under the vigorous and determined leadership of Churchill, Britain refused even to think of capitulation. On the contrary, she worked feverishly to increase her defensive strength, carried on a lively diplomatic activity, and cast around energetically for new allies. As a result, all hopes that Germany's leaders might have had for the speedy conclusion of a compromise peace acceptable to all parties – though the matter had never been thought out very carefully – were now dissipated. Germany could retain what she had so far achieved only if she were prepared to use further armed force, and in consequence her leaders felt that she must continue to take military action or lose the political initiative.[2]

The most radical solution of the problem was hurriedly to improvise plans for a landing in England.[3] After a certain amount of hesitation Hitler finally agreed to regard the invasion of Britain as a practical possibility, but the more his naval, military and Luftwaffe commanders went into the details of the planning and preparations which would be necessary, the more they realized what enormous difficulties an invasion would involve. For one thing, in view of the weakness of the German Navy, they came to the conclusion that an invasion could be successful only if the Luftwaffe could first succeed in winning command of the air, or at least clear air superiority, in the Channel area and over southern England.[4] Thus the war in the air over Britain now became directly related to the plans to stage an invasion. However, unlike the commanders of the other military Services and of OKW as a whole, the Luftwaffe commanders did not at first regard their task exclusively from the standpoint of preparation for an invasion. On the contrary, as we shall see later, they were inclined to regard their operations against Britain as independently conceived and executed, though, of course, in choosing their targets they certainly did to some extent take the invasion into account.

During the campaigns in Poland and France, the beginning of the Luftwaffe offensive coincided with the beginning of the invasion by the German Army. Swift and powerful Luftwaffe attacks quickly destroyed the Polish air force, and the French air force was so crippled from the start that the Luftwaffe enjoyed air superiority, if not complete command of the air, throughout the operations. In other words, after the enemy air force had been destroyed, or

73

at least crippled, and its ground organization dislocated, the German Army, with close support from the Luftwaffe, pushed forward and occupied the enemy's airfields. This procedure could obviously not be used against Britain, and so air warfare – to over-simplify the matter – took the form prophesied by the Italian air theorist General Douhet: offence in the air coupled with defensive measures by other arms, though neither side could call on the sort of resources Douhet had in mind when he developed his theories. For the first time in history an attempt was made to use air power to cripple an enemy to such an extent that he would not thereafter be in a position to offer any serious resistance – in fact it was even hoped that air action alone could force him to sue for peace.

A period of seven weeks lies between the victorious end of the campaign in France and the beginning of the Luftwaffe attack on Britain. These seven weeks were devoted to the necessary expansion of the ground organization to enable the Luftwaffe to carry out the task it had undertaken; including regrouping the Luftwaffe squadrons and briefing them on their objectives. But the very fact that the commanders of the air fleets and air corps to be committed against Britain had also to use this period for drawing up plans for the attack on Britain is proof enough that even after the end of the campaign in France the Luftwaffe Operations Staff had still no very clear idea as to how air warfare against Britain was to be effectively carried out. In order to help us to understand what actually happened we must first take a look at such plans for air operations against Britain as did actually exist, and grasp how it came about that the Luftwaffe command was so unsure of itself.

The Luftwaffe's Plans

The possibility that Britain might, after all, be one of Germany's enemies was first taken into account in the plans of the Commander-in-Chief OKW, Field-Marshal von Blomberg, in June 1937.[5] As German leaders were well aware that Germany's military situation would be very greatly worsened, if not made altogether impossible, by Britain's participation, Hitler was prepared to do a very great deal to ensure Britain's neutrality. However, as insurance against the worst, Germany's military, naval and air leaders were instructed to draw up plans for use should diplomacy fail to persuade Britain to remain neutral. But in the Hossbach memorandum of November 1937 there are no details about war against Britain. Hitler felt quite certain that in the event of a conflict between Germany and Czechoslovakia, Britain would remain neutral.

On May 30th, 1938, some sections of the general plans for war of June 24th, 1937, were replaced by a fresh draft. In particular, the military operations planned against Czechoslovakia were now to be put into execution as quickly as possible in order to present other powers with a *fait accompli* and make any intervention quite hopeless. Should there be a clash in the west, then purely defensive operations were provided for. And in the corresponding directive of OKW for the year 1939–40 issued on April 3rd, 1939, there were only provisions for defensive air operations in the west in the event of a war with Poland. However, there was an addition to this directive which contained instructions for a campaign on the part of the Navy and the Luftwaffe against the enemy's economy. The Luftwaffe was instructed to prepare plans to destroy the food, raw material and productive resources of the enemy, including his war production.

On May 23rd, 1939, Hitler communicated certain ideas to his military leaders, and these ideas later became the basis for still further plans. The main concept was that in view of her absolute dependence on imports, Britain could be forced to surrender by cutting off her supplies. It was not supposed that a quick victory could be won by Luftwaffe action alone; the destruction of the British fleet was envisaged as well and it was to be followed by a campaign against her overseas supply lines. Should Britain intervene in a conflict between Germany and Poland, then the German Army was to occupy areas important as bases for naval and Luftwaffe operations against her. By occupying Holland and Belgium and defeating France in the field, the German Army could create the preliminary conditions for a victorious war against Britain. Thus these ideas of Hitler contain one of the basic concepts of Germany's conduct of the war, and one which came to the fore again and again, namely that Britain could be defeated by cutting her overseas supply lines.

The conclusion of the Russo-German Non-Aggression Pact of August 23rd, 1939, greatly improved Germany's military situation. But even at this late stage there were still no plans for an offensive in the west, only for purely defensive measures in the event of Anglo-French intervention in a German-Polish conflict. The cause of this omission is to be found in the fact that Germany's armaments were still incomplete and certainly far from adequate for a big war. Army organization was to be complete by 1943; the Navy and the Luftwaffe targets were even further off. After the signing of his treaty with Soviet Russia, Hitler felt quite sure that at the worst he would have to cope with no more than a formal declaration of war in the west. In the light of the inadequacy of Germany's armament preparations – which was, of course, no secret for Hitler – his decision to attack Poland makes sense only from this point of view. Göring's attempts to ensure peace in August 1939, and his impulsive observations when he heard that the date for the attack on Poland had been finally fixed, and again when he heard of the declarations of war by Britain and France, are a clear indication that he was under no illusions about the weakness of the Luftwaffe in any offensive war. As Commander-in-Chief of the Luftwaffe his estimate of its capacities was based on detailed studies sponsored by Luftwaffe Group Command 2 (which later became Air Fleet 2) and by the Luftwaffe General Staff.

Up to the beginning of 1938 there were no plans at all for air warfare against Britain, and it was not until the middle of February 1938 that Luftwaffe Group Command 2 was instructed to draw up proposals for action in the event of

Britain's intervening in a war in the west. In the following autumn Luftwaffe Group Command 2 presented two memoranda which made it quite clear that any air war against Britain could have nuisance value only and under no circumstances exercise any decisive effect on the course of a war. It was pointed out that the range of Germany's available bombers would not permit an effective air war against Britain from Germany's Friesian bases. The memoranda went on to say that for such a purpose bases in Holland and Belgium would be essential. It is very interesting to note that right up to the outbreak of war the Luftwaffe staged none of the usual map exercises to test the possibilities of air warfare against Britain.

An evaluation of the situation drawn up by the Luftwaffe Operations Staff, and presented in August 1938, sheds a good deal of light on the way the Luftwaffe subsequently waged the war in the air against Britain. It declares that in the given circumstances there could be no hope whatever of securing a decision by an attack on the enemy's war economy by the Luftwaffe and the Navy. The essential task of the Luftwaffe must therefore be to guarantee the ground forces freedom of operative action.

A study carried out by Operations Branch I of the Luftwaffe General Staff in May 1939 provides us with certain valuable indications, and it makes it clear that the given numerical strength, equipment and training of Luftwaffe Air Fleet 2 would not permit it to secure a quick decision against Britain in the air. At the same time it was pointed out that no decision could be obtained by air attack on Britain's overseas supplies because all her important western and southwestern ports were out of Luftwaffe range. Because of the increasing strength of the air defences no decision could be hoped for by terror attacks on London. On the contrary, such attacks were more likely to produce the opposite effect and undesirably strengthen the national will to resist. The study also held out little hope of success in a show-down with Britain's fighter arm with a view to securing better conditions for a general attack at a later date, because conditions favoured the defence and the losses of the attacking forces were likely to be prohibitively high. This form of air warfare was generally regarded with distrust and misgiving; it would play into the hands of the enemy and distract the attention of the Luftwaffe from its really vital objectives in Britain. The most favourable target for air attack in Britain was her aircraft industry, the study went on. Port and harbour installations and oil storage tanks could also be attacked with profit. On July 9th, 1939, Luftwaffe Air Fleet 2 was given instructions in accordance with this study as to how it should wage air warfare against Great Britain in the event of hostilities. The main targets listed were sites of war industries and supply centres.

In July 1939, Lieutenant-Colonel Schmid, Chief of Intelligence of the Luftwaffe Operations Staff, presented a detailed study of Britain's air strength to Göring. It pointed out that given further systematic development, the RAF could be as strong as the Luftwaffe by 1940. The preliminary condition for any successful air war against Britain was the destruction of the Royal Air Force and the aircraft industry which supplied it. Only after this had been carried out successfully would it be worth while to attack Britain's ports, harbours and shipping. Further, such big objectives would require powerful Luftwaffe forces, and the task would be so arduous that it would not be possible to fix any date by which the campaign could be concluded. The study finally pointed out that because of the well-known ability of the British for improvisation, and their general moral toughness, air attack alone might not secure their surrender, in which case the British Isles would have to be invaded and occupied. This study obviously foresaw very accurately what was to happen in 1940. In post-war literature on the subject the Luftwaffe has almost invariably been accused of making light of its task and exaggerating its prospects of success. The fact is that the Luftwaffe Command held very realistic views concerning its capacities and had a very clear idea indeed of what its weaknesses were likely to be.

We have dealt in some detail with questions relating to the Luftwaffe leadership before the outbreak of the Second World War, since they obviously have a direct bearing on what happened subsequently during the actual Battle of Britain.

From the beginning of the campaign against Poland until the beginning of the Battle of Britain the use of the Luftwaffe against Britain was stepped up only by degrees. Germany's leaders were very much interested in avoiding any serious fighting in the west, until Poland was defeated, and for the time being, therefore, attacks on Britain were forbidden. It was well known that any attacks on London itself were entirely a matter for Hitler in person. All that was allowed was weather reconnaissance over the midlands and the southern counties. On September 10th, 1939, permission to attack British naval forces if they ventured into the neighbourhood of German naval bases or of German minefields was given. Then on October 18th, permission to attack enemy naval units at anchorage was extracted. But it was not until November 1st that the Luftwaffe was allowed to attack enemy convoys. At the end of November, the Luftwaffe Operations Staff discussed the possibility and usefulness of a surprise air attack on Britain. In the end nothing came of this for fear of RAF reprisals against German territory. Even after the RAF had attacked Wilhelmshaven in December 1939, Hitler was unable to make up his mind to step up the air war against Britain because conditions in general were not regarded as favourable. On January 17th, 1940, OKW ordered certain measures at sea and in the air in connection with the coming offensive in the west, but at the same time it struck a cautious note: 'In the interests of the conduct of the war as a whole it is not desirable that anything should be done to step up the air war against Britain to the full until suitable bases have been obtained and until strong forces are available for the purpose.'

It was quite obvious that so long as this view was held nothing could be done, particularly as the Luftwaffe would have enormous difficulties to cope with if any attempt were made to wage an air war against Britain from north

German bases. The situation was to change fundamentally only after the victorious conclusion of the German offensive in the west.

Hitler explained the necessity for the attack on Holland, Belgium and France by calling attention to Germany's unfavourable geographical situation. Bases in these countries were essential if air and submarine warfare were to be waged effectively, otherwise the U-boats would have to make long cruises and the Luftwaffe long flights before they could go into action. When Holland and Belgium, and perhaps parts of the north coast of France, were in German hands, Germany's situation in a war with Britain would be vastly improved. Directive No. 6 for the prosecution of the war contained a significant paragraph. On November 29th Hitler once again insisted that the best way to defeat Britain, Germany's main enemy, was to cut off her supplies and cripple her production. If the German Army were able to capture and occupy some part of the Channel coast, then the Navy and the Luftwaffe would be in a much better position to bring this about. The basic idea of the conduct of the war against Britain is underlined again here: Britain's will to resist could be broken by an all-out war against her supplies.

The discussions which took place concerning Germany's plan of operations and the date on which it was to be implemented showed very clearly that Germany had entered the war in 1939 without any very clear idea of how it was to be fought. When Britain rejected his peace offer made after the conclusion of the campaign against Poland in the autumn of 1939, Hitler felt that an even clearer demonstration of Germany's strength was necessary in order to bring Britain to her senses, persuade her to conclude peace and to tolerate German hegemony on the continent. This demonstration was to be the military defeat of the Western Allies in Europe, and that should, in Hitler's view, be the end of the war. Once again there was no carefully worked out plan showing how this should be achieved. However, Hitler felt confident that once the job was done Britain would see reason. As it turned out, he was wrong. Defeated on the continent, and with her allies defeated too, Britain was still not prepared to give up; Germany's triumphs in Poland, Norway and France made no difference, so all that remained was to wage war directly and exclusively against Britain herself.

Incidentally, the destruction of the British Empire was not part of Hitler's general political conception. He could see clearly enough that its collapse would not benefit Germany, and that other powers were much more likely to derive advantages from it. Rather hesitantly, therefore, he now turned his attention to the plans for an invasion of Britain. Even when he had more or less made up his mind to launch an invasion, he was still worried about the dangers which he thought he could see threatening Germany from the east. For one thing, Germany was very dependent on supplies of oil from Rumania, and for another he was disturbed at the increasing demands of the Russians. His lively imagination did not need much prompting to imagine the dangerous situation that could develop if Germany had her hands full with an invasion of

Britain and was therefore not in a position to oppose Russian advances in the east. In this situation, and in view of his keen anxiety about the political effect of any military set-back, he insisted that every avoidable risk be eliminated before an invasion of Britain. In the end he decided against an invasion because in his view the preliminary conditions for the certain success of a landing were unobtainable.

Even after the successful conclusion of the campaign against France, a detailed plan for the prosecution of the war was once more clearly absent. The next stage of the planning – an invasion in 1940 and the defeat of Britain on her own ground – had to be drawn up hurriedly. Hitler was a man in a very great hurry indeed, because he already had a vast project in mind for 1941, namely the destruction of the Soviet Union. We must keep in mind this background against which the Battle of Britain developed.

We need not go into any details here of the plans and preparations made for a landing in Britain, though we must certainly take into consideration the close connection between the Battle of Britain and Operation 'Sea Lion', or 'Seelöwe', the code name for the invasion. In particular, we shall have to examine the question whether the air war against Britain was carried out as a preparation for invasion, or whether the Luftwaffe was out to obtain a decision against Britain by air warfare alone. First of all, therefore, let us briefly review the operations of the Luftwaffe from the ending of the offensive in the west to the beginning of the Battle of Britain.

On June 30th, 1940, eight days after the signing of the armistice with France, Göring issued a general directive[6] for the air war against Britain, from which the following is an extract: 'The operational use of the Luftwaffe against Britain will demand the closest co-ordination between Air Fleets 2, 3 and 5, both in synchronization and in the choice of targets. Generally speaking, therefore, orders to the individual air fleets will include definite targets and times of attack. In this way it is hoped, in addition to whatever material effect can be caused, to dislocate the defence by presenting it simultaneously with as many different tasks as possible.

'Once the units have been regrouped in their new bases, adequate flak and fighter cover provided, and arrangements perfected for uninterrupted supplies and efficient transmission of orders, systematic action will begin against such targets and groups of targets as the Ob.d.L. will decide from time to time. Until then, and in addition to bringing the units up to a complete state of readiness:

'(a) active operations against Britain are to be confined to nuisance raids by relatively minor forces on industrial and RAF targets. Such attacks are to be carried out during suitable weather when surprise is possible, and also in daylight by single aircraft or in pairs. If such operations are to be successful it is essential that the targets to be attacked should be very carefully studied both on the map and from the target data. For the time being heavy civilian casualties are to be avoided if possible;

'(*b*) air crews are to be systematically briefed on their new field of operations. Reconnaissance flights and small group missions will at the same time test the strength and organization of the enemy defence.

'1. *Objectives*

'When regrouped and in a full state of readiness the Luftwaffe will aim:

'(*a*) to create the conditions necessary for a successful campaign against the enemy's war industry and supply lines by defeating his air force, destroying his ground organization, and disrupting his aircraft industry, thus defending Germany's own *Lebensraum*;

'(*b*) to dislocate Britain's supplies by attacking ports, and harbour installations, ships bringing supplies into the country, and warships escorting them.

'These two tasks are to be carried out in concert and not treated separately. So long as the enemy air force remains in being, the supreme principle of air warfare must be to attack it at every possible opportunity by day and by night, in the air and on the ground with priority over other tasks.'

This document shows clearly that after the destruction of the RAF, the aim of the Luftwaffe was to smash Britain's supply organization and war industry. However, its leaders felt that it would be inadvisable to begin such a struggle before the necessary preparations were completed. First of all, an adequate ground organization had to be built up, then the units had to be regrouped, and only when all these preparations had been thoroughly carried out would there be any chance of waging a successful air war against Britain. Thus they were very well aware of the difficulties they would have to cope with, but what was lacking – as happened so often on the German side during the Second World War – was a proper appreciation of both the German and the Allied situation.

On July 11th Göring issued a further directive,[7] this time for operations against British shipping, for nuisance attacks generally, and for briefing air crews on their new target areas.

On July 21st Göring, who had in the meantime been promoted to Reich Marshal, conferred with the commanders-in-chief of Air Fleets 2, 3 and 5. His instructions were that until the real air battle began only minor forces were to be sent against Britain. Strong forces might be used only for attacks on convoys and naval units in Scapa Flow. Target priority on land should be given to the British aircraft industry. It is interesting to note that Göring expressly forbade his planes to bomb port and harbour installations on the south coast, which would be required intact by an invading force at a later date; this indicates the connection between the Battle of Britain and the proposed Operation 'Sea Lion'. In discussing the use to be made of the 9th Air Division, he expressly forbade the laying of mines along the south coast. It is obvious, therefore, that at this stage the Luftwaffe reckoned with the possibility of landings in Britain, and was choosing its targets accordingly.[8]

The Luftwaffe Operations Staff knew about the preliminary invasion discussions going on in the Wehrmacht's Operations Staff as early as June 25th, 1940, and its technical Staff Officer, Major Freiherr von Falkenstein requested the Operations Staff of the Luftwaffe to examine the Wehrmacht proposals, which were to be set before Hitler in the next few days. The Luftwaffe Chief of Staff, General Hans Jeschonnek, refused this request because in his view Hitler was not then contemplating any attempt to cross the Channel. But later on the situation changed, and orders were issued by OKW which left no further doubt as to Hitler's desire that preparations should now be made for an invasion of Britain.[9] However, the most important condition for an invasion was still command of the air over southern England.

If the orders issued by Luftwaffe command did not at first always reflect the intention to invade, the main reason for this was that the destruction of the RAF was the primary and all-important objective of Luftwaffe operations. Once this objective had been secured, then the characteristics of aerial warfare would make a sudden change of individual target and an alteration of the main weight of attack possible. Nevertheless, the Luftwaffe also formally set itself the task of covering those objectives insisted on by the German Army and Navy as the essential conditions for an invasion: namely, command of the air over southern England and the crippling of the British fleet.

With regard to the latter objective, on July 21st Göring extended the targets listed on July 11th; in addition to attacks on shipping in the Channel and along the east coast, he specified that the British fleet should also be attacked whenever possible. However, the main aim of Luftwaffe operations was still as before. Air armament production was to be attacked only as a subsidiary target. The objective of the preliminary battles was to secure a permanent weakening of morale, material and personnel in the British fighter force. Once this had been obtained the bombers and dive-bombers would be able to attack RAF ground organization under much more favourable conditions.

The actual start of the Battle of Britain was considerably delayed. There were various reasons for this. For one thing, the heavy demands made on the Luftwaffe during the campaign in France and Flanders had naturally weakened it; for example, the number of front-line bombers available fell from 1,102 on March 30th, 1940, to 841 on June 29th. 635 of these were lost, though this number included all planes which suffered more than 10 per cent damage. By the time the big air attack on Britain started, the number of aircraft ready for action had been increased once more, to 949. In the months of April, May and June the Luftwaffe lost 2,784 planes, including 231 short-range and 106 long-range reconnaissance planes, 579 fighters, 216 twin-engined fighters and night-fighters (Me–110 and Ju–88), 976 bombers, 187 ground attack aircraft, 242 transport planes, 90 seaplanes, and 67 communications aircraft.[10] The Luftwaffe's preliminary aim now was to build up the necessary ground organization and to replenish its units both in personnel and equipment. Very many units were still stationed on distant German airfields and it was not possible to transfer them to the west until the airfields in the newly-occupied western territories had been enlarged to receive them. All these measures took time.

During this period of intensive preparation the Luftwaffe, generally speaking, held its fire, flying only nuisance raids against railways, docks, storage depots, aircraft factories and airfields, though the 9th Air Division was also used for mining waters adjacent to ports and harbours, and river estuaries, and for attacks on shipping. During July 1940 the Luftwaffe flew 5,376 individual missions (not including fighter missions), and dropped only 1,473 tons of bombs. 135 planes were lost, but 293 enemy planes were claimed as having been destroyed during these operations. In addition 223,000 GRT of shipping were claimed as sunk, though the actual number is now known to have been 70,193 GRT. 363,000 GRT was reported as having been damaged.

The Contact Phase

The period between the end of the campaign in France and the beginning of the big air battles is generally referred to in German war histories as the 'contact' phase. Although during this period it became quite clear that the RAF fighter planes were every bit as good as the Luftwaffe fighters, it was also obvious that generally speaking their fighter pilots were avoiding battle as far as possible. The reason for this was not far to seek: those responsible for the RAF were determined to husband their fighters for the time when Germany either sent over powerful bomber formations or attempted an invasion. The result was that the Luftwaffe enjoyed command of the air by default in those areas it penetrated with reasonably strong forces, but it was unable to force a decision and make this permanent. The discussions which took place at this time about intensifying the air war suggest that Luftwaffe High Command was under no illusions.

Although operational plans had been drawn up for Air Fleet No. 2 before the war, there was still no generally accepted idea of the best methods of attack on Britain. To some extent this was probably because no one had ever foreseen such a favourable situation as now existed after the complete defeat of the Allies in Europe.

Following a discussion between Göring and his Air Fleet commanders on July 21st, 1940, Air Fleets 2 and 3 drafted proposals for the conduct of the air war against Britain, basing their suggestions on studies carried out by their own Air Corps. The Luftwaffe Operations Staff met on July 29th to discuss these proposals. On August 1st the Air Fleets presented revised proposals. Göring considered them, and on August 2nd, he gave the final order to intensify the air war against Britain.

The proposals made by I and VIII Air Corps are still extant.[11] VIII Air Corps's proposals were limited chiefly to operations in its own area. A further link between the Battle of Britain and Operation 'Sea Lion' now becomes visible in the proposals of I Air Corps, which mention a new task in addition to the primary one of winning the command of the air, namely the protection of troops being ferried across the Channel and close support for the landing operations. The most interesting contribution on the conduct of the air war against Britain came from II Air Corps. Writing after the war, General Paul Deichmann, who was Chief of Staff of II Air Corps during the Battle of Britain, recalls that the proposals he submitted to Air Fleet 2 (to which II Air Corps was attached) included the following: 'German bomber squadrons must not be committed against objectives in the interior until the enemy fighter arm has been materially weakened. The enemy, however, is in a position to prevent this. In view of the short range of German fighter planes, which extends little beyond London, German bombers cannot attack airfields beyond this range if those airfields are defended by fighter planes. However, there is a way in which Britain's fighters can be got into the air, and that is to attack London. For a variety of reasons London is so important to the British that they would throw in their last fighter to defend it. Thus by attacking London we can force the British fighters to accept battle. Once Britain's fighter arm has been weakened in this way, we can use our bomber squadrons to attack other important objectives with impunity. As I was told soon afterwards by the Luftwaffe Chief of Staff, General Jeschonnek, this idea was adopted as the basis for the first phase of the Battle of Britain. But when it came to the point, Hitler forbade us to attack London, and so our plans broke down.'

Deichmann's proposal was a clear-sighted estimate of what was to happen later. In view of the evasive tactics adopted by the British, the only chance the Luftwaffe had of forcing Fighter Command to accept battle was to attack the British capital.

On August 1st, 1940, by which time the Luftwaffe had practically concluded its preliminary discussions, OKW issued general instructions for intensifying the war against Britain both at sea and in the air:

'In order to establish the necessary conditions for Britain's final defeat it is my intention to intensify both air and sea war against the British Motherland. To this end I therefore order the following:

'1. The Luftwaffe will use all the forces at its disposal to destroy the British air force as quickly as possible. Luftwaffe attacks must be primarily directed against enemy planes, their ground organization and their supply system, and also against the aircraft industry, and factories producing anti-aircraft equipment.

'2. Once local air superiority has been won the air war will be turned against the enemy's ports, and in particular against food-supply organization and food-supply centres in the interior. In view of our future plans, operations against south coast ports and harbours are to be kept to a necessary minimum.

'3. Air attacks on enemy warships and merchant shipping may therefore be kept to a minimum in the interests of the above instructions, except where particularly favourable opportunities arise; or where the success of the operations ordered in para. 2 above can be consolidated; or where such attacks are considered necessary for the training of bomber crews for future operations.

'4. This intensified air warfare must be so waged that it always remains possible for the Luftwaffe to provide adequate support to naval operations against favourable targets of opportunity. Further, the Luftwaffe must be fully available for Operation "Sea Lion".

'5. I reserve to myself the decision with regard to terror attacks as reprisals.

'6. August 5th is the first day on which this intensified air war may begin, but the exact date is to be left to the Luftwaffe and will depend on how soon its preparations are complete, and on the weather situation.

'At the same time, the Navy will be allowed to intensify its own operations.

(Signed) Adolf Hitler
K(eitel).'

These instructions for the stepping up of sea and air warfare against Britain suggest that the object is no longer to make the British Government more inclined to negotiate. There is also no suggestion that Britain can be forced to sue for peace because of air and sea warfare alone. On the contrary, it is made very clear that the aim is 'to establish the necessary conditions for Britain's defeat'. One passage expressly insists that the Luftwaffe must at all times be fully available to support Operation 'Sea Lion'. However, as we shall see, the Luftwaffe High Command did not interpret these instructions to mean that the aim of its operations must be to create the conditions necessary for a landing. And yet this is the only interpretation which can be placed on the text as it stands. In addition, as early as June 25th, the Luftwaffe Operations Staff had been informed that OKW was considering the possibility of an invasion of Britain. In particular, Directive No. 16 specifically laid down the tasks of the Luftwaffe in the event of landing operations: it was to fight off all interference by enemy planes and at the same time give close support to the landing operations themselves. This job of preventing the RAF from interfering with landing operations would naturally be much easier to carry out if the Luftwaffe had already succeeded in materially weakening the RAF before landings were attempted, or, better still, if it had succeeded in destroying the RAF altogether. Weakening or destroying the RAF was thus for the time being the immediate aim and the Luftwaffe concentrated on it. Certainly at this early stage it was thought just possible that a decision against Britain could be obtained by operational air warfare, though as yet experience provided no answer to the question whether this was possible with the means available.

Two days before Directive No. 17 was issued, OKW intimated to Göring that his preparations for the big attack on Britain should be so made that the attack could begin within twelve hours of his receiving the order from Hitler. However, the operational planning of the Luftwaffe was being held up by the need to co-ordinate the various proposals made by the Air Fleets for the

Chronicle IV

January

to

May 1941

Politics		Conduct of the War
Neutrals	Axis Powers and their Allies	Axis Powers and their Allies
January: The Japanese Admiral Yamamoto acts on his own initiative in ordering a study of the possibilities of a carrier attack on Pearl Harbour.		January 10th to 11th: Heavy German air on Malta convoy. January 11th: Führer Directive establishes G armoured force in Libya.
	January 14th: Meeting of Hitler and Marshal Antonescu. January 19th to 20th: Meeting of Hitler and Mussolini: German decision to attack Greece.	
	January 30th: Chief of Finnish General Staff visits OKH (Army High Command HQ).	February 8th: German convoy leaves Nap
		February 12th: General Rommel arrives in T
March 1st: Bulgaria joins the Three-Power Pact.		March 2nd: German troops enter Bulgaria
		March 9th: New Italian offensive in Greece
March 25th: Yugoslavia joins the Three-Power Pact. March 27th: Military *putsch* in Belgrade.	March 27th to March 29th: Japanese Foreign Minister Matsuoka visits Berlin.	March 16th: Italian offensive bogged down March 19th to 20th: Heavy German air r London. March 27th: Führer Directive for the atta Yugoslavia.
April 3rd: *Coup d'état* in Iraq. April 5th: Soviet Union and Yugoslavia sign a Pact of Non-Aggression.		March 31st: Italo-German counter-offens North Africa. April to December: Third phase of Battle Atlantic (1.86 million GRT sunk). April 6th: German Balkans campaign.
April 13th: Soviet Union and Japan sign a Treaty of Friendship and Non-Aggression.		April 16th to 17th: Air raid on London. April 17th: Capitulation of Yugoslav Army April 19th: Heavy air raid on London. April 21st to 23rd: Greeks sign capitulation
	April 24th: Discussion between Hitler and the Hungarian Regent, Admiral Horthy.	April 28th: Sollum captured.
May 6th: Stalin becomes Chairman of the Council of People's Commissars.	May 10th: Rudolf Hess, Deputy-Führer, flies to Britain. May 13th: Hitler's decree for martial law in the 'Barbarossa' area (Eastern Front).	May 10th to 11th: Heavy air raid on London
May 15th: Pétain broadcasts on Franco-German collaboration.	May 18th: Italo-Croat Treaty cedes parts of Yugoslavia and almost all the Dalmatian islands to Italy.	May 16th: Italian forces in Abyssinia surren May 17th to 18th: First air mines dropped i Canal. May 20th: German parachute landings on May 24th: Battleship *Bismarck* and cruiser *Eugen* sink the battle-cruiser *Hood*. May 27th: Sinking of the *Bismarck*. May 28th: British evacuate Crete.

Conduct of the War	Politics	
The Western Allies	The Western Allies	Neutrals
		January 6th: US President Roosevelt on the 'Four Freedoms'.
		January 13th: Greek Government rejects Britain's offer of troops.
ary 19th: British offensive against Eritrea.	January 20th: British Defence Committee decides to occupy Benghazi and the Dodecanese and establish strategic reserves for use in the Balkans.	
ary 22nd: British capture Tobruk.		
ary 24th: British march into Abyssinia.		
		January 29th: Secret Anglo-American Staff talks open in Washington.
uary 6th: British capture Benghazi.		
uary 9th: British Task Force 'H' bombards Genoa.	February 10th: Diplomatic relations with Rumania broken off.	
uary 11th: RAF raids Hanover (189 planes). First use of four-engined heavy bombers (against Rotterdam).		
uary 15th: British take Chisimaju in Somaliland.	February 24th: British War Cabinet approves proposed expedition to Greece.	
uary 25th: British capture Mogadiscio.		
ch 4th: British raid Lofoten.		
ch 5th: First British troops leave Egypt.		
ch 7th: British troops from Egypt land on Volos and in Piraeus.		
ch 16th: Berbera (British Somaliland) recaptured.		March 11th: Lease-Lend comes into force.
ch 28th: Sea battle off Cape Matapan (three Italian cruisers sunk).		
l 6th: British occupy Addis Abbaba.		
		April 7th: US Operational Plan 'Rainbow 5' (US strategy towards the Axis Powers): 'Europe first'.
l 8th: British occupy Massawa (Eritrea).		April 9th: Danish Ambassador grants US Government air bases in Greenland.
l 15th to 16th: British destroyers smash Axis North Africa convoy.		
l 24th: British evacuate Greece.		April 21st to 27th: Military discussions in Singapore between Holland, Australia, New Zealand and the United States.
2nd: Fighting between British and Iraq forces.		
8th to 9th: RAF attacks Hamburg and Bremen (359 planes).		
16th to 19th: Duke of Aosta capitulates with his forces at Amba Alagi in Abyssinia.		
		May 27th: President Roosevelt declares 'Unlimited National Emergency.
30th: Fighting in Iraq ceases.		

The Battle for Crete 1941

BY KARL GUNDELACH

*The Development of the European Situation from Autumn 1940,
and the Decision to attack Crete*

The German victory in France, Belgium and the Netherlands had driven Britain from western Europe, and at the same time considerably diminished her influence in southeast Europe, whose states, all backward in the matter of modern armaments, sought to avoid a clash with the strongest military power on the Continent.

The tension between Hungary, Bulgaria and Rumania in the Balkans had been relieved by the Vienna arbitration decision imposed by Germany and Italy – without Soviet Russia – on August 30th, 1940. Although Rumania lost most as the result of this decision, she nevertheless sought closer relations with Germany, because she recognized clearly that with Britain powerless on the Continent Germany was the only power strong enough to protect the rest of her territory – even against Soviet Russia. Hitler was prepared to meet Rumanian wishes up to a point because, for one thing, he was interested in the Ploesti oilfields, on which to a very great extent depended Germany's ability to continue the war. In October, a German military mission under General Hansen and a Luftwaffe mission under General Speidel arrived in Rumania. Germany was also anxious to explore the possibility of involving Rumania in the campaign against Russia, which was already under consideration.

While this was going on in eastern Europe, the Battle of Britain was still raging in the west, though the disappointing situation there had already caused the postponement of Operation 'Sea Lion'. As we have seen, the postponement was decided on not only because the Luftwaffe had failed to gain command of the air in the Battle of Britain,[1] but also because Germany's naval chiefs were very doubtful about the whole undertaking; and, in the last resort, because Hitler himself was inwardly none too confident of the outcome.

Germany was interested in securing peace in southeast Europe, because of its economic importance and her own military plans. Italy should have recognized the wisdom of this, particularly as her drive into Egypt, which had started on September 13th, was already bogged down at Sidi Barrani. But instead of concentrating all his efforts in the Mediterranean, where Britain was now weak enough to make a vigorous attack promising, Mussolini turned

99

against Greece, which he invaded on October 28th. For one thing Mussolini had allowed himself to be provoked by Germany's measures in Rumania, and for another – badly advised by his Foreign Minister, Ciano – he anticipated a quick success. It is well known now that Germany was completely taken by surprise by Italy's action, which she found most unwelcome. It is late in the day, and perhaps rather pointless, to add one more voice to the many which have criticized the separate and divergent war efforts of the Axis powers, but one thing seems certain: quite apart from the personalities of the two chief actors, and apart from political reasons – for example, consideration for Mussolini's position in Italy – it was for military reasons impossible at that time to shift the main weight of operations to the Mediterranean.[2] All the essential conditions for doing this successfully were absent. However, it must be pointed out that Hitler was repeatedly urged to do just this, particularly by naval and military advisers – for example, by Admiral Raeder, though the Navy was even weaker in the Mediterranean than elsewhere.[3]

Führer Directive No. 18, signed by Hitler on November 12th, 1940, that is on the day of Molotov's visit to Berlin, clearly reflects the uncertainty which prevailed in the autumn of 1940, after the failure of the Luftwaffe in the Battle of Britain, the postponement of Operation 'Sea Lion', and the unexpected and unwelcome outbreak of war in the Balkans. In this directive, Hitler examines every possibility for waging war against his main enemy, Britain, and reviews the whole European situation as it appeared to him then: Germany's relations with France, and the possibility that France might be persuaded to join in the war against Britain; the attitude of Spain and Portugal to Operation 'Felix' (the proposed attack on Gibraltar and on the Canary and Cape Verde Islands); and Germany's contribution to the Italian offensive against Egypt. The directive then turned its attention to the southeast and the east.

Foreseeing the difficulties which Italy would encounter as the result of a winter campaign against Greece, and realizing the chance this would offer Britain to regain a foothold on the Continent, Hitler instructed his Army C.-in-C., von Brauchitsch, to make preparations to 'attack, if necessary, *Greek territory* from Bulgaria and occupy it to the north of the Aegean Sea, thus providing the Luftwaffe with bases from which to operate effectively, particularly against those British *air bases* from which *Rumania's oilfields* could be threatened.'[4] Recognizing the importance of Turkey's role, 'the discussions and military movements are to be based on the use of a force amounting to about ten divisions.' In order to speed up the necessary deployment measures the military mission in Rumania was to be strengthened as soon as possible. Göring was similarly instructed to strengthen the Luftwaffe mission in Rumania, and to make preparations to establish Luftwaffe units in the southeast Balkans; he was also to establish an aircraft reporting service on the southern frontier of Bulgaria. Referring to the great problem of Russia, which was to affect the whole Balkan campaign, and in particular the Battle of Crete, the directive observes: 'Political discussions have begun with a view to clarifying

Russia's attitude in the immediate future. Irrespective of the outcome of these discussions, all oral instructions regarding preparations in the east remain valid and such preparations are to be continued.'

By the middle of November the Italians had been forced on to the defensive in Albania, and were having difficulty in holding their positions. The first German assistance was afforded by a German air transport group, but it was already clear that very much more would have to be done.

Führer Directive No. 20 was signed on December 13th, 1940, and in it Hitler lays down the general lines of the offensive Germany now planned against Greece (Operation 'Marita'). It will be discussed here only because it underlined the ideas which subsequently led to the attack on Crete.

The directive begins by pointing out that the threatening situation in Albania made it doubly important that Britain's efforts to establish air bases under cover of a Balkan front should be prevented, since from such bases she could menace both Italy and the Rumanian oilfields. The first objective of the German offensive was to be the seizure of the Aegean coast and the Salonika basin; however, it might be necessary to continue the offensive by way of Larissa and the Isthmus of Corinth and occupy the whole of Greece. The Luftwaffe's particular mission – to be carried out 'as far as possible' – was 'to seize British bases on the Greek islands by parachute and airborne landings'.

Once the objectives of the offensive were fully attained, the forces involved would be withdrawn 'for use elsewhere'. This illuminating phrase indicates the direct connection of these operations with the projected campaign against Russia. In fact, five days later, on December 18th, Hitler signed Führer Directive No. 21 – 'Barbarossa', the operation against Russia.

The attack on Greece was originally planned for March 1941, by which time it was thought the weather would be favourable. However, the start of the offensive was delayed, at first because of the diplomatic negotiations with Bulgaria, whose territory was needed in order to get at Greece, and then because of the political upheaval in Yugoslavia on March 26th–27th. In the end, the Wehrmacht could not move until April 6th, and its deployment had to be hurriedly improvised. All these measures were cramped by lack of time owing to the imminence of the campaign against Russia, plans for which had, in the meantime, taken on firmer shape. Even so, the original date for this offensive, May 15th, 1941, had to be abandoned, and a new date fixed for four weeks later.

By the end of March, the proposal for airborne landings to seize the Greek islands, contained in Operation 'Marita', had got as far as practical measures for the seizure of Lemnos.[5] The Cyclades were to be captured only after the area around Athens[6] had been occupied, and the terrain was regarded as particularly difficult for such an attack.[7]

By March 26th, 1941, as part of its preparations, the Luftwaffe had ordered the Süssmann detachment (2nd Reinforced Parachute Regiment, with artillery, anti-aircraft batteries, engineers and signal units; commanded by Lieutenant-General Süssmann), together with the staff of the 7th Air Division, to Bulgaria.[8] In Bulgaria these forces were entrusted with the execution of the operations and placed under the command of VIII Air Corps.

However, the Luftwaffe forces in Bulgaria were needed to support the drive across the frontier against the Greek Army and the British Expeditionary Force, which meant that they would not be available for parachute and airborne landings, so action was postponed.[9]

The course of the campaign made it unnecessary for paratroops to seize the isle of Lemnos, but on April 26th, 1941, 2nd Parachute Regiment was success-fully dropped, together with heavy weapons, over the Isthmus of Corinth. The bridge over the canal there was destroyed by a chance hit from an enemy shell which detonated the demolition charge; however, an improvised bridge was quickly built. With losses of only 63 dead, 158 wounded and 16 missing, the parachutists managed to capture 21 officers, 900 British and 1,450 Greek troops.

Apart from opening up the Peloponnese, which brought the fighting to a more rapid conclusion, and safeguarding the important sea route Constanza–Bosphorus–Corinth for the Axis powers, this action made striking use of the parachute troops, and – together with previous experience in Holland and Belgium – indicated the principles which guided their use.

We do not propose to discuss whether the idea of seizing Crete from the air came from the staff of Air Fleet 4, though its commander, General Löhr, suggested the idea to Göring on April 15th,[10] or whether General Student, commander of XI Air Corps, was its originator.[11] It is certain, however, that while the operations in Greece were already proceeding, Student met Göring on April 20th to report, and that the next day, after a further report to Hitler, the decision to carry out Operation 'Merkur', or the seizure of Crete from the air, was taken.[12]

A study carried out by the Wehrmacht Operations Staff[13] expressed the view that in the present phase of the war the capture of Malta should, in view of the island's more central situation, be given priority over the capture of Crete, but at that time Hitler's strategic ideas tended more and more eastward, in view of the coming campaign against Russia. His attention was therefore concentrated more on the Balkans, the eastern Mediterranean, Egypt and the Middle East. His directive says quite clearly that the object in seizing Crete was to make the island an air base against the British in the eastern Mediterranean.

Although Directive No. 28 does not expressly deal with any strategic intentions behind the seizure of Crete, we may nevertheless assume that at the crucial discussion on April 21st, General Student expressed the same ideas to Hitler that he stressed in his battle report after the successful seizure of the island.[14] He records that Crete had to be taken because in the last resort its capture was the only way to safeguard the vital sea route Constanza–Corinth–

Italy for the Axis after the ejection of the British from the mainland, and to protect Hitler's supplies of Rumanian oil – 'a constant source of anxiety' to him.[15] In German hands the island would: (*a*) practically exclude the British Fleet from the Aegean; (*b*) represent a material weakening of Britain's position in the eastern Mediterranean; and (*c*) provide a favourable base for Luftwaffe attacks against Egyptian objectives, and in particular against the Suez Canal.

Hitler's orders specified that the attack on Crete should begin on May 15th, and the operation was entrusted to Göring. The brunt of the undertaking was to fall to the Airborne Landing Corps, supported by Luftwaffe formations already based in the Mediterranean area. The 22nd Division, which had already distinguished itself in the west, was also to lend support. However, this division happened to be in the Bucharest area and it proved impossible to bring it up in time because all available transport was urgently needed for the preparation of Operation 'Barbarossa', the attack on Russia.[16] A little later, General Ringel's reinforced 5th Mountain Division was brought in instead.

Anxiety concerning the projected campaign against Russia can be sensed throughout the whole of Directive 'Merkur'. Hitler noticeably hurried the preparations for the operation; and all units involved were obviously expected to get along with such forces as were already at hand: 'transport movements must under no circumstances delay deployment "Barbarossa",' and after the operation the Airborne Landing Corps was immediately to be released 'for use elsewhere'.

Thus from the very beginning there was great pressure as far as time was concerned, and this continued throughout the whole operation, leading to constant improvisations. Unfortunately this had serious consequences, because with airborne and parachute operations accurate timing is essential for success. However, the planners were greatly heartened by the brilliant victory over British troops in the Balkan campaign, and they probably felt quite confident that this new task would also be successfully accomplished.[17]

Military Geography in Crete

As the fifth largest island in the Mediterranean and the largest in the Aegean, Crete occupies a central position. To the west, Malta and Sicily are its nearest neighbours; to the east Cyprus, and beyond Cyprus Syria. To the northwest, the fingers of the Peloponnese reach down towards the island, and the distance between Cape Malea and Cape Spatha is barely sixty miles. To the north, Crete itself closes the entrance to the island-dotted Aegean Sea. To the northeast, less than 100 miles away, lies the island of Rhodes and the island world of the Dodecanese, and immediately behind them, Turkey. To the south, about 200 miles away, lies the coast of Cyrenaica between Tobruk and Sollum. The island is thus about 350 miles from Alexandria and the Nile Delta – less than the distance between Sicily and Tripoli.

The topography of the island determined the nature and extent of the defensive measures adopted by the British, and also, directly or indirectly, the conditions under which the battle for the island was fought. It may, therefore, also be said to have largely determined its course and its outcome.

Crete is about 160 miles long from east to west and, on an average, something like 20 miles wide. However, the narrowest part, at Ierapetra, in the east, is only about 7 miles across, while the widest part is about 37 miles. Four chains of mountains make up the island's main features. In the west, the White Mountains extend for about 50 miles, and reach a height of about 7,000 feet. Next comes the Ida massif, which is almost as high; and then, farther to the east, the Lasithi Mountains, about 6,000 feet high. Farthest to the east is the Sitia range, which rises to a height of about 4,500 feet and covers practically the whole of the eastern peninsula. All these mountains are steep and barren. They determine the direction of the rivers, the nature of the coastline, the woods and the vegetation; and, to some extent, the climate. On the whole, the watershed lies nearer to the south coast, where there are few ports, and those few are small. The coastal strip in the south is narrow, and because the ground slopes steeply down to the sea there are no good anchorages. Most of the rivers of Crete flow northwards, scouring their way through deep valleys and representing a very serious obstacle to any lateral troop movements. In the north, the land slopes more gradually to the sea; and along the coast, particularly in the neighbourhood of the capital Canea, there are long, narrow plains. The best ports and harbours are on the north coast: Suda Bay, Retimo and Heraklion, but even these are not large, and are equipped to meet only the ordinary needs of the island. Suda Bay, which is sheltered to the north by the Akrotiri peninsula, is by far the most important anchorage on the island, and can accommodate heavy warships. At the same time, it is also an ideal base for flying-boats. This valuable naval strong-point can be guarded from the dominating heights of the 1,500-feet Akrotiri plateau, which falls steeply away to the sea.

Apart from these ports and harbours the only coastal places worth mentioning are the fishing villages on the south coast: Sfakia, Tymbakion and Ierapetra – but only in order to underline their inadequacy as ports, a point which was to prove of some importance during the battle. The lack of shipping facilities on the south coast meant that the British troops in Crete had to be kept supplied through the ports and harbours on the north coast, which were much more vulnerable to attack from the air. At the same time, the British naval and supply ships had to steam considerably longer distances in order to reach them.

In 1941, the Greeks and the British had nearly finished building a number of air bases in the neighbourhood of these north-coast ports and harbours, but they were really hardly more than forward airfields.

Heraklion airfield was the best of them, and it could take all types of planes. Maleme airfield, about ten miles to the west of Canea, was still unfinished, and it was suitable only for fighter planes. Retimo was in an even worse state. Yet these airfields were to be the hard-won prizes of the battle. Because there were so few of them, and because they were so inadequate, it was very difficult for the defenders to put up adequate air cover – and this would have been the case even if the British had not been so very short of planes. A further important factor which affected the struggle was the highly vulnerable situation the defenders faced in the north of the island.

Traffic conditions and communications were deplorable. Just as the airfields determined the extent of the air support which could be provided, and the capacity of the ports determined the speed at which troops, equipment and supplies could be unloaded, so traffic and communication facilities determined how the supplies landed could then be distributed; this had a direct influence on the course of the battle.

Thus the fact that the island's most important roads were, like its ports and airfields, all in the north determined not only the objectives of the German attack, but also the measures adopted by the British defence, including the concentration of its forces along the north coast. In addition, the road network on the island could easily be kept under observation from the air.

As a result the various British forces were without effective communications, and it was impossible to concentrate them rapidly to meet the main weight of the attack when that had been recognized. Another disadvantage was that their various strong-points could be isolated from each other with comparative ease. There was only one east–west road on Crete, and vulnerable defence points lay dotted along it at some considerable distance from each other: Maleme, Suda Bay, Retimo and Heraklion, each of which the defence had to hold with the aid of supplies through the ports. Although this road was the best on the island, it was very poor by European standards. It was so narrow that heavy lorries could not pass each other. There were many sharp bends, particularly in hilly terrain; there was not a single bridge which could take a seven-ton load; and, finally, the greater part of the road was visible from the sea.

Nor was there any network of auxiliary roads running parallel to this one main road; those to the south were very bad indeed, and few in number, and only four of them ran across the island. Of these, the wretched track which went nearly to Sfakia was to prove of some importance for the outcome of the battle, because of its position. The three existing narrow-gauge railway lines were of local importance only, and were no help at all to the defence.

Telephone communications were not too bad, and almost every village was linked to the network. This was an important matter for the defence, because the British troops evacuated from Greece had had to leave most of their equipment behind. However, the main telephone wires ran along the coastal road, and so were extremely vulnerable.

Early summer in Crete is characterized by clear skies and bright sunshine, and April and May, 1941, were no exception. The weather was ideal for the operations of an air force which enjoyed command of the air, as did the Luftwaffe. However, along the slopes on the north side of the island there were many vineyards and olive or almond groves, and these offered the defence ample cover and camouflage, and made air reconnaissance very difficult. Finally, the area between Maleme and Canea, the scene of the chief engagements, consists largely of a chain of hills extending to the sea, with deep, narrow, gorge-like valleys between them, with only here and there a broader valley. This terrain certainly offered advantages to retreating troops, but it forced counter-attacking troops to keep mainly to the coastal road, easily outflanked by German airborne landings.

To sum up, Crete is an island which is unsuitable for landings from sea and air in the south, west, and east, but open to them in the north. Even to the north, the position of the coastal road and the good harbour of Suda Bay meant that only the area from Maleme to Canea and on to Suda Bay was really suitable for landing operations on a large scale.

The British in Crete

Up to the Evacuation of Greece

Such was the general situation when the British landed in Crete on October 29th, 1940, the first time since 1913, when the island became a Greek possession, that foreign troops had set foot on its soil.

How did this development come about? The British had always kept a close eye on Crete and were to some extent responsible for the fact that Turkey had to give up Crete in 1913 in favour of Greece, a small neutral state.

Because of its geographical situation, the island was always of strategic importance for naval purposes, and with the great development of aircraft after the First World War this strategic importance had increased still further. With the outbreak of war in 1939, the island was obviously a potential threat to neighbouring territories and, in particular, to sea communications between the eastern and western Mediterranean – provided it were in the hands of a country with sufficiently powerful naval and air forces. The neutrality of Greece, whose independence was guaranteed by Britain and France in April, 1939, after the Italian occupation of Albania, was at first in Britain's interest, but this changed when Italy entered the war on Germany's side. With their eye on the Italian base at Rhodes in the Dodecanese, and on the possibility of using Suda Bay as a tanker station for the Allied naval forces operating in these waters far away from the main British naval base at Alexandria, the British Chiefs of Staff decided as early as April 25, 1940 – with French agreement – to occupy the island immediately if Italy entered the war.[18] Within a very few days – May 21st – the British had secured the consent of the Greek Government to an Allied occupation of Crete should war break out between Italy and Greece. By May 30th plans for the occupation of the island were complete, but the unexpectedly speedy collapse of France deprived the British of their resources for the project. On July 27th, the British abandoned the plan for the time being, influenced by a desire not to be the first to violate Greek neutrality – though the threatened launching of Operation 'Sea Lion' no doubt also had something to do with it.

On September 13th, 1940, Marshal Graziani began his North African drive towards the Egyptian frontier, but it very quickly came to a halt at Sidi Barrani. At the same time, there were clear indications in Albania that Italy was preparing to attack Greece. As a result, on October 4th further discussions took place between the Greeks and the British, who were regrettably 'unable to make any promises', though, in fact, a battalion, later increased to a brigade, from the Middle East was offered. As early as the end of September the Commander-in-Chief Middle East had urged that under all circumstances Suda Bay, Canea, Heraklion, the Gulf of Mirabella and the Sitia Peninsula must not be allowed to slip out of British control, but all he had in mind for his own contribution was air force support – perhaps reinforced later by Fleet Air Arm planes.

During the course of October it became clear that Graziani was not likely to get much farther eastward, and as British strength in the Mediterranean had increased, it became possible by October 21st to prepare a small force to help the Greeks should they be attacked. The likelihood became a fact on October 28th, when Italian troops marched into Greece from Albania. Previously there had been merely the question of safeguarding Crete, that is Suda Bay and an air base; now it was necessary to help Greece. This obligation represented a further grievous burden on Britain's resources, which already seemed stretched to the limit. The British Admiralty was primarily concerned with safeguarding the important naval base, and Churchill himself was contemplating developing the island into 'a second Scapa Flow'.[19] But the Army, in particular Sir John Dill, Chief of the Imperial General Staff, opposed the transfer of any forces to Greece which might be needed for the defence of Egypt, and they were able for the time being to leave it to the Navy, which sent part of the Mobile Naval Base Defence Organization,[20] to the island to reinforce the two battalions which had already landed there on October 29th. However, the political situation soon compelled Britain to make greater efforts to assist Greece, and by the end of November there were already three squadrons of the RAF in Greece, together with relatively weak covering ground forces. At the beginning of December the equipment for a fourth squadron was handed over to the Greek Air Force.[21] Churchill, in particular, was very much in favour of these moves; he remembered the importance of the Allied Balkan Front during the First World War, and he was anxious to retain a military foothold in southeast Europe. Forces from Egypt were therefore sent to Greece.

We do not propose to discuss at any length the British forces sent to the Greek mainland or the diplomatic negotiations with the Greek Government which preceded that move; all we are interested in is the direct effect of this decision on the defence of Crete, though the latter cannot be understood except in connection with the ebb and flow of events in the whole of the Middle East.

In accordance with the original intention of turning the island into a second Scapa Flow, the relatively weak forces then available were concentrated in and around Canea and in Suda Bay. Everything else had to be left to the Greeks.

However, British troops later took over the defence of the island as a whole, in order to release Greek troops for the Albanian front. At first, the intention was to bring ANZAC units[22] from Egypt, but as an offensive against the Italians was then being planned on that front – it was launched on December 9th, and met with brilliant success – no reinforcements of any real strength could be withdrawn from the Middle East. From November 19th to the middle of December, not more than about 1,000 men were brought in, though the local British commanders already had the possibility of an air attack on Suda Bay in mind, and regarded such places as Maleme, Retimo and Heraklion as vulnerable landing spots!

On February 8th, British forces took El Agheila on the edge of the Great Sirte, thus completing the conquest of Cyrenaica and taking 130,000 prisoners. On February 19th, Brigadier Galloway arrived in Crete as the fourth C.-in-C. Crete since November 1940. He was to establish himself in Suda Bay and the area, take charge of all British forces on the island, prepare certain operations which were being planned against the Dodecanese, and make arrangements for adding another division to island defences if a worsening of the situation in Greece should make this necessary. But on March 7th Brigadier Galloway was sent to Greece, where British troops had landed at Piraeus and Volos to head off the expected German attack under Field-Marshal List, whose forces had marched into Bulgaria on March 2nd. Thus the British kept their word to the Greeks and provided what assistance they could, even though it meant not following up their successes against the Italians in North Africa.

In the second half of March, the Italian Naval High Command (Supermarina), acting under instructions from the Armed Forces High Command (Comando Supremo), itself under pressure from the German military authorities, had to launch an attack on British convoys steaming from Egypt to Greece. On March 26th, protected by destroyers, six explosive boats, a new small battle unit developed by the Italian Navy, carried out a daring raid on Suda Bay, destroying the British cruiser *York* and two transports.

The next day an Italian battle fleet consisting of 1 battleship, 6 heavy cruisers, 2 light cruisers and 13 destroyers put to sea under the command of Admiral Iachino, with the intention of attacking British convoys believed to be to the south of Crete. The German X Air Corps co-operated with the Italian air force to provide air cover for the fleet, and to carry out reconnaissance in the eastern Mediterranean. However, owing to operational errors and technical signals defects, no effective co-operation between the ships and the planes was achieved. The result was that while the presence of these Italian naval forces was quickly discovered by British air reconnaissance units, Admiral Iachino was completely in the dark and quite unable to shake off his British shadowers. There are various indications that the British had been expecting something of the sort since March 25th. In any case, they re-routed their convoys and sent out the Mediterranean Fleet of 3 battleships, 1 aircraft carrier, 4 light cruisers and 13 destroyers under Admiral Cunningham, to meet the Italians. Thanks to the skilful use of planes from the aircraft carrier *Formidable*, and land-based planes from Maleme in Crete, the British succeeded in torpedoing first the Italian battleship *Vittorio Veneto* and later the cruiser *Pola*. They were not sunk, but the damage greatly reduced their speed. The Italian battleship succeeded in evading her pursuers, but the British forces caught up with the *Pola*. On March 28th off Cape Matapan, to the southwest of the Peloponnese, the *Pola*, the cruisers *Zara* and *Fiume*, and two destroyers which came to the *Pola's* aid, were reduced to smoking hulks. This was the first time that naval radar was used in night fighting, and it enabled the British to discover the whereabouts of the Italian ships. In the end, the Italian vessels were given the *coup de grâce* by torpedoes fired at close range by British destroyers. It was not surprising that this new heavy blow, coming so soon after the carrier-based raid on Taranto in November 1940, had a paralysing effect on future Italian naval activity.[23]

In this first period of British occupation, Crete served as a transit base for the RAF and the Navy. The Army was a garrisoning force only, and in charge of air defence. On April 2nd, four days before the beginning of the campaign in Greece, General Wavell decided that the growing importance of Suda Bay for troop and air movements in support of actions on the mainland required its development into a proper naval base. He was probably also persuaded that the presence of the Luftwaffe in Bulgaria made it impossible to establish a base farther north.

The British commanders in Crete had already formed a very good idea of the sort of attack they would probably have to face on the island, and from March 27th on exercises directed towards repulsing parachute attacks, particularly on Maleme, had become routine.

On April 15th, Major-General Weston, who was now the sixth British C.-in-C. Crete, saw that in view of the rapidly worsening situation on the mainland he would soon be faced with the task of defending the island against attack, and he therefore informed his superiors of the resources which he would need, including infantry, aircraft, efficient airfields and supplies.

On April 21st, an armistice was signed between German and Greek troops in Epirus. On the same day, the Middle East Joint Planning Staff[24] came to the conclusion that an invasion of Crete from the air would be launched only when it could be combined with a supporting attack from the sea, and that this could be expected three or four weeks after the evacuation of British troops from the mainland (which began on April 24th). The course of events proved this estimate to be correct. Three fresh, full-strength and fully equipped brigades, with corresponding artillery support, were regarded as necessary to defend Crete. The forces evacuated from Greece were to be withdrawn to Egypt. During the evacuation the requisite strength of the RAF was estimated at three squadrons of fighters, the level not to fall below two squadrons. The existing anti-aircraft artillery was to be reinforced by three further heavy batteries.

General Wavell was faced with a series of difficult problems throughout the Middle East. The offensive against the Italians in Abyssinia had been going on since the previous March. Addis Ababa fell on April 5th, and on May 16th the main Italian forces under the Duke of Aosta surrendered. The remaining Italian forces, some 23,000 men, did not capitulate until the following November 28th.[25]

On April 3rd a pro-Axis government seized power in Iraq under Rashid Ali al-Gelani, and relations between Iraq and Britain worsened rapidly. On April 30th, Iraqi forces began to besiege the airport at Habbaniya, the most important British base in the country. The only way to assist the besieged was by air, and all supplies or bomber and fighter reinforcements had to come from Egypt.[26] The Luftwaffe also took some part in the fighting, though with very inadequate forces, 9 He–111s of No. 4 Squadron, 4th Bomber Wing, and 3 Me–110s of 76th Ground Attack Wing.[27] Nevertheless, on May 16th an attack by three He–111s did more damage than the whole Iraqi air force had managed to do,[28] and in consequence the RAF had to fly in further precious reinforcements from Egypt.[29]

This was the place from where they could least be spared. Advance elements of the German Afrika Korps arrived in Tripoli in the middle of February, and after a successful preliminary reconnaissance on March 24th they rallied the Italians, and began a threatening forward move on March 31st. Under the brilliant leadership of Rommel, they took Agedabia on April 2nd and Benghazi on April 4th. On April 7th, they surrounded and captured a strong British force near El Mechili, and on April 8th they invested Tobruk, which from then on had to be supplied from the sea. Bardia fell to Rommel on April 9th, and Sollum on April 13th, and here the advance finally halted. As all available British forces were extended to the full, all that could be done in reply was to send out the Mediterranean Fleet to cut the Italo-German supply lines to North Africa. The aircraft and submarine forces stationed at Malta were not strong enough for the purpose and Admiral Cunningham despatched four destroyers on April 11th, which won the first success off Kerkenna on April 16th with the destruction of an Italian convoy of five ships escorted by three destroyers. At the insistence of Churchill, who was prepared to sacrifice the battleship *Barham* as a blockship, on April 21st Admiral Cunningham sent his battleships to bombard Tripoli in order to put the port out of action for a while.[30]

In view of the difficult situation on all fronts, General Wavell decided that apart from a mountain battery no further troops should be sent to Crete for the time being, and that the question should be reviewed when the British forces in Greece had all been evacuated. However, he did order that the anti-aircraft defences of the island should be increased to six heavy and three light batteries, and that supplies for two months should be sent to the island.

This decision on the part of General Wavell, imposed on him by lack of troops, meant that the British troops which had been defeated in Greece, including the Australians and New Zealanders, had to be sent into action once again in the Battle of Crete. After their arrival on the island the situation developed too swiftly for fresh troops to be brought in to help defend the island. The British had to make the best of a bad job – and the situation *was* bad.

In addition, the build-up of the defence went much too slowly. The already difficult situation was made worse by the necessity of defending Alexandria and the Suez Canal. The original intention of raising levies amongst the civilian population after the evacuation of the last Greek units in February 1941 proved impossible, because there were just no weapons available with which they could be armed and trained.

This general shortage of arms and equipment also explains why the minimum anti-aircraft equipment which, in the previous November, had been promised to Crete, had not been supplied by the beginning of the evacuation of Greece. For example, there were only 16 heavy anti-aircraft guns on the island instead of the promised 32, and of the promised 72 searchlights there were only 24. However, the 24 light anti-aircraft guns originally asked for had been supplemented by a further 12. Nevertheless, even when we take into consideration the fact that by the time the battle for Crete opened this anti-aircraft defence had been increased by a further 16 heavy guns, the defences of the island against air attack must be regarded as very inadequate indeed, particularly as the lack of fighter planes made the air superiority of the Luftwaffe even more overwhelming. On November 13th, when it was decided to hold Crete 'whatever might happen on the mainland',[31] the General Staff had rightly assumed that the attack would in all probability come from the air, but there were just no fighter planes to cope with it.

In fact, by the end of March there was not a single RAF plane on the island, and there had been no discussions about co-operation with the Fleet Air Arm, which had a few squadrons of obsolescent planes available,[32] or with the Army. Nor had anyone discussed the all-important question of extending and developing the airfields, so crucial to the defence of the island.

Apart from a few Sunderland flying-boats in Suda Bay, whose job was chiefly to help in the evacuation of troops from Greece to Crete and on to Egypt, the first really effective air force units did not arrive in Crete until April 18th, when they flew in from Greece. More arrived between April 22nd and 24th, including perhaps a dozen Hurricanes, but these planes were now hardly battleworthy, and with the resources available in Crete it was scarcely possible to make them so. All available aircraft were engaged on convoy protection, and so not in a position to prepare for the expected invasion.

In face of these harsh facts, the demands of the planners of Middle East Command on April 21st for three squadrons of fighter planes became purely **academic**. Crete had now been occupied by the British for six months; but the existing garrison of 6,100[33] was totally inadequate to repulse the expected attack. There was no systematically prepared plan of defence; the anti-aircraft and coastal defences were far below the strength originally regarded as necessary; transport facilities were poor; communications were bad; supplies were not available in sufficient quantity; there were no proper quarters for the troops; the existing airfields were inadequately equipped and prepared – and, worst of all, the planes to use them were not available.

British Plans after the Evacuation of Greece

Apart from those evacuated by air, 50,732 men were brought from the mainland of Greece by the British Navy between the nights of April 24th–25th and April 30th–May 1st.[34] In accordance with instructions, the majority of these men were landed in Crete so as to speed up the evacuation. As the authorities had decided to give priority to saving man-power, all arms and equipment, apart from rifles and machine-guns, were left behind. A minority of the evacuated units was carried straight to Egypt; unfortunately for the defence of Crete, this included the 6th New Zealand Infantry Brigade, which would have proved very useful, whereas the relatively large numbers of artillerymen and other specialized troops who were carried to Crete without equipment represented little more than an additional burden.

The evacuation was a success, and it provided further proof of the efficiency of the British Navy. It was carried out under constant pressure from numerically superior German forces, and with complete command of the air in the hands of the Luftwaffe.

Although it had originally been intended to transfer the exhausted men to Egypt, the new commander in Crete, General Weston, had to make the best of what forces he had available, and he hurriedly stopped up the worst gaps in the defences. The situation had become much more urgent now, because with the whole of Greece in German hands the danger of an invasion of Crete seemed imminent.

On April 28th, General Freyberg, commanding the New Zealand forces, arrived in Crete with parts of the NZ Expeditionary Force. Freyberg supposed that for him Crete was merely a transit on his way to Egypt, but two days later General Wavell visited the island, inspected its defences, and appointed Freyberg C.-in-C. of all British and Greek forces there. General Freyberg was now the seventh military commander in Crete since the previous November. He was also the last, and certainly a man capable of making the best out of a grim situation which was the result of a series of stop-gaps and half-measures, of British weakness and German strength. His appointment, and the fact that the New Zealand forces were to remain on the island instead of being transported to Egypt, led to certain difficulties with the New Zealand Government, which not unnaturally now demanded that its forces should be provided with everything necessary for the job they were being asked to do, or, alternatively, that the decision to hold the island under all circumstances should be reviewed. Churchill had to intervene personally before the difficulties could be composed.

On April 17th General Wavell had received permission from London to prepare for the evacuation of the Greek mainland and to regroup his forces with a view to the defence of Crete, at the same time using as many Greek forces for the task as possible, and, for political reasons, establishing the Greek King and the Greek Government in Crete.[35]

As early as April 27th, C.-in-C. Middle East received information of German preparations on the Greek mainland which indicated that the attack on Crete was to be delivered by sea as well as by air, and the next day at a session of the British War Cabinet Churchill declared that the Germans intended to use Crete and Rhodes as air bases in order to drive the British out of the eastern Mediterranean and to attack shipping off the Egyptian coast.[36] This, he went on, was a preliminary stage to a further attack on Egypt proper. At the same time, he expressed doubts as to Britain's ability to resist a prolonged attack on Crete.

This misgiving merely reflected the doubts generally held by the military experts. The advantages and disadvantages of defending Crete were carefully weighed up; the question was whether the forces which would have to be used for the defence of the island might not be better employed in North Africa in an attempt to reconquer Benghazi.

As Commander-in-Chief in the Mediterranean, Admiral Cunningham probably tipped the scales with his estimate of the general situation on May 1st. In his view, it was essential that the Germans should be denied the possession of Crete for as long as possible, because its airfields would make it easy for the Luftwaffe to increase the pressure on Malta and make it more difficult for the Navy to keep that island supplied. The Luftwaffe would be able to operate in much greater strength off the coasts of North Africa; and the possession of Crete would make it much easier for the Germans to use light surface craft to attack Cyprus. The presence of the RAF in Crete would have no effect on the campaign in the African desert, but was certainly essential if the island itself was to be held.

From this point on there was no further discussion as to whether Crete should be held or not. The decision had been taken. However, it is probably true to say that it was taken under the pressure of events; the British really had very little choice. With the occupation of Greece, German forces were firmly established in the southeast of Europe; they were in North Africa; they had already set foot on Egyptian territory; in Iraq they were intervening in support of the pro-Axis premier al-Gelani; in Syria General Dentz was affording assistance to Luftwaffe planes on their way to Iraq; and, finally, Malta had been under constant attack since the beginning of the year from X Air Corps. The Luftwaffe already enjoyed air superiority; everything possible must be done to deny it further favourable bases from which it could still more effectively support the expected German drive to the Middle East.

Further discussion on Crete was only about how to get in the necessary material and equipment, since by now there was a sufficient force of men on the island. In a message to Churchill on May 5th, General Freyberg declared that he felt confident that he would be able to hold the island with his troops against an airborne attack – provided he were given adequate artillery, sufficient supplies and a certain number of fighter planes. But because not enough planes were being manufactured in Britain, and also because the airfields in Crete were in any case quite inadequate, the Chief of Air Staff, Air Chief Marshal Sir Charles Portal, opposed any permanent transfer of planes to Crete, and was prepared to approve only forward landing fields for fighters there. No doubt he was influenced by the heavy losses the RAF had already suffered in Greece. On May 9th, the remnants of the RAF which had flown into Crete from the Greek mainland totalled only 24 planes in Maleme and 12 in Heraklion, and most of those badly needed repairs for which there were no adequate facilities on the island. By May 13th General Freyberg had 6 Hurricanes at his disposal. On May 17th he received another 10, but by this time Luftwaffe pressure on the island was so intense that they had to be flown back to Egypt to save them from destruction. On May 19th, the day before the attack on Crete began, the last 4 Hurricanes and the last 3 Gladiators left Crete for Egypt.[37]

Hoping that the air strips might come in useful later, the defenders did not destroy them altogether, but merely blocked them, and this proved a great advantage to the invaders in their airborne landings.

It also proved very difficult to bring tanks to stiffen the defence of the island. Owing to the heavy tank losses suffered in Greece and against Rommel's Afrika Korps, and to the still uncertain situation in Iraq,[38] General Wavell was able to provide only 16 light tanks and 6 infantry support tanks; and that only with great difficulty and thanks largely to the daring success of the Royal Navy's convoy 'Tiger', which succeeded in bringing 238 tanks and 43 Hurricanes through the Mediterranean.[39] In this matter he was hard pressed by Churchill, who showed a great personal interest in Operation 'Scorcher'.[40]

Hardly was the evacuation of Greece completed, when the Navy had to concentrate on the new tasks imposed on it by the necessity of defending Crete, bringing in primarily supplies but also troops. Between April 29th and May 20th, it succeeded in landing 15,000 tons of supplies. On the night of May 15th, it landed a force at Heraklion, and on the night of May 18th another at Tymbakion on the south coast of the island. These operations had to be carried out under cover of darkness, because Luftwaffe pressure during the daylight hours was rapidly increasing; facilities at Suda Bay were now so restricted that Alexandria, which was over 400 miles away, had to be made the base for all fleet operations in connection with Crete.

The British Mediterranean Fleet in May 1941[41]

4 Battleships:	*Queen Elizabeth, Barham,* Warspite,* Valiant**
1 Aircraft Carrier:	*Formidable**
8 Cruisers:	*Gloucester,† Fiji,†, Orion,* Ajax,* Perth,* Dido,* Naiad,* Phoebe,* and three obsolescent cruisers: *Coventry, Calcutta,† Carlisle.**
1 Minelayer:	*Abdiel.*
30 Destroyers:	*Napier,* Nizam,* Kandahar, Kingston, Kimberley, Kelly,† Kashmir,† Kipling, Kelvin,* Juno,† Janus, Jervis, Jackal, Jaguar, Nubian,* Isis, Imperial,† Ilex, Hero, Hotspur, Hereward,† Hasty, Havock, Griffin, Greyhound,† Decoy,* Defender, Stuart, Voyager, Vendetta.*
2 Sloops:	*Auckland, Flamingo.*

†sunk and *damaged during the fighting.

In order to be prepared for all eventualities, part of the British Mediterranean Fleet was always at sea, and another force was held in constant readiness to put out at once should the operations of the warships already at sea be hampered by shortage of fuel. Between May 15th and May 20th, Admiral Cunningham divided his available forces into four groups:[42] Force A, consisting of two battleships and five destroyers, operated to the west of Crete; Force B, consisting of two cruisers and two destroyers, operated to the northwest of the island; Force C, consisting of two cruisers and four destroyers, operated to the east of the island; and Force D, consisting of two cruisers and four destroyers, operated off Retimo to forestall any landing attempts there.

In addition to these forces, there were two more battleships in reserve at Alexandria, the aircraft-carrier *Formidable* (though it had only four planes ready to take the air), two cruisers and a number of destroyers. By this time, only seven motor torpedo boats were actually operating from Suda Bay.

May 17th was regarded as the most likely date for the Germans to start their landings. General Freyberg decided, after a careful inspection of his resources and an appraisal of the expected German attack, that four points would be vital for the defence: the three airfields and the area around Suda Bay. His judgement of the situation was more than an inspired guess; it was based on advance knowledge of the actual German intentions. By April 26th the Intelligence Service knew that there were to be airborne landings; and by May 6th it knew the main details, including the likely date of the attack.[43] This was the first time during the Second World War that the British were in the relatively happy position of knowing the intentions of the enemy in advance.

General Freyberg realized that the distances between these four vital defence points, the shortage of transport and the poor state of communications, meant that the four sectors would have to be made as self-contained as possible. From May 3rd, therefore, he distributed his forces as follows:[44] 8,024 men at Heraklion under Brigadier Chappel; 6,730 men at Retimo under Brigadier

Vasey; 14,822 men at Suda Bay under Major-General Weston; and 11,859 men at Maleme under Brigadier Puttick.

In addition to these forces there were 405 men on his own staff, and another 800 ('Layforce') who had landed between May 24th and May 27th, so that in all he commanded a total force of 42,640 men, including 10,258 Greeks. The fighting value of the Greeks was not very high, however; they were demoralized, disorganized and poorly equipped.

Equipment and supplies were General Freyberg's biggest headache, because all supplies had to come by sea, and the ports and harbours were under constant Luftwaffe attack. At first it proved possible to bring in and unload 700 tons a day at Suda Bay, but later on only ships with a speed of over thirty knots (cruisers and destroyers) could be used, as these could steam in and out under cover of darkness. As a result, the volume of supplies unloaded at Suda Bay fell to 100 tons a day (it was calculated that between 20,000 and 30,000 tons a month were needed to supply the garrison of Crete). By May 19th, thirteen wrecked vessels were lying in the harbour at Suda Bay, and the anti-aircraft batteries were quite unable to keep the Luftwaffe planes away.

However, despite all these difficulties, preparations for the defence went forward vigorously: defensive positions were built, strong-points were camouflaged, dummy positions were laid out to deceive the enemy, and the best possible use was made of the difficult terrain, so that when the attack finally came the Germans suffered very heavy losses indeed. The defenders were well prepared in another respect: they knew the enemy they would have to face; everything had been done to make them familiar with the German airborne troops and parachutists and their battle tactics, and to indicate the probable course of the battle. From May 17th the garrison was in the utmost possible state of preparedness. The enemy intentions were known, and there was no question of any strategic or even tactical surprise.

The German Plan of Attack

Operation 'Merkur', the first independent Luftwaffe operation in which all three arms of the Wehrmacht co-operated, was entrusted to Air Fleet 4 under General Löhr, which included VIII Air Corps under General von Richthofen, and XI Air Corps under General Student. The supporting naval operations were in the hands of Flag Officer Southeast, Admiral Schuster.

VIII Air Corps, under General von Richthofen, had taken a prominent part in the operations on the Greek mainland, and it was therefore already well acquainted with conditions in general. Most of the units which made up XI Air Corps under General Student had to be brought in from Germany, where they had been in garrisons or training camps. Despite great difficulties, chiefly technical, the very inadequate lines of communication in the Balkans, and the transport demands of Operation 'Barbarossa', XI Air Corps was successfully concentrated in the neighbourhood of Athens and ready for action by May 14th. Ten wings of Ju–52s, with 502 planes, had been assembled to transport the parachute and airborne troops.

But the ground organization was neither ready nor adequate to carry out its task. As the few available airfields had to be shared by VIII Air Corps' bombers, dive-bombers and fighters, XI Air Corps was left with the airfields at Corinth, Megara, Tanagra, Topolia, Dadion, Eleusis and Phaleron. The excessive concentration of planes on these very poor airfields greatly hampered the execution of the attack on Crete. The almost incredible volume of dust which was raised made formation take-offs within a reasonable space of time almost impossible. XI Air Corps used ground fire-fighting equipment in an effort to lay the dust, but without a great deal of success.

All supplies had to be brought to the ports of Piraeus and Corinth with whatever shipping space was immediately available. Supplies were hampered by mines and the operations of hostile submarines and, despite the tireless efforts of Flag Officer Southeast, they did not start arriving until after May 17th. Further delays occurred in unloading these supplies because dock and port facilities had been severely damaged, and a proper labour force was not available. After that, there were further delays before the supplies could be sent on. But the real bottleneck of the operation was the supply of fuel for the Luftwaffe. In the period from May 17th to May 20th, 792,000 gallons of fuel had to be brought up for the use of XI Air Corps, enough for three operations for ten Ju–52 groups. The units of VIII Air Corps had also to be supplied.

The delay in the arrival of the supply ships and the difficulty of supplying the airfields with fuel made it necessary to postpone the start of operations, first to May 18th, and then to May 20th. In addition, the signals network was by no means satisfactory.

However, the concentration in and around Athens of the operations staffs concerned proved advantageous; a good deal of the inevitable friction could be quickly settled. Similarly, the presence of the Luftwaffe Chief of Staff, Jeschonnek, led to speedy decisions from the C.-in-C. Air Force.

Once its forces had been regrouped and prepared for action, VIII Air Corps performed various essential preliminary tasks. It provided air cover for the supply ships against submarines and surface craft; reconnoitred the whole of the sea area involved; attacked enemy transport and warships around Crete; attacked Crete itself – for example, shipping in Suda Bay; and attacked RAF ground organization and anti-aircraft positions. These operations not only inflicted casualties and damage on the enemy, but they led to command of the air over the island,[45] an essential condition for the success of the subsequent airborne landings.

The Luftwaffe also fortified a number of islands as part of the general operations against Crete: Cythera and Anticythera were developed as anti-aircraft points; Melos as a centre for supplies and the air-sea rescue service; and Scarpanto as a base for fighters and dive-bombers.

The operations staffs had to depend primarily on information supplied by

German Intelligence (Canaris, its head, took charge himself) and by air reconnaissance for their knowledge of the strength and positions of the enemy. In fact, the picture pieced together from these sources was untrue in a number of important particulars. For one thing, the British forces were about three times as strong as had been supposed. Those units which had fought on the mainland were certainly below strength, and had lost all their heavy equipment – though some tanks were landed later; but they were ready for action, and fought with great tenacity and courage. Those in charge of the operations against Crete were also mistaken about the attitude of the island population – it had even been regarded as possible that their desire for peace might persuade the British to evacuate Crete voluntarily. In fact, the civilian population, particularly in western Crete, actively supported the British in their resistance to the German invaders.

Wherever the terrain permitted the landing of forces by air or sea, the defences had been systematically prepared with much skill and with a considerable amount of material and equipment. Many highly defensible strong-points were established around the crucial airfields and along the north coast, and, acting in full knowledge of German parachute-troop tactics, the defence had carefully prepared all areas inland which could be used by the invading forces. As most of these places were flat and low-lying, the heights around them were occupied and strongly fortified. The olive groves in those areas regarded as suitable for airborne and parachute landings were occupied by snipers, in order to keep the whole area under fire and inflict the heaviest possible losses on the attackers. All defensive strong-points were so well camouflaged that even with the aid of detailed air photographs and daring low flying it was very difficult to identify them. Incidentally, the reconnaissance squadron of the XI Air Corps lost three section leaders on such low-flying missions. But despite all efforts, a number of points apparently reliably identified as anti-aircraft positions subsequently turned out to be decoy sites with wooden 'guns'. The real positions were elsewhere, and very successfully camouflaged.

These inaccurate estimates of the enemy's strength and the misjudgement of his positions by the higher German staffs were often reflected in the beliefs of the German troops involved: the Greeks 'wouldn't fight any more', the Tommies were 'demoralized' and 'wouldn't show much fight' once the attack started.[46]

This erroneous estimate of enemy strength endangered the success of the whole operation, and resulted in excessively high losses for XI Air Corps.[47]

In view of the efficiency of British Intelligence, and since German parachute troops had already been committed near Corinth, there was no hope of a strategic surprise. But even tactical surprise in the nature of the attack, its strength and its timing was not obtained. Thanks to active and efficient espionage in Greece, the concentration of parachute troops and Transport Wings in the neighbourhood of Athens and the loading and sailing of shipping became known in full detail to the enemy. As a result, British naval forces based on Alexandria were at sea in the neighbourhood of Crete from May 15th, and by May 17th the British forces on Crete were fully alerted to meet the attack, which was expected in the early morning hours.

There were various ways of attacking Crete:

(*a*) Air Fleet 4 could concentrate all its efforts on seizing the western part of the island – from Maleme to Canea – and then use the conquered territory as a base from which to seize the rest of the island. This plan permitted the strongest possible concentration of forces, and swift and absolute superiority at the decisive point, even if the enemy should prove stronger than had been assumed; and the full and undivided support of VIII Air Corps was certain. But it was possible that during heavy and perhaps lengthy fighting in the mountains, the enemy, being in possession of airfields in the east, and perhaps also Suda Bay, could increase his defensive power. In view of overwhelming German superiority in the air, such enemy reinforcement would have been possible, if at all, only to a very limited extent during the day; though, of course, it would hardly have been possible to prevent night landings.

(*b*) XI Air Corps could attack simultaneously about seven points on the island, including the most important: Maleme, Canea, Retimo and Heraklion. The advantage of this proposal lay in the 'swift and sudden' occupation of all crucial points on the island; if this succeeded then the conquest of the rest of the island would be speedy and complete. However, the forces were not strong enough to attack so many different points, and the capacity of the available transport planes (twelve men at a time) was inadequate. In particular, VIII Air Corps would not be able to lend equally effective support at all landing areas simultaneously. Should strong enemy resistance be encountered, success was doubtful.

(*c*) Göring's ultimate orders for the attack represented a combination of these two variants. The invading forces were to ensure the conquest of the island by rapidly seizing possession of the four most crucial points. XI Air Corps was to commit strong advance detachments of parachutists and assault troops in a surprise attack from the air to seize the airfields and the most important towns on the island. In order to obtain full support from VIII Air Corps (and above all, full fighter support), the attack was to be carried out in stages. The first wave was to go in at 07.15 hours in the west, its main objectives being the airfield at Maleme and the town of Canea. The second wave was to go in at 15.15 in the east, taking Retimo and Heraklion as its main objectives. These two waves were to be supported by reinforcements of parachute troops and by airborne landings, and also by landings from the sea, until the whole corps was on the island.

Success for this plan would mean that from the very first day the occupation of the three airfields and Canea (including Suda Bay) would make it impossible for the enemy to use his air strength against the landings, or undertake any considerable troop movements between crucial points. The forces available for the operations to be carried out by XI Air Corps were divided into three groups:[48]

(*a*) Western Group, under Major-General Meindl, was to seize possession of Maleme swiftly and suddenly in the first attack, and hold the airfield for subsequent airborne landings;

(*b*) Centre Group, under Lieutenant-General Süssmann, was also part of the first wave, and its task was to seize Canea and the village of Suda in order to dislocate the defence and put the main harbour of the island out of action. By 15.15 the second wave was to have taken the town and the airfield of Retimo.[49]

(*c*) Eastern Group, under Lieutenant-General Ringel, also part of the second wave, was to seize the town and airfield of Heraklion by parachute drops, and then hold the airfield open for the subsequent airborne landing of mountain troops.

In the early morning of the first day of the attack, VIII Air Corps was to carry out preliminary operations to destroy the still existing British air forces on the island, and silence the ground defences. It was also entrusted with protecting the approach and landing of the first two waves of XI Air Corps, and supporting its subsequent operations. Finally, VIII Air Corps was to protect the shipping engaged in the operation, and destroy enemy naval forces in the neighbourhood of Crete.

Flag Officer Southeast was to send minesweepers and motor sailing vessels so that the first flotilla could put in to the west of Maleme in the evening of the first day of the attack, while the second flotilla could put in to the east of Heraklion on the evening of the second day. The steamers were to be ready to put out as soon as Suda Bay was reported free of mines and enemy forces.[50]

The plan of attack, which had been worked out to the last detail, offered every hope for the speedy capture of Crete. The success of the invasion depended on the capture of three airfields. Should the capture of any one of the three run up against unforeseen difficulties, there was always the possibility of switching to one of the other airfields already in German hands. In this way, success seemed certain.

Critical Moments in the Battle for Crete

The preliminary attack[51] was launched between 05.30 and 06.00 hours by VIII Air Corps, against the airfields of Maleme and Heraklion and against the anti-aircraft defences around these airfields and in Canea. Following this, and immediately before the beginning of the air landings, a new attack by VIII Air Corps began at 07.15, with a view to pinning down the enemy at the landing places. Although the defence had made its preparations very carefully, only seven Ju–52s were lost out of a total of 493 engaged.

The first wave of the attack by XI Air Corps went according to plan as far as the time of the landing operations was concerned, but for a number of reasons (heavy anti-aircraft fire, pilots losing their way, and so on) the chosen landing places were not always reached. Western Group (Maleme) and Centre Group (Suda village and Canea) each landed half of the 1st Battalion Assault Regiment in gliders. Three companies were to land around enemy anti-aircraft positions and put them out of action. In two cases, this plan was successfully carried out. The rest of the wave followed closely on their heels in parachute drops.

The drops met fierce resistance from enemy infantry, whose strength had not been recognized from the air. This resistance was particularly heavy on the slopes to the south of Maleme airfield, where terraced defensive positions had been built. Enemy fire was so intense that many paratroopers were killed in the air and others were killed immediately on landing, while very many of those who did land alive were unable to reach their weapon containers. One battalion of the Assault Regiment was landed too far to the east. The attack launched by Centre Group against the heights of Akrotiri, which command Canea and Suda Bay, and against the village of Galatas, failed completely.[52]

The situation was complicated by the fact that Western and Centre Groups lost their commanding officers at the very outset. Lieutenant-General Süssmann, in command of Centre Group, was killed at the start of operations when his glider crashed on the island of Aegina,[53] and the commander of Western Group, Major-General Meindl, was seriously wounded shortly before the landing.

These developments did not become known back at the Operations Rooms until the afternoon, because when the transport aircraft returned safely (1·4 per cent losses) and the reports came in from VIII Air Corps, the impression was that 'the first wave had gone in successfully according to plan'. Air Landing Corps HQ in Athens at that time had no news at all from the dropped parachute units. Towards midday, a message came from Centre Group reporting that the attack on Canea had been discontinued after heavy losses. Western Group reported that heavy fighting was still proceeding, and that its commander had been wounded. Because of the first optimistic impression, the second wave was sent in as planned, and as a result there were further errors and set-backs.

The transport planes were back at their bases in Greece between 09.00 and 10.00 hours, but it proved impossible to get the Ju–52s ready for a second sortie by 13.00. The start of individual groups of Ju–52s was delayed by as long as three and a half hours because of the difficulty of refuelling, because crashed planes had first to be removed from the runways, and because the dust clouds on the overtaxed airfields were so thick that not even the use of fire-fighting apparatus could give much relief. In consequence the squadrons started in the wrong tactical order, and instead of arriving at their destinations together, they arrived haphazardly between 15.00 and 18.00 hours. The battle report of XI Air Corps notes that telephone communication between the individual airfields was frequently interrupted, and that it was therefore impossible for commanders to discuss the delays and make arrangements for a new joint starting time. The Officer Commanding No. 2 Special Duties Bomber Group (Paratroop transport planes)[54] reports that he was aware of this situation immediately after landing with the first wave. As no contact could be established with his own immediate superior, the Area Operations Officer attached to XI Air Corps, he telephoned direct to Corps HQ, requesting that the start of the second wave be delayed. If any decision was arrived at, the unfortunate fact is that it did not reach the transport groups. In the same way, there were no further arrangements with VIII Air Corps.[55]

Its bomber formations were over objectives in Retimo and Heraklion at 15.00 hours as originally planned, in an attempt to destroy anti-aircraft positions, or at least keep down their fire. Immediately afterwards, single- and twin-engined fighters flew in to protect the drop and overwhelm the defence. Owing to their short range, these planes were unable to stay over the operations area after 16.15, and thus the major part of the forces were dropped without fighter protection.

The task of Centre Group, now under the command of Colonel Sturm, was to capture the airfield at Retimo and then drive towards Suda Bay. The task of Eastern Group, under the command of Colonel Bräuer, was to capture the town and the airfield of Heraklion, and hold the latter for subsequent airborne landings.

Both groups suffered heavy losses because, as was the case of the first wave, they were dropped in the centre of strongly held and well camouflaged defensive positions. The enemy's task was made much easier because the transport planes arrived unsystematically.[56] Some inexperienced transport crews made errors and carried out their drops in the wrong places, and this led to still further confusion amongst the attackers. There were also heavy losses in material because many paratroopers were unable to reach their supply containers.

All these circumstances combined to thwart Centre Group in its efforts to capture the airfield at Retimo, while its attempt to drive towards Suda Bay broke down under heavy enemy fire. Because planes were out of action both during and after the first wave, Eastern Group made contact with the enemy with 600 fewer men that originally planned. The delays in starting were particularly bad here, and they added to the difficulties so that it was really not surprising that this group also failed to attain its objectives. All that Colonel Bräuer could do was to gather his dispersed men under cover of darkness and launch them against the airfield the next morning.

The review of the battle situation on the evening of May 20th showed that at all four points where paratroops had been dropped the enemy was considerably stronger than had been expected. Not one of the three airfields had been captured, and the situation in Crete was critical. The position at Maleme seemed more favourable, and later in the day it was even reported – erroneously – that the airfield had been captured, although still under enemy artillery fire. It was now absolutely necessary to capture at least one of the three airfields, in order to carry out the proposed airborne landing of the 5th Mountain Division. In the present situation this could only be Maleme, which was nearest to the Luftwaffe bases in Greece; although it was considerably smaller than the airfield at Heraklion, it seemed to offer the best prospects for the attacking forces. 'In brief, at Maleme the battle of Crete was lost and won,' writes the historian of the Royal Air Force.[57] How did this come about?

Hill 107 to the south of the airfield proved to be the key point of the local defences, though at first its importance was not recognized from aerial photographs.[58] It was therefore attacked only by a reinforced company, under Major Koch, in gliders, and the attack was repulsed with heavy losses. On landing, Major-General Meindl, commander of Western Group, immediately recognized the strength of the enemy position, which ran along the river bed of the Tavronitis from the western edge of the airfield over the western slope of Hill 107 southward. He at once added four companies to the frontal attack in the direction of the airfield, and two more from the south to envelop the hill position. The area around Maleme was held by the 22nd New Zealand Battalion under the command of Lieutenant-Colonel Andrew. When his communications and signals system broke down, he felt that he could no longer exercise effective command over his men; he therefore withdrew his forces, under strong pressure, at night. This 'retreat from Maleme' resulted in the loss of Crete.[59]

During the course of the day, the British Commander-in-Chief, General Freyberg, came into possession of instructions sending the 3rd German Parachute Regiment into action. This order, together with his own view of the general situation, gave him a very good idea of what was likely to happen, and during the night he reported to General Wavell that if the Navy could thwart the expected invasion by sea (which was supposed to be the main German force) his own forces were sufficiently strong and in a good enough position to cope with all possible attacks from the air. However, he did point out that, as the result of heavy enemy air attacks, his communications and signals system was functioning badly. But when he made this report he did not know how bad it was; for example, he did not know that the 22nd New Zealand Battalion had withdrawn from Maleme, and that as a result a yawning gap had opened in the most vulnerable part of his defence. Had he known he would undoubtedly have moved heaven and earth to save Maleme by bringing up reinforcements under cover of darkness.

When the heavy attack General Student expected during the decisive night of May 20th–21st did not materialize, so that the shot-up and exhausted remnants of the Assault Regiment were given a respite even during the early hours of May 21st, he decided to concentrate all efforts on Maleme, and thus tipped the scales. One of the factors which led to this decision was the excellent wireless connection the regimental signals officer had in the meantime – despite the loss of a good deal of his equipment – succeeded in establishing with Airborne HQ in Athens.[60]

During the morning of May 21st, some Ju's managed to land on the beach at Maleme (suffering damage), bringing arms and ammunition; and one Ju managed to land on the airfield itself. However, the runway was still under such intense infantry and artillery fire that although everything was ready for the landing of the Mountain Battalion it had to be postponed again. The only way to reinforce Western Group and strengthen its efforts to get the airfield completely under its control was by further parachute drops, and this was done; by approximately 17.00 hours Maleme itself was captured and the German hold on the airfield consolidated. This was achieved with very effective support from VIII Air Corps, which enjoyed absolute command of the air and carried out constant attacks on anti-aircraft positions, enemy strong-points, and so on. In the meantime, from 16.00 hours, the first groups of a reinforced Mountain Battalion were landed on the airfield in face of continued artillery and machine-gun fire. A good many Ju–52s were destroyed in the process, but it was now possible to count on further landings, the exploitation of the successes so far obtained, and a drive to make contact with Centre Group near Canea and Suda Bay on May 22nd. The next objective was to extend the bridgehead at Maleme and drive the enemy out of his naval strong-point at Suda Bay, where fast vessels were still bringing in supplies under cover of night. On May 21st, transport planes succeeded in bringing munitions to Centre Group, but an attempt to take the high ground around Galatas was beaten off. The attacking forces were considerably weakened by losses, and they could do no more than hold the positions they had won and pin down enemy forces.

The German forces remaining near Retimo beat off repeated enemy attacks, and with the aid of munition and other supplies they succeeded in maintaining their positions, though with some difficulty.

Eastern Group, near Heraklion, was split into two. With close support from VIII Air Corps, the troops to the west tried to penetrate into Heraklion itself, but after a promising start the attack came to a standstill in the face of powerful enemy resistance, and those elements which had actually succeeded in penetrating into the town had to be withdrawn. The other group, to the east, led by Colonel Bräuer, attempted to capture the airfield itself, but without success. The attack was hopeless without heavy weapons, and because of its failure the Airborne Corps was unable to land parts of the 5th Mountain Division in Heraklion as planned.

However, thanks to the capture of Maleme, XI Air Corps reported by the evening of May 21st that the critical point had been passed, and orders were issued for the consolidation of the German positions at Maleme and for launching the attack on Canea. General Ringel, commander of the 5th Mountain Division, was now given command of Western Group. The following day three battalions of his division were landed on Maleme airfield.

The Battle against the British Fleet

One of the chief problems of the attack on Crete was the speedy supply of heavy weapons. The only satisfactory way to bring these in was by sea, and motor sailing vessels and merchant ships were made available for the purpose. The attempts to carry out this task and at the same time prevent the British Navy from landing reinforcements on Crete, led to the first 'air-sea battle' of the Second World War. As they were so clearly inferior in the air, the British hoped to make up for this by using the strong naval forces they were in a position to commit in the eastern Mediterranean. They felt that the Germans would find it impossible to capture Crete by air alone, and they therefore anticipated that an attempt would be made to bring in strong German forces by sea.

As we have already mentioned, VIII Air Corps had received general instructions to keep the sea around Crete under constant observation in the preparatory phase of the battle, and to attack all enemy shipping encountered in the area. It reported that in carrying out these instructions it had sunk or damaged twenty-seven ships by May 20th.[61]

Two motor sailing vessel flotillas put out from Piraeus and Chalcis according to plan, escorted by the Italian torpedo boats *Lupo* and *Sagittario* and carrying about 2,300 mountain troops and heavy equipment.[62] By the evening of the first day of the attack on Crete, they had reached their operational starting point, Melos, and Flag Officer Southeast was requested by Air Fleet 4 to do everything possible to ensure the landing of the first of the motor sailing vessel flotillas near Maleme before the fall of darkness on May 21st. The German authorities made another attempt to persuade the Italian fleet to put out in order to draw British naval forces away from the Crete operations, but Rome refused.

During the night from May 20th–21st, British naval units passed round Crete to the east and through the Cythera Channel to the west, combed the sea to the north of Crete, and sailed along the northern coast of the island. During these operations the airfield at Scarpanto was bombarded from the sea, but without causing a great deal of damage. Strong forces of VIII Air Corps, which had been held in reserve for just such a possibility, attacked the departing British naval units in the morning of May 21st, sinking the destroyer *Juno* and damaging the cruiser *Ajax*.[63] While continuing its operations to the south of the island VIII Air Corps was able to report by 09.00 hours that the sea to the north of Crete was free of enemy naval forces, and about midday the first of the motor sailing vessel flotillas continued its course from Melos towards Maleme. However, in the afternoon it was spotted by RAF reconnaissance planes and in the night it was attacked by a newly arrived British naval force consisting of the cruisers *Dido* and *Orion*, with the *Ajax* and four destroyers. Thanks to the gallant efforts of the Italian torpedo boat *Lupo* (Commander Mimbelli), which received eighteen direct hits, and to the fact that the flotilla immediately dispersed in all directions, only ten vessels were sunk. The remainder took refuge on the south coast of the Peloponnese.[64] The problem of getting heavy weapons and reinforcements into Crete was still unsolved; the second convoy was immediately recalled, but not before it was attacked on the morning of May 22nd by a second British task force consisting of the cruisers *Perth*, *Naiad*, *Calcutta* and *Carlisle* with two destroyers. Two boats were sunk, and it was only thanks to the Italian torpedo boat *Sagittario* (Captain Cigala), and repeated attacks by Luftwaffe squadrons immediately brought up that losses were kept so low. To support the attacking naval forces, Admiral Cunningham now sent out a third task force consisting of the battleships *Warspite* and *Valiant*, the cruisers *Gloucester* and *Fiji* and seven destroyers. Throughout the day of May 22nd there was constant heavy fighting between these British task forces and planes of VIII Air Corps supported by bombers and dive-bombers of X Air Corps. The cruisers *Gloucester* and *Fiji* and the destroyer *Greyhound* were sunk, the cruiser *Naiad* and the battleship *Warspite* were badly damaged, and the AA cruiser *Carlisle* and the battleship *Valiant* sustained minor damage. The British Navy thus had to pay a high price for its successes against the German convoys. Attacks by the reinforced VIII Air Corps the next day, May 23rd, resulted in the loss of two further British destroyers, the *Kashmir* and the *Kelly*, which were sunk to the south of Crete. The Luftwaffe leaders were still not sure whether the British ceded them victory in this engagement, 'aircraft against warship in narrow seas', but on May 24th Admiral Cunningham told London frankly that in view of the weight of the Luftwaffe attack his forces could no longer operate in daylight in the Aegean or in Cretan waters. Any attempt to prevent the enemy landing troops and supplies from the sea must entail heavy losses for the fleet in the eastern Mediterranean. However, London was still quite sure that the Germans would find it impossible to take Crete from the air, particularly as they had captured only one airfield, that of Maleme, so the reply received in Alexandria was quite uncompromising: the British Navy and the RAF must take every necessary risk to prevent the Germans from landing further reinforcements in Crete; in pursuance of these instructions British naval forces were to be committed in daylight against convoys to the north of the island and suffer whatever losses might be involved. Only experience could show how long this could continue.

However, despite these instructions it was impossible to send further warships from the western Mediterranean to Crete because Force 'H' stationed at Gibraltar, the whole of the Home Fleet, and every available vessel had to be mobilized to hunt down the German battleship *Bismarck*, which was at large in the Atlantic.

However, night operations and the movement of reinforcements to the north coast of Crete were continued on May 24th–25th. On May 26th, even the aircraft carrier *Formidable* appeared on the scene, and raided the airfield on the island of Scarpanto with the twelve planes she now had at her disposal. But in the afternoon she was heavily attacked by German bombers and received two direct hits, while the destroyer *Nubian* lost her stern. The next day the battleship *Barham*, which was attached to another task force, was attacked and damaged to the southeast of Caso.

All these operations demonstrated very clearly that a fleet cannot operate without adequate air cover in waters within range of a superior enemy air force, except at the price of very heavy losses.

Continuation and Conclusion of the Battle for Crete

As a result of the British decision to defend Crete at all costs, RAF planes coming from Egypt now appeared in the sky over the island once more, and in particular they attacked the airfield at Maleme. Hurricanes provided with supplementary fuel tanks even landed on Heraklion airfield. But these efforts met with little success, particularly as, for the first time, the Germans had succeeded that same evening in transferring fighters to Maleme.

On the evening of May 22nd, General Ringel took command in Maleme, reorganized his forces, and began mopping-up operations in the western part of the island in order to prevent any threat to his base from the west and the south. Castelli fell on May 25th.

For his drive towards Canea and Suda Bay in the east, he divided his forces into two groups: one consisting of his mountain troops, which were to fan out southward and make their way forward over difficult mountain territory; the other group, the paratroopers, was to advance along the coast.

Thanks to this drive by the mountain troops, it proved possible to link up with Centre Group to the west of Canea by the evening of May 23rd, and thus the first important success was achieved in the German effort to out-manœuvre the defence by a strong enveloping movement on the right wing.

During the next few days after May 24th, further reinforcements were systematically sent to General Ringel's group to enable him to carry out his intentions. To what extent he could be reinforced depended on the number of transport planes available, and on the amount of supplies required by the other battle groups engaged on the island. The only way to relieve the over-burdened air transport groups and to bring in heavy weapons such as tanks was still by sea in daylight under the protection of strong air escort and after the whole sea area in question had been thoroughly reconnoitred. The first German success in this respect was obtained after the anti-aircraft defences of Melos and Cythera had been strengthened; on May 28th, a tug brought two lighters into Maleme carrying four tanks. On the whole, therefore, the British Navy did prevent the Germans from bringing in reinforcements and supplies by sea in the critical days of the battle for Crete. At night the British Navy had complete command of the sea, and the advance of General Ringel's forces through the mountains, which avoided losses but took a great deal of time, might well have given the British an opportunity of landing important reinforcements in Suda Bay if the Luftwaffe had not kept a close watch for any shipping movements by day, pouncing on any such attempt at once. As it was, only the fastest enemy ships could undertake the round trip to Suda Bay during the night, and even then only part of their journey was out of reach of the Luftwaffe. Very few such vessels were available, and those that were could carry only a few hundred men.

The Ringel Group came to a halt on May 24th before the strongly fortified enemy positions at Galatas. It was here, on the plateau to the west of Canea, that General Freyberg had concentrated all his forces in the Suda Bay area. It was the last barrier before these two decisive points, and it was here that the final battle for Crete was fought. On May 25th, the RAF once again intervened in the battle by attacking Maleme airfield with bombers and long-range fighters from Egypt. However, these air attacks against what was now the key German base on the island were too weak to be effective, and too late to change the situation. All the same, the situation at Maleme was far from satisfactory; planes were constantly crashing on landing on the relatively small airfield, and the confined space available was narrowed still further by wreckage. However, a landing party equipped with captured enemy tanks succeeded in clearing away obstacles fairly rapidly.

Thanks to their efforts, it proved possible to bring in the necessary reinforcements for the Mountain Division, and on May 26th a further regiment of the 6th Mountain Division was landed. After this, the operation to break the enemy's resistance proceeded according to plan. On May 26th, after a concentrated attack by units of VIII Air Corps on Canea, German troops succeeded in penetrating the enemy's positions to the west of the town; the following day his resistance at Canea was definitely broken, and the town was captured. Suda Bay was captured on May 28th. The following day, Retimo was relieved and contact made with Eastern Group around Heraklion.

On May 22nd, the Italians judged the situation on Crete to be sufficiently favourable to allow them to take part in the conquest of the island, and they proposed to contribute one armoured company. This expeditionary force of reinforced regimental strength landed on May 28th in Sitia, and then advanced on Ierapetra without meeting with much resistance. Its objective was to make it impossible for the British to withdraw to the east of the island and evacuate any considerable forces there. The landing had no effect whatever on the outcome of the battle for Crete.

By the morning of May 26th, it was quite clear to General Freyberg that the loss of Crete was now only a matter of time, and he communicated his views to General Wavell, C.-in-C. Middle East, at the same time informing him that during the non-stop fighting and the concentrated bombing attacks of the past few days the British forces on Crete had reached the limit of human endurance. If permission to evacuate were given at once, it would prove possible to save some of the forces engaged. He added that of course he would continue to do his best if it were felt that every hour was important for the situation in the Middle East.

Wavell answered that this was, in fact, the case. Churchill, who was also consulted, still insisted that victory in Crete was absolutely necessary and called on Wavell to send decisive aid to Crete. But the hard facts of the case could not be denied; and as this reply came from London, Wavell received news that a further convoy for Crete had been compelled by heavy Luftwaffe attacks to turn back to Egypt.

On the island itself, the situation of the defenders had greatly deteriorated during the course of May 26th, and on the following day General Freyberg ordered preparations for evacuation from the small harbour of Sfakia on the south coast. Two battalions of commando troops under Colonel Laycock were landed at Suda Bay on the night of May 26th–27th, and these fresh troops fought a determined rearguard action which made it possible for the surviving defenders to make their way from Maleme and Canea to the south coast of Crete. In the meantime, all thought of retreat to Retimo and Heraklion was disposed of by the German drive eastward.

The evacuation of something like 4,000 men from the harbours of the north coast during the night of May 28th–29th cost the British Navy the loss of the destroyers *Hereward* and *Imperial* with 800 men. They were both sunk while trying to pass through the Kaso strait. At the same time the cruisers *Ajax*, *Orion* and *Dido* were damaged. All that was left to the defenders was to try to escape from the south coast of Crete.

The collecting point for the evacuation was at Sfakia, a small fishing village at the foot of an almost perpendicular rock face which was over three hundred feet high and negotiable only by one steep goat track. During the day, the men awaiting evacuation had to hide from the attacks of the Luftwaffe as best they could, while in the mountains behind them there was bitter fighting between their rearguard and the pursuing German mountain troops along the completely inadequate road in the bare, arid, trackless terrain to the south. Later, General Freyberg was to refer to this road as the *via dolorosa* of the British forces.

In the four nights beginning with the night of May 28th–29th, a fleet of British cruisers, destroyers and merchant vessels took off a total of 17,000 men. Half the British expeditionary force was taken from the open beaches during the few short hours of the night; a really masterly performance which was not sufficiently recognized by the commanders of Air Fleet 4 at the time.[65] From the beginning of the operation, the night of May 31st–June 1st was fixed as the final day of the evacuation. It was felt that any further loss and damage to the Mediterranean Fleet would prove too heavy. As it was, the naval losses of the British in the evacuation from Sfakia, apart from damage to the cruiser *Perth* and to three destroyers, were increased by the loss of the AA cruiser *Calcutta*, which was sunk a hundred miles off Alexandria by a Ju–88. The three squadrons of RAF fighters left in Egypt were used by Air Marshal Tedder for convoy protection duties during the daylight hours, and this prevented even worse losses.

British casualties are usually put at about 15,000 in dead, wounded and prisoners, but a more reliable report places them at 15,743.[66] In addition, the Navy lost 2,011 men. It is now possible to make a reliable estimate of German losses during the Crete operation, and they are very much below the original estimate made by Churchill of 'more than 5,000 parachute troops killed', and a total of 15,000 dead and wounded. A careful perusal of all official and other sources puts them at 6,580 dead, wounded and missing, out of a total of 22,000 men engaged in the operation.[67]

Although, as we have said, this number was considerably below Churchill's estimate, it was nevertheless higher than the entire German losses throughout the whole of the Balkan campaign, which amounted to a total of 5,650 dead, wounded and missing.[68] At that relatively low price, Germany purchased a unique victory, and one which made the German conduct of operations on land appear almost invincible.

The Importance of Crete for the Subsequent Course of the War

If the British historians are right when they say that the war in the Middle East was becoming more and more a battle for airfields, and that the main significance of territorial gains or losses was to what extent they placed the two air forces in a more or less favourable situation towards Alexandria, Cairo, the Suez Canal, Benghazi, Tripoli and the supply lines across the Mediterranean, then the loss of Crete was a heavy blow for Britain's position in the Middle East. Further, the loss was suffered at a time when the British badly needed a victory, if only for reasons of prestige. In Iraq, the insurrectionary government of al-Gelani had been defeated with some difficulty; in Syria, preparations were being made to take action against General Dentz, who was loyal to the Vichy Government; on May 15th, General Wavell had started a drive to relieve Tobruk, but it had failed completely, losing all the hard-earned gains within a very few days more; and on May 27th, Halfaya had fallen to German troops.[69] The Mediterranean Fleet, which had suffered heavy damage during the battle for Crete, now faced the prospect of a still more serious situation, because with Crete on its northern flank and Cyrenaica in the south both in German hands, every attempt to send a ship to Malta, or to venture into the Mediterranean for any reason whatever, would amount to running the gauntlet of Luftwaffe attacks. In addition, the Italian fleet was practically untouched by the air-sea battle for Crete, and it still consisted of four battleships and twelve cruisers.[70] British Middle East Command judged the situation to be so serious that a similar German attempt to capture Cyprus was regarded as likely, and ways and means of bringing up the necessary forces and equipment to defend the island were being considered – though neither men nor material were available for the next two to three months.[71] Behind Cyprus was Syria, Iraq – and even Persia. They too would lie open to the attacks of German airborne forces. Crete might well be the 'first stepping-stone' – just as later on the Americans were to hop across the Pacific from island to island.

British war historians unanimously believe that the very high losses suffered by his parachute troops in Crete dissuaded Hitler from ever using them on a large scale again, so that in this way a tactical British defeat can be reckoned as a strategic success.[72]

There is, however, no reliable evidence that the defence of Crete by the British substantially delayed the opening of the campaign against Russia and thus affected the outcome of the 1941 offensive. General Student[73] reports that on July 17th, 1941, at a reception for holders of the Knight's Cross, Hitler observed to him: 'Crete proved that the days of the parachute troops are over. The parachute arm is one which relies entirely on surprise. In the meantime the surprise factor has exhausted itself.' This conviction may well have materially influenced him in his refusal to countenance Operation 'Hercules'[74] in the summer of 1942, which was the plan to capture Malta by air attack as Crete had been captured. He was too doubtful about its success. If this is the case then General Student's own words that Crete was 'the grave of Germany's parachutists' were true in a double sense.

At this juncture it should be pointed out that both during the campaign against France and in the battle of Crete, Germany used her parachute troops operatively on a big scale, whereas the Allies used theirs – for example, in Normandy, and rather later on at Arnhem – only in close tactical co-operation with land operations.

The battle of Crete suddenly exposed the dependence of modern naval power on command of the air, and it showed that a fleet without strong air support is condemned to impotence. This was made very clear in Admiral Cunningham's final report on the operations, which pointed out that the Mediterranean Fleet had to pay a very high price for such successes as it obtained. The losses and damage it suffered would, he said, have been quite natural if they had been inflicted in a big naval engagement, in which the enemy fleet could have been expected to suffer even greater loss and damage. But no enemy fleet had been engaged in these operations; the battle had been between ships and planes.

The operations which succeeded in capturing Crete without the support of a strong fleet might have been expected to persuade Hitler that the situation in the Mediterranean was favourable for further operations, but he had decided on the campaign against Russia, and in his 'Middle East' Directive, dated May 23rd, 1941, he expressly postponed the decisive offensive on Britain's position between the Mediterranean and the Persian Gulf, including an attack on the Suez Canal, to the period *after* the successful conclusion of Operation

'Barbarossa',[75] the attack on Russia. Directive No. 31, dated June 9th, 1941, i.e. between the campaigns, dealt with the situation in the southeast. Crete was regarded as occupying a special position from which the Luftwaffe would be able to fight an air war in the eastern Mediterranean to support operations in North Africa. In the meantime the organization, consolidation, safeguarding and supplying of this base was declared to be the most important task in the southeast area. These ideas were set out at greater length in the draft of Directive No. 32 of June 11th, dealing with preparations for the period *after* Operation 'Barbarossa', which was to include 'a concentric attack on the British position in the Mediterranean and the Near East', using 'the new sea route' from south Greece.

But the subsequent course of the war made these plans for southeast Europe irrelevant. For the time being, operations in the Mediterranean were much less important than the happenings in Russia. The ambitious plans in which this dearly-bought island of Crete was to serve as a spring-board were never carried out, and the island fell into a kind of enchanted sleep for the rest of the war. The Luftwaffe no longer had sufficient forces to make use of the advantages Crete offered as a base in the eastern Mediterranean. It even proved impossible to use Crete as a supply base for the armies in North Africa, as had been intended, because the Greek railways were just adequate to keep the garrison supplied, and no more; and, in any case, no shipping was available for the purpose. So the subsequent role of Crete during the war was a typical example of the axiom that a favourable geographical position need not necessarily be a favourable strategic one, and that it must first be made so by efficient communications and the investment of adequate material resources. However, the possession of Crete did close the Aegean to the enemy and safeguard the sea route Constanza–Bosphorus–Corinth–Italy, so the island continued to represent a latent threat to Britain's positions in the Mediterranean and the Near East.

In the end, Britain was able to strengthen her position in the Middle East once more, and – with the assistance of her allies – she then captured North Africa, defeated the Afrika Korps and knocked Germany's Italian ally out of the war altogether.

Chronicle V

June

to

December 1941

	Politics		Conduct of the War
Neutrals	Axis Powers and Japan		Axis Powers and Japan
	June 6th: OKW issues 'Commissar Order'.		
			June 11th: Führer Directive No. 32 (draft Germany's strategy after the conclusio Operation 'Barbarossa'.
	June 15th: Croatia joins Three-Power Pact.		
	June 18th: German-Turkish Treaty of Friendship signed.		
	June 22nd: Italy and Rumania declare war on Russia.		June 22nd: German attack on Russia.
			June 29th: Capture of Riga.
			June 30th: Capture of Lemberg.
			July 10th: End of the dual battle Byelostok–M 323,898 Russian prisoners taken.
July 23rd: Franco-Japanese Treaty on Indo-China.	July 17th: Hitler's decree on the administration of the newly-occupied eastern areas.		
			July 26th: Italian surprise raid against Malta
	August: Tokyo map manœuvres test operational plans drawn up by the Admiralty and General Staff.		
			August 21st: Führer directive: attacks to north and south of the battlefront.
			August 29th: Finns capture Viborg.
	September 1st: Discrimination against Jews in Germany: introduction of the Yellow Star.		
	Beginning of September: Joint Admiralty and General Staff Planning Conference in Tokyo draws up final war plans.		
	September 15th: 'Peenemunde Project' (rockets) given top priority.		September 19th: Kiev captured.
			September 24th: Battle of Kiev ends; 65 Russian prisoners.
	October 3rd: Decree introducing forced labour for Jews in Germany.		October 2nd: Beginning of the Battle for M(('Typhoon'). First phase.
	October 18th: General Tojo replaces Prince Konoye as Prime Minister.		
	November 3rd: Pearl Harbour attack included in Japanese naval plans.		
	November 5th: Conference in presence of Japanese Emperor decides to put Pearl Harbour plan into execution unless agreement with the US reached by November 25th.		November 14th: U. 81 sinks British aircraft c Ark Royal off Gibraltar.
			November 15th: Opening of the second ph; the Battle for Moscow.
			November 16th: Capture of Kerch.
	November 25th: Bulgaria, Croatia, Denmark, Finland, China (Nanking), Rumania and Slovakia join Anti-Comintern Pact.		November 25th: U. 331 sinks British batt Barham off Sollum.
	December 1st: Japan decides to go to war.		December 17th: Naval battle between Britis Italian convoy covering forces in the G Sirte.
	December 7th: 'Nacht und Nebel' decree issued, imposing savage penalties for sabotage, etc., in occupied areas.		December 19th: Hitler takes over supreme mand of the German Army. Italian u water charioteers sink two British battl in Alexandria Harbour.
	December 11th: Germany and Italy declare war on United States. Italo-German agreement on joint prosecution of the war.		December 21st: Heavy Luftwaffe attacks on I
			December 27th: Capitulation of Hong Kong
			December: After heavy air attacks, Jar forces land in Malaya (8th); North I (8th to 10th); the Gilbert Islands Guam (10th); South Luzon (11th); Borneo (17th); Mindanao (20th); Li Gulf (21st) and Wake Island (22nd).

Conduct of the War	Politics	
stern Allies and the Soviet Union	Western Allies and the Soviet Union	Neutrals

7th: Anglo-French troops march into Syria.		
12th to 13th: Heavy British air raids on the Ruhr.		June 16th: Roosevelt orders closing of all German consulates in the United States.
21st: Allied forces occupy Damascus.		
	June 30th: Formation of the National Defence Committee in the Soviet Union.	July 7th: US marines land in Iceland.
	July 12th: Armistice in Syria. Russo-British agreement on the joint prosecution of the war.	
	July 18th: Stalin asks Britain to open a Second Front.	
0th: British carrier-borne air raid on Petsamo.		
		August 1st: US Government declares oil embargo against 'aggressors'.
st 7th: Stalin becomes supreme Soviet commander.		August 2nd: USA begins to send supplies to Russia.
	August 16th: Communist Party Directive for Russian war economy 41/42.	August 14th: Roosevelt and Churchill proclaim the 'Atlantic Charter'. US Atlantic Fleet takes over Denmark Straits patrol and the escorting of fast Allied convoys in the western North Atlantic.
st 25th: British and Russian troops enter Iran.		
st 28th: Baltic Fleet evacuates Reval and uffers heavy losses from minefields in the Gulf of Finland.		
		September 4th: Greer incident.
nber 17th: US destroyer groups escort Allied ist North Atlantic convoys.		September 11th: Roosevelt issues 'shoot first' order: US warships to open fire without warning on German and Italian warships.
nber 18th: British submarine *Upholder* sinks vo large Italian troop transports.		
er 16th: Russians evacuate Odessa.		October 9th: Nuri-es-Said forms new Iraqi Cabinet friendly to Great Britain.
nber 8th to 9th: British 'Force K' to the west f Malta destroys Italian convoy to North frica.		November 13th: US Congress votes for arming of merchant ships and their use in transporting supplies to Britain.
nber 18th: British counter-offensive in North frica.		
nber 29th: Russian counter-attack on the outhern front (Rostov recaptured).	December 4th: Pact of friendship and mutual assistance signed by the Polish Government in exile and the Soviet Government.	November 25th: USA sends 'Ten-Point' Note to Japan. Japanese regard it as an ultimatum making a breach inevitable.
ber 5th: Soviet counter-offensive opens up efore Moscow.	December 6th: Great Britain declares war on Hungary, Finland and Rumania.	November 27th: 'War warning' sent to all US Commanders outside the United States.
ber 7th: Surprise Japanese attack on the US leet in Pearl Harbour, without a declaration f war.	December 8th: United States declares war on Japan.	
ber 10th: British relieve Tobruk.		
ber 14th to 22nd: British warships under aptain Walker escorting Gibraltar convoy G. 76 sink five German U-boats.	December 22nd: Beginning of the first Washington Conference (Roosevelt and Churchill).	

The Battle for Moscow 1941

BY RUDOLF HOFMANN

Preliminary

When Hitler launched the German Army against Russia on June 22nd, 1941, he felt confident that he could break the military power of the Soviet Union before the end of the year. Once this was done his rear would be protected, and he could turn against Britain and her allies, including perhaps, after 1943, the United States, and bring the war to a successful conclusion. The more Britain tightened the blockade around Europe, the more important Russia's rich material resources became for Germany's war industries, and the more important Russia's grain production became for the feeding of Germany's population. But in the last resort it was ideological differences which made Hitler feel that sooner or later the two countries must clash, and persuaded him to attack Russia at a time of his own choosing. Russia certainly harboured no immediately aggressive intentions, because she first had to modernize her air and armoured forces. In any case, she was used to achieving political successes without firing a shot. There was nothing to tempt Stalin to abandon his tried and trusted policy and run the risk of an aggressive war against Germany, particularly as the German Wehrmacht was now very strong. On the other hand, Germany's steady transfer of her forces to the east had not gone unnoticed, and Stalin was preparing the country as best he could to fight a war of defence. The initiative was therefore unquestionably in Hitler's hands, and he felt that he was in a position to risk a war on two fronts for a while, being firmly convinced that the German Army, with the great advantage of its experience in the previous blitz campaigns and the high morale derived from victory, could readily destroy 'the giant with the feet of clay' within the year 1941. He had chosen the end of the muddy weather in the spring – that is to say, about the beginning of May – as the earliest possible date for the invasion, but the unexpected Balkan campaign involved a delay of between five to six weeks, since the victorious troops there – chiefly the highly mobile units – had to be brought back and regrouped.

Hitler now had new allies in Finland, Hungary and Rumania. Italy was also Germany's ally, but there was little hope that she would take any active part in the campaign, at least for the time being. She still had her hands full in North Africa. She had suffered heavy losses there, and her retreat had been brought to a halt only with the assistance of German troops. On April 13th, Japan signed a Neutrality Pact with Russia, thus upsetting the balance of forces in the Far East, and giving Russia an opportunity of withdrawing some of her forces from the Far East to Europe. On the other hand, it was in Hitler's interests that Japan should have her hands free to attack Singapore as quickly as possible, and so pin down British forces there.

Hitler explained the necessity of his Russian campaign to the German people by stressing the danger of Bolshevism, pointing out that now was the most favourable moment for dealing with that danger once and for all. He said it was Germany's historic mission to save Western civilization from this threat. People sensed the new great sacrifices they would be called upon to bear, though, of course, they did not realize the extent of the catastrophe which was to come.

For the attack, OKW had ordered that: 'Operations are to be carried out in such a manner as to destroy the mass of the Russian Army in the west, by driving armoured spearheads forward to prevent the withdrawal into the vast expanses of the country of any remnants of her forces still capable of putting up a fight.' According to the Führer Directive of December 18th, 1940, the 'ultimate objective' of the attack was to cut off Asiatic Russia from Europe along a line from Archangel to the Volga.[1]

It was assumed that Russia would make use of both the field fortifications she had erected behind her old frontiers and of those behind her new ones, some of which had been recently strengthened; and at the same time take advantage of numerous rivers and water-courses favourable for defence, before finally accepting battle with her main forces in the area to the west of the Dnieper and the Dvina. Russia's military leaders would, it was thought, attach particular importance to holding the air and naval bases in the Baltic provinces, and anchoring a southern flank on the Black Sea as long as possible. For this, they would probably be prepared to commit strong forces. In the event of an unfavourable outcome of the battle to the south and north of the Pripet Marshes, the Russians would probably seek to halt the German advance on the Dnieper–Dvina line.

In resisting German attempts to break through, and if it later became necessary to withdraw their endangered forces to the Dnieper–Dvina line, the Russians would undoubtedly commit strong forces supported by armour.

The first objective set by OKH, within the general framework of its assigned task, was to break through the Russian front in the west by swift and deep drives with its mobile units, both north and south of the Pripet marshes, and then to exploit the break-through to destroy the enemy forces thus separated from each other.

South of the Pripet Marshes – Army Group South, Field-Marshal von Rundstedt: strong armoured forces from the Lublin area were to break through quickly in the direction of Kiev, and were to cut the communications of the enemy forces in Galicia and the Western Ukraine by seizing the Dnieper crossings at and below Kiev; at the same time they were to ensure freedom of movement for subsequent co-operation between Army Group South and the German forces operating in northern Russia, or for new operations in southern Russia.

North of the Pripet Marshes – Army Group Centre, Field-Marshal von Bock: mobile forces from the Warsaw and Suwalki area were to drive forward swiftly in the direction of Smolensk; the subsequent break-through to be exploited by wheeling strong mobile forces northward to co-operate with Army Group North, Field-Marshal von Leeb, in its advance from East Prussia in the general direction of Leningrad, destroying the enemy forces operating in the Baltic provinces; there they would link up with the Finnish Army, and perhaps with German forces brought in from Norway, to crush the last enemy resistance in northern Russia, thus safeguarding freedom of movement for further tasks – perhaps in co-operation with the German forces operating in southern Russia. In the event of any sudden and complete collapse of enemy resistance in northern Russia, the wheeling movement could be abandoned in favour of a direct drive on Moscow. . . .

Active co-operation could be relied on from Finland and Rumania on both flanks of the advance. The form this co-operation was to take, and the unification of these forces under German command, would be decided according to circumstances. The task of Rumania's forces would be to co-operate with the German forces deployed there, to pin down enemy forces and to afford auxiliary service in the rearward areas. The task of Finland would be to liquidate the Hangö base as quickly as possible, and to cover the deployment of German forces in north Finland; then, not later than when Army Group North crossed the Dvina, to make a concerted attack on the Russian forces on the Finnish southeast front, with the focal point to the east or the west of Lake Ladoga according to the request of OKH.

'Active co-operation on the part of Sweden is unlikely, but it is not impossible that she might allow the use of her railways for the German deployment in north Finland and for keeping the German forces supplied.'[2]

Encouraged by the success of frontier battles, the three Army Groups[3] all reached their first operational objectives, the Dnieper–Dvina Line, by the middle of July, and here and there even went beyond them. While the two outer Army Groups were pushing the enemy back frontally, Army Group Centre inflicted great damage on the Russian forces in a series of encircle- ment battles. However, successful as they were, these operations did not break the resistance of the enemy. It was seen quite early on that the Russian commanders were again and again able to throw new forces into the battle, and that 'the giant with feet of clay' was not going to be destroyed as easily as had been thought. On the contrary, the Russians fought back with grim determination, and they were very skilfully led. On July 14th Stalin issued a rousing appeal to the Russian people to resist the invader with all the means in their power, including partisan warfare. At the same time he appealed to the British, who were now his allies, to lend him aid. Although Britain was

TABLE I

Strengths of the German and Soviet Armies and Air Forces on the Eastern Front in 1941

Germany (including High Command Reserves)		Soviet Union (estimated) (Western Front only)	

ARMY

Germany		Soviet Union	
Infantry divisions	118	Infantry divisions	118
Mechanized divisions	15¼	Cavalry divisions	20
Armoured divisions	19	Mechanized and armoured brigades	40
	152¼	138 divisions and 40 brigades	

In addition: about 16 Finnish, 15 Rumanian, 3 to 4 Hungarian, and 3 Italian divisions, though these were not available until the summer.

AIR FORCES

	Bombers	Fighters	Recon-naissance		Bombers	Fighters	Recon-naissance
Air Fleet 4	360	210	30		1,800	2,000	800
Air Fleet 2	490	390	30		(incl.	(incl.	(Largely
Air Fleet 1	270	110	50		800	250–300	obsolete)
Air Fleet 5	40	10	10		modern)	modern)	
(Finland)							
	1,160	720	120				

A total of 2,000

An estimated total of 8,000, with 6,000 on the Western Front.

quite unable to comply with his request to open new fronts against Germany in France and Norway, he was given an assurance that arms and supplies would be delivered in increasing quantities.

Up to the end of July, the German Eastern Front moved steadily farther and farther eastward to the accompaniment of increasingly bitter fighting. Army Group South succeeded in encircling and destroying strong enemy forces in the Uman basin. Army Group Centre closed the ring around Smolensk, and began to withdraw parts of Panzer Groups 2 and 3 from the front for regrouping and replacements. Army Group North pushed on towards Leningrad, with a view to establishing contact with the Finns as soon as possible. However, despite all the undoubted successes, the general balance of the operations was not altogether satisfactory. In previous campaigns the tactic of driving armoured spearheads deep into enemy territory had created the preliminary conditions for swift victory, but it did not have the same results on the Eastern Front, primarily because in the vast spaces of the Russian steppes the advancing mechanized troops were not sufficiently powerful to seal off the encirclements they were in a position to achieve; they had to wait for the infantry to come up. At the same time, the Russian soldier continued to fight on obstinately even if he were encircled, thus giving his leaders time to bring up new forces from the rear. These long and bitter struggles on two fronts began to exhaust the strength of the mobile units, and led to unforeseen shortages of manpower and material. However, the men in the field still retained a confident sense of their superiority. Unfortunately, by this time there was dissension at the top. Differences of opinion existed between Hitler and OKH about the further conduct of operations, and this naturally delayed the ultimate decisions. Before long the men in the fighting line became aware of the trouble.

While the exclusive aim of OKH was to destroy the enemy's military forces, Hitler was anxious to pursue primarily political and economic objectives. OKH and the senior field commanders were in no doubt whatever that the decisive blow must be delivered against Moscow, if only because the main forces of the enemy lay in that direction. Russia's whole railway and communications network was centred on Moscow, and the loss of the capital would greatly hamper the freedom of movement of the Russian forces. The Russians knew this too and they had therefore to concentrate the strongest possible forces to defend their capital. Hitler, however, was anxious to drive southward in order to secure the rich grain fields of the Ukraine, the Donets industrial basin and the prosperous Crimea, while in the north, for political reasons, he was anxious to link up as quickly as possible with the Finns to the east of Lake Ladoga. But if such aims were to be paramount it would be necessary to spread out the German forces instead of concentrating them, and they were already thin enough on the ground. It meant, for example, that Army Group Centre would have to defend something like 450 miles of front with its infantry units alone, while giving up the mass of its mobile units to Army Groups North and South. This denial of all logical strategy was a hard blow, not only for OKH but also for the commanders in the field. OKH's intention to continue to drive towards Moscow (OKH Memorandum dated August 18th, 1941) was side-tracked by Hitler's decision of August 20th, to turn strong forces of Army Group Centre southward so that the inner wings of Army Groups Centre and South now sought to encircle the enemy in the battle of Kiev and cut off his retreat to the east. The tone of the Führer Directive of August 21st, 1941, to Brauchitsch, C.-in-C. Army, is clear evidence not only of the differences of opinion which existed between him and OKH but also of his intention to impose his own will more and more ruthlessly on the conduct of operations.[4]

The material results of the battle of Kiev were the destruction of at least five Russian armies (according to Wehrmacht reports, 650,000 prisoners were taken, together with 3,500 guns and 900 tanks), the joining of the two inner wings of Army Groups Centre and South, and the forward drive of the north wing of Army Group South across the barrier of the River Dnieper. On the other side of the balance sheet was the time the operation had taken: it was not until September 30th that Army Group Centre was ready to continue its operations against Moscow. Almost two precious months had been lost.

Even while the battle of Kiev was going on, much against the wishes of OKH, Brauchitsch never lost sight of his real aim, Moscow, although Hitler was intent on his old objectives in the south. The final opportunity to secure a decision before the year ended was now at hand, and to refrain from an attack on Moscow meant inevitably to extend the war into the following year. Although the season was now far advanced the risk just had to be taken, and under the pressure of the general situation everything had to be staked on this attack. Timoshenko's army group had to be destroyed, and the way to Moscow opened. This time Hitler did bow to the cogent arguments of OKH, and even agreed that the objective was sufficiently important to justify the concentration of all available forces on the wings of the main front (Army Groups South and North).

On September 6th, he issued Führer Directive No. 35,[5] instructing Army Group Centre to prepare 'as quickly as possible (end of September) for an attack on Moscow'. At the same time, Army Group South was instructed – even before the battle of Kiev was over – to exploit the enemy's weakness and drive to the east and southeast. Despite the fact that it had to transfer Panzer Group 4 to Army Group Centre, Army Group North was instructed to close the ring around Leningrad and advance over the Valdai Hills to the southeast of Lake Ilmen, and drive northeastwards. It was not foreseen at the time that after promising beginnings both these actions would come to a halt through lack of reserve strength, and ultimately end in humiliating set-backs.

The Attack on Moscow

The ideas of Hitler's intimate circle about the strategic situation in September 1941 can be seen in a memorandum issued by OKW with his approval[6]. Here is the gist of it. It was becoming doubtful whether it would be possible to break Russia's resistance before the end of 1941. Should it prove impossible after all, then at least 1942 must see the destruction of Russia's power to wage war – as a preliminary condition to persuading Britain to sue for peace. Thus the defeat of Russia was Germany's immediate objective; only when this was achieved would it be possible to concentrate all forces against Britain. There was still some hope that, despite the recently signed non-aggression pact, Japan might still attack Russia; but there was no hope at all, for the moment, that Turkey and Spain would abandon their neutrality and come into the war on Germany's side. However, once Turkey felt convinced that Russia was going to be defeated, the situation could change, and this was also true of Spain, once she could see that the Axis positions in the Mediterranean were quite secure. The possibility of contact between Britain and Russia through Iran gave rise to some misgiving, particularly as at the moment there was no means of preventing it. Turkey found it disturbing too. In the meantime Britain was strengthening her hold on the Suez Canal, while the position of the Italo-German forces in Libya was becoming more and more difficult. The only hope of changing this situation was to bring about a radical improvement of the supply lines across the Mediterranean. Britain would do her best, with the help of the United States, to prevent Franco-German co-operation, destroy the Axis bridgehead in North Africa, and seize the whole coast of North Africa in order to obtain command of the Mediterranean by sea and air. At the same time, the Mediterranean would be opened to the Americans through French Morocco (Casablanca) and French West Africa (Dakar). This would greatly curtail the strategic possibilities for the Axis powers, and if the blockade were still further tightened it might drive Italy to the point of collapse. Britain was thus pursuing two great aims: first of all, to strengthen Russia's will and capacity to resist by sending her supplies via Iran, and at the same time to thwart Germany's attempts to seize the Caucasian oil wells; and second, sooner or later to seize the whole of West and North Africa.

Germany must therefore wage war with the following objectives:

(a) her first and most urgent aim must be to bring about the collapse of Russia, and all possible forces which could be dispensed with on other fronts must be committed to this task;

(b) only after Russia had been knocked out of the war would it be possible to concentrate all forces against Britain in the Atlantic and in the Mediterranean – perhaps with the use of French and Spanish bases;

(c) political and military relationships with France and Spain must therefore be improved. France must be encouraged to strengthen her position in West Africa in order to resist Anglo-American intervention there; and

(d) the blockade of Britain must be tightened by stepping up U-boat operations with Luftwaffe support.

Even after the collapse of Russia, an invasion of Britain would be contemplated only if all other means of bringing the enemy to his knees should fail.

The conclusion drawn from these considerations was logical enough: an attempt must be made during the current year to break Russia's main military forces, which were likely to be encountered on the way to Moscow.

With this objective in view, OKH planned to take the strong Russian forces to the east of Smolensk in a pincers movement. Mobile units advancing on the wings were to close the pincers behind Vyazma. Only when the forces thus encircled had been destroyed was the drive on Moscow to proceed. The plan of attack developed by Army Group Centre in close co-operation with OKH depended primarily on what forces, and in particular what mobile forces, could be contributed by the neighbouring Army Groups. OKH proposed one armoured and two mechanized divisions from Army Group South, and Panzer Group 4 with three armoured and two mechanized divisions from Army Group North; and, in addition, various GHQ troops, including heavy artillery and self-propelled guns. To bring up Panzer Group 2 and the 2nd Army, which were engaged 125 miles away in the battle of Kiev, would have meant an excessive expenditure of time and energy, so it was decided to establish a second focal point in the south, with Panzer Group 2 reinforced by two infantry corps. A factor which once again heavily influenced these considerations was the question of close co-operation between armour and infantry. Relying on past experience, it was decided to subordinate the armour to the infantry armies. Only the more distant Panzer Group 2 was placed directly under Army Group Centre. Much was expected of the operations of this armoured group, because it was thought that it would be driving into a relatively weak defence which might allow a break-through in the direction of Moscow.

The almost uninterrupted fighting since June 22nd, together with the tremendous distances covered, had placed a great material strain on the attacking forces, and in particular on the mobile units. The clouds of dust which arose on dry days, and the tenacious mud whenever it rained heavily, led to numerous delays and breakdowns. In the short respite during the battle for Smolensk, there had been time to overhaul vehicles to some extent, but the supply of spare parts and MT was still inadequate. Hitler had allotted only 300 tank engines to the whole of the Eastern Front, and no new tanks at all. It was quite clear that the long journeys which many of them now had to make to their new operational positions would result in more breakdowns, and that for the time being it would be impossible to make them good. For example, after the battle for Kiev, Panzer Group 2 had only 30 per cent of its tanks, though Panzer Groups 3 and 4 were rather better off. Casualties, particularly in officers and NCO's, were high, and some infantry divisions had lost up to a third of their original strength. Because of the long distances to be covered from Germany, the few new drafts which were provided arrived only very slowly at the front.[7] Some compensation for these defects was provided by the high morale of the troops, who still felt themselves superior to the enemy and were prepared to put all they had into battle.

Supply lines had become longer and longer, and the capacity of mechanized transport had greatly declined. The railways were still in operation as far as Smolensk and Toropez, but they could not carry enough traffic to keep the widespread fronts adequately supplied. However, it did prove possible to bring up sufficient supplies to dumps near the front to meet the estimated requirements of the front-line troops.

The main force for the defence of Moscow opposite Army Group Centre was the 'Western Command' (from July 2nd with Marshal Timoshenko as C.-in-C. and HQ in Vyazma). This command consisted of 6 armies with 45 infantry, 6 armoured and 3 cavalry divisions. Held in reserve were 5 further armies. Facing the southern end of the Army Group Centre front was the 'Bryansk Command' with 3 armies with a total of 20 infantry, 3 armoured and 3 cavalry divisions. As official Russian figures are not available it is impossible to say whether this estimate, made by OKH and the Army Groups concerned on the basis of intelligence at the time, was really accurate.[8]

What is quite certain, however, is that some of these forces had already been engaged in battle and had been badly mauled, so that they were no longer at full battle strength. However, the Russians still seemed able to throw in fresh units repeatedly.[9] Even though these latter were not always fully equipped and fully trained, the Russians succeeded in building up a very strong front before Moscow, and the attacking German forces were faced with the task of breaking it up before there could be any thought of capturing Moscow. Despite many defeats and heavy losses in men and material, the fighting qualities of the Russian troops were still very high. In particular, the new Russian T–34 tank, which was appearing on the battlefield in increasing numbers, proved a hard nut to crack with the anti-tank weapons the German troops were using. The Russians had built a deep network of defensive positions, with their focal point along the Smolensk–Moscow road, and much of the civilian population had been conscribed to help in the work. It was already quite clear that, even though divisions had been transferred both north and south, the hard core of the Russian army was still barring the way to Moscow (according to Russian statements more than 40 per cent of all Russian troops on the Western Front were concentrated for its defence.[10]

Army Group HQ had ample time to study the tasks it had been assigned, and to give appropriate instructions to the commanders-in-chief of the armies and armoured groups engaged, while the troops were moving forward and taking up their new positions. The Russians still occupied their strengthened defensive positions opposite the 4th and 9th Armies, and from time to time they exerted pressure by launching local attacks, but it seemed fairly clear that, for the time being at any rate, they were not capable of launching operations on a really big scale. On September 26th, Army Group Centre issued the following order (extract) for the attack:[11]

'1. After a long period of waiting Army Group is about to advance to the attack again;

'2. *The 4th Army*, with Panzer Group 4 under command, will attack with its main thrust on both sides of the Roslavl–Moscow road. After breaking through, the Army will wheel with strong forces against the Smolensk–Moscow motorway on both sides of Vyazma, at the same time safeguarding the eastern flanks;

'3. *The 9th Army*, with Panzer Group 3 under command, will break through the enemy positions between the motorway and the Bieloi area and press on to the Vyazma–Rzhev railway line. The main drive will be made in the direction of Kholm by mobile forces with continuous strong infantry support. It is then intended, east of the Lower Dnieper, to turn towards the motorway at and to the west of Vyazma, at the same time protecting its eastern flank. The northern flank of the army must also be safeguarded. The road leading from Yetkino to Bieloi will be captured and used to bring up supplies;

'4. On *the inner wings of the 4th and 9th Armies*, between the Yelna area and the motorway, feint attacks will be launched so long as there is no possibility of an advance on these fronts; and concentrated drives with limited objectives will be launched in order to pin down enemy forces as far as possible;

'5. *The 2nd Army* will protect the flank of the 4th Army. For this purpose it will break through the Dezna position with the main weight on its north wing, and drive in the direction of Sukhinichi-Meshchovsk. The Army will protect itself against attack from the direction of the town and industrial area of Bryansk. Any possibility of capturing the latter by a sudden attack, and in particular its railways and bridges, should be seized irrespective of the dividing line with Panzer Group 2;

'6. Deploying presumably two days before the beginning of the attack, *Panzer Group 2* will drive forward over the Orel–Bryansk line. The right wing will rest on the Scop and Oka sectors. Its left wing will roll up the Dezna position from the south, and dispose of the enemy in the south-east Dezna bend in co-operation with the 2nd Army. The town and industrial area of Bryansk is to be taken by mobile forces, if possible in one attempt. Otherwise it should be sealed off for the moment and taken later by XXXV Army Corps in co-operation with the Luftwaffe;

'7. *Dividing lines . . .*

'8. *Army Group South* will advance its north wing (6th Army) in a general eastward direction to the north of Kharkov. *Army Group North* will use the 16th Army to secure a lake line, north of Lake Shedanya to Lake Ilmen;

'9. Reinforced *Air Fleet 2* will destroy the Russian air force opposite the Army Group, and give all possible support to the attack of the armies and the armoured groups. Attacks on industrial objectives in the Moscow district are subordinate to these tasks, and will be carried out only when the general situation on the ground permits. In order to hamper the movement of enemy supplies and reinforcements, the railways leading eastward from the line Bryansk–Vyazma–Rzhev will be persistently attacked;

'10. I shall fix the day and the time of deployment in accordance with the instructions I issued to commanders-in-chief on September 24th.

'Signed von Bock.'

This meant that the 4th Army, with Panzer Group 4, was to break through the enemy front on both sides of the Smolensk–Moscow motorway and then turn in towards Bryansk, while the 9th Army, with Panzer Group 3, was to drive forward in the direction of Cholm and then turn in to Vyazma to the east of the Upper Dnieper and make contact there with Panzer Group 4. The 9th Army would have to protect its own north flank, because the south wing of Army Group North had insufficient forces available for the purpose. For the moment, all the infantry corps of the 4th and 9th Armies had to do was pin down the enemy frontally, and they were to go forward only when the two armoured groups had pushed far enough forward to close the trap from the rear. The operational drive of Panzer Group 2 and the 2nd Army was to take place farther south and, for the time being, without any connection with the drive towards Bryansk; the 2nd Army was to break through the Dezna position to the northwest of Bryansk and advance on Sukhinichi, while Panzer Group 2 was to attack from the Gluchov area across the line Orel–Bryansk. The enemy in the Bryansk area was to be encircled and destroyed by the inner wings of Panzer Group 2 and the 2nd Army. After this the objective was to drive deep into the area to the southwest of Moscow. As Panzer Group 2's deployment point was far off, the group needed extra time in order to get to the main offensive front on schedule. It therefore had to deploy two days before the other elements of the Army Group launched their attacks. Flank protection to the south was to be secured by the advance of the north wing of Army Group South beyond Oboyan. The Army Group reserves were relatively weak, and consisted of one armoured division, one mechanized infantry regiment and one mechanized brigade.

The concentration and deployment of the forces brought in from north and south did not proceed without difficulty. Panzer Group 2, which had to turn away from the battle for Kiev, had first to conquer its deployment area, and a number of divisions of the 2nd Army were held up for some time. The units detached from Army Group North were very late in arriving, and their route crossed the east-west communications of the 9th and 4th Armies. In order to expedite matters, OKH took charge of this movement. As there was no time to be lost, Army Group Centre decided that the attack should be launched on October 2nd, despite the fact that the preliminary deployment had not altogether been concluded. Panzer Group 2 was to deploy on September 30th. An Order of the Day issued by Hitler underlined the great significance of the operations and concluded: 'The last great decisive battle of this year will deal a crushing blow to the enemy, and also to Britain, the instigator of the whole war. In destroying our enemy here, we shall be destroying Britain's last ally on the Continent. At the same time we shall ward off a danger not only to the German Reich but to the whole of Europe, a danger more terrible than anything since the days of the Huns and the Mongol incursions. During the coming weeks, therefore, the German people will be more closely behind you than ever.' And the next day he announced to the German people and to the world: 'I say this today because for the first time I am entitled to say it: the enemy is already broken, and will never be in a position to rise again.'

Officers and men were well aware of the significance of this decisive hour, and they were all prepared to give their utmost in a final effort. The operation's code name, 'Typhoon', indicates very clearly the expectations and the hopes which were attached to it.

The Battle for Moscow was launched on the appointed date: October 2nd, 1941. Panzer Group 2 succeeded in breaking through the southern wing of the enemy, and covering its unprotected southern flank approached Orel on October 3rd, whilst at the same time its left wing turned on Bryansk. The other armies also went over to the offensive, and in unexpected drives on both sides of the Moscow motorway they tore deep gaps in the Russian front. Very soon, two great cauldrons began to take shape, the one in the south around Bryansk, the other in the north around Vyazma. But the Russians accepted battle, and sent all their available reserves to the front. They fought desperately, but were unable to prevent the pincers formed by the two armoured groups from closing round Vyazma on October 7th, so that large elements of three Russian armies were trapped. The German generals had learned from previous experience, and this time the eastern edge of the cauldron was effectively sealed off, so that by October 13th mopping-up operations in the cauldron were completed. To the south, Panzer Group 2 (renamed '2nd Panzer Army' on October 6th) took the urban area of Bryansk from the east, but the lack of a second armoured claw made itself felt here, and bravely as the 2nd Army fought it could not make up for it. Here, as at Vyazma, three Russian armies were trapped, but it was not possible to close the ring tightly to the north of Bryansk, and large numbers of the trapped units, which attacked repeatedly in their efforts to break out, succeeded in escaping. At the same time, the 2nd Panzer Army sought to gain further ground in the northeast, but on October 6th, the spearhead of XXIV Panzer Corps, which was being used for the essential operational drive on Tula, came up against strong enemy resistance and large numbers of T–34 tanks, and the German advance was temporarily halted.

The inner wings of the 2nd and 4th Armies drove forward through the gap which had been torn open between Bryansk and Vyazma, in the direction of Moscow via Sukhinichi. The 9th Army also gained ground slowly in the northeast.

On October 7th, the Army Commander-in Chief, Field-Marshal von Brauchitsch, paid a visit to Army Group Centre HQ to discuss further developments. By this time, Army Group South had encircled strong enemy forces at Mariupol and advanced its north wing in the direction of Kharkov. Satisfactory front-line reports were also coming in from Army Group North, whose forces had captured the island of Saaremaa on October 6th. Brauchitsch was therefore able to concentrate his attention on the prospects of Army Group Centre, whose operations – thanks to excellent preparation and the high morale of the troops – had gone like clockwork. The main thing now was to pursue the enemy in the direction of Moscow with all the forces not actually required to contain the enemy in the cauldrons. It was hoped that this time the forces available would be sufficient for both tasks simultaneously: to conclude the mopping-up operations in the cauldrons and at the same time to continue the drive towards Moscow.

In accordance with the terms of the discussion which took place on October 7th, therefore, OKH[12] ordered the continuation of operations in the direction of Moscow. The 2nd Panzer Army was to drive forward to Tula; the 4th Army, with two new corps under its command (XII and XIII), was to drive on towards Kaluga and at the same time use whatever forces Panzer Group 4 could spare to destroy the Russian fortifications at Mozhaysk. Simultaneously, mopping-up operations in the two cauldrons had to be concluded; the Bryansk cauldron by the 2nd Army, and the Vyazma cauldron by elements of the 4th Army. The 9th Army – and here the views of von Bock differed from the orders of OKH – was to drive forward to Sychevka using forces of Panzer Group 3 as a screen towards the northeast, and then be ready to move with all its available forces in the direction of Kalinin or Rzhev. So while OKH wanted to dispose of the enemy in front of the inner wings of Army Groups North and Centre, whose advance was hanging fire, von Bock wanted to relieve the north flank by a drive with all possible forces towards Moscow.[13]

Hardly had this order been given when there was a sudden change in the weather, though even then everything still went well with the German pursuit groups. The men knew what was at stake, and they fought their way forwards through deeper and deeper mud. But although ground was still being won, the rate of advance was slowing down. On the south wing, in particular, where the operations of the 2nd Panzer Army drive had promised to cut off Moscow very rapidly from the south, the advance now came to a stop. The first snow fell. A shortage of fuel, which had to be brought forward on the bombed unmetalled road which ran from Orel to Tula and was pitted with craters now full of mud, delayed the advance. Inside the Bryansk cauldron the enemy was exerting heavy pressure on the western flank of the 2nd Panzer Army, and considerable forces had to be detached to meet it. For the moment, therefore, the forward drive did not get beyond Mtsensk. By the middle of the month, mopping-up operations in the cauldron were finished and the important supply road to Orel via Bryansk was reported clear of the enemy. However, for the time being it was unusable, owing to the destruction of numerous bridges and severe damage to the road surface carried out by the trapped Russians inside the cauldron. Precious days passed before the 2nd Panzer Army could be supplied in order to continue the attack.

By the middle of the month, advanced elements of the 4th Army (XIII Army Corps) reached the area to the east of Kaluga, and its left wing approached Mozhaysk. But now fresh Russian troops appeared opposite the 4th Army front, and here and there they even took the offensive, seriously hampering the movements of the German forces. By October 14th, the rearward elements of the 4th Army had finished mopping up the Vyazma cauldron, and started to regroup for an advance eastwards. The 9th Army had been given instructions to drive via Rzhev towards Kalinin, probably with the idea of bringing forward the inner wings of Army Groups Centre and North, and at the same time relieving the north flank for the drive on Moscow and cutting the important

Moscow–Leningrad railway line. But once again it was a movement that spread out rather than concentrated forces, and it would probably have been better to commit Panzer Group 3 between Klin and the Volga Dam. Taking advantage of the reservoir, the Panzer forces would then have been able to get considerably closer to Moscow, while the 9th Army infantry could have established contact with the south wing of Army Group North. Panzer Group 3 now found itself engaged with strong enemy forces around Kalinin instead of driving forward swiftly and vigorously as far as possible towards the northern outskirts of Moscow.

All the same, a good deal had been achieved, and in the middle of the month there was optimism amongst both officers and men about future prospects. The German forces were already practically two-thirds of the way to Moscow, and the result of the double battle had been an unexpectedly big success. An Order of the Day issued by Army Group Centre claimed the capture of 673,000 men, 3,500 guns of all calibres and 1,200 tanks.[14] It was estimated that 8 Russian armies consisting of 73 infantry and cavalry divisions and 13 armoured divisions or brigades, had been destroyed. As early as October 9th, the Chief of the Reich Press Office had publicly announced that the military decision in the east was already taken, and that Russia was defeated. This was splendid news for the German people, and it was readily accepted and believed. The Russians had certainly suffered a very heavy defeat and the Soviet Government transferred its seat to Kuybychev, about 560 miles to the east of Moscow on the Volga, though Stalin remained behind with a small staff. A million inhabitants were evacuated, and the factory workers toiled feverishly to put the capital into a state of defence.[15]

At about the same time, Army Group South also scored a success. It had succeeded in encircling strong Russian forces at Mariupol, and its 17th and 6th Armies had made good progress. A note in Halder's diary dated October 8th, is illuminating; it puts the total losses of the German Army in the east since the beginning of the operations (June 22nd) at 564,727, i.e. 16·61 per cent of the total force of 3·4 million men engaged. On the same day, Halder summed up the German prospects of taking Moscow as follows: 'The enemy will attempt to bring up still further forces to defend Moscow, particularly from the north. But units gathered hurriedly from here and there will hardly prove adequate to ward off the serious threat our drive represents, so that with reasonably good leadership and reasonably good weather we should succeed in encircling Moscow.' This optimism did not seem excessive at the time, but unfortunately the future showed that it was.

On October 14th, OKH issued a new directive ordering Moscow to be closely encircled. The 2nd Panzer Army was to sweep round Moscow and seal off the enemy capital from the south, southeast and east, while the 4th Army with Panzer Group 4 was to do the same in the west, northwest and north and make preparations for a subsequent drive by mobile units to the north of and beyond Moscow. The degree of confidence behind these operations can be judged from

Hitler's instruction forbidding the acceptance of any offer from Moscow to capitulate.[16]

In committing its forces to carry out the encirclement of Moscow according to its instructions, Army Group HQ had particular misgivings about its right wing, because the left wing of Army Group South was not advancing towards Oboyan as arranged, but farther south towards Byelgorod. The result was that a gap about fifty miles wide opened between the inner wings of the two Army Groups, and there was every reason to fear that the enemy would exploit it. Army Group Centre therefore decided to use the 2nd Army, which was now disengaging at Bryansk, to protect the south flank of the 2nd Panzer Army, and send it forward along the line Yeletz–Stalinogorsk. At the same time, the south wing of the 2nd Army was instructed to take Kursk. This manœuvre involved a regrouping: XXXIV and XXXV Corps, which had been attached to Panzer Army 2, now had to transfer to the command of 2nd Army, which, at the same time, had to transfer XLIII and LIII Corps to the 2nd Panzer Army. OKH's directive for the north wing provided for the concentrated forces of the 9th Army to advance via Kalinin northwards, in order to destroy the enemy forces there in co-operation with the south wing of Army Group North (16th Army). But the Russian forces at Kalinin resisted obstinately and Russian reinforcements were brought up from all directions in defence of this important junction. The south wing of Army Group North was very slow off the mark because: 'The enemy is still standing firm opposite the centre and left wing of the 16th Army.'[17]

When OKH issued its ambitious directive for the encirclement of Moscow it probably hoped that the forces engaged in the operation would manage to cope somehow or the other with the weather. If it began to freeze rather earlier than expected, so much the better; that would solve the problem. But, in fact, the weather was disobliging, and from the middle of the month large-scale troop movements were hopelessly bogged down in the soft ground. In such circumstances it was impossible to carry out the operations in the spirit of the recent instructions. The autumn weather in Russia was very unfavourable for military operations, but it was the particular nature of the terrain that turned the situation into a catastrophe that profoundly affected the future prosecution of the war. When the skies opened, the rivers overflowed their banks and vast areas were turned into a sticky morass. As none of the roads – with the one exception of that from Minsk to Moscow – was solidly built, their condition was soon no better than that of the surrounding agricultural land into which they almost imperceptibly merged. None of the roads was good even under ordinary conditions, and they were altogether inadequate for the traffic involved by large-scale troop movements; but with such weather they were soon broad bands of squelchy clay which clung like glue to any vehicle that attempted to move along them. Men and animals struggled forward, often knee deep in the clinging mud. Frequently they reached the point of exhaustion, and dead horses became an increasingly common sight. The mechanized units were no better off. Their vehicles sank into the mud up to their hubs and stuck fast. The only vehicles with a chance of moving at all were those with broad caterpillar tracks, and, until their fuel was exhausted, these slowly and laboriously towed other vehicles and guns along the roads. The result, of course, was a complete failure of supplies. It was impossible to bring them up on time. Only limited supplies could be brought up by air. Tractors and light horse-drawn carts, such as could be found in large numbers in the surrounding countryside, were widely used, and everything possible was done to get the necessary minimum of supplies up to the troops in the front line.

There was scarcely enough fuel for the supply detachments, and the troops had to live on potatoes dug up in the surrounding fields. Even the main motor-way from Minsk to Moscow, which was still unfinished in places, and was now crammed with masses of vehicles, soon became little more than a ribbon of mud and water-filled craters. In consequence, traffic came almost to a stand-still, and a whole infantry division had to be set aside to maintain the road as well as possible. In the end, the German divisions were spread out over hundreds of miles of territory, while thousands of motor vehicles were bogged down, impatiently awaiting the arrival of cold weather – the only thing which could free them from the mud. The men were, of course, used to Western European roads, and for them it was like being in the grip of a natural catastrophe; with the best will in the world, and despite all their efforts, they were unable to cope satisfactorily.

To some extent the enemy was also hampered by the same difficulties, but – to the great disappointment of the Germans – he proved more mobile in such circumstances. His light vehicles and his lorries, which had a greater ground clearance and were all fitted with mud chains, were better suited to such weather conditions, which were in any case by no means unfamiliar to his men. And he enjoyed another great advantage: apart from bringing up reinforce-ments he was for the time being not interested in mobility. In any case, for bringing up fresh troops he had the still intact railway network on the other side of Moscow and behind his own lines at his disposal. The mud, which so desperately hampered German movements, helped him, and gave him time to bring reinforcements to his front line.

However, the attack was still proceeding, though in this exhausting struggle against the weather and against a tough enemy who fought obstinately, progress was very slow. All the same, up to the beginning of November there was still progress, and so the commanders did not despair nor did their men flag; they both knew that though great tactical successes had been won the operative results had still to be achieved, though they felt that they were now within grasping distances.

The 2nd Panzer Army had only the Orel–Tula road[18] at its disposal, and it had concentrated the major part of its armour under XXIV Panzer Corps together with Infantry Regiment 'Grossdeutschland', and these units had been supplied with sufficient fuel, even at the expense of the rest. On

October 24th, they drove forward from Mtsensk towards Tula, which was reached on October 30th. However, the attacking forces were not strong enough to take the town against the obstinate Russian defence, particularly as XLIII Army Corps advancing from the west was halted near Alexin. This meant that the eastern flank of the 2nd Panzer Army was now excessively attenuated. For the moment, no attempt was being made to attack it, but the movements of troop trains from the east were observed. The Army therefore ordered LIII Army Corps to turn behind the armoured spearhead to protect the eastern flank. At the same time, the 2nd Army was gradually advancing in considerable depth along the Kursk–Novosil line, so that the danger from the southeast seemed more or less satisfactorily countered.

The 4th Army, which was to drive forward to Moscow from the west, found itself under increasing pressure from fresh Russian troops (the 49th, 43rd, and 33rd Armies), and in the southern sector of its front it was unable to push forward beyond the River Oka in the Serpukhovo–Nara area. Its northern wing, represented by Panzer Group 4, fought its way forward as far as the Mozhaysk–Volokolamsk line against the 5th and 16th Armies.

On the 9th Army front, Panzer Group 3 was held up at Kalinin by the 30th and 31st Armies, but with its infantry corps it succeeded in establishing a thin front to the north against the 29th and 22nd Armies, with contact westward to Kalinin and a loose contact with the 16th Army west of Ostashkov.

By this time the front line commanders were unanimously of the opinion that the general attack could be continued only with drier weather, when movement would be possible on and off the roads. And, in any case, the much-extended divisions would have to close up and bring up their artillery, which was largely bogged down in the rear. In other words, everything now depended on the weather, and for the moment 'General Mud' was in command.

In this pause in the fighting imposed by the weather, the Supreme Command issued new instructions ordering the two Army Group wings to renew their divergent operations. On October 23rd, OKH ordered the 2nd Army, reinforced by mobile units from the 2nd Panzer Army, to advance towards the Don, with its right wing on Voronezh, in order to forestall a possible drive by fresh Russian forces from this area and to destroy them in co-operation with the northern wing of Army Group South. On October 29th, this order was fortunately withdrawn,[19] but only after Field-Marshal von Bock had vigorously expressed his opposition to it because it would dilute the strength of his southern wing's attack.[20] Instead, OKH now ordered that the surprise drive on Moscow should be started again as soon as possible, and that the railway lines from Moscow southward should be cut.

Thus Army Group HQ was relieved of the anxieties created by the first order, but on October 30th came surprise instructions[21] to destroy the Russian forces between the Volga and Lake Ladoga. With this in view Army Group was to use Panzer Groups 3 and 4, and the strongest possible infantry support, to capture the area north of Moscow, and from there it was to send armoured units towards Rybinsk, and after that towards Vologda! At the same time, the lines of communication of the northern Russian forces were to be cut and destroyed. Such ambitious objectives were something of a *cura posterior* for Army Group HQ, particularly as the first part of these future operations coincided entirely with its own views: the immediate trouble was the northern drive beyond Moscow. Once this had been successfully carried out it would be possible to think of what came next! *Army Group HQ* never had more than the *one* aim, an aim it never abandoned – and that was *Moscow*.

It is depressing to read the diaries of von Bock and Halder, and to see how from October to November spirits fell and optimism declined, finally disappearing altogether. Not that they gave up, or resigned themselves to defeat because of the forces of nature; indeed, they desperately sought ways and means to circumvent them. How enviously von Bock observed the progress which was being made in the Crimea! – thanks to sunshine and the dry steppes.[22] The C.-in-C. of 4th Army, von Kluge, personally described to Hitler the enormous difficulties the weather created for all transport movements, difficulties which Hitler had not altogether understood from the written reports alone.[23] The stiffening of the Russian front – it was reported that General Zhukov had taken command on the Moscow front on October 10th, with General Sokolovsky as Chief of Staff, and Bulganin as a member of the Front War Council[24] – the launching of local offensives, reports of the arrival of fresh troops from Siberia, the formation of improvised units from Moscow's industrial workers,[25] and the feverish erection of defensive positions around the capital,[26] all indicated that the Russians were determined to defend their beloved Moscow to the last, and that there was no flagging in their determination or the toughness of their resistance.

In the meantime, at OKH and Army Group HQ there was very good reason to regard their own position with some anxiety. As a result of heavy losses, all the infantry divisions engaged were something like 2,500 men short, or approximately one-third of their effectives,[27] which naturally meant a corresponding drop in their fighting potential. The infantry strength of the armoured units was down by about 50 per cent, and the fighting potential of the armoured regiments by between 65 and 70 per cent. Thus, on an average, an armoured division was about 35 per cent of its normal strength. This was a depressing but not altogether surprising state of affairs, because in the previous four months all units had been grossly overtaxed, and it had not been possible to provide them with adequate replacements in manpower or material. Morale, too, was suffering and the disappointment of the men was obvious: boastful propaganda had proclaimed that the enemy was already defeated and that the war was already won, whereas the men in the field knew that in reality Russian resistance had stiffened. However, their courage was as great as ever and their spirit was unbroken.

The supplies of the German forces depended on narrow, long-drawn-out and extremely vulnerable lines. It is true that during October the railway lines had been brought into working order again, and that trains were now running eastward as far as Bryansk, Vyazma and Rzhev, but the track was by no means at the highest pitch of efficiency, and the repair or rebuilding of damaged or destroyed installations and bridges took a long time. All in all, therefore, supply capacity remained far below expectations. Russian partisans were becoming a growing nuisance, and in the sparsely patrolled rearward areas it was relatively easy for them to attack supply trains and sabotage railway installations. The utmost exertions on the part of the supply organization were necessary to get even the bare minimum of necessary supplies to the railway termini, from where they very often had then to be carried over long distances by damaged and inadequate road transport to the front-line troops. But now, on the verge of winter, no winter clothing for the troops had been brought up, and there was no anti-freeze mixture for the mechanized transport.

Air Fleet 2, under Field-Marshal Kesselring, had vigorously supported the operations of Army Group Centre throughout, and in doing so had suffered heavy losses in men and material. In his memoirs Kesselring says: 'The climatic difficulties of the Russian autumn did the rest: there was rain and mist, and it was very cold. Pilots, including close-support fighter pilots, could only attack when they could see the targets, and the larger targets were scarce. After the encirclement battles of Bryansk and Vyazma, large-scale troop movements were only rarely observed. . . . The enemy strongpoints were isolated little bunkers dotted over the countryside, and they were extremely difficult for fast-flying planes to sight and hit, particularly in bad weather. The T–34 tanks were appearing in increasing numbers, and they were mobile even in the worst ground and weather conditions. To deal with them demanded the utmost from ground-attack pilots flying low over woods, hills and villages. At the same time, our fighter pilots were constantly called on to protect our troops against strafing by low-flying Russian planes, as otherwise morale would have suffered. Successes were few and far between, because the opportunities were so fleeting. Actually anti-aircraft and anti-tank fire was a better defence, though because the terrain was so unfavourable and lacked adequate cover even this was of limited value. No matter how often and resolutely our pilots attacked, the conditions were so difficult that their efforts were never decisive.'[28]

Before long High Command had to decide whether, in the difficult circumstances, there was any point in continuing the attack on Moscow at all, particularly as conditions were fast becoming almost impossible. However, so long as there was the slightest hope that a decision could be forced before the end of the year, everything possible had to be done. The memory of the Battle of the Marne still haunted the minds of Germany's military leaders. They were afraid of letting the chance of victory slip through their fingers at the last moment once more, so in full consciousness of what was involved, and despite the inadequacy of the means available, they took the risk of continuing the campaign. There was something else which disturbed them and made them more willing to risk everything in a last great effort: if it were decided not to go over to the offensive, how could the much extended front be held throughout the winter months? The numerous gaps and weaknesses in the line were an open invitation to the enemy to break through. The German flanks were long, and there were no reserves to reinforce them. At the same time, the front line was close up to Moscow, a great railway junction, and the Russians were in a position to switch their forces here and there at will, while the German troops were pinned down in open country. In such circumstances only one decision was possible: what chance there was had to be taken, and the offensive continued. This was the decision the German High Command finally adopted, and in so doing it agreed with the view of the C.-in-C. at the front, who was anxious to make the best possible use of the expected spell of mild frost before the advent of deep winter. This spell of mild frost actually arrived at the beginning of November.

The plan of attack called once again for an envelopment battle and the closing of the pincers. After taking the junction of Tula, the 2nd Panzer Army was to drive directly northeast towards Kolomna. It was regarded as almost inevitable that during these operations it would have to use a considerable part of its strength to protect its own lengthening east flank, since the weak 2nd Army was hanging too far back to undertake the task. The 2nd Army was to move forward towards Yelets and Yefremov to make contact with the northern wing of Army Group South, which had come to a halt near Byelgorod, and so undertake flank protection in depth. In the north, the 9th Army with Panzer Group 3 was to drive eastwards to the Volga Canal and then wheel towards Moscow as the left arm of the pincers movement. Here, too, strong forces would unquestionably have to be detached as flank protection. The 4th Army, with Panzer Group 4 on its north wing, was to attack directly towards Moscow. Behind it were the two divisions which were all Army Group had in the way of reserves.

When the expected frost arrived in the first days of November and turned the slush into ice, von Bock insisted on the earliest possible deployment in order to have as much time as possible for operations before the dreaded winter snow came, but, in fact, the supply situation made it necessary to postpone the attack. Finally, November 15th was fixed for the north wing and Panzer Group 4, and November 17th for the south wing. Unfortunately, it was impossible to fix the start of the new offensive for the 4th Army, but it was calculated that the Russians would be compelled to call off their continuous attacks when strong pressure on their wings forced them to draw off forces both to right and left. Then the 4th Army would also be able to move forward towards Moscow.

Army Group Centre launched its last offensive according to plan. Thanks to clear frosty weather preliminary successes were certainly attained, but the advance was not as swift as had been hoped, and it was not long before severe cold set in, with temperatures down to 20° Centigrade below zero. Both men and horses suffered terribly, and engines stalled. By the end of November, the situation was roughly as follows: on the south wing the 2nd Panzer Army had encircled enemy forces in Stalinogorsk and pressed on as far as Gonovo-Michailov. However, the spearhead driving northward (17th Panzer Division) had been brought to a halt to the south of Kashira by newly arrived Russian forces. More and more fresh troops were reaching the front from Siberia, and the Russian attacks were increasing in strength[29]. In particular, their pressure on the flanks was putting the thin line of German armour into a critical situation. Tula had still not been captured, though as General Guderian insisted: 'Until we were in possession of this communications centre and its airfield we had no hope of continuing to advance either northwards or eastwards'.[30]

2nd Panzer Army HQ wanted the 4th Army to drive over the River Oka eastwards at once, and thus give Guderian's attack more elbow room, but this it was unable to do because it had its hands full defending itself against fierce Russian attacks. The idea of advancing farther was out of the question. On November 28th, therefore, Army Group HQ ordered the 2nd Panzer Army to halt its drive to the north and to take Tula instead. At this point, an attempt to destroy the railway tracks between Ryazan and Kolomna, and so stop or delay the Russian reinforcements, which were moving towards the front line, proved a failure. Towards the end of November, the 2nd Army reached the area to the east of Kursk, but here, too, enemy resistance was noticeably stiffening.

The forces on the north wing reached the Volga between the dam and Kalinin fairly quickly. For reasons of command, Panzer Group 3 was subordinated directly to Army Group. After heavy fighting it drove past Klin towards the Volga Canal, which it reached on November 28th. It actually succeeded in establishing a small bridgehead, but before long it was compelled to surrender it again under overwhelming enemy pressure. For the time being it was impossible to wheel southwards on Moscow, because Russian pressure on the left flank on the west bank of the canal was steadily growing. After heavy fighting, Panzer Group 4, which was carrying out a parallel attack, managed to advance as far as Istra, from where – exploiting the element of surprise – it succeeded in pushing forward a division from the northwest to within eighteen miles of the northern periphery of Moscow, but this move quickly came to a halt in the face of violent enemy counter-attacks.

The left wing of the 4th Army won little ground along the motorway. On November 29th, it looked as though the enemy had withdrawn forces from the front and sent them against the north wing, and Army Group approved the 4th Army's proposal to attack on December 1st. But it was too late. The Russians had made good use of the respite granted them by the mud to bring up fresh troops from the interior, and thus strengthen their resistance – the non-aggression pact with Japan even allowed them to take troops away from the Far East. No less than 34 fresh divisions arrived on the Eastern Front, and no fewer than 21 of these were committed on the front of Army Group Centre.[31] In addition to these fresh, well trained units, all of which were

adequately clothed and properly equipped for a winter campaign, the enemy also threw many hurriedly improvised groups into the battle. Some of these were made up of units which had been badly mauled in the previous fighting. In the meantime, their ranks had been filled up by the recruitment of untrained men, some of them from amongst the Moscow workers. Within a very few days of their renewed attack on Moscow, the German troops could feel that Russian resistance had greatly strengthened. Their will to resist was stronger too; they no longer surrendered, as they had often done before, instead they fought on until they were wiped out. The German troops were now suffering very severely from the intense cold, but there was nothing at all they could do about it, and frost-bite cost them heavier losses than the enemy did. Engines and all automatic weapons froze, and so did locomotive boilers, which then burst. Fewer supplies than ever were reaching the front line. Fuel, in particular, was in increasingly short supply. On November 27th, the Quartermaster-General at OKH admitted frankly: 'We have come to the end of our resources in both men and material.'[32] What was to have been a strategic battle now disintegrated more and more into individual tactical engagements. All reserves had been committed, and Army Group HQ was no longer in a position to help. On December 1st, von Bock, the C.-in-C., sent a teleprinter message to OKH,[33] describing the general situation in the following urgent terms:

'The queries and reports repeatedly forwarded to OKH about the dangerous situation which has arisen have brought the decision that the attack should be continued even at the risk of annihilation. Every tactical possibility will, of course, be exploited in the attack which is now proceeding, but it has to be conducted primarily as a frontal operation, because, as already reported, there are not sufficient troops available for carrying out any large-scale encircling movements, while large-scale movements of any kind are out of the question. In further heavy fighting the attack will probably result in limited territorial gains, and enemy forces will certainly be destroyed, but *any strategic results are very unlikely*. The idea that the enemy forces opposing Army Group would 'collapse' is an illusion, as the fighting during the past fourteen days has shown. To remain before the gates of Moscow, on which the rail and road network of almost the whole of eastern Russia converge, means heavy defensive fighting against a numerically far superior enemy. The forces available to Army Group are not sufficient to sustain this even for a limited period. And if the improbable should happen and further ground be won, the forces available would not be even approximately sufficient to envelop Moscow and at the same time defend the envelopment against counter-attacks from the south-east, the east and the northeast.

'It is therefore difficult to see what sense there is in continuing the operation, or what objectives it could have, particularly as the moment is now very near when the strength of the troops will be utterly exhausted. What is to happen then must be decided now. Army Group is holding a front approximately 600 miles long, with only one division, and a weak one at that, in reserve behind the lines. In this situation, and in view of its heavy losses in officers, and its greatly declining battle strength, it could not withstand a systematic and organized attack. In view of the failure of the railways there is no possibility of preparing this extended front for an adequate defensive struggle or of keeping it properly supplied in such a struggle.

'I do not know the intentions of OKH, but if Army Group is to survive the winter and defend itself adequately then the strongest possible reserves must be brought up so that any enemy break-through can be sealed off promptly, and exhausted divisions can be withdrawn from the front line for rest and replacement. Another absolutely essential proviso is that the railway service should be made more reliable, so that the front-line troops can be regularly supplied and stores built up. If these two conditions cannot be complied with adequately, then a shorter and more easily defensible line should be chosen without delay and thoroughly prepared in advance for accommodation, supplies and defence, so that when the time comes it can be occupied within a very short space of time.'

The same evening General Halder confirmed receipt of this teleprinter message. Its 'general gist' was, he said, no different from 'the almost daily reports coming in for some time about the condition of the troops, reports for which OKH was grateful. Today's letter (von Bock's) was the clear and logical summary. OKH would lose no time in putting its point of view in writing once more to OKW.'[34]

Halder's diary contains the following entry for December 1st, 1941, after a discussion with von Bock: 'To break frontally through prepared enemy positions is a tremendous task for troops which have become numerically weak. But they are now so weak that it is no longer possible to use them in this way. They have to work their way forward in small tactical thrusts. All attacks have to be launched frontally. . . . I must stress that we too are anxious about the wastage of our forces. But we must try to defeat the enemy with one last effort. Should it ultimately become clear that this is impossible, then we shall have to think again.' Instead of directives to think again the next few days produced inquiries from Hitler, criticizing minor points, and proffering advice which a battle-experienced field-marshal like von Bock really did not need. In the end, von Bock began to wonder anxiously whether Hitler was properly informed about the situation. He therefore adopted the unusual step of ringing up Hitler's military adviser, General Jodl (Chief of Wehrmacht Operations Staff) and giving him a very sombre picture of the condition of the troops. But the hoped-for order to halt the attack did not arrive. However, he was given general permission to break off the attack at the point when it became quite clear that there was no longer any hope of success for the costly offensive.[35] This point, whose determination had now been left to the discretion of Army Group itself, was not long in coming.

The attack launched by the 4th Army across the Nara was at first successful, and, exploiting this, Panzer Group 4 also managed to go forward a little; but then these gallant troops came to the end of their tether. Panzer Group 3 was also exhausted; its attempt to wheel to the south broke down in mined marshland, and the attacks on its eastern flank from the direction of the Moscow Canal grew steadily heavier. On December 3rd, the 4th Army had to be withdrawn from Narofominsk to its starting point. On December 5th, the Army Group Commander ordered Panzer Groups 3 and 4 to break off contact with the enemy and withdraw during the next few days to a shorter line from Istra to the east of Klin. The position of the 2nd Panzer Army was no more favourable. Tula was almost encircled and Alexin had been captured, but enemy pressure on the thinly held and very zigzag front to the north and east was steadily increasing, and it was clear that a critical situation might arise at any moment. Army Group therefore approved General Guderian's decision on December 5th to call off the attack, withdraw his forces from the salient and straighten his line.

The temperature had now dropped to 30° Centigrade below freezing, and the withdrawal of the 2nd Army in the next few days involved the loss of a good deal of equipment owing to engine failure in the extreme cold. On the south wing, the 2nd Army had reached Tim and was advancing on Yelets and Yefremov, but there was no co-ordinated front. Individual battle groups had been pushed forward to seize road or rail junctions, whichever was considered the more important at the moment, but between these groups there was 'open country', and it was not long before the enemy began to infiltrate into the gaps. It was a real piece of luck that for the time being he had no really strong forces with which to exploit the strategically important area at the Army Group boundary.

Two-thirds of all forces available were engaged along the 175-mile sector of the Moscow front between Venev and Dmitrov, while the remaining third was distributed along the threatened flanks, the northern one of which swept back to the northwest. There were no worthwhile reserves for a front 750 miles long! The 255th Division stood alone behind the north wing of the 4th Army, and in the vast hinterland there were scattered another four security divisions protecting supply and communication lines against increasing partisan activity. It was an unexampled situation calculated to give rise to the greatest anxiety.

During the next few days, Army Group's biggest headache was to establish an adequate defensive line on the shortest possible front. Was the enemy likely to allow sufficient time for the manœuvre? As late as December 4th, OKH Intelligence Section Foreign Armies (East) still calculated that 'at the moment' the Russians were not strong enough 'to carry out a large-scale offensive', and that for this purpose they would have to bring up considerably larger forces. But once again it was seen that the Germans had been harbouring illusions: the Russians chose their time well, and launched a counter-offensive. At first the main pressure was directed against the 2nd Panzer Army near Venev, against Panzer Group 3 on the Moscow Canal, and against the right wing of the 9th Army near Kalinin.

The Russian Winter Offensive

In the meantime, what was the situation in the other theatres? In North Africa, the Axis Powers were paying dearly for their omission to seize the island of Malta as part of their general preparations in the Mediterranean. Throughout the autumn the importance of Malta as a submarine and air base increased steadily, and British operations from the island against German and Italian trans-Mediterranean convoys were so successful that almost half the supplies despatched to North Africa along this route were sent to the bottom. In consequence, the shipping and supply situation of the Axis Powers in the Mediterranean began to grow precarious. In the autumn of 1941, Britain had command of both the air and the sea in the western Mediterranean, and in consequence the German Supreme Command was compelled, very reluctantly, to transfer to Italy a part of Air Fleet 2 from the Eastern Front, where German forces were still battling desperately to force a decision against the Russians. German and Italian submarines inflicted heavy losses on the British Mediterranean fleet, and Malta was pounded by constant Luftwaffe attacks. In North Africa, Rommel began to disengage at Tobruk (December 7th) and withdraw westward. The battle there, which had swayed first one way and then the other, had been costly for both sides. So far, Britain had not succeeded in sweeping North Africa clear of the Axis forces, and in particular her victories had not persuaded the French forces stationed in North Africa to come over to the Allies. On the whole, therefore, the situation in the Mediterranean theatre was still in the balance.

Japan's attack on the United States, and her declaration of war on Great Britain (December 8th, 1941) seemed a ray of hope for the Axis Powers. Britain's position in the Far East was now dangerously threatened. However, the ruthless attack on Pearl Harbour proved a double-edged weapon, because it roused public opinion in the United States, not only against the Japanese aggressor but against the Axis Powers as well. Up to that time, President Roosevelt had been by no means certain that he could carry Congress with him in a declaration of war on the Axis Powers; a convincing reason was necessary for such action. Now he had it, and there was no need for him to worry any more on that score. In any case, a few days later Germany and Italy themselves declared war on the United States, giving as their reason the fact that from mere breaches of neutrality in the beginning the United States had now begun to commit openly warlike acts against the Axis Powers. Because of Japan's entry into the war, Britain was clearly going to find herself strongly engaged in the Far East, and would therefore be unable to commit all her strength in North Africa. An even more important factor was that the United States now needed the major part of her war production for her own use, and was therefore compelled to cut down supplies of arms to Britain and Russia until such time as her economy had been geared to war production. Finally, Hitler now hoped that he would be given the greatly desired respite in which to force a decision in Russia, after which he would have his hands free in Europe, with no threat to his back from the east.

On the German Eastern Front the objective of Army Group South was the Don, and with it the Donets Basin with its large-scale heavy industry, and then the rich peninsula of the Crimea. By the middle of November, the 11th Army had reached and invested Sevastopol, but there it found itself halted. The 6th Army took Kharkov on November 2nd, and soon afterwards reached the Donets Basin. The drive carried out by the 1st Panzer Army (the new name for Panzer Group 1), and to its north the 17th Army, took Stalino on October 20th; but then Russian resistance stiffened. In addition, the weather turned muddy, and the armour could advance only slowly. The Russians brought up fresh forces from Caucasia and went over to the offensive. They were so successful that the German forces had to abandon Rostov, which had been captured on November 29th, and withdraw over the Mius, suffering heavy losses. Here, too, German strength was not adequate for the very distant objectives of the operations. Despite this sharp set-back, it proved possible to retain the greater part of the Donets Basin and bring the Russian counter-offensive to a halt. Field-Marshal von Rundstedt, who had foreseen the Rostov set-back and opposed Hitler's standstill order, was replaced as C.-in-C. of Army Group South by Field-Marshal von Reichenau (December 3rd, 1941).

The south wing of Army Group North was halted by the Russians at the Valdai Hills. It reached Tikhoin by the middle of November, but at the beginning of December a Russian counter-offensive forced it back behind the Volkhov. Despite violent Russian attacks, the northern 18th Army managed to hold Schlüsselburg. Fierce battles to capture Leningrad and destroy the Russian bridgehead at Oranienburg (25 miles long and 12 miles wide) failed to attain their objectives, and both remained in Russian hands. Thus, the German forces had failed in their efforts to link up with the Finnish forces at Lake Ladoga, and this was a great disappointment for the Finns. In expectation of a rapid German victory over Russia they had called up every man capable of bearing arms, but now pressing economic needs made it necessary to demobilize a good many of them and send them back into the fields and factories. Many units had then to be amalgamated. Nevertheless, the Finns gallantly continued to hold the envelopment front to the northwest of Leningrad, and the Svir sector.

The average strength of the divisions under Army Group Centre had now fallen to about half their normal complement. The heaviest losses were amongst officers and NCOs. Lieutenants were now often in command of battalions and sergeants in charge of companies. Intense cold, between thirty and forty degrees Centigrade below freezing, resulted in heavy losses from frostbite; and the situation was worsened by the fact that many of the men were still without winter clothing, and often had to bivouac in the open. The campaign launched in Germany by Goebbels to collect winter clothing for the troops on the Eastern Front was exploited by the Nazi Party leaders, who blamed the

Wehrmacht, which was regarded with increasing jealousy and suspicion.[36] The army horses also suffered greatly in the intense cold, particularly because there was an acute shortage of oats owing to the breakdown of supplies. The fodder available locally was chiefly hay and straw, and the poor beasts had no proper nourishment with which to resist the intense cold.

Mechanically, things were in no better shape. There was an equally acute shortage of fuel and winter oils, and in consequence, armour and motor vehicles were immobilized and wireless stations ceased to function. Twenty-six goods trains daily were required to keep Army Group supplies at an acceptable level, but in this critical period when so much was at stake no more than eight, or perhaps ten at the utmost, got through. This was primarily because the capacity of the railways – never very high – had been greatly reduced by war damage, and was being still further reduced by partisan sabotage. In addition, the intense cold was constantly putting locomotives out of commission. The long distances between the railway unloading points and the front line had to be covered by already badly mauled supply columns, often with improvised sledges. Some supplies were flown in, but only an insignificant amount. The supply service as a whole was in the grip of a paralysing crisis.

In short, the men were at the end of their tether, and in the subsequent fighting local withdrawals often turned into panic-stricken flight. The sudden and unexpected change for the worse caused great disappointment, and there was a growing lack of confidence amongst the men in their military leaders, who were obviously dithering and quite unable to make up their minds. However, generally speaking, and despite the tremendous pressure and the many deficiencies, the morale of the men remained high. Army Group and commanders were all well aware of the difficult situation from the time that fortunes suddenly changed in favour of the enemy, and allowed him to marshal his forces for a counter-offensive.

Undoubtedly, the Russian military leaders had counted on the advantage that the severe winter weather would inevitably give them. They had brought fresh troops[37] to the Moscow area[38] – obviously unobserved by Luftwaffe long-range reconnaissance. Judged by German standards, many of these units were not fully battleworthy, but what they lacked in quality they made up for in numbers, which were overwhelmingly superior. Both the Russians and their animals were used to wintry conditions, and, in addition, their needs were unbelievably frugal. Their clothing and their means of transport were both well adapted to the hard weather, and they enjoyed the inestimable advantage of short supply lines. Above all, the knowledge that they had saved Moscow, their beloved capital, from the hands of the enemy was a tremendous boost to their morale. In these circumstances, the Russian leadership decided that the time had come to launch a counter-offensive where it suited them, to take the initiative out of German hands. On December 5th, 1941, the so-called 'Kalinin Front' under General Koniev, followed on December 6th by the 'West Front' under General Zhukov, went over to the offensive.

TABLE II

Comparative Military Strength on the Eastern Front in December 1941
(according to Soviet Sources)*

		Soviet Union	Germany
Troops		1·5	1
	(November)	(1·2)	(1)
Guns and Mortars		1·1	1
	(November)	(1)	(1·7)
Planes		2	1
	(November)	(1·7)	(1)
Tanks	(End of October)	(1 [382])	(1·6 [750])
		=1	2·5
Anti-tank Guns		1	2

When the first German withdrawals began, the difficulties became immense. The all-pervading snow, which hardly permitted any movement at all beyond the roads, themselves kept clear only with difficulty, made it impossible for the German forces to retire for more than a few miles at a time without leaving valuable material and equipment to fall into enemy hands. However, even in these conditions the Russians were much more mobile, and they pressed hard on the heels of the German rearguards, using infantry units wearing snowshoes to overtake the retreating Germans. They also attacked the retreating columns on the flank, and so kept the Germans fighting all the time, depriving them of the respite they urgently needed. German unit commanders did their best to overcome the difficulties by improvisations on the spot, but by December 8th Hitler had still not realized that there had been a fundamental change in the tactical situation. In Directive No. 39, he ordered the German forces to withdraw to shorter defensive lines to be chosen by Brauchitsch. At the same time, the armour and mechanized units were to be withdrawn for rest and replacements. This new and shorter defensive front was to solve the problem of accommodation and make supply conditions easier. The text of this directive shows very clearly that, sitting at his table in his well-heated bunker, Hitler had no idea of the real conditions prevailing at the front. Heaviest enemy pressure was being exerted on Panzer Group 3, and the Russians had already broken through its front and reached the railway line Klin–Kalinin. Army Group therefore despatched a small battle group, consisting of one regiment of the 255th Division and one Army Engineer Battalion, in the direction of Klin. However, because of the crowded roads this force went forward only very slowly, and Panzer Group 4 had to help. So far the 9th Army had succeeded in sealing off the Russian break-through to the southeast of Kalinin, and it had sent a division from its left wing against Kalinin. This whole sector was now in flames! On December 8th, Army Group placed Panzer Group 3 under Panzer Group 4, in order to establish a unified command.

*This form of comparison is typical of Soviet Russian war reporting. Exact figures are avoided. (Boltin, p. 30.)

Although the fighting had been bitter and heavy, the withdrawal movement of the 2nd Panzer Army had gone according to plan, though the loss of a good deal of material and equipment had been unavoidable. The chief anxiety here was caused by the twelve-mile gap to the southwest of Tula, between XXIV Panzer Corps and XLIII Army Corps on the one hand, and the 2nd Army on the other. The weak and attenuated front of the 2nd Army had already been penetrated by numerically superior enemy forces near Yelets.

Army Group was unable to be of very much help, and on December 8th it informed OKH that it was not in a position to repulse a large-scale Russian offensive, no matter where it might be launched. At the same time, it asked for the speedy sending up of reserves. But where was OKH to take reserves from? There were none available anywhere. OKH was itself in sore difficulties; not only was it deeply concerned about the situation at the front, but the differences of opinion between Hitler and the General Staff, which was in favour of greater elasticity, were rapidly widening into an abyss. Hitler was growing more and more distrustful, and the atmosphere was becoming increasingly hostile. 'C.-in-C. Army is now little more than a messenger boy,' complained Halder in a diary entry dated December 7th, and he went on: 'But the worst feature of all is that the Supreme Command does not understand the condition of the troops, and thinks patching and botching will do when, in reality, radical decisions are called for.' Hitler would bypass von Brauchitsch and deal directly with the Army Group commanders, and even with the commanders in the field; and OKH was repeatedly cut out altogether. After a good deal of exhausting and irritating vacillation, Army Group was at last given freedom of action, and it immediately ordered that a line Kursk–Orel–Medyn–Rzhev should be prepared as a 'winter position' to fall back on. The announcement on December 10th that a number of divisions were to be transferred from the west was not allowed to affect von Bock's decision, since, at the best, they could not arrive for weeks.

In the period up to December 18th, new crises kept flaring up at various points on the front. The main body of Panzer Group 3 was in danger of being cut off. Panzer Group 4 found both its flanks being taken in a pincers movement. On the 9th Army front, a numerically greatly superior enemy succeeded in extending his break-through to the southeast of Kalinin. The south wing resting on the Volga dam reservoir had to be pulled back, and preparations were begun to evacuate Kalinin (December 14th). Only the 4th Army was still holding its position, and it successfully used its last reserves to seal off local Russian penetrations. To the west of Serpukhovo, a large-scale Russian offensive was expected at any moment. To the west of Tula, the enemy had widened the existing gap and was exerting pressure southwestward. An attempt to close the gap was made by committing the already battle-weary 137th Division. By December 13th, the 2nd Panzer Army had begun to withdraw. Its chief anxiety was its deep flank in the south, where the Russian break-through had already extended so far that two divisions were cut off and enemy cavalry was moving northwards across their rear. In order to establish a unified local command in this area, Army Group placed the 2nd Army under command of 2nd Panzer Army (Guderian's Force). The danger points at which success for the enemy was almost within grasp could already be seen plainly enough. Brauchitsch clearly recognized the situation when he arrived at Army Group HQ in Smolensk on December 13th. In the circumstances it was easy to convince him that a gradual retreat to the 'winter position' was unavoidable. However, he did not feel himself entitled to give the necessary order for the withdrawal, and on December 14th he met Hitler in order to obtain his agreement for the retreat. Hitler was prepared to agree to local withdrawals by Panzer Groups 3 and 4 and the 9th Army in the Kalinin area, and to an evasive movement by Guderian, but he forbade any other surrender of territory until the rearward line had been fully prepared. But this meant that the main Army Group forces still had to stay where they were. It appears that, after the return of Brauchitsch from the front, Hitler did finally begin to realize both the position at the front and the perilous state of the troops, and to recognize the deadly danger which was now beginning to threaten the German forces. But he also knew that, thanks to very clever propaganda, he still enjoyed the confidence of both the soldiers and the people; indeed, that any word he cared to utter would carry great weight and help to strengthen morale. On December 16th, therefore, he ordered the soldiers in the field to offer 'fanatical resistance'[39] to the enemy, and on the following day he insisted both to Field-Marshal von Bock and to General Guderian that the territory already won must be held at all costs. The most important part of his order reads: 'No major withdrawals may be carried out. They lead only to the irretrievable loss of heavy weapons and equipment. At the risk of their own lives, commanders and their officers must force their men to fanatical resistance, irrespective of whether the enemy may have broken through the flank or at the rear. Only by waging war in this way will it be possible to gain the necessary time to send reinforcements from home and from the west, as I have ordered. Only when reserves have arrived in rearward positions can a retirement to these positions be envisaged.' In a subsequent paragraph he promised the despatch of replacement battalions – partly by air – for seriously weakened divisions. He also promised that during the course of January five divisions would be sent to the Vitebsk front; and by the middle of January, a further two divisions and two replacement divisions were to be ready on the eastern frontier of the Reich. At the same time he instructed Göring to send four bomber, one twin-engined fighter and six transport wings to reinforce VIII Air Corps.

This order made any voluntary withdrawal henceforth impossible, but primitive as the measure was, it did take account of the immediate danger, and it was loyally obeyed by both officers and men. On December 19th, three days after this order was issued, Field-Marshal von Brauchitsch, who was suffering from a serious heart complaint, resigned from his position as C.-in-C. Army. Hitler then took over the supreme command of the Army with the words: 'Anybody can issue a few tactical orders. The task of a C.-in-C. is to educate the army in the National-Socialist spirit. I don't know of any general in the army who could carry out such a task to my satisfaction.'[40]

At the same time, the suggestion was conveyed to Field-Marshal von Bock that it would be a good idea if he took leave of absence and enjoyed a protracted 'rest'. On December 19th, Field-Marshal von Kluge, commander of the 4th Army, took over in his place. At first, he experienced some difficulties with his army commanders, who resented Hitler's interference, and felt that their freedom of action was being restricted and their sense of responsibility undermined. In fact, von Kluge was by no means a yes-man, and he did not hesitate to put forward his own views against Hitler where necessary, but he ruthlessly enforced Hitler's order that the army must 'hold on at all costs'. It was Guderian's unwillingness to submit to this order which led to his removal on December 25th, but personal friction between him and von Kluge seemed to have played a part too. From now on, there was no withdrawal of any sort unless it had previously been approved by Hitler himself. But this meant that local commanders had no freedom of action at all, whatever the situation, and urgent decisions which should have been taken on the spot and immediately carried out had first to be sent back through the usual channels for approval. It therefore frequently happened that the approval arrived far too late, and in the meantime the men were paying for the delay with unnecessary loss of life and equipment.

The aim of the Russian Supreme Command was to break off and destroy the two German armoured tentacles seeking to encircle Moscow from the north and the south. For this purpose two strong forces were operating simultaneously. This was to be followed by an enveloping movement on each outer wing ending in the destruction of the whole Army Group, which was in the meantime being kept occupied frontally by holding attacks.[41]

This 'holding' operation was carried out by launching constant attacks at all points along the front. The Russians were anxious to find by repeated probing the boundary lines in the German front, and to exploit them by systematic small-scale and large-scale attacks. Such 'probing' attacks were sometimes carried out by a single battalion on a short sector of the front, and sometimes by several divisions at a time on a broader front. These attacks were usually preceded by an artillery barrage, but not always. Surprise night attacks alternated with mass attacks launched in waves, sometimes after artillery fire lasting for several days. Such operations were often conducted after an enormous expenditure of shells of all kinds, but in particular by the greatly-feared salvo guns – the so-called 'Stalin organs' – and the hardly less feared, because highly effective, mortars. The losses suffered by the advancing Russians in the defensive fire laid down by the German defenders were enormous, but when one attacking force had been bled white in an offensive, the Russians just brought up fresh divisions and started the operation all over again. On the whole, the Russian methods of attack were not particularly ingenious.

Their unit commanders were not sufficiently imaginative or flexible to exploit their successes on a big scale.[42] But along the whole front there was no 'quiet sector', such as was typical of the trench warfare of the First World War.

It is not necessary to deal in any detail with these Russian holding tactics, but they must be understood if the significance of the large-scale encirclement battles is to be grasped, because it was with these holding tactics that the Russians sought to prevent the German defence from taking any reserves out of the front line to meet Russian pressure elsewhere. On the whole these tactics were successful, but they had to be paid for at a very high price.

The long, deep flank of the advanced spearhead of 2nd Panzer Army ran right back to Army Group periphery, and offered the Russians ample opportunities for attacks. They flung three armies against 2nd Panzer Army, and another two armies against the 2nd Army. At the same time, their 50th Army, reinforced by three cavalry divisions, was thrust into the gap between 2nd Panzer Army and the 4th Army. On December 20th, the Russian advance was halted along the line Tim–Livny–Odoyev, and the two surrounded German divisions succeeded in extricating themselves, but not without suffering very heavy losses. Neither division had more than seven companies left, and they had lost all their artillery. A new attempt at a big break-through was expected in the direction of Orel, where fresh enemy forces were reported coming up three columns abreast from the direction of Yelets. Only loose contact existed with the north wing of Army Group South (6th Army), and the reinforcements promised by Army Group South came up only very slowly, and were not strong enough when they did arrive (one corps, with not quite two infantry divisions). Thus, when the Russians launched a new offensive on December 20th, the situation began to look very critical. 22 Russian infantry divisions and 5 brigades attacked 8 weakened German divisions at Livny and Verkhova (thirty miles north of Livny). Under this pressure, 2nd Panzer Army and the 2nd Army withdrew to a line to the west of Tim–Mtsensk and the south of Belev ('Winter Position'), and by dint of desperate efforts succeeded in holding it for the time being.

The Russian attempt to break through at Orel was beaten off, but the situation on the northern wing was still extremely dangerous. Russian forces were streaming into the gap, and they included strong cavalry forces (Guards Cavalry Corps) and ski and sledge troops, which captured Kosielsk. An attack by XXIV Panzer Corps into the enemy's southern flank, proposed by the commander of 2nd Panzer Army, was approved too late, and when it was finally launched it was held up on December 27th near Belev. The Russians now took advantage of the opportunity to clear the way to Sukhinichi and Yukhnov. The aim of the Russian drive to Yukhnov was to take the south wing of the 4th Army in a pincers movement, and the situation this created was extremely precarious. German forces originally brought forward to close the gap on the Oka front now had to go straight into action the moment they tumbled out of their railway trucks. XLIII Army Corps, now under 4th Army

Command, turned its wing to the northwest near Kaluga in order to avoid envelopment by Russian cavalry. On December 26th, XL Panzer Corps was sent into the gap, which was by now about forty miles wide, in order to re-establish contact between the two armies. The forces engaged, the 10th Armoured and the 10th Mechanized Divisions, each with a combat efficiency of about a regiment, made only slow progress. It was essential for the Germans to hold Yukhnov, because the supply line of the 4th Army went through the town. To defend it, therefore, a line was quickly established to the south of the town with what forces happened to be available at a moment's notice: the 19th Panzer Division was withdrawn from the front, and a draft-conducting battalion was brought up by air.

The south wing of the 4th Army was anxious about its deep flank, but the situation in front was serious too, and the Russians were pressing forward relentlessly. A heavy drive against the boundary between XLIII and XIII Army Corps broke through the front, cut off XLIII Army Corps and then turned in on Malo-Yaroslavets. Under persistent pressure, Hitler finally agreed to allow the Army a limited amount of freedom of action on the right wing and in the centre, so that the centre could slowly withdraw to the Protva sector to the south of Malo-Yaroslavets. But Russian pressure did not relax. On December 29th, Russian forces broke through the front of LVII Army Corps (north wing of the army), and now both wings of the 4th Army were left in the air, so that the Army was threatened with being dislodged from its supports altogether. Army Group now bombarded Hitler with requests for permission to withdraw along the whole front, but Hitler turned a deaf ear to its entreaties, and on January 1st, 1942, he gave orders that the northern front of the 4th Army must stand fast under all circumstances, and that the salient driven into the German lines on the north wing, must be straightened out again. But the heavily pressed 4th Army was no longer strong enough for this. On January 2nd, Army Group therefore ordered 4th Panzer Army[43] to attack from the north and thus close the gap between the two armies. But once again it was too late; the favourable moment had been missed.

By the end of December, Panzer Groups 3 and 4 – fighting against three Russian armies – had managed to stabilize the position in the Ruza and Lama sectors, though the withdrawal of Panzer Group 3, which had only a single, icy road at its disposal, was hampered by very heavy snow-storms and proceeded only very slowly, particularly as from time to time Russian forces which had broken through had to be driven off before the road could be used. The north wing of Panzer Group 4 made contact with the 9th Army, but the attacks which had been going on persistently day after day since December 20th at this boundary line were met by an almost exhausted defence, which at last gave way. By the end of the month, however, with the aid of a few reserves from Panzer Group 3 the break-through was sealed off. Nevertheless, the situation in face of an overwhelmingly superior enemy was still critical, and at any moment a renewed break-through was feared. The two Panzer groups had been very badly mauled, but at least they had succeeded in getting back to their shortened lines still intact. Despite all their efforts, the Russians had not succeeded in destroying them. But von Kluge's hope that he would be able to form reserves from the two Panzer groups was disappointed, because heavy snow-storms, coupled with a shortage of fuel, temporarily immobilized them.

The front of the 9th Army now bent back westward, and each weakened division had to hold between ten and twenty-five miles of the line. Not surprisingly, the situation tempted the Russians to make a drive southwards to thrust deep into the rear of the whole Army Group and encompass its destruction. With the four armies, including numerous fresh divisions at their disposal, the Russians were entitled to feel that this aim was well within their grasp. At first, the right wing of the 9th Army was able to withdraw slowly, a little at a time, abandoning Kalinin, keeping its front intact and maintaining contact with its neighbour on the right. But then the full weight of the Russian attack hit the right wing and centre of the 9th Army. The repeated requests of Army Group for permission to withdraw to the prepared 'Winter Position' were obstinately refused by Hitler, who was prepared to allow only such 'withdrawals' as were made inevitable by enemy pressure, and who continued to demand that every village and every strongpoint should be defended to the last. On January 2nd, he even issued an order forbidding the 9th Army to abandon 'one inch of ground', but this naturally made no difference to the facts of the situation; the front in the direction of Rzhev was now broken, and with this a new danger arose. Powerful enemy forces seemed to be concentrating against the boundary with Army Group North in the Ostashkov area. The inner wings of the two army groups formed only a quite loose, thin, defensive line, and it was obvious that the new drive was to be directed against this sector.

Thus, as the New Year began two main focal points began to crystallize amidst the welter of local danger spots everywhere. It was clearly at these two points that the Russians were hoping for tactical successes. It was obvious that these two points would see the main concentration of the Russian forces for the execution of their plan: the destruction of Army Group Centre. At the southern point, the Russians would aim to drive past Sukhinichi towards Vyazma or Smolensk, after widening their penetration, and at the northern point they would aim to rip open the Army Group boundary and execute a fatal enveloping movement in the rear of 9th Army. Characteristically, the Russians had brought their main forces to these two points in order to commit an overwhelming superiority of fresh troops against the thin and battle-weary German front, and thus be certain of achieving their aim as quickly and surely as possible.

Owing to heavy battle losses and the ravages of frostbite, there was a desperate shortage of manpower in the German lines, and the length of front to be defended bore no reasonable relation to the number of fighting men available for the purpose. In some places the 'front line' consisted of isolated strongpoints, and there was no defence in depth at all. It was often impossible to build defensive positions, because picks could not penetrate the deeply frozen ground, which could only be broken by high explosives. Every man capable of bearing arms was combed out from the HQ staffs, supply columns and rearward services, and sent into the front line, but this measure was a counsel of despair and could no more mend matters than the isolated reinforcements brought up by air.[44] There was a desperate shortage of fighting men, and nothing could be done about it.

In this situation, Russian numerical superiority was overwhelming. At the same time the Russians were more mobile and better adapted to winter movement. Strong groups infiltrated through the German lines and suddenly appeared in their rear. Reinforcements were then rushed through the holes torn in the German lines, so that often they became big gaps that the inadequate German reserves were quite unable to seal off. The order not to give an inch of ground meant that the men were repeatedly involved in hand-to-hand fighting from which they could extricate themselves only after heavy losses. It was now the ordinary front line officers who were urging withdrawal while there was still time.

It was snowing all the time now, and this meant that the roads constantly had to be cleared in order to bring up that minimum of munitions and food without which the men could not hold on at all. The railways had to cope as well with the troop transports which were now starting to come forward, and under the combined strain they almost came to a standstill. The airfields were covered in deep snow, and air operations tremendously difficult.

Desperate appeals for assistance were now coming from all parts of the front, where the nerves of senior and junior officers alike were stretched to breaking point. Army Group was near enough to it all to have some idea of what was happening, but Hitler, far back in his East Prussian HQ, still realized nothing. Von Kluge did his best to convince him that the front, which was already torn open at many points, could be held only if those in command at the break-through points were granted greater freedom of movement and allowed to act at once on their own judgement; von Kluge pointed out again and again that the longer the delay in giving them this absolutely essential freedom, the greater would be the unnecessary losses in men and material. Army Group could form reserves again only if it had a shorter front to defend; and then it would be able to close the gap at Yukhnov. Hitler's reply was that in such a situation even a tactically-limited withdrawal could bring the whole front tumbling back, and this would mean enormous losses in material and equipment. On the other hand, he argued, if the German forces fought for every inch of ground then the Russians would be bled white. Hitler had his way, of course, and in an order dated December 28th, 1941, he set out the reasons why, in his view, it was absolutely necessary to defend every inch of ground, and gave his instructions for the further conduct of the war on land and in the air.[45] The men at the front listened to such 'directives' with mixed feelings, but they obeyed.

In the meantime, the Russians were seeking to extend their penetration in the Sukhinichi area in all three directions. On January 3rd, the ring around Sukhinichi was closed, and the trapped garrison – 4,000 men of the Gilsa Group – put up a tough defence. The Russians now shifted their main pressure to the west and the south, and threatened to envelop the north wing of 2nd Panzer Army. This, for the moment, was the most dangerous point. On January 4th, the German command decided to hem in the penetration by attacking simultaneously from south and north. The 208th and 211th Divisions were coming up via Bryansk, and a further division was promised. 2nd Panzer Army brought up elements of the 10th Mechanized Division, and bent back the left wing (LIII Army Corps) still farther. The 4th Army, anxious to keep open the arterial road to Yukhnov, had secured the town fairly successfully with parts of the 10th Panzer Division and one or two battalions. For the moment, it was quite impossible to withdraw any further reserves from its front, because the 43rd Russian Army was advancing westward, having broken through the front of LVII Army Corps. Thus 4th Army was being surrounded on both flanks and being compressed into a confined area; in this extremely critical situation General Hoepner, commander of 4th Panzer Army, took upon himself the responsibility of issuing the order to retire to a shorter line, since it was perfectly clear that unless this were done the enemy would break through his lines. He was immediately relieved of his command and ignominiously dismissed from the Wehrmacht. Hitler deliberately made an example. of him 'pour encourager les autres'! By January 11th the situation again became very critical when the Russian 1st Guards Cavalry Corps broke through the thin covering lines to the south of Yuchnov and drove forward across the arterial road in the direction of Vyazma. By really desperate efforts, the enemy was temporarily forced back again and supply traffic could continue once more, at least for the time being. The urgency of this situation persuaded Army Group to let the counter-attack from the south go forward without waiting for the deployment of all the forces chosen. On January 16th, relatively weak German forces assembled in temperatures of 40° Centigrade below freezing for a drive on Sukhinichi, and by January 24th they had succeeded in driving a small spearhead far enough forward to make contact with the trapped Gilsa group. But a new and disagreeable surprise was not long in coming: the Russian 61st Army broke through to the south into the rear of LIII Army Corps. The next day, this new Russian advance was halted, but the plan to cut off the Russian forces with a twofold envelopment movement had to be abandoned because adequate forces to carry it out were not available.

Some radical decision was urgently necessary on the German side. On January 2nd, the 39th Russian Army broke through to the northwest of Rzhev and captured a good deal of territory to the south in the direction of Vyazma, thereby threatening the German communications at Sychevka. Elements of the 216th and 339th Divisions were flown up to form a new front and co-operate with the SS Cavalry Brigade to cut the enemy's rearward communications.

But the Russians now hurled new forces (the 29th Army) into the break-through area, and on January 10th strong Russian forces attacked the 3rd Panzer Army near Volokolamsk, where there was heavy fighting. Thanks to a daring attack by the 1st Panzer Division, the Russian advance was brought to a halt near Suchevka. But in the meantime (on January 9th, the previous day), Russian forces had broken through at the boundary between the two Army groups at Ostashkov, and were still streaming unhindered through the gap.

The pressure maintained by the Russians at both break-through points – Sukhinichi and Rzhev – and the constant reinforcements brought up there, clearly indicated by the middle of January that the Russian aim was to encircle Army Group Centre in the Vyazma area. Without further reserves, the German situation had become untenable. To bring in reserves from the Reich or from the west would take too long; in view of the poor transport conditions, they would certainly arrive too late. All that remained was the possibility of accumulating forces as reserves by shortening the battle front. After almost endless discussions between von Kluge and Hitler,[46] the latter finally agreed on January 15th that the centre of the front should be allowed to withdraw step by step to the previously prepared winter position. But Hitler imposed one condition: the gap between the 4th Army and the 4th Panzer Army must be closed before the withdrawal began. After that, the sealing off of the break-through at Rzhev was to be regarded as the most urgent task of the moment, and at the same time the arterial road in the south was to be kept clear of the enemy until his break-through could be dealt with by a German offensive. The 2nd Army was placed under Army Group South, in order to relieve Army Group Centre of its anxieties in that direction; in addition, Army Group South would now have the responsibility of itself doing something to counter the Russian pressure from the Voronezh area.

On January 15th, Army Group Centre gave the order to abandon the salients at Kaluga (4th Army), Rusa (4th Panzer Army) and Volokolamsk (3rd Panzer Army), and, in the period from January 18th to 24th, to withdraw the whole front through various temporary lines to the final winter position.

In fact, during the following weeks the German plans were upset so often and so completely by the Russians that the anxieties of Army Group never ceased. The situation frequently looked worse than ever, and the persistent Russian attempts at encirclement caused crisis after crisis, which could often be resolved only at the very last moment by the gallantry of the German troops engaged. By this time the nerves of all those in command were strained to the limit. Here we can do no more than give a general sketch of the situation.

General Model took command of the 9th Army in the middle of January, when its previous commander, General Strauss, was compelled to resign for reasons of health. Model's energetic personality soon began to make itself felt. While the eastern front of the Army Group carried out a systematic withdrawal to the winter line, the separated left wing of the 9th Army (XXIII

Army Corps) managed to restore contact with the VI Army Corps; XLVI Panzer Corps from the south contained the enemy and finally encircled strong forces of the Russian 29th and 39th Armies to the west of Rzhev. Attempts by the Russian 30th Army to break through the German front north of Rzhev, and link up with the encircled 29th and 39th Armies (seven divisions), were beaten off. However, it proved impossible to hold up a drive by the 11th Russian Cavalry Corps which penetrated almost as far as the motorway to the west of Vyazma; though quickly concentrated units managed to defend this important supply line and keep it clear for Army Group and the 9th Army. The situation became more threatening than ever when Russian airborne troops were landed to the south and west of Vyazma to cut the German supply lines.

The gap at what had been the boundary of the Army groups was now something like sixty miles wide and the Russian 3rd Assault Army was driving forward in a westerly direction towards Velikiye-Luki, while to the south the 4th Assault Army was advancing towards Velizh and Demidov. Both these armies originally formed part of the Russian 'Northwest Front', but on January 21st they were transferred to the 'Kalinin Front'. The obvious intention of these forces was to drive the encircling arm still farther southward, to cut off German rearward communications, and to cover their own west flank by the advance on Velikiye-Luki. Towards the end of January, the German Command deployed the 246th Division against Bieloi, which was encircled on January 27th. However, two days later the Russians succeeded in relieving the town, and they then secured it firmly against all further attack. The 83rd Division was now brought up and committed against Velizh and Velikiye-Luki, and the 330th Division via Rudnia against Demidov, while behind came the 205th Division. These units, and other forces scattered over this wide area, were taken over by LIX Army Corps, which was sent into action on January 16th, and was thus able to provide some general protection for the important rail and road communications in the Vitebsk and Velikiye-Luki area. On February 1st all these units, which were still arriving in dribs and drabs, were put under 3rd Panzer Army and given the task of holding up the enemy drive southwards. Velikiye-Luki had to be left to look after itself.

It proved impossible to close the gap between the 4th Army and 4th Panzer Army before the withdrawal to the winter line, and on January 18th the Russian 33rd Army unexpectedly broke through and drove from the northeast towards Yukhnov, coming to within about ten miles of the town. Counter-attacks from both north and south in an effort to seal off the break-through made some progress at first, and the two forces came within about six miles of each other, but then the attack died away from sheer exhaustion. But the Russian forces were at the end of their tether too, and on February 3rd, when new German forces were brought from the front, it proved possible to cut the rearward connections of the Russian forces already nearing Vyazma. It was high time, because in several places Russian Cavalry units had again broken through the arterial road defences to the southwest of Yukhnov. In heavy fighting, a patchwork XL Army Corps succeeded in clearing the roads so that supply convoys could be resumed, although still under Russian fire.

Sections of the Russian 33rd Army and the Cavalry Guards had broken through the German lines, and at first it proved impossible to bring them to battle. In the extensive forest area, they joined with parachute and airborne troops which had been continually dropped since January 18th, and with the partisans, who were becoming more and more active; these forces represented a very disagreeable threat to Army Group's rear. The fight for the arterial road continued, and those Russian forces which had been cut off sought to join up with the main Russian forces driving through from the east. However, the German defence lines held, and gradually the Russian offensive petered out. The Russian forces had exhausted themselves, and had suffered tremendous losses. The successful withdrawal to the winter line and the defensive successes obtained near Yukhnov and Rzhev were the first practical steps to the formation of a new defensive front. The German Command, which was expecting further reinforcements during the course of February, now regarded the worst danger as having been overcome. It calculated that before the advent of the muddy weather, which was to be expected in the middle of March, it would be able to launch a successful offensive to push back the Russian salients and to dispose of the acute danger threatening the important supply line Smolensk–Vyazma.

Prospect and Retrospect

After the first encirclement battles, the distant objective, Moscow, came closer and clearer. From the time of the battle of Smolensk, the operational ideas of Army Group Centre were almost exclusively concentrated on this one objective to the exclusion of all else; primarily, because it would naturally play the decisive role in the operation. Army Group Commander, Field-Marshal von Bock, clung to this idea, even when the clash between Hitler's ideas and the military aims of OKH, which we have previously described, began to make itself felt in the front line. Hitler's decision on August 21st, 1941, that the battle for Kiev must be fought first, with the acceptance of all the far-reaching aims behind this, did not lead to the desired results: neither the loss of the Donets Basin nor the encirclement of Leningrad materially weakened the fighting strength of the Russian armies; and by then the German Eastern Front was stretched out over enormous distances. If OKH had been able to persuade Hitler to accept its proposal that immediately after the battle of Smolensk all forces should be concentrated for a drive against Moscow, then, looking back, we may reasonably conclude that after the troops had been rested, which was, of course, essential, they could have been re-deployed for the new offensive towards the end of August – i.e., after the flanking threat from the Gomel area had been dealt with. The double battle Vyazma–Bryansk would then have been fought five weeks earlier, and the subsequent drive on Moscow would have taken place in dry weather and under much more favourable conditions; at this earlier date the Russians would not have been able to bring up sufficient reserves or put their capital into such a state of defence. It is true, of course, that if this proposal had been carried out, considerable dangers would have developed on the flanks, particularly from the south. But they could have been countered readily enough if the north wing of Army Group South had kept in close contact with Army Group Centre. Similarly, perhaps Army Group North should not have set its sights on Leningrad, but have considered an advance over the Valdai Hills eastward. Any flanking threat would thus have been forestalled, and the centre of the German Eastern Army would have been able to concentrate more specifically against Moscow. There is good reason to believe that Army Group Centre would have been able to reach the Moscow area, and even Moscow itself, where it would at the same time have met the main military strength of the enemy, who would automatically have accepted battle before Moscow.[47] There is now little point in speculating whether, if this had been the case, the Russians might have been prepared to put out peace feelers since, after all, Hitler's declared aim was the destruction of Bolshevism. In any event, one thing is quite certain: the fatal mistake of the whole risky campaign on the Eastern Front was to underestimate the enemy in every important respect – politically, economically and militarily. Russia's potential military strength was very much greater than Germany's leaders, and Hitler in particular, had supposed or allowed for. The summer and autumn battles on the Eastern Front quickly convinced OKH and the commanders in the field that they were faced with a very different enemy than any they had encountered in their previous campaigns in Poland, France and the Balkans. The tough obstinacy of the Russian soldier, his indifference to whether his flanks were in the air or not; the repeated and unexpected arrival of fresh forces, even after the heaviest losses in men and material; the enormous Russian numerical superiority; and the vast spaces involved – all these things added up to something unique in German experience. At the very latest, by the time the turning point came in the Battle for Moscow, the OKW must have realized that a very dangerous undertaking had been started with inadequate forces. Thus, in the last resort, it was not the delay caused by the unexpected Balkan campaign, nor the precious time wasted by the Kiev digression, nor the slush and mud which rendered the terrain impassable in late autumn, which led to the first significant turning point in the military history of the Second World War: it was the misjudgement of the politician and 'strategist' Hitler. It was this that set his military commanders an impossible task, and provided them with forces too weak to accomplish it.

During the tremendous Russian counter-offensive, involving fierce fighting for many months, both sides performed prodigies of skill and valour such as would previously have been regarded as impossible. In the three months of battle, the Russians hurled in 117 new divisions,[48] and all the German forces had to put against them was the exhausted front of Army Group Centre, feebly reinforced with nine divisions in all![49] It still seems a miracle that the unequal odds of this life-and-death struggle did not bring about the complete collapse of the German centre. It has been suggested in military literature that it was Hitler's order to 'hold on at all costs' which saved Army Group Centre and the whole German Eastern Front from the fate which overtook the Grand Army of Napoleon. There is no more than a very limited amount of truth in this contention. It is quite certain that any withdrawal under pressure is inevitably coupled with a certain loss of equipment and material, and it is also true that a retreat over long distances with demoralized forces involves the danger of a panic. But, in fact, the German forces were not demoralized. Their feeling of superiority was badly shaken in December, but it quickly recovered; and when it was necessary to seal off enemy penetrations it was very often the men themselves who took the initiative. The 'hold on at all costs' policy was extremely costly in manpower, and it led to a galloping decline of military substance that could not be halted because there were no reserves of any account. There was no question of any 'long' retreat, because in the middle of December the 'winter position' was not more than about fifty miles behind the front line. The operations carried out by the 2nd Army, 2nd Panzer Army and the 9th Army, which were either already in, or very near, the winter line by the end of December, show that the withdrawal had been carried out without losing a great deal of material and equipment, and certainly without adversely affecting the morale of the troops. The arguments put forward by Hitler in favour of his tactics were therefore not altogether cogent. There is also no obvious reason why the withdrawal should not have been carried out earlier. Of course, if Army Group had withdrawn at an earlier date it would still not have been able to evade the decision sought by the enemy, but at the very least it could have fought the battle under much more favourable circumstances, since withdrawal to a shorter line would have made it possible to gather reserves; and, another important point, it would have been much closer to the vital supply lines.

Thus, there is a good deal of evidence to suggest that a withdrawal to the winter position in December could have been carried out quite smoothly. Hitler's argument that his tactics would exhaust the Russians sooner and more thoroughly is also unconvincing, because it overlooks the fact that the German forces also had to pay an enormous price in blood and suffering. A very little consideration will show that there is really no basis for the suggestion that only Hitler's 'hold on at all costs' order saved the Army Group front from collapse. It also seems likely that Hitler's order was due less to military considerations than to anxiety for his own prestige: an unscrupulous but very skilful party propaganda campaign had built him up as 'the greatest military genius of all time', and in the circumstances he felt he simply could not afford to retreat.

There was another factor which began to play an increasing part in the development of the situation. Once he had taken over the command of the Army, Hitler took the reins more and more into his own hands; in fact he degraded OKH and the subordinate commands to 'mere messenger boys'.

The proposals of von Kluge for a more elastic (and more efficient) conduct of the war were obstinately rejected. At the same time, all the old tried and trusted military principles that had served Germany so well throughout her history were now contemptuously dismissed as old-fashioned and out of date; Hitler's distrust of the General Staff became more and more marked. This led to a disastrous course of action, particularly as Hitler concluded from any success of his 'hold on' policy that it must be 'a universal panacea for all future military operations. . . . Adroit leadership and skilful manœuvring were replaced by the unintelligent exercise of brute force on principle; the Nazi tactic of political uproar was transferred to the battlefield. . . . The sound principle that in a critical situation the men in the front line can be called upon to exert their last ounce of strength was turned into a permanent and absolute rule.'[50]

The final result of the battle for Moscow was to bring both sides temporarily to the end of their strength.[51] Neither side succeeded in attaining its objectives. The Germans did not capture Moscow, though for a while it looked almost within their grasp, and the Russians did not succeed in disintegrating and destroying Army Group Centre. By the spring of 1942, the German forces along the whole of the Eastern Front had been brought into a battleworthy condition again, and their mobility was restored by bringing up new men, material and equipment. But even this was not enough to enable them to launch an offensive along the whole of the front, which was now 1,700 miles long. The only hope of enforcing a decision now was to concentrate the armour and the mechanized units on one sector of the front. Only then could there possibly be sufficient strength – with the assistance of Germany's allies (Rumania, Italy and Hungary contributed a total of about thirty-five divisions) – to win the victory.

However, the military and political significance of the Battle for Moscow is that the original great plan to subjugate Russia within a period of from three to five months was a failure, and this failure closed the period of Germany's 'blitz' campaigns. In 1939, Hitler, the statesman, claimed credit for the fact that Germany need fight on one front only. Now the war on two fronts was an unalterable fact; not only that, but the determination of the Allies to fight on to victory had now received great psychological reinforcement. After winning an uninterrupted series of manifest victories, the German Wehrmacht had now suffered a manifest military defeat. The German arms had lost their aura of 'invincibility'.

The all-important question for the further course of the war on the Eastern Front was whether Hitler and his closest advisers had learnt the lessons of the winter campaign of 1941–42, and were prepared to draw the necessary conclusions for the conduct of the war in 1942.

Chronicle VI

January

to

October 1942

	Politics		Conduct of the War
Neutrals	**Axis Powers and Japan**	**Axis Powers and Japan**

Neutrals	Axis Powers and Japan	Axis Powers and Japan
		January (throughout): Heavy Luftwaffe attack on Malta.
		January to July: Fourth phase of the Battle of the Atlantic; almost 3,000,000 GRT sunk.
		January 11th to February 7th: Operation 'Pauken schlag' or 'Drumbeat'; German submarine sink 142,373 GRT off the USA.
	January 18th: Military alliance between Germany, Italy and Japan.	January: Japanese troops land in the Celebes, New Ireland, Bougainville, New Britain, Borneo Ambon. Offensive against Burma begins.
	January 20th: 'Wannsee Conference': Jewish problem to be settled by 'emigration' – and 'other measures'. Systematic destruction of five million Jews by the end of the war.	January 21st: Rommel launches counter-drive to recapture Cyrenaica. German forces reach El Gazala.
	Beginning of February: Secret session of Germany's leading scientists, under chairmanship of Göring, decides production of atom bombs impossible during the next few years.	
	February 8th: Speer appointed Minister for Munitions.	February 9th to 15th: Japanese capture Singapore
		February: Japanese landings on Sumatra, Bali and Timor.
		February 12th to 13th: German warships *Gneisenau Scharnhorst* and *Prinz Eugen* steam through the Channel.
		February 19th: Heavy Japanese carrier-borne air raid against Port Darwin.
		February 27th to March 1st: Naval battle in the Java Sea, followed by landings on Java.
		February 14th: Japanese naval plan for operation in the Indian Ocean.
		March: Japanese land in New Guinea and the Andaman Islands.
		March 8th: Dutch East Indian forces capitulate
	March 21st: Sauckel appointed Commissar for Labour Mobilization (7.5 million foreign workers and 30 million German civilians engaged in German economy).	April 2nd to May 10th: Intensified Luftwaffe attacks on Malta.
		April 4th to 9th: Big Japanese carrier-borne air raids on Ceylon and coastal towns along the Bay of Bengal.
		April 5th: Führer Directive No. 41 for the summer offensive 1942.
		April 16th: Japanese plan of operations for 'the second phase of the war'.
		April 20th: Demyansk encirclement broken.
	April 26th: Hitler demands full powers from Reichstag to take all measures necessary for the welfare of the German people.	
	April 29th: Conference between Hitler and Mussolini at Berchtesgaden, on the conduct of the war in the Mediterranean.	April 29th: Japanese cut Burma Road near Lashio
		May 4th to 8th: Sea-air battle in the Coral Sea.
		May 4th: Wehrmacht High Command gives instructions for Operation 'Hercules' – the capture of Malta.
		May 5th: Japanese land on Corregidor.
		May 5th: Japan; Directive No. 18 for the Midway Operation.
		May 8th to 15th: Kerch peninsula captured.
		May 15th to July 1st: Japanese offensive in Chekiang against US air bases.
		May 17th to 25th: Battle of Kharkov.
		May 23rd: Withdrawal of German U-boats from the US east coast.

Conduct of the War	Politics	
Western Allies and the Soviet Union	Western Allies and the Soviet Union	Neutrals
January: First plans for a landing in North Africa.	January 1st: Washington Pact; twenty-six Nations agree not to make a separate peace with Germany. November 22, 1941 to January 14th, 1942: Washington Conference ('Arcadia'). January 15th: General Wavell takes over ABDA Command. January 28th: First US troops arrive in Britain.	
February 8th: Soviet forces close the Demyansk cauldron.		
March: Start of British air raids on German factories and U-boat bases. March 8th: Fall of Rangoon. March 28th: British raid St Nazaire. March 28th to 29th: Heavy RAF attack on Lübeck.	March 17th: General MacArthur appointed Allied Supreme Commander in the southwest Pacific. April 1st: US Secretary of State for War proposes a landing in northern France.	
April 18th: Doolittle leads US air raid on Tokyo. April 23rd: First of five successive RAF night raids on Rostock.	April 8th to 17th: Discussions in London between Harry Hopkins and Churchill. General Marshall visits London. April 14th: Project for the invasion of Europe adopted: landing in 1943.	
May 5th to 7th: British landings on the north coast of Madagascar. May: Convoy system introduced on eastern seaboard of the United States.		

	Politics		Conduct of the War
Neutrals	Axis Powers and Japan		Axis Powers and Japan
	May 26th: Heydrich, Reich Protector of Bohemia and Moravia, assassinated. May 29th: Hitler receives Subhas Chandra Bose, leader of the anti-British movement in India. May 30th: Luxembourg incorporated into the German Reich.		May 26th: Beginning of the last German offens. in North Africa ('Theseus').
June 1st: 'Yellow Star', introduced into France and Holland			June 7th to July 4th: Capture of Sevastopol.
	June 10th: Czech village of Lidice wiped out as 'retaliation' for Heydrich's assassination. June 12th: Himmler gives his approval to a 'German Eastern Plan', the driving of the East European peoples out of their territories.		June 12th to 16th: 15 out of a total of 17 ships two British convoys sunk on the way Malta.
			June 20th to 21st: Tobruk captured.
			June 28th: Beginning of German offensive aga the Volga and the Caucasus. July 1st to 10th: Luftwaffe and U-boats sink out of 32 ships in Allied convoy to Murmar July 19th: Main weight of the German submar campaign again transferred to the Nc Atlantic convoy routes. July 21st: 4th Panzer Army crosses the Don. July 23rd: Führer Directive No. 45. Army Grou retakes Rostov.
			August 1942 to May 1943: Fifth phase of Atlantic Battle. Convoy battles in the Nc Atlantic. 3.8 million GRT sunk.
			August 9, 1942: Night naval battle off Savo Isla Japanese success. German forces capt Maykop and Piatigorsk. August 10th: Operation 'Pedestal'; British M. convoy badly mauled. August 15th to 19th: U.507 attacks Brazi coastal shipping.
			August 18th to 19th: Anglo-Canadian raid Dieppe. August 21st: Reichs war flag planted on to Mount Elbrus. August 23rd to 25th: Carrier-borne air battl east of the Solomons broken off with result. August 30th to September 3rd: North Afr front hardens after failure of Rommel's offensive. September 1st to 15th: 6th Army and 4th Pa Army fight their way into Stalingrad f the north and west. September 6th: Novorossisk captured. September 12th: Laconia incident. U.156 bom by US plane whilst picking up survivors September 25th: General Halder, Chief of A General Staff, resigns. General Zei succeeds him.
	September 30th: Whilst launching the Winter Aid Campaign, Hitler announces that the German soldier will give up nothing of what he has won.		October 3rd: Stalingrad suburb Orlovka captu October 7th to 17th: German U-boats operate Cape Town. 114,000 GRT sunk. October 10th: Luftwaffe reopens offensive ag Malta. October 14th: German forces attack the Dzer sky tractor works at Stalingrad. October 18th: Hitler issues 'Commando' orde October 26th to 27th: Sea-air battles off S Cruz. Tactical success or Japanese.

Conduct of the War	Politics	
...estern Allies and the Soviet Union	Western Allies and the Soviet Union	Neutrals

	May 26th: Molotov in London; conclusion of a Soviet-British Pact. May 29th to June 1st: Molotov in Washington.	
30th to 31st: RAF 1,000 bomber raid on Cologne. 1st to 2nd: RAF 1,000 bomber raid on Essen. 3rd to 7th: Japanese defeat in air-sea battle off Midway Island.		
12th: First attack of USAAF on Ploesti oilfields.	June 11th: British Cabinet decides no landing in northern France until sufficient forces available. Agreement incorporating principles for mutual aid signed by US and Soviet Union. June 18th to 26th: Second Washington Conference (Churchill–Roosevelt).	
25th to 26th: RAF 1,000 bomber raid on Bremen.		
10th: Russian High Command brings up 62nd and 64th Armies for the defence of Stalingrad.	July 18th to 25th: Discussions in London between Churchill, Harry Hopkins and representatives of the US and British General Staffs. July 23rd: Roosevelt supports British proposal to land first in North Africa. July 24th to 25th: Decision goes in favour of Operation 'Torch', the Allied landing in North Africa. August 6th: General Eisenhower appointed C.-in-C. for Operation 'Torch'.	
24th: British and US General Staffs agree to postpone invasion of Europe. Preparations for North African landing, Operation 'Torch', peeded up. ...st 7th to 8th: US troops land on Guadalcanal. Turning point in Pacific war.		
...st 17th: First attack by 8th USAAF from ...ases in Britain. Twelve B–17 'Flying Forresses' bomb Rouen railway station. ...st 18th to 19th: First raid led by 'Pathfinder' ...ircraft on Flensburg.	August 12th to 15th: Discussions in Moscow between Stalin, Churchill and Roosevelt's representative, Harriman. August 18th: General Montgomery appointed C.-in-C. British 8th Army in Egypt. August 28th: Brazil declares war on Axis Powers.	
...nber 22nd: General Eisenhower fixes ...ovember 7, 1942, for Allied landing in North ...frica.		
...er 4th: Representatives of Russian High ...ommand meet in Stalingrad to discuss ...perations. ...er 9th: Sole authority of Russian military ...mmanders restored. ...er 11th to 12th: Naval battle off Cape ...sperance between US and Japanese cruiser ...rces ends in US success. ...er 23rd: British offensive at El Alamein ...gins.		

The Decision in the Mediterranean 1942

BY WALTER WARLIMONT

The decision in the Mediterranean was brought about by the victory of the British 8th Army at El Alamein and the landing of the Allies in French North Africa; both events took place in November 1942. But in a wider sense, the events of the previous few months also belong to this decisive period. In the constant fluctuation which marked the conflict in the Mediterranean from the beginning, it sometimes looked as though the Axis Powers were within grasping distance of a strategic victory of immeasurable consequence, but in the end the scales tipped definitely and finally in favour of the Allies. However, the Italo-German offensive of the spring and summer of 1942 must also be counted as part of 'the decision', even if one merely regards its real or supposed failures and omissions as 'the beginning of the end'.

Any investigation of the events of the war in these latitudes must proceed from the basis that from the start the general situation gave the Anglo-Saxon powers a great advantage. For one thing, the peoples who live on the Mediterranean seaboard are used to British dominance; and for another, the Allies began with a number of very important strongpoints in their hands. This Allied superiority, the extent and importance of which can hardly be overestimated, was underlined by the fundamental difference in the original strategic objectives of the combatants. From the beginning, the British regarded the Mediterranean as the lifeline of their empire, and their objective was to secure control of the sea and the air, and, if possible, the control of North Africa as a whole.[1]

On the other hand, after the costly failure of the Italians in their first attempt to attack the Suez Canal at the end of 1940, the Axis Powers confined themselves to defending the core of the Italian North-African colonial empire in Tripolitania. Even then, it was only after a good deal of hesitation that Hitler finally agreed to provide the necessary German aid to his Italian ally – and this was done primarily for fear that if the Italians lost their colonial bridgehead in North Africa it might cause them to lay down their arms and abandon the Axis altogether.[2]

The feeble and nerveless beginning of Axis operations in North Africa was suddenly and unexpectedly transformed when Rommel appeared on the scene in the spring of 1941. With the support of X Air Corps, which had been transferred to the Mediterranean only a few months previously, he pulled the relatively small Axis forces together and led them in a dashing advance right up to the frontiers of Egypt. Taken together with the occupation of the whole of the Balkans, which was carried out at the same time, and in view of the attack which was about to take place in Russia, Germany was now in a position to think more ambitiously about the Mediterranean. Hitler began to consider a pincer movement whose southern arm would thrust forward from North Africa through Egypt deep into the Middle East, and break up the British Empire.[3]

But before any such ambitious plans could take practical shape, the Italo-German forces in North Africa were hurled back to their starting positions in the Gulf of Sirte area. This was the beginning of 1942, and the winter crisis was in full swing on the Eastern Front. In addition, thanks to Pearl Harbour, the United States was now at war with the Axis Powers. This disappointing reversal of fortunes, and the heavy and increasing losses along the Mediterranean supply line which had preceded it,[4] made it clearer than ever that the Mediterranean theatre of war was controlled from the sea – and there the British had recovered command. X Air Corps had been transferred to the eastern Mediterranean to support the Balkan campaign, and was subsequently left there against all sensible advice to the contrary. With the aid of fighters flown in from carriers in the western Mediterranean, the British succeeded in turning Malta into a naval base of considerable strength once more. In the autumn of 1941, 'Force K', with first two and then four cruisers, supported by a number of destroyers, was able to operate in the Mediterranean across the Axis supply line to North Africa. The Italian fleet was unable to bring its still existing numerical superiority to bear against this threat.[5]

Naval Strengths in the Mediterranean in November 1941
(Ships ready for action only)

Type	Italian	British Mediterranean Fleet (Alexandria)	Force K (Malta)	Force H (Gibraltar)
Battleships	5	3		1
Aircraft Carriers				1
Heavy Cruisers	3			
Light Cruisers	8	6–8	2–4	1
Destroyers	34	21		7
Submarines	46+6	11	12	6

German

Quite apart from its lack of battle experience, the Italian fleet sadly lacked an effective air force. It was also without radar, already being used by the British. On top of all this came a chronic shortage of oil fuel, and this made Italy's naval leaders – already inclined to caution because of previous heavy losses – more cautious than ever.

Considerable German air strength – Air Fleet 2 under the command of Field-Marshal Kesselring, who was appointed C.-in-C. South on November

28th – had to be brought in to redress the balance in the air; a balance which soon after turned into German air superiority in the central Mediterranean. A big change also took place in the comparative naval strengths, and for the same reason: German U-boats were transferred to the Mediterranean – six in September and October, and a further twenty in November and December. There was also increased activity on the part of the Italian fleet. German submarines sank the aircraft carrier *Ark Royal* and the battleship *Barham*, and also the cruiser *Galatea* after she had been hit by an Italian torpedo. With their 'human torpedoes' (the 'sea-swine' or *maiale*) the Italians penetrated the defences of Alexandria and put the battleships *Queen Elizabeth* and *Valiant* out of action. Then 'Force K' sailed into a minefield laid down by Italian cruisers north of Tripoli. The cruiser *Neptune* and a destroyer were sunk, and the cruisers *Aurora* and *Penelope* suffered heavy damage. These losses robbed the Mediterranean fleet of all its heavy units, and the British Admiralty was unable to replace them, because for the time being the new theatre of war in the Far East demanded all available naval forces.

The advantage secured by the Axis Powers at sea and in the air, with the subsequent improvement of the supply situation, allowed Rommel to make another bid for victory; and once more he set out towards Egypt. He drove forward on January 21st, 1942, right into the middle of British forces preparing for a further advance. The British were taken completely by surprise and routed, and within a very short space of time Rommel's forces had reached Derna, halfway between Benghazi and Tobruk. The Italians were half-heartedly carried along with this tremendous offensive drive, but it encouraged Germany's leaders to revert to their ambitious project of the previous year, linking it this time with plans for a further offensive in the Caucasus.[6]

The inherent weakness of this development, in which strategic considerations limped along in the rear of tactical success, was glossed over by Rommel's brilliant victory in the desert, and it was optimistically assumed that Rommel's tremendous reputation and his undoubted skill as a leader in the field would more than compensate for the steady increase of enemy strength which was to be expected. In the same way, Luftwaffe superiority in the air was expected to compensate for the weakness of the Axis at sea; and, in particular, to dispose of the island of Malta, which had in the meantime proved itself the most dangerous strongpoint of the British in the Mediterranean.

The Axis Powers seek to force a Decision
(April to September 1942)

The decisive events of 1942 were introduced on April 2nd by a powerful Luftwaffe offensive, supported by the Royal Italian Air Force, against Malta. The preliminary condition for carrying out the task which now devolved on C.-in-C. South, 'to create a powerful centre for the Axis in the Mediterranean as the basis for a further development of Axis strength',[7] was the destruction of Malta's military installations. The island, right in the middle of the Axis line of supply to North Africa, was to be made, and kept, harmless. But just as the strengthening of the Luftwaffe at the beginning of the year came too late to prevent the Axis set-back in North Africa, so the air battle now launched against Malta came too soon for the proposed landings, which were to seize the island for the Axis and provide a really secure basis for far-reaching operational plans throughout the eastern Mediterranean area.

The Luftwaffe offensive against Malta had been going on for almost a month before the two Axis leaders met in Berchtesgaden (April 29th and 30th) to discuss future objectives in the Mediterranean, and the timing of the further conduct of the war there.[8] There was no joint Axis operational staff, and all attempts to form one failed because the two dictators secretly distrusted each other. Therefore, at rare meetings such as this, they had to discuss not only fundamental matters of joint strategy, but very often the technical background as well.

As the joint meeting showed, the Italians were resolved in future operations to maintain the cautious reserve that they had already shown since the beginning of the year towards Rommel's renewed offensive in Libya. On the German side, Hitler revived the old plan to drive across Egypt – which he regarded as 'ripe for revolution' – and beyond, in order to encircle the British position in the Middle East. But Mussolini and his Chief of General Staff, subsequently Marshal Cavallero, were unwilling, for the time being at any rate, to agree to go beyond the Libyan-Egyptian frontier. They also came to the conference determined to insist that 'the conquest of Malta' was the really essential condition for the continued prosecution of the war in North Africa, and that the Axis must therefore adopt this as its immediate objective. However, as they – and the Germans too – realized that the island could no longer be captured swiftly by a *coup de main*, and as, further, they announced that they would not be ready to take part in a systematic attack by landing on the island for another three months, to accept their standpoint meant practically the abandonment of all hope that the Axis Powers could ever resume the offensive in North Africa. In the meantime, the British were preparing to forestall an Italo-German attack in Libya by themselves driving forward to force a decisive battle on their enemies. Whereas Malta was one more reason for the Italians to hesitate, it was one more reason for the British to speed up their plans. For them, to save Malta in this indirect fashion meant to ward off a 'catastrophe'; which is how Churchill regarded the possible loss of the island with its 30,000-man garrison and several hundred guns. Its loss would frustrate all his future plans for the Mediterranean, and even for the defence of the Nile Valley.[9]

After detailed military discussions, the Axis heads of State finally decided that 'for the time being' Rommel's armour should attack in North Africa at the end of May, take Tobruk if possible, and then continue its advance no farther than the Egyptian frontier; by which time – mid-June, or at the latest by the full moon in July[10] – Operation 'Hercules', i.e. the capture of Malta, could be carried out.

Now although this decision seemed to be the only one possible at the given moment, if the Axis Powers were not to lose the initiative entirely by further procrastination, it suffered very obviously from all the inadequacies and imperfections that had dogged the conduct of the war in the Mediterranean from the start. The agreement was still further undermined by disappointments and unspoken reservations. Rommel himself was not present at the conference, but he had managed to get confirmation of the date on which he wanted to set his armour in motion, though he was very disappointed when he subsequently learned that there was no intention of trying to take Malta beforehand. In the same way, Field-Marshal Kesselring, C.-in-C. Air Fleet 2, saw himself robbed of the culmination of his successful air offensive – the capture of Malta. On the other hand, the Italians were forced to agree to a decision which ran counter to their own plans. Hitler had always opposed the idea of landing on Malta. He was against it when it had first been broached over a year before, and his consent now was probably very grudging. He insisted, for example, that strong forces of Air Fleet 2 should be withdrawn immediately after the attack on Malta had been launched on May 10th, in order that they could take part in the coming summer offensive on the Eastern Front. Within a matter of ten days, on May 21st, he seems to have given up the idea altogether, since in his own intimate circle he now declared that Operation 'Hercules' was to be prepared merely 'psychologically'.[11]

Although the German paratroops which had in the meantime been transferred to southern Italy were left there, the decision against an attempt to capture Malta by airborne operations had already been taken. Hitler shied away even more violently now from any attempt at a landing than he had from an invasion of Britain in 1940, and for the same reasons: he did not regard the available forces, particularly at sea, as adequate to the task, and he was not prepared to risk a failure. In any case, in his view Malta was not all that important, as he was firmly convinced that Rommel's new offensive would take Tobruk; then the Italo-German supply line across the Mediterranean could run under the protection of Crete to this harbour, so conveniently near to the front line. And when, a little later, two British convoys to Malta were almost completely destroyed by combined Italo-German naval and air forces, he advanced the further argument that the Axis should not deliberately deprive itself of such an opportunity for inflicting heavy losses in ships, men and supplies on the British.[12]

This, however, did not alter the fact that in the spring of 1942 the German High Command had ambitious plans for a drive far into the Middle East which depended on a doubtful supply line across the Mediterranean, a few Libyan harbours of low capacity, and a small strip along the coast of North Africa. But there was another important difficulty that year: there were no longer adequate forces in the Balkans for a joint drive from there. There was also no longer any hope of drawing Turkey into the war on the side of the Axis, and the Arab states in the eastern Mediterranean had fallen back into their traditional reliance on British colonialism, and were now serving the Western Allies as a rest and rehabilitation centre for their reserves. To the west of the Axis deployment area, Spain seemed more and more inclined to interpret her voluntarily adopted policy of 'non-belligerence' to the detriment of her Axis friends. On the flanks and in the rear of Axis operations lay French North Africa, whose importance Axis policy failed to recognize and continued to neglect, with the result that this area threatened to drift completely out of the always weak military orbit of the Axis.

On May 26th, just one month after the conference in Berchtesgaden, Rommel launched his new offensive in the desert according to plan and on time, using the German Afrika Korps (one armoured and one light division with 333 tanks) and the Italian XX Corps (one armoured and one mechanized division with 228 tanks) against the British XXX Corps (two armoured divisions and one mechanized brigade). The Italian X and XXI Corps, with four infantry divisions, were given the task of pinning down the British XIII Corps, with its three mechanized divisions. Strong forces of Air Fleet 2 had been regrouped and brought up to support the attack, and there were 542 German planes against the 604 of the Desert Air Force.[13] In the meantime, German and Italian naval forces held Malta in check so that, thanks to a now almost uninterrupted supply line, it was possible to accumulate supplies sufficient to last the Axis troops in North Africa for a month. However, it proved impossible to establish the really big dumps in North Africa which had been planned. The maintenance of supplies was therefore still dependent on regular and uninterrupted transport across the Mediterranean by sea followed by long distances overland, during which a proportion of the supplies, and in particular the fuel, was used before it arrived at its destination.

Rommel's new attack anticipated the enemy's own offensive by a few days only. The British forces were liberally supplied and well equipped, particularly with munitions; they were also superior to the Italo-German armies in mechanization and in numbers, and to some extent in the quality of their armour. In other ways, the respective forces on land and in the air were more or less equal.

From the start, the more optimistic hopes were frustrated when the enveloping wing of the German armour reached out southwards but found itself halted soon after the start of its attack by the 1st Free French Brigade, which defended its positions at Bir-Hakeim with grim determination. In this situation, the Italian High Command was inclined to be satisfied with preliminary successes, and to turn its attention prematurely to the attempt to capture Malta, but on June 11th and 12th a renewed attack by German land and air forces succeeded in capturing the desert fortress. This was followed by bitter fighting for the British strongpoint 'Knightsbridge'. The success of the operations was then crowned on June 20th by the swift capture of the fortress of Tobruk.

A day later, Rommel, now promoted to Field-Marshal as a reward for this new brilliant victory, was once again at the gates of Egypt, and this time the situation was much more favourable than it had been a year before, when the fortress of Tobruk, manned by picked British troops, was like a painful thorn in the flank and rear of relatively weak Axis forces. Now Tobruk was in Axis hands, and serving as a collecting point for tens of thousands of prisoners of war. In addition, tremendous quantities of supplies were captured, and the harbour was almost undamaged, so that the supply position was very much better. There seemed very little resistance ahead now. The powerful British 8th Army with its strong reserves held ready for an attack, with its artillery, its anti-tank guns and its tanks, seemed to have melted away.

Disputed Decisions

The speed and the scope of Rommel's victory were not calculated to encourage Germany's leaders to carry out the cautious decision they had just come to with their Axis partner: on the contrary, they were far more inclined to continue the victorious course of events. The Italian High Command, on the other hand, was very anxious that the plans jointly agreed to should now be carried out, and it therefore insisted that Rommel's army should stand on the defensive on the Egyptian frontier. Perhaps with a presentiment of what was to come, Mussolini, at Cavallero's suggestion, sent a letter to Hitler on June 21st, urging him to consolidate the success achieved and turn to the attack on Malta before going any further.[14] But quite different views now prevailed at German HQ, and as soon as he received the news of the capture of Tobruk, Hitler reverted once more to the decision of May 21st, and declared in the presence of his military advisers that any attempt to capture Malta was 'once and for all' out of the question – quite clearly the British must immediately be chased on to Suez.

Thus, neither the urging of his victorious commander in North Africa, nor the support of the Wehrmacht Operations Staff and the German Naval Operations Staff, was necessary to persuade Hitler to 'advise' Mussolini in favour of following up Rommel's victory, and this was done in a communication dated June 22nd and addressed to Mussolini personally.[15] Without bothering to waste even a word on Malta, Hitler allowed the enthusiasm of the moment to carry him away, and insisted that 'a historic turning point' had now been reached, and that it could be of 'decisive importance' for the outcome of the whole war. The British 8th Army had been 'practically destroyed'. It was unlikely that such a situation would ever arise again in that theatre of operations, and 'the swiftest and most complete exploitation' of the advantage was urgently necessary. This required 'uninterrupted pursuit' until the British forces had been totally destroyed, before they could be strengthened by reinforcements and the situation once again changed 'to our disadvantage'. This time 'Britain could be deprived of Egypt', while the capture of Sevastopol opened the way to an advance through the Caucasus 'to overthrow the whole Middle-Eastern edifice of the British Empire'. Appealing once again to 'the historic hour', which he insisted had now struck, Hitler concluded by assuring his fellow dictator that 'the goddess of good fortune in battle approaches the leaders of men but once, and whoever fails to seize her in his arms will not often be able to reach her again thereafter'.

Behind the orotund phraseology of this correspondence, which sought to replace the far-sighted planning of the joint staffs with something quite different now the decisive moment had arrived, one can once more see the fundamental divergence in the strategic aims of the Axis coalition partners, and, closely related to this, the difference in their methods of war. While the German leaders, emboldened by the great preliminary successes in the east and the south, were raising their sights far out into the Middle East, Rome insisted that the Axis bases in the Mediterranean should first be made safe – and at the same time, of course, the Italian empire in North Africa. The same clash of interest and methods was reflected in the leadership on the spot. On the basis of earlier experience, the Italians were disinclined to seek new successes by advancing still further, until the question of supplies seemed fully safeguarded. German HQ, on the other hand, firmly believed that, with the supposed disintegration of the British 8th Army, the tactical conditions were now ripe for a victorious drive into Egypt. It also believed that the supply situation was more hopeful than ever before, particularly when Rommel declared that for general supply purposes his forces could draw on the great British dumps he had captured, that for munitions and fuel they could draw on Tobruk, and that there was now a large number of captured British lorries for the general overland transport of supplies. In addition, he could use the narrow-gauge railway line to Egypt.[16] If the Axis successes continued, and the Axis forces were soon in Alexandria and along the Suez Canal, then Malta – isolated far behind the fronts – would soon lose its importance.

On the other hand, the Italian High Command was far from ready to play its part in the campaign to capture the island. It is true that writing on June 21st Mussolini assured his ally that Italy's preparations were far advanced, but at the same time he demanded no less than 70,000 tons of oil fuel in order to ensure the effective co-operation of the Italian Navy. For this reason alone, quite apart from the probable intervention of the enemy, who had in the meantime reinforced his air forces on Malta by flying in planes from carriers in the western Mediterranean, it really did not look as though when the 'final and most favourable moment' arrived – the Italians were now in favour of August – it would be possible to take advantage of it. If this should turn out to be the case, then, as Mussolini pointed out in his letter, the operation would have to wait until the following spring.

This examination of the possibilities shows clearly that in those late June days of 1942 the Axis leaders were not being asked to decide between Malta and Suez, but merely whether Rommel's forces should stay where they were or go forward. To stay put would mean abandoning the full exploitation of Rommel's

An Anglo-French transport column destroyed by the Luftwaffe outside Dunkirk.

British and French soldiers waiting to be taken off the beach at Dunkirk.

Above: Evacuated British soldiers on board a rescue ship looking back at burning Dunkirk. In the background, a hospital ship.
Below: British destroyers loaded with hundreds of evacuated soldiers making fast at Dover.

General (later Field-Marshal) Gerd von Rundstedt, Commander-in-Chief of Army Group A at Dunkirk.

Vice-Admiral (later Admiral) Sir Bertram Ramsay, Flag Officer, Dover, who commanded the evacuation.

General Hans Jeschonnek, Luftwaffe Chief of Staff.

Air Chief-Marshal Sir Hugh Dowding, Air Officer Commanding-in-Chief, Fighter Command.

Above: A Heinkel 111 bomber above the Thames on September 7, 1940.
Below: The business area around St Paul's after a Luftwaffe attack.

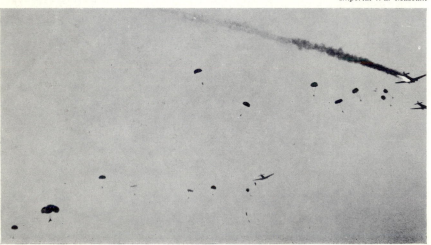

Above: German paratroops being dropped by three Junkers 52 planes over Maleme.
Below: German paratroops being dropped over Heraklion. On the right, a Junkers 52 hit by anti-aircraft fire. In the left bottom corner a parachute carrying supplies.

Above: German infantry with self-propelled guns before Moscow (mid-December 1941).
Below: Snowstorms impeding the supply columns in the Kalinin area (end of December 1941).

Landing craft bringing supplies ashore from vessels lying in the roads of Arzeu.

victory, and this would have been a gross violation of a cardinal principle of German tactics. If this were done it would mean giving the enemy back his freedom of movement, and making sure that sooner or later the Axis Powers would lose the initiative again. It is probably not too much to say that the German commander on the spot, who had already on two occasions turned a reconnoitring drive into a large-scale offensive, would in any case, and irrespective of whatever orders he received, have exploited the spirit of victory to force through his own intentions by some means or other.

As a matter of fact, on June 22nd, before he had officially been given a free hand, Rommel, who could in any case hardly have acted any differently, ordered his forces to continue the pursuit of the enemy to Sidi Barrani, about fifty miles beyond the Libyan-Egyptian frontier.[17] In the meantime, a certain modification of Italy's standpoint had taken place – so much so that Mussolini was now anxious lest the Axis success might not be 'exploited to the full', and he was therefore far more inclined to trust Rommel's judgement than that of his own advisers.[18] Hitler's letter was, in fact, merely pushing open a door which was already ajar, and it gave the Comando Supremo an opportunity to abandon its opposition to the German plans. Encouraged by American reports from Cairo about the great chance now open to Rommel, and by wireless messages picked up from the French warships interned in Alexandria to the French Admiralty suggesting that the British were about to evacuate the harbour, the Italian Comando Supremo on June 23rd began to issue a series of new orders instructing its forces to join in the pursuit of the British into Egypt towards the Suez Canal.[19] Cairo was to be taken *en passant*, and for the time being Alexandria was to be invested. Even Field-Marshal Kesselring, who had at first raised serious objections because of the difficulty of ensuring supplies across the Mediterranean and because of the air situation that was likely to develop in the event of further action against British bases in the valley of the Nile, now willy-nilly accepted the new decision. Mussolini was so confident that he flew to North Africa himself, and had a white horse flown over too, in order that when the time came to march into Cairo he could ride on it at the head of his troops.

The Axis successes were to continue only for a few days beyond this peak point. Advancing over the Libyan-Egyptian frontier on a broad front, the Italo-German armoured divisions succeeded in pushing the British back very rapidly to Sidi Barrani and to the fortified areas of Mersah-Matruh. Then, on June 30th, they suddenly came up against unexpectedly strong resistance at the fortified position of El Alamein. After a further three days of heavy fighting, Field-Marshal Rommel, and with him his staffs, were compelled to recognize that the pursuit which had now been going on since the middle of June had come to an end – a temporary end only, it was presumed. After six weeks of movement and heavy fighting, the attacking forces began to show signs of exhaustion. Rommel had arrived at El Alamein with only 55 tanks, 15 armoured scout vehicles, 77 guns of various calibres, 65 anti-tank guns (including 8·8 cm.

anti-aircraft guns) and about 2,000 infantrymen in the three German divisions. The fighting strength of the Italian armoured units was even less, and their two infantry corps were lagging behind far in the rear. It appeared that the enemy had reacted with unexpected speed and was now occupying long-prepared positions between El Alamein and the Qattara Depression. His forces consisted of eight South African, New Zealand and Indian brigades, with fresh and rested men equipped with large quantities of US supplies, including armour and mechanized artillery. The retreating 1st British Armoured and 50th British Mechanized Divisions were now safely ensconced behind this fortified line.[20]

At the same time, the changed balance of air strength feared by Kesselring had also come about, and the situation was beginning to look threatening. Whereas during the course of Rommel's offensive the number of sorties flown by the Luftwaffe continued to decline, and additional difficulties were encountered because of the greater distance between the airfields and the front, the British succeeded in increasing the number of sorties flown by the Desert Air Force from 354 on May 27th to 780 on July 3rd.[21]

However, Rommel still felt confident that after a short pause for rest and regrouping, and with the reinforcements that had hurriedly been flown out to him, and the arrival of new supplies by sea, he would be able to enforce a decision. But two weeks later, in the middle of July, after supply-line losses had risen again, and indecisive fighting had produced very little result, he had to submit to bitter necessity and go over to the defensive.

On July 20th, Mussolini left Derna, where he had been waiting impatiently for the entry into Cairo, and returned to Rome. Simultaneously Churchill was able to announce that Egypt was out of danger. In fact, the position was so changed that Rommel himself was now urging that he should be allowed to break off contact with the enemy and retreat to his frontier positions; and he was as insistent as he had been just a short month previously, when he had urged the continuation of the pursuit. He was so keenly aware of the change that had come about in the situation that when his request was turned down, and no further worth-while reinforcements were forthcoming, he even began to consider the abandonment of the whole of Italian North Africa. However, these ideas were unanimously rejected in Germany, and even more vigorously by the Italians. Both Axis Powers were still confident that they could retain the initiative and reach their objectives in a new offensive as soon as the necessary reinforcements had been brought up.[22]

As there was no other source from which reinforcements could be obtained, the Italian Comando Supremo and OKW reached a joint agreement in the middle of July to draw on the forces being concentrated for use against Malta and send them to Egypt as quickly as possible.[23] As early as July 7th, Cavallero instructed the Operations Staff at work on the Malta project to postpone the plans for an attack on the island and to prepare instead for a transfer of the forces concerned to Tunisia. Now that the pursuit in Egypt had come to a halt, the Chief of Comando Supremo feared more than ever that the British would carry out landing operations in French North Africa and organize a drive into Tripolitania from there.[24] The last chance of capturing Malta was now abandoned, and there was no further question of turning the island into an Axis stepping-stone to North Africa.

Rommel approved of the orders issued in the meantime by the Comando Supremo, and when the author of this chapter visited him at the end of July in his battle headquarters about eight to twelve miles to the west of El Alamein, he found Rommel convinced of the necessity of resuming very soon the offensive against Egypt. There was no further talk of retreat.[25] During his visit, the author received a lasting impression of the intensity of the fighting on land and in the air, fighting which in the exposed desert now showed all signs of developing into a battle of material.

In the following weeks a complete volte-face occurred, in that the Italian High Command as well as the German C.-in-C. South, Field-Marshal Kesselring, correctly appreciating the ever-growing strength of the enemy, pressed for an offensive as soon as possible, whereas Hitler and OKW were in favour of leaving it to Rommel to decide whether he would after all be able to keep to the date which he had provisionally fixed as the end of August for launching his new offensive. The operational aims laid down in the Italian directive of August 17th were that Rommel should first defeat the enemy to the west of the delta, then capture Alexandria, and, with the harbour as a base, press on towards Cairo and the Suez Canal.[26]

A race by sea and air now started between the two camps, to bring in as much material and as many reinforcements and supplies as possible for the renewed clash which was coming. In this respect, the Western Allies had a clear advantage, because although their supply line around Africa was a very extended one it was, at least, practically free from enemy interference. How different Allied Middle East Command would have found things, if the Axis Powers had managed to persuade the Japanese to follow up their successful carrier-based raid on Ceylon by permanently committing strong naval forces to the Indian Ocean, instead of completely neglecting all the strategic possibilities implicit in the Three-Power Pact![27] The supply lines of the Axis Powers from southern Italy across the Mediterranean to Libya and through Greece to Cyrenaica, were certainly very much shorter, but they were subject to constant attack from Alexandria, and in particular from Malta. As soon as the Italo-German air and sea attacks, which included minelaying, subsided, the British, who had withdrawn the 10th Submarine Flotilla from Malta at the beginning of May, now (mid-July) transferred it back to the island; and by the middle of August they had managed to increase the number of aircraft stationed on the island, including heavy bombers, to 250. At the same time, they succeeded in taking a convoy carrying supplies and equipment of all sorts into Malta, escorted by no less than 2 battleships, 3 aircraft carriers, 7 cruisers and 24 destroyers, though they certainly had to pay heavily for this success.[28] For months the Axis forces had managed to keep the ring around Malta tightly closed, but now it had been broken, and the Western Allies found themselves once more in a position to attack the Mediterranean transports of the Axis right into the smallest ports and harbours, inflicting very serious damage and heavy losses; while at the same time they could transport men and supplies into the numerous and efficient ports and harbours of the nearby Nile and Suez Canal without Axis interference. According to Italian calculations, in the last few weeks of August alone, the British succeeded in unloading no less than 500,000 GRT in northeast Africa, whilst all the Axis Powers could set against this enormous total was 13,000 tons.[29]

Field-Marshal Rommel had often been accused of paying too little attention to the question of supplies, but this time at least he was determined not to move until the minimum volume of supplies he had laid down as necessary for the attack were guaranteed, and in particular his requirements in fuel. But under strong pressure, and – as he said himself afterwards – against his own better judgement, he agreed to launch his offensive on August 30th in return for a firm promise that the still lacking quantities of fuel would be made available by the time he needed them.[30] But after a few preliminary successes the new offensive was halted, and by September 1st Rommel was compelled to call off his attack. Two days later he ordered his men to withdraw to their original positions. The requisite supplies of fuel had not reached the front line as promised. At the same time, the surprise factor was lost through the long delay caused by unexpectedly extensive British minefields; meanwhile the attacks of the superior Desert Air Force were now so intensive that they threatened to undermine the morale of even a veteran force like the Afrika Korps.[31]

In this situation, Rommel and the German leaders now gave up the idea of any further offensive plans, but the Italian Comando Supremo, supported by Field-Marshal Kesselring, continued to insist that after repulsing the British counter-offensive, which was expected at any moment, the Axis forces in North Africa should go over to the offensive once more in order to seek a decision. But the preliminary condition for this – and here the Italian and German views agreed completely – was that these forces should at least succeed in maintaining their positions before El Alamein.[32]

November 1942
The Western Allies force the Decision.
The Allied Plans for North Africa

At the insistence of Churchill, far-reaching plans had been in preparation in Britain since the summer of 1941 to clear up the situation in the Mediterranean once and for all. According to these plans,[33] the November 1941 offensive of the 8th Army against Cyrenaica (Operation 'Crusader') was originally to have been extended towards Tripoli (Operation 'Acrobat'). It was hoped that the success of this offensive would persuade the French C.-in-C. North Africa, General Weygand, to turn his back on Vichy. If they were successful in this, the British proposed to reinforce Weygand's troops with an armoured division and three infantry divisions from Britain (Operation 'Gymnast').

When the recall of General Weygand made any hope of assistance on his part illusory, Churchill proposed at the 'Arcadia' conference, held in Washington (December 23rd, 1941, to January 14th, 1942) after the entry of the US into the war, that Operation 'Gymnast' should if necessary be carried out against French opposition. President Roosevelt approved of the idea, because it seemed to offer the possibility of obtaining a military success against Germany even in 1942. This operation was now given the new code-name of 'Super-gymnast', and fixed for May 1942.

However, during the course of the second half of February, it became clear that owing to the urgent requirements of the Pacific theatre it would not at that time be possible to provide the shipping space needed for Operation 'Super-gymnast', while the set-back suffered by the 8th Army in Cyrenaica diminished the prospect of co-operation from east and west. On March 3rd, the Combined Chiefs of Staff therefore decided that the potentialities of Operation 'Super-gymnast' should, for the time being, be investigated as a study only.

In the middle of April 1942, General Marshall, US Army Chief of Staff, flew to London with Roosevelt's personal representative, Harry Hopkins, to discuss long-term strategy in Europe with the British Chiefs of Staff, and to come to some agreement. Marshall proposed that sufficient forces be gathered in Britain as soon as possible in order to launch a large-scale invasion of northwest France, since in his view this was the only way in which a decisive offensive could be launched against the vital centres of German power. However, an examination of the situation revealed that no such operation could possibly be carried out before 1943. But as the Western Allies were unwilling to remain inactive for that length of time – particularly because the Russians were pressing for the opening of a Second Front as quickly as possible – the discussion reverted to the operational possibilities for 1942, though no definite decision was reached. Marshall favoured a landing near Brest or Cherbourg in the autumn of 1942, with the limited objective of depriving the Germans of one or other of the French northwest peninsulas (Operation 'Sledgehammer'), at the same time compelling them to withdraw forces from the Eastern Front. This operation would also have the advantage of giving the Allied forces battle experience. However, Churchill, supported by the Chiefs of Staff, put forward certain ideas of his own. For a long time he had favoured landings either in North Africa or Norway (Operation 'Jupiter'). He and his advisers felt that it would be too risky to attempt a landing on the continent, the 'heart of Fortress Europe', with inadequate forces. Their national instinct for 'the indirect approach' made them favour an attack against the softer enemy flank as the more likely to promise success.[34]

For the time being, the question remained undecided, and even Churchill's visit to Washington in June 1942 did not clarify the situation – no doubt partly because of the catastrophe which had come upon the 8th Army in North Africa, including the fall of Tobruk.[35]

In the middle of July, General Marshall, Harry Hopkins and Admiral King, the US Chief of Naval Operations, flew to London for further discussion; the situation on the Russian front called for a quick decision on the operations for 1942. The Americans were anxious to persuade the British to give up the idea of the operations they were proposing under the code-name 'Super-gymnast', and to accept the US proposal for Operation 'Sledgehammer' instead. General Marshall objected that the proposed landing near Casablanca would bring the Russians no relief, and he also feared that Operation 'Super-gymnast' would use up forces he would prefer to see kept for his proposed invasion of northwestern France in 1943 (Operation 'Round-up'). Admiral King also opposed Churchill's North African proposal, because in his view the establishment of a new convoy route to Morocco would mean an unnecessary exacerbation of the already critical shipping situation. He also felt it would be dangerous to withdraw aircraft carriers from the Pacific in support of such an operation.

The first meeting took place on July 20th, and the Americans found themselves faced with spirited resistance to their proposals from Churchill, who argued very cogently that Operation 'Sledgehammer' would quite certainly render Operation 'Round-up' impossible, whereas there was every likelihood that Operation 'Super-gymnast' would bring about the decisive turning point in the Mediterranean, and thus in the Middle East, and at the same time relieve pressure on the Russian southern front. In the subsequent discussions of the Chiefs of Staff, the opposing views clashed again. While the British were unwilling to accept Operation 'Sledgehammer', there was an increasing tendency amongst the Americans to say 'well, if nothing can be done this year in Europe we'd better concentrate all our forces in the Pacific'. In this apparently hopeless situation the American representatives now turned to Roosevelt for further instructions, and on July 22nd he ordered them to abandon the proposal for Operation 'Sledgehammer' and to come to some agreement with the British which would allow US troops to go into action in 1942. In the end Churchill was given a free hand for Operation 'Super-gymnast', and, with a new code name – Operation 'Torch'[36] – it was agreed to on July 24th–25th.

Everything was to be ready by the end of October, and Operation 'Torch' was to be co-ordinated with an offensive by the 8th Army at El Alamein, for which reinforcements, large quantities of equipment and material, and further RAF squadrons were sent out. During a visit he paid to the Near East at the beginning of August 1942, Churchill also cleared up the command situation by removing the hesitant Auchinleck and replacing him by General Alexander, who became C.-in-C. Near East. General Gott was to have taken command of the 8th Army, but after his death General Montgomery was sent out instead.[37]

The Situation of the Axis Powers

The abandonment of the offensive in North Africa, followed shortly afterwards by the breakdown of the German offensive on the Eastern Front, brought about a disagreeable change in the general picture for the Axis Powers: after what had looked like promising superiority everywhere there was now a situation of dangerous strain, objectives seemed far distant and the means of attaining them inadequate. The Axis lines were more attenuated than ever before. The offensive spearheads in Egypt and north of the Caucasus stretched out like two great arms, but the power was no longer behind them and there was no longer any hope that they could operate in strategic concert. Elsewhere, too, there were unmistakable signs of a threatening change in the situation to the disadvantage of the Axis Powers. The strength of the Allied forces, increasingly reinforced by the US, compelled the Axis strategists to reconsider and limit their aims for the further prosecution of the war. Merely going over to the defensive under enemy pressure could obviously be no more than the first step. In itself it was not enough, and further measures were necessary, including a systematic withdrawal from fronts which were too far forward, to nearer, shorter and more favourable lines; reserves had to be collected, and the whole supply system put on a more efficient basis. But these obviously necessary measures were not in fact taken, and any attempt to think soberly and take the objective facts of the military situation into account was frowned on, and even condemned as weakness and defeatism. Instead, Hitler put forward his own personal recipe: 'hold on at all costs!', 'defend every inch of ground!'. Without any new strategic aims, and without an intelligence service adapted to the new situation, this was equivalent to dependence on what the enemy did; it left the initiative in his hands and ensured that he had valuable advantages for the coming decision.

By September, all signs in the Mediterranean indicated that before very long the British 8th Army would once more be strong enough to launch a powerful counter-offensive against the Axis forces at El Alamein. At the other Mediterranean focal point, the island of Malta, the strength of the enemy both at sea and in the air was increasing so rapidly that Marshal Cavallero now declared that the 'neutralization' of this British Mediterranean strongpoint was 'a matter of life and death' for the Axis Powers.[38] The Italians also believed that an Anglo-American attack on Tunis was now more likely than ever, though the Germans – despite their own earlier suggestions – did not attach a great deal of importance to the danger except to warn Rome in July 1942, against any premature steps which might drive French North Africa into the arms of de Gaulle and thus of the Allies.[39] Hitler was more interested in Crete, an island to which, despite all experience since its capture in May 1941, he continued to ascribe 'a dominating influence' in the eastern Mediterranean, with particular reference to the battle for Egypt. At his instance, quite large forces of all kinds were now sent to the island, together with large quantities of equipment and material, in order to fortify its coasts after the example of the 'Atlantic Wall'.[40]

In the meantime, however, the Axis forces in North Africa were closely concentrated opposite El Alamein, in a narrow strip of desert less than forty miles across, and there was hardly any connection between them and Crete at all. Behind the Axis lines the Libyan countryside had been swept almost bare in order to send as many men as possible up into the front line. Losses along the Mediterranean supply line began to rise menacingly again, and, as a result of the generally tense situation, reinforcements for Rommel's Panzer Army were limited to reinforcements of men and a minimum of heavy weapons, though enormous numbers of landmines were brought in. In March, the Italians strengthened their forces by the despatch of two further infantry divisions from Italy.

Although his army had not been strongly reinforced, Field-Marshal Rommel, when towards the end of September he was ordered by Hitler, for reasons of health, to take leave, seemed first in Rome and then in Berlin very confident in the defensive strength of his forces; certainly, he was not considering any voluntary withdrawal of the Axis forces. On the contrary, both he and his second-in-command, General Stumme, declared confidently that the defence against the expected British attack would be conducted in a definitely offensive spirit, and that should a favourable opportunity arise, the German forces would not hesitate to go over to the offensive themselves. In fact General Stumme still thought it a practical possibility to talk of 'the destruction of the 8th Army and a drive towards Alexandria'.[41] Hitler himself was more cautious in his judgement, but he too stressed the advantages of the German position at El Alamein, which was unique in the North-African desert because of its shortness and because its southern flank was safe from envelopment.

By comparison with such optimism, the misgivings expressed by both commanders because of the growing superiority of the enemy in the air – misgivings underlined by those who had visited the front line – did not bulk large; particularly as Göring was inclined to take the slightest expression of doubt about Luftwaffe superiority as a personal insult. But at this juncture Field-Marshal Kesselring was compelled to admit in Rome that, because of his obligation to provide air support for the North African front, he had not enough forces to keep Malta under the constant pressure which the Italians demanded. According to an entry in Cavallero's diary for September, Kesselring told him that the Luftwaffe crews were on edge, over-strained and suffering from 'Malta sickness'.[42] However, on October 10th, after supplementing if not greatly reinforcing his strength, Kesselring and the Italians jointly began a new series of systematic air attacks on Malta. But after a few days it was seen that the results obtained did not outweigh the losses suffered; and so, on Göring's intervention, followed by that of Hitler himself, the new attempt to 'neutralize' Malta was abandoned. The only alternative now was to strengthen the air escort provided for his Axis convoys in the Mediterranean.[43]

No doubt it was because of this new failure to tame Malta that, on October 20th, both dictators independently expressed their views on the subject. Mussolini declared himself in agreement with Cavallero that it would have been better to launch landing operations in June to capture the island, *provided that the preparations had been concluded.*[44] Hitler's view was quite uncompromising: he declared to his entourage that it was quite impossible to capture such fortified islands.[45]

El Alamein

By the middle of October, Montgomery had assembled his forces for the great offensive, including XXX Corps, consisting of a British, an Australian, a New Zealand, a South African and an Indian division, XIII Corps with one armoured and two infantry divisions, and X Corps with three armoured divisions. In addition, there were two armoured brigades, and two Free French and one Greek Brigade. In all, there were 150,000 men and 1,114 tanks; against this, Rommel had two German and two Italian armoured divisions with three German and five Italian infantry divisions, making a total of 96,000 men and between 500 and 600 tanks.[46] On October 9th, the Allied air force began the systematic bombing of supply bases, harbours and airfields in southern Italy and behind the Axis lines in Cyrenaica, using 500 bombers from Egypt and Malta.

On October 23rd, the 8th Army launched the long expected attack against the Axis positions at El Alamein, while at the same time destructive blows were delivered against Axis shipping to North Africa. Despite the great superiority of the enemy, particularly in ammunition, which soon determined the picture of the battle in the desert, it was some days before the leaders of the Axis Powers allowed their deceptive confidence in the strength of the defensive position at El Alamein to be shaken. Even Kesselring had gone on record a little earlier as saying that the British offensive in North Africa was being undertaken more for political than military reasons, and that it could hardly hope to bring about any fundamental change in the situation in Egypt.[47] Rommel, who took over command on the spot when his second-in-command, General Stumme, was killed on the first day of battle, reported on October 26th that an increasing shortage of fuel was hampering the movements of his armour, still his strongest weapon even in defence, and followed this the next day by reporting that after uninterrupted fighting and heavy losses the situation was becoming critical; but even then the higher-ups were still quite confident that in the end a defensive success was certain.

It was only on October 30th that misgivings arose, when Rommel reported that if the British kept up their enormous pressure much longer, then the resistance of his own forces must crack, after which – when his reserves had been exhausted – there would be nothing to stop the enemy driving westward as far as he liked. Suddenly, all the disadvantages of taking up a position too far forward became alarmingly clear. First of all, it was impossible to bring up enough munitions to have any hope of holding it, and secondly, it was impossible to bring up enough fuel to permit a swift and adroit withdrawal. In view of these disagreeable revelations, and with the knowledge, shared with Rommel, that there was nothing to speak of behind the Axis lines on which a retreating army could fall back, the Chief of the Italian Comando Supremo concluded that the only possible thing to do was to hang on despite all the dangers involved. But how little confidence he had in a satisfactory outcome can be seen from an entry in his diary: 'Have the impression that this is the end of the army. . . . What is to happen when the front breaks – when the army which the Duce himself commands is defeated and destroyed?'[48]

But then, while the fierce fighting went on unabated, there seemed suddenly to be a change for the better, and on November 1st, after having inspected the situation on the spot, Kesselring felt that the worst of the crisis had already been overcome. At the same time, Count Ciano noted in his diary that Mussolini was in good spirits, a circumstance he put down to 'the favourable development of operations' in North Africa. But these happy impressions were soon effaced by further and less favourable reports that persuaded the Comando Supremo in Rome to issue an order, on November 2nd, that the position at El Alamein was to be held 'at all costs'.[49] Late in the afternoon of the same day, Hitler also felt it desirable to send a wireless message of vehement encouragement to Rommel, urging him to stand firm. Prefacing his remarks by an expression of complete confidence both in the army in North Africa and its great leader, Hitler declared once again that in such a situation there could be 'no other thought but that of holding out and refusing to yield one inch of ground'. Then, after solemnly promising to exert every possible effort to provide the necessary supplies and equipment, he concluded by addressing the Field-Marshal in person: 'It would not be the first time in history that the stronger will has prevailed over the bigger battalions. You can show your troops only the way to victory or death.'[50]

However, before this long coded wireless message could be taken down, decoded and passed on to Rommel, the latter had already decided – at 22.00 hours on November 2nd – to carry out an orderly withdrawal. After a battle lasting eleven days, during which the British had kept up a massive bombardment of the Axis position with inexhaustible supplies of munitions, Rommel decided, in defiance of the orders repeatedly given to him, that it was his duty to withdraw his forces intact from El Alamein rather than hang on and condemn them to destruction.[51]

He has himself described the situation on the morning of November 3rd for us: 'Our vehicles moved westward in close order. Italian infantry marched off.' Then at 13.30 Hitler's wireless message arrived from Supreme HQ.[52] Probably in the belief that this message had been sent in reply to his despatch of the previous evening informing Hitler of his decision to withdraw, a despatch which was not sent off until the withdrawal had begun, Rommel allowed himself to be persuaded – once again against his better judgement – to halt the withdrawal and to take up the fight again. But hardly twenty-four hours had passed before he was compelled to break contact with the enemy once more, and withdraw westward without waiting for further orders – this time for good. 'Those two days,' he wrote later, probably referring to the period from early afternoon on November 3rd to November 4th, 'decided our fate, because in a very short time we lost nearly 200 tanks – the remains of our armour arm – and the greater part of our Italian units. With this, we were deprived of the possibility of conducting a mobile fighting retreat. By this time the army was so badly mauled that the only thing to do was to continue evasive action.'

The report in which Rommel acknowledged Hitler's wireless message presented the state of the army in a rather more favourable light. At this time, he still hoped that a more mobile conduct of the war, coupled, as he added, with a struggle for every inch of ground, would continue to inflict heavy losses on the enemy, and at the same time make it unnecessary to abandon the whole of North Africa. Despite this clear hint of what would happen if the worst came to the worst, Rommel's despatch, supplemented by the verbal report of a staff officer hurriedly despatched to HQ, gave the German Supreme Command the impression that at the very worst the retreat would stop at the Libyan-Egyptian frontier. In this belief, which seemed to find confirmation in the corresponding orders issued by the Italian Comando Supremo, Hitler was prepared to approve of Rommel's decision to retreat.[53] However, his resentment needed some outlet, so it descended in full force on two officers of the Wehrmacht Operations Staff who were – quite unjustly – blamed because he had not been informed of Rommel's intention to withdraw early enough to intervene and prevent it.

The sustained indignation about this supposed omission to inform Hitler in time, and the general obscurity which continued, not only about the condition of Rommel's army but also about his immediate intentions, prevented OKW from realizing that with Rommel's retreat from El Alamein a far-reaching decision affecting the whole North African theatre had been taken. The important thing was not that the Italo-German army was once again in retreat, but that this time there would be no about-turn. Although it had been fought with all available resources, the North African campaign had to some extent been colonial in character; but El Alamein had developed into a typical battle of material in which no military genius on the part of the commander, and no amount of courage on the part of the men, could make up for the catastrophic situation brought about by the failure of the overseas supply lines. Further unfavourable factors were the irremediable weakness of Italian armaments, and the increasing rate at which the Eastern Front was sucking up Germany's few remaining reserves and leaving very little over with which to reinforce the Mediterranean Axis front: a few tanks, a few batteries, one or two battalions and a few planes were all that could be spared. The failure of the Italian fleet was another factor which allowed the situation to change so definitely in favour of the Western Allies – the heavy ships of the Italian Navy had taken refuge from constant air raids in the northern harbours of the Tyrrhenian Sea. Montgomery was not far out when he declared in his Order of the Day issued on October 23rd before El Alamein: 'The battle which is about to begin will be one of the decisive battles of history. It will be the turning point of the war.'[54]

The Allied Landings in North Africa

But still greater and even more irrevocable decisions were also being prepared in the western Mediterranean. During the preparations for Operation 'Torch' it had been decided – after certain misgivings had been suppressed – to extend the landings beyond French Morocco far into the Mediterranean area, taking in the harbours of eastern Algeria. The immediate objectives, after overcoming French resistance, which was regarded as likely to be of little account, were to occupy Tunisia, if possible by the end of the year, and then – in co-operation with Montgomery's 8th Army – to destroy the Italo-German forces in North Africa. In this way, a springboard would be created for operations against the southern flank, or what Churchill called the 'soft underbelly', of 'Fortress Europe'. For the British, in particular, the success of these plans would relieve them of all further anxieties in the Mediterranean. Their hegemony in the Near and Middle East would once more be restored, and their hold on valuable oil deposits re-established; at the same time, the shortening of Britain's overseas supply lines would mean a very important strategic gain in tonnage and shipping space.

Side by side with very thorough military preparations for the first great landing, there were systematic efforts to create a 'fifth column', and for this purpose there was a great increase in US consular personnel throughout French North Africa. The result was a growing movement amongst the French to open the doors voluntarily to the Western Allies. By the end of October, contacts with numerous highly-placed officers and officials in the French Army and administration were so close that General Clark of the US Army, who was later to have a high command in the actual landing operations, was able to go to North Africa to discuss plans with officers in key positions in the French colonial forces. They were prepared to hamstring the coastal defences at the critical moment, and thus allow the forces of the Western Allies to land without resistance. By this time (from October 20th), the convoys were already at sea on their way to North Africa from both Great Britain and the United States. The Commander-in-Chief of the whole undertaking was General Eisenhower.[55]

The possibility that North Africa might one day offer the Western Allies a useful springboard for a leap across the Mediterranean and an attack on the European mainland had already been repeatedly discussed in Germany, but attempts during the armistice negotiations with France towards the end of June 1940 to secure a firm grip on the French possessions in North Africa were unsuccessful, as in the following December were negotiations with Franco to secure Spanish agreement for an attack on Gibraltar. Negotiations opened at about the same time in the hope of establishing close military collaboration between the Wehrmacht and the remaining forces under French command did not advance beyond what looked like promising beginnings, and they were now quite dead, partly because the suspicious obstinacy of Hitler and the jealous watchfulness of Mussolini made it impossible to offer sufficiently generous military concessions; and partly also because all political accommodation was refused. Ever since December 1941, the Germans were forced to accept the situation that, whether they liked it or not, the defence of French North Africa was solely in the hands of the French. At the same time, there was clearly no serious guarantee that France's colonial forces would be able to withstand the superior forces of their former allies – or would be willing to do so even if they could. All that existed was a few control commissions, chiefly Italian, whose activities were limited to matters arising out of the armistice agreements; thanks to these commissions, though the French took little notice of them, there was a certain loose contact.

In this situation it was remarkable that in June, and again in September, 1942, Marshal Pétain, his Premier Laval, and other members of the Vichy Government, approached the German authorities with the suggestion that there should be further discussions aimed at stronger defensive measures in French North and West Africa.[56] It may be, of course, that in taking this step the French Government was moved chiefly by a desire to keep the war as far away as possible from the territories under its control – and perhaps there was even privy knowledge of the intentions of the Western Allies. All the same, Germany's interest, stressed once again by Grand Admiral Raeder in particular, lay in the same general direction. However, as far as it is possible to discover now, the French were not even accorded the courtesy of an official reply to their suggestion. It even appears that Jodl, the Chief of the Wehrmacht Operations Staff, was not aware of the new French offer when he informed Hitler on October 15th of 'the increasing number of reports of imminent Anglo-Saxon landings in West Africa', and followed this up by urging that 'the French Government should be allowed to strengthen its defences in North Africa by sending further troops from the Motherland'. Once again Hitler refused to give the necessary permission. He probably felt that it was sufficient to justify his refusal, as he had probably justified his silence about the previous French diplomatic feelers, by pointing out that 'the Italians regarded every reinforcement of French troops in North Africa with the utmost distrust.'[57] The fact that by this time the Italians themselves were preparing to repulse Allied landings in Tunisia was ignored.

The information in the possession of OKW at this juncture was so vague that, for example, in his message to Mussolini a few days later (October 21st), Hitler did not even mention it. He was thinking exclusively of Belgium and France, and perhaps Norway, when he expressed the hope that 'they – the British – will land at some spot where we can prepare them a really annihilating reception'.[58] Still suffering from this delusion, he instructed General von Rintelen in Rome the very same day to remind the Italian Government of his warning uttered the previous July – with the same argument as three months earlier – against any action in Tunisia, which he still regarded as premature. This message went on to say that, while OKW certainly expected landing attempts, probably at Dakar, but perhaps also on the Atlantic coast of Morocco, it regarded 'the danger of similar operations on the Algerian–Tunisian coasts as less likely' – an opinion supported by quoting a general report on the situation issued the previous day by the German Naval Operations Staff, declaring roundly that 'the enemy will not attempt a landing on the Algerian–Tunisian coast because the danger from the air and from the French fleet is too great'.[59] Two days later, when the first reports of the start of the British attack at El Alamein began to come in, Hitler observed that in his opinion 'the greatest danger was in the western Mediterranean area', but in this connection he was not thinking of Northwest Africa at all, but – quite astonishingly and probably because of an air raid the previous night on Genoa – of Corsica![60]

But independently, and quite unmoved by the vacillation in high places, the Wehrmacht Operations Staff declared in one of its regular 'Reviews of the General Situation' that, from the standpoint of the enemy, French North Africa was the most favourable, and therefore the most likely, area for the attack the Western Allies were known to be preparing. Apart from the sparse reports, which had proved insufficiently impressive to arouse Hitler's otherwise only too willing attention, this judgement was based primarily on general political, military and strategic considerations. The shortage of all 'hard' news on the point can be seen from the fact that this 'Review' supposed that the Allied landing attempts could hardly take place before the spring of 1943.[61] Perhaps for this reason, and perhaps also because Hitler had already rejected such views, this appreciation by the Chief of the Wehrmacht Operations Staff was pigeonholed and ignored.

The Italians, on the other hand, who were quite naturally closer to events in the Mediterranean than the Germans, were finding their fears of an irruption of enemy forces into French North Africa increasingly confirmed by the reports of their own intelligence service. At the same time, they were well aware of the great threat this would represent, not only to the Axis forces in North Africa but to their own colonial empire. During his short stay in Rome at the end of September, Rommel had expressed similar anxieties. Impressed and disturbed by these reports, Mussolini exhorted his military chiefs at a meeting on October 4th to think of Tripolitania as well as El Alamein, suggesting that the Italian forces there should be reinforced in order to occupy Tunis before the Western Allies landed. A few days later, on October 9th, Count Ciano noted in his diary after a discussion with the chief of the Italian intelligence service: 'All reports and indications suggest that the Anglo-Saxons are preparing to land in North Africa.'[62]

Hitler seems to have received some inkling of these matters, for he now warned Rome once again against taking any premature measures against Tunisia. Once more his warning voice seems to have carried sufficient weight to intimidate the Italian Comando Supremo, which, like the Wehrmacht Operations Staff, probably expected the Allied landings to take place at a later date. In any case, it went against its own better judgement – and even Mussolini's exhortations – and bowed to that of Hitler. It is a fact, anyway, that in his discussion with General von Rintelen following the German warning of October 21st, Marshal Cavallero referred merely to the prospects of coming to an understanding with the French colonial army in Tunisia, though it is true that in conclusion he did say that in the event of failure the Axis Powers would have to act 'quickly and independently'. On October 23rd, when Montgomery was already in position at El Alamein, Cavallero noted in his diary that 'the enemy could attempt to launch a decisive blow in Africa', but he does not appear to have done anything further about the Axis plans for the defence of Tunisia. And on November 1st, in his answer to Hitler's message, Mussolini does not even mention Italian anxieties about French North Africa.[63]

Hitler's already firmly held opinions were to bedevil the situation still further, and make the misunderstanding even more complete, when news came in on October 31st that twenty-one merchant ships had arrived in Gibraltar. At first, both the Germans and the Italians assumed that there was to be another attempt to force a supply convoy through to Malta, and German Supreme Command saw no reason to change its views even when during the next few days, which were made very tense by the happenings at El Alamein, unquestionably reliable reports came through to the effect that strong naval forces also were assembling at Gibraltar; reports which were followed shortly afterwards by a message that a big convoy had left Gibraltar harbour and sailed out into the Mediterranean. But, probably on account of Hitler's intervention, it was not until November 4th that even in Rome the authorities began to suspect that this might be the beginning of landing operations in French North Africa.[64] After further close observation of the situation during the next couple of days, Mussolini himself came round to this view on November 6th – only to find that Hitler still refused to agree with him. In fact, on that date Hitler communicated his views to Kesselring through Göring: Corsica or Sardinia, perhaps even Derna and Tripoli, i.e. coastal points far beyond the Sicilian narrows, would be the objective – if, indeed, any landing operations were planned at all. In any case, French North Africa – which, in common with the Italians, Kesselring thought the most likely objective – did not come into question. Hitler's views, incidentally, had the support of the German Naval Operations Staff. Germany's admirals felt that the most likely objective for landing operations was Tripoli, and, to a lesser extent perhaps, Italy herself or the Italian islands, but certainly not French North Africa. Although, in the meantime, no less than 190 ships had been counted, it was still thought that the whole scare might be only another massive attempt to force a convoy through to Malta. By the afternoon of November 7th, Hitler had come to the conclusion, though for no ascertainable reason, that 'large-scale landing operations with perhaps four or five divisions' were intended for Tripoli or Benghazi. In consequence, General von Rintelen was instructed to approach the Italian Comando Supremo with the exhortation that it should 'do everything possible to defend these places, including the erection of barricades'.[65]

In the meantime, the first naval counter-measures were being prepared. The big convoys had remained unsighted in the Atlantic, partly through lack of adequate air reconnaissance and partly because what U-boats there were in the area were engaged in attacking a Sierra Leone convoy, but now the Axis submarines in the western Mediterranean, nine German U-boats and twenty Italian submarines, were hastily concentrated for an attack on the Allied armada. The Italian fleet was once again unable to put to sea and join in the action, partly because its light forces were still engaged in convoy work between Italy and North Africa, and partly because it lacked both oil fuel and air cover. Hitler's suggestion, made through Göring, that Mussolini should issue an Order of the Day calling on the Italian Navy to prove worthy of 'this historic hour', revealed complete ignorance of the situation of his Italian ally, and his appeal naturally fell on stony ground. German Air Fleet 2 was still largely in the eastern desert, where strong forces were in action in support of Rommel. Replying to an almost desperate appeal from Göring that he should call on his airmen to strain every nerve to attack the Allied convoys uninterruptedly, by day and by night, and destroy them and their escorts, particularly the aircraft carriers, Kesselring made it quite clear that his pilots would be able to intervene effectively only within range of the Sicilian narrows. Even in this situation, he was given no reinforcements.

Finally OKW ordered a higher state of preparedness with a view to occupying the still unoccupied area of France as a further counter-measure. This was done not – as was frequently supposed – because an Allied landing on the French Mediterranean coast was feared, but in order to prevent French forces from joining the enemy.

The Germans took no further counter-measures against an invasion of French North Africa. And, as far as can be discovered, the Italians did nothing either, despite their correct estimate of the situation and of Allied intentions; and no attempt was made to seize the big Tunisian harbours at the last moment, admittedly a very difficult task. The order which transferred an infantry division to Sicily was intended merely to strengthen its defence. At the same time, it was Rome which still had the greatest doubts about the alleged readiness of the French to put up a serious defence against Allied landings. The Germans seemed prepared to rely on Vichy's word, given long before in very different circumstances, that France would defend her North African possessions against *any* attacker.

Dawning Realization and First Counter-measures

During the twelve hours which still remained between midday on November 7th and the Allied landings in the following night, Hitler, accompanied by Keitel, Head of OKW, and Jodl, Chief of the Wehrmacht Operations Staff, with their adjutants, was travelling by rail from East Prussia to Munich, to attend the customary annual celebrations with the 'veteran fighters' of the National Socialist Party. That evening at 19.00 hours, when the situation was discussed with Hitler at a conference on his special train, Jodl made one more attempt to interpret Allied intentions in the western Mediterranean. In all probability, only a few of the latest, more important reports were then available. In any case, he came to the conclusion that the Allies would attempt landings at the ports and harbours of Cyrenaica with the intention of destroying Rommel's army. At the same time, there might be an attempt to recapture Crete in order to seize another important strongpoint in the eastern Mediterranean, cut off Rommel's army from its sources of supply and thus indirectly encompass its destruction. Finally, probably in connection with one or other of these objectives, the Allied intention was to reinforce and supply the island of Malta.

Jodl's opinion was that a landing in Tripoli or Sicily was unlikely, and that an attack on French territory in North Africa was very improbable. In this latter particular, he was completely at odds with his own staff, but the reason he gave for his opinion – thus reversing Hitler's own fears with regard to the Italians – was that if the Allies did anything of the sort they would finally drive the French over to Germany's side. This was, it must be admitted, a quite extraordinary misreading of the situation. Hitler, as Supreme Commander of the Wehrmacht, expressed general agreement with these observations, though he felt that there was a higher degree of probability in favour of a landing in Sicily. He also considered it possible that the expected thrust might be delivered also against Corsica, as from there the enemy would be in a more favourable position to deliver a mortal blow against northern Italy.

The general atmosphere of smug satisfaction and misplaced confidence was a little shaken when someone – who it was is not recorded – informed the conference that a further study of Allied naval movements indicated that there was obviously no intention of setting a course through the Sicilian narrows during the night. By day – which was another thing the conference felt confident about – the Luftwaffe would be able to prevent the convoy from sailing through. For similar reasons, the possibility of an attack on the big Italian islands was also considered unlikely. After this, the only possibility that remained was the one they had all been busily rejecting for days, right up to the last moment: namely, a landing in French North Africa – the possibility, even probability, Mussolini had been stressing all the time in the face of repeated German discouragement.[66]

At about 02.00 hours the following morning, the first reports reached the special train on its journey to Munich: Anglo-American landings in the harbours of French North Africa had begun. Although the possibility had been a probability for some hours now, the news when it came made such a profound impression that Hitler recalled it eighteen months later during a discussion of an imminent invasion in the west; and Keitel, repeating his master's words as usual, or even taking them out of his mouth, declared, though not altogether accurately: 'We didn't even dream of it. Right up to the last day we were sure they were going through (the Sicilian narrows). . . . And then suddenly they turned about and made for the coast.'[67]

Those on board the special train now came together again in the early hours of the morning and discussed the painful surprise the night had brought. In the meantime, the train stood in a siding of a Thuringian railway station. They were awakened from their complacency now, and brought face to face with the harsh fact that the Western Allies had once again taken the strategic initiative – and in a very awkward place too. Obviously, far-reaching decisions were called for.

Shaken by this new blow, which followed so quickly on El Alamein, even this circle was unable to ignore the grim question whether in the circumstances it would be possible to retain a foothold in North Africa at all. Clearly, such a far-reaching decision could not be arrived at without the Italians, who were even more directly concerned, and so such a thought, entertained by a part of the Wehrmacht Operations Staff which had remained behind in East Prussia, and supported by the first reports, was immediately rejected. The main reason for this swift decision was probably a realization of the very serious political and strategic disadvantages the abandonment of North Africa would bring with it. However, the immediate and very real question as to how, if at all, this new Allied offensive could be dealt with, receded very much into the background. It looked as though the French were the only people who could do anything at all in this dangerous situation, and Hitler was now prepared to make generous offers, though none of them had any real content. At all events, they were immediately sent off to Vichy in the hope of encouraging French resistance. There was, of course, nothing more to be done beyond what had already been decided in the way of counter-measures at sea and in the air, because there were no other German forces available anywhere in the neighbourhood, and Hitler still felt that the Italians should be kept away from French colonial territory.[68]

The first thing that occurred to the Italians, also, in this situation was that only the French were in a position to do anything; so, embracing the German plan, Mussolini declared himself ready to conclude an alliance with Vichy. From what Cavallero confided to his diary on the point, it is clear that he attached grotesquely improbable hopes to this policy: 'The French fleet can put out from Toulon within the hour. I hardly dare hope for it, but if it does happen then the war is won'. The Chief of the Comando Supremo now turned his attention to a plan which had been worked out by his staff during the past four months to seize Tunisia, though now as a forestalling action. But, as in the case of Malta, it was quickly seen that it was not merely Hitler's repeated opposition which stood in the way. There was no need for Cavallero to go into the question in any great detail before turning the plan down. As he noted in his diary, there were neither sufficient ships nor sufficient vehicles, and the shortages made the project altogether impossible. But a little later, after a talk with Kesselring, who no doubt promised him assistance, we find him noting in his diary: 'Our intervention in Tunis is the only way to save Tripolitania.' There is no doubt that he was now thinking of crossing the Sicilian narrows to seize Tunis; the original idea of driving forward overland from western Libya had been abandoned – in all probability, because there was an acute shortage of both men and transport.[69]

Hitler called a conference for November 9th, in Munich, and the Italian and French Foreign Ministers were hurriedly requested to attend. By the time the conference met, the situation was already clear enough to make it obvious that there was no hope that the far inferior French forces would be able to put up any serious resistance. Those officers of the French colonial forces who were co-operating with the Western Allies had been able to cause confusion amongst the defenders; but no more than that, chiefly because the Western Allies, extremely anxious to keep the time and the place of the landings a secret as long as possible, had not kept them properly informed. These pro-Allied elements did not succeed in preventing resistance, and there was fighting at almost all the landing points. As the French naval commanders had not been taken into the confidence of the conspirators, it was on a considerable scale in some places. In the neighbourhood of Casablanca and Oran, French coastal batteries, naval units and parts of the army put up a fight against far superior Allied forces which went on for several days in some places. During the course of the fighting 1 cruiser, 6 destroyers and 7 submarines were sunk or disabled at Casablanca, and 4 destroyers and 2 submarines at Oran, all French. In all, 115 of the French defenders were killed. In Algiers, however, resistance ceased at the instructions of Admiral Darlan, C.-in-C. of the French Forces. He happened to be in the town in the afternoon of November 8th, for personal reasons, and when it became clear that the attack was on a large scale he ordered the French defenders to cease firing. But it was not until midday on November 10th that, after securing the approval of Marshal Pétain by means of a code unknown to the Germans, he succeeded in stopping all fighting.[70]

In the meantime, Hitler's confidence in his own ability to deal with the situation without French assistance had grown. The new basis for the strategy of the Axis Powers in the western Mediterranean was to be the immediate establishment of a bridgehead in Tunisia, the occupation of the whole of France, and a landing in Corsica. However, the only German forces available for the Tunisian bridgehead were three divisions, two of them scattered over occupied France, and not fully ready for action, and the third in process of formation in Germany. But meanwhile, in the weeks before their arrival, all the

Axis Powers could muster were very weak forces, primarily the staff troops of C.-in-C. South, supported by a few motor assault boats and a few planes. The Italians were to come in only after the French division in Tunis had been persuaded to co-operate in joint resistance. For once, there was no need for anxiety about transport, because the sea route to Bizerta and Tunis was, as Göring pointed out, 'a mere panther's leap', and the German Naval Operations Staff also thought it 'an easy task' to use this short sea route. It was taken for granted that there would be plenty of shipping space available in the ports and harbours of southern France. This was all more or less arranged before it was possible to ask Laval, who arrived late from Vichy, for his agreement.

Such was the background of the orders issued from Munich on November 10th. Field-Marshal Kesselring, who was formally seconded to Mussolini, took command over the new theatre in addition to Air Fleet 2. His instructions were 'to establish a bridgehead in Tunisia' before the enemy could get there. After that, having once concentrated the necessary forces, he was to drive westward, taking harbour after harbour on the way and chasing the enemy forces back to their ships. Rommel's army, still fighting for its life twelve hundred miles away, was informed that henceforth the supply line over the Mediterranean would be secure and Rommel was urged to bring the British advance to a halt as soon as possible and as far as possible to the east. At Hitler's express instructions – even in this situation – Crete was to be reinforced with the same urgency as North Africa.[71]

Despite all the troubles of the late autumn of 1942, these plans and orders were calculated to create the impression that the power of the Axis was still unbroken and that its leaders continued to be completely confident. Immediate developments even seemed to confirm this deceptive picture. Though they were very weak, the Italo-German forces in Tunisia did very quickly succeed in establishing some sort of loose front, and the hopes of a very greatly superior Allied force were frustrated then and there, and even for some months to come. Throughout November, at least, supplies were brought in along the new, greatly shortened line without loss, although the amount carried in one month was hardly as much as the Anglo-American forces in North Africa were receiving in a day.

The German High Command was once again – as so often in the past – inclined to overestimate these preliminary successes, and attach too much importance to its own determination to strain every nerve in the new situation, and too little to the quite clearly calculable and inevitable worsening of the situation in the future. The characteristic failure of all Hitler's leadership in this period became visible once again: the necessary minimum of supplies and equipment for carrying out his instructions, and attaining the objectives he set, was not made available. Before long, supply losses as a result of sinkings began to rise dangerously again, and the balance of forces changed more and more in favour of the enemy. Once again, the limits of Axis naval capacity were revealed, even on this relatively short seaway. Finally, there was an obstinate unwillingness to recognize that the successful Allied landing, even regarded purely as a strategic manœuvre, coupled with a steadily growing superiority in the air, must in the near future render the whole Axis position in North Africa untenable.

Certainly, the attempt to establish a bridgehead in Tunisia had to be made, since, as far as could be seen, this was the only hope of helping Rommel, who was still retreating, and of getting his forces back to the European mainland. The quicker his forces were withdrawn from the Egyptian frontier and brought back to Tunisia, the better the chances would be. But this, of course, was in direct contradiction to the orders they had received, though the only practical purpose the Tunisian bridgehead could still serve was to facilitate the evacuation of Rommel's forces.

In view of the decisive inferiority of the Axis Powers at sea and in the air, it would not have made much difference by this time if Hitler had followed the advice given to him by Mussolini at the beginning of December 1942, after Stalingrad, namely that 'the chapter of the war begun with the attack on Russia now has no further point' and should be closed in some way or other 'in order to release forces for the west and the Mediterranean'.[72] Quite apart from the fact that it was now very unlikely that the Russians would be willing to come to terms, it would have been impossible to send further forces across the Mediterranean to Tunisia – not to speak of carrying out Mussolini's other idea of 'taking the Allied advance in North Africa in the rear' by going through Spain.[73] The fact is that at the beginning of the fourth year of the war, the Axis lacked all the necessary means for carrying out operations of this kind; operations that had, incidentally, also been suggested by the German Admiralty.[74]

In the same way, it was all very well to decide to hold Tunisia 'at all costs' because of its unquestionably high strategic importance; the harsh fact was that to do so would have required larger forces than the Axis now had available. Strategically speaking, any attempt to carry out this decision meant fighting a battle that was already potentially lost when the Western Allies successfully landed in French North Africa. The destruction and capture of the North African Axis armies, including many divisions of the highest fighting quality, brought the war in North Africa to an end in the middle of May, 1943. At the same time, the Axis lost all hope of defeating the Allies in the coming struggle for the European coasts of the Mediterranean.

Chronicle VII

November 1942

to

February 1943

Politics		Conduct of the War
Neutrals	Axis Powers and Japan	Axis Powers and Japan
		November 3, 1942: Hitler orders Rommel to 'l on at all costs' in North Africa.
		November 5th: Retreat of Italo-German fo begins in North Africa.
		November 10th: First German airborne land in Tunisia.
November 12, 1942: Vichy French cease resistance in North Africa.		November 11th: German troops occupy the so of France (Operation 'Anton').
		November 24th: Hitler forbids German force Stalingrad to attempt to break out, promises supplies and relief.
November 27th: French fleet scuttles itself in Toulon. French Army in Metropolitan France disbanded.		November 27th: Field-Marshal von Mans takes over the command of Army Group L
		December 12th: German drive to relieve Stalin begins. This was to come to a halt t miles away.
December 24th: Assassination of Admiral Darlan, Head of Civil Affairs in French North Africa since December 1st.	December 27, 1942: Formation of the so-called 'Smolensk Committee' – later known as 'The Liberation Army' – under the leadership of the Russian General Vlassov.	December 31st: German task force fails in at on British Murmansk convoy.
	January 20, 1943: German-Japanese economic agreement.	
	January 27th: Labour mobilization order in Germany for waging of total war.	January 30, 1943: Following on Murm convoy failure, Admiral Raeder resign Supreme Commander of the German N
	January 31st: Grand Admiral Dönitz appointed Supreme Commander of the German Navy.	February 1st to 8th: Japanese evacuate Gu canal.
		February 2nd: Remnants of the German 6th encircled in Stalingrad surrender.
	February 5th: Italian Foreign Minister, Count Ciano, resigns.	
	February 18th: In a speech in the Berlin Sports Palace, Goebbels calls for 'total war'. The Scholls (brother and sister) distribute a leaflet calling for the re-establishment of Germany's honour and a struggle against the National Socialist Party.	February 21st: German counter-offensive beg Kharkov.

Conduct of the War	Politics	
estern Allies and the Soviet Union	Western Allies and the Soviet Union	Neutrals
mber 7 to 8, 1942: Anglo-American forces and in Algiers, Oran and Morocco.	November 5, 1942: Armistice in Madagascar.	
mber 12th to 13th: British forces capture Tobruk. mber 12th to 15th: Naval battle off Guadal-anal. mber 19th: Soviet counter-offensive at Stalin-grad begins. mber 20th: British 8th Army captures Ben-ghazi. mber 23rd: German forces encircled in Stalingrad.	November 15th: General Giraud appointed French Commander-in-Chief in North Africa.	
mber 30th: Soviet offensive opens up in the Caucasus. mber 4th: First attack of 9th USAAF on Naples. mber 16th: Soviet offensive across the Don n the direction of Chir–Rostov, against the th Italian Army. mber 20th to 21st: Mosquito aircraft attack argets in Germany, using 'Oboe' long-range adar,	December 2nd: Fermi starts up the first atomic reactor in Chicago.	
	December 29th: General Juin suc-ceeds General Giraud as French Commander-in-Chief in North Africa.	
ry 8, 1943: Russians call on 6th Army to urrender. ry 10th: Russians begin liquidation of 6th rmy in Stalingrad. ry 13th to 18th: Russians establish land ontact with Leningrad. ry 14th: First area-bombing attack on German submarine base at Lorient.	January 14 to 21, 1943: Casablanca Conference. Roosevelt and Churchill call for 'uncondi-tional surrender'. Landing in Sicily decided. January 21st: Defeat of Germany's U-boats given priority on list of Allied war aims.	
ry 27th: First daylight attack by 8th USAAF n Germany (Wilhelmshaven). ry 30th to 31st: First use of British radar pparatus H.2.S in raid on Hamburg.		January 29, 1943: Turkish President meets Churchill in Adana.
ary 5th to 9th: Russians take Kursk and yelgorod. ary 14th: Russians take Rostov.	February 5th: Conference between Churchill, Eisenhower, de Gaulle and Giraud in Algiers.	

The Battle for Stalingrad 1942–3

BY WALTER GÖRLITZ

November 19th, 1942, the day on which Soviet armour, followed by masses of infantry, overran the 3rd Rumanian Army in the frozen snow-covered steppes of the Don is generally regarded as the beginning of the Battle for Stalingrad proper. Rightly or wrongly, this battle has long since taken on a legendary character in both German and Russian war literature. It is regarded as the turning point of the Second World War, and because of this, questions of importance to the war as a whole are involved.

The question which first arises is whether one can examine the battle of the encirclement of the German 6th Army, which opened on November 19th, 1942, and culminated in the surrender of the remnants of that army on February 2nd, 1943, without dealing with the preliminary situation. Actually what happened occurred in two stages: the march on Stalingrad in the first place, and then the battle for control of the town.

It was in November 1941, that Hitler first considered the idea of capturing the industrial and inland waterways centres on the Volga.[1] The project was linked up with a plan to drive forward in the south to the Caucasus, weather permitting, and capture the Maykop–Groznyy oilfields. On November 13th 1941, at a conference in Orsha, General Halder, Chief of the Army General Staff, communicated these proposals to the commanders of the armies attached to Army Group South.[2] General Paulus was then deputy Chief of General Staff, and was thus well acquainted with these ideas of Hitler. The generals now gave way to Hitler, who insisted that the war against the Soviet Union should be waged not purely strategically, but on the basis of political, ideological and economic calculations. Hitler was anxious to hit the ideological and military-economic centres of his 'political enemy', and for him these were first of all Leningrad, as the 'breeding-ground' of Bolshevism, and secondly the areas of south Russia and the Caucasus with their rich agricultural, coal, ore and oil resources. Hitler's calculations, based on ideological considerations, clashed with the ideas of the General Staff, since the latter thought along traditional political-strategic lines and regarded the capture of Moscow, the enemy capital, as the main objective.[3] There was also a conflict between Hitler, as the Supreme Commander of the Wehrmacht, and OKH; this was resolved only after a serious internal crisis while the campaign was in full swing. In fact, the whole 1941 operation against Russia was influenced by such discord.

219

During the winter battle for Moscow in December 1941 it had become quite clear that the enemy's resistance and his determination to fight on had by no means been broken. For the first time since the outbreak of war, the victorious advance of the German armies had been brought to a halt. Up to December 1941 the German losses in killed, wounded and missing totalled 765,415 men, or approximately 24 per cent of the original strength of 3·2 million men.[4]

It was out of the question to resume the attack along the whole front again. In fact, it was even doubtful whether an offensive of any sort was possible, or, indeed, desirable, and it was suggested that perhaps it might be better to wear down the enemy (whose reserves of manpower and material were unknown) in a series of holding operations. In view of Hitler's temperament, and the fact that he felt very strongly that Russia must first be 'knocked out' before he could force Britain to her knees, it is not surprising that as Supreme Commander of the Wehrmacht he should decide that the offensive must be resumed; and that it must be resumed on that part of the front on which it was thought that Russia's war economy could be most seriously damaged, while at the same time opening up new sources of materials for Germany's own war economy.

Leaving aside calculations as to the importance of the Trans-Ural Siberian area in the transformation and reorganization of Russia's arms industry, this undoubtedly meant the Donets and Don Basins, the great railway centre of Stalingrad on the Volga, with its big tank- and gun-producing factories, and the Caucasian oilfields. General Halder recommended that if there were to be any further offensive it should be against Moscow,[5] but his recommendations no longer bore much weight with Hitler. In considering a general drive towards the Volga there was also the prospect of capturing Saratov, an important railway junction which, like Moscow, allowed the Russians to switch troops to and fro readily. From Saratov there were railway communications to the Trans-Ural industrial area, and Allied supplies were brought up to the front from Archangel on the White Sea and from Persia and Siberia via Saratov.[6]

But for Hitler the most important objective was the capture of the Caucasus with its oilfields, as this would ease Germany's over-strained fuel situation. Linked up with this project were other very ambitious but rather vague ideas – it might, for example, be possible to break into the Near East through the Caucasus while simultaneously General Rommel and the Italo-German armies in North Africa occupied Egypt and captured the Suez Canal. These two operations together could shatter the power of the British Empire, particularly as the operations of the Japanese in Southeast Asia had already caused the British great losses.[7]

The Southern Offensive

Führer Directive No. 41 for the summer campaign of the year 1942 was issued on April 5th, 1942, in the period in which RAF Bomber Command was preparing for its first big attacks on German domestic targets. This Führer directive listed two objectives: in the north, besieged Leningrad was finally to be captured and the land connection with Germany's Finnish ally established. But Operation 'Northern Light', which was the attempt to capture Leningrad and make contact with the Finns, was only a secondary consideration; the big objective was in the south, the break-through into the Caucasus.

This offensive in the south was planned to unroll in four stages. The 2nd Army and the 4th Panzer Army were to break through to Voronezh on the Don; the 6th Army was to break out of the area to the west of Kharkov and destroy the enemy forces to the west of the Don in co-operation with the 4th Panzer Army, which would turn southward along the Don in order to encircle the enemy there. After this, the 4th Panzer Army and the 6th Army, under the command of Army Group B, would co-operate with Army Group A (1st Panzer Army and 17th Army) to encircle Stalingrad. Army Group B was to drive forward down the Don in a southeasterly direction, whilst Army Group A would advance from the area to the east of Taganrog–Artemovsk across the lower Donets to the northeast. The fourth phase of the summer offensive was to be the march southward to the Caucasus.[8]

The main instrument of the undertaking as a whole was to be Army Group South, and the first phase of the operation was given the code name 'Blue'. In 1942, Field-Marshal von Reichenau suffered a stroke at his headquarters in Poltava, and had to return to Germany, where he died in Leipzig, a very premature end for such a skilful and energetic leader. He was replaced by Field-Marshal von Bock, who had commanded Army Group Centre until shortly before Moscow.

It must be borne in mind that according to the original plans for the offensive it was to be carried out by stages, because the requirements exceeded the forces of a single army group and at the very least, presupposed the provision of strong reserves, which were, in fact, never made available.

Preliminary conditions for the start of the summer offensive were the clearing up of the situation in the Kerch peninsula and the Crimea, where the enemy was still holding on in spite of the winter campaign, and the elimination of the large enemy penetration in the neighbourhood of Kharkov, which had also existed since the winter campaign.

The task of capturing the Kerch peninsula and the strong fortress of Sevastopol was given to the 11th Army under General von Manstein. The undertaking was carried out during the course of May and June and concluded with the capture of Sevastopol, an achievement for which von Manstein was rewarded with the marshal's baton.

In the middle of May 1942 the Soviet C.-in-C. on the 'Southwestern Front', Marshal Timoshenko, at the head of – according to German estimates – twenty infantry divisions, numerous cavalry brigades and fifteen armoured brigades, drove forward right into the middle of the German preparations for an advance and temporarily achieved a deep penetration in the Kharkov area. Timoshenko's offensive was brought to a halt by counter-attacks against the deep flanks of the advancing enemy carried out by the 1st Panzer Army under General von Kleist, the 6th Army under General Paulus, and Chief of Staff Major-General Arthur Schmidt, together with Rumanian, Hungarian, Italian and Slovakian units, with the support of Air Fleet 4. According to the concluding report of OKW, 20 infantry divisions, 7 cavalry divisions and 14 armoured brigades of the enemy were destroyed in this counter-action, and 240,000 prisoners taken.

The spring battle for Kharkov was of great importance for the tactics of General Paulus, who had taken over command of the 6th Army in January 1942. In disagreement with the Chiefs of Staffs of the Army and the Army Group, General Schmidt and General von Sodenstern, General Paulus and the C.-in-C. of Army Group South, Field-Marshal von Bock, insisted that the Russian penetration should be halted by immediate counter-measures. But OKH, like the staffs of Army Command 6 and Army Group Command, was of a different opinion. General Halder always quite rightly regarded the spring battle for Kharkov as his biggest success. He had his way in the matter, allowed the enemy attack to roll close up to Kharkov, and then made a counter-drive into its deep flank. General Paulus regarded Kharkov as an example of the fact that at a critical juncture OKH was sometimes in a better position to judge a general situation than individual army commanders.[9]

At the end of June 1942, while Field-Marshal Rommel was grouping his 'Panzer Army Africa' for a drive against the El Alamein positions, Army Group South, under Field-Marshal von Bock, went over to the offensive in southern Russia. Along a front of some 500 miles there were here deployed the German 2nd, 6th, 11th, and 17th Armies, 1st and 4th Panzer Armies, 2nd Hungarian Army under General Jany, which was not yet up to strength, the Italian Expeditionary Corps and Group Wietersheim. East of Kursk, the 2nd Army, 4th Panzer Army (General Hoth) and the Hungarians were combined in an army group under command of General Freiherr von Weichs zur Glon. At this time, von Bock's reserves consisted of two German infantry divisions and six satellite divisions, some of which were still moving into position. 11th Army was still engaged in the Crimea.

And as though a malicious fate were giving a broad hint, a particular misfortune occurred after the battle of Kharkov. On June 19th, the Operations Officer of the 23rd Panzer Division (XL Panzer Corps under the command of General Georg Stumme) was shot down in his Storch aircraft between the German and Soviet lines. Unfortunately, he was carrying one or two Corps orders for the offensive deployment and these fell into enemy hands. Hitler was furious at this mishap, and General Stumme was recalled and court-martialled. Security measures were tightened up, and it was once more announced that in Hitler's view no officer should ever know more than was absolutely necessary in order to carry out his particular assignment. Severe punishment was threatened for anyone violating this principle.[10] Hitler's attitude in such matters was diametrically opposed to the traditional methods of operation still formally in use. His insistence on his point of view meant that the C.-in-C. of an army or an army group was unnecessarily hampered, his field of vision narrowed, and his ability to judge called into question. Under this new ruling he was not officially supposed to have the slightest interest in the situation on the front as a whole even in his own area of operations, not to mention those on other fronts, or the situation at home! It was not long before this sort of thing began to have its effects, particularly in November and December.[11]

The forces of Army Group South began their attack on June 28th, 1942. Between July 4th and 6th, the Weichs Group captured the greater part of the town of Voronezh, and it was noted that in this operation the enemy did not adopt the typical Russian tactic of holding on to the last, but evacuated Voronezh on his own initiative (with the exception of the university quarter in the north of the town). This behaviour was due to new instructions issued by Stalin for more elastic tactics aimed at cutting down losses by withdrawing when necessary. On the German side changing instructions and repeated direct intervention by Hitler indicated a disturbing uncertainty on the part of the Supreme Commander of the Wehrmacht and the Army.

Originally Hitler had ordered that Voronezh was to be taken in the first phase of the operations, but von Bock made no secret of his opinion that this particular operation was a waste of time, so in the end Hitler left it to the discretion of Army Group HQ whether to take Voronezh or not. But when von Bock, who had changed his views in the meantime, took advantage of an opportunity offered him, Hitler ordered that a Panzer corps of the 4th Panzer Army should wheel away to the southeast.

Thus the second operational phase laid down by Directive No. 41 was started by a single Panzer corps (XL) before the first phase of the operations had been brought to an end. The absence of XL Panzer Corps was keenly felt at Voronezh, and, in addition, because the available supplies of fuel were inadequate, it proved impossible to carry out the task which devolved on the Panzer Army as a whole; namely, to prevent the Russian forces moving back under the attack of 6th Army and escaping eastwards over the Don. This 'strategy of half-measures' was to remain characteristic of the whole summer campaign.[12] And it must be remembered that these operations on the Don were also intended to consolidate the long northern flank for future operations between the Don and the Volga and in the Caucasus.

On July 10th, 1942, a regrouping of the German forces in south Russia came into operation. The previous Army Group South was now divided into Army Group B (Field-Marshal von Bock) with the 6th German, 2nd Hungarian, and 8th Italian Armies, and the 3rd Rumanian Army, which was still in process of formation under command. The new Army Group A, under the command of Field-Marshal List, with 17th Army, and, from July 14th on, the 4th Panzer and 1st Panzer Armies, was to undertake the operations against Stalingrad.

According to Directive No. 41 this was the third phase of the operations, and forces of Army Group B driving down the Don were to unite in a pincer movement with the forces of Army Group A (List), which were to advance from the Taganrog–Artemovsk area across the lower reaches of the Donets and Don towards Stalingrad and the Volga. As the plan to send two armies across the lower Donets aroused certain tactical misgivings, the deployment was changed. Army Group A was set in march in a northerly direction, and on July 14th, it established preliminary contact with Army Group B near Millerovo. With this the idea of a pincer movement against Stalingrad was abandoned.

By this time the enemy was beginning to show signs of exhaustion, but at the same time there were also indications that his withdrawal was planned and systematic.

On July 16th, 1942, Hitler, together with the Operations Staff of the Wehrmacht and the Army General Staff, moved to advanced HQ 'Werwolf', near Vinnitza in Podolia (Western Ukraine), which had been set up in spruce woods along the Vinnitza–Shitomir road. For a long time Hitler had been dissatisfied with Field-Marshal von Bock's conduct of affairs, and now von Bock was removed for good and General Freiherr von Weichs was appointed commander of Army Group B in his stead.

At this time Hitler still seriously believed that the Russians were at the end of their tether, having drawn no conclusions from the falsity of his similar belief in the autumn of the previous year. Even before the transfer of Führer HQ from East Prussia to Podolia, Hitler once again intervened in operations. On July 13th, he ordered that the two Panzer Armies 1 and 4 should attack with 17th Army (General Ruoff) in the direction of Rostov. This meant nothing less than the breaking off of the attack on Stalingrad.

Hitler was quite convinced that the Russian 'main forces', which were retreating before the 6th Army and XL Panzer Corps on the Don, could be encircled between the Don and the Donets and destroyed in a great battle before they could retreat via Rostov in the direction of the Caucasus. This was wishful thinking. According to reports of the German Intelligence Service, by coincidence a council of war had taken place in Moscow on this same July 13th, and it had been decided to withdraw the Russian forces to Stalingrad, the Volga and the Caucasus in order to force the Germans to fight another winter campaign.

The next day the two German Panzer armies were beyond the Donets between Kamensk-Shakhtinski and the Upper Chir, and they were thus in an ideal position for a swift drive against Stalingrad. But they were ordered to wheel away from this favourable position to take part in an encirclement battle, which was, in fact, unlikely to take place.

As a deviation from the original plans, it was now decided that the sole force to carry out the attack on Stalingrad would be the 6th Army. It is highly probable that the 'main operation', the conquest of the Caucasian oilfields,

Above: Führer discussion in Poltava before the German summer offensive of 1942. From left to right: Field-Marshal Keitel, C.-in-C. Wehrmacht; General von Sodenstern, Chief of Staff, Army Group South; General Freiherr von Weichs, commander of the 2nd Army; Hitler; General Paulus, Quartermaster-General, Army General Staff; General von Mackensen, commander Panzer Korps III; Field-Marshal von Bock, C.-in-C. Army Group South.
Below: General Freiherr von Richthofen (left), Commander of Air Fleet 4, discusses the commitment of his forces with General Paulus,

German infantryman in a snow-covered trench in Stalingrad in January 1943.

German infantry finally takes the bitterly contested Hill 102

British convoy conference. The Convoy Commodore explains Admiralty orders to the captains of the merchant vessels in the convoy and the measures he intends to take to protect the convoy.

Above: U-boat travelling at top speed tries to dodge the bombs of a Liberator. Below: A U-boat forced to the surface by depth charges is machine-gunned by a Liberator.

Official USAF photograph

Official USAF photograph

Allied air 'Interdiction campaign'. Above: A Havoc of the 9th Air Force attacks supply lines on the Cotentin Peninsula.
Below: Destruction caused by air attack at a railway junction in Normandy.

Above: German self-propelled gun passing crippled Russian T 34 tank.
Below: German 7.5 cm (Pak) anti-tank gun in action against advancing Russian tanks.

Field-Marshal Model (right), C.-in-C. of Army Group B, visits General von Manteuffel, commander of the 5th Panzer Army (left). Major-General Thomale (centre).

Soldiers of a German armoured spearhead with captured Americans. In the centre a German soldier carrying the German

was now occupying Hitler's imagination. Vacillation and uncertainty in the giving of orders were again noticeable, and for a while the 4th Panzer Army was kept standing in bridgehead positions south of the Don.[13]

On July 23rd, 1942, the 1st Panzer Army and 17th Army took Rostov. There was no longer any question of the imagined 'encirclement battle'; the enemy was already well on his way towards the Caucasus in full retreat.

While the 6th Army advanced across the upper reaches of the Chir towards the Don loop at Kremenskaya, Hitler put his cards on the table. Führer Directive No. 45 of July 23rd, 1942, provided that Army Group A, with Army Group Ruoff (17th Army and the 3rd Rumanian Army), should advance towards Batum on the Black Sea. The 1st and 4th Panzer Armies were to take the oilfields of Maykop–Groznyy and then seize the line Tiflis–Baku – Operation 'Mouse'. Army Group B received instructions to take Stalingrad with 6th Army and to prepare the Don as a defensive line – Operation 'Siegfried'. 11th Army, under Field-Marshal von Manstein, was sent north to take Leningrad. Despite the enormous strain imposed once more on all available forces two mobile divisions were sent back to France.

The front line of the two army groups in south Russia in the Rostov–Tsymlyanskaya–Voronezh area was already about 750 miles long, but if they were to reach the desired Batum–Baku–Astrakhan–Stalingrad–Voronezh line, then the German southern front would be approximately 2,500 miles long – and would have to be held in spite of steadily diminishing forces, a lack of urgently-needed replacements, and a constant shortage of fuel! This latter difficulty certainly played a role in the decision to send the two mobile divisions back to Europe. In view of the difficult fuel situation it was very doubtful whether it would have been possible to use them at the focal point of the operations. At the same time, Hitler feared an Allied invasion of northern France to relieve pressure on the Russians, so back they went to France.

The issue of Führer Directive No. 45 underlined the strange dispositions of the summer offensive of 1942. The attack by a series of stages, which was the arrangement at the beginning of the offensive, was now abandoned in favour of two offensives starting in different directions: towards Stalingrad and towards the Caucasus – despite the fact that originally these two undertakings had no connection with each other. For example, it was not necessary that Stalingrad should be captured in order to occupy the Caucasus, nor vice versa.[14]

However, Hitler was still firmly convinced that the Russians were at the end of their tether, though, in fact, they were suffering far fewer losses, and the German forces were taking far fewer prisoners. The Russians were obviously pursuing delaying tactics. Hitler also believed that the capture of the Caucasian oilfields would deliver a decisive blow to Russia's armaments industry.

But in fact something quite different was taking place on the Russian side of the fence. The vast reorganization of the armaments industry in eastern Russia and in the Trans-Ural area and Siberia was approaching its end. Production figures for tanks, guns and the multiple rocket guns, known as

'Stalin organs', were rising. An Order of the Day issued by Stalin on July 1st, 1942, was captured on the sector of LII Corps. It was couched in a serious but fatherly tone, and frankly admitted great Russian losses in men and territory, including agricultural areas and industrial centres. Then it went on to say solemnly – without threat or reproach – that any further retreat could mean the end of Russia. All sources are in agreement that the psychological effect of this Order of the Day, and the measures which followed it in order to consolidate Russia's defensive capacity, was very powerful.[15] Major-General Schmidt, of 6th Army, had the impression that from August 1942 Russian resistance stiffened once more, whereas in the preceding weeks there had been frequent signs of disintegration in the ranks of the retreating enemy.

On the German side supply difficulties made themselves very keenly felt once more, for the German forces were now operating in vast areas. As there was no proper road network, all the supplies for the two German army groups had to be carried by two railway lines which ended in Kharkov and Stalino (these were later extended beyond Rostov), a time-wasting operation because the Russian gauge had to be adapted to the German width. The Army Quartermaster-General sought to establish a system of supply points from which columns of lorries could take over, but the constant changes of disposition ordered by Führer HQ, which moved armies here and there like battalions on old-fashioned manœuvres, caused new confusion. On the whole, it was possible to feed the men off the land, but the supply of munitions, and more especially the supply of fuel, became more and more critical. Even Air Fleet 4 had to help out with hastily organized columns of lorries.[16]

All the same, Führer Directive No. 45 did form a new focal point for the available German forces. Three German armies were allotted to the conquest of the Caucasus, and a single German army, the 6th, was not only to take Stalingrad but also prepare the Don front as a defensive line. With this, Hitler's objective, Stalingrad, was brought into the centre of the picture, and with it the 6th Army and its command. The tragedy of Stalingrad, the tragedy of the 6th Army, began with a long and involved prelude.

At the beginning of the century Stalingrad, then known as Tsaritsyn, was a small town with no more than 55,000 inhabitants, but it was of some importance as a distribution centre for oil, grain, timber, wool, fish and salt. In still earlier times Tsaritsyn, situated where the Don and the Kalmuck steppes meet along the land narrows between the two great rivers of eastern European Russia, was the starting point of the defensive line against the Asiatic horsemen of the steppes. Since the days of the Revolution the town has borne the name of the all-powerful ruler of the new Russia, Joseph Vissarionovich Djugashvili, known as Stalin. The change of name in 1918 commemorates the fact that he defended and held the town against the army of the Don Cossack hetman, Krasnov.

Thus one-time Tsaritsyn certainly held special memories for Stalin. The fighting against the Cossack bands of Krasnov represented the beginning of his military career and the beginning of his fame, though he had been sent south with no military mission but as special commissar for the Volga grain collection. However, Hitler over-estimated the psychological and ideological importance of the town for the Russians, though, in fact, since those early days the economic importance of Stalingrad as a trans-shipment and production centre had enormously increased. The town, situated in a flat, treeless area scored by deep ravines, had now a population of half a million and extended about twenty miles on either side of the Volga between Kuperossnoya in the south and Rynok in the north. It had become an important economic centre with industrial suburbs, railway installations, factories and great administrative buildings. It produced large numbers of tractors, tanks, and guns and it was a trans-shipment point for oil supplies from the Caucasus. Despite its undoubted importance, however, the capture of Stalingrad and the interruption of shipping on the Volga did not (as the future showed) mean that Russia's war economy and transport system had been damaged to anything like the extent Hitler had supposed.

The man whom Hitler had entrusted with the capture of Stalingrad, General Paulus, was to find that the campaign on the Volga would bring him the highest military honours, including the marshal's baton, but also an agonizing crisis of conscience. Paulus was well aware that Hitler attached great importance to the capture and holding of 'the keystone on the Volga' in conjunction with the capture of the Caucasian oilfields. Paulus had been Chief of the General Staff of the 6th Army under Field-Marshal von Reichenau, and he was on the Army General Staff from September 1940 to January 1942. He had taken part in drawing up the plans for the attack on Russia in 1941, and in the first discussions for the 1942 campaign.

Paulus, who was the son of a minor official, had worked his way to the top by industry and determination. He was regarded as a highly-educated and very conscientious general staff officer whose every decision was preceded by thorough and careful preparation and study. He was, in fact, the ideal Chief of Staff for a supreme and vigorous commander-in-chief prepared to take responsibility, a man, in short, like Field-Marshal von Reichenau. It is reported that when Hitler once said that he could storm the gates of heaven itself with the 6th Army, von Reichenau replied: 'But not with me as Commander-in-Chief!'[17]

This sense of supremacy, deliberately cultivated by von Reichenau, was lacking in Paulus; in fact, later on, at the height of the crisis, he observed quietly, 'I'm not von Reichenau.' In his own Chief of Staff, Major-General Arthur Schmidt, the son of a Hamburg merchant, he had an ideal aide. Schmidt was an energetic, clear-sighted officer who was never afraid to take responsibility. Despite what has sometimes been said, the two men worked together in complete harmony up to a certain point in the final phase.[18] Both men were general staff officers, both were educated outside the sphere of politics, in accordance with the tradition of the Reichswehr. Neither of them was remotely interested in any form of political action; for many months both men had been completely absorbed in their own job, that of conducting the war in south Russia. And each was greatly hampered both in his judgement and his actions by the maxims of the art of leadership as understood by Hitler.

Hitler's Change of Plans

On July 30th, 1942, just one week after the issue of Führer Directive No. 45 on July 23rd, Hitler carried out his last radical disposition in the planning of this double-pronged campaign. The 4th Panzer Army, commanded by General Hoth, which had just won a bridgehead over the River Manych and taken Proletarskaya on its advance towards the Caucasus, was suddenly placed under the orders of Army Group B, and ordered to wheel round and advance south of the Don through the Kalmuck steppes towards Stalingrad and the Volga in co-operation with 6th Army. With this the last attempt to form focal points was abandoned.

To complete the general dissipation of forces, Army Group Centre was given instructions on August 11th, the month of the decisive offensive operations 'Siegfried' and 'Mouse' against the Volga and the Caucasus, to begin Operation 'Whirlwind'. The 2nd Panzer Army was to attack near Sukhinichi in order to iron out the Russian salient in the Sukhinichi–Yukhnov area. However, Army Group Centre was now in a critical situation because of Russian penetrations in the Sychevka–Subzov–Rzhev area where the 9th Army and 3rd Panzer Army were operating. On August 19th, an Anglo-Canadian landing force attacked Dieppe, and this greatly concerned Hitler though, in fact, it was no more than a large-scale reconnaissance in force. On August 22nd Operation 'Whirlwind' was called off; the attack had failed. The next day, August 23rd, on which Army Group Centre reported heavy Russian attacks, Hitler ordered the launching of Operation 'Northern Light', the attack on Leningrad, on September 14th.

According to the calculations of the Foreign Armies (East) Department of the General Staff, on August 15th the Russians had 254 infantry divisions, 83 infantry brigades, 13 cavalry divisions and 68 armoured brigades at the front, a fighting force equal to approximately 222 German divisions. Enemy reserves were estimated at 73 infantry divisions, 66 infantry brigades, 20 cavalry divisions and 86 armoured brigades.[19]

On the Volga–Don front, the 4th Panzer Army, which had had to give up a Panzer Corps (XXIV) to the 6th Army, a further Panzer Corps (XL) to Army Group A, and the 'Grossdeutschland Division' to the army in the west, still had XLVIII Panzer Corps with one armoured and one motorized division, the IV Corps with two infantry divisions, and the VI Rumanian Corps with, for the moment, two divisions. And the 6th Army, which was to carry out the main two-pronged attack (north and south) in the great Don loop, had XIV Panzer Corps, VIII and XVII Corps, and XXIV Panzer Corps and LI Corps.

As a result of the constant regrouping and the siphoning off of large quantities of fuel for the undertaking against the Caucasus, it was not until

August 7th that the army succeeded in defeating the main Russian forces in the great Don loop – about twelve infantry divisions and five armoured brigades – and forcing the Don crossing. In the meantime, the 4th Panzer Army fought its way – against obstinate enemy resistance and in the teeth of repeated fuel supply difficulties – across the River Aksay in the Kalmuck steppes and into Abganerovo in the direction of Krasnoarmeysk on the Volga to the south of Stalingrad. Russian resistance was so persistent that for the time being the 6th Army had to give up another armoured and an infantry division to Hoth.

Because of the relative weakness of the two attacking German armies the Russians succeeded in strengthening the defences of Stalingrad by building improvised field works. German sources like to talk about Stalingrad as a 'fortress' with an inner and an outer defensive ring, but in fact this description is rather misleading. The defensive preparations were in the hands of Major-General Tolbukhin, who was later to become a marshal and to capture Budapest and Vienna.

On August 19th, 1942, General Paulus found himself at last in a position to give the order for the attack on the town itself. In accordance with a directive issued by Army Group B, this provided for the seizure of the land bridge between the Don and the Volga to the north of the railway line Kalach–Stalingrad. Part of the German forces were to seek contact with Hoth on the uplands to the west of Stalingrad. For the moment, no detailed instructions for the occupation of the urban area on the Volga were issued because Army HQ did not know whether the enemy had sufficient forces to undertake a protracted defence of Stalingrad.[20]

Three days later, on August 21st, the 6th Army forced the Don crossing on both sides of Vertyachi; and on the evening of August 23rd, units of XIV Panzer Corps reached the Volga near Rynok on the northern edge of the sprawling urban complex.

The next day, in Führer HQ at Vinnitza, so to speak in the first flush of victory, Hitler discussed the preparations for Operation 'Northern Light' with Field-Marshal von Manstein, who at the same time witnessed a violent and astonishing attack by Hitler on his Chief of General Staff, Halder.[21]

But before this, on August 20th, the attack of the 4th Panzer Army under Hoth had come to a stop on the heights to the east of Tundutovo railway station before the uplands of Krasnoarmeysk. This high ridge of land, which was strongly defended by the Russians, dominated the Volga bend and was the southern keystone of the defence of Stalingrad. The forces of the 4th Panzer Army proved too weak to capture the heights between Krasnoarmeysk and Beketovka, and had to seek contact to its left with the 6th Army. Thus it proved impossible to carry out the two-pronged attack as originally planned. On September 3rd, German and Rumanian units under Hoth succeeded in capturing the Volga heights on the western edge of Stalingrad. They then went down to the Volga and on September 10th reached the area between Yelshanka and Kuperossnoya on the Volga to the south of Stalingrad. It proved impossible to capture Beketovka, which later became one of the starting points for the Russian counter-offensive.

Many of the judgements made during these anxious weeks later proved to be accurate. Even before the attack in the great Don loop started, Paulus had had lively discussions with Army Group B as to how the flanks of the more and more extended offensive prong were to be protected. He had pointed out that the northern flank was insufficiently covered, and that the offensive power of the drive must diminish as forces were taken away for the purpose of flank defence. The daily log of the Wehrmacht Operations Staff notes as early as August 16th, 1942, that the Führer was anxious lest Stalin might repeat the 'standard Russian attack' of 1920. In that year the Red Army had attacked across the Don into the Serafimovich area towards Rostov, and defeated the White Army of General Wrangel.[22]

But there was always a big gap between the accuracy of Hitler's momentary impressions and the conclusions he came to as a result of his anticipations; and at this particular time his strategic conceptions bore no relation to the forces that were available. In fact, on August 20th, the Russians did launch an attack across the Don with quite considerable forces, driving into the 8th Italian Army, which was guarding the deep northern flank of the German 6th Army, and in the first few days this attack met with a good deal of success. Despite splendid individual achievements, such as the attack of the famous Savoy Cavalry Regiment against Russian infantry and artillery at Isbushensky, the fighting value of many Italian units turned out to be unsatisfactory. The intervention of German forces, XVII Corps, was necessary before the situation could be restored.[23]

General Paulus and his Chief of Staff were extremely worried about the situation on the Italian sector, and they had every cause to be. It so happened that the successor of Paulus as deputy Chief of Staff at OKH, General Blumentritt, was on a visit to the front of the 6th Army, and in order to show him, how well founded were his reports and warnings about the northern sector Paulus asked him to inspect the 8th Italian Army. As Paulus himself recorded this was exceeding his authority, according to Hitler's instructions.[24]

The strange illusions still harboured by the supreme leadership in those days can be seen very clearly from a report delivered by Göring on August 28th, 1942, in Vinnitza. According to Göring, General Freiherr von Richthofen, C.-in-C. of Air Fleet 4, had personally inspected the Stalingrad area, and there could no longer be any question of strong enemy forces being in the neighbourhood. Richthofen had received the impression that the enemy lacked any sort of unified command.[25] At that time the North Group of the 6th Army was having a difficult time in the Kotluban area, while XIV Panzer Corps was held up for a very critical week near Rynok on the Volga. The German forces were not strong enough to exploit their preliminary successes rapidly; neither, for the time being, were the Russian forces, which consisted primarily of the 62nd Army under General Vassily Ivanovitch Chuikov, 'the legendary sixty-second', strong enough to launch a large-scale planned counter-offensive. But the Russians had not given up.

On the same day, August 28th, Army Group North reported a Russian counter-attack, and two days later Hitler could see a crisis developing for Army Group A on the northern edge of the Caucasus. The attack there had come to a standstill, which was small wonder, but Hitler was furious and brusquely summoned Field-Marshal List to Vinnitza to explain himself.

Between September 1st and September 15th the 6th Army and the 4th Panzer Army fought their way forward step by step, despite increasingly heavy losses, into the confusion of suburbs, factory sites and railway installations of Stalingrad, in a battle which was to last two and a half months and to become more and more reminiscent of the bitter battle of attrition for Verdun in the First World War. Gradually the German forces captured the greater part of the town, but the Russians still kept hold of part of the Volga bank in the five-mile-long centre of the town; and, in particular, they still held the decisive crossing, the ferry at Krasnaya Sloboda.

In the meantime, after violent altercations with General Jodl, Chief of Wehrmacht Operations Staff, who had just made one of his rarely permitted visits to the front and had returned to confirm Field-Marshal List's assessment of the situation, Hitler recalled List and decided to conduct the operations of Army Group A himself from Vinnitza in the hope of saving the 'main operation', which was Operation 'Mouse'.

While the battle for Stalingrad was still undecided, Hitler carried out an extraordinary but very typical piece of propaganda strategy: Stalingrad was proclaimed to the world as a great German victory. When Hitler went to Berlin at the end of September to open the Winter Relief Campaign for 1942–3 he announced that the German offensive had four objectives: the seizure of the last great Russian grain area, and of the 'last remnant' of Russia's coal, the capture or cutting off of Russia's oil supplies, and the closing of the Volga as a Russian supply line. Referring to Stalingrad he declared: 'And you may be quite certain that no one will be able to get us out now.'

Addressing a great demonstration in the Berlin Sports Palace at the beginning of October, in honour of Germany's rural population, the Supreme Commander of the Luftwaffe, Reichsmarshal Göring, declared confidently that from now on everything would get better. There was no longer any reason to fear the coming winter campaign in the east; the prospect had lost all its horror. 'This time we are immune. We already know what a Russian winter is like.'

In this speech Göring also referred to the German General Staff, because in the meantime constant differences of opinion concerning the conduct of the war on the Eastern Front had led Hitler to dismiss General Halder on September 24th, 1942, and appoint General Zeitzler as the new Chief of the Army General Staff. Göring declared that this National-Socialist General Staff Officer was merely an 'assistant' to the Commander; and he thanked God that

Germany had plenty of first-class generals. Anyone who did not come up to scratch or was not ruthless enough, or strong enough, would be summarily dismissed.

On November 8th, 1942, Hitler himself delivered a speech in the Löwenbräu Cellar in Munich at a meeting in celebration of the *Putsch* of 1923. Once again he announced the capture of 'this gigantic trans-shipment centre' and declared it to be a great German victory. He insisted that he had wanted to capture the place because in doing so he could cut off thirty million tons of Russian supplies. 'And do you know what?' he asked rhetorically. 'We're modest; we've got it.'

With such utterances, trumpeted out into the world by the German radio, the political demagogue Hitler robbed the Generalissimo Hitler of all room to manœuvre; in fact, this circumstance played a very important role in all the decisions subsequently taken. With his public assurance that 'we hold Stalingrad', Hitler was both right and wrong. The German forces did 'hold' Stalingrad; the traffic on the Volga was interrupted, and all armament production in the town had ceased. On the other hand, they did not hold it completely, because the 62nd Russian Army was clinging on grimly to a bridgehead on the Volga, and it was increasing in strength with every passing week.

Once again it might formally be said that at this turning point of the war in those early months of 1942, the German forces held a great deal, but from another angle their hold was very precarious. They were tied down on the Volga and were not strong enough to protect either the northern flank in the Kotluban area or the southern flank in the Krasnoarmeysk–Beketovka area adequately. Army Group A had driven into the northwest of the Caucasus and had captured one or two small oilfields in the Maykop–Groznyy area, and established a bridgehead over the Terek, but it had not reached the Batum–Tiflis–Baku line. In North Africa Rommel's Panzer Army was not strong enough to break through the British lines at El Alamein and drive eastward towards the Nile. And on the home front, RAF Bomber Command had carried out, during the spring, huge and devastating raids on Lübeck, Rostock and Cologne, and its offensive was still being vigorously continued. More and more reports of 'terror attacks' on German towns were coming in.

On September 12th, 1942, General Paulus paid a visit to the Führer's HQ in Vinnitza. He pointed out the weaknesses of the German front at Stalingrad and in particular that the flanks were inadequately safeguarded. He suggested that German divisions should be brigaded with the forces of the Axis satellites in order to strengthen their backbone, and asked for the preparation of German reserves so that they could intervene if necessary. Similar demands and warnings were to be made again and again by the 6th Army. At the end of September, they were repeated through the liaison officer of OKH with the 6th Army, Major Menzel; and later on through highly-placed visitors such as General Ochsner, General Fellgiebel and General Schmundt. In order to illustrate just how serious the situation was, General Paulus took his visitor, General Schmundt, up into the northern front, where the enemy had just succeeded in making a deep penetration over the Don into the lines of the 376th Division, so that Schmundt could see for himself what was happening.[26]

However, we must not ignore an important psychological factor, though it is very difficult to explain now that the strange personality of Hitler is no longer present. The fact is that again and again Hitler succeeded in a quite extraordinary fashion in restoring the confidence of officers from the front who came to see him in Vinnitza. Officers of a sensitive nature like Paulus were particularly subject to Hitler's almost magical influence. In addition, of course, so far everything had gone very well indeed. The German forces on the Eastern Front had overcome one critical situation after another. The German soldier and his leaders had proved superior to the enemy again and again. Even in this summer campaign the German forces had once again brought off the practically impossible.

Paulus returned to the front firmly convinced that the Führer attached fundamental importance to the capture of Stalingrad, the 'keystone on the Volga'. He had made a good impression on Hitler, who thought him a reliable man and had already decided to appoint him Chief of the Wehrmacht Operations Staff, or even as Head of OKW in the near future; as soon in fact as the fighting around Stalingrad had come to an end. During his visit to the front in October, General Schmundt hinted to General Paulus that before long he would be given another and more important task. His successor as Commander-in-Chief of the 6th Army would be General von Seydlitz-Kurzbach, the commander of LI Corps, another general who enjoyed the particular confidence of the Führer. General Paulus happened to be married to a high-born Rumanian lady, and it was proposed to appoint him deputy commander of the planned German-Rumanian Army Group Don on the Volga, which was to be commanded by the Rumanian Chief of State, Marshal Antonescu.

Before his enforced retirement General Halder did his best to render a final service to his still active colleagues by insisting that the wedge-shaped front at Stalingrad was a military impossibility, but Hitler dismissed his warnings as pedantic and hyper-critical. All the same, as the War Diary of Wehrmacht Operations Staff records repeatedly,[27] Hitler did recognize that the inadequate protection of the flanks of the 6th Army represented a danger, though he drew no conclusions from his own knowledge. By September at the very latest the German High Command had to decide what it really wanted: Stalingrad, or to advance into the Caucasus. One or the other would have to be abandoned; it was not possible to have both. It was also necessary to concentrate all possible reserves on the southern East Front in order to consolidate the initial successes there. But none of these things was done.

One of the last War Diary entries under General Halder's régime records that 'gradual exhaustion' was making itself felt in the attacking spearhead at Stalingrad.[28] The 6th Army had fought itself to a standstill and the average company strength had sunk to sixty. An armoured division had now only between sixty and eighty tanks capable of action. By the end of September, we find Halder's successor, General Zeitzler, recommending that the Stalingrad offensive be called off. General Paulus was also in favour of this step, but in the meantime he called for three fresh infantry divisions. The only reinforcements he received were five sapper battalions specially flown out to him to assist in the exhausting and costly house-to-house fighting in the town. Hitler still insisted that the battle must go on until the enemy had been thrown back over the Volga for good.

However, in October and November two Rumanian armies, the 3rd under General Dumitrescu and the 4th under General Constantinescu, were sent to strengthen the wings of the 6th Army, the one to the north and the other to the south. But these armies consisted exclusively of infantry and cavalry. They had no heavy weapons and no effective anti-tank equipment. As a reserve behind the 3rd Rumanian Army on the northern flank, the 6th Army released XLVIII Panzer Corps, whose units, the 14th Panzer Division and the 29th Motorized Division, were otherwise engaged. But the forces allocated to the Corps command, the 2nd Panzer Division with about forty tanks, most of them light, and the 1st Rumanian Armoured Division with about forty-five light Czech Skoda tanks, did not represent a very powerful fighting force.

In the meantime, bitter house-to-house fighting was going on in Stalingrad together with a struggle for possession of the big factories, the Dzerzhinsky tractor works, the Barrikady artillery works, and the Red October blast furnaces.

At his HQ in Vinnitza the Führer finally decided to abandon Operation 'Northern Light', i.e., the attack on Leningrad. During October, more and more reports began to come in of big concentrations of Russian forces to the east and north of the Volga and the Don on both sides of Stalingrad. In the Stalingrad area the Russians formed two 'fronts' (Army Groups). In the south there was the 'Stalingrad front', under General Yeremenko, and in the north there was the 'Don front', under General Rokossovsky. It was not difficult to see that the enemy was planning a pincer movement. The Commander-in-Chief of the 6th Army and his chief of staff both realized this and gave the appropriate warnings, but their own hands were tied.

As far as we know – and not a great deal is known – these Russian operations were conducted by the first deputy Defence Commissar, General Zhukov, assisted by his representative General Vassilevsky. Both of them were members of STAVKA, which was the Russian General Staff under the leadership of Stalin himself. The deputy leader of STAVKA up to November 1942 was Marshal Shaposhnikov, a one-time general staff officer of the Tsar. When Shaposhnikov retired for reasons of health, his place was taken by General Zhukov, a skilful commander. Unfortunately, Soviet publications still do not give any clear picture of how decisions were taken, how plans for their execution were made, or what the Russians thought of their German enemy and his methods.[29]

By the end of October, the Russian preparations were only too obvious. During the discussions which took place at the Führer's HQ, Hitler was greatly worried by the thought that the Russians would attack the Italian forces on the Don. As a result, he issued all sorts of instructions: for the building of defensive positions behind the Don front; for air attacks on Russian attempts to throw bridges across the Don, and on suspicious preparations to the north of the Don; for the transfer of newly-raised Luftwaffe Field Divisions to the sectors held by the armies of the Axis allies; and so on – without ever asking whether all, or, indeed, any of these instructions could actually be carried out.

In the meantime, the British in Egypt had gone over to the offensive against Rommel's forces, and at the beginning of November Rommel was compelled to withdraw to the Libyan–Egyptian frontier. Towards the end of October, General Zeitzler received reports describing a big Russian propaganda campaign about large-scale operations against the invader, which were said to be imminent, but he was unable to make up his mind how much of it was propaganda and how much of it was fact.[30] Manstein, who visited Hitler at the Führer's HQ at Vinnitza on October 25th and 26th, after the great defensive battle at Lake Ladoga, was told that 11th Army would probably be sent into the Vitebsk area. Hitler expected a big Russian attack in the central sector. If he were to leave his advanced HQ at Vinnitza, then Manstein would take over Army Group A. For next year, it appeared, Hitler was thinking of a drive beyond the Caucasus into the Near East.[31]

For the time being, it was proposed to split up the area under the command of Army Group B, which at the moment had no less than seven armies to control. The German and Rumanian armies on the Volga–Don front were to be grouped together as 'Army Group Don' under the command of the Rumanian Chief of State, Marshal Antonescu. 6th Army HQ was inclined to think that this measure might be helpful and at last provide some relief. The influence of Antonescu, of whom Hitler thought highly, ought, it was hoped, to be strong enough to make sure that the equipment of the Rumanian wing armies would be completed at last. For the time being, however, nothing seemed to have any effect; neither the warnings of General Dumitrescu, C.-in-C. of the Rumanian 3rd Army, nor those of the German Army Mission in Rumania (General Hauffe). In fact, even Antonescu's own urgings achieved nothing, and Paulus, who had set some store by the intervention of Dumitrescu, was doomed to disappointment: the formation of Army Group Don as originally planned was fated to remain on paper. Events beyond their control now moved quickly.

For the time being, therefore – before the November catastrophe – Army Group B with its HQ in Starobelsk on the Aidar, a tributary of the Donets, continued to control no less than seven armies; reading from the right to the left wing they were: the Rumanian 4th Army, the 4th Panzer Army, the 6th Army, the Rumanian 3rd Army, the Italian 8th Army, the Hungarian 2nd Army and the German 2nd Army. Far in the south in the Kalmuck steppes, in the neighbourhood of Elista, one single motorized German division maintained contact with Army Group A. The reserves of Army Group B consisted of XLVIII Panzer Corps and a single infantry division behind the Italian front.

In the middle of November 1942, General Paulus received a wireless message from Hitler: he, the Führer, expected one last effort from his tried and trusted 6th Army and its gallant men to capture the whole bank of the Volga in the urban area of Stalingrad.[32]

In the meantime, Hitler had left his HQ in Vinnitza and withdrawn to the 'Wolfsschanze', or 'Wolf's Lair', near Rastenburg. From there he now left for Munich to take part in the Nazi anniversary celebrations on November 8th and 9th. After that, he went on to his permanent quarters at the Berghof, Obersalzberg. When he arrived there, disagreeable news reached him from the Mediterranean: Rommel's army was in full retreat into Libya. On November 8th, strong Anglo-American forces had landed in Morocco, Oran and Algiers. As a result, Operation 'Anton', the occupation of the whole of France, was launched on November 11th, and Italian and German units were hurriedly sent to Tunisia. Stalingrad, far away in the already wintry Volga steppes, now seemed an affair of secondary importance. Then on November 19th, the Chief of the Army General Staff reported from East Prussia that the Russian offensive, 'long expected by the Führer', had begun.

At five o'clock in the morning of November 19th, 1942, after heavy artillery preparation, the 21st and 65th Infantry Armies and the 5th Tank Army (according to German estimates two armoured and two cavalry corps and about forty infantry divisions) advanced out of the bridgeheads at Kletskaya and Serafimovich to attack the Rumanian 3rd Army. Strong forces of tanks with infantry in close support quickly broke through the Rumanian front. The attack, which had deliberately been launched far from the left wing of the 6th Army, carried the Russian armour deep into the snowy steppes behind the rear of the Rumanian Army and by evening the Russian spearhead was about thirty-seven miles behind the broken front on the upper reaches of the River Chir.

Army Group reserve, XLVIII Panzer Corps, was immediately committed, but it was not to have any decisive effect. This corps, which was immediately bombarded with several different orders from Hitler at the Berghof via Army Group B assigning it new battle tasks, soon found itself in fuel difficulties, and by November 21st it had lost about half of its eighty or ninety tanks in isolated and ineffective counter-drives against the enemy.

On November 20th, the Russian 51st and 57th Infantry Armies advanced from the Beketovka area to the south of Stalingrad to attack the Rumanian 4th Army, which proved unable to stand up to the weight of the attack.

Hitler's first measure in these critical days on the Eastern Front was a reshuffle of generals. General von Kleist was given command of Army Group A, and Field-Marshal von Manstein was to form Army Group Don out of the HQ staff of 11th Army and take command of the German and Rumanian forces in the Volga–Don area. But Manstein happened to be away from his HQ inspecting the front lines of Army Group Centre. The weather would not allow him to fly, and Russian partisans twice held up his train by putting mines on the line, so for the moment he was practically out of it. He did not arrive at General von Weichs's HQ in Starobelsk until November 24th, and by that time the decisions had already been taken.

Before serious research into the protracted series of Stalingrad battles began, the situation was bedevilled by the accounts published just after the war which insisted on regarding everything that happened from the angle of the German Resistance Movement. These accounts also provided us with the legend of Stalingrad. In particular they represent that as soon as the threatening encirclement on the Volga became evident General Paulus should have withdrawn his forces at once – just as General Litzmann and General von Scheffer-Boyadel did at Brczeziny in 1914 during the great autumn battle in Poland, in order to avoid threatening encirclement. More than that, General Paulus should have behaved 'like Field-Marshal Yorck'.*

This independent action would then have given the signal for the plotters gathered around the dismissed General Beck to overthrow the Hitler régime.

Let us leave legends on one side. As commander of the Prussian auxiliary corps with the broken and defeated *Grande Armée*, Yorck von Wartenburg was in a very different position from that of Paulus at Stalingrad. And, let us remember, neither Paulus nor his Chief of Staff, Major-General Schmidt, was in the least politically-minded. Even if they had had any intention of acting politically, in the situation as it was, it would have been absolutely impossible for them to do so under the relentless pressure of the enemy.

Let us face the situation without prejudice, just as it was, and ask ourselves soberly how much Paulus and Schmidt actually knew about the general situation in those November days and under what conditions they came to their decisions. Only when we have done this shall we be entitled to ask whether they acted rightly or wrongly.[33]

From November 19th to November 21st, Paulus and Schmidt were in their HQ at Golubinskaya on the Don, and throughout this period they had no clear idea that their units might possibly be encircled. They both supposed that there would be Army Group measures against any such eventuality, and that deployment instructions for a counter-blow against the Russian break-through would remedy the situation. After all, critical situations had arisen before during the campaign on the Eastern Front. This is a point which should not be forgotten. German military commanders were accustomed to feeling confident. Similar views were held at HQ 4th Panzer Army.

---

*The reference is to Count Yorck von Wartenburg (1759–1830), a Prussian nobleman who commanded the corps Prussia was compelled to send against Russia. However, being convinced of the ultimate defeat of France, he neutralized the Prussian Army by the Convention of Tauroggen; an immensely popular step which nevertheless almost caused him to be court-martialled. He was saved by the Treaty of Kalisch, which brought Prussia over to the side of the Allies against France.—*Translator.*

On the evening of November 19th, Army Group B ordered the 6th Army to cease all offensive operations in Stalingrad and concentrate mobile units under the command of XIV Panzer Corps (General Hube) behind its left wing to the west of the Don in order to counter-attack.

It was only on November 21st that the two men in Golubinskaya realized the deadly seriousness of their situation. Russian tanks which had originally driven forward in the direction of Kalach, where they had met with opposition, causing them to turn away, now appeared only a few miles from Army HQ. But worse even than this, other Russian tanks of the northern attacking group seized the Don bridges at Kalach and thus cut the 6th Army's supply line. At midday, HQ was transferred to the railway station at Gumrak to the west of Stalingrad, and for the time being the C.-in-C. and his Chief of Staff went to Nizhne-Chirskaya on the Don to superintend the consolidation of the Don front.

The question they now faced was not so much what ought to be done, but what *could* be done. Unless a southern front could be built up very quickly, there was a danger that the army would be taken in the rear and destroyed. The same thing was necessary even if there were to be any break out southwards in order to link up with those parts of Hoth's army which had been pushed away. However, there could be no question of any attempt at a break-out until the units of the 6th Army fighting on the west bank of the Don (XI Corps and XIV Panzer Corps) had crossed eastwards over the Don; in other words, certainly not before November 26th. For the moment the obvious thing to do was to form a 'hedgehog' in order to gain time for a regrouping before any attempt was made to break out.

On the afternoon of November 21st, Major-General Schmidt spoke to the Chief of Staff of Army Group B, General von Sodenstern, and informed him that as far as the Rumanian 3rd Army was concerned the situation was catastrophic. General von Sodenstern was unable to send any help and told the Major-General bluntly: 'You'll have to do the best you can on your own'.

Paulus now got in touch with Army Group HQ Starobelsk and proposed that the 6th Army should withdraw to the Don–Chir chord position. Army Group was about to give permission for this move when in the evening of November 21st special instructions were received from OKH concerning the 6th Army. Their gist was that Stalingrad and the Volga front must be held at all costs. At the same time, strong forces were to be concentrated west of the Don for a counter-attack. It was stressed that large-scale counter-measures were being taken and that further instructions would follow.

Quite clearly, a 'hedgehog' had to be formed unless the 6th Army were to run the risk of destruction from the rear. It was also necessary if adequate preparations were to be made to abandon the previous position successfully. In the meantime, the 6th Army would have to be supplied from the air. However, all the Luftwaffe commanders concerned – General von Richthofen, commander of Air Fleet 4, Major-General Fiebig, commander of VIII Air

Corps at Stalingrad, and Major-General Pickert, commander of the 9th Flak Division – were unanimously of the opinion that an adequate air lift over an extended period was impossible because the transport aircraft available had not sufficient capacity for the job.[34]

For the moment, General Paulus and his Chief of Staff were chiefly interested in the problem of saving their men and retaining their own freedom of action rather than in holding their position. The C.-in-C. of the 4th Panzer Army, General Hoth, arrived in Nizhne-Chirskaya early in the morning of November 22nd on his way to Army Group B. He too had only a very general idea of the fate of his units, which had been split up and forced in two different directions by the Russian south group, which had in the meantime itself divided into two groups. IV Corps (General Jaenicke) had withdrawn to the 6th Army, and the majority of the Rumanian forces were flooding back through the Kalmuck steppes in the direction of Kotelnikovski.

The Encirclement of the 6th Army

It was on this day that strong Russian armoured units coming from the northwest and the southeast joined forces in the southwest flank of the 6th Army in the Marinovka–Kalach area, where there were only improvised defences. The 6th Army was now surrounded, and it was clear that unless something effective were done quickly the encirclement could develop disastrously. At 14.00 hours Paulus and his Chief of Staff flew from Nizhne-Chirskaya to their new headquarters at Gumrak station, inside the cauldron which was now beginning to form. It was already impossible to hold on to the positions to the west of the Don, where XI Corps (General Strecker) and XVI Panzer Corps (General Hube) were engaged in heavy fighting, so in defiance of OKH instructions these units were ordered to withdraw to the eastern bank. Heavy fighting was also proceeding on the south front where IV Corps was engaged, but on the north front, where LI and VIII Corps were engaged there were merely holding attacks of no great strength to cope with.

On the afternoon of November 22nd, when Paulus and Schmidt were still trying to decide the best thing to do in the very difficult circumstances, and whether, in fact, it would prove possible to hold the cauldron at all, new instructions arrived from OKH, through Army Group, insisting that the 6th Army must hold on to its positions until further notice. On reading these instructions Paulus turned to his Chief of Staff and said: 'We've still time to decide what's to be done about this, so let each of us think it over for himself. Meet me again in an hour and let me know what you feel.'[35]

The two men met again in an hour's time and discovered that they had come independently to the same conclusion: the whole 6th Army must attempt to break out to the southwest. But time would be necessary before such a break out could be prepared – at least until November 26th.

Paulus now consulted his Corps Commanders and found that they were of the same opinion: everyone was in favour of a break out. In the afternoon Paulus had a discussion with General von Seydlitz-Kurzbach of LI Corps, who was profoundly alarmed by the situation and demanded immediate action without waiting to consult either Army Group or OKH.[36]

One can no doubt discuss at length whether and to what extent the efficiency of modern means of communication over long distances, permitting direct intervention on the part of the OKH, and making it possible for the man on the spot to refer back to OKH, affects initiative and sovereignty of action. Old Moltke once said with what now sounds like foreknowledge that the really unfortunate commander was the one with a telegraph line behind him.

In the case of General Paulus we must remember that he was an extremely conscientious man, and that, in addition, he was well aware of the importance the supreme leadership attached to the whole operation on the Volga. In such circumstances, therefore, to act on his own initiative would necessarily appear premature to him, as in general he was not well informed about the situation as a whole, or about the situation of Army Group A in the south in particular.

In the evening of the same day, November 22nd, the voice of Hitler once again floated over the ether in the shape of a wireless message direct to 6th Army HQ. The gist of it was just the same: 'Hold on! The Führer expects . . .' But there was no specific suggestion as to how this was to be done. That night Paulus reported the situation once more, and he summed up his own views under five headings. First of all it was doubtful whether it would be possible to hold a hedgehog position in the wintry steppes without prepared positions. Second, the forces at his disposal were not strong enough to hold a sufficiently large area. Third, the supply situation was already critical, and a continuous air lift seemed out of the question. Fourth, all Corps commanders were in favour of a break out to the southwest. Fifth, in conclusion, he asked for immediate freedom of action. This report went to Army Group B and to OKH.

For the next thirty-six hours not a word was heard in Gumrak from the Führer's HQ. This was probably because in the evening of November 22nd Hitler set off by special train from Obersalzberg to Leipzig, from where he took a plane to his 'Wolfsschanze' HQ in East Prussia.

In the meantime, Paulus several times asked his superiors at Army Group B for freedom of action. General von Weichs and General von Sodenstern both agreed with the view of the men on the spot, Paulus and Schmidt, but they also both felt that it would be premature to take any decision without previously obtaining the agreement of OKH. However, in a teleprint to General Zeitzler, General von Weichs declared that he was wholeheartedly in favour of a break-out being attempted by the 6th Army, adding that in his view it would be impossible to keep the Army adequately supplied by an air lift.

Paulus and Schmidt reckoned that if the order for the break-out could be given on November 24th, the actual attempt could be launched on November 27th. Then Gumrak heard from Starobelsk that von Manstein was preparing for the 6th Army to break out of its encirclement; and, it must be remembered, von Manstein enjoyed an almost legendary reputation.

When Hitler arrived in his 'Wolfsschanze' HQ on November 23rd, it was up to the new Chief of the General Staff, General Zeitzler, to take up the cudgels on behalf of the 6th Army,[37] and this, in fact, he did during the routine evening Situation Conference that day; urging the views of Paulus and Schmidt, which coincided with his own, with all the cogency he could. It would, he declared, be a crime to stake everything on one card and allow a whole army – 400,000 men was the figure estimated by OKH – to be ultimately encircled with doubtful hope of relief. That night after the conference Zeitzler rang up General von Sodenstern in Starobelsk and informed him that he believed that he had succeeded in convincing Hitler, and that the order for the 6th Army to break out could be expected the following day.

In the meantime, an act of personal initiative and therefore disobedience had already taken place in the 6th Army. On November 23rd General von Seydlitz ordered parts of his Corps to evacuate their well-prepared winter positions in the Yersovka area and withdraw to a position five miles farther back; but he had not informed the 6th Army Command of what he intended to do. The withdrawal took place to the accompaniment of rather theatrical scenes: von Seydlitz burnt his own baggage, and the troops destroyed all superfluous stores, or such stores as they considered to be superfluous. The tragic features of the affair was that the enemy drove on relentlessly and almost completely destroyed the 94th Infantry Division as it withdrew.

It was only on November 24th that von Seydlitz reported the circumstances to Schmidt as Chief of Staff, adding that his intention had been to make it easier for Paulus to decide on a break-out. This behaviour was tantamount to mutiny, and had Paulus not been such a mild and understanding superior, Seydlitz would certainly have faced a court martial. However, Hitler's order of November 24th placed the northern and eastern edges of the perimeter under the command of this same General Seydlitz, without, of course, affecting the ultimate responsibility of Paulus as Commander-in-Chief of the 6th Army. Nothing was known at Hitler's HQ of the arbitrary action of von Seydlitz; and the order concluded by saying that he, von Seydlitz, would be held responsible to the Führer for holding the front. Paulus passed on this order to Seydlitz, who, although he felt that the final decision should be left to the men on the spot, replied to Paulus's question of what he thought of the order by saying that he could see no alternative but to carry it out. It remained for Manstein to restore some order to this odd situation.

Heavy fighting was still proceeding on the Don and on the developing southern front, and in the meantime Paulus and Schmidt waited impatiently in Gumrak for orders from Starobelsk, while in Starobelsk they were waiting no less impatiently for a call from Zeitzler. Finally, at about 10.00 hours on November 24th General von Sodenstern telephoned OKH. The laconic answer he received was that the Army Group would have to wait. . . .

According to notes made by Major-General Schmidt, an order arrived in Gumrak at 08.38 hours direct from OKH, giving detailed instructions for the formation of 'hedgehogs'. Stalingrad and the bank of the Volga were to be held at all costs. At the same time, the 6th Army was informed that strong forces (4th Panzer Army) were preparing to fight their way through and snatch victory from the jaws of defeat. The relief operations were to start at the beginning of December. Until then Air Fleet 4 would supply the 6th Army by means of an air lift.

That morning, far away in the 'Wolfsschanze' HQ, Reichsmarshal Göring had announced through his Chief of Staff, General Jeschonnek, that the Luftwaffe would make itself responsible for keeping the encircled 6th Army supplied. It is said that this guarantee was given despite urgent warnings that Air Fleet 4 – indeed, the Luftwaffe as a whole, which already had to keep the Tunisian bridgehead supplied – just did not have the necessary number of transport aircraft available to operate such a large-scale air lift.

Prestige strategy had already played a fatally influential role in the original decision to capture Stalingrad, and now Göring's personal prestige policy did the rest. He was well aware of the extent to which his own reputation and that of the Luftwaffe had sunk in Hitler's eyes, and here, he felt, was an opportunity to push himself to the fore again. At the same time, the situation was complicated for Hitler personally by the fact that there had been a tremendous amount of propaganda about Stalingrad and its capture; and the retention of the city was now linked up with a lot of irresponsible promises and grandiloquent boasts. If there were any retreat now the halo of the People's Tribune would be tarnished, and the zealously propagated idea that 'the Führer is always right' would receive a severe blow. In these circumstances, Göring's totally irresponsible offer to keep the encircled 6th Army supplied by means of an air lift was very welcome. Thanks to these various factors, General Zeitzler lost his battle on behalf of Paulus and the 6th Army.

In the meantime, the situation was so grave that Army Group HQ in Starobelsk was considering whether to give the 6th Army permission to break out without waiting for higher instructions, but then the Chief Signals Officer reported that a message had been picked up from the Führer's HQ for the 6th Army with the personal assurance that he, Hitler, would keep the encircled Army supplied and see that it was relieved in good time.

Neither Army Group HQ at Starobelsk nor 6th Army HQ in Gumrak was in a position to know just what forces OKW and OKH could gather for the counter-measures which were promised. Hitler's idea that the horizon of a commander-in-chief should be kept as narrow as possible now bore bitter fruit. In considering the psychological situation in November 1942, one must not forget that the Führer and Supreme Commander of the Wehrmacht was still something of a miracle man. After all, up to this time Hitler had very often been proved right. In addition, Paulus also had confidence (and it was not misplaced) in the new Chief of the Army General Staff. No doubt, too, he also

remembered that at Kharkov in the spring OKH had turned a battle that looked as if it was sliding into defeat into a great victory.

The chief concern of Paulus himself was to save the army for which he was responsible from the destruction which now threatened it; at the same time, from his days at OKH as deputy Chief of Staff, he was very well aware of the great importance Hitler attached to the Volga campaign. A wireless message now arrived from Manstein, the future Commander-in-Chief of Army Group Don, and therefore the future superior of Paulus, recommending that Stalingrad and the Volga front should be held. At this moment, then, any disobedience on the part of Paulus would have been disobedience against his superior at Army Group, and not merely a demonstration against a far-off Hitler. At the same time, Paulus was well aware of Hitler's obstinacy; if he, Paulus, acted as he thought fit, then within a matter of hours he would probably be relieved of his command. In this most critical situation his men would then be confused by orders and counter-orders, and it was they who would chiefly have to suffer for any disobedience on his part. Confiding in his Chief of Staff, Paulus declared that he would not hesitate to risk his head for his men, but he could see no sense in it.

In retrospect it is perhaps easy enough to judge, to judge lightly or harshly, and say that after all the right thing for Paulus would have been to take the responsibility for a break-out by the 6th Army. It is on record that Paulus did feel at the time that left to himself he could have solved the problem. But had he acted on his own responsibility and without a full knowledge of the situation as a whole, he would have cut the ground from under the Supreme Commander. 'Such action against the plans of the overall commander must, if practised systematically, result in anarchy.' This was his firm conviction in the situation as he knew it at the time. He knew, too, that his Chief of Staff agreed with him. If we reject all barren political speculation and strictly judge the obligations of conscience, it is still impossible to say that in the given situation Paulus had a greater obligation to his conscience or that it urged him to act otherwise than he did.[38]

In any case, the 6th Army was now encircled. The fate of four Army corps, one Panzer corps, fourteen infantry divisions, three motorized divisions, three armoured divisions, one Rumanian infantry and one Rumanian cavalry division, and numerous other units, special groups and various services was at stake. On paper, the 6th Army totalled approximately 330,000 men; the actual strength was rather less – something like 300,000 men. Of this strength some units were outside the actual cauldron; for example, the supply services of the armoured and motorized divisions on the Chir, men on leave, training units, guard troops, supply and signals units, and so on, totalling approximately 80,000 men. In all, about 220,000 men were surrounded, together with 100 tanks, 1,800 guns and 10,000 vehicles of various kinds.

On his way to his new HQ in Novocherkassk, Manstein appeared at Starobelsk on November 24th in the hope of getting a better idea of the general situation. The decisive moment was already past then, and Manstein had to make the best of a situation he had not created – indeed, he had been able to exercise no influence at all on its development. Personally,[39] he felt that OKH had been wrong not to give Paulus a free hand to act as he thought fit when he asked for it on November 19th. At the same time, he thought Paulus had committed a psychological error when he asked Hitler for permission to break out of the encirclement. He should have taken the responsibility for leading his Army out of the trap. However, in his memoirs he frankly admits that to have attempted a break-out in November would have involved more risks than establishing 'hedgehogs' and waiting to be relieved.

The War Diary of Wehrmacht Operations Staff for November 25th records the Führer's 'confidence' concerning the position of the 6th Army; though it was, of course, doubtful whether the air lift could really supply the encircled army with the 700 tons of supplies it needed every day. Air Fleet 4 had only 298 transport aircraft available, and for such a lift something like 500 would be needed.[40]

The position of the 6th Army was by no means regarded as hopeless; and, indeed, it was far from hopeless, but everything now depended on two things: adequate supplies from the air, and the timely launching of relief operations.

At first the 6th Army asked for 700 tons daily of rations, ammunition and fuel, but then it set its minimum demand at 500 tons daily. Göring, Jeschonnek and the Chief of Air Transport, General Morzik, all felt that to organize an air lift to supply 300 tons a day was within the bounds of possibility, but even this lower estimate presupposed certain conditions which were not, in fact, present: namely, a sufficiently large number of transport aircraft; a sufficiently large ground organization outside the cauldron (the two nearest airfields, Tazinskaya and Morosovskaya, 150 and 125 miles away from the cauldron respectively, were obviously not adequate); and at least four secure landing-fields inside the cauldron itself.[41] If, over and above all this, the particular difficulties of the Russian winter are taken into account, it becomes clear that Göring's guarantee was either an irresponsible piece of bluff, or that his calculations were very wrong indeed.[42] Actually, the supplies carried to the 6th Army by the air lift amounted on an average to 104·7 tons daily. On one occasion, during the critical days of December, almost 300 tons were flown in during a single day, but this was exceptional. The truth is that the Luftwaffe was faced with an impossible task, and its efforts to fulfil it were paid for with the loss of 488 aircraft and 1,000 air crew, many of them key-men who could only be replaced at such short notice by instructors from the flying schools. But the sacrifice was not altogether useless, and perhaps the greatest achievement of the Stalingrad air lift was that it proved possible to evacuate 42,000 wounded men and a great number of highly-trained specialists of various kinds.

Manstein finally arrived in his new HQ at Novocherkassk on November 27th. The forces available on the spot were so inadequate that the guard duties for the new Army Group HQ had to be undertaken by a battalion of Cossack volunteers. For the moment, all that the new commander had at his disposal were his high reputation and his brilliant abilities, and an HQ echelon – but no fresh divisions.[43]

Before setting out for his new HQ, Manstein sent a wireless message to Paulus – to which we have already referred – assuring him that everything possible would be done to 'dig him out of it'. Everything now depended on whether the army could hold the Volga and the northern front in accordance with the orders of the Führer and at the same time concentrate sufficiently strong forces to 'cut out' at least a temporary supply lane for itself towards the southwest.[44]

But by its transfer to the command of Army Group Don, and its temporary encirclement, the 6th Army was now involved in even greater events: there was the struggle to establish a new defensive front on the Don and the Chir from the remnants of the 4th Panzer Army and the two Rumanian armies; and in addition the safeguarding of Army Group A's supply lines – and perhaps its line of retreat, because for the time being Hitler had obstinately left it isolated on the edge of the Caucasus. Manstein was certainly right when he declared that though the 6th Army was his chief headache, it was by no means his only one. For example, there was still a danger that the enemy, correctly recognizing that for the time being the 6th Army had lost its freedom of movement, would exploit the opportunity to concentrate all his mobile armoured forces and make a drive through the German lines towards Rostov on the Don. This would mean the threat of a 'super-Stalingrad' – the encirclement of Army Group A far to the south between the Kuban and Terek rivers.

Manstein was unable to fly into the cauldron to see the Stalingrad situation for himself because the situation on the Don–Chir front – which had only just been restored with the help of special battle groups – was still so uncertain that he felt he ought not to leave Novocherkassk. However, towards the end of November he sent his Chief of Staff, Major-General Schulz; and at the beginning of December his Operations Officer, Colonel Busse. Both Paulus and his Chief of Staff, Major-General Schmidt, made it abundantly clear to the two visitors that it would be impossible to maintain their position in Stalingrad indefinitely. According to Major-General Schmidt's account, Colonel Busse told him that Manstein was of the same opinion, but that so far no one had been able to persuade Hitler to change his views.[45]

The ultimate fate of the 6th Army now depended on the course of the relief operations, which began on December 12th, 1942. For these operations Manstein had the forces under General Hollidt, taken over from Army Group B, consisting of three infantry divisions, two Luftwaffe field divisions, and XLVIII Panzer Corps, which had been reorganized with two disivions, and LVII Panzer Corps withdrawn from Army Group A, with the badly mauled 23rd Panzer Division, and, finally, the 6th Panzer Division, recently transferred from France, which was fully up to strength and had 160 armoured vehicles. The 17th Panzer Division was also attached to this Corps, but too late. LVII

Panzer Corps and the regrouped 4th Rumanian Army, with two weak Corps, were placed under the 4th Panzer Army.

The Hollidt Group was instructed to stop the Soviet attacks on the Chir in the great Don loop and then move from the west to the relief of the 6th Army. These instructions were never carried out because these forces found themselves tied down the whole time in endless defensive actions. Hoth's 4th Panzer Army was to advance from the Kalmuck steppes in the Kotelnikovski area to relieve the 6th Army from the southeast.[46]

Two relief and break-out operations were operating together here and they must be carefully separated: the one was known as Operation 'Wintergewitter', or 'Winter Storm'. This was the Hoth drive which began on December 12th, 1942. The other was Operation 'Donnerschlag' or 'Thunderclap'.

The objective of Operation 'Winter Storm' was to re-establish contact with the 6th Army, which, on its part was to make a drive to meet Hoth with an armoured break-out group. At the same time, the 6th Army was expected to hold its previous position on the land tongue between the Volga and the Don. The idea of Operation 'Thunderclap' was that the 6th Army should gradually disengage and be prepared for a total break out as soon as Hoth's forces had come close enough.

Between the latter and the encircled 6th Army were strong Russian forces consisting of the 51st Army, the 2nd Guards Army, an armoured corps, a mechanized corps, three motorized corps, a cavalry corps, two infantry divisions and an armoured brigade. The enemy had particularly strengthened the heights overlooking the Karpovka–Rakotino sector, a likely spot for the Germans to choose in an attempt to break out of the encirclement. In addition, between December 16th and 18th there were numerous Russian holding attacks at various points around the perimeter.

In the meantime, the 6th Army prepared a break-out group under General Hube with between fifty and eighty tanks to co-operate in the execution of Operation 'Winter Storm'. However, the fuel situation was very unsatisfactory; the air lift was working so ineffectively that this armoured group had fuel for less than twenty miles. This meant that Hoth's forces would have to reach the heights near the village of Businovka, about that distance as the crow flies from the perimeter, before the armoured break-out group could make its effort at all. It also meant that Hoth would have to provide the encircled army with everything that could not be brought in by air, including all kinds of supplies, and in particular fuel.

The Critical Phase

On December 19th the critical moment came closer. In very heavy and costly fighting against numerically superior Russian forces in the Kalmuck steppes, Hoth's armoured spearhead fought its way as far as the Mishkovo area, just over forty miles from the perimeter held by the encircled 6th Army.[47]

Manstein now thought it time to order the 6th Army to join in 'Winter Storm', so at 18.00 hours on that day it received instructions to send the armoured break-out group into action 'as soon as possible'. Manstein pointed out in his orders that the situation might make it necessary to start Operation 'Thunderclap' immediately on the heels of Operation 'Winter Storm'. Preparations must therefore be made for Operation 'Thunderclap' at once. However, this operation was not to be started without express orders. The background to this was that at 14.35, a few hours previously, Manstein had asked General Zeitzler for permission to allow the 6th Army as a whole to attempt a break out.

In these critical hours and in the days that followed, Paulus and Schmidt felt that they were not being kept properly informed of what was going on. It was impossible to read Manstein's intentions from the teleprinter conversations which took place with Army Group Don between 17.50 and 18.30 hours on December 19th. Paulus reported that he had sufficient fuel to allow his tanks to move twelve miles, and no more. At 18.15 Manstein informed him through his Chief of Staff that the overall situation had not changed. Paulus asked whether he could begin psychological preparations for Operation 'Thunderclap', and Manstein answered laconically: 'Wait for this evening's contact.'[48]

Between 20.40 and 21.00 hours the two Chiefs of Staff, of the Army and the Army Group, discussed the situation. Schmidt explained that a drive beyond the Donskaya–Tzaritza line southward was impossible if at the same time they were supposed to hold the 'Fortress'. The best that could be managed was a short drive forward by armoured forces across the Donskaya–Tzaritza line – and even then they would have to be ready to return speedily behind the perimeter if necessary, to act as a sort of 'fire brigade'. If the 6th Army were expected to hold on to Stalingrad, Schmidt went on, then it could deploy only when LVII Panzer Corps reached the Businovka area. Schulz replied that he thoroughly understood and appreciated this.

It was quite clear that Paulus and Schmidt – and in fact, Manstein himself – regarded Operation 'Thunderclap', i.e., the total break out – as the only possible solution. But Hitler was not prepared to give his permission, no matter what the circumstances. 6th Army HQ reckoned that, allowing for systematic regrouping, gradual withdrawal from other perimeter fronts, and the necessary stratagems to mislead the enemy, about five days would be required before the 6th Army would be in a position to carry out Operation 'Thunderclap'. About 1,000 tons of additional supplies, including ammunition, fuel and food would have to be flown in, and the aircraft bringing in the supplies could fly out about 8,000 seriously wounded men on the return journey. However, it became quite clear that Paulus and Schmidt were not prepared to carry out Operation 'Thunderclap' on their own against Manstein's explicit instructions; and it also became clear – though in this we have to rely to some extent on conjecture – that at this point Manstein felt that he could not possibly order Operation 'Thunderclap' on his own initiative against the wishes of OKH (probably because of the very delicate situation on the Don–Chir and Caucasian fronts).

Copies of the teleprinter conversations indicate that on December 20th and the following days the discussions on the situation continued. Schmidt pointed out that Operation 'Winter Storm' was still possible, provided that Operation 'Thunderclap' followed immediately, but Major-General Schulz could only reply that OKH had still not given permission for the break-out.

Manstein's attention was now partly distracted by a further catastrophe: in the north the enemy broke through the front of the Italian 8th Army on the Don; and on December 22nd Manstein had to ask OKH for permission to detach the 23rd Panzer Division from Operation 'Winter Storm' in order to commit it on the Don front in an effort to restore the situation there.

Late in the afternoon on December 23rd, Manstein once more asked Paulus by teleprinter if he could still carry out Operation 'Thunderclap' provided that extra supplies of fuel and food were sent in during the next few days. On the assumption that there was no alternative, Paulus replied: 'I can't judge from here whether the relief of the Army is at all possible in the foreseeable future, so the sooner we try to break out the better, as far as I'm concerned. Incidentally, may I regard this conversation as authority to start Operation "Thunderclap"?' Manstein replied: 'I am not yet in a position to give you such authority. . . . But what I want to know is whether you think you can force your way through to Hoth?' Paulus replied: 'There's nothing else to do.'[49]

On Christmas Eve, 1942, General Schulz and General Schmidt were in touch between 17.05 and 17.15 hours. Schulz informed Schmidt that though there was still no decision from OKH with regard to the 6th Army, the Field-Marshal (Manstein) had instructed him to tell the 6th Army to make up its mind that Operation 'Thunderclap' would be the solution. However, better weather was needed before the necessary extra supplies of fuel and food could be flown in. A further urgent request for considerable reinforcements had also been made.

On Christmas Day the last hope disappeared. Owing to the disaster which had overcome the Italians on the Don, and because of a new deep Russian penetration into the left flank of Army Group Don, Manstein, who had no proper reserves, found himself forced to regroup his forces. The 6th Panzer Division had to be sent into action in the new battle sector, and the rescue of the 6th Army was now a forlorn hope. It had been placed in this hopeless position first of all by the ill-conceived summer campaign and then by the over-optimistic decisions of the Supreme Commander in November, and now its fate was sealed in the reorganization of the German South Front to cover the retreat of Army Group A from the Caucasus to the northwest towards Rostov. Though General Paulus knew little enough about the general situation, it was not difficult for him to see this coming.

The only question that remains for some future historian to answer is whether in those dark December days of Christmas 1942, Paulus, seeing that it was quite clearly impossible to hold the position on the Volga, and seeing that it was now equally clear that the air lift could not keep him supplied, should have taken the initiative and made an attempt with his army to break out of the encirclement. Should he have extricated his army, without regard to Manstein (whom he greatly respected), without regard to the consequences of such an action to his neighbours in the field, and without regard for whatever decisions the far-off Führer HQ might have come to?

One thing is quite certain: a decision to attempt to break out would have mobilized the utmost strength and moral determination of his men, who were well aware of the deadly danger which threatened them, but who certainly did not feel themselves defeated, still less 'betrayed'. In all probability, and in accordance with an old military tradition that existing stocks of supplies are always underestimated, it would probably have been discovered that there were reserves of ammunition, and even fuel, of which the headquarters staff were ignorant. The decisive factor was, of course, the shortage of fuel. Unfortunately something else was also quite certain: the greater part of the heavy material, and the sick and wounded, would have had to be left behind. Finally, it would be no cut-and-dried affair: any attempt to break out to the southwest into the wintry steppes would be a very risky business. In fact, no one can now say for certain whether an attempt at a break out would have succeeded or not, whether the badly mauled units would have managed to link up effectively in a new rear front, or whether the powerful armoured forces of the enemy would have cut the retreating German columns to pieces in the open steppes before they had a chance of reaching safety. However, in such a situation men like Field-Marshal von Reichenau or Field-Marshal Model would have done their utmost to save their armies.

But a man like Paulus was too conscientious to shoulder such a great burden of responsibility on his own – and this very conscientiousness tortured him with a number of agonizing questions. Was there, in fact, any way of saving his army at all? Was he even entitled to take the responsibility for endangering the whole German southern front with its three Army Groups B, Don and A for the sake of a highly problematical attempt to save his own army? And if he did attempt a break out, might not his army be destroyed in any case before it could save itself? In short, was there any sense at all in trying to break out?

The fate of the 6th Army became certain on December 25th, 1942, Christmas Day. The sacrifice in Stalingrad has often been dismissed as useless, but it cannot be too often stressed that a dividing line must be drawn between the unfortunate preliminaries to the whole operation, and the deeds and sufferings of the army between December 25th, 1942, and February 2nd, 1943. At one time the 6th Army was holding 143 large Russian formations, infantry divisions and armoured brigades; and even towards the end it was still holding down between 50 and 60 such large enemy forces. By their heroic and determined resistance, which won the greatest respect of the enemy, those men compelled the Russians to concentrate large forces against them instead of driving after strategic objectives in the rear of the German forces, and in this way they rendered an invaluable service to Germany's military operations on the Eastern Front.

The story of the last stand and the annihilation of the 6th Army in the slowly constricting perimeter around the ruins of Stalingrad has often been told. The epic stand has even been a subject of fiction, but rarely presented in a worthy fashion. In accordance with contemporary literary taste, those German authors who did take Stalingrad as a subject were far more interested in a description of the terrible misery and suffering which accompanied the end of the 6th Army, than in the fact that in a hopeless situation, in bitterness and desperation, tens of thousands of men, generals, officers and other ranks, fought to the last and died worthy of their calling.

It was typical of Hitler that right to the end he did his best to give the encircled army new confidence, though before long it was against his better knowledge. At the end of the year, when General Hube flew out of Stalingrad to the Führer's HQ to give a first-hand report on the situation, he was assured that OKH was preparing a great new relief offensive from the west; that the air lift – which had almost completely broken down by this time – was to be reorganized on a broader basis; and that the men in Stalingrad could expect to be relieved in the second half of February. The preliminary condition for all this was the restoration of the Southern Front and the withdrawal of Army Group A from the Caucasus. Provided only that the 6th Army held out in Stalingrad, what threatened to be a defeat could still be transformed into a great German victory.

Manstein now found himself in a really tragic situation for any conscientious general: for the time being he had to rely on the encircled 6th Army to hold out – he even had to order it to do so. But at least by so doing he was relieving Paulus of the ultimate responsibility. In this situation Paulus did what was required of him to the very last. In agreement with all his Corps commanders, he rejected the Russian demand of January 8th, 1943, for the surrender of the 6th Army. This demand prefaced the Russian general offensive against the encircled 6th Army on January 22nd. Without consulting Führer HQ, Paulus rejected the recommendation of his superior, Manstein, that, in the words of his Chief of Staff, Schmidt, he should 'make preparations for the end', meaning that he should leave it to units which were no longer capable of fighting to arrange their own surrender, though by this time Manstein was not so desperately dependent on the sacrifice of the 6th Army as he had been earlier on.[50]

The end came on January 31st, after the Russians had succeeded in cutting the German-occupied area into two. Paulus, who had just been promoted Field-Marshal, and Major-General Schmidt, his Chief of Staff, surrendered when the Russians appeared in the Red Square before the last HQ of the dying 6th Army in Stalingrad, and the men who had been concentrated to defend it laid down their arms without waiting for orders. On February 2nd General

Strecker, who commanded the remnants of XI Corps in the northern area, also surrendered. From January 22nd on there had been no point in further sacrifice, but it was in the nature of Paulus that he was unable to diverge from the path he had once taken. In this way a field-marshal, twenty-four generals and about 90,000 men were carried off into a captivity which was little more than a different form of death. Right up to the last moment Hitler had forbidden any kind of capitulation, and he now felt that Paulus had not behaved as he should have done. Paulus had failed on the verge of immortality, he observed; he should have shot himself.

Stalingrad has been described again and again as the decisive battle of the war on the Eastern Front, and even of the whole Second World War. A sober estimate will show that the Battle of Stalingrad does not deserve this high place in history. A very little later, in the middle of February, during the third battle of Kharkov, the German Army demonstrated that its aggressive spirit was by no means broken. It was during this battle that Manstein carried out one of his most brilliant exploits; sealing off the Russian penetration by a counter-offensive from the rear. It was only with the failure of the summer offensive 'Citadel', and after the battles for Kursk and Byelgorod, that the initiative on the Eastern Front finally went over to the enemy and stayed with him until the end of the war.

However, Stalingrad certainly was a turning point in the Second World War; a psychological and political turning point. The victory of the Russians at Stalingrad greatly increased their confidence.[51] Conversely, confidence in the leadership of Hitler amongst the satellite and neutral powers began to decline, particularly with Mussolini. The foreign political consequences of the Stalingrad disaster were very great, even though their full effect was not felt until later.

The psychological consequences of the defeat for the German people were even more profound. Despite the fanatical appeals of Goebbels for 'total warfare' it was after the Stalingrad disaster that the mystical and often incomprehensible confidence in 'the Führer' as a genius who could do nothing wrong finally began to fade. It was from this point on that a common front began to form amongst some of the younger officers of the General Staff against the senseless and dishonourable conduct of the war by Hitler, and to press more and more for action. Since Stalingrad, and right down into our own day, there has been a distrust of any form of leadership, of the principles of the soldier, of honour, obedience, manly dignity and self-sacrifice, because they were so obviously abused and perverted by Hitler. But, objectively speaking, such ideals were not evil then, nor are they evil now.[52]

And thus, because of its lasting effects, the battle of Stalingrad was more than a German military defeat. It became a political event. In the summer offensive of 1942 Hitler wrongly mixed propaganda and politics with strategy. He had to pay for this error in the end – and so did the whole German people.

Chronicle VIII

March

to

December 1943

	Politics	Conduct of the War
Neutrals	Axis Powers and Japan	Axis Powers and Japan
		March 5th: Army High Command issues Ctional Order No. 5 for 'the conduct of th during the next few months'.
	March 13th: Time-bomb placed in Hitler's aircraft by Resistance supporters fails to explode.	March 16th to 20th: Biggest convoy battle war; 42 German U-boats sink 21 Allied totalling 140,942 GRT. Only one U-boa
		March 25th: Japanese plan of operation fo 'third phase'; defensive.
	March 26th: Goerdeler's secret memorandum for the generals on the necessity of a *coup d'état*	March 28th: German withdrawal from the M Line (Tunisia).
		April 15th: Hitler gives the order for Ope 'Citadel'.
		April 18th: Admiral Yamamoto, C.-in-C. Japanese Combined Fleet, killed.
	April 19th: SS troops surround Warsaw ghetto.	May 5th: Six German U-boats lost attack convoy, four others badly damaged.
	May 6th: Jews in Warsaw ghetto rise. 50,000 killed.	May 13th: Army Group Tunisia surrender of the fighting in North Africa.
		May 24th: C.-in-C. U-boats calls off action Atlantic convoys, after several costly f
		June to August: Sixth phase of Battle Atlantic.
		June 25th: Start of Operation 'Citadel' fi July 5th.
		July 5th: Operation 'Citadel', last German sive on the Eastern Front, launched.
		July 15th: Operation 'Citadel' halted.
	July 19th: Hitler and Mussolini meet in Feltre.	
	July 24th to 25th: *Coup d'état* in Italy. Badoglio head of government. Mussolini arrested.	
		August 18th: General Jeschonnek, Luftwa of Staff, commits suicide.
August 29th: Danish Navy scuttles itself.		August 25th: First use of guided bomb Bay of Biscay.
September 9th: Italian fleet escapes to Malta.	September 8th: Italy's capitulation announced.	September 10th: German troops occupy R
	September 12th: Mussolini freed by German parachutists on the Gran Sasso.	
	September 18th: Italian Republican Fascist State founded.	September 20th to 22nd: First use of homing torpedo against warships Allied convoy.
		September 24th: German troops evacua ensk.
		September 30th: Japanese defence line w to the Marianas and the West Caroli
		September 1943 to May 1944: Seventh ph Battle of the Atlantic.

Conduct of the War	Politics	
...stern Allies and the Soviet Union	Western Allies and the Soviet Union	Neutrals

...2nd: Aircraft of the 5th USAAF destroy ...panese convoy in the Bismarck Sea. ...5th to 6th: RAF Bomber Command opens ...w offensive against Ruhr.	March 1st: Atlantic convoy conference opens. March 7th: Stalin made a Marshal by Supreme Soviet.	
...26th: Naval battle off the Komandorsky ...lands. ... March to December: First use of escort ...rriers, very-long-range bombers and 'sup-...rt' groups for convoy protection. ...th: British 8th Army makes contact with ...d US Corps in Tunisia.		April 13th: Bodies of 4,000 Polish officers discovered in mass graves at Katyn.
...th: RAF Bomber Command attacks the ...hne and Eder dams. ...th to 26th: First Allied convoy through the ...diterranean. ...h: RAF reaches the 100,000-ton mark in its ...cks on Germany.	May 12th to 25th: 'Trident' Conference in Washington. May 15th: Dissolution of the Communist International founded in 1919.	
...a: Heavy US air attack on Spezia. ...t to 22nd: First RAF 'shuttle' attacks from ...ain and North Africa. ...h: US troops land on Rendova and New ...rgia in the Solomons. ...to 10th: Allied forces land in Sicily.	June 10th: 'Point-blank' Plan gives target priority to German fighter airfields and aircraft works, in preference to U-boat bases and works.	
...a: First Allied air attack on Rome. ...n to August 3rd: 'Round the clock' air ...k on Hamburg by 3,000 bombers. ...st: 9th USAAF attacks Ploesti. ...5th: Russians recapture Orel and Byel-...d. ...5th: US landing on Vella-Lavella in the ...mons. ...7th: US aircraft bomb Schweinfurt. ...of the fighting in Sicily. ...7th to 18th: RAF bomb Peenemünde.	July 12th to 13th: 'National Free German Committee' formed in Moscow. July 16th: Roosevelt and Churchill appeal to Italian people to lay down arms. August 12th to 24th: Quebec Conference. August 25th: Southeast Asia Command under Lord Louis Mountbatten.	
...r 3rd: British landing in Calabria. ...r 9th: Allied landing at Salerno. ...r 13th: British landing at Kos (Dodeca-...., French landing in Corsica. ...r 17th: Russians recapture Bryansk.	September 3rd: Italian surrender instrument signed.	
...1943: First Allied strategic air attacks ...Italian bases.		

Politics		Conduct of the War
Neutrals	Axis Powers and Japan	Axis Powers and Japan
		October 3rd: German troops land on Kos. ning of the reconquest of the Dodecanes
		October 9th: German troops evacuate bridgehead.
		November 14th to 16th: First 'Walter' mental U-boats in service.
		November 16th: Leros captured.
		November 22nd: Samos captured.
	December 2nd: Call-up of German youth for war tasks.	December 2nd: Last blockade-runner from reaches France.
		December 5th: Hitler orders highest prio Me–262, to be used as a fighter-bomb
		December 7th: Last U-boat pack in the Atlantic dispersed after renewed failu
		December 25th to 26th: Sinking of the battleship *Scharnhorst* in the Arctic S

Conduct of the War	Politics	
estern Allies and the Soviet Union	Western Allies and the Soviet Union	Neutrals
ber 6th: Russian break-through at Nevel.		October 12th: Portugal grants bases to the Allies in the Azores.
ber 14th: US daylight raid on ball-bearing works in Schweinfurt; 60 out of 228 bombers hot down.	October 13th: Italy declares war on Germany.	
er 23rd: Russian break-through on the ower Dnieper.	October 18th to 30th: Moscow Conference.	
mber 1st: Crimea cut off by Russian Dnieper rive.		
JS troops land at Bougainville.		
mber 5th: US carrier-borne air raid on Rabaul.		
mber 6th: Russians recapture Kiev.		November 9th: Establishment of UNRRA.
nber 20th: US forces land on the Gilbert slands, Tarawa and Makin.	November 22nd to 26th: 'Sextant' Conference in Cairo.	
nber 28th: British troops cross the Sangro in taly.	November 28th to December 1st: Teheran Conference. Date for Normandy landings fixed for May 1944.	
	December 3rd to 6th: Second Cairo Conference. 'Matterhorn' Plan for air attack on Japan from Chinese bases.	
nber: 8th USAAF flies record number of issions against German territory with 3,546 ombers.	December 12th: Agreement signed between Soviet Union and Czech Government in Exile.	

The U-Boat War
Against the Allied Supply Lines

BY JÜRGEN ROHWER

By the beginning of 1943, the Western Allies had obtained the strategic initiative on almost all fronts. In June 1942 the first '1,000-bomber raids' on Cologne, Essen and Bremen showed very clearly that the German Luftwaffe could not hope to equal the offensive strength of the Anglo-American air arm. At the same time, the Japanese, by the loss of their carriers at the battle of Midway Island, were deprived of their most effective weapon, and from August 1942 they were forced on the defensive. Finally, the last few months of 1942 saw the turning point in favour of the Western Allies in the Mediterranean, with the battle of El Alamein and the landing of the Allies in North Africa; and the turning point on the Eastern Front in favour of the Russians, with the battle of Stalingrad. But the longest battle of all, the Battle of the Atlantic, had not yet reached its culminating point.

Britain's vital supply lines were at stake in this, the most important battle of the supply war – with German naval and air forces attacking British coastal shipping, mines being laid across Britain's seaways, air attacks on British ports, Britain isolated from the Continent by the occupation of Norway and France, and war at sea and in the air in European waters and in the oceans against Allied and neutral shipping. Germany's most effective instrument for waging this war was the U-boat, and this weapon bore the brunt of the battle of the Atlantic, lasting as it did nearly sixty-nine months, though sometimes supported by battleships, cruisers, auxiliary cruisers, long-range bombers and Italian submarines.

The German Navy and the Supply War

Ideas as to how this supply war should be waged varied considerably in German naval circles in the years before the war broke out.[1] It was not until the autumn of 1938 that the German Admiralty formed a Planning Committee to study the problems of naval warfare against Britain. Previously, the prosecution of naval warfare against Britain had been regarded as practically impossible, given the relationship of strength laid down in the Anglo-German Naval Agreement of 1935, and in view of the great material requirements of such warfare. But Captain Dönitz, who was commander of the German submarine arm at the time, had very much earlier arrived at the conclusion

259

that, in developing the submarine arm, he would have to reckon primarily with the possibility of a war against Britain's supplies. On the assumption – which proved to be correct – that in the event of war Britain would immediately adopt the convoy system which had so effectively protected her shipping during the First World War, Dönitz began to experiment as early as 1935, and in the subsequent years, with the so-called 'group' or 'wolf-pack' tactic. He felt that the only way to cope with the concentration of enemy shipping and escort strength in the convoys was by the close tactical control of a U-boat group or 'pack'. With the intention of adopting this tactic if it ever came to the point, Dönitz called for the biggest possible U-boat building programme the Anglo-German Naval Agreement would allow, and within the framework of this programme the building of the greatest possible number of medium-sized U-boats (Type VII), which seemed to him best suited to convoy attack. But OKM* felt that in any future war the U-boat would still have to operate on its own. It therefore preferred to build bigger submarines with respectable artillery performance and the ability to stay at sea for long periods. The idea was that such submarines would be able to wage a cruiser war against enemy shipping in distant waters. This difference of opinion between Dönitz and OKM in the years before the war resulted in a slowing down of the U-boat building programme

German U-boat Building before the War

	Laid down:	1935	1936	1937	1938	1939	Total Sept. 1st, 1939	On Order
Type I	Large	2					2	
Type II	Small	20	4	4	2	2	32	
Type VII	Medium	4	6	9	2	4	25	35
Type IX	Large			6	4	3	13	19
Type X	Minelayers							4
Type XI	U-Cruisers							4
	Total	26	10	19	8	9	72	62
	Already completed	14	21	1	9	12	57	

The investigations of the Planning Committee led OKM to adopt two possibilities for waging naval warfare against Britain. The first was for an attack on Britain's merchant shipping to be carried out with U-boats and pocket battleships. This plan had the advantage that it could be put into execution fairly rapidly, though as an attack on only one front its chances of success were not rated very highly. The second plan, the building of a large fleet, was more costly and would take longer to carry out; but at least it would give Germany a well-balanced navy of real fighting capacity, and thus enable her to wage war not only against Britain's merchant shipping but also against the British fleet, whose strength would be split up by its task of protecting

Oberkommando der Kriegsmarine, abbreviated OKM = German Admiralty.

shipping in many different places simultaneously. Hitler, assuring Grand Admiral Raeder, Supreme Commander of the German Navy, that this fleet would not be needed before 1946, decided in favour of this second, or Z Plan,[2] and steps were taken to put it into operation at once. Orders were given for the immediate building of 6 super-battleships, 3 battle cruisers, 6 light cruisers and an appropriate number of light craft. In addition to the 72 U-boats already completed or in course of construction, this plan proposed the building of 27 U-cruisers, 47 large U-boats (Type IX), 75 medium U-boats (Type VII) and 28 small U-boats (Type II).

Dönitz, as commander of Germany's U-boat arm, was not in favour of these proposals. He was afraid that Britain would not stand idly by and watch the completion of such a big naval-building programme – with the result, he feared, that war might break out before its completion. In that case, Germany would have neither her fleet nor an adequate number of U-boats. On the basis of map manœuvres carried out during the winter of 1938–9, Dönitz had come to the conclusion that he would need at least 300 ocean-going U-boats, of which about 100 ought to be kept in the actual area of operations, if Germany were to have any chance of winning real success in her supply warfare against escorted convoys.[3] He still felt that Type VII, the medium-sized U-boat, was best suited to this purpose, and he proposed that it should be built in a proportion of 75:25 to all other U-boats. But it was not until after exercises simulating operations against enemy convoys in the summer of 1939, which conclusively proved his point, that he succeeded in persuading OKM to accept his views. However, before anything could be done about it, war actually broke out, and found the German Navy quite unprepared to wage the envisaged war against Britain's supply lines. The planned battleships and cruisers were not yet ready, and so far the German Navy consisted of only 3 pocket-battleships and 57 U-boats; and only 2 of the pocket-battleships and 23 of the submarines were ready for immediate service in the Atlantic.

The Battle of the Atlantic 1939 to 1942
Individual Operations in British Waters

In the first phase of the Battle of the Atlantic (September 1939 to March 1940),[4] those German U-boats which were ready for action operated individually in the eastern North Atlantic between Gibraltar and the Hebrides, with the focal point of their attack to the west of the English Channel and the Bay of Biscay, where the Allied Atlantic shipping lanes began to bunch together. The three attempts which were made in the first autumn and winter of the war to put the tactical ideas developed before the war into operation, and to attack Allied convoys with groups of U-boats controlled by a strategic command on land and directly commanded by a tactical commander in one of the U-boats, were a failure because the number of U-boats in the operational area at any one time was too small. The few new U-boats coming into service were only enough to make good losses, and to keep the number of U-boats capable of operating in the Atlantic more or less stable at twenty or so. But, apart from the first strong wave in September 1939, there were rarely more than a third of them actually at sea at any one time, because of the excessive period they had to lie in dock while their teething troubles were being dealt with, owing to insufficient shipyard workers having been allotted to U-boat repair work. Because of the long voyage which had to be made round Britain, there were rarely more than six or eight U-boats in the area of operations at the same time; usually there were between three and five, and sometimes even fewer. Despite excellent individual achievements, real success was impossible with so few U-boats, particularly because of the limits on U-boat activity imposed by international law,[5] which were withdrawn only gradually. Frequently, too, the torpedoes failed to function.

These U-boat operations in the first phase of the Battle of the Atlantic succeeded in sinking 148 ships with a total GRT of 678,130. For some months they were supplemented by operations carried out in the North and South Atlantic by the pocket-battleships *Deutschland* and *Admiral Graf Spee*, which sank 57,051 GRT of Allied shipping; by the operations of smaller U-boats with torpedoes and mines against shipping off the east coast of Britain (267,443 GRT); by minefields laid by destroyers (226,989 GRT); and by mines laid and bombs dropped by the Luftwaffe in November and December 1939 (64,596 GRT).[6]

In April 1940 the war against Britain's supply lines was interrupted by the necessity for concentrating all available Atlantic and North Sea U-boats to co-operate in the invasion of Norway. These U-boat operations were a complete failure. A great number of attacks were launched against enemy battleships, cruisers and troop transports, but although they were pressed home with great daring and determination they all failed because the depth-keeping mechanism fitted to their torpedoes did not function accurately, and because the magnetic fusing mechanism failed owing to insufficient tests of these new types of weapons under war-time conditions.[7] The temporary uncertainty concerning the reason for these torpedo failures, and the resulting flow of orders and counter-orders, created confusion and undermined the confidence of U-boat commanders and their crews; and Dönitz had some difficulty in re-establishing their fighting spirit and determination. His efforts to rekindle their enthusiasm were assisted by the fact that in June and the beginning of July, after the pause imposed by the necessary overhaul after the Norwegian undertaking in May, the U-boats arriving in their operational areas to the west of the English Channel and the Bay of Biscay found a large number of promising targets. Allied escorts were being strained to the limit by the necessity of evacuating troops from the French mainland, and ordinary Allied shipping was inadequately protected. As a result, almost all the U-boats returned home with many sinkings to their credit.[8] The general development of the military situation in Europe, together with the prospect of obtaining new U-boat bases on the French Atlantic coast, did the rest, and morale in the U-boat service rose buoyantly so that when it entered the second phase of the Battle of the Atlantic (July 1940 to March–May 1941), spirits were high.

Pack Operations in the North Channel

The situation had now changed very considerably.[9] It was true that for the time being there was no hope of any rapid increase in the number of U-boats available; in fact even a reduction had to be temporarily accepted, in order that the U-boats made available in this way could take part in the big training programme which was to supply the crews for the rapidly increasing number of U-boats to come into commission from the spring of 1941 onwards. However, this reduction in the number of U-boats available was made up for by a considerable shortening in the length of time they needed to reach their operational areas – thanks to the acquisition of new bases on the French Atlantic coast. In the same way, the time necessary for repairs and overhaul was also cut down, so that it was now possible to get more out of each U-boat. Germany's U-boat warfare was still further favoured by the fact that from July 1940, owing to the danger from the air, the British were compelled to re-route all their incoming and outgoing shipping through the North Channel between Ireland and Scotland. A shipping bottle-neck inevitably developed here, and U-boats,` operating either close together or in more open order, usually found good targets very quickly, used up their torpedoes and returned home. The summer and autumn months of 1940 also offered particularly favourable opportunities for U-boat warfare against Britain's convoys because strong destroyer forces had to be kept in readiness to defend the country against the threat of invasion. However, this very favourable situation could not be taken full advantage of, owing to the lack of effective long-range air reconnaissance, which could have spotted convoys bringing important supplies to Britain while they were far enough out in the Atlantic to allow the U-boats between twenty-four and forty-eight hours to concentrate and intercept them before they entered the North Channel. The few U-boats available – usually there were less than ten in the operational area at one time, and two of these had to take up positions far to the west of the area to serve as 'weather ships' – were not in a position to close the gap completely, particularly in view of their limited horizon. It was therefore largely a matter of luck if a U-boat sighted a convoy early enough for it to summon the other U-boats by sending out shadowing reports and homing signals. The few convoy battles which did come about, and the high tonnage losses sustained by the British[10] in them, are quite sufficient to give some idea of what could have been done in these months with effective long-range reconnaissance and more U-boats. An attempt to make up for the lack of U-boats by using Italian submarines, which had been transferred from their bases in the Mediterranean to Bordeaux in September, was a failure. In the few months during which this was tried out, there were actually more Italian submarines than German vessels available, but not once did any group operations take place against a convoy sighted by Italian submarines. This was primarily because they were accustomed to the quite different tactical conditions of the Mediterranean, and their crews were not trained for such closely controlled and mobile operations. Dönitz therefore abandoned the attempt to organize tactical co-operation, and from December 5th the Italians were left to operate on their own within the general framework, and some of their submarines did in fact register outstanding successes.[11]

At the beginning of January 1941, when the 1st Wing of 40 Bomber Group, which was equipped with long-range Focke-Wulf Condor aircraft, was allotted for tactical co-operation, a new opportunity for improving U-boat tactics arose. However, there were very few such long-range aircraft available, and in consequence only one or two reconnaissance flights as far as the North Channel were possible daily. It always took quite a while before several U-boats could be brought in simultaneously against outbound convoys sighted there; and, in addition, operations were greatly hampered by uncertain navigation on the part of the aircraft.[12] In the meantime, too, the British convoy system had succeeded in emerging from its weakest period, because the disappearance of the invasion threat had released convoy escort ships from the Channel for service elsewhere. Further, the numbers available for escort duties had been increased by taking over fifty old US destroyers, and by putting into service modern anti-submarine corvettes built in Britain and in Canada. There was also a noticeable increase in Coastal Command patrolling, and this forced U-boats more and more out of coastal waters. The result was that U-boat operations in February and March 1941 were by no means as successful as those in the autumn of 1940 and it soon became clear that the diminishing effectiveness of the individual U-boats was not, in fact, due to the exceptionally long period of bad weather in the winter months. The sudden loss of five U-boats in March, including three of the most successful commanders,[13] after a period of three months in which not a single U-boat had been lost, made it clear to Commander U-boats that any further operations close to the North Channel were unlikely to be profitable, and so the U-boats were compelled to shift their positions farther westward.

With this, the second phase of the Battle of the Atlantic came to an end; and, as the table opposite illustrates, all in all it was the most successful not only for the U-boat arm, but for all the other forces engaged, including the auxiliary cruisers everywhere, the battleships and cruisers in the North and Central Atlantic, and the long-range planes operating in the waters to the west of Britain and as far as Gibraltar. The results obtained in all these ways were supplemented by minelaying, attacks by the Luftwaffe and light surface forces on British shipping around the British Isles (547,886 GRT), and the Italian successes in the Mediterranean (68,520 GRT).

Allied and Neutral Shipping Losses in the Second Phase of the Battle of the Atlantic

Month	German U-boats	Italian submarines	Auxiliary Cruisers	Heavy Surface Units	Long-range Bombers
July 1940	38—194,922		11—67,494		
August 1940	54—283,386	2—13,593	11—61,767		2— 8,973
September 1940	52—265,737	3— 7,669	8—65,386		
October 1940	61—344,513	4—15,591	4—30,539		2— 6,420
November 1940	34—173,995	1— 4,866	9—74,923	8—60,332	7—34,806
December 1940	39—229,501	7—27,976	5—25,904	3—20,971	1— 4,360
January 1941	17— 98,702	7—41,150	20—78,484	3—18,783	15—61,068
February 1941	42—207,649	3—14,705	1— 7,031	16—76,752	22—79,955
March 1941	44—243,622	2— 7,863	4—28,707	17—79,838	3—12,307
Ships	381	29	73	47	52
	2,042,027	133,413	440,235	256,496	207,889

Combing Pack Operations across the North Atlantic

In the third phase of the Battle of the Atlantic (April to December 1941),[14] the brunt of the campaign was more and more clearly borne by the U-boat arm. The auxiliary cruisers now began to suffer their first losses,[15] and the successes per ship and time at sea began to decline. In particular, the operations of heavy surface units[16] against the Atlantic convoy routes came to an end with the return of the battle cruisers *Scharnhorst* and *Gneisenau*, the heavy cruiser *Admiral Hipper* and the pocket-battleship *Admiral Scheer* in March, the failure of the *Bismarck* and *Prinz Eugen* group in May,[17] and the mopping up of the far-flung supply organization of ships and tankers by British naval search groups in June.[18] At the same time, the use of long-range aircraft against British shipping was countered by catapulting Hurricane fighters into the air from British merchant vessels, by the increased provision of anti-aircraft guns, and by the appearance in September of the first auxiliary aircraft carrier *Audacity*, on the Gibraltar route. As a result of improved defences, the light surface craft, aircraft and minelaying around the British Isles also met with fewer successes (256,152 GRT), although this decline was more than made up for by increased German and Italian successes in the Mediterranean, particularly during the campaigns in the Balkans and against Crete (481,153 GRT), and by heavy Allied shipping losses in the Far East when Japan entered the war in December (431,673 GRT).

At the beginning of 1941, a number of large (Type IX) U-boats were put into commission, and towards the end of February three of these vessels were despatched to the Freetown area. Two previous experiments with U-boats operating singly had shown that such vessels could be supplied from surface ships. Four more were sent out in the following April. The voyages of this first wave of 'south U-boats', which replenished their supplies of fuel, torpedoes and so on from auxiliary cruisers and supply ships, were amongst the most successful submarine operations of the whole war.[19]

**Allied and Neutral Shipping Losses in the Third Phase of the
Battle of the Atlantic**

1941	German U-boats	Italian submarines	Auxiliary Cruisers	Heavy Surface Units	Long-range Bombers
April	46—260,414	3—18,052	7—56,885		10—35,502
May	63—349,620	4—25,918	3—15,002		4—25,121
June	60—305,734	6—20,376	4—17,759		4— 7,762
July	17— 61,471	7—43,851	1— 5,792		
August	22— 67,638	2— 9,902	3—21,378		2— 7,189
September	54—208,822	1— 434	2— 8,734		
October	33—176,059				4— 4,103
November	18— 85,028				
December	12— 67,603				
Ships	325	23	20		24
Tonnage	1,582,389	118,533	125,550		79,677

The good results obtained in the south up to June tended to conceal the change which had come about in the meantime on the North Atlantic convoy routes. On March 26th, the U-boat patrol-lines, which had previously been posted in the relatively narrow area before the North Channel, were shifted into the area to the south and west of Iceland.[20] The British convoy routes were drawn as far north as possible, in order to take every advantage of the protection afforded by RAF Coastal Command stationed in Iceland. In addition, the British Admiralty now began to disperse the convoy routes as far as possible over the central North Atlantic. Owing to this tactic, and to the fact that there were still too few U-boats available, though their numbers were now gradually beginning to rise, it was impossible to cover all the convoy routes effectively, particularly as the British were beginning to take increasing advantage of their radio D/F service to locate and avoid recognized U-boat lines. Towards the end of May, thanks to a big increase in the numbers of available escort vessels, the British succeeded in giving their convoys protection along the whole of the North-Atlantic route. As the technique of oil-fuelling at sea was not yet adequately developed, the escorting vessels had to be relieved several times on the voyage, but nevertheless they greatly hampered the U-boat attacks, particularly when some of the convoy vessels were equipped with the first, still somewhat primitive, radar devices.

On May 8th, in an effort to improve the technique of convoy locating, Dönitz began an experiment with a wider search sweep instead of the previous more stationary patrol-lines, but this new tactic produced only sporadic successes.[21] On June 21st, after having waited patiently for a long time but in vain for sightings, it was decided to spread the available U-boats out more loosely over a wide area of the North Atlantic, in the hope of making it more difficult for the convoys to avoid the U-boat patrol-lines. After a few days this did lead to a big convoy battle,[22] but the difficulty of bringing U-boats up quickly enough over great distances to within range of their targets before the enemy had time to strengthen his convoy protection was still very great, and for this reason this form of operation also proved unsatisfactory.

By this time, the Condor aircraft of the Luftwaffe's 40 Bomber Group had become more experienced, and they had managed to improve their navigational and shadowing methods considerably, so from the middle of July a new attempt at tactical co-operation between the Luftwaffe and the U-boat arm was carried out against the Gibraltar–Britain route, which lay well within air range. Since the end of May, Italian submarines had been operating with some success in the southern sector of this area. Almost every week after this convoys were sighted – either through the good offices of agents in southern Spain, air reconnaissance or U-boats – and each time packs of from six to twelve U-boats were sent into action against them. However, these convoys were usually so strongly protected (for example, HG.73 by ten escorting vessels instead of the usual four or five) that despite air reconnaissance contact was repeatedly lost, and very few commanders, and then only the most experienced, were able to manœuvre their U-boats into position for an attack.[23] Later, it was also realized that the successes obtained by these attacks were being grossly over-estimated owing to the failure to recognize that this route was used almost exclusively by rather small vessels (from 1,000 to 3,000 GRT). All in all, therefore, the months of July and August saw the North Atlantic U-boat operations sink to their lowest level of effectiveness, and it looked almost as though the defence had won the race against the attack, particularly as successes in the south, where U-boat operations had previously been very promising indeed, were no longer obtainable because shipping kept within the Pan-American security zone, which was respected by Germany.[24]

It was during this period that the increasing number of U-boats in action began to make itself felt for the first time. In August, the new U-boats coming off the stocks allowed the formation of a 'North Group', in addition to the packs operating on the Gibraltar route. When this 'North Group' had grown to between fifteen and seventeen vessels, Dönitz ordered them to comb the area from Iceland in the direction of Greenland–Newfoundland. The result of this operation was the sighting of Convoy SC. 42 off Cape Farewell, and the biggest convoy battle so far took place. Twenty ships were sunk out of a total of sixty-three before fog descended to save the convoy from annihilation. This success encouraged Dönitz to form further such groups, and in the following weeks up to the beginning of November they sailed across the North Atlantic in four successive waves; they took part in a number of operations against convoys, but without repeating the great success achieved against SC. 42.[25]

United States Intervention

While all this was going on, there were a number of very serious incidents with US warships.[26] In carrying out Roosevelt's policy to undertake everything 'short of war' to help Britain, a policy which had already led to the Destroyer–Naval Base Deal in September 1940 and to the Lend Lease Act of March 1941, the US Navy was doing everything it could to lighten the British Navy's burden without actual participation in the war. In order to justify the presence and behaviour of US warships in the western North Atlantic, the frontier of the Western Hemisphere, which had previously been laid down as the Pan-American security zone, was now pushed farther eastward: on April 18th to 30° W, and on June 14th to 26° W. US warships had instructions to shadow all Axis vessels sighted to the west of this line, and to make running reports concerning their positions. On July 7th, US troops landed in Iceland to relieve the British units stationed there. On July 15th, Icelandic waters were included in the Western Hemisphere, and a strong force was based on Hvalfjord to guard the Denmark Strait through which all the heavy German surface units had formerly broken through into the Atlantic.[27] Further, Allied ships were able to join the US supply convoys to Iceland, which used the same routes as the British transatlantic convoys.

That in these circumstances there had been no serious incidents in July and August was due on the one hand to the fact that the main weight of U-boat operations up to this time had been on the Gibraltar route, and on the other to the strict instructions issued personally by Hitler that incidents were to be avoided under all circumstances.[28] Because it was impossible to distinguish the former US destroyers now sailing under the British flag from their US sister ships, the grotesque situation arose of Dönitz having to forbid any action against destroyers – which were, of course, the worst enemies of the U-boats – except in self-defence.[29] At the Atlantic Conference between Roosevelt and Churchill in August, it was agreed that from the middle of September US escorts should guard the fast British HX and ON Convoys to the west of 26° W. And on September 4th the *Greer* incident[30] provided Roosevelt with the pretext to issue his 'open fire' orders, giving permission for US warships to attack Axis ships. Towards the end of September and at the beginning of October, the North Atlantic routes were more or less free of U-boats, which had returned to base after a number of convoy battles, so it was October 17th before any serious incident occurred. It was then that the US destroyer *Kearny*, which had intervened with its escort group in a convoy battle which had been going on for over thirty-six hours, was torpedoed by *U. 568*.[31] A fortnight later, *U. 552* torpedoed and sank the US destroyer *Reuben James*, which was part of the escort of Convoy HX. 156. With these incidents, relations between Germany and the United States became so strained as to be practically indistinguishable from a state of war, though war was not declared.

Further incidents were avoided only because the critical situation in the

Mediterranean required the sending of a strong force of U-boats there, and the concentration of every available Atlantic U-boat in the Gibraltar area. This concentration of U-boats meant that in December, when the Japanese attacked Pearl Harbour, an action which came as a complete surprise to Germany's leaders, there was not a single U-boat available for speedy despatch to the American coast – although previously, on September 19th, 1941, Dönitz had suggested starting the war against the United States with a 'Paukenschlag', or 'a roll of drums'.[32] In fact Dönitz had to ask urgently again and again before he was able to secure the gradual release of the submarines from the Gibraltar area, where, owing to a concentrated defence, the supply war was proving unprofitable both in terms of tonnage sunk and losses sustained.[33]

How Dönitz Used his U-boat Strength

For Dönitz, the ultimate and decisive criterion for the use of the U-boat weapon was the quickest possible sinking of the greatest possible enemy tonnage, and tonnage that was potentially useful to the enemy. As time was working for the enemy, with his steadily growing shipbuilding capacity, and as the number of U-boats available (ninety at the end of December 1941) was still far below what he regarded as the necessary minimum of 300 vessels if any real success were to be obtained, Dönitz felt that to use U-boats for any purpose which would diminish their effectiveness in the tonnage war was bad tactics. He wanted his U-boats to be used 'economically', that is to say, at those points where in the given circumstances they could sink the greatest possible tonnage of enemy shipping in the shortest possible space of time.[34]

However, the German Naval Operations Staff thought it necessary to use U-boats for other tasks occasionally: to create a strategic diversion, for reconnaissance purposes, to protect blockade runners, and so on;[35] and to help in critical situations such as that in the Mediterranean towards the end of 1941 – where their intervention was not without tangible success.[36] But Hitler's intuition – he sensed the danger of a British invasion of Norway after a number of British Commando raids – led to what Dönitz regarded as a useless waste of U-boats on tasks which were not properly their own, at a time when they were urgently needed in the Atlantic.[37]

It is unquestionable that the retention of one-third and more of the number of U-boats available for active service (30 out of 90 at the end of December 1941; 39 out of 115 at the end of March 1942) in the Mediterranean and northern waters, where in view of the much smaller volume of Allied shipping using these areas their effectiveness was, at best, only a fraction of that of the U-boats operating in the Atlantic (GRT per day at sea), very adversely affected the figures for tonnage sunk in the fourth phase of the Battle of the Atlantic (January to July 1942), although the conditions for U-boat operations were once again relatively favourable. It was certainly a blunder to withdraw such a large percentage of the front-line U-boats from the supply war in which they were the only effective weapon left. The U-boats in the Mediterranean and northern waters were kept there primarily as a threat to Allied surface craft, a threat which did tie down strong escort forces. This effect could certainly have been obtained with a considerably smaller number of U-boats; at the same time, surface craft and planes could – if their efforts had been systematically co-ordinated – have produced better results than U-boats in the tonnage war in this particular area.

Individual Operations off North and Central America

It was five weeks after the declaration of war against the United States when the first U-boat arrived off the American coast. Instead of the proposed 'roll of drums', the first attack was delivered by only five U-boats. The activities of these U-boats, which operated individually in relatively large areas, were particularly successful because the US defence completely lacked experience in anti-submarine warfare, and because coastal shipping was still proceeding almost as in peace-time. Dönitz therefore immediately decided to send all available U-boats into this 'virgin area', which had for the time being, despite the long voyage necessary to get there, become the area in which U-boats could most economically operate.[38]

In January and February it was primarily the bigger Type IX U-boats which operated first in the area off Cape Hatteras and then in the Caribbean, and returned home with figures of from three to nine sinkings each. The medium Type VII U-boats, with their limited range, were confined to the sea areas off Newfoundland and Halifax, which were much less profitable hunting-grounds because of the fogs and the stormy weather often met with there, and also because the British defences were stronger and more experienced. However, the engineer officers of these medium-range U-boats soon found ways to increase their fuel storage capacity, and thus their range. They also saved fuel by cruising at the most economical speeds on the way to their operational areas. As a result, at the end of February these U-boats also appeared off New York, in March off Cape Hatteras, and in April even in the Florida Strait, where they achieved considerable success for their size. The latter operations and, indeed, most of the operations of the Type IX U-boats in the Caribbean, the Antilles and the Gulf of Mexico, were made practicable only when the first U-tankers came into service at the end of March.

These U-tankers had been put on the stocks in the spring of 1940, thanks to the foresight of Dönitz, and they came into service just at the moment when it was necessary to send U-boats into areas in which, because of inadequate fuel storage capacity, they would not otherwise have been able to operate long enough to use their full complement of torpedoes, which had been increased by building upper deck compartments.[39] Such a U-tanker was able to carry a reserve of up to 600 tons of fuel, and could thus keep twelve Type VII U-boats supplied for four extra weeks, or five Type IX U-boats supplied for eight extra weeks at sea. In this way, Type VII U-boats were now able to operate in the Antilles area and off West Africa, and, with two refuellings, even in the Caribbean area, while there were now no limits at all to the range of the Type IX U-boats in the Atlantic. The use of these U-tankers meant, in particular, that despite the very considerably longer voyages which were necessary to get to these far-distant seas it was still possible to reckon that at any one time 50 per cent of the U-boats at sea would actually be in their operational areas.

The US defence system took unexpectedly long to adapt itself to the problems created for it by the presence of not more than between eight and fifteen U-boats operating from Halifax to Trinidad.[40] It was weeks before the US authorities even realized that all beacons should be dowsed; and it took months before any kind of black-out was introduced along the coasts, before US merchant captains realized that their irresponsible wireless chatter was providing the U-boats with valuable information, and before there was any real evidence that something was at last being done to introduce some sort of war-time control. It also proved very difficult to keep in check the enthusiasm of private plane and ship owners, who were anxious to take part in the hunt for U-boats. It was only hesitantly that the Americans accepted the assistance offered to them by the British, who, in addition to sending anti-submarine corvettes and planes, also slowed down the rhythm of their North Atlantic convoys organization in order to release escort vessels for the Western Atlantic. It was the end of April before the Americans, pressed all the time by the British, finally began to organize their shipping into convoys; first in the northern section to Cape Hatteras, and then from the middle of May along the whole of the eastern seaboard. The effect of this measure was soon felt. Sightings dropped almost to nil, and in their situation reports U-boat commanders now began to note more and more frequently: 'no traffic'.

These situation reports, which were usually very detailed, together with the reports of the wireless monitoring service, gave Dönitz an idea of the general situation and a basis for his tactics. There was, of course, always the danger that the enemy would succeed in getting a radio bearing on a U-boat sending home such a detailed report; but the risk had to be run, as otherwise it would have been impossible to organize a swift, efficient and elastic policy for using the given U-boat resources at any time in accordance with the current sea-traffic situation.

On May 23rd, Dönitz had to withdraw his U-boats from US coastal waters, where they had been operating so successfully, but the slow reaction of the defence gave him every reason to hope that there would be no fundamental change in the situation for a while, and that in the next new moon period, which was in about a fortnight, he would be able to launch a new offensive with freshly supplied U-boats along the whole American seaboard.[41] However, it was in this period that he ordered the first minelaying operations to be carried out in American coastal waters, and such an action was always a sign that the chances of the submarines were diminishing.

The decline of U-boat successes along the eastern coasts of the United States was compensated for in May and June by particularly outstanding successes on the part of a strong group of Type IX U-boats in the Caribbean Sea, the Gulf of Mexico and the Antilles, where five Italian submarines were also operating with good results.[42] But in July the Americans extended the convoy system to the Caribbean, and in August they finally gathered the various convoy routes into what was known as the 'interlocking convoy system'. Even now, some U-boats managed to get within attacking distance of these convoys, which were guarded chiefly by light escort vessels. However, the development of coastal air patrols began to make life so difficult for U-boats in these waters that they had to be withdrawn to the Trinidad area and eastward, where the favourable conditions created by the bunching of the sea routes lasted for an unexpectedly long time, whereas the defence in the Freetown area, which U-boats now began to work again, recovered relatively quickly after the first unexpected U-boat successes.

U-boat Successes in the Atlantic (January to August 1942)
(Number of Ships and GRT sunk)

Month	US East Seaboard	Gulf of Mexico	Caribbean	Antilles	North Atlantic	Central Atlantic	Italians
January	23—142,320				25—128,718		1— 5,473
February	31—199,695		18— 88,981	5— 18,938	15— 95,617		4—23,670
March	48—274,295		3— 20,131	11— 55,563	8— 26,430	9—52,857	12—74,120
April	43—250,813		7— 49,396	7— 40,564	3— 15,744	2—11,534	3— 16,990
May	34—137,960	26—150,277	29—117,319	19— 85,946	15— 82,879		3—18,833
June	29—132,341	18— 83,444	39—177,625	18—113,369	18— 91,355		6—23,865
July	21—112,910	15— 48,991	12— 60,544	11— 29,685	8— 56,932	15—96,416	
August			20—109,087	21—110,911	38—202,189	16—72,826	5—27,762

Measured by absolute figures for sinkings, the most successful period of the U-boat war against Allied supplies was now over. The losses sustained by the enemy during this period were particularly painful because of the unusually high percentage of big tankers amongst the ships sunk. The result was a strict rationing of domestic petrol consumption in the United States, in order that military needs could be at least approximately satisfied. The supply difficulties of the Allies were increased by other large losses:

(*a*) by losses following on the occupation of southeast Asia by the Japanese (444,736 GRT);

(*b*) by Japanese attacks on Allied supply lines (519,736 GRT);[43]

(*c*) by German auxiliary cruisers (139,135 GRT);

(*d*) by Italo-German action in the Mediterranean (115,291 GRT);[44]

(*e*) by German attacks on the Murmansk convoys (307,831 GRT);[45]

(*f*) by continued sea, air and minelaying operations, despite growing defence measures, in British coastal waters (184,783 GRT).

All Allied strategic planning in the year 1942 was bedevilled by the critical shortage of shipping space, and its brightest prospects were hampered by this factor.[46]

Convoy Battles in the North Atlantic Flare up Again

Operations against convoys occasionally took place as early as the spring of 1942, when U-boats on the way to the American seaboard, or on passage from Norway to France, came across convoys and were able to bring up other U-boats in the neighbourhood.[47] These operations, and the information obtained by the wireless monitoring service, indicated that the convoys were obviously using the Great Circle once more.

In fact as soon as the British realized that U-boats were no longer being systematically used against their convoys they once again began to send them along the shortest route, because for one thing the danger of falling in with U-boats on this route was hardly greater than in other parts of the North Atlantic, and for another the shorter distance saved a good deal of time. This new situation seemed to offer Dönitz an opportunity to make better use of his forces, and he gathered together a number of U-boats which happened to be putting out simultaneously, formed them into a single pack and sent it along the Great Circle route from the North Channel to Newfoundland to comb the area. If the pack fell in with one or more convoys it could rapidly discharge its stock of torpedoes and then turn for home, otherwise it could refuel from a U-tanker to the south of the Newfoundland Bank and continue its voyage down the American seaboard.[48]

On May 11th, even before this first pack, 'Hecht', had fully grouped, a convoy was sighted, and in the first night seven of its ships were sunk. When the six U-boats concerned arrived at their supply tanker on May 25th after a second operation, which had been frustrated by fog, the situation along the US coasts had so deteriorated that Dönitz decided that they should continue their operations on the convoy routes in an eastward direction. Three convoys moving west were sighted successively, and five ships sunk. These experiences, and the results of three operations carried out on the Gibraltar–Freetown route by U-boats which happened to be available, suggested that the prospects for a continuation of the convoy battles were relatively favourable. The reports of U-boat commanders on their return to base confirmed this suggestion. Incidentally, Dönitz always attached great importance to these personal reports by U-boat commanders, and the discussions which followed them were always conducted with great frankness on both sides. It was certainly these uninhibited discussions with his commanders that saved Dönitz from losing contact with the grim realities of front-line action, and helped to forge a bond of union between him and his staff on the one hand, and the commanders and crews of the U-boats on the other.

At the beginning of July, U-boat 'Wolf' pack gathered at a spot about 600 miles to the west of the North Channel to operate in the same way as 'Hecht' pack had done. It was to comb the convoy routes in a westerly direction, and after re-supplying and refuelling it was to proceed, according to the given situation, to the American eastern seaboard or into the Caribbean area. But by the middle of July, it was already quite clear that any operations conducted along the American seaboard, even in the new moon period, were no longer likely to be profitable. Dönitz therefore did not hesitate to draw the appropriate conclusion, and on July 19th orders were issued to shift the focal point of the struggle back to the North Atlantic convoy routes once more. It was easier for him to come to this decision because there was every prospect that after the U-boat flotillas in the Mediterranean and the Arctic Sea had been brought up to strength, there would be an increasing supply of front-line U-boats coming into service, and this would allow the successive formation of new packs to operate to the west of the North Channel.[49]

On the basis of experience in the most recent operations, and in order to commit his available U-boat strength as efficiently and economically as possible in the given situation, Dönitz formulated new rules for the fifth phase of the Battle of the Atlantic (August 1942 to May 1943):[50] to gather the U-boats putting out from Germany and France into a pack on the east side of the North Atlantic, but on the periphery of the area covered by enemy coastal patrols stationed in Northern Ireland and Iceland, and to let the pack move steadily westward combing the most recently noted convoy routes and the routes along which other information suggested that convoys might be met. It was hoped that during this operation the pack would soon come across a convoy moving westward. Should this prove to be the case they could then pursue it across the whole breadth of the Atlantic, and refuel from a U-tanker stationed to the northeast of Bermuda outside the normal traffic routes. The re-supplied U-boats would then form a new patrol-line in the Newfoundland Bank area, in the hope of making contact in the same way with convoys moving eastward. After the end of the convoy battle on the eastern side of the Atlantic, those U-boats still well stocked with fuel could come together to form a new pack, while those U-boats which were short of fuel or torpedoes, or were damaged, could return to their French bases. Dönitz certainly did not agree with the views of Raeder and the German Naval Operations Staff that only the eastward-bound, loaded convoys were worth attacking, because if this view were adopted only one convoy operation per voyage would be possible, and thus the effectiveness of each individual U-boat would decline considerably.

On the basis of this general scheme, which was elastic enough to be adapted to any given situation and to the weather, a three and a half month cycle of convoy battles now began, in which good results alternated with bad according to the weather and the strength of the convoy escorts. These operations, which would last four, six and even eight days, with only short pauses from time to time, imposed a great strain on both commanders and their crews, and demanded a high standard of training and determination; and many of them were, of course, newcomers to the game. When a convoy was reported, the attacking U-boats, in defiance of wind and weather, had then to manœuvre themselves close enough, despite the evasive action taken by the convoy, to launch a surface attack under cover of darkness. But a sudden change of the convoy's course shortly before the attack would frequently frustrate days of effort; or U-boats would be driven away from their prey by the watchfulness of the escort vessels, and contact would be lost. Then the whole operation had to be started again from scratch, often to be defeated finally by the arrival of air cover or the sudden onset of the fog which was so frequent off Newfoundland.[51]

The British soon realized that the expected systematic attacks on convoys had started again, but for some reason or other they did not react to the situation as quickly as Dönitz expected. The biggest difficulties of the Allies were first of all the general shortage of shipping space, which made it necessary to secure the quickest possible turn-round of ships, and secondly the lack of escort vessels. The number of these latter was increasing, but not fast enough to keep pace with the steadily increasing demand for their services everywhere. On the North Atlantic route alone, 78 destroyers and 156 corvettes had to be available if each of the monthly four fast HX. and ON. and two slower SC. and ONS. convoys was to be adequately protected. With an average-sized convoy of 50 ships, at least 7 escort vessels were required so that each 'escort group' had to consist – allowing for the docking periods which were necessary from time to time – of 3 destroyers and 6 corvettes. Because of the shortage of suitable tankers and the inadequate equipment of the escort vessels for refuelling at sea, escort vessels had to be relieved two or three times on the voyage from New York to the North Channel, so that with the narrowest possible calculation of the time stages, eight 'escort groups' were required for each protective stage; in addition, two other groups were needed for the further stage to Iceland. These vessels were based on Halifax and Boston for the western sector (New York–49° W), on St John's and Argentia for the central sector (49° W–22° W), on Hvalfjord for the Iceland sector, and on London-derry, the Clyde and Liverpool for the eastern sector (22° W–North Channel). Despite all the shipbuilding which was going on, it was not always possible to maintain these figures in the second half of 1942, because big convoy operations on the Murmansk route (PQ. 17 in July and PQ. 18 in September) and in the Mediterranean ('Pedestal' in August), and, finally, Operation 'Torch', made further additional demands. Thus until the problem of refuelling at sea was solved, the Allied convoy system had no alternative but to send the convoys along the Great Circle route, and to attempt to evade known U-boat positions by taking minor tactical evasive action.[52]

As long as there was only one U-boat pack of between 12 to 18 vessels operating on the North Atlantic route this was possible, and from the middle of August to the beginning of September this led to rather longer pauses between sightings. But then the number of U-boats in the operational area rose to 20, 30 and (in the middle of October) 40. With these numbers, one or two patrol-lines could be set up simultaneously on both the west and the east side of the North Atlantic, and then by appropriately controlling their movements the observed routes of enemy convoys could be covered. At this time U-boat operations were greatly assisted by the fact that the wireless monitoring service was often able to provide Dönitz with decoded Allied wireless signals indicating the routes followed by convoys, so that U-boats could be directed there in good time.[53]

The result was that in September and October there were a great many convoy battles. If the first sighting took place in the centre of a patrol-line so that the other U-boats were in a favourable position, or if it proved possible to call up a second pack and achieve a concentration of between 15 and 20 U-boats, then the losses of the convoy were usually very heavy but, of course, a storm could always beat up unexpectedly, or fog descend, to put an end to operations and save the convoy. On the other hand, operations which took place as the result of casual sightings were usually much less successful because in such circumstances it was very rarely possible to achieve the necessary concentration of U-boats against the convoy. Whereas in 1940 the presence of anything up to half a dozen U-boats was enough to present the escorting force with insoluble problems, now two or three times that number were able to get at their target only if conditions were favourable. To some extent this was due to the fact that the escorting vessels were now being increasingly equipped with radar.

The Use of U-boats in Distant Waters

While the Type VII U-boats concentrated on the operations against convoys, it was necessary to find new spheres of operation for Type IX U-boats, which on account of their size were easier for the escort vessels to deal with, and therefore less suited to anti-convoy operations. If any particular area became unprofitable for U-boat operations because of Allied defensive measures and the adoption of the convoy system, Dönitz transferred the focal point of operations – always according to his principle of 'economic investment' – to areas where a fair amount of traffic but relatively weaker defence was to be expected. In view of the highly inadequate information available about the conditions to be expected, it was often a question of giving the thing a try-out; sometimes such an experiment would meet with unexpected success: for example, the sending of two U-boats into the St Lawrence River in September. On the other hand, such an experiment could well end in failure, as witness the sending of two U-boats into the Gulf of Guinea in October. In the autumn, U-boat commanders were still finding the most favourable conditions for their operations in the area to the east of Trinidad. On the other hand, the introduction of the convoy system into the Freetown area in October led to a decline of U-boat successes there.

The political, strategic and tactical problems which arose, and the differences of opinion between OKW, the German Naval Operations Staff and Dönitz in connection with this exploitation of 'virgin' areas, were not always very happily settled, as two examples from this period will show.

During the spring of 1942, it became more and more clear that Brazil was not only granting bases on her territory for the use of US air and naval forces, but that she was beginning to arm her merchant vessels. Therefore when, on May 28th, it was officially announced that Brazilian planes had attacked and bombed U-boats, the German Naval Operations Staff asked OKW on the following day for permission to treat all Brazilian shipping as hostile, and to use unrestricted armed force against it. At the same time it instructed Dönitz to draw up a plan for a surprise U-boat attack on the Brazilian coasts in the event of a declaration of war by Brazil. But Hitler was unwilling to wait for this eventuality; he was in favour of declaring war and opening hostilities with a powerful U-boat attack. Dönitz therefore worked out a plan to be put into operation in the period between August 3rd and August 8th, 1942: ten U-boats, supported by one U-tanker, would suddenly penetrate into the harbours of Santos, Rio de Janeiro, Bahia and Recife, destroy all the shipping they could find, and then, after having mined the harbours, operate against merchant shipping along the coasts. In this way Dönitz calculated that his U-boats would be able to sink the greatest possible tonnage in this active and previously untouched area, in which, of course, defensive measures would exist hardly at all. In fact, as far as he was concerned these subsequent sinkings were the only justification for the whole operation. The plan was approved by Hitler on June 17th, but the German Foreign Office objected to it on account of the reaction to be expected from the other still neutral states of South America, and on June 29th Hitler withdrew his approval. The U-boats which had already been sent out to put the plan into execution were diverted to the Caribbean.

During the course of July, attacks by Brazilian planes on U-boats were repeatedly reported; and, in addition, there was further confirmation that the Brazilians were arming their merchant ships. Therefore, on August 7th, as a 'reprisal' the *U. 507* was given 'a free hand' to operate along the coast of Brazil. Between August 15th and August 19th this U-boat sank six vessels.[54] This was politically unwise, because it gave Brazil a welcome pretext for declaring war, which her government did on August 28th; and it greatly damaged Germany in the eyes of the other South American states. If the plan which had been worked out by Dönitz had been carried out as originally intended, it could hardly have had more unfavourable political consequences, and its operational effects in the tonnage war would have been worth while, whereas the operational value of the *U. 507*'s performance was negligible.

The Cape Town area now seemed to offer particularly favourable chances for surprise operations in a 'virgin' field, but Dönitz felt that in view of the 6,000-mile journey which would be necessary before U-boats could operate in this area it would be an economic proposition only if the U-boats concerned seized every chance to attack and sink Allied shipping. On the other hand, the German Naval Operations Staff felt that if the U-boats told to operate in the Cape Town area went in for sinkings on the way the all-important surprise factor would be prematurely sacrificed; and in this case the surprise factor was particularly desirable, because Cape Town was the focal point of the supply line to Egypt. At the same time, it judged the strategic effect of these proposed U-boat operations in direct connection with events in the Mediterranean and on the Eastern Front, whereas Dönitz insisted that the strategic effect lay almost entirely in the quickest possible sinking of the greatest possible amount of tonnage, and that the place where it was sunk was of subordinate importance.[55]

The controversy ended in a compromise, and one which was certainly unfavourable in this particular case: the U-boats sent to the Cape Town area were given permission to attack large warships and troop transports *en route* but not other shipping. In this way they were compelled to let many opportunities pass unexploited, but at the same time they came across an unusually large number of troop transports, and these they attacked,[56] so that the surprise factor was sacrificed after all. However, the effect of this was not so great as it might have been, because the slow and inadequate reaction of the defence off South Africa allowed this first operation, and the following missions of the bigger Type IXd U-boats, to develop very successfully.[57]

Operation 'Torch' and its Effects on the U-boat War

The Allied landings in North Africa on November 8th took the German leaders by surprise.[58] In the first week of November, unusually large numbers of warships and merchant ships were reported to be concentrating at Gibraltar, but all indications seemed to suggest that the Allies were preparing to send a new big supply convoy through to Malta. In accordance with this interpretation of the concentration observed at Gibraltar, 27 Italian and 8 German submarines were now sent to the western Mediterranean. In addition to the 4 U-boats sent to the Mediterranean in October, 6 further U-boats were given orders on November 4th to go there as replacements for lost vessels. Just at this time, Convoy SL. 125 attracted the attention of all available U-boats to the west of Morocco and Gibraltar, and in a seven-day battle 12 of its ships were sunk – with the result that the big invasion convoys with their escort vessels, under way at the same time, got through without even being sighted (apart from one or two reports which were incorrectly interpreted).

As soon as the first news of the landings came in, Dönitz ordered all available U-boats between the Bay of Biscay and Cape Verde to assemble as quickly as possible off the Moroccan coast. After a discussion with the German Naval Operations Staff, a similar order to assemble in the Gibraltar area was sent to all U-boats in the North Atlantic which had good stocks of fuel.[59] When the first U-boats arrived off Casablanca on November 11th, they found land- and carrier-based air patrols and sea defences so strong that only two U-boat commanders managed to penetrate into the Fedala Roads, where they sank four troop transports. The other vessels promptly sought safety in the harbours which had been made available to them in the meantime, so when U-boat reinforcements arrived there were no targets for them.

On November 4th, the 'Dolphin' U-boat pack passed through the Straits of Gibraltar, meeting with surprisingly little difficulty, and, together with U-boats coming from Italian harbours, they attacked ships lying in the Algiers and Oran Roads, and also the first of the returning convoys.[60] The U-boats brought back from the North Atlantic arrived on November 12th. One or two of these U-boats, whose commanders were particularly experienced, were fortunate in their attacks on warships and merchant shipping,[61] but unusually strong air patrols and efficient naval defences forced the others to dive for safety again and again. The losses thus occasioned, and the increasing frequency of reports from U-boat commanders concerning hot pursuit and damage to their boats, compelled Dönitz to issue orders on November 18th and again on November 21st for the U-boats, assembled under the code-name 'West Wall', to withdraw westwards, at first only a little, but then considerably farther. In this situation, the instructions of the German Naval Operations Staff that twenty U-boats should operate to the west of Morocco and Gibraltar, and that further Atlantic U-boats should be sent into the Mediterranean, no longer made any sense.

In the meantime, Dönitz had received reports of successes from the commanders of those U-boats with a limited fuel storage reserve which had remained in the Atlantic and made contact with Convoy ONS. 144. He immediately came to the conclusion that the Allies had been compelled to reduce the escort strength of their Atlantic convoys for the benefit of the invasion convoys, and that therefore for the time being there were particularly favourable opportunities for U-boat operations on the sea routes from the United States to Britain. Such opportunities had to be exploited at once. However, Naval Operations Staff could not make up its mind to grant his repeated requests in this matter, because it regarded sinkings obtained against the supply convoys to North Africa as much more important. Finally, on November 26th another compromise was arrived at: Dönitz was allowed to sweep the route America–Gibraltar westwards with the remainder of the 'West Wall' U-boats. However, in view of the facts that only very few of the U-boats were still ready for action, that little reliable information was available concerning traffic on this route, and that the sea areas to be combed were very wide, it was clear that no very great degree of success could be hoped for except by chance.[62]

The Convoy Battles of the Winter 1942–43

After a search lasting several weeks, during which one or two ships sailing singly were sighted and sunk, but no convoy was contacted, Naval Operations Staff finally (December 23rd) withdrew the orders which kept the U-boats tied to the Gibraltar area. Together with losses and damage, and the sending of vessels into the Mediterranean, this policy resulted in an 'absence of U-boats' in the North Atlantic in the second half of November. The situation was made worse by the fact that those U-boats which had attacked Convoy ONS. 144 were down to their last few hundred gallons of fuel, and stormy weather made their refuelling very difficult. It was only at the beginning of December that it became possible to form new active packs in the North Atlantic by sending out U-boats from French and German bases. But by this time the Allies had got over their temporary weakness in this area, and the first operation, against Convoy HX. 217, was a failure, despite the fact that it was helped by a new special apparatus installed on board one of the attacking U-boats which could pick up conversations between the escort vessels, and although it proved possible to bring a total of twenty-two U-boats into action. Visibility was bad, and many of the U-boats did not succeed in sighting the convoy at all before they were driven off altogether by the arrival of air patrols in unusually large numbers. In the two following weeks, U-boat operations, based to some extent on Allied code messages deciphered by the wireless monitoring service, continued to be a failure, but this was chiefly on account of heavy storms with hail and snow. It was only towards the end of December that a new, important success was obtained. When mist suddenly lifted, a U-boat pack which had been following Convoy ONS. 154 for several days unexpectedly found itself within the outer defences of the convoy, and the inner defences were not strong enough to deal with the swift succession of attacks the U-boats were able to launch.[63]

As most of the U-boats involved had now used all their torpedoes and had to turn for home, there was once again a pack of only thirteen U-boats in the operational area when the New Year opened. Their numbers were insufficient to make sightings, particularly as the British had returned once more to their previous tactic of spreading the convoy routes over the whole of the North Atlantic.

This was made possible by the fact that the number of escort vessels available was steadily increasing, but also because escort vessels could now be refuelled from tankers in the convoy, and the 'escort groups' could be used much more rationally and effectively. At first Dönitz had put down the lack of sightings in this period to the succession of troughs of low pressure which moved over the Atlantic more frequently than ever this winter, but by the middle of January he realized that the British had returned to their old tactics – incidentally no one in Germany had any idea why they had abandoned them for so long.[64] Dönitz hoped to be able to cope with the return of this previous situation towards the end of January when he would have considerably more U-boats available; and, in fact, by January 22nd it proved possible to form three packs of 7, 17 and 18 U-boats. But once again heavy storms upset his plans, and two convoys slipped through unsighted despite the fact that many U-boats spent days searching for them. A few days later the *U. 456*, which was on her way out into the Atlantic, fell in by chance with Convoy HX. 224, shadowed it for three days amidst heavy storms, and then managed to attack successfully. A seaman who was fished out of the water was interrogated, and his incautious replies were immediately radioed to Dönitz, and proved to fit in with his daily checked convoy time-table. Thanks to this unexpected information, it proved possible to concentrate twenty U-boats against the following slow Convoy SC. 118. In a bitter convoy battle which lasted for five days the attacking U-boats succeeded, despite all the efforts of an unusually strong escort force of 12 vessels supported by increasing air cover, in sinking 13 ships. 3 of the U-boats were themselves destroyed, and 2 others severely damaged either by bombs or depth-charges.

For the first time after such a big operation, there was now no 'absence of U-boats', thanks to a stream of reinforcements arriving from France and Germany which quickly filled the gaps. In the second half of February, a pack returning home and another pack on the way out were involved in convoy operations, but owing to heavy seas and unfavourable starting positions the results of these operations were not satisfactory. But at the same time the radio bearings on the defensive air patrols gave away the position of Convoy ON. 166, which was pursued for over a thousand miles by a U-boat pack. In all, fourteen of its ships were sunk. It was possible to carry on these three operations simultaneously thanks to the presence of two U-tankers, and from February 21st to March 5th no fewer than twenty-seven U-boats were refuelled in this way.

During these winter months, U-boat operations in the more distant area of the Atlantic had greatly declined. For example, there were very few U-boats operating to the east of Trinidad, off Freetown and along the South African coast; and it was only towards the end of January that a new U-boat pack arrived in these waters. Towards the end of January 1943, it was only off the coast of Brazil that there were more U-boats than before. In fact, Dönitz regarded it as useful to despatch another pack together with a U-tanker into this still relatively favourable area. On its way out, this pack fell in with Convoy TM. 1 off the Azores, and in operations which were waged with great skill and a good deal of luck the convoy, which was on its way from Trinidad to Gibraltar, lost seven out of a total of nine tankers. As some of these tankers were hit five or six times by torpedoes from different U-boats before they sank, the U-boat commanders unwittingly exaggerated their success in their reports. As a result, Dönitz decided that operations against convoys in the Azores area were likely to prove profitable. However, although the pack was strengthened to fourteen U-boats he had to recognize after many weeks of fruitless search that the problem of making contact outside the range of enemy air-cover was a very difficult one indeed, in view of the wide possibilities of evasion at the disposal of the enemy; at the same time, mobile operations nearer to the shipping bottle-neck of Gibraltar were no longer profitable because air patrols equipped with radar were now too strong and active there.[65]

Culmination and Turning Point in the Battle of the Atlantic
(Spring 1943)

How the Germans saw the Situation

German experiences in the winter convoy battles had suggested that though conditions for U-boat operations against Allied convoys were becoming increasingly difficult, it was still possible to achieve successes given a sufficient number of U-boats. Dönitz, who had in the meantime been appointed Supreme Commander of Germany's Navy in succession to Grand Admiral Raeder, was determined to meet this situation by an intensified U-boat building programme. Thanks to his new position and to the relationship of trust and confidence he managed to establish with Hitler,[66] Dönitz soon succeeded in obtaining the necessary personnel and material. But was there any sound basis for his confidence?

The tonnage war was a monstrous race between the sinking of Allied shipping, particularly by U-boats, and the shipbuilding capacity of the Allied shipyards. According to an estimate drawn up by the German Naval Operations Staff in the summer of 1942, the latter would amount to approximately seven million GRT during 1942. Actually the shipyards of Great Britain, the British Empire and the United States built 7,182,000 GRT in that period, so the estimate was very accurate. Thus if the shipping space at the disposal of the enemy was to be reduced, at least 600,000 GRT would have to be sunk monthly. Figures available to the German Naval Operations Staff at the beginning of 1943 suggested that total Allied shipping losses in 1942 had been 11,667,000 GRT.[67] But these figures proved to be exaggerated, and in reality the losses had been 7,699,000 GRT, so that although the target of 600,000 GRT monthly seemed to have been exceeded by almost 400,000 GRT, it was actually exceeded by only 41,600 GRT. Figures drawn up by the German Naval Operations Staff estimated that Allied shipyards would build 10·8 million GRT in 1943 (the actual figure was 12,384,000 GRT), so that a monthly average of 900,000 GRT would have to be sunk in order to prevent any increase in the shipping space available to the enemy. But even this figure was below the average monthly sinkings thought to have been obtained in 1942. Taking into consideration the fact that very little change had taken place in the percentage of destroyed U-boats or in the effectiveness of the individual U-boats since the summer of 1942, and as the number of U-boats available for operations on the North Atlantic convoy routes was rapidly rising, it was not unreasonable to suppose that it would still be possible to wage the tonnage war successfully in the future.[68]

However, although his general estimate of the situation was favourable for continued U-boat activity, Dönitz did not fail to recognize that there were dangers, though they were as yet still on the horizon, and he did not omit to underline them.[69] They referred chiefly to the technical progress being made by the Allies in anti-submarine warfare. Clearly, this progress had to be countered in good time. However, it was by no means an easy matter, because the new technical departures introduced by the Allies made themselves felt only in action. The careful training of U-boat commanders to observe every little detail of any change in the behaviour of the enemy and to report it back at once, together with the patient sifting and study of all the numerous incoming reports, was all that Germany's own scientists and technicians had as a basis on which they could develop their own counter-measures.

The biggest headache for the U-boat Command was the system of radar location now being increasingly used by air patrols. Even in the early summer of 1942, U-boats on their nightly surface cruises in the Bay of Biscay frequently found themselves suddenly and unexpectedly picked out by searchlights from patrolling planes and subjected to bombing attacks. This first Allied air offensive against the U-boats was frustrated by equipping them with the simple 'Metox' receiver which picked up the impulses of the ASV. II radar device (wave-length 169 cm) used by the British at the time. By the beginning of October, all U-boats were so equipped. At the same time, this 'Metox' receiver allowed U-boats to evade radar location by hostile surface craft. However, reports which began to come in in February 1943 gave rise to the suspicion that the enemy was now using some other method of detection for which the 'Metox' apparatus offered no protection.[70]

This innovation appeared particularly menacing because the few Ju–88 C7's which were allotted to the Commander Air Forces Atlantic were hopelessly inferior to the British Beaufighters, and were no longer in a position to provide the U-boats with protection during their voyage across the Bay of Biscay. The Luftwaffe was unable to make better aircraft available. As a counter-measure, the U-boats were then equipped with more powerful anti-aircraft guns, first with two 2-cm flak 38, instead of one 2-cm flak C/30, but this proved ineffective against the heavy four-engined Allied bombers and flying-boats.[71]

The range of these planes steadily increased throughout the year 1942, so that the 'hole', 'black pit', or 'air gap', in the Atlantic where the convoy battles took place grew smaller and smaller. The result was that less and less time was available for attacking the convoys, and as experience had shown that the best time for attacking was in the first two nights before the enemy had a chance of bringing up reinforcements for his escort groups, it became more and more important for the convoys to be picked up as early as possible, whichever side they were leaving from. Unfortunately it was still not possible to count on any long-range air reconnaissance for this purpose. The very few machines which might have performed such work, the He–177s and the BV–222s, were either still coping with their teething troubles or were being used fully elsewhere. But the increased range of the enemy air patrols, and their equipment with radar devices, meant that the U-boat patrol-lines could more easily be located and therefore evaded by the convoys. On the other hand, to adopt a more open order would have been tactically unfavourable, and have offered much less chance of sightings. All that remained, therefore, was to make it more difficult for the convoys to evade the U-boat patrol-lines by increasing the number of U-boats operating, and extending the lines. In order to obtain as quickly as possible the increased number of U-boats necessary for this purpose, Dönitz decided to use the new Type IX U-boats, which were now coming into the Atlantic, on the North Atlantic route.[72]

From the standpoint of improved technique, the introduction of the new FAT (*flächenabsuchender Torpedo*, or zigzag runner) and a new magnetic torpedo pistol in December promised to increase the accuracy of torpedo attack from a longer range and from less favourable angles.

Operative and Technical Problems of the Allies

In order to counter Germany's U-boat offensive in US waters, and the resultant heavy losses of Allied shipping, and to meet the threatened flare-up of convoy battles in the North Atlantic, the summer of 1942 saw the formation of the Anti-U–boat Warfare Committee in Britain. In addition to various Ministers, Chiefs of Staff, US representatives and so on, a number of scientists were co-opted on to this committee, which was under the chairmanship of Churchill himself. At the first meeting of the new committee in November, Churchill declared that it was formed to step up anti-submarine warfare, to wage it under unified leadership and according to uniform principles, and to see that the required numbers of ships and planes and the required amount of materials were made available.[73]

It had been quite clear for a long time that as far as Britain was concerned the most dangerous weapon the enemy had was the submarine, but opinions as to how this menace could best be countered were by no means unanimous. It had even taken some time before Britain's naval leaders were entirely convinced that the best way of meeting the U-boat peril was by the introduction of the convoy system. And even when by the end of 1942, and particularly after the impressive experiences of that year, it was established beyond all doubt that the convoy system did offer the best protection for shipping and that it really did keep down losses from U-boat action, no naval officer or RAF pilot was particularly happy with a defensive mission in which he stood a chance of coming face to face with the enemy only on the tenth, twentieth or perhaps even fiftieth mission – and perhaps even not at all! In consequence there were repeated demands – particularly from the RAF – to be relieved of 'the useless attrition' of convoy duties in order to fight the U-boats more offensively.

At the beginning of February, Air Chief Marshal Sir Philip Joubert was succeeded as A.O.C.-in-C. Coastal Command by Air Marshal Slessor (later Sir John), who immediately instructed the RAF Operations Research Station to get to work on a statistical analysis of the air missions flown from June 1942 to February 1943. A break-down of this analysis showed that in this period an average of twenty-nine hours flying on convoy protection duties resulted in a U-boat sighting, whereas the so-called offensive missions flown as part of the patrolling operations over the Bay of Biscay ('Bay Patrol') up to September required an average of 164 hours flying time for one sighting. And after October (that is, after the general equipment of U-boats with the 'Metox' apparatus), the Bay Patrol average was very greatly increased, to 312 flying hours for one sighting.[74]

The result of these investigations clearly confirmed the contention of Commander-in-Chief Western Approaches (C.-in-C. WA), Admiral Sir Percy Noble, and his successor (from November 1942) Admiral Sir Max Horton, that the best way to fight the U-boat was still through the convoy system.

However, as long as the number of escort vessels available for each individual convoy was small, the tactic of fighting the U-boat through the convoy system had its limitations. For example, if the convoy escort commander had reason to fear further U-boat attacks he was unable to release a single one of his few escort vessels to chase a located U-boat right up to the kill. He had to content himself with forcing the U-boat to dive and withdraw, so that for the time being it no longer represented a danger to the convoy it was his duty to protect, while keeping his weak forces together for fear of a further U-boat attack. There is little doubt that very many U-boats owed their escape from apparently hopeless situations to this tactical necessity imposed on their enemy, who had to break off the pursuit and return to his position to protect the convoy.

This very unsatisfactory situation led to the idea of the support group, which consisted of a number of anti-submarine vessels operating independently without any specific objectives to defend, and which could therefore be used at will to go to the assistance of particularly threatened convoys. Ships belonging to these 'support groups' would be able to keep tabs on a once located U-boat and 'starve it out', so to speak, to the kill. It was not until September 1942, that the number of escort vessels available allowed Admiral Sir Percy Noble to form such a group, and it was placed under the command of one of Britain's most experienced U-boat hunters, Captain F. J. Walker. But very soon after this came Operation 'Torch' and the demands it involved upset the support group plan – much to the regret of Churchill, who had set his heart on it.[75]

But it was not only the actual number of escort vessels available which counted, and Admiral Sir Percy Noble was never tired of pointing out that it was much more important to have well-trained crews used to working in close co-operation as members of such a group than to have less well trained but numerically stronger groups. More than one irritating experience, and the far above average successes of one or two group commanders like Captain Walker with their experienced crews, underlined the correctness of this judgement.[76]

There was also lively controversy concerning the role of the RAF in fighting the U-boat menace. In Britain all flying units with the exception of the Fleet Air Arm were grouped in the RAF, which had formed Coastal Command for patrol service over the sea. In April 1941, after long and involved discussions, Coastal Command was subordinated to the Admiralty for operational purposes, but only through C.-in-C. Coastal Command. The tactical co-operation of the naval and air groups was then assured by the close co-ordination, and even amalgamation, of their respective commands in Area Combined Headquarters. For example, the naval command responsible for the eastern North Atlantic 'Western Approaches' and 15 Group, Coastal Command, shared a joint operations room.

However, Coastal was the youngest and weakest Command of the RAF, and such supplies priority as it enjoyed limped far behind that of Bomber Command. The result was a good deal of friction as to how the long-range (LR) and very long-range (VLR) aircraft, of which only very few were available at first, but which were, of course, essential for closing the 'black pit' in the middle of the Atlantic, should be allotted between the various claims, and – as in the United States – the government had to intervene to settle the vexed question.[77] The following table shows how few aircraft were available for protecting the North Atlantic convoy routes at the beginning of February 1943, by comparison with the number available elsewhere:

Aircraft available for Atlantic Convoy Protection
(February 1943)

Based on:	VLR	LR	Medium	Short-range	Totals
Scotland and Northern Ireland	9	60			69
Iceland	9	11	12	24	56
Greenland		2	8	4	14
Newfoundland and Labrador		34	24	70	128
Bermuda		12			12
US Eastern Coast		70	100	144	314
Gulf of Mexico and the Caribbean		42	132	126	300
Brazil		20	20	12	52
Gibraltar and Morocco		43	20	42	105
West Africa		18		20	38
South Africa				32	32
Grand totals:	18	312	316	474	1,120

In the United States the problem of air force commitment was still further complicated by the fact that the air force, which was under army command, sought to be recognized as a third arm and adopted the slogan: 'everything that flies belongs to the Air Force!' In the emergency of the year 1942, the US Army Air Force formed a number of anti-U–boat units from the material and personnel available, but this was followed by long and not altogether fruitful discussion as to how they should be used. The US Navy was in favour of the convoy system, with air cover as far as possible, but the airmen disagreed, arguing that at the best of times escort work was a wasteful and ineffective procedure. They were in favour of more offensive operations, which they summed up in the slogan: 'Find! Attack! Sink!' The clash was not resolved until July 9th, 1943, when as the result of a little 'horse-trading' all anti-submarine air patrols were placed under naval command, while as compensation the US Navy had to cede a corresponding number of planes to the Air Force from its share of production.[78]

The difficulties created for Allied planning by the serious situation in the Battle of the Atlantic made the problem of fighting the U-boat menace one of the chief items on the agenda of the Casablanca Conference.[79] The conference decided that victory over the U-boat was the essential preliminary condition for all further large-scale operations, and that for the time being, therefore, the main weight of the Allied war effort should be directed to finding a solution for this problem. This meant priority for the building of merchant shipping and escort vessels, at the expense of the landing craft so urgently necessary if the projected invasion of Europe and the operations against Japan were to be carried out. At the same time, any increase in the number of U-boats available to the enemy had to be prevented by all possible means. In addition to the planes already directly engaged in the Battle of the Atlantic, this meant that Britain's strategic bombing force, i.e. Bomber Command, and the US 8th Air Force had to be used to hamper the U-boat building programme.

The British Admiralty had for a long time been calling for massive bombing attacks on the German U-boat bases around the Bay of Biscay, but without being able to persuade Bomber Command, which regarded the suggestion as an attempt to distract it from its main aim, the waging of an increasingly intensive bombing war on Germany. And quite apart from this, Air Chief Marshal Harris, Air Officer Commanding-in-Chief, Bomber Command, thought there was very little likelihood of obtaining decisive results in this way, because the U-boats were well protected from bombs in the strong concrete bunkers of Brest, Lorient, St Nazaire, La Pallice and Bordeaux.[80] A further argument against the proposal was that such heavy bombing could not be carried out without causing many casualties among the French civilian population. If there were to be any specific bombing of this kind, Sir Arthur Harris was in favour of attacking the German ports and harbours in which the U-boat building yards were situated. Admiral King, the US Chief of Naval Operations, also felt that this would offer the best prospects of worthwhile success. In addition, there was the possibility of bombing those towns in which ancillary equipment for U-boat building was manufactured. In 1942 Bomber Command had already flown about 7,000 missions with 11,000 tons of bombs, or about 20 per cent of the total, against these two groups of targets.[81] The situation was now so serious that not only was the U-boat building industry placed at the top of Bomber Command's priority list (January 21st, 1943), but the misgivings about bombing attacks on French ports and harbours were overruled, and on January 14th Bomber Command flew the first of a series of large-scale area-bombing attacks against Lorient, against which some 2,000 sorties were flown by the middle of February. The following table gives some idea of the massive attacks launched by RAF Bomber Command and the USAAF against the U-boat bases.

Bombing Attacks on U-boat Bases and Building Yards[82]

Month	Biscay Bases			German Yards		
	No. of Aircraft Sorties	Tons of HE Bombs	Aircraft Losses	No. of Aircraft Sorties	Tons of HE Bombs	Aircraft Losses
January 1943	666	744	31	167	317	13
February 1943	1,744	2,184	30	1,119	1,550	46
March 1943	646	1,250	6	539	981	15
April 1943	148	544	9	1,041	1,572	59
May 1943	364	707	22	548	1,152	35
Totals:	3,568	5,429 +3,704 tons incendiaries	98	3,414	5,572 +4,173 tons incendiaries	168

The direct result of all these attacks was absolutely nil; not a single U-boat was destroyed or even damaged. However, a great deal of devastation was caused in the towns attacked, and this did result in a certain slowing down of U-boat building, and particularly repair time-tables.

Another important problem also gave rise to a good deal of discussion in the Allied camp at this time. There were many voices which attributed much of the trouble for the Allies in the Battle of the Atlantic to the lack of central direction. Whereas, for example, the U-boat attack was centrally directed and controlled, the defence suffered from a plethora of directing and controlling bodies, with overlapping competences and authority. As far as the British were concerned this problem had been more or less resolved, thanks to the close co-operation which now existed between the Admiralty and Coastal Command with their Area Combined Headquarters, but on the other side of the Atlantic there were so many parallel US and Canadian naval, air and naval-air commands without any co-ordinating central body that, in the words of Sir John Slessor, it was a miracle that anything got done at all.[83] Because of this chaos, people like Field-Marshal Smuts and Air Chief Marshal Sir Philip Joubert had as early as 1942 proposed the appointment of a Super-Commander-in-Chief for the whole of the Atlantic. Others, following a suggestion of the US War Secretary Stimson, were in favour of a unified command for at least all the flying units involved. But obviously advantageous as this idea might seem, it proved impossible to overcome national jealousies and the rivalries between the various services involved.[84]

However, the Atlantic Convoy Conference, convened at the instance of Admiral King on March 1st, did succeed in laying down spheres of responsibility for convoy protection in the North Atlantic. This conference decided that the Change of Operational Control – known as the 'Chop Line' – which had been between 35° and 25° W, should be shifted on April 1st to 47° W., and to the west of this line a newly formed Canadian 'Northwest Atlantic Command' now took over the control and protection of all convoys, while eastward movements were still under the control of C.-in-C. Western Approaches. The US escort groups were withdrawn from the North Atlantic, and the Tenth Fleet, newly formed under Admiral King to control all anti-submarine measures in the American sphere, took over full responsibility for all routes from America to Gibraltar and Morocco, and from the Caribbean to Britain. At the same time, new convoy time-tables were introduced and new arrangements made for the allotment of the long-range and very long-range aircraft and the aircraft carriers for convoy work. The High-Frequency Direction Finder network was also developed and extended. No agreement was arrived at concerning the US flying units stationed in Morocco, as Admiral King was not prepared to place them under the control of Coastal Command operating from Area Combined Headquarters at Gibraltar. The result was an expenditure of flying hours out of all proportion to the U-boat danger at any time, and in view of the great shortage of air-cover in the North Atlantic this was particularly irrational.[85]

But the Battle of the Atlantic was to reach its dramatic culmination before these organizational changes, the allotment of new ships and aircraft, and the introduction of new weapons and devices, such as the Leigh Light combined with centimetre radar (ASV. III or H.2S), rocket-firing, carrier-based aircraft, the new 'Hedgehog' depth-charge salvo firer, and the acoustic homing air torpedo could have their effect.

The Culmination of the Battle of the Atlantic

The First Three Weeks of March 1943

During the second half of February, a large number of new U-boats sailed out into the Atlantic, so that despite the three convoy battles which had just ended, there were nevertheless three packs of U-boats immediately available for service. On March 5th, there were no less than fifty U-boats operating in the North Atlantic in a number of extended patrol-lines. Although from time to time sections of these patrol-lines were discovered by Allied aircraft, and measures were taken against them, their exact extent remained unclear to the Allies. Dönitz was well aware of the danger and kept the positions fluid, while at the same time the U-boats concerned did their best to avoid radar discovery by the use of their 'Metox' apparatus. Most of the U-boat operations at this time were considerably hampered by great storms sweeping across the Atlantic from west to east. However, the German wireless monitoring service was able to pick up a number of valuable hints of Allied shipping intentions, and this allowed a number of very promising operations to be launched, in which more distant U-boat packs were called to join. The result was that in the next few weeks all fast HX. and almost all slow SC. convoys were attacked – sometimes with considerable success.

The following account of the operations against Convoy HX. 229 and Convoy SC. 122 gives a typical general picture of these battles.[86]

Convoy SC. 122 put out from New York on March 5th. Owing to storm damage, six out of its 60 vessels had to put into Halifax on March 8th, the day on which HX. 229, which consisted of 40 vessels, put to sea. On March 12th and 13th, the 'Western Local Escorts' were relieved off St John's by the 'Ocean Escort Groups', which consisted of two destroyers, one frigate and five corvettes for Convoy SC. 122, and four destroyers and one corvette for Convoy HX. 229. The original intention had been to send both these convoys along the northern route past Greenland and Iceland, but on March 12th and 13th various reports came in from escort planes and vessels protecting Convoy ON. 170, which was sailing the same route in the opposite direction, concerning the locating of U-boats and the picking up of U-boat wireless signals in the area. So at the last moment it was decided to switch the two convoys to the southern route, and the Convoy Commodores were given the necessary instructions by wireless.

On March 11th and 13th, Dönitz had ordered the discontinuance of operations against Convoys HX. 228 and SC. 121 because they were too near to land, and on March 14th and 15th the U-boats concerned, which still had good supplies of fuel, were instructed to form two new patrol-lines. These were given the code-names of 'Stürmer' (18 U-boats) and 'Dränger' (11 U-boats). Both these packs were joined by a number of new U-boats which had sailed into the Atlantic from German and French bases. Dönitz now instructed 'Dränger' pack to operate against HX. 229, whose change of route orders had been picked up and decoded by his wireless monitoring service. On March 14th, the monitoring service also deciphered the very detailed new instructions sent out to Convoy SC. 122. With this valuable information in his possession, Dönitz decided to withdraw 'Raubgraf' U-boat pack, which had been vainly seeking Convoy ON. 170 in the area between Newfoundland and Greenland in very bad visibility, and send its nine U-boats off at top speed to take up their position in a concentrated patrol-line across the now known new course of Convoy SC. 122; at the same time, he corrected the movements of the two U-boat packs, 'Stürmer' and 'Dränger'.

However, because of the stormy weather, the 'Raubgraf' pack was unable to get into position in time, and by the evening of March 15th Convoy SC. 122 was already to the east of the patrol-line. Convoy HX. 229, which was sailing on a somewhat more southerly route, passed the southern end of the patrol-line on the evening of March 15th. The U-boat farthest south, *U. 91*, spotted a destroyer on an eastward course, with visibility at about five hundred yards; and a little later it heard a broad band of noise on its listening apparatus.

Together with three other U-boats in the southern part of the 'Raubgraf' patrol-line, it received instructions to hunt for Convoy SC. 122, which was believed to be in the neighbourhood. During the night, the remaining U-boats of the pack were sent off eastward in order not to fall behind the convoy. However, in all probability both convoys would have evaded the attention of the 'Raubgraf' pack but for the fact that in the morning of March 16th *U. 653*, which was on her way home, accidentally fell in with Convoy HX. 229.

As soon as he had received the report of *U. 653*, Dönitz despatched eight U-boats of the 'Raubgraf' pack, two other U-boats which had just replenished their fuel supplies from a U-tanker stationed in the neighbourhood, and eleven of the southern U-boats of the 'Stürmer' pack to the scene. It was calculated that the first U-boat could arrive by nightfall, and the last on the morning of March 17th. Six other U-boats of the 'Stürmer' pack and the U-boats of the 'Dränger' pack were ordered to set course in order to form a patrol-line ahead of the located convoy, which Dönitz believed to be Convoy SC. 122, or to attack Convoy HX. 229, which was also expected. In the afternoon he received a report from his monitoring service – a report which, incidentally, proved to be erroneous – to the effect that Convoy HX. 229 had once again been re-routed to the northern route, so he sent all the remaining U-boats against the convoy which had already been sighted.

A big storm moving westward and heavy following seas made things very difficult for the escort vessels, and the merchant ships found it no easy matter to keep their positions in the convoy. For example, the anti-submarine trawler *Campobello*, one of the vessels escorting Convoy SC. 122 actually capsized; and individual ships and groups of ships lagged behind from both convoys. At midday on March 16th, the first U-boats of the 'Raubgraf' pack made contact with stragglers from Convoy HX. 229, and by the evening eight U-boats had made contact with the convoy. Between 23.00 hours and 06.30 hours the following morning, *U. 603*, *U. 758*, *U. 435*, *U. 91* and *U. 600* got close enough to launch surface attacks under cover of darkness (*U. 435* twice), and eighteen or nineteen hits were scored on various vessels, as a result of which six were sunk and four others badly damaged. The following day *U. 91* gave all these damaged vessels the *coup de grâce* in underwater attacks.

In the same night, six of the U-boats from the 'Stürmer' pack coming from the north made contact with Convoy SC. 122, but without being able to get into position for an attack during the night. At first Dönitz had erroneously taken the first reported convoy to be the HX. 229, but then it became clear to him from the reports of the U-boats on the spot that there were two convoys of which the first and slower was the SC. 122. The second and faster convoy must therefore be the HX. 229. However, the great differences in the position reports of the various U-boats, whose accuracy was affected by the stormy weather and the low visibility, caused some uncertainty in the movements of the U-boats, which were now closing in from great distances.

On the morning of March 17th, all the vessels of the 'Raubgraf' pack with the exception of two, and four out of the five U-boats which had been on their way home, had to break off the operation either because they had no more torpedoes or because their fuel was running short, so contact with the enemy was temporarily lost. However, the weather now improved, and with better visibility five U-boats from the 'Stürmer' pack, and another U-boat which had replenished its supplies, succeeded in making contact again. Between 12.00 and 17.00 hours, the *U. 665* and the *U. 228* managed to get into position to launch underwater torpedo attacks against Convoy HX. 229, while *U. 384* and *U. 631* simultaneously attacked Convoy SC. 122. As a result, four further vessels of the convoys were sunk. Liberators operating from Iceland and Northern Ireland now began to provide air cover. Within a very short space of time the U-boats were forced to dive, and contact with the enemy was once again lost. During the following night only two U-boats succeeded in renewing contact: *U. 338* sank two vessels from Convoy HX. 229, and *U. 305* sank a vessel belonging to Convoy SC. 122. In each case the U-boats had to launch second, underwater attacks to finish off the crippled ships.

During the day of March 18th, the weather brightened temporarily, but then there were snow-storms, and out of the thirty-two U-boats operating against the convoys only nine got within sighting distance, and they were forced to dive either by the reappearance of air-cover in the early morning, or by the action of the escort groups. In the meantime, the escort had been strengthened by vessels from other convoys which were not endangered. Only *U. 221* under Lieut.-Commander Trojer, an officer particularly experienced in convoy operations, managed to get within the escort-ring and sink a couple of ships belonging to Convoy HX. 229.

During the night of March 18th–19th, the faster Convoy HX. 229 had closed up so rapidly that the two convoys made a very large collection of ships within a relatively small space, and in the meantime the escort had increased to a total of eighteen vessels – British, Canadian and US destroyers, British frigates and sloops, British and Canadian corvettes, and US Coastguard cutters. Some of these vessels had arrived at full speed from Iceland. The result was that although it was bright moonlight, only *U. 666* of all the many U-boats which made contact once more was able to launch a successful attack, while seven U-boats were driven away by depth-charge attacks.

At dawn on March 19th, strong air-cover began to operate from bases 600 miles away, and most of the U-boats were prevented from getting close enough during the hours of daylight. Sunderland flying-boats and Liberators made bombing attacks on seven U-boats; the *U. 384* was destroyed and the *U. 338* badly damaged. However, four U-boats – *U. 441*, *U. 608*, *U. 527* and *U. 663* – managed to launch underwater attacks during the day, and reported seven hits though only two ships were badly damaged. These two were finished off later in the day by torpedo attacks from *U. 523* and *U. 333*.

As the prospects for operations on March 20th did not look particularly favourable, because the convoys were now well within the reach of air cover,

Dönitz ordered the U-boats to break off the attack at dawn and withdraw westward. That morning, the two last U-boats in contact with the enemy, *U. 441* and *U. 631*, were bombed and so seriously damaged that they had to return to their bases.

With this the biggest and, from the standpoint of the U-boats, the most successful of all the convoy battles came to an end. According to the reports of the U-boat commanders, 32 enemy vessels were sunk, making a total of 186,000 GRT, and nine other vessels badly damaged. Dönitz was particularly pleased with this success because it had proved possible to bring 75 per cent of the total of 38 U-boats, which were joined by another six U-boats either on the way out or on the way home, into contact with the convoys despite bad weather and unfavourable attack conditions. 19 U-boats had been able to launch repeated attacks, and no less than seven of these vessels were on their first operational mission. Although experience had once again confirmed that the first night offered the best chances, nevertheless a surprisingly large number of U-boats had managed to launch successful underwater attacks during the hours of daylight, despite the increasingly strong air and sea defence. And this altogether excellent result had been obtained with the total loss of only one U-boat. The obvious thing was now to exploit this favourable situation to the full.

What was the situation from the standpoint of the Allies? Both convoys entered the North Channel on March 22nd. 100 ships had left New York, but only 69 had arrived. 21 vessels with a gross tonnage of 140,842 had fallen victim to the U-boat attacks, and the remainder had either sunk in the heavy storms or been compelled to put back owing to heavy damage. But that was not the full extent of the catastrophe. The two previous convoys had lost a total of 18 ships. In the last ten days of February, 28 ships had been sunk, representing a total of 183,650 GRT; in the first ten days of March, 41 ships had been sunk, representing a total of 229,949 GRT; and in the second ten days a further 44 ships, representing a total of 282,009 GRT, had been sunk. Altogether, March threatened to outdo very considerably even the previous November. And what made these new figures appear so menacing to the Allies was the fact that whereas previously 70 ships had been sunk while sailing on their own, and only 39 while sailing in convoy, during the first twenty days of March out of a total of 85 ships sunk by U-boats no less than 67 had been sunk while in protected convoys, including 41 on the North Atlantic route.

What would happen if losses continued at this high rate? In view of the increasing number of U-boats coming into service, it was now pointless to try to avoid a located U-boat position by re-routing, as this merely led the convoy into the arms of another U-boat pack. How could the morale of the merchant navy crews be sustained if each convoy regularly lost six, eight and even twelve ships? It might be necessary to abandon the convoy system altogether, though in three and a half years of war it had been the backbone of Allied strategy in the Atlantic. The U-boats never came nearer their object of cutting the connections between the Old World and the New than they did in the first twenty days of March 1943.[87]

Looking back at this critical situation Captain Roskill, the historian of the British Navy, asks: 'Where could the Admiralty turn if the convoy system had lost its effectiveness?' And he goes on to say: 'They did not know; but they must have felt, though no one admitted it, that defeat then stared them in the face.'[88]

March 21st to April 20th – the Pendulum Swings Back

While Berlin was gleefully studying the situation, and London was doing the same with less enthusiasm, the pendulum swung in the other direction over the Atlantic with a suddenness that surprised everyone. What had happened?

Many post-war publications, particularly in Germany, have created the impression that this decisive change of fortune was brought about entirely as a result of radar; but this is not so, as a closer examination of the events in the North Atlantic from the end of March to the beginning of May 1943 will show. Radar had, in fact, been used for some years by both sides, and it was not radar which decided the Battle of the Atlantic, but a combination of many factors. The introduction of a new radar device was only one of them. Let us therefore analyse the events of these weeks, in order to recognize what share the individual factors had in the Allied victory over the U-boats.

The immediate practical result of the Atlantic Convoy Conference was that the US Navy now formed its first support group for service on the North Atlantic route. This was at the beginning of March, and it consisted of the escort carrier *Bogue* and five destroyers. In that same month, the support group crossed the Atlantic for the first time with Convoy HX. 228, and was present at an attack by the U-boat pack 'Neuland' on the convoy without being able to do much about it. The weather was so stormy that it was almost impossible for planes to take the air; at the same time tactical mobility was greatly hampered because the carrier was placed in the middle of the convoy and the destroyers were part of the escort and not in a position to act independently. It took two more such frustrating convoy experiences before the Americans at last recognized the advantages of the *independent* support groups favoured by the British, and then they adopted the same tactics.

C.-in-C. Western Approaches had been compelled again and again to postpone the formation of these support groups, because he simply did not have the necessary escort vessels available. It was only the abandonment of traffic on the Murmansk convoy route during the summer months of 1943 which made it possible for the Admiralty to lend C.-in-C. WA two extra destroyer flotillas of the Home Fleet for his purposes. This loan made it possible for Admiral Max Horton to form the first five of these support groups during the course of March 1943, and the US *Bogue* group then linked up as the sixth.

These groups were composed as follows:[89]

1st Support Group: Captain Brewer, R.N., in the sloop *Pelican*; the ex-Coastguard cutter *Sennen*; and the frigates *Rother, Spey, Wear* and *Jed*;

2nd Support Group: Captain Walker, R.N., in the sloop *Starling*; with the sloops *Cygnet, Wren, Kite, Whimbrel, Wild Goose* and *Woodpecker*;

3rd Support Group: Captain McCoy, R.N., in the destroyer *Offa*; with the Home Fleet destroyers *Obedient, Oribi, Orwell* and *Onslaught*. The aircraft carrier *Dasher* was to have been attached to this support group, but she was lost on March 27th owing to a petrol explosion on board;

4th Support Group: Captain Scott-Moncrieff, R.N., in the destroyer *Milne*; with the Home Fleet destroyers *Matchless, Eclipse, Impulsive, Icarus* and *Fury*. In May, the aircraft carrier *Archer* was attached to this group;

5th Support Group: Captain Abel Smith, R.N., in the carrier *Biter*; with the Home Fleet destroyers *Inglefield, Obdurate, Opportune* and *Pathfinder*;

6th Support Group: Captain Short, US Navy, in the carrier *Bogue*; with the US destroyers *Lea, Greene, Belknap, Osmond-Ingram* and *George E. Badger*.

Such support groups were to demonstrate their worth for the first time in support of Convoys SC. 123 and HX. 230, which were faced – according to radio information – with a strong U-boat pack waiting for them in the 'air gap' to the southeast of Cape Farewell. This was the 'Seeteufel' pack, which had been searching vainly since March 21st for Convoy ONS. 1, identified by the monitoring service, and was now on its way to meet Convoy SC. 123, with which it expected to make contact on March 25th. The head of this convoy sailed into the centre of the U-boat patrol-line on the evening of March 26th, and both *U. 564* and *U. 663* sent out contact signals. The commander of the latter U-boat also reported sighting a carrier 'of the *Illustrious* class'. Actually it was the US carrier *Bogue*, which was sailing with the convoy. The 3rd Support Group under Captain McCoy was also with the convoy, and thanks to the new High-Frequency Direction Finder, HF/DF, or more familiarly, the 'Huff-Duff',[90] the U-boat was immediately located and forced to dive before further signals could be sent out to indicate the course and speed of the convoy. As all the evidence so far available suggested a convoy proceeding westward, Dönitz ordered his U-boats in this direction. Convoy SC. 123 therefore broke through the U-boat patrol-line without being identified. When there were no further indications of any U-boats in the neighbourhood of Convoy SC. 123, the support group was sent back at top speed to Convoy HX. 230, which was following on.[91]

Dönitz assumed that this convoy would attempt to evade the known U-boat position to the southeast of Greenland, and another U-boat position between Ireland and Newfoundland – which, according to a message picked up and deciphered by the monitoring service from a US U-boat situation report, the enemy had also located – probably by steering a course between them; he therefore ordered the 'Seewolf' pack in the south to set course at full speed northwards. His assumption was correct, and a little later the northernmost

U-boat of the 'Seewolf' pack sighted Convoy HX. 230. The whole 'Seewolf' pack, with a total of twenty-eight U-boats, was then also sent on to the convoy. Thanks once again to the new Huff-Duff device, the destroyers of the 3rd Support Group located three signalling U-boats during the night and forced them to withdraw in the middle of their signalling. On the morning of March 28th, a hurricane set in and any operations against the convoy were rendered impossible. However, the convoy itself was scattered by the hurricane and it lost a number of ships, including that of the Convoy Commodore himself. But the U-boats were also battered by the enormous waves, and had trouble keeping themselves above water. Only one of them managed to fall in with and sink a straggler from the convoy.

Unfortunately, there was only one U-tanker available at this time, and it was just able to supply the most needy of the U-boats with fuel for their return voyage. The result was that in the first ten days of April, the number of U-boats operating in the Atlantic was considerably reduced, despite the fact that Dönitz sent all the U-boats available, including the Type IX boats, into the North Atlantic to fill the gap.[92]

At the beginning of April, U-boat pack 'Löwenherz' with fourteen U-boats was positioned to the southeast of Cape Farewell. On April 4th, it managed to make contact with Convoy HX. 231, but C.-in-C. WA succeeded in guiding Convoy SC. 124 and the westward convoys around the U-boat positions. Despite a favourable tactical starting position and calm weather, the U-boats, most of which were on their first operational mission, were unable to do much against the experienced Escort Group B.7[93] under Commander Gretton. Out of the eight U-boats that sighted the convoy in the first night, only two were able to get into a position to fire their torpedoes. During the following twenty-four hours, only one or two U-boats succeeded in maintaining contact with the convoy. Six ships, including three stragglers, were sunk. On April 5th, the 5th Support Group with the carrier *Biter* arrived on the scene, and air-cover from Icelandic bases began to be available. Within a very short time *U. 632* and *U. 635* were sunk by a Liberator and the frigate *Tay*, and four other U-boats were so severely damaged that they had to turn for home. The rest of the U-boats were forced away from the convoy.

The operations in the middle of April when U-boat pack 'Adler' attacked Convoy ON. 176, 'Lerche' pack attacked Convoy HX. 232, and eight U-boats on their way out attacked Convoy HX. 233, which took a wide southerly course, were not particularly successful, owing to the speedy provision of air-cover and to very heavy seas. The actual results were greatly over-estimated by Dönitz; the defence pounced as soon as a torpedo was fired and it became more and more difficult to check results accurately.

April 21st to April 30th—the Turn of the Tide

During these weeks Dönitz was amazed and shocked to discover from deciphered American U-boat situation reports how accurately informed the Allies now were concerning the U-boat positions. As we know today, this was the result of constant analysis carried out by the Operational Research Sections, for whose work Professor Blackett and Lord Cherwell were largely responsible in Britain, and Dr Vannevar Bush in the United States. The same task was carried out in Germany by one or two officers of Dönitz's staff '*en passant*'.[94] This did not matter a great deal so long as the monitoring service was in a position to provide such excellent information. Not only did Dönitz frequently receive deciphered convoy courses, providing him with valuable information for his own dispositions, but thanks to his knowledge of the U-boat situation reports, which the monitoring service also provided, he was able, so to speak, to 'think with the enemy' and calculate the Allied evasive actions in advance. The great thing was to set up the U-boat positions at the last possible moment along the expected convoy routes, and thus give the enemy no time to issue re-routing orders. At this period the Battle of the Atlantic was by no means settled, and at the end of April the number of U-boats operating in the area was to reach a record height.

U-boat Distribution on May 1, 1943

	Type VII B/C	Type VII D Mine-layers	Type IX B/C	Type IX D	Type XIV U Tankers	Total
U-boats available in in the West	124	3	48	10	8	193
Number at sea	81	2	32	10	5	130
Number on the North Atlantic routes	79	2	17		3	101

The appearance of the support groups greatly hampered U-boat operations against the convoys. However, it was still possible – particularly when there were no carriers in the neighbourhood – to bring sufficient U-boats into contact with the convoys. With persistence, tactical skill, and unflagging concentration – plus a slice of luck – they would manage to get into firing positions, often after days of manœuvring. And when several U-boats attacked simultaneously, thus splitting up the defence, the attack usually met with success. But such operations were still possible only in a relatively narrow area of 200 to 600 miles which was not covered by long-range Catalina and Sunderland flying-boats, the normal Liberators II and III and the Flying Fortresses, based on Newfoundland, Iceland and Northern Ireland. The aim of the Allies was therefore to close this 'air gap' by providing an adequate number of very long-range aircraft.

After the very heavy Allied shipping losses in March, President Roosevelt ordered a revision of the allotment of the Liberator I aircraft. The investigation showed that of 112 such aircraft handed over to the US Navy, 70 were engaged in the Pacific area, while not a single one of them was based anywhere in the North Atlantic to the west of Iceland. As a result of this investigation, 255 Liberators were now taken from the US Army Air Force, the US Navy and RAF Bomber Command for service in the North Atlantic.[95] In this way, the number of VLR aircraft available rose from 20 at the end of March to 41 in the middle of April, and to about 70 during the course of May. Of these, fourteen were based on Ballykelly in Northern Ireland, twelve on Reykjavik in Iceland (all of them part of the RAF's 120 Squadron), thirteen at Gander in Newfoundland (ten Squadron of the RCAF), and six attached to the US Navy at Argentia in Newfoundland. The remainder of the aircraft belonged to the US Army Air Force and were stationed primarily in Newfoundland and Nova Scotia, but these latter could not be regarded as real VLR aircraft because their range was shorter, and most of them were equipped with H.2S radar apparatus not specially adapted for use over the sea.

In the next few weeks the VLR Liberators of 120 Squadron based on Iceland were to play a leading role. This was seen clearly for the first time during the U-boat operations against Convoy HX. 234.[96] Thanks to deciphered routing instructions and to a U-boat situation report of April 18th, Dönitz identified evasive movements northwards with a view to avoiding U-boat pack 'Meise'. However, he waited to the last moment before moving his U-boats until, travelling at top speed, they would just be able to take up their positions across the course of the expected convoy. In this way, they caught not only Convoy HX. 234 but also Convoy ONS. 3, which was steaming in the opposite direction. During the first night the U-boats were unable to manœuvre into position, and the next day Liberators from Iceland forced all eleven U-boats away before they could attack, though, thanks to the very accurate contact reports of *U. 306* (Lieut.-Commander von Trotha), they all managed to get into the neighbourhood of the convoy.

On April 23rd, while on her way to attack Convoy HX. 234, the *U. 732* accidentally fell in with Convoy ONS. 4, which was taking evasive action on a more southerly course. She immediately took up the pursuit, together with four other U-boats of the 'Meise' pack. Dönitz also decided to send the 'Specht' pack, which had been waiting in vain for Convoy SC. 127, after this new convoy. The operations which followed saw the first serious encounter between U-boats and a carrier group – the 5th Support Group with the carrier *Biter*, whose Swordfish aircraft soon forced the leading shadowing U-boat to dive. After an unsuccessful attack, *U. 191* took over the task of maintaining contact, and while using her radio for this purpose she was located, thanks to the Huff-Duff device, by the leading vessel of Escort Group B.2, the destroyer *Hesperus* under Commander Macintyre. This destroyer raced towards the *U. 191* at top speed sending up huge bow-waves. The U-boat dived but was immediately located by Asdic. Conditions were very favourable for locating, and the *U. 191* was unable to elude the attentions of the experienced operators on board the destroyer. Neither evasive action nor the discharge of chemical substances was of any avail, and after surviving several attacks, in which the new 'Torpex' depth-charge and 'Hedgehog', the new depth-charge salvo firer, were employed, the *U. 191* received two hits and sank.[97]

The following day, *U. 404* made contact with the support group, which had in the meantime drawn away to a distance of almost thirty miles from the convoy. Visibility was poor, but on the morning of April 25th she succeeded in getting a shot at a carrier, which was described as of the *Ranger* type, but from a great distance. After eleven minutes four detonations were heard and two spurts of flame observed. Commander von Bülow submitted a cautious report, underlining that the sinking could not be regarded as certain, and this was forwarded by the C.-in-C. U-boats to OKW. However, the commander's warning did not prevent the Nazi propaganda apparatus from joyfully proclaiming the sinking of the carrier. Actually the torpedoes detonated before reaching the *Biter*, which suffered no damage. On the same day, one of the Swordfish aircraft from the *Biter* spotted the *U. 203*, which happened to be in the neighbourhood on her way back to base. *U. 203* managed to dive and avoid the attentions of the aircraft, but the destroyer *Pathfinder* immediately took up the pursuit and continued the hunt relentlessly until she finally destroyed the U-boat.

April 30th to May 6th. The ONS. 5 Disaster

In the following days the number of U-boats operating against the North Atlantic convoy routes was to reach its highest point of the whole war: 60 U-boats formed four extended patrol-lines. 'Star' pack with 16 vessels was to the southwest of Iceland lying in wait for Convoy ONS. 5; 'Specht' pack with eighteen vessels was combing the area to the northeast of Newfoundland for Convoy SC. 127; while to the south of 'Star' was the newly-formed 'Amsel' pack, consisting entirely of vessels which had just put out. This pack was moving in a southwesterly direction to meet Convoy HX. 235. The fourth pack, 'Drossel', which also consisted of new vessels and inexperienced crews, was out to take part in a new attempt at combined operations with air reconnaissance to the west of Spain and the Bay of Biscay against the Gibraltar route.[98]

But the Allies had obviously got very accurate wind of these various positions, because the awaited convoys were safely guided round them. Only Convoy ONS. 5 was sighted. This was by *U. 650*, which was on the northern end of the 'Star' pack patrol-line. But owing to poor visibility, near-hurricane weather, radio disturbances and navigation difficulties, most of the U-boats failed to make contact with the convoy, whose ships had been riding out the heavy seas for several days. On April 30th, the monitoring service once again picked up and deciphered a positional report, this time referring to Convoy SC. 128. Despite the danger from the air, Dönitz decided to combine the 'Specht' and 'Amsel' packs and set up a crescent-shaped line on May 1st across the likely convoy routes. But Canadian air reconnaissance recognized the threatening danger. The convoy was guided around the western end of the patrol-line, while a small diversionary group attracted the attention of the waiting U-boats by firing flare shells and signal rockets. When contact broke down Dönitz combined the 'Specht' and 'Star' packs, returning from the abandoned operation against Convoy ONS. 5, into a very tight patrol-line 'Fink' across the supposed course of the enemy.

On the afternoon of May 4th, he was just about to abandon the search for Convoy SC. 128, which had obviously made good its escape, when, approaching from the north, the delayed Convoy ONS. 5 steamed right into the middle of the patrol-line. By a stroke of luck the initial tactical situation was uniquely favourable for the attack: 30 U-boats were extended within short distances of each other on either side of the convoy, and in addition there were eleven other U-boats of the 'Amsel' pack, which had in the meantime been spread out around Newfoundland, not far ahead of the convoy. Dönitz's staff now looked forward with high hopes and great expectations to the operations of the first night.

The convoy itself had been badly battered by the hurricane, and its escort – Escort Group B. 7 under Commander Gretton – had experienced the greatest difficulty in getting 30 of the ships into line again in the frequent snow flurries. The remainder – ten or twelve stragglers – had been formed into two groups and were sailing in the rear of the convoy. During the work of collecting the stragglers, the escorting destroyers had used up a great deal of their fuel, and in the prevailing heavy seas it was impossible for them to replenish their supplies. The result was that by May 4th, it had been necessary to dismiss four destroyers of the escort group one after the other. But this was not all; the 3rd Support Group, which had come up in the meantime, had to go too, including Commander Gretton's own ship, the *Duncan*. As the destroyer *Vidette* and the corvette *Pink* had been assigned to protect the stragglers, Lieut.-Commander Sherwood, who was now Escort Commander, had only his own frigate *Tay*, the corvettes *Sunflower*, *Snowflake* and *Loosestrife*, two anti-submarine trawlers and two destroyers *Offa* and *Oribi* with which to protect the convoy proper. Air protection for the convoy was provided by Canso flying-boats of 5 Squadron RCAF from Gander, and in the afternoon one of these flying-boats bombed and sank the *U. 630* just as she was about to attack one of the stragglers. The *U. 438* was also attacked but she was able to beat off the attack with her 2-cm flak.

Late in the afternoon the wind dropped and the weather improved, and so before darkness fell five U-boats managed to make contact. In the night six others came up. During the evening, *U. 125* had managed to attack and sink one of the stragglers, and now under cover of darkness *U. 628* and *U. 952* attacked almost simultaneously. Then *U. 264*, *U. 358* and *U. 707* attacked one after the other, and *U. 264* made a second attack. During these attacks they sank six further ships (reported as ten).

When it grew light on May 5th, Lieut.-Commander Sherwood tried to drive off the attacking U-boats by sending the destroyer *Oribi* at top speed parallel and to the rear of the convoy, but there were too many U-boats in the pack. In the meantime, however, the corvette *Pink* had made seven attacks with the Hedgehog against *U. 192*, which she finally succeeded in destroying. Nevertheless, during the course of the day a total of 15 U-boats reported contact with the convoy. Two of them, the *U. 584* and *U. 266*, launched successful underwater attacks and sank a further five ships. As things stood, Dönitz expected even greater success during the course of the second night.

But then, a couple of hours before nightfall, fog set in with visibility down to about 500 yards, and now the escort vessels with their centimetric radar devices, which the U-boats could not detect in operation, held an advantage. While their radar screens allowed them to spot the U-boats as they approached, the latter themselves were blind. Again and again, when they came in to attack they found their way barred by escort vessels operating with Asdic and radar location apparatus. Thanks solely to her superior speed the *U. 267* escaped destruction by gunfire from the corvette *Loosestrife*, which suddenly appeared out of the fog. *U. 638* discharged her torpedoes, but her targets succeeded in evading them. When the corvette *Loosestrife* raced up she dived but was destroyed by a pattern of depth-charges. The *U. 125* was rammed just behind the conning tower by the destroyer *Oribi* which suddenly pounced on her out of the fog. Taking advantage of the fog the commander of the *U. 125* managed to shake off the destroyer, but after sending out an SOS the damaged submarine was located by the corvette *Snowflake*, which raced up and sank her by gunfire. The destroyer *Vidette* sank the *U. 531* with a Hedgehog salvo. *U. 533* was rammed by the corvette *Sunflower* and badly damaged. In the meantime, the 1st Support Group arrived with five vessels. The leading vessel *Pelican* promptly located the *U. 438* by radar, opened fire and then sank the diving U-boat with depth-charges. The *U. 267* escaped the *Sennen* by the skin of her teeth and made off with her conning tower full of holes. In the morning, the Western Local Escort Group arrived.

The critical situation in which the pack now found itself gradually became clear to Dönitz from the reports of the commanders. By 04.00 hours, contact with the convoy had been lost completely, and by then fifteen of the surviving U-boats had reported as many depth-charge and six gunfire attacks. Dönitz therefore decided to break off the operation. Six U-boats had not reported at all and four others were very badly damaged, and this was quite sufficient to justify second thoughts about the situation.

The War Diary of May 6th[99] records:

'(*a*) Enemy radar devices operated both from the air and from surface vessels very greatly hampered the operations of individual U-boats, and in addition they provide the enemy with an opportunity, which he is obviously not slow to use, of discovering the preparatory positions of the U-boats and then seeking to evade them. The U-boat is now threatened with the loss of its most important advantage: the difficulty of being located.

'(*b*) The enemy's air force can now provide air-cover for convoys over almost the whole area of the North Atlantic, and we must expect that before long the remaining gaps will be closed by land-based aircraft or by the use of auxiliary aircraft carriers.

'This form of escort operations, when carried out with large numbers of aircraft in a wide area around a convoy, has always resulted in U-boats falling hopelessly astern of convoys and being unable to register any further successes – particularly when there is skilful co-operation between the sea and air defence.

'(*c*) Operations against submerged U-boats with new methods of location, and attacks with apparently more powerful depth-charges, have also grown more intense.

'(*d*) U-boat operations are being made more difficult by the increasing number of escort vessels available to the enemy. On our part we have made a start with the magnetic torpedo pistol, Mk. 2, the Falke, an acoustic torpedo and zigzag-running torpedoes, but so far there is no really effective weapon available.

'In conclusion it must be recognized that at the moment U-boat operations are more difficult than ever before. However, every effort is being made with all possible energy to equip U-boats with improved weapons, and thus facilitate their operations.'

This report on the general situation shows clearly that the C.-in-C. U-boats and his Staff did not fail to recognize the causes of the unsatisfactory and costly operations of the past few weeks, even though it was still to some extent in the dark about one or two technical questions with reference to the new locating equipment and weapons now being employed by the enemy. Despite the sinkings reported, the operation against Convoy ONS. 5, with the loss of six U-boats, was still regarded as a very painful defeat. However, in the ups-and-downs of warfare both sides have to reckon with such disagreeable set-backs, above all when particularly unfavourable circumstances, such as in this case the sudden onset of fog, supervene to give the advantage in battle to the enemy. One such defeat was certainly not sufficient to justify any fundamental change of policy. The bitter experiences of the next fourteen days were necessary for that.

May 7th to May 24th, 1943 – Collapse of the U-boat Offensive

When operations against Convoy ONS. 5 were broken off, Dönitz had left only eighteen U-boats still ready for action, out of the packs he had committed. These vessels were now formed into the 'Elbe' pack, to the east of New-foundland. The twelve U-boats of 'Amsel pack 1' and 'Amsel pack 2' were amalgamated farther south into 'Rhein' pack. From messages deciphered by his monitoring service, it became clear to Dönitz that the enemy had discovered the positions of these two packs, because Convoy HX. 237 and Convoy

SC. 129 made a wide detour southward to avoid them. He therefore gave 'Rhein' pack orders to proceed at full speed in a southeasterly direction, in order to take up its position across the course of Convoy HX. 237; while 'Drossel' pack, which was off Cape Finisterre, was instructed to move westwards. 'Elbe' pack, which could no longer be sent to intercept the fast Convoy HX. 237, was sent off at full speed southeastwards to intercept the following convoy, SC. 129.[100]

U. 359, which was stationed on the southern end of 'Rhein' pack, actually sighted Convoy HX. 237 on May 9th, but as soon as she had sent off her contact report she was forced to dive by a destroyer. A close patrol-line was now formed ahead of the convoy, but the convoy passed through it unobserved after an aircraft from the *Biter*, which was with the 5th Support Group reinforcing Escort Group C. 2, had forced the *U. 454*, in the path of the convoy, to dive. Pursuing a straggler, *U. 403* made contact with the convoy again. She was able to beat off a Swordfish with her flak, but was forced to dive when a destroyer came on the scene. The monitoring service again provided valuable information by managing to decipher a message indicating the convoy's position on May 11th. The result was that by evening a number of U-boats had found the convoy once more. Three stragglers were caught and sunk, but the attacking U-boats were unable to break through the protective cordon and attack the convoy proper. Again and again, they tried to beat off the aircraft with their flak, and *U. 230* even shot down a Swordfish, but again and again they were forced to dive by destroyers and corvettes which were swiftly called up by the aircraft to deal with them, and actually managed to destroy most of them. *U. 89* was destroyed by the *Broadway* and the *Lagan*, which were called to the spot by a Swordfish; after being badly damaged by a Liberator from Northern Ireland, *U. 456* was destroyed by the *Pathfinder*, which had also been brought on the scene by a Swordfish; *U. 753* was destroyed on May 13th by the *Lagan* and the *Drumheller*, brought up by a Sunderland flying-boat.

When it became clear, on the morning of May 13th, that all the attacking U-boats had been forced away or destroyed, the 5th Support Group turned away and went westward to the assistance of Convoy SC. 129, whose position had been reported by *U. 504* on the evening of May 11th. It was now being hard pressed by the U-boat pack 'Elbe'. This convoy was protected by Commander Macintyre's Escort Group B. 2. *U. 402* managed to get close enough to the convoy to launch a successful underwater attack, as the result of which two ships were sunk, but she was then damaged by a pattern of depth-charges. The leading escort vessel *Hesperus* located *U. 223* by radar during the night, as she approached from the rear of the convoy and sought to come into a position to attack. Macintyre himself – using the naval glasses he had taken from the renowned U-boat Commander Kretschmer as war booty – spotted the U-boat in process of diving. His own vessel carried out several depth-charge attacks, and the badly damaged U-boat was forced to surface. A dramatic duel now took place. *U. 223* made several attempts to torpedo the *Hesperus* while the latter tried to sink the U-boat by gunfire, by shallow-set depth-charges and, finally, by ramming her. But when all this failed to dispose of the damaged U-boat, which was just about afloat, Macintyre decided to leave her to her own devices in the hope that she would founder. He raced back at top speed to his convoy, which had steamed ahead during the encounter and was being hard pressed by numerous other U-boats. Actually, *U. 223* managed to limp back to her base.

Macintyre and the *Hesperus* arrived just in time, because according to radio signals which were picked up at least twelve U-boats (the number was correct) were trying to get into favourable positions ahead of the convoy for underwater attacks by day, or surface attack by night. During the following thirty-six hours, the escort vessels were constantly dashing here and there, following various radar and Huff-Duff bearings. Towards midday, the *Hesperus* sank the leading shadowing U-boat, the *U. 186*, with two depth-charge attacks. *Whitehall, Heather, Sweetbriar*, and *Clematis* simultaneously spotted a couple of U-boats, and made for them, but the U-boats managed to escape because their surface speed was faster than that of the relatively slow corvettes. Towards evening *Hesperus* and *Whitehall* co-operated in hunting three U-boats, all of which they forced to dive. They had no time to continue the pursuit, because darkness was falling and there were still other U-boats in the neighbourhood. In the night, *Whitehall, Hesperus* and *Heather* located three U-boats with their radar apparatus and forced them away. Not a single U-boat was able to get into position for a further attack. Huff-Duff and the centimetric radar apparatus now made it possible for a skilfully handled escort group to defend the convoy against a whole pack of U-boats on its own! When, towards evening on May 13th, the *U. 642* reported the arrival of a carrier, Dönitz decided to break off the operation the following morning at dawn. Shortly after this, *U. 266* was sunk by a Liberator of 86 Squadron.

On the southern route at this time, the 'Elbe' and 'Rhein' U-boat packs were pursuing Convoy HX. 237 and Convoy SC. 129. Dönitz now formed the packs 'Donau 1' and '2' to the southeast of Cape Farewell, out of U-boats which had just arrived. Their patrol-lines were extended northwards by the 'Iller' pack, which had chased Convoy ONS. 7 in vain. When the monitoring service reported that Convoy HX. 238 had obviously evaded the position in the south, Dönitz interpreted a deciphered situation report to mean that the following Convoy SC. 130 would probably use this route, so he ordered seventeen U-boats of the 'Donau' pack southwards. Shortly after midnight on May 19th, *U. 304* sighted the convoy. The weather was calm, and in the short moonlit night two U-boats managed to come up. By the morning, seven U-boats had made contact, and during the course of the day another six arrived.[101]

However, at daybreak Commander Gretton, who was Escort Commander, ordered the convoy to change course 90° southward, with the result that the U-boats, some of which had already taken up favourable positions for a submerged daylight attack, were left in the rear. They had just surfaced in order to regain their advantage when the first Liberator, T of 120 Squadron, arrived. In the very first attack, *U. 954* was bracketed with bombs, and sunk. On its way to the convoy, the aircraft located five other U-boats in a very short space of time and dived down on them from the low-lying clouds. As it had no more bombs it called up the convoy escort vessels to deal with the submerging U-boats. The frigate *Tay* seriously damaged *U. 952*, and together with Commander Gretton's ship *Duncan*, the corvette *Snowflake* sank *U. 381* after several runs over her. Two other U-boats succeeded in escaping on the surface from the slower corvettes *Pink* and *Sunflower*. Towards midday, the 1st Support Group raced up to the convoy from the rear. The frigates *Wear* and *Jed* immediately spotted two surfaced U-boats about fifteen miles away from the convoy. One was *U. 209*, which fired her torpedoes as she submerged. However, she was quickly located by the *Jed* and the *Sennen*, and destroyed by a Hedgehog attack. In the meantime, the *Duncan* had frustrated an attack by *U. 707* and damaged her badly. At about this time, the second Liberator, P of 120 Squadron, arrived and spotted no less than six U-boats, all of which it forced to dive. In the afternoon, two other Liberators, O and Y of the same squadron, came on the scene and spotted two groups of four and two U-boats, and attacked three of them. The last contact U-boat was forced away from the convoy shortly before darkness by the frigates *Jed* and *Spey*. Vigorous zig-zagging by the convoy now left the U-boats still farther behind. *U. 92* was the only attacker which managed to manœuvre herself into a favourable position for an attack and under cover of darkness she discharged her torpedoes, but they all missed their targets. By morning all contact had been lost. During the course of the day the air-cover was considerably strengthened, and U-boats were compelled to dive on fourteen different occasions. Dönitz was now compelled to break off operations. This convoy had sailed right through a U-boat patrol-line without losing a single vessel.

In the meantime, Dönitz had ordered twenty-one vessels to form a patrol-line, 'Mosel', on the evening of May 21st, in the hope of intercepting Convoy HX. 239, whose position had been discovered by the monitoring service. Dönitz came to the conclusion that Convoy HX. 239 was to be re-routed farther southward in order to avoid his U-boat positions, and he therefore shifted the line accordingly. However, before Convoy HX. 239 arrived, the U-boats lying in wait sighted Convoy ON. 184 approaching. It was protected by Escort Group C. 1, reinforced by the 6th Support Group with the carrier *Bogue*. On the evening of May 21st, *U. 231* was bombed by an Avenger and so badly damaged that she had to turn back to base for repairs. The destroyers *Osmond-Ingram* and *St Laurent* forced two other U-boats to dive, and the convoy was able to pass unscathed through the gap thus torn in the U-boat line. On the morning of May 22nd, another Avenger spotted *U. 468*, which was, however, able to beat off the attack with her 2-cm flak.

It was not until midday that the *U. 305* was able to send out the first contact report, whereupon Dönitz called up those U-boats of the 'Donau' pack which had survived the attack on Convoy SC. 130. But during the day, *U. 305* was attacked three times by aircraft from the *Bogue*, and was so badly damaged that she had to withdraw. In the afternoon, *U. 569* was attacked and sunk by two Avengers. The following morning, Convoy HX. 239 reached the 'Mosel' patrol-line somewhat farther south. It was protected by Escort Group B. 3, reinforced by the 4th Support Group with the carrier *Archer*. One of her Swordfish aircraft sighted the *U. 468* and kept her under observation out of range of her flak, at the same time calling up a destroyer, from which the *U. 468* succeeded in escaping. The *U. 218* managed to extricate herself from a similar tight corner. *U. 752* spotted another Swordfish – it happened to be the only one equipped to carry rockets – and dived, but too late. While at periscope depth she was hit by rockets from the Swordfish and forced to surface. This was the first time rockets had been used against U-boats. With her flak armament the U-boat managed to hold off three Martlet fighters, but then as the destroyers *Keppel* and *Escapade* came up she scuttled herself. Once more five U-boats had been lost without a single success to show for it. It was obviously pointless to continue operations against a convoy which was so strongly protected.

Dönitz himself summed up the results of these operations in the War Diary of May 24th:

'During the past few days circumstances have arisen which confirm the present critical situation in the U-boat war and underline the need for radical counter-measures. . . . 14 U-boats were lost in the Atlantic in February, 13 in March and 12 in April, and up to May 22nd the total of losses of this month has reached 31; and in all probability, another two vessels have been lost as a result of the operations against Convoy HX. 239.

'Losses, even heavy losses, must be accepted if they are accompanied by proportional success in tonnage sunk. But in May one U-boat was lost for every 10,000 GRT sunk, where not so long ago one U-boat was lost for 100,000 GRT sunk. Thus our losses so far in May have reached an intolerable level.

'The enemy air force played a decisive role in inflicting these high losses. This was due to the increased use of land-based and carrier-borne planes, together with the opportunities for surprise afforded to the enemy both day and night by his improved location devices.

'In the operations of pack 'Donau', aircraft prevented the U-boats from delivering their attack, and at the same time they prevented anything but a desultory and temporary maintenance of contact. Similarly, the presence of a strong force of enemy aircraft prevented the 'Mosel' pack from establishing any proper contact at all, although it is likely that at least one convoy passed the patrol-line.

'The intolerable burden of the losses we have sustained and the failure of our recent convoy operations call urgently for radical measures to equip our U-boats with improved offensive and defensive weapons.'

Dönitz drew the only possible conclusion from the facts, and called off the convoy battle in the North Atlantic. A few U-boats without a very large fuel capacity were to remain in the area and give the impression that strong U-boat packs were still in the neighbourhood, but in fact the remainder of the available U-boats were to be withdrawn to the area west of the Azores.

The decision in the Battle of the Atlantic had gone to the enemy.

Conclusion

The Causes of the U-boat Collapse

A closer analysis of the individual operations which took place between March 20th and May 24th, 1943, will show very clearly that the Allied victory over the U-boats was not due to any single weapon or technical device, but to a combination of factors. The most significant of these factors were:

1. The development of the radio location network, which now permitted all messages and signals to be picked up without fail, even when wave-lengths were frequently changed; and the steady extension of air reconnaissance far out into the North Atlantic by aircraft equipped with centimetric radar (ASV III, H.2S.), a system which the U-boats were unable to detect in operation. In these two ways, the Allies were able to obtain a fairly accurate picture of the U-boat positions and re-route their convoys, though, in fact, this re-routing was usually countered by corresponding U-boat movements made possible by the high degree of efficiency shown by Germany's monitoring service in breaking into Allied air and wireless communications;

2. The equipment of escort vessels with the High-Frequency Direction Finder (Huff-Duff), made it possible for escort vessels and aircraft to drive off those U-boats seeking to keep contact with the convoys for the U-boat pack;

3. The equipment of the escort vessels and aircraft with centimetric radar provided them with a clear picture of the situation on their screens even in bad visibility, and allowed them to spot U-boats advancing on the surface to the attack under cover of darkness, whereas the U-boats had only the eyes of their look-outs to serve them;

4. The strengthening of the escort groups for convoys threatened by U-boats by bringing up special support groups. First of all, this made it more difficult for U-boats to come into position for an attack; secondly, it made systematic pursuit possible right to the kill once they had been located, without weakening the protection of the convoy while the hunt was proceeding;

5. The appearance of aircraft carriers with the support groups, together with the provision of VLR aircraft, allowed the Allies to bridge the dangerous 'air gap' in mid-Atlantic. The extension of air-cover during the whole time a

convoy was at sea made it impossible for U-boats to manœuvre effectively to get ahead of a convoy;

6. The introduction of new weapons such as the Hedgehog salvo firer for depth-charges, the Torpex depth-charge for greater depths, the shallow set depth-charges, and, finally, the equipment of aircraft with rocket-firing apparatus, all combined to increase the effectiveness of the Allied anti-submarine measures very considerably;

7. Finally, the intensive scientific exploitation of all available data, both Allied and enemy, by the Operational Research Sections shed a good deal of valuable light on important tactical and strategic questions, and it was in this latter period that the fruits began to be harvested.

One is inclined to assume that the U-boat war on the Allied supply lines was finally crushed by 'the overwhelming sea and air defences of the two great naval powers'.[102] But anyone who accepts this explanation will be very much surprised to find the same names mentioned again and again in descriptions of the convoy battles from the Allied side: whether the names are those of Escort Commanders such as Commander Gretton, Commander Macintyre and so on; or the names of ships such as *Biter*, *Hesperus*, *Tay*, *Snowflake*; or mere designations such as 'Escort Group B. 2', or 'B. 7', or the '1st or 3rd Support Group'; or '120 Squadron' of RAF Coastal Command. It is, of course, quite true that in 1943 the number of ships and aircraft available to the Allies for combating the U-boat menace was considerable greater than before. Even so, there were never more than these six support groups, with their two or three carriers supported by about 40 Liberators, in assosication with the 12 ocean escort groups. And amongst these, only a few groups, ships and aircraft actually won the decisive success against the U-boats; they justified Sir Percy Noble's contention that numbers alone do not decide, but the training, ability and teamwork of the crews, ships and units engaged. By effectively using the weapons placed in their hands as a result of close co-operation between their military and political leaders, their science and their technology, they won the Battle of the Atlantic, and their victory represented one of the most important turning points in the Second World War.

Why was the U-boat War Continued?

But victory in the North Atlantic for the Allies did not mean the end of U-boat warfare. For two more years, the U-boats continued the struggle under material and moral conditions which became more and more difficult, right to the bitter end. Since the war it has been asked more than once why the U-boat war was not broken off in the summer of 1943.[103] During the last two years of the war the U-boat question was repeatedly the centre of discussion among leading circles in Germany; it was examined again and again, and decided again and again, in accordance with the changing conditions. As far as we are concerned here, however, the only question at issue is whether the decision not to break off the U-boat warfare in the summer of 1943 was correct or not.[104]

The first thing to answer is why that decision was taken. The answer must be based on the data available to Dönitz and the U-boat Staff at the time, on their picture of the situation, and their reasonable expectation of subsequent developments.

In a report made to Hitler on May 31st,[105] Dönitz ascribed the critical situation which had arisen in U-boat warfare chiefly to 'the very considerable increase of enemy air-cover' in conjunction with a 'new locating device' which is apparently also being used by surface vessels'. The gist of his assessment of the situation was: 'We have fallen down on a technical problem, but we shall find a solution'. Somehow the U-boat must be equipped with apparatus to counter the new enemy location device; in addition, the U-boat must be given new weapons to enable it to fight successfully against its deadliest enemies, the aircraft and the destroyer.

The first requirement was very difficult to fulfil so long as nothing was known about the nature of the new enemy location-finder. However, the radio wave indicator known as the 'Hagenuk-Wanze' which was introduced in August 1943, and the 'Naxos' detector apparatus introduced in the following October, did a great deal in this respect, and their operation was soon reflected in a sharp drop in U-boat losses. And as far as the aircraft was concerned, considerable improvements in the anti-aircraft equipment of the U-boat were introduced at the end of May and the beginning of June, and their promise was soon confirmed in practical experience: the *U.441*, the first U-boat equipped as a flak trap, shot down a Sunderland flying-boat. The *U.758*, the first U-boat equipped with the 2-cm quadruple flak, successfully beat off several attacks by carrier-borne aircraft. And as a more effective counter to the destroyer, there was the improved acoustic homing torpedo known as the 'Zaunkönig', which was on the point of being put into service. With these new weapons at his disposal Dönitz looked forward confidently to being able to resume the battle against the convoys with some hope of success in the late summer.

However, there was some doubt as to whether the U-boat tonnage war could be effectively stepped up again.[106] Naval Operations Staff experts reckoned that up to May 30th, 1943, the Allies had lost approximately 30 million GRT and had built about 15·5 million GRT to replace it – the real figures were rather less favourable to Germany, namely 21·5 million GRT and 16·5 million GRT respectively. But one way or the other, Dönitz was right in thinking that the Allies had a good deal of leeway to make up, and that Germany must strain every nerve to see that they did not succeed in making it up. Shortage of shipping space was the bottleneck which was delaying all the Allied attempts to carry out large-scale amphibious undertakings.

But in Dönitz's opinion, the supply war would have to be continued even if victory in the tonnage war was impossible – because 'it tied down enemy forces which were very considerable indeed'.[107] This argument that the U-boat war tied down very large enemy forces was reinforced when Germany's monitoring service discovered that strong forces of 15 and 19 Groups, Coastal Command, had taken part in the devastating attacks on Hamburg towards the end of July 1943, whereas previously they had been completely occupied by the war against the U-boat menace.[108]

Finally, it must not be forgotten that all the decisions that were taken in these weeks were influenced to some extent by the hopes and expectations placed in the construction and development of new U-boat types. There was, for example, the fast electric Type XXI U-boat and the 'Walter' U-boat; these new U-boats were expected to revolutionize submarine warfare. At that time it was reckoned that a large number of Type XXI U-boats would be ready for service in the summer and autumn months of 1944. In the meantime, unless U-boat activities were continued there was a danger of losing touch with enemy defensive developments and tactical methods.

Accepting this view of the general situation – which must be set against the background of the Allied demand for unconditional surrender with all its obvious implications – together with very promising arms and shipbuilding developments, and the encouraging results (over-estimated incidentally) of the first new U-boat operations in September 1943 against Convoy ON. 202 and Convoy ON. 18, the decision arrived at by Grand Admiral Dönitz in the summer and autumn of 1943 could hardly have been any different; the U-boats would fight on!

It was quite clear to Dönitz that the fight could not be continued with half measures; as many U-boats as possible must be provided, and they must be as efficient as possible. In consequence, a U-boat building programme to put all previous programmes into the shade was adopted. At the same time, and despite the misgivings of some more conservative designers, the method of sectional building was adopted, simply and solely because it was the only method which promised to provide a sufficient number of U-boats within a relatively short space of time.

Looking back on it now, can we say that the decision of the summer of 1943 was 'correct'?

From numerous statements made since by leading political and military figures in the Allied camp, we know today that the general ideas of Dönitz concerning the U-boat tonnage war were certainly 'correct'. There is, for example, Captain Roskill, the official naval historian, who declares that Dönitz was unquestionably right in his belief that defeat or victory would depend on whether he could sink British merchant shipping – whether tramps, liners or tankers – more quickly than the British could replace them by building other ships.[109] But at the same time this statement of the position also makes it quite clear that the upshot of the Battle of the Atlantic would remain uncertain only so long as the U-boats, in combination with the other weapons and resources of the Axis Powers, still had a sporting chance in the race against the productive capacity of the Allied shipbuilding yards.

It was in May 1943 that Dönitz began to harbour the first doubts as to whether, in fact, they did have such a chance. Despite this, in the following summer the decision was taken to continue the U-boat tonnage war – but only after long and serious debate in the U-boat Staff, during which every aspect of the problem was discussed, all the pros and cons weighed up, due consideration given to the reports of the U-boat commanders themselves, and a general estimate of the political and strategic situation and its tactical demands adopted.

And even if the U-boats did not and could not win the tonnage war, there was still no other weapon which could so effectively hamper and delay Allied plans for an invasion of France as the U-boat could. From Allied war literature we know that the problem of shipping space was the decisive factor in fixing the invasion date, and that a powerful flare-up of the U-boat war in the winter of 1943–4 would probably have made it impossible to carry out the invasion in June 1944. And it can truly be said that the situation as seen in the summer of 1943 did hold out reasonable hope that it would be possible in the near future to renew successfully operations against the Allied convoys.

Finally, it was indisputable that a successful continuation of the U-boat war would tie down large, if incalculable, enemy forces which would otherwise be used in the bombing war against Germany, or for attacks on Germany's own sea communications. The following figures, which can be extended *ad infinitum*, prove the case conclusively: for example, in April 1943, when the Allied anti-submarine effort was at its peak, aircraft (chiefly four-engined machines) based on airfields in Great Britain flew 2,459 missions for convoy protection and U-boat patrols. But in April 1945, when there were comparatively few U-boats operating in the area, 6,314 missions were flown. In the spring of 1943, the normal escort force protecting a convoy in the North Atlantic consisted of from seven to nine vessels, and in the event of a support group's coming in to reinforce the escort this might increase to perhaps one carrier and eighteen escort vessels. But in October 1944, the two convoys on the Murmansk route, Convoy JW. 61 and Convoy RA. 61, were protected by no less than three carriers, one cruiser and up to 32 escort vessels.

Looking back, therefore, we may say that the decision arrived at in the summer of 1943 to continue the U-boat war was correct. The hope that the U-boats would be able to renew the convoy battles successfully in the six winter months of 1943–4, however, came to nothing; but this was due to brilliant technical improvisation on the part of the Allied defences, the speed and effectiveness of which could hardly have been foreseen.

The tragedy of the German U-boat during the Second World War was that from 1939 to 1942 the U-boat weapon was never strong enough to live up completely to the hopes placed in it. And when, in the spring of 1943, the numbers of U-boats available reached, for the first and only time, the approximate level which Dönitz had declared in the summer of 1939 to be essential if there were to be any real chance of winning the tonnage war, it was too late.

By this time the Allied anti-submarine defences had become so strong and so effective that, in the end, it was the Allied shipbuilding yards which won the tonnage war. It was this that laid the basis for the subsequent total victory of the Allies over Germany.

Chronicle IX

January

to

May 1944

	Politics		Conduct of the War
Neutrals	Germany and Japan		Germany and Japan
			January 21st: 'Little blitz' against Britain.
			January 28th: Encirclement battle of Che~~ commences.
			February: First German U-boat equipped the 'Snorkel' device sails into the A~
			February 4th: Japanese offensive in Burm. lift to supply those Allied units cut of
	February 11th: Plan of the German Resistance Movement to assassinate both Hitler and Himmler by a bomb explosion abandoned, because Himmler did not appear as expected.		February 14th to 18th: Last attempt at a ~ U-boat-pack operation in the North A~ with air reconnaissance.
			February 22nd: Loss of Krivoi Rog.
			February 23rd: End of encirclement ba~ Cherkassy.
	March 9th: Plan to shoot Hitler during a situation conference.		March 8th: Japanese attack Impal ju~ Burma.
			March 13th: Loss of Cherson.
	March 19th: German troops occupy strategic points in Hungary.		
	March 21st: Finland rejects Russian peace offer.		
	March 22nd: Hungary 'gleich-geschaltet' under Minister-President Sztojay.		
	April 12th: Finnish parliament rejects Russian peace terms.		
			April 17th: Japanese offensive to deprive A~ of air bases in China.
			May 3rd: Japanese Plan 'A' for the de~ West New Guinea, Palau and the M~
			May 5th to 12th: Germans evacuate Se~ and Cherson. 150,000 men evacuate~ and air since April.
	May 15th: Field-Marshal Rommel and General von Stülpnagel plan to arrest Hitler and bring him to trial.		
			May 20th: Hitler orders C.-in-C. Army Centre to hold on 'at all costs'.
	May 30th: Bormann encourages the lynching of Allied airmen.		

The Invasion of Normandy

BY FRIEDRICH RUGE

Germany's central position between the leading European powers, and her long and tragic role as the European battlefield, have made her people very much aware of all aspects of land warfare and land power. As a consequence, the implications of sea power and naval operations have been largely over-looked and inadequately taken into account by German political and military thinking. It is almost forgotten that on two occasions Prussia survived only because she was an ally of England, in the Seven Years War and in the Napoleonic Wars. After 1900, when Germany started building up a strong navy she became fleet-conscious to some extent, but not sea-conscious. The fighting of millions of men on immense land-fronts from 1914 to 1918 again over-shadowed the events at sea, and especially the distant blockade which strangled her. Her coasts were never threatened, coastal defence measures and methods were tried out only on the coast of Flanders, not quite 30 miles long, against frequent British bombardments and some raids. Some experience was also gained in the defence of the Dardanelles, where German units co-operated with the Turkish army and navy.

By the Treaty of Versailles (1919), the German armed forces were restricted to an army of 100,000 men and a small navy; neither planes nor submarines were permitted. Another war against England seemed unthinkable; all military preparations centred on creating a minimum defence against land attack. The Navy manned the remaining coastal batteries, but there was little interest in possibilities of amphibious warfare because nobody expected any landing operations against the German coastline, about 600 nautical miles long and mostly on the Baltic – which could be reached only via the Danish narrows; the remainder, on the North Sea, was protected by narrow islands, shifting sands, and difficult weather conditions.

The Development of German Coast Defence in the West, 1940–1

The situation changed when the spring campaigns of 1940 doubled the territory under German control and increased the length of coastline to approximately 3,500 miles (smaller islands excluded), for the most part open to direct attack from the sea. At that time, the British were far too weak for any large-scale operation, but the Germans had to protect their new submarine bases in western France, the ports where ships and barges for Operation 'Sea Lion' were assembled, and shipping routes all along their newly acquired coasts, against raids and attacks from the air and the sea. On land, this had to be done by erecting coastal and AA batteries around the main ports, particularly the submarine bases, and medium batteries along the coasts. An immense amount of labour and material was needed for this scheme, which had to be spread over years. Because of the complete disarmament after 1918, there were hardly any reserves, especially of heavier naval guns. Because of this, a number of batteries were transferred from the Baltic and the North Sea to the coastline from northern Norway to southwestern France. Work was started at the narrowest part of the Channel as protection for the units crossing to England in the event of Operation 'Sea Lion'. Altogether, the following naval batteries were erected there:

Grosser Kurfürst	Four 280mm guns at Cape Gris Nez
Friedrich August	Three 305mm guns near Wimereux
Lindemann	Three 406mm guns west of Sangatte
Todt	Four 381mm guns south of Cape Gris Nez

In addition, some army coastal batteries of calibres up to 280mm were placed here, and quite a number of smaller batteries. Incidentally, most pictures of the so-called Atlantic Wall were taken in this region.

Hitler gave priority to two other large programmes. He was obsessed by the idea that the British would try to regain a foothold in Norway, and he ordered strong fortifications to be built there. By 1944, the inner and outer defences of the Narvik–Harstad area consisted of about 40 batteries, 7 of them of heavy calibres up to 406mm. The port of Bergen and its approaches were protected by 7 heavy batteries with 21 guns of 210 to 280mm, 8 medium batteries with 34 guns of 127 to 155mm, and 18 light batteries with 66 guns of 88 to 105mm. Altogether, there were 350 coastal artillery batteries in Norway, of 88mm to 381mm guns.[1]

This did not prevent Hitler from initiating an eight-year plan for fortifying the Channel Islands. Every month, 90,000 tons of material were to be transported to the islands, and 32,000 workmen were moved there. By 1944, they had finished 11 batteries with 38 heavy guns of 210 to 305mm calibre, but no airfield was finished, although several were planned. In view of the position of the Channel Islands, this was a waste of men and material sorely needed on the mainland for defences, submarine bunkers, and, later, V–1 installations. So the defence plans had to be far more modest: they provided an average of 2 heavy and 3 medium batteries for each major base and 2 medium batteries for the smaller ports.

The sum of these plans was far beyond the strength of the Navy. Therefore, in summer 1940, the Army Coastal Artillery was formed. Within a year, 171 batteries were ready, 98 of them in Norway, with 62 more under construction there. This sounded more effective than it actually was, for many of the guns were old and unprotected, with scratch crews not trained in firing at naval targets.

1941–2

The failure of the attack on Russia and the entry of the USA into the war created entirely new and dangerous circumstances. The best method of fighting the Western Allies was still the U-boat war, mainly conducted from the bases on the Bay of Biscay, causing a loss of $\frac{1}{2}$ to $\frac{3}{4}$ million tons of shipping every month. The bulk of the Army and the Luftwaffe operated in the east, where the drain on manpower and material was enormous. In the west, there remained only 33 infantry divisions, many engaged in training, and weak air and naval forces (except the submarines). OKW took account of the state of affairs in the Führer Directive No. 40, dated March 23rd, 1942,[2] concerning the powers of command on the coasts. It stated that all the European coasts were seriously exposed to the danger of Allied landings which, even with limited objectives, would seriously affect the German plans. All troops of the three Services were to be fully prepared for defensive action and counter-attacks under one responsible commander; all forces, even the German civil authorities in the zone of occupation, should be committed by him, and this commitment *'must lead to the collapse of the enemy attack, if possible before but at latest upon the actual landing'*. This is particularly interesting in view of the desperate and only partially successful efforts of Field-Marshal Rommel two years later to co-ordinate action in this way. Directive No. 40 then ordered improvement of the fortifications and strongpoints all along the coasts, and a uniform definition of coastal sectors (never fulfilled in France at least). It ended by nominating those responsible for the various coasts, the priorities to be observed, and the tasks of the Luftwaffe and Navy. It did not commit itself to naming the areas which might be selected by the Allies for landing operations.

Raids by British commandos, successfully undertaken at the end of December, 1941, against small bases in Norway, were probably the direct incentive for these orders. Their importance was underlined by the much larger raid on the port installations of St Nazaire at the mouth of the Loire on March 28th, 1942. Carried out cleverly and courageously, it achieved some success; but it was more instructive for the defenders, because it showed them their weak points. The experience gained at St Nazaire greatly helped in repelling the attack on the town and port of Dieppe on August 19th, 1942; this raid was an almost complete failure, and gave further valuable hints for the improvement of the coastal defences.

The main lesson drawn from the St Nazaire and Dieppe raids was that in the event of a large landing operation the Allies would *not* directly attack one of the larger ports, but would land on the open beach and try to take the port from the rear.[3] Views differed on how to oppose the first landings, as will be shown later. In any case, the minimum defences of the major ports had to be finished first, to make them safe from raids.

In an evaluation of the situation dated July 20th, 1942, OKM expressed the opinion[4] that an Allied landing operation might be expected in northwestern France, with the limited objective of destroying the submarine bases of Brest, Lorient, and St Nazaire, possibly preceded by the formation of a temporary bridgehead in the Seine Bight. Measures for better protection of the submarine bases were taken.

The Allied Plans

In view of the incomplete state of the defences, the limited strength of the German troops in France and their lack of training and preparation, there can be little doubt that the Allies could have gained a bridgehead in France in 1942 with comparatively weak forces. Actually, the Americans wanted a limited operation to be undertaken against the Cotentin Peninsula or a similar point (Operation 'Sledgehammer'), to be followed in the spring of 1943 by a large operation, with six divisions, in the area between Le Havre and Boulogne.[5] However, the British were against a limited operation in France proper, and the Americans eventually consented to the invasion of North Africa, although this was bound to require such an effort that the cross-Channel attack would probably have to be postponed to the spring of 1944.

The landings in North Africa in November 1942 were a success. In May 1943, all Axis resistance in Tunisia was ended; in July, the Allies landed in Sicily, in accordance with the plans agreed upon at the Casablanca Conference in January 1943. Another decision made there was not to undertake a cross-Channel attack in the same year, because by the middle of September not more than 21 to 24 British and American divisions could be ready in England, as against 44 German divisions in France. No date was fixed at Casablanca for that attack. A date was mentioned for the first time when the conference of the Combined Chiefs of Staff at Washington in May 1943 set May 1st, 1944, 'as target date for an operation to secure a lodgement on the Continent from which further offensive operations can be carried out'.[6]

German Measures in 1943

To the Germans, the invasion in North Africa came as a strategic surprise which cost them an excellent army, a valuable position, and a considerable amount of material. The landing in Sicily in July, followed by that at Salerno in September 1943, increased the strain on their manpower and material resources, by creating the Second Front in Europe and removing Italy as a belligerent. If the Germans gained time for preparing the defence of France, they did not benefit from it as much as they should have done. Their various high commanders realized the dangers of the situation, and tried to make the best of the rather inadequate means at their disposal.[7] However, there was hardly enough co-operation and determination to exploit all possibilities to the utmost.

Field-Marshal von Rundstedt, Supreme Commander West and C.-in-C. Army Group D, was the area commander responsible under Directive No. 40 for co-ordinating all military, and even Party and civilian, efforts. In the opinion of his staff, the invasion fleet would take the shortest route across the Channel; this narrowed the danger zone to its eastern part, approximately from the mouth of the Somme to the estuary of the Scheldt. Between these two points, therefore, there was a heavy concentration of infantry divisions, together with the strong group of heavy batteries in the Calais–Boulogne sector. To the west, the defence forces were spread out very thinly, particularly so in the western part of the Seine Bight. One weak division held over thirty miles of excellent landing beach. For long stretches there were only observation posts, with nothing between and little behind them. In Brittany, the forces were still weaker, but there were few good landing beaches, all the rest being rocky and open to westerly gales.

Even in the erection of the heavy batteries, the coast of the Channel west of the Straits lagged behind all other areas. While the Channel Islands had a surfeit of heavy guns, the five main bases on the Bay of Biscay had only two heavy batteries (the second, at the mouth of the Gironde, still under construction), Cherbourg had only one 240mm battery ready; Le Havre had no heavy guns, only a 170mm battery. At Gréville, west of Cherbourg, and at Octéville, north of Le Havre, batteries of three 380mm guns each were under construction, but work on them had been begun so late that they were not ready by June 1944; they would have been very useful, although not decisive.

On the whole, there seems to have been a fatalistic acceptance of the deteriorating situation, and a lack of alertness in looking for possible improvements. This was aggravated by the absence of an integrated plan to exploit every available means of developing defensive strength to the full. On November 3rd, Hitler issued Führer Directive No. 51,[8] which frankly referred to the losses in Russia and the increasing threat of an invasion in the west. It pointed out the vital importance of France for continuing the war, considered a landing in Denmark as possible, and continued: 'I have therefore decided to strengthen the defences in the west, particularly at places from which we shall launch our long-range war against England. For those are the very points at which the enemy must and will attack' (a conclusion and also a diversion from the main issue typical of Hitler); '. . . stationary weapons will be heavily concentrated in points of main defensive effort at the most vulnerable coastal sectors. . . . Should the enemy nevertheless force a landing . . . the counter-attack will prevent the enlargement of the beach-head, and throw the enemy back into the sea . . .' Then followed details for strengthening the defence forces in men and material, and directives for the Luftwaffe, the Navy, and the SS. In short, Directive No. 51 repeated Directive No. 40 in a more urgent tone and for an area restricted to the coasts from Denmark to France, although

Norway cropped up in the orders for the Navy, which was asked 'to get ready numerous submarines for the northern seas areas', with a temporary weakening of the submarine forces in the Atlantic.

These orders were accompanied by an innovation. When they were issued, Field-Marshal Rommel, at that time C.-in-C. of Army Group B in Upper Italy, received instructions to inspect the defences in northwestern Europe, beginning in Denmark, and going on to the Artois, the Cotentin, the Netherlands, and Brittany; he was to report on their state of readiness, and suggest possible improvements. For this task, he retained the staff of Army Group B, which in a somewhat reduced and modified form was designated as an 'Army Group for Special Employment'.

Place and Date of the Invasion

Before D-day, the German high staffs did not agree where and when to expect the invasion. The intelligence service fell for the Allied radio deception which placed a fictitious US 14th Army and the existing British 4th Army in southeastern England, facing the Pas-de-Calais across the Straits of Dover.[9] The Navy was less impressed by this apparent concentration opposite the Boulogne–Calais area than the Army, because it knew how easily the direction of large transport movements can be changed at sea. Most HQs expected the attack where it could be supported by the thousands of fighters based on southern England. That was the coast between the Scheldt River and eastern Brittany. Denmark was too far away from England for fighter protection, and its west coast too open to the prevailing westerly winds. The Skagerrak, by which the sheltered east coast could be reached, seemed sufficiently secure after two heavy batteries (380mm guns) had been erected and strong minefields had been laid.

OKW believed all the time that the invasion would come across the Straits of Dover and did not change this opinion even in the first weeks after the actual landing in the Seine Bight. Army Group D (von Rundstedt) chose the beaches on either side of the Somme. They were excellent for getting ashore, although very open to the sea. Field-Marshal Rommel at first supported the Somme idea, but soon changed over to the Seine Bight as being better protected. The activities of the Allied air forces, which in April and May attacked all the bridges and railways leading into Normandy, destroying most of them, also strongly indicated the Seine Bight. Furthermore, the Allies had left it un-mined in contrast to the heavily mined waters east of Le Havre. The Scheldt, which at first seemed possible, was heavily mined, too, and its hinterland almost completely neglected by the Allied air forces.

Actually, the Allies after almost two years of research and study selected the area between the Vire and Orne rivers – for its good beaches, its distance from known Germany army reserves and fighter airfields, its good terrain for airfield construction and its proximity to the large port of Cherbourg. The Combined Commanders proposed it first in February 1943.[10]

The defenders expected the invasion to start with a rising tide, one to two hours before high water, about two hours before daybreak, in a not too dark night (half moon), and, of course, with little wind and sea.[11] The actual requirements of the Allies were somewhat different: three hours before high water (to be able to see the beach obstacles), one hour after the beginning of daylight (to have time for preliminary bombardments from the sea and the air) and with moonlight on the preceding night so that airborne troops could be landed correctly near their targets.[12] As to the date, the attack was expected from the end of March on, whenever the weather and the other conditions seemed suitable. Every afternoon, the German troops were informed whether a landing was considered as very probable, probable, possible, or improbable.

Rommel Starts his Inspection

In the first half of December 1943, Field-Marshal Rommel, with his small staff of experts from the three Services, had inspected the defences, or rather the lack of defences in Denmark. Why he was ordered to begin there has never been explained. He gained valuable experience, but he could not start work in France before December 20th, and time was of the essence. In France, the impressions were the same as in Denmark, only on a much larger scale. The main points were:

The Army forces were barely adequate for a vigorous defence, the Luftwaffe and Navy very weak. There was no uniform defence plan, except for the major ports, and even in these not all necessary measures had been carried out. The three Services did not co-operate enough in many details. No agreement had been reached on the principles of the use of artillery in coastal defence. The Army wanted the batteries placed behind the coast for indirect fire; the Navy wanted them on the coast for direct fire. The infantry was not mobile, owing to lack of motor transport. There were not enough mines on land and in the water. Almost every commander had his own ideas, not always very clear, on how to defend his area.

The Army in the West in 1943–4

By the late autumn of 1943, forty-nine German divisions were stationed in the west; they were of greatly differing character, personnel and material strength, and fighting value. Some infantry divisions had been in France since 1940, and had been used to train replacements for the east or south. They had a hard core of experienced officers and non-commissioned officers, but many of them had been wounded and were not completely fit for active duty. In the west, replacements were either very young, or rather old. The average age of the German Army was 31·5 years, i.e. *six* years older than the US Army in 1943.[13] In fact, the average of one division was 37 years. The state of health was indifferent; men suffering from specific ailments, mainly of the stomach, were concentrated in one static division.

The 'indigenous' or 'static' divisions were stationed on the coast, in order to combine training and guarding the beaches. Not all had the normal strength of three regiments of three battalions each. Some were composed of two regiments and a further battalion, others of three regiments of which two had two battalions only. There were some battalions, stationed mostly in Brittany, formed of Cossacks or Tartars; south of the Gironde were some Indians. The Channel Islands were garrisoned by the reinforced 319th Infantry Division, some tanks, an AA brigade and naval coastal artillery: 40,000 men in all.

In areas further inland, there were always a number of divisions resting after severe losses; some others were in the process of formation. The number of armoured divisions fluctuated with the tides of the war in the east. In March 1944, only one fully mobile armoured division was left in France, the 21st Panzer Division. From then on, their strength was rapidly increased again until the beginning of June, when there were 58 divisions in the west, 10 of them armoured (including the 17th SS Panzer-Grenadier Division).

The Air Force in the West in 1943–4

Curiously enough, two types of infantry divisions were part of the Luftwaffe, the 'Air Force Field Divisions' (*Luftwaffenfeld-Divisionen*) and the Parachute Divisions. The first had been formed in 1942 from the excess of Luftwaffe ground personnel. They were meant to replace the severe losses of the Russian campaign. Their men were good, they were well armed, but most of their officers and non-commissioned officers also came from the Luftwaffe, and lacked the training and experience for fighting in mobile operations. In Russia, they had suffered heavily without achieving much. It would have been much better to put them into existing infantry units as a kind of blood transfusion, but Göring considered them as part of the Luftwaffe and would not let them go.

The same was the case with the paratroops. They were an *élite* arm, on an equal status with the SS, tough, well trained, excellently equipped for land fighting, and were never again used from the air. In the spring of 1944, 3rd Anti-Aircraft Corps of the Luftwaffe was relieved from its static duties as local AA defence and sent to training camps for a short course of instruction in more mobile warfare. Then three of its four regiments were stationed near the coast in the Somme area, the fourth in the vicinity of Bayeux, changing their positions almost daily.

The Luftwaffe was said to have between 200,000 and 300,000 ground and airfield personnel in the west. Its strength in aircraft was so low, however, that it had to give up the airfields near the coast and move into the interior of France. In the second half of 1943 and in 1944, the attempt was made to resume the air attacks on England. In January 1944, the 'England Attack Command' (*Angriffsführer England*) had at its disposal 524 planes (about 90 per cent twin-engined bombers), of which 462 were operational. From January 21st to May 29th, they undertook 29 attacks on England, 14 alone on London, with an average of 200 aircraft. Losses were high, results meagre. The British called it 'the baby blitz'. The last attacks were carried out at the end of May 1944 by 66, 65, and 51 aircraft. The strength of the attacking forces had sunk to 181 planes (107 operational).[14]

The Navy in the West in 1943–4

For offensive purposes, the Navy had become the weakest of the three Services. In 1943, the submarine war had broken down because the submarine types used by the Germans were outmoded by Allied technical development. When they travelled on the surface, they were located by planes and ships equipped with radar. Under water, they were too slow to escape the specially formed anti-submarine forces once they had been located by their improved Asdic. The 'snorkel', a breathing-tube, was being installed in the existing submarines to enable them to proceed submerged with their diesel engines. This minimized the danger from radar, but only a completely new type of submarine with a highly increased underwater speed (17 knots as against 6) had any prospects of operating successfully again. Two types (XXI and XXIII) were being rushed through the designing rooms and the shipyards, but the first boats could not be ready before the winter of 1944–5. In the meantime, the Navy had in the west:

about 100 obsolete submarines
8 destroyers and large torpedo-boats
5 small torpedo-boats
30 motor torpedo-boats
about 500 minesweepers and patrol vessels of little fighting value

Ashore, the Navy manned the coastal and AA batteries around the major ports, and a number of radar stations on the coast. It had a good communications system, and some well-trained transport battalions. In addition, there were some naval training battalions in the Netherlands, Belgium, and southeast France, where they relieved army units from garrison duties.

All the naval personnel ashore that did not man the guns were organized in 'alarm units' for local defence in case of airborne landings or raids. In theory, everybody was trained and armed for close combat, but there was little time for training, and weapons were scarce.

The Plans for Defence

There was no doubt that a successful defence would be difficult with the means available. Obviously, the armoured divisions with their great mobility and striking power were the strongest weapon, and the outcome would largely depend on their use. All high-ranking commanders agreed that in theory it would be best to smash the attack before or when it reached the beach. However, neither von Rundstedt nor von Sodenstern (C.-in-C. 19th Army in southern France, one of the best planners of the General Staff) nor Geyr von Schweppenburg (C.-in-C. Armoured Forces West from the end of 1943) believed in this possibility. Their plan was to do as much harm as possible to the approaching landing fleets by the fire of the guns near the coast, and to hamper the actual landing by a rather thin cordon of troops stationed there. The enemy forces which were bound to gain beach-heads were to be counter-attacked by the local reserves. The enemy was expected to overcome this resistance, too, and was then to be thrown back into the sea by the concentrated motorized forces.

Whereas von Rundstedt visualized this decisive phase of the invasion battle near the beach, von Schweppenburg planned that it would be farther inland, with his armoured divisions hidden in the forests of southern Normandy and around Paris. Von Sodenstern, who realized the decisive influence of the overwhelming Allied strength in the air, planned an 'interesting variation' in 1943.[15] He proposed to lure the Allies into the area between the Seine and Loire, west–northwest of Paris. Here, the German armoured forces were to be ready to spring the trap.[16]

Rommel approached the problem from a different angle. He had great experience in mobile warfare with armoured forces. He also had recent experience – in contrast to the other generals – with the greatly improved Allied tanks, and particularly their anti-tank weapons, and he knew what it meant to fight without an adequate air force. He did not think movements at night impossible, but he expected them to be too slow to be decisive, particularly with the short nights of summer. Moreover, he visualized the political as well as the military side of the war. He knew that there was no hope of winning, but hoped that the war could be brought to a tolerable end. Any kind of beach-head in the West would mean a third front, because it would be impossible to get the Allies out again even if they suffered a set-back in the battle with the armoured forces. He was sure that, with their superiority, they would break out sooner or later, with disastrous results for the Eastern Front, too.

So he looked for a way to defeat the landing on the beach, and to win a respite which could be exploited politically. During his tour of inspection in Denmark, he planned a defence which used and integrated everything the three Services could offer without neglecting the strength of the armoured troops. He planned to oppose the landings by a belt about three miles deep composed of strongpoints surrounded by minefields. They were to be manned by the infantry and defended by more and better protected artillery, with the armoured divisions stationed behind this belt in such a way that the guns of their forward units could shell the beach. In this way, the infantry would have armoured support as soon as they were attacked. Rommel was a great believer in close co-operation of infantry and armour. The divisions on either flank of the attacked area would form the reserves and, with the good roads in France, be speedily available.

Forward Defence in the Water

This defence system had the disadvantage of too little depth. Rommel planned to make up for it by extending the defence far into the sea, placing obstacles in shallow water and various types of naval mines in deeper water. The underwater obstacles consisted of tank traps, stakes slanting seawards, tetrahedra and rails, with mines, if possible, or with iron 'tin-openers', all designed to wreck enemy landing craft. The obstacles began just under the high-water line; later they were extended seawards when labour and material became available. Owing to the great difference between high water and low water in the Seine Bight (over twenty feet) this scheme needed an immense amount of work and material and was far from finished in June 1944. Nevertheless, the obstacles accounted for the greatest part of the losses of landing craft on D–day.

From August 1943 to January 1944, 16 minefields had been laid between Boulogne and Cherbourg, slightly south of a line of minefields in the middle of the Channel, dating back to 1942 and probably no longer operative. After that not a single mine was laid in the Seine Bight in spite of the unceasing demands of Army Group B on Navy Group West to strengthen the defences with naval mines. This was due more to ineffective command structure and divergence of opinions on the probable place of the invasion than to lack of material or minelayers.

The Navy had developed a simple and effective mine for shallow water, the KMA (Coastal Mine A), but the first few thousand were laid in the Dieppe area and south of the Gironde and not at all in accordance with Rommel's wishes. Navy Group West planned to lay anchored mines by torpedo-boats and large minesweepers, although they could have used the motor torpedo-boats and, particularly, small fast minesweepers (R–boats), which had already carried out numerous minelaying operations of this sort in previous years. The larger vessels suffered heavily from sea and air attacks and from mines on their way to Le Havre, where they were to take the mines on board. Their first excursion was planned for the night before D–day but cancelled owing to the weather conditions. Navy Group West prepared, under the name of 'Blitzsperren' (lightning barrages), a system of minefields to be laid by all available vessels as soon as the attack was recognized as being imminent. Army Group B protested against this dubious measure, but to no avail. Most of these fields were laid on D–day but, as was to be expected, not a single one in the attack area where they were needed most, for the enemy forces arrived there before the minelayers were ready. Therefore, a very important part of Rommel's plan for the defence was not executed. Even a few hundred mines in the Seine Bight could have caused losses and considerable delays, as was shown later.

Strengthening the Defences on Land

At first, Rommel had the right of inspection only, and could give advice but
not orders. Locally, the troops accepted his ideas eagerly, but the higher staffs
did not. This caused delays which could not be afforded in that critical situation.
Rommel therefore applied to Hitler to be given command, and was made
C.-in-C. of the 7th Army (from the Loire to the Orne), the 15th Army (from
the Orne to the Scheldt) and the 88th Army Corps (in Holland). He was put
under Field-Marshal von Rundstedt, but his orders to inspect the defences
of the other areas remained unaltered. Von Schweppenburg, C.-in-C. Armoured
Forces West, was directly under von Rundstedt, parallel to Rommel, as was
Colonel-General Blaskowitz, for the southwest and south of France. Neither
von Rundstedt nor Rommel could give any orders to Field-Marshal Sperrle,
C.-in-C. 3rd Air Fleet, or to Admiral Krancke, C.-in-C. Navy Group West,
nor were they permitted to move any of the armoured and other divisions
without asking Armed Forces High Command (OKW). To add to the difficulties, the 'Fighting Area' (*Kampfgebiet*) and with it the jurisdiction
of Army Group B and the armies defending the coast, did not reach more
than twenty miles inland. All the interior was under a military governor who
resided in Paris and received orders partly from OKW and partly from
von Rundstedt.

Rommel tried to overcome all these obstacles with great energy. He soon
got the building of strongpoints and the laying of mines going at a good pace.
It took some time to increase the deliveries of mines. So his engineers designed
simple gadgets to convert heavy shells into mines, and to produce makeshift
mines from material on hand. Up to the end of 1943, 1·7 million land mines
had been laid in France. In 1944, over 4 million were laid, with a target of
50 million more.

Getting more guns to the coast and putting all the artillery there under
bomb-proof shelters was slow work. The Navy contributed its last reserves,
two batteries of 210mm guns and two of 150mm guns, in the winter 1943–4.
They were split between the 15th Army and the 7th Army, with the result that
one 210mm battery was placed near Calais where it was hardly needed. The
other went to Marcouf on the east coast of the Cotentin peninsula, and was the
only heavy battery which could and did fire against the invasion forces.
Armour to protect the larger guns was unobtainable, and concrete was in short
supply owing to the demands for the Channel Islands, the submarine pens and
the missile sites. As a result, quite a number of army coastal batteries had no
shelter by the end of May and were withdrawn to concealed positions more
inland. The shelters, particularly those of naval design, withstood bombardments well. Dummy batteries attracted a great many Allied air attacks and
helped the real guns to survive. By D–day, the numerous air attacks had
destroyed only 8 guns in the Pas-de-Calais, 5 in the Seine–Somme area and
3 in Normandy.[17]

To prevent gliders from landing, stakes were to be erected in the open areas in the 'Rommel belt'. Rommel was not much afraid of airborne landings farther inland, providing that they could be prevented from reaching the coast and getting into contact with their own forces there.

The Situation immediately before D–day

These measures amounted to a considerable increase in the defensive strength in the West, though they were started rather late and, for various reasons, had an additional delay of several weeks in the area of the 7th Army, i.e. where the invasion struck. By the end of May, the 84th Army Corps estimated that its programme of construction was about half complete. On the east coast of the Cotentin Peninsula, strongpoints and resistance nests were spaced about 875 yards apart; between the Orne and Vire rivers, 1,300 yards. In the sector of 352nd Infantry Division, only 15 per cent of the shelters were bomb-proof.[18] Yet it gave a good account of itself in the battle, and prevented the Americans from winning a deep bridgehead on the first day. If work had started two or three months earlier, the situation would have been quite different.

Rommel tried in vain to get some kind of offensive action against the invasion forces gathering in the south of England. The Luftwaffe directed 14 of their 29 attacks against London, and only a few of the others against the embarkation ports on the south coast. His request for dropping pressure mines from the air in the area of Portsmouth and Southampton was turned down by OKW, as well as his request for the V–1 missile attack to be opened. The launching installations were ready, but Hitler wanted to wait until a certain volume of fire could be kept up.

The Navy could do nothing with their obsolete U-boats, but sent destroyers, large torpedo-boats and motor torpedo-boats to the attack. Two large torpedo-boats were lost, as against one Canadian destroyer. Motor torpedo-boats surprised a landing exercise, sank two landing ships and damaged a third, inflicting great loss of life. The motor torpedo-boats could have carried quite a number of mines into the swept channels.

Towards the end of April, air reconnaissance showed a concentration of shipping, landing craft, and warships in the Portsmouth–Southampton area with an estimated capacity for carrying 3 divisions, in the Plymouth–Brixham area with a capacity for $2\frac{1}{2}$ divisions, in Falmouth for 1 division. The last reliable photos were made on May 24th, and confirmed the picture gained in April. The Germans estimated that shipping for at least sixteen divisions had been assembled in southern England. In addition, a great many 'Mulberries', the artificial harbours, were photographed, and identified as 'large landing-stages'. In the two weeks before D–day, not a single reconnaissance plane got through.[19]

Almost the only bright spot in the dark defence picture was the increase in armour and efficient divisions after March 1944. At the beginning of the year there were 823 tanks, assault guns, and self-propelled anti-tank guns; their number rose to 1,600 at the end of April, and to almost 2,000 at the end of May, excluding weapons of French and Russian make. On D-day, there were 9 armoured divisions in the West, plus 1 mechanized division (17th SS Panzer-Grenadier Division). Two parachute divisions and one parachute regiment were ready for combat. The AA Corps was getting into shape. Of the 58 divisions under the orders of von Rundstedt, 33 were static or reserve units, i.e. rather immobile and suited for limited tasks only.

In accordance with his overall plan, which in principle had been approved by Hitler, Rommel tried to increase the number of divisions in or behind the 'Rommel belt'. He succeeded only in part. The 352nd Infantry Division was moved to the coast, and took over the western half of the front between Vire and Orne. The 91st Airborne Division (weak in heavy weapons) was moved into the Cotentin Peninsula; one regiment of the AA Corps went to the Bayeux area.

It was a different tale with the paratroops and the armoured forces. The two para-divisions were stationed in northern Brittany, and only the 6th Parachute Regiment at Lessay-Périers in the southwest of the Cotentin Peninsula. OKW decided to order three armoured divisions to southern France (9th, 11th, and 2nd SS); to assign three to Army Group B for tactical control, von Schweppenburg remaining responsible for their training (2nd, 21st and 116th); and to form a 'strategical' reserve of the last four (1st SS, 12th SS, Panzerlehr, 17th SS Panzer-Grenadier). This was a bad compromise which could not be expected to work, particularly with the existing command structure and the divergence of opinions between Rommel and von Schweppenburg. The latter had gone personally to OKW to plead for his idea of keeping the armoured divisions far back, and evidently had carried part of his point, thus destroying another mainstay of Rommel's plan without getting his own fully approved in exchange.[20]

Even the areas for the divisions under the tactical control of Army Group B were determined by OKW, the Somme for the 2nd, north of the lower Seine for the 116th, and the Orne for the 21st. As a result, only the 21st Panzer Division was in the area where Rommel expected the blow to fall. He pleaded in vain to move Panzerlehr and 3rd AA Corps up between the Orne and the Vire, the 12th SS Panzer to straddle the Vire, and to have a rocket-launching brigade stationed west of the Orne. They would have been exactly in the right places to counter the invasion, and would have left seven armoured divisions to form von Schweppenburg's mobile assault group. Incidentally, these dispositions planned by Rommel were the best proof that he had a good idea where the Allies would strike. His requests were not granted, however, and on June 5th, 1944, he left his headquarters in La Roche Guyon, on the Seine forty miles northwest of Paris, for Berchtesgaden, in order personally to support his request. Westerly winds were blowing, low clouds made reconnaissance and landings from the air almost impossible; therefore nobody on the German side expected the invasion in the next two or three days.

The Allied Attack

On the other side of the Channel, the meteorologists were better served with weather data, and gave the Supreme Allied Commander a more reliable picture to base his decisions upon. On June 3rd, when all troops were aboard, the weather situation started to deteriorate into a series of depressions moving across from the west. D–day had been scheduled for June 5th, but in the early hours of June 4th so much cloud was predicted for the following day that the air force would not be able to operate effectively. General Eisenhower therefore decided to postpone the operation for twenty-four hours. On Sunday night (June 4th), the forecasters expected the rain front over the Channel area to clear up soon, with tolerable conditions till Tuesday morning (June 6th). On the strength of this forecast, General Eisenhower decided to go ahead on Tuesday, because otherwise it would have been necessary to postpone the operation to June 19th at least. It was one of the truly great decisions of military history.

There was no need for General Eisenhower to ask for permission when with a few words he set the immense machinery of the invasion forces in motion. The command organization of the Allies was simple, with clear responsibilities at every level, and much better than that of the Germans. Alliances very often are cumbersome to handle, and it took some time to find the best form and the right men for Operation 'Overlord'. Experience previously gained in the war helped considerably, from the luckless ABDA Command (American–British–Dutch–Australian) in Southeast Asia in the winter of 1941–2, through the staff organizations for the invasions in North Africa, Sicily, and Italy to COSSAC (Chief of Staff to the Supreme Allied Commander designate) as predecessor of SHAEF (Supreme Headquarters of the Allied Expeditionary Force); this came into being on January 15th, 1944, with General Eisenhower (who had been Supreme Allied Commander in the Mediterranean) taking over as Supreme Commander on February 13th. General W. Bedell Smith was appointed as his Chief of Staff, and three Commanders-in-Chief were under him, responsible for all planning and for all Allied forces of their own service: General (later Field-Marshal) Montgomery as C.-in-C. 21st Army Group responsible for the planning of the ground operations and their execution until the Supreme Commander had transferred his headquarters to France, which was expected for about D+90; Air Marshal Sir T. Leigh-Mallory as C.-in-C. Allied Expeditionary Air Force; and Admiral Sir Bertram Ramsay as C.-in-C. Allied Naval Expeditionary Force.

Co-operation at all levels was much facilitated by this practical organization. When there was friction, unavoidable in an undertaking of that size, as much depended on the human qualities of the Supreme Commander as on his military efficiency. The choice of General Eisenhower by the Combined Chiefs of Staff was very fortunate in this respect, too.

Thirty-eight divisions had been assembled in England to take part in

Operation 'Overlord', which within ninety days after the first landings was to conquer France north of the Loire River and west of the Seine up to Paris. It was to be complemented by an invasion of the Mediterranean coast of France, but this operation, although on a much smaller scale, had to be postponed to the middle of August owing to an insufficiency of landing ships.

On D–day, five assault divisions were to be put ashore; from west to east, two US divisions at Utah and Omaha beaches as the van of US 1st Army under General Omar Bradley, then one British at Gold beach, one Canadian at Juno, and one British at Sword, these three leading the British 2nd Army under General Dempsey. The five divisions were reinforced by armour and AA units and several battalions of commandos and rangers. The assault was to start with two US airborne divisions dropping into the Cotentin Peninsula directly behind Utah beach, and one British immediately east of the Orne River downstream from Caen. Within six days, 7 more divisions were to be put ashore, in the following six days 5 more and a number of armoured battalions and brigades. The Allied air strength was composed of 3,500 heavy bombers, 2,300 medium and light bombers, and 5,000 fighters. For airborne operations, there were nearly 1,400 troop carriers and 3,300 gliders.[21]

An immense fleet now began to move out of the ports and roadsteads and across the waters upon which another proud armada had sailed 356 years before to seek victory and to meet with defeat. 4,266 landing ships and landing craft assembled in five double columns converging on Z Area, thirty miles south-southeast of Portsmouth. They proceeded on parallel courses along the swept channels and steered for the five assault areas. They were attended by a great many tugs and other auxiliary vessels, and protected by no fewer than 702 warships (apart from the minesweepers), made up as follows:

>   6 battleships
>   2 monitors with 15-inch guns
>   2 cruisers
> 119 destroyers and escort destroyers
> 113 sloops, frigates, and corvettes
> 80 patrol craft, anti-submarine trawlers, and gunboats
> 360 motor launches, motor torpedo-boats and motor gunboats

In the previous weeks, the Allied air forces had flown up to 5,500 bomber missions daily over Germany, accompanied by 5,000 fighters. At the same time, they had shifted the target of their attacks to the plants producing aircraft fuel, with the result that production fell from 175,000 tons in April to 156,000 tons in May, and to only 53,000 tons in June, a development which was of decisive influence on the German reaction in the air.[22]

In the night before D–day, the silent columns of ships were overtaken again and again by large formations of planes. The transport planes carried 13,000 parachutists to France. The British were the first to touch French soil, at 02.00 hours; the Americans landed a few minutes later. At the same time, 1,100

British and Canadian night bombers attacked the coastal batteries between Le Havre and Cherbourg, followed at daybreak by about 1,000 American heavy bombers attacking coastal targets during the half-hour before the first waves of landing craft reached the beaches. Then, the navies took a hand, with their thirty large ships and about 100 destroyers and gunboats opening fire to destroy what remained of the defence installations. On the whole, the result of these massive bombardments was disappointing. Hardly any of those guns completely protected with concrete shelters were knocked out; even the smaller gun positions and troop shelters were not all put out of action. As far as can be ascertained, no more than 14 per cent of the gun positions in the invasion area were destroyed.[23]

The work of the twenty-five flotillas of minesweepers had been thorough, not a single ship was damaged by a mine with the exception of one minesweeper, although quite a few mines were encountered and swept in the old German minefields in the middle of the Channel. Minesweeping is a slow business at best, and had to be begun in good time, Therefore, early in the afternoon of June 5th, the fleet minesweeping flotillas started sweeping the ten channels leading south from Z Area, less officially called 'Piccadilly Circus'. When clear, each channel was marked by lighted Dan buoys, up to eighty for one channel.

Two of the minesweeping flotillas came in sight of the French coast in the late afternoon, but kept on sweeping in the direction of the German look-outs. The 14th Flotilla sighted the coast almost three hours before it grew dark and approached it for more than two hours, until the crews could make out houses and other objects with the naked eye. Nothing happened. The 16th Minesweeping Flotilla sighted the coast at a distance of eighteen miles and approached to eleven miles, with the same lack of reaction from the German side.[24]

So far, it has proved impossible to find out if these flotillas were sighted by the German watchers on the coast, and, if so, what action these took. In any case, no report seems to have reached the higher staffs. No attempt at air reconnaissance was made on June 5th, and owing to the apparently bad weather conditions, the 7th Army had not even been put on the alert. For the same reason, Navy Group West cancelled not only the intended minelaying operation but also all patrols by motor torpedo-boats and gunboats. A kind of coma appears to have descended on all those who might have changed the course of events by realizing some hours earlier what was happening. Even one very late, last possibility which fate offered was turned down. On the evening of June 5th, C.-in-C. West (von Rundstedt) as well as the 15th Army picked up messages sent by the BBC, evidently to alert the French resistance movement. The 15th Army ordered the highest degree of readiness for its troops, but neither C.-in-C. West nor Army Group B nor the 7th Army took any steps. Early on June 6th, the general in command of 91st Airborne Division was on his way back from a map exercise held by the 7th Army at Rennes when the first paratroopers descended from the clouds. He was killed in the ensuing fight.

The US paratroops landed in a far too wide area, fifteen by twenty-five miles, and found themselves dispersed to such an extent that they had great difficulties concentrating even against the few German troops in the interior of the Cotentin. They failed in their main objective, namely to cut off the peninsula from the south, and it took them up to two days to make contact with the troops that had landed on the beach. The British paratroops were dropped very accurately east of the lower Orne, and within a few hours succeeded in seizing their objectives, the bridges over the river and the Caen canal.

The air landings and the bombardments had alarmed the German troops on the coast, and when the first waves of landing craft came in between 06.30 and 08.00 hours, they met with stubborn resistance in many places. However, at Utah, the westernmost beach, the forces landed about a mile too far to the south by mistake, and in this way found a much weaker spot than the original attack area. Omaha beach, east of the Vire, was the best defended part of the coast. Here, the well-trained 352nd Division had taken over two months ago, a change which had not been discovered by Allied intelligence. On D–day, the beach-head remained shallow and unconnected with the British-Canadian beach-head to the east. Everywhere, underwater obstacles caused losses, or at least considerable damage; many tanks were lost in the water or on land mines ashore. In spite of local resistance, great masses of assault troops reached the shore because there were no reserves behind the thin defences along the beach, and there was no heavy artillery to fight the rocket ships and destroyers which bombarded the strongpoints at close range.

The German Countermeasures

German reaction higher up was far too slow, as a result of the faulty command structure. The 15th Army requested the alerting of the 12th SS Panzer Division as early as 02.45 hours, and Army Group B (where the Chief of Staff, General Speidel, acted vigorously in the absence of Rommel) gave orders to Armour Group West (von Schweppenburg) to move this division to positions on either side of Lisieux, about fifteen miles behind the coast. At 09.40 hours, C.-in-C. West cancelled these orders because OKW had not yet agreed. No decision had been reached yet about the Panzerlehr Division, which was stationed about seventy miles from the coast to the south of the 12th SS Panzer Division. At 14.32 hours, OKW eventually released the 12th SS to fight with the 7th Army, and at 15.07, it put the two armoured divisions under the orders of 1st SS Panzer Corps. However, they were too far away from the battlefield to attack on the same day. As was to be expected, they were seriously hampered by attacks from the air and by damage to roads and bridges, and suffered considerable losses before going into action. Units of the 12th SS were in position to fight late on June 7th, but both divisions could not start their counter-attack before June 9th. By that time, the Allies had landed masses of men and material, and were ready to give armoured forces a hot reception.

Only the 21st Panzer Division could participate in the fighting on D–day. At first, it moved to positions east of the Orne to attack the British airborne troops there. The preparations took longer than Army Group B expected, because the mass of the division had been kept deeper inland than was compatible with the orders it had received from Rommel. Before it was ready, the situation west of the Orne had deteriorated to such an extent that General Marcks, commanding the 84th Army Corps, gave orders to the 21st Panzer Division to attack west of the Orne. This meant passing through the town of Caen, and cost time and some losses. Nevertheless, when the division eventually started its attack in the late afternoon it almost reached the sea near Riva Bella. Then it fell back because the British landed glider troops on both banks of the Orne. 'In this way, a momentous service was rendered to the enemy and an initial success was not exploited.'[25]

The only other reserve on hand, the 915th Reinforced Grenadier Regiment (Battle Group Meyer) of the 352nd Division was not successful either. Stationed south of Bayeux, it was alerted by the 84th Army Corps at 04.00 hours, and sent to the Carentan–Isigny area where large-scale airborne landings had been reported, erroneously as it turned out later. With the 12th SS Panzer Division in that area, as requested by Rommel, or a division in the second line as in the Pas-de-Calais, the 84th Army Corps would have had no cause to feel alarmed for its rear. As things were, the 915th Regiment moved twenty miles to the west, partly on foot, partly on bicycles and worn-out French lorries, while the British landed all along the coast to the north and broke through the thin line of defences at Rivière, about ten miles northeast of Bayeux. The battle group now received orders to countermarch, and joined the fight late in the afternoon, worn out and strung out, in an area which it could easily have reached in the morning in full strength and much closer to the coast.

Neither the Luftwaffe nor the Navy succeeded in bringing any relief to the hard-pressed defenders. The forces of 3rd Air Fleet, with a nominal strength of 900 planes, of which 500 were operational, suffered so much from air attack themselves that no more than 319 sorties were flown on D–day. Twelve times fighter-bombers tried to reach the beach-heads, but they were intercepted and had to jettison their bombs. The ratio of strength was about 1:50, success correspondingly meagre.

The Luftwaffe Command had planned to send the following reinforcements to the West following an invasion:

19 fighter wings	(full complement of a wing =
2 fighter-bomber wings	27 planes + 9 reserve)
5 bomber wings	
8 night fighter wings	
2 close-reconnaissance wings	

and the necessary staff to operate them. Actually, however, the powerful Allied air-shield prevented aircraft movements before the late afternoon of D–day, and even then hampered them considerably. Twenty-two fighters started from Cologne at 20.00 hours for Villacoublay near Paris, ran into Allied fighters in bad weather and failing daylight, with the result that only two reached their destination – most of the others crash-landed. On the following day, only one plane of the twenty-two was operational. By June 10th, 3rd Air Fleet had a strength of 1,300 planes (756 operational). Despite all efforts, their number sank slowly but surely thereafter. On the same day, there were only 408 day and night fighters in Germany (264 operational) and 175 obsolete two-seater aircraft (100 operational) which had no chances whatsoever against the Allied long-range fighters.

Early in the morning of D-day, the Navy sent four old torpedo-boats from Le Havre against the invasion fleet. They fired torpedoes which missed the battleships *Warspite* and *Ramillies* and sank the Norwegian destroyer *Svenner*. Then they turned back, in view of the overwhelming odds. The large destroyers stationed on the Bay of Biscay attempted to get into the Channel but were intercepted near the island of Ouessant, where two of them were put out of action in a night engagement on June 9th. No U-boats reached the Channel in the first three decisive days of the invasion.

The Situation after Three Days

On D–day, the Allies succeeded in forming beach-heads of different sizes and depth in all five attack areas, but did not reach the target line set for that day at any point. The German defence had not been altogether unsuccessful, as shown by the following figures:

	Target for D–day	Actually landed	Ashore on June 18th	July 3rd	July 29th
men	107,000	87,000	629,000	929,000	1,566,000
vehicles	14,000	7,000	95,000	177,000	333,000
material (tons)	14,500	3,500	218,000	586,000	1,603,000

On Omaha beach, no more than 100 tons were unloaded as against 2,400 planned.[26] This deficit of 20 per cent of the men, 50 per cent of the vehicles and over 70 per cent of the material, with the ensuing grave shortage of ammunition, could not be exploited by the Germans, partly because of the Allied mastery of the air and well-directed fire from the sea, and partly because they could not fill the vacuum created behind their first-line divisions by placing the reserves too far back.

Rommel, who reached his headquarters late on June 6th, at once requested that regimental combat teams from the 15th Army be sent to the eastern beach-head to be followed by all the infantry divisions which held the second line in the Pas-de-Calais. With the exception of one division (346th), this was declined by OKW, which still expected a big landing operation there; it was again turned down a week later. In the second half of June some of these divisions were at last released.

Rommel also asked for the 319th Infantry Division from the Channel Islands, for part of the infantry division in Brittany, and for the four armoured divisions stationed in central and southern France, because the beach-heads could be contained only with very strong forces. These requests were declined, too, only to be granted weeks later when it was too late. As a result, only the 1st SS Panzer Corps with the 12th SS Panzer Division and the Panzerlehr Division reached the battlefield in the first three days, together with the 346th Infantry Division from the right bank of the Seine. The strength of the Allies increased rapidly; on June 10th they held a well-defended continuous beach-head deep enough to protect the landing beaches from artillery fire and to build landing strips for fighters. On June 11th, US troops took Carentan and opened the main road between Omaha and Utah forces. With their reinforcements painfully straggling up, the Germans were unable to prevent this development. Armoured counter-attacks on June 7th and 8th made limited progress only, and at such cost that on the whole the Germans were hard put to hold any coherent line inland. There was no hope of relieving various strongpoints still holding out in the coastal zone. In agreement with Rommel, von Schweppenburg went on the defensive until he could reassemble the three armoured divisions and, together with the 2nd Para-Corps coming up from Brittany, mount a massive attack to split the beach-head. On the evening of June 10th, however, RAF bombers completely destroyed von Schweppenburg's headquarters. His chief of staff, many officers and men were killed; he himself was wounded, and his staff put out of action for several days. SS General Sepp Dietrich, commanding the 1st SS Panzer Corps, took over for him, but had to postpone the counter-attack. The Third Front had become a fact, and the fate of the Third Reich was sealed.

The main reason for the failure of the German defence was lack of a single, clear-cut plan, carried out under the responsibility of a single, experienced commander. Considering the overwhelming strength of the Allies and the heavy strain on the German armed forces in the other theatres of war, it is doubtful if they could have entirely beaten off the invasion in Normandy. The difficulties of the Americans at Omaha beach and the progress made by the 21st Panzer Division late on D–day showed, however, that there were possibilities in Rommel's plans.

In the following weeks, the Luftwaffe dropped about 1,600 mines in the Seine Bight causing much trouble and the loss of, or heavy damage to, at least forty-three vessels. Timely minelaying by Navy Group West could have created the same amount of trouble and, in addition, loss of valuable time on D–day. With two armoured divisions, the 3rd AA Corps and some other reinforcements in the attack area there would have been a good chance of restricting the initial success of the Allies to some shallow lodgements on the coast. Nobody can say what would have happened then.

The Conspiracy against Hitler

The impending military defeat in the West and the heavy reverses in the East made it clear to a group of patriotic Germans, united against Hitler, that time was running out if they wanted to avert a complete catastrophe for their people. They were diplomats, politicians of various former parties, noblemen, labour leaders, high officials and officers, who had seen through Hitler and had combined to overthrow the dictatorship and to end the war. In the West, Field-Marshal Rommel, Colonel-General von Falkenhausen, the Military Governor of Belgium, General von Stülpnagel, the Military Governor of France, General Speidel, the Chief of Staff of Army Group B, and a number of prominent staff and reserve officers belonged to this group. Field-Marshal von Rundstedt had been informed and was in full agreement, but said to Rommel: 'You are young, the people know and like you, you'll have to do it.'[27] As the first step, Hitler was to be removed. Rommel wanted to arrest him and put him before a German court of law; others wanted to kill him outright. There was to be a provisional government by politicians, not by the military. In spite of the Allied demand for 'unconditional surrender', it was hoped that sober political thinking would prevail when the evacuation of the occupied Western countries was offered in order to facilitate negotiations.

Rommel had put himself unreservedly at the disposal of the conspirators. He knew the grave difficulties that lay ahead. He knew that atonement had to be made for the crimes of the National Socialists, and that the conditions of the Allies would be harsh. But he was convinced that continuing the war would be to the advantage of the Communists and to the detriment of Western civilization. From that time on, he played a most difficult double part, conducting military operations to the best of his ability in order to retain a position for negotiations, and at the same time waiting for the right moment to act against the usurper and for his country.

The Fight for Cherbourg

After securing the initial beach-head, the overall plan of the Allies was to drive down to the Loire and then to wheel eastwards to the Seine as far as Paris, in order to gain space for building up the operations against Germany itself. They planned to create the impression that they intended to break through in the Caen area on the eastern flank of the beach-head, while the actual break-out was to take place on the western flank, in the southern part of the Cotentin Peninsula. They calculated that it would take ninety days to cross the Seine and reach Paris.

Although the two artificial harbours (one off Arromanches at Gold beach, the other off St Laurent at Omaha beach) were each building up a capacity of handling 6,000 tons of supplies a day, it was imperative to take at least one large port, better two, as quickly as possible, because 54,000 tons had to be unloaded daily.[28] The original plans had foreseen the fall of Cherbourg on D+8, that of Brest on D+35. This proved impossible, however, and the operation to cut off the Cotentin Peninsula and to take Cherbourg could not be started before June 14th.

For the Germans, it was not difficult to guess that Cherbourg would be one of the first targets. This was confirmed by various US orders which fell into their hands. Fully appreciating the importance of a big port for the Allied build-up, Rommel intended to concentrate forces for the protection of the Cotentin Peninsula and of Cherbourg. Hitler and OKW knew better, however. They saw the main danger in the zone of Caen, and ordered the bulk of the armoured divisions there, 520 tanks and 43 infantry battalions as against 63 battalions with only 70 tanks for all the rest. They were not strong enough to prevent the US VII Corps from fighting its way across the peninsula from June 14th to 18th. The 7th German Army planned to direct as many units as possible to the south, but could not do so owing to repeated orders from Hitler forbidding the least move to the rear. They were all cut off, with the exception of a battle group of the 77th Infantry Division under Colonel Bacherer which broke through on June 19th, and a naval transport battalion which had taken ammunition to Cherbourg. In the evening of July 31st, the same battalion witnessed the Americans rushing towards Rennes and Brest while hidden between the two enemy columns in the hilly country just south of Pontaubault. Again it got away.

After reaching the west coast of the Cotentin Peninsula, the VII Corps turned north, with the VIII Corps facing south to meet any counter-attacks that might come. On the German side, General Marcks, the able commander of the 84th Army Corps, had been killed near the front by a shell from an American fighter. He was succeeded by General Fahrmbacher, who had commanded the 25th Army Corps in Brittany. No counter-attacks were possible, for reinforcements and supplies came up slowly and with great losses. The railways were practically paralysed, the roads under constant attack from the air, all troop movements took several times longer than under normal conditions.

The far-reaching effect of the invasion battle became evident when Hitler cancelled an attack that had been planned at Kovel on the Eastern Front, and released the 2nd SS Panzer Corps for operations in the West. Needless to say, it took weeks to move to Normandy. In the meantime, the great Soviet summer attack broke loose and the 2nd SS Panzer Corps was bitterly missed. As usual, Hitler stubbornly denied all freedom of action, and gave orders to hold every bit of ground.

At the urgent request of the two Field-Marshals, he came to the West (for the first time since 1940) and met them on June 17th near Soissons, in a concrete bunker built in 1940 as headquarters for the invasion of England. He sharply criticized the measures of the local commanders, and gave strict orders to hold the 'fortress' of Cherbourg at any price. After a short introduction by

Rundstedt, Rommel gave a candid and uncompromising evaluation of the situation, predicted the fall of Cherbourg almost to a day, and requested permission to operate more flexibly and to bring up reserves from the other parts of the coast. Hitler did not answer directly, but talked about the decisive effects of the V–1 fire on England which had been opened the day before. Rommel then gave an unvarnished picture of the political situation and urged Hitler to end the war. Hitler closed the meeting by telling him: 'Don't concern yourself about the progress of the war but look after your invasion front.'[29]

Hitler had promised to see some of the commanders who had been in the invasion battle, yet he left France a few hours later, allegedly because a V–1 missile with steering trouble had circled back and detonated near his bunker. He ordered the two Field-Marshals to report to him in the morning of June 29th at Berchtesgaden. They had to wait until night, before they were admitted, and were not allowed to discuss the situation, but had to listen to his rantings about the speedy decision which would be brought about by the new 'miracle weapons'. By that time the Russian offensive, started on June 20th, had shattered a large part of the Eastern Front, Cherbourg was in American hands and the remnants of the four divisions cut off in the Cotentin Peninsula were in captivity. The only glimmer in the dark situation was that the port had been damaged far more than the Allies had thought possible, with little damage to the city and to the installations vital for the inhabitants. The US evaluation of the harbour was: 'The demolition of the port of Cherbourg is a masterful job, beyond doubt the most complete, intensive and best-planned demolition in history.'[30]

Attempts to Contain the Beach-head

Just as the Americans cut off the Cotentin Peninsula and started their advance northwards on Cherbourg, a sudden gale from the northeast sprang up in the Channel, contrary to all meteorological experience for that season. It blew from June 19th to 23rd, drove 800 vessels ashore, mostly landing craft, wrecked the artificial harbour at Omaha beach (the other, somewhat protected by the Calvados Reef, remained intact and was used all through the winter), and – worst of all – completely interrupted unloading for four days running.

The Germans did not exploit this disaster, however, partly because they had no clear picture of the Allied set-back, partly because their reinforcements were still very slow in coming up. The regimental battle group of the 77th Infantry Division, which was stationed in Brittany about 100 miles to the southwest, took three days to cover thirty miles by train, suffering considerable losses in men and material. Then it had to march for another three to five days until it reached the battle area. Those parts of the battle group of the 265th Division which went by road covered the 180 miles to the front in five days, but their heavy weapons and equipment needed seven days for the first 100 miles by train. Then they had to proceed by road, too.[31]

OKW had not yet released any divisions of the 15th Army, yet on June 20th it gave orders to concentrate six armoured divisions for a counter-attack in the direction of Bayeux to cut the beach-head in two. The British positions east of the Orne were to be taken simultaneously. These plans were far too optimistic, in view of the transport situation. Neither could the six divisions be assembled quickly (1st SS, 9th SS, and 10th SS had not yet arrived, Panzerlehr and 12th SS were in the front line and had to be relieved by infantry divisions which were not yet available) nor could enough ammunition be brought up – 14,000 tons were required. On June 28th, General von Schweppenburg, as C.-in-C. of the 5th Panzer Army, with a new staff, was to take over the front from the Drôme River (between St Lô and Caumont) to the sea east of the Orne with the 47th, 1st SS and 2nd SS Panzer Corps, and the 86th Infantry Corps, which was to be moved up from the 1st Army in southwestern France. The 7th Army was to hold the line from the Drôme to the west with the 2nd Parachute Corps, the remnants of the 84th Corps and the reinforcements that might arrive.

British attacks on June 25th and 26th, planned to bypass Caen to the south, upset the German plans for relieving and assembling their armoured forces. On the morning of June 29th, a local American attack pinned down the battle group of the 2nd SS Panzer Division, with the result that in the afternoon of the same day von Schweppenburg only had the 2nd SS Panzer Corps (the 9th SS and the 10th SS) for his attack. After a slight initial success against the British bridgehead over the Odon River, it came to a standstill the same night. On June 28th, Colonel-General Dollmann died of heart failure and was succeeded by SS Colonel-General Hauser.

After the inconclusive meeting at Berchtesgaden on June 29th, OKW gave orders to cancel all attacks and to hold on everywhere. Hauser and von Schweppenburg in their turn sent proposals to Army Group B to evacuate the Caen pocket and to form south of the town a line which was shorter, easier to defend and out of range of the naval guns. These reached further inland than had been expected, because now there was nothing to prevent the big ships from taking up positions close inshore. They liked to fire from behind an old French battleship which had been scuttled in shallow water to serve as a breakwater for the Arromanches artificial harbour. By that time the Allies had found and studied some pressure mines which German aircraft had dropped on land by mistake. In the water they could not be swept, but they did not work against ships proceeding at very slow speed. To be compelled never to do more than a few knots was a nuisance, but much better than being blown up.

Rommel supported the request of the two army commanders; von Rundstedt approved of it, too, and sent it to OKW early on July 1st. On the same day, OKW rejected the proposals, and Hitler repeated his orders to hold everything at all costs. On the following day, von Rundstedt and von Schweppenburg were relieved of their commands and sent home. Their successors were Field-Marshal G. von Kluge as Supreme Commander West and C.-in-C. Army Group D, (not Rommel, as might have been expected) and General H. Eberbach as C.-in-C. 5th Panzer Army. Both were experienced and first-rate commanders, but von Kluge had been on the Russian front from 1941 to 1943, and then on sick leave after a serious accident. Now, he had been in Hitler's headquarters for two weeks and arrived in France with the same curious and unrealistic optimism which many people showed when they had been exposed to Hitler's personal influence for some time. In his case, this attitude was enhanced by the far too optimistic evaluation of the Allied strength by OKW and by his staff. The report of Supreme Commander West dated July 3rd estimated that so far 225,000 to 250,000 men and 43,000 vehicles had been landed, whereas the actual figures were 929,000 men, 177,000 vehicles, and 586,000 tons of material.[32]

Naval Attempts to Relieve the Situation

On June 15th, a heavy air attack on Le Havre put out of action the 4 remaining torpedo-boats, 10 motor torpedo-boats, and 15 minesweepers and patrol boats, and damaged many other small craft. The bombers approached by daylight in close formation at a comparatively low altitude, and remained entirely undisturbed because the AA artillery ashore had strict orders from 3rd Air Fleet not to fire at approaching aircraft under any circumstances. The reason was that on the same evening a Luftwaffe attack on the invasion fleet was planned, with Le Havre as the rendezvous. Two days later, a number of light craft were destroyed or damaged in Boulogne harbour by bombers. The remaining motor torpedo-boats carried out many attacks, but hardly ever got through to the larger ships because the Allies guarded the flank of the invasion area with numerous gunboats and motor torpedo-boats. Long-range torpedoes with a circling mechanism probably accounted for two destroyers and damaged a cruiser and a repair ship.[33]

German submarines penetrated into the Seine Bight from the middle of June. Forty-three left bases in Norway and on the Bay of Biscay with orders to attack shipping in the central Channel and the Seine Bight. Of these, 12 had to return prematurely owing to mechanical defects or damage by depth-charges, 10 were sunk before reaching their area of operations, 8 were destroyed there, and only 13 returned to their bases after operating in the Channel. They succeeded in sinking:

> 7 warships, from destroyer escorts to anti-submarine trawlers
> 2 LSTs (landing ships tanks)
> 1 LCI (landing craft infantry)
> 13 transports totalling 55,000 tons

They damaged:

> 1 frigate
> 6 transports totalling 49,000 tons

Operating in the Channel was rendered difficult by the strong and very irregular currents. On July 7th, after having been under almost continuous pressure from Asdic and depth-charges for thirty hours, *U. 763* had completely lost its bearings and eventually found itself in Spithead Roads off Portsmouth. Without sighting any remunerative targets and without being discovered, the U-boat got out again and back to its base.[34]

On July 5th to 6th, the Germans attacked for the first time with one-man torpedoes, sinking two minesweepers. Two nights later, a similar attack damaged the old cruiser *Dragon* so seriously that she was scuttled as an additional breakwater. On August 3rd, they sank a destroyer and a mine-sweeper; they were followed by explosive motorboats which sank one landing craft. In attacks by German small assault craft, scuttled hulks serving as breakwaters at Arromanches were torpedoed, among them the old battleship *Courbet*. On the whole, these attacks were only successful at first, when they came as a surprise. The British, who bore the brunt because the attackers came from the east, soon found efficient ways of dealing with the new menace, and the German losses mounted, without any corresponding success. In the first month after D-day, the Allies lost 261 vessels destroyed or damaged by enemy action, as against 606 by the weather.[35]

Military and Political Crisis

A visit to the front quickly convinced Field-Marshal von Kluge that the reports on the severity of the fighting and the superiority of the Allies in almost every respect had not been exaggerated. The British took Caen on July 10th, breaking through the positions of the 16th Luftwaffe Field Division which was too inexperienced in this kind of warfare. The attack was stopped south of the town. Then the Americans began to hammer at St Lô. The attacks were generally introduced by 1,000 and more bombers, softening up the German positions. Losses in men and material were very high, replacements few and far between. From June 6th to July 23rd, the Germans lost 2,722 officers and 110,357 non-commissioned officers and men, of whom no more than 10,078 had been replaced.[36] The losses of the Allies for the same period were estimated at 117,000. They were fully replaced.

In view of this situation, Field-Marshal Rommel sent a very grave evaluation of the situation through Supreme Commander West to Hitler. He described the Allied superiority and the rapid whittling away of the German forces. He predicted the Allied break-out within two to three weeks at most, and finished by saying: 'Our men are fighting heroically, but the unequal struggle is nearing its end. I must request you at once to draw the necessary conclusions from this situation. I feel it my obligation as C.-in-C. of my Army Group to say this plainly.'[37] This message was a last attempt to bring Hitler to his senses. If it failed – which was to be expected – it would make Rommel morally free to act against the dictator. Like many high military commanders, he found himself in a desperate conflict. He had sworn his oath to a man whom he recognized more and more as a usurper and a criminal, he knew the Allied demand for unconditional surrender, and he felt himself responsible to the German people and to Europe. As a rule, high commanders are isolated in war. In this situation where no satisfactory solution could be seen, each had to solve these moral problems entirely by himself, according to his conscience and his knowledge. Bitter inner struggles were fought during the invasion battle. They were closely interrelated with it, and have to be taken into account when analysing the German military operations.

On July 17th, Rommel visited several staffs at the front. When he received news of the American attack on St Lô, he hurried back to his headquarters. On an open stretch of road, two fighters fired at his car and killed the driver. Rommel was flung out and suffered four fractures of the skull. Tough as he was, he survived, but he was completely out of action on July 20th when Colonel Count Stauffenberg made an unsuccessful attempt on Hitler's life. At first Hitler was reported dead. In Paris, army units arrested the secret police (SD) without difficulty; the commanders of several armoured divisions were ready to join the conspirators; even some of the SS commanders were expected to turn against Hitler. However, Field-Marshal von Kluge could not make up his mind to take the decisive step, and to put himself at the head of the uprising in the West. It was difficult for him because he was not as well known or as well liked as Rommel, who probably was Hitler's strongest and most dangerous opponent, capable of 'carrying the terrible double weight of war and civil war on his shoulders.'[38] The opportunity was lost, the secret police were released, General von Stülpnagel, the Military Governor, tried to kill himself and was later executed. Von Kluge, not yet suspected, took over as C.-in-C. Army Group B, in addition to his duties as Supreme Commander West. A chance to end the war had passed: Hitler's despotism increased, if possible, and the fighting went on relentlessly. What Rommel had gained in time was lost by the change in command and by the interference of the dictator.

After a feint to the southwest of Caen, Montgomery launched a massive attack on July 18th in a southeasterly direction, understood by SHAEF to aim at a complete break-through, but actually meant as a local battle of attrition[39] to destroy as much German fighting strength as possible without endangering the 'eastern bastion' of the beach-head, as Montgomery called his position around Caen.[40] Despite air preparation on an unprecedented scale by 1,000 British and 1,500 US heavy bombers, the attack stuck fast in a deep defensive zone prepared by Rommel. A first line of infantry had to absorb the initial shock; they were supported by tanks immediately behind, then a line of strongpoints with anti-tank guns, backed by strong artillery in concealed positions, then another line of strongpoints with the remaining armour as mobile reserve some miles behind. 12,000 tons of bombs did not succeed in cracking this formidable obstacle. The British enlarged their bridgehead around Caen, but could not break through, and suffered heavy losses in tanks. Rain set in, the mud made tank operations difficult, and on July 20th, Montgomery ordered his armoured divisions to pull out of the fighting.

The Break-out

The bad weather compelled the Americans, who had taken St Lô on July 18th, to postpone for several days their final offensive to break out of the beach-head. It started on July 25th, preceded by heavy air attacks which practically annihilated the German defences, which were not so deep here as in the Caen area. At first Bradley made slow but sure progress; then his advance gained momentum. Co-operation between reconnaissance aircraft, fighter-bombers, armour, and infantry was excellent. By using tanks with hedgecutters, the Americans gained a mobility in the '*bocage*' country which the Germans did not have. On July 28th, they took Countances, cutting off part of the 7th Army; on the 30th, Avranches; and they broke out into Brittany on the following day. Von Kluge had sent the 2nd and the 116th Panzer Divisions from the Orne to the Vire after the British attack had been stopped, but they arrived too late. The 3rd Air Fleet concentrated its scanty bomber force on the bridge at Avranches, in a vain attempt to cut the only main road the Americans could use for their advance. General Patton (US VIII Corps) moved seven divisions in three days through this bottleneck. They streamed fanwise into Brittany, took Rennes on August 4th and reached Vannes on the Bay of Biscay on the same day, thus cutting off the peninsula. The US division advancing on Brest lost a day by mopping up a pocket at Dinan instead of bypassing it. When it arrived before that important port on August 7th, the Germans had managed to bring into the town enough of the units dispersed all along the coasts to beat off the first attack and to defend it until September 18th. As a result, the port could not be used by the Allies on D+35 as planned. PLUTO (Pipe Line Under The Ocean), first laid in August and September from the Isle of Wight to Cherbourg, helped partly to overcome the logistic difficulties caused by the lack of ports, the destruction of railways and roads, and the great demands of the mechanized Allied armies. Later, four pipelines were laid from England to Cherbourg, and sixteen to Boulogne.

Other US divisions struck southeast and then east, and approached Le Mans on August 7th. With superior mobility on the ground and supremacy in the air, they were in a good position to envelop the battered German forces. Von Kluge and his army commanders planned to fall back on a shorter line (roughly Seine–Yonne–Swiss frontier) and to slow down the Allied advance by energetic rearguard actions with their remaining mobile units. From a military point of view this was the best that could be done. Yet Hitler, entirely unapproachable after the attempt on his life, refused to consider this plan, and gave strict orders to assemble the armoured divisions for a concentrated attack in the direction Mortain–Avranches to cut off the American forces which had broken out. He promised support from several hundred fighters, but none arrived when the counter-attack was launched on August 7th. Early in the day, in foggy weather, the 2nd SS Panzer Division made good progress, took Mortain and covered about half the distance to Avranches, followed by what remained of the 116th, 2nd, and Panzerlehr Divisions. The other divisions were fully occupied in protecting the flanks of the German wedge. After a few hours, the weather cleared up, and the German advance was completely stopped from the air. The 2nd SS had to fall back slowly under the pressure of strong American forces. After forty-eight hours, the Germans were again in their initial positions, but now the British began to attack from the north, the Americans from the south. Hitler ordered the assault to be renewed and again forbade any retreat; as a result, after ten days of desperate fighting the remnants of the 5th Panzer Army and the 7th Army were almost completely encircled by the Allies in the Falaise pocket. Von Kluge ordered the retreat without Hitler's permission; the remnants of the armoured forces and the 2nd SS Panzer Corps opened a narrow corridor through which a considerable number of his men escaped, leaving behind the dead and wounded, most of their material and at least 45,000 prisoners. Von Kluge was then superseded by Field-Marshal Model, and he committed suicide on his way back to Germany.

On August 18th, the Allies crossed the Seine at several places, among them La Roche Guyon, where up to that day an echelon of the headquarters of Army Group B had been stationed. On August 25th, Paris was taken over intact by the Americans from General von Choltitz, who had refused to obey Hitler's orders to blow up all the bridges and destroy the city. The 15th Army, kept immobile too long, had failed to set up a new line of defence and was drawn into the general débâcle. The invasion battle had turned into an overwhelming Allied victory which cost the Germans at least 400,000 men and immense quantities of material. The road into the heart of Germany seemed open to the Western belligerents.

Mediterranean Sideshow

In August 1943, at the Quebec Conference, the proposal of the 'Overlord' planners for a diversion against the Mediterranean coast of France was accepted in principle. The underlying idea was to contain German troops there and to improve logistics by taking the big ports of Marseilles and Toulon. At the Teheran Conference in November 1943, Stalin showed great interest in that supplementary enterprise, evidently because to execute it forces would be needed which otherwise could be used by his Western Allies for an operation in northeastern Italy or the Balkans with the aim of reaching Austria or Yugoslavia before the Russians. For political reasons, Churchill would have liked this thrust more to the east, but he did not convince Roosevelt. Consequently, Operation 'Anvil' was agreed upon and carried through as a landing in southern France, although in the course of the preparations it became evident that it could not be undertaken simultaneously with 'Overlord' owing to lack of landing ships. Eventually it was fixed for August 15th, its first-line strength at 3 US and 4 French divisions (mostly from the Italian front), supported by 5,000 aircraft, 800 warships and 1,300 other vessels, with 3 more US divisions to follow. 450,000 men in all were landed.

The 19th German Army, shorn of its armour, had to guard a coastline of more than 300 miles with seven infantry divisions (four of them 'static'), about 200 aircraft and practically no navy. Behind it, there was a country full of Resistance fighters, and the Germans needed a considerable part of their troops to safeguard their communications.

The amphibious part of 'Anvil' was preceded by the usual massive bombardments from the air and sea, and by the drop of 2,000 parachutists in the rear of the coastal zone. Naval aircraft from nine carriers supplied direct air support. These preparations had been so effective that there was hardly any resistance when the first units of US VI Corps landed between Toulon and Cannes. The Americans pushed rapidly inland up the valleys of the Durance and the Rhône, to prevent the 19th Army from forming a consolidated front. The Germans, hopelessly outnumbered, retreated at once, with the exceptions of the garrisons of Toulon and Marseilles. The French took the first on August 22nd, the second on August 28th. The port installations had been demolished thoroughly. *U. 230*, the last German submarine in the Mediterranean, at the time under repair in Toulon, was hastily patched up. It went to sea to attack the US ships bombarding Toulon, but did not get within range.

German motor transport was in short supply, but this was to some extent compensated for by a flotilla of shallow-draught landing craft, which accompanied the retreat up the Rhône as far as possible, carrying stores and fuel, assisting army units in crossing the river, and using their guns against aircraft and Maquis. Leaving much material and 24,000 prisoners behind, the 19th Army passed the gap between the right wing of the 'Overlord' forces and the Swiss frontier before the US VI Corps could close it. Reinforcements were brought together west of Belfort, and put up a stout resistance. These events seem to show that Operation 'Anvil' was undertaken in the wrong place at the wrong time. The logistic problems could have been solved better by using the 'Anvil' forces for taking ports on the Bay of Biscay, where Lorient, St Nazaire, La Pallice, and Royan (blocking Bordeaux) were held by the Germans to the end of the war, or for opening the Schelde more quickly. Left to their own devices, the few German divisions in southern France, badly equipped and cut off from their supplies, would not have been able to influence the course of events to any extent, certainly less than they did in defending southwestern Germany after having been chased up the Rhône valley by the troops landed in southern France.

Conclusion

When the Allies occupied Brittany, reached the Loire, entered Paris, and crossed the lower Seine, they were slightly ahead of their original schedule. They had recovered the time lost at the beginning because of the German defence and the gale of June 19th, and were in position for the attack on Germany proper. There was one important exception, however: their logistics could not keep up with the rapid advance of their masses of men and vehicles, because they still had to unload most of their supplies on the beaches. One of the two Mulberry harbours had been virtually destroyed; Cherbourg, taken behind schedule, was more damaged than expected; Brest was still in German hands, as were all the larger harbours on the Bay of Biscay.

It proved impossible to bring up sufficient supplies for a full-strength offensive to the Rhine. The Americans had to slow down their advance; the British pushed on to Antwerp, practically cutting off the 15th German Army in Flanders, but failed to attack it at once. Thus the Germans were given time to form a beach-head on the southern bank of the Scheldt. This enabled them to transport the mass of the 15th Army across the river, and to use it for the defence of the frontier. A British attempt to take Arnhem by airborne troops failed after heavy fighting, and the waterway to Antwerp and the road to Holland (with its large ports) remained closed. The Germans found a breathing space, and recovered enough to build up a defence between Holland and Switzerland which could not easily be overrun. The invasion battle was definitely ended.

Unified command, supremacy in the air, sea power, technical superiority, and good co-operation at most levels, ensured an Allied victory in the invasion battle. Lack of flexibility in some phases, and the failure to secure a sufficient logistical basis, prevented them from turning that victory into winning the war outright.

On the German side, Hitler's wishful thinking, his interference in the operations, an unsound command structure, lack of co-operation at the highest military levels, material deterioration of the Luftwaffe and the Navy, and a general overtaxing of military strength, were the factors that primarily contributed to the defeat. German bravery and resourcefulness, sacrifices and obedience, were not enough to compensate for these defects. Yet there was a man who might have changed the outcome of the invasion battle. He found a strategy for this first great 'tri-phibian' defence operation, which he tried to solve by integrating everything the three Services could offer. Nobody can say for certain what the result would have been if Rommel had had his way. The British military expert, Captain Liddell Hart, says: 'It is probable that the Germans' only hope lay in checking the invasion at the outset, and that if they had waited, their intended counter-offensive would have been broken up by the overwhelming Allied air force.'[41] And this is Chester Wilmot's opinion: 'By temperament Rommel was an improviser, and in battle he was inclined to be impetuous. But his close and accurate study of the Allied technique of invasion, and the practical counter-measures which he ordered, reveal abilities in the spheres of planning and organization for which he has been given too little credit by either his fellow generals or his opponents. It was fortunate for the Allies that Rommel had not begun his task six months earlier, and that his plans were not wholeheartedly endorsed by his superiors nor thoroughly carried out by his subordinates; for even as it was, the problem of invasion became more formidable and more hazardous every week that passed.'[42]

Chronicle X

June

to

August 1944

Politics		Conduct of the War
Neutrals	Germany and Japan	Germany and Japan
		June 1944 to May 1945: Eighth phase o Battle of the Atlantic. June 4th: German forces evacuate Rome.
		June 10th: Destruction of French villa Oradour by Waffen SS. June 12th: Beginning of bombardment of L by V–weapons.
June 17th: Proclamation of the Republic of Iceland. (Separated from Denmark, May 25th).	July 18th: Tojo Government in Japan resigns. General Koiso forms a new Cabinet. July 20th: Colonel Count Stauffenberg makes bomb attempt on Hitler's life at 'Wolfsschanze' HQ in East Prussia. Hitler meets Mussolini for the last time. SS Reich Führer Himmler C.-in-C. Reserve Army.	June 21st: Thousandth V–1 launched a London. June 26th: Fortress Cherbourg capitula Allies. June 28th: First fast electro-U–boat (Type put into service.
		July 12th: German forces evacuate Vilna.
		July 17th: Field-Marshal Rommel wound strafing Allied aircraft. Japanese operational plans 'Sho 1 to defence of the line Philippines–Formosa and the Kurile Islands.
August 2nd: Turkey breaks off diplomatic relations with Germany.	August 1st: Hitler issues kinship hostage order, making members of a family responsible for the actions of any individual member. Mannerheim new Finnish President. August 5th to 6th: Last meeting of Hitler and Antonescu.	August 4th: German forces evacuate Flore August 6th to 7th: German counter-attack Mortain–Avranches.
	August 17th: Field-Marshal Keitel visits Mannerheim in order to prevent defection of Finland. August 23rd: Coup d'état in Rumania. Antonescu arrested. August 25th: Bulgaria abandons Axis.	August 30th: German forces evacuate oilfields.

Conduct of the War	Politics	
stern Allies and the Soviet Union	Western Allies and the Soviet Union	Neutrals

6th: D–day. Allied invasion of northern rance begins. 0th: Russian offensive on Karelian front. rst US 'Super-Fortress' raid on Japan from hengtu, in China.	June 9th: Government changes in Italy; Bonomi Cabinet formed.	
15th: US landing on Saipan (Mariana ands).		
9th to 20th: Air-sea battle off the Philippine ands. Large-scale sabotage by Russian rtisans behind Army Group Centre lines.		
2nd: Russians begin large-scale offensive ainst Army Group Centre. lied offensive in Burma reopens.		
0th to July 1st: RAF Bomber Command rries out first area-bombing attack in sup-rt of Allied troops at Caen. d: Russians recapture Minsk.	July 1st to 22nd: Bretton Woods Conference. July 11th: US Government recog-nizes de Gaulle's Committee of National Liberation.	
th: Russian offensive against Army Group orth Ukraine and Army Group North. th: First use of napalm bombs in Normandy. st: US forces land on Guam in the Marianas. 4th: US forces land on Tinian in the arianas. st: Allied forces break through at Avranches. 1st: Warsaw rising.	July 21st: Formation of the Polish National Liberation Committee. August 2nd: Soviet Government recognizes Polish Communist Lublin Committee.	
7th: First Britain–Russia shuttle bombing Germany. 13th to 20th: Battle of the Falaise pocket. 15th: Allied troops land on French Medi-ranean coast. 20th: Russian offensive opens against ny Group South Ukraine. 21st: Allied troops take Florence. 24th to 25th: Free French troops liberate is.	August 11th: Churchill meets Tito in Naples. August 21st to October 9th: Dum-barton Oaks Conference. August 30th: Rumania declares war on Germany.	

The Collapse of Army Group Centre in 1944[1]

BY HERMANN GACKENHOLZ

After having secured a pledge from his Western Allies at the Teheran Conference that their landing in northwest France would take place not later than May 1st, 1944, Stalin promised that a big Russian offensive would also be launched at this time. If the decisive battle against Germany were about to take place, then, for political reasons if no others, the Soviet Union would have to take part in it. In any case, the Russians were determined not to allow the initiative they had seized in July 1943 at Orel to slip from their hands. As the odds had changed in their favour, they looked forward to the coming winter battles with confidence. The fact that the situation developed in a way even more favourable to them than could have been foreseen at the Teheran Conference was largely due to decisions which the Germans made, or rather, failed to make.

Since the landing of the Allies in Italy, and with the constant threat of an Allied invasion of France, Germany now had to face the probability of fighting on several fronts. More than half the forces available were still on the Eastern Front, it is true, but the remainder were now tied down by the necessity of defending 'Fortress Europe' on all sides. In the second half of 1943, even the Eastern Front, though it was hard pressed by superior enemy forces, had to surrender units to reinforce OKW theatres in Italy, the Balkans and France; OKH, whose operations were limited to the Eastern Front, had to get on as best it could with the forces left to it. Acute tensions were inevitable under such circumstances, and they began to make themselves felt as early as the autumn of 1943 when the Russians resumed their offensive, which had been interrupted for a short period only by the mud, on a 600-mile front, and won a victory of great tactical importance which culminated on November 6th in the recapture of Kiev.

With the beginning of the Russian winter offensive at the end of December 1943, the whole German Eastern Front from the Crimea to Leningrad began to waver once more. The focal point of these Russian operations was clearly in the south, where the reconquest of the Ukraine, with its economic resources, was a profitable objective. However, in the middle of January 1944 a second focal point formed in the north, when a Russian attack broke the encirclement of Leningrad and then extended southward, forcing Army Group North to withdraw to a previously prepared position running from Polotsk through Opotchka and Ostrov, along the western bank of Lake Peipus to the bridgehead at Narva. Thanks to Field-Marshal Model, who was temporary C.-in-C. at the time in the place of Field-Marshal von Küchler, the German withdrawal which began on February 18th, 1944, despite Hitler's unwillingness to agree to a withdrawal of any sort, could at least be carried out according to a prearranged plan.

Army Group A (Field-Marshal von Kleist) and Army Group South (Field-Marshal von Manstein), whose positions in the Ukraine extended far to the east in the Dnieper bend, were immediately seriously threatened by the Russian drive from the Kiev area. However, Hitler rejected all the reasonable proposals for relieving the intolerable pressure on the heavily engaged troops and helping the formation of reserves. These proposals included the evacuation of the Crimea and the Dnieper salient, but advocated a vigorous rearguard battle. Up to the end of February 1944, the two Army Groups managed to hold a line extending from Kherson to Vinnitza. From here to the Pripet Marshes, there was a deep gap in which Brody, Lutsk and Kovel were held as isolated strongpoints. Although the encirclement which threatened the left wing of Manstein's Army Group South was clearly visible on any map of the daily situation, Hitler was determined that German troops should remain in the neighbourhood of the Crimea, which was already cut off, and he ordered that resistance should continue along the whole extended front, which now ran almost entirely from east to west. But then, in March, the inevitable happened: the concentrated force of the Russian attack shattered Manstein's weakened divisions, and pushed beyond Chernovitz right up to the Carpathians, while from the north Russian forces broke through into Moldavia and Bessarabia.

In this situation, Hitler issued a new directive,[2] dated April 2nd, 1944, in which he gave instructions for the future conduct of the battle: 'The Russian offensive in the southern sector of the Eastern Front has shot its bolt. The Russians have exhausted and dissipated their forces. The time has now come to bring their advance to a standstill for good. To this end, I have ordered far-reaching measures.' These measures included remaining in the Crimea and holding the following line 'under all circumstances': the course of the Dniester eastward to Kishinev–Yassy–the eastern exits of the Carpathians as far as Kolomea–Brody–Kovel. In fact the beginning of the mud, which came rather late that year, did give the Germans a respite, and a new front arose more or less along the line laid down. Between the Carpathians and the Black Sea it was manned by Army Group Southern Ukraine (previously Army Group A), and north of the Carpathians by Army Group Northern Ukraine (formerly Army Group South). Large Rumanian forces manned part of the line held by Army Group Southern Ukraine. Field-Marshals von Kleist and von Manstein, who were regarded as a nuisance by Hitler because they were men of independent judgement, were now dismissed and replaced by General Schörner,

Army Group Southern Ukraine, and by Field-Marshal Model, who had been specially transferred from Army Group North, Army Group Northern Ukraine. Without openly admitting it, Hitler's directive showed the result of the fighting which had taken place during the winter of 1943–4: the Russians had broken the encirclement of Leningrad, recaptured the Ukraine, and advanced up to the gates of the Balkans in northern Rumania, and to the gates of central Europe in eastern Galicia. The recapture of the Crimea, which Hitler had obstinately refused to evacuate in time, could not be prevented: after the fall of Sevastopol, the last German defenders were overwhelmed on the Chersonese peninsula on May 11th, 1944.

Compared with the decisions which had been fought out in the south and north of the Eastern Front in these winter months, the fighting in the centre had not been of any great importance. In a series of defensive battles, Army Group Centre (Field-Marshal Busch) had managed to retain the positions it had occupied after its retreat to the 'Panther' line in the autumn of 1943. It held the line on the east bank of the Dnieper between Stari-Bishov and Orsha, and it defeated repeated attempts by the Russians to seize the strip of land between the Dnieper and the Dvina, and held them in heavy fighting before Vitebsk and in the battles for the supply route at Orsha. The flanks of this salient, which bellied eastward, were threatened in the north near Polotsk, and also, and perhaps even more so, in the south. Owing to the withdrawal of Army Group South, it was found necessary at the beginning of 1944 to set up a thinly manned defensive flank in the Pripet Marshes. When the Russian drive towards Kovel threatened the rearward communications of Army Group Centre through Brest, its C.-in-C. decided on his own initiative to concentrate all available reserves at Kovel, even at the cost of weakening his front facing east. On April 5th, 1944, these forces, under the command of LVI Panzer Corps General Hossbach, relieved 'fortress' Kovel, which was already invested. After this, they pressed on as far as the Turya sector, where they re-established contact with the left wing of Army Group Northern Ukraine (formerly South).

Towards the end of April, the spring mud and the operational pause which the Russians themselves needed brought a period of quiet to the Eastern Front. Once again, though the picture was deceptive, there was an uninterrupted front line extending from the Black Sea to the Gulf of Finland. Although the Chief of Wehrmacht Operations Staff, General Jodl, was able to console himself with the thought – first expressed on November 7th, 1943, in view of the coming winter campaign – that none of the enemy's successes had had a 'directly fatal effect', there was no mistaking the weakness of this new zig-zagging and inadequately manned front line: it was not strong enough to resist a really determined Russian offensive bent on enforcing a decision. It was not the extent of the lost territory which was of primary importance, but that owing to Hitler's insistence that it should be held despite increasingly heavy sacrifices Germany's forces on the Eastern Front had suffered heavy losses in both men and material. The fighting strength of the various units had fallen to a dangerously weak level, and by the end of 1943 no less than thirty of the 200 divisions on the Eastern Front had had to be disbanded or amalgamated. Even so, a great number of those still in existence as divisions had lost more than half their effectives. Various attempts were made to bring the units up to strength in men and material, but there were not even sufficient reserves to relieve even temporarily the overtaxed infantry. Only the armoured divisions could be withdrawn from the front line for resting and replacements.

In the spring of 1944, the front still ran deep through enemy territory. If the line had been radically straightened and shortened, and all unimportant salients requiring large numbers of men abandoned, reserves could have been formed and there would have been room to manœuvre. At the beginning of 1944, Jodl himself had advised Hitler to withdraw German forces on the Eastern Front to the shortest possible line between the Black Sea and the Baltic from Odessa to Riga. His idea was to free troops and create a reserve not only on the Eastern Front, but also – in view of the threat of invasion in the West – a 'Central Reserve' of some twenty divisions under Wehrmacht command. Hitler refused to listen to such suggestions; at that time, he was still determined to hang on to the Crimea and the Dnieper salient, and, because of Finland, he was also unwilling to give up ground in the Baltic; in addition, he wanted the Baltic as an exercise area for the new U-boat types. But even *after* the winter campaign he was still unwilling to give up an inch of conquered territory without being forced to do so. At the same time, he simply refused to recognize the superior strength of the Russians, and so his directive of April 2nd expressly ordered the defence of the line he had laid down. He refused to agree to a withdrawal of Army Group Centre from the dangerously bellying salient it was holding, despite the fact that its northern and southern flanks were both seriously threatened. He also refused to allow Army Group Southern Ukraine to withdraw to a shorter line between the mouth of the Danube and the Carpathians, though this would still have adequately controlled access to the Balkans.

Hitler's obstinacy in all these matters appears quite incomprehensible (if, indeed, any of his behaviour can be rationally understood), because in the situation he could only expect a speedy renewal of the Russian offensive operations – probably timed to coincide with an Anglo-American landing in France. The result of the winter campaign had led to a heavy concentration of Russian troops in the western Ukraine, and in Hitler's view, which was shared by both his OKW and OKH advisers, the big Russian summer offensive must be expected here, particularly as the Russian advance to the east of Lemberg in eastern Galicia had been halted only with great difficulty. Using this sector as a springboard, the enemy could drive forward to the southwest into the Carpathians, thus opening up the way to Warsaw, and lifting the centre and the northern wings of the German Eastern Front off their hinges.

This estimate of the enemy's intentions suggested, indeed, a grave threat to the whole military situation of Germany, and perhaps it was this that so obsessed German leaders that they were unable to free themselves from the idea even when it became evident that the factors which had determined the estimate were no longer operative. In any case, all the available German reserves were concentrated in Galicia to meet the enemy threat, including the majority of the armoured divisions, a step which denuded other sectors of the front.

The first big blow was expected against Army Group Northern Ukraine. This was also Field-Marshal Model's opinion, and at OKH they felt quite sure that 'once again focal point would meet focal point'. However, it should have been fairly obvious that the enemy was unlikely to choose the strongest part of the German line to launch the offensive by which he hoped to secure a decision. Another very necessary and obvious conclusion was not drawn from this view of the situation: namely, if the other Army Groups were to be left without reserves, they should at least have been given permission to make their own arrangements to get on without them. What actually happened was that, without reserves, they were given strict orders to hold their lines at all costs.

It is not too much to say that the germ of the new heavy defeat inflicted on the German forces on the Eastern Front in the summer of 1944 was contained in this one-sided view of the enemy's intentions, coupled with the inconsistency of the operational decisions taken to cope with them. The whole front was excessively strung out. The reserves were – as was soon to be seen – wrongly placed. At the same time, the Army groups were forbidden the expedient of waging a war of mobile defence. In such circumstances, the defeat and collapse of Army Group Centre in the summer of 1944 was not surprising. It must be regarded and judged as the first and most disastrous of a series of catastrophes.

On the whole, Army Group Centre had fought successfully throughout the winter of 1943–4, and had repulsed all the Russian attacks against the front it was holding. Both officers and men had come out of this fighting with increased confidence, but they had failed to recognize that the real decisions had been fought out elsewhere – in the south and the north of the Eastern Front – and that in this period their own sector had been of only subordinate significance.[3] Be that as it may, there was general confidence that they could continue to cope with any Russian attacks of the kind they had grown used to since the autumn of 1943 – and they did not expect anything different. All previous Russian attacks had been launched successively against various parts of the front, so that Army Group C.-in-C. had been able to switch reserves from the sectors not threatened, to reinforce the defence at the critical points.

This successful tactic had last been adopted when the situation in the Kovel-Brest sector became difficult. Army Group C.-in-C. had concentrated his reserves on the deep southwest flank at the expense of the main front facing east. 8 divisions, including 2 armoured divisions, had been concentrated at Kovel, out of the 45 divisions which made up the Army Group at the time. Thanks to this concentration, the threat to Army Group's rearward communications through Brest had been disposed of, 'strongpoint' Kovel had been relieved, and contact established with the 4th Panzer Army, the left wing of Army Group Northern Ukraine. Although the results justified this decision and the risks involved, it still remained a fact that the east front of the Army Group was inadequately manned. The 9th Army, the 4th Army and the 3rd Panzer Army, had to hold with thirty-two divisions a front nearly 450 miles long. In addition, operations on this front were hampered by Hitler's orders that so-called 'strongpoints' should be set up, because this tied down considerable forces and impeded mobility from the start. Hitler was so keen on these 'strongpoints' that their commanders had to take a special oath to him that they would not abandon them without express permission, and that, failing such permission, they would hold out to the last. At the same time, they were given the right to call on all other fighting detachments that happened to come into their area, to assist them in the defence of their strongpoints, which were, incidentally, not all that strong, and were reinforced with improvised materials. Hitler believed that these 'strongpoint' tactics would tie down large forces in the event of a break-through, and that the enemy supply lines would be so affected that the driving force of the offensive would be dissipated. Bobruisk, Mogilev, Orsha and Vitebsk had been declared such 'strongpoints', in the front-line area, and a front-line division had been assigned to each, except Vitebsk, which was considered so important that three divisions were allotted for its defence.

The Army commanders pointed out in vain that in the event of an enemy break-through the already torn front would be still further weakened by immobilizing considerable forces in this way, and that it would then hardly be possible to restore the front again even by an ordered withdrawal. This was true in particular of the 3rd Panzer Army, whose commander, General Reinhardt, pointed out that if three of his divisions (out of a total of ten) were tied down in Vitebsk, he would not be in a position to form a new front to the west of the town, unless fresh reinforcements were available. In his opinion, therefore, 'the interest of the front as a whole' ought to be placed above the interests of such 'strongpoints'. However, he was unable to get his point of view accepted by Army Group C.-in-C., Field-Marshal Busch, who accepted Hitler's arguments as to the value of these 'strongpoints', and insisted that Hitler's orders should be carried out: 'The strongpoints will tie down such large enemy forces that the absence of the divisions allotted to their defence will not materially affect the defence of the front as a whole.'[4]

In view of the almost impossible thinning out of the forces manning the east front of the Army Group (each division had a sector of approximately fifteen miles to defend!) the Army commanders involved had suggested as early as April 1944 that their battle instructions should be modified. There were two ways of withdrawing from the salient in order to occupy a shorter line which could be satisfactorily held with fewer men: (1) the 'minor' variant – a withdrawal to the Dnieper position built by the 4th Army, which could be satisfactorily defended against armoured forces, and could, if necessary, be extended northwards from Orsha to Polotsk by the 3rd Panzer Army in the so-called 'Tiger' position to the west of Vitebsk; (2) the 'major' variant – a withdrawal to the tactically equally satisfactory chord position along the Beresina, which would save about 150 miles in the Bobruisk–Polotsk line.

It seemed best to carry out a previously prepared withdrawal shortly before the beginning of the Russian offensive, since in this case the enemy offensive would be thrown out of gear, and he would be compelled to make time-wasting re-dispositions. Army Group had already made a start by consolidating the Beresina position. As well as releasing considerable forces, it would also make it possible to combat the partisan menace more effectively in the areas to the rear of the 4th Army; and this was a very important point, because partisan activity was on the increase, and might well be extremely dangerous in the event of an enforced retreat through the trackless wooded area on both sides of the Beresina.

On May 20th, 1944, Field-Marshal Busch visited Führer HQ to report on the general situation. In particular, he stressed the dangerous lack of proportion between the forces available and the length of front to be held, and suggested that in order to remedy this situation he should be allowed to shorten his lines by an ordered withdrawal into either the Dnieper or the Beresina position. His suggestion was rejected out of hand, and Hitler made the cynical remark (deliberately calculated to affect Field-Marshal Busch's thinking) that he, Hitler, had not previously supposed that Busch would turn out to be one of those generals who were always glancing back over their shoulders. The gibe struck home, all the more because Field-Marshal Busch happened to be one of those higher officers who really believed in the 'historical mission' of Hitler and National Socialism on behalf of the German people, and who therefore looked up to the Führer with utter devotion. There is good reason to believe that this disagreeable experience had a definite influence on the Field-Marshal's subsequent behaviour. The doubt deliberately expressed by Hitler concerning the personal character and loyalty of the Field-Marshal may well have driven the latter to demonstrate how 'loyal' he was by accepting all the orders of the dictator without making the slightest objection, and then forcing them through against the better judgement of his fellow generals – perhaps, indeed, even against his own.

In any case on May 24th, 1944, he informed his army commanders that it was 'Hitler's unshakable will' that the east front of the Army Group line was to be defended and held at all costs. He also told them that Hitler had forbidden any attempt to prepare lines in the rear to retire to in case of need, and that, instead, he had insisted on 'the increased consolidation of the present positions with the concentration of engineering and construction units in the main battle zone.' This insistence on the previous instructions that the line must be held at all costs had been expressly underlined by a special directive of Hitler issued on May 23rd. At Army Group HQ it was thought that it might be possible to carry out these orders, because as far as could be seen for the moment there was nothing to indicate acute danger to the main Army Group front, which faced eastwards. On the whole, the general picture of enemy dispositions pointed to concentrations around the inner wings of Army Group Northern Ukraine and Army Group Centre in eastern Galicia.

Since the beginning of May, OKH had been planning to set up a reserve army behind the left wing of Army Group Northern Ukraine. As General Zeitzler, Chief of the Army General Staff, declared on May 5th: 'We should then be in a position to do something when the expected large-scale enemy attack does come.'[5] But throughout the whole month the question of forming this force remained in abeyance, and in the end nothing came of it. Instead, on May 29th, OKH placed LVI Panzer Corps, which was in the Kovel sector, under the command of Army Group Northern Ukraine, a measure taken under the still accepted assumption of a large-scale Russian offensive in Galicia and the ensuing necessity of concentrating all available reserves with this Army Group. But this measure gravely depleted the strength of Army Group Centre: at one blow it lost almost all its armour and a third of its GHQ troops, including its special assault gun brigades. The C.-in-C. of Army Group Centre immediately pointed out that this would make it impossible for him to adopt the tactic which had proved so valuable in previous battles: namely, to counter the development of enemy focal points by bringing up reinforcements in good time. The C.-in-C. maintained that it had certainly been necessary to take the risk of thinning out the main front of the Army Group towards the east in order to restore the situation in the Kovel–Brest sector, but while this had been acceptable as a temporary measure it was intolerable as a permanent one, because the formation of reserves from the forces remaining was impossible.

The 'enemy situation' report of June 4th, 1944, noted that 'at any time the enemy could strengthen his local concentrations on the east front (of Army Group Centre) by switching his very considerable reserves'.[6] Even if the enemy were intending to launch mere holding or diversionary attacks, which was the opinion at the time, the situation was critical enough, because the only reserves Army Group Centre had available were one division with the 4th Army and another one with the 3rd Panzer Army. This was the first warning of the danger, and OKH could not ignore it altogether, particularly as during the next few days the 'enemy situation' reports became much more disturbing. From June 10th, unmistakable reports began to come in showing that very strong Russian forces were being brought up to the main Army Group Centre front with the following focal points: (1) opposite the 9th Army on both sides of the Beresina for an enveloping attack on Bobruisk; (2) opposite the 4th Army to the east of Mogilev and along the supply route at Orsha; and (3) opposite the 3rd Panzer Army on both sides of Vitebsk.

The extent of these preparations, which were obviously of an offensive nature, the appearance of well-known, *élite* troops at the various focal points along the front, or their readiness in reserve (for example, the 5th Guards

Armoured Army held near Smolensk as an operational reserve) – all these things suggested enemy intentions far exceeding the originally supposed local objectives and pinning-down attacks. In addition, there was the sudden massing of the enemy air force: something like 4,500 planes had been brought up into the neighbourhood of the front line. Everything suggested that the Russians had determined to dispose once and for all of the salient which bellied out eastward, particularly as they must have known very well that it was only very thinly held. 'A sober and unprejudiced appraisal of the situation made it impossible for Army Group HQ to suppose that, in view of the extended linear front it was manning, it could possibly cope, without adequate reserves, with the expected large-scale attack.'[7] However, the question of what to do in this critical situation went beyond the responsibilities of Army Group HQ, and rested primarily with Germany's Supreme Command.

At the discussion which took place at OKH HQ on June 14th at which all the Army Group and Army Chiefs of Staff were present, only Army Group Centre was in a position to submit clear proofs that strong Russian forces were massing along its front. No other Army Group (not even Army Group Northern Ukraine) had observed such infallible indications of preparations for an offensive in the neighbourhood of its front lines. However, although by this time the Russian preparations were already quite obvious, it was still impossible to detach either Hitler or OKH from their obstinate belief that the focal point of the Russian summer offensive would be in Galicia and that any operations against Army Group Centre would be in the nature of introductory and subordinate moves. The only concession made to the warnings given by Army Group Centre was that on June 14th the 20th Panzer Division was ordered to Bobruisk behind the front of the 9th Army. Even on June 20th, the Chief of OKW, Field-Marshal Keitel, declared in a lecture on the general situation delivered to a conference of National Socialist Indoctrination Officers in Sonthofen that the Russians would not attack until the Western Allies (whose forces had landed in Normandy on June 6th) had obtained greater successes. In any case, the focal point of their operations was to be expected in the south, and not on the front held by Army Group Centre.[8] The result of such views was that the Supreme Command made none of the decisions required to counter the critical situation in which Army Group Centre now found itself; it was neither reinforced in order to make it better able to meet the great Russian challenge when it came, nor was it given freedom of action which would have allowed it to fight a mobile defensive battle and if necessary withdraw to tactically more favourable positions which could be held with fewer forces.

It is hardly possible to reproach C.-in-C. Army Group Centre for not having warned the Supreme Command in good time or with sufficient vigour concerning the dangers which were developing on his front. All the reports, requests and proposals met with the stereotyped reply: the situation on the Eastern Front as a whole did not permit any change in the present orders (defence of the advanced line) or any change in the general dispositions (the provision of reserves, for example). It has been suggested[9] that if the C.-in-C. had been more adamant in his remonstrances something might have been achieved, but this is very questionable; though it must be admitted that his psychological dependence on Hitler certainly did make him less forthright and less able to secure the acceptance of his own views. But even if a different, a stronger and more independent, personality had been in command of Army Group Centre at the time, it is doubtful whether, in view of the nature and structure of the Supreme Command in the summer of 1944, he would have been able to make his influence more strongly felt; Supreme Command was then completely dominated by Hitler.

The lack of insight shown by the Supreme Command, and its rejection of all suggestions to cope with the threat, created a certain spirit of resignation in Army Group Command. After all, what else remained now but to wait and see how things would develop? Moreover, Army Group Centre did not do anything even to prepare more mobile defensive tactics on its own responsibility. In face of a situation which was growing more and more critical, it practically surrendered any possibility of leadership.[10] But initiative was not to be expected of Army Group C.-in-C. 'on his own responsibility', in view of the strict orders of his 'Führer'. However, Army Group Centre did feel confident that when the circumstances arose it would be given the necessary freedom of action. For the rest, it relied on the toughness of its troops in defence, a quality which they had already demonstrated to the full in the past. Both the driving power and the objectives of the expected Russian offensive were underestimated, and this was because the commanders in question had been given no opportunity of adequately acquainting themselves with the progress the Russians had made in tactical leadership, organizational efficiency and armaments.

The Battle of White Russia

The prelude to the 'Battle of White Russia' was wide-scale action by the partisans, whose strength in the areas to the rear of Army Group Centre at that time was estimated as being in the neighbourhood of 240,000.[11] On the night of June 19th, 10,500 demolitions sabotaged all railway communications to the west of Minsk. Control squads managed to discover and dismantle 3,500 other charges. Although no irreparable damage was done, the sudden action, which demonstrated very clearly that the partisans were a well-organized and centrally led force, held up supply traffic for twenty-four hours, and more at some points.[12] The connection between this swift sabotage operation and the now completed Russian deployment opposite the east front of Army Group Centre was too obvious to be ignored, and the launching of the Russian offensive was regarded as immediately imminent.

This 'offensive to free White Russia',[13] known in Soviet war literature as 'the fifth blow' of the year 1944, was directed by Marshal Zhukov. 'As representatives of Supreme Command HQ', as the Russians put it, Marshal Zhukov and Marshal Vassilevsky, Chief of the General Staff, were responsible for co-ordinating the operations of the 'Fronts'.[14] A number of these so-called 'Fronts', which may be regarded as approximately equivalent to the German Army groups, were engaged in the offensive: the 1st White Russian Front (General Rokossovsky); the 2nd White Russian Front (General Sakharov); the 3rd White Russian Front (General Cherniakovsky); and the 1st Baltic Front (General Bagramyan), with the following forces at their disposal:

(*a*) *Opposite the 9th Army:* the right wing of the 1st White Russian Front with 23 infantry and 7 armoured divisions, facing XLI Panzer Corps to the south of the Beresina, and 27 infantry and 6 tank formations facing XXXV Army Corps to the north of Rogachev;

(*b*) *Opposite the 4th Army:* the 2nd White Russian Front, with 16 infantry and 2 armoured divisions facing XXXIX Panzer Corps on both sides of the road from Ryassna to Mogilev; the left wing of the 3rd White Russian Front with 25 infantry and 11 armoured divisions facing XXVII Army Corps along the motor-road Moscow–Minsk to the north of Orsha;

(*c*) *Opposite the 3rd Panzer Army:* the right wing of the 3rd White Russian Front, with 18 infantry and 9 armoured divisions facing VI Army Corps on the Sukodrovka sector to the southeast of Vitebsk; and the 1st Baltic Front with 29 infantry and 8 armoured divisions facing IX Army Corps on both sides of the River Obol to the west of Vitebsk.[15]

The concentration of strong forces on both wings of the offensive front showed clearly enough that the Russian High Command was aiming in the first place to attain the objectives for which the Russian armies had fought in vain during the winter battles of 1943–4. It hoped to succeed now by means of a massive superiority, and at the same time to create the necessary conditions for further operations. For example, in the north the 3rd White Russian Front and the 1st Baltic Front were to co-operate to capture the narrow stretch of land between the Dvina and the Dnieper, with its two cornerstones Vitebsk and Orsha, and then to drive on westward: the 1st Baltic Front towards Lepel, and the 3rd White Russian Front towards Borisov. In the south, the 1st White Russian Front was to make a concentric attack on Bobruisk and prise it out of the German defence line, and thus open the way into the area north of the Pripet Marshes. Compared with these focal points on the wings, the forces of the 2nd White Russian Front in the centre were relatively weak. It was their task to make a frontal attack on the German forces on the east bank of the Dnieper, force them back over the river, and then drive on from Mogilev towards Beresino. The Beresina line – Lepel–Borisov–Beresino–Pukhovichy – could be regarded as the first operational aim of the Russian offensive. Beyond this line the next objective was certainly the recapture of the provincial capital, Minsk, after which the offensive would probably be carried on towards Molodechno and Baranovichi. Just how this was to be done depended no doubt on the development of the situation as a whole, and we shall therefore have to leave open the question as to whether the Russians had already planned the encirclement of the German 4th Army as part of their concentric drive on Minsk. The Russians were certainly not in a position to make such an accurate estimate of what the Germans would do in reply to their offensive.[16]

On the whole, the Russian deployment was in accordance with the estimate of Army Group Centre *before* the beginning of the offensive; and this was true not only of the focal points and the direction of the drives, but also of the forces engaged. The only thing which had not been recognized fully in advance was the powerful concentration on the 1st Baltic Front to the northwest of Vitebsk. In agreement with the estimate of Army Group North, it was supposed that the 1st Baltic Front would attack in a westerly direction towards Polotsk. As the German front to the west of Vitebsk was particularly thinly held, and as there were virtually no reserves there, a very serious situation soon developed for the 3rd Panzer Army.

The Russian offensive opened on June 22nd, 1944, the third anniversary of Operation 'Barbarossa'.[17] On the first day, the attacks were confined to the front held by the 3rd Panzer Army on either side of Vitebsk, but then the operations extended southward: on the following day they included the 4th Army front, and the day after that, the 9th Army front. The Russian attack was launched in stages, possibly because they wanted to make concentrated use of their air power, and this misled the Germans, even though the difference in timing was not very great. Because the attack was launched in this way, the German Army commanders continued to believe for a day or so that it was merely a question of 'holding attacks'.[18] In consequence, there were new and time-wasting discussions between Army Group HQ and OKH which fatally delayed the swift decisions which were now necessary.

From the beginning, the fighting indicated that the Russians were out to secure a decision. This was evident not only in their overwhelming superiority in artillery, ground-attack aircraft and armour, but in their new battle tactics, which took the German troops and their leaders by surprise. A new feature of the fighting was the appearance of strong formations of ground-attack aircraft in support of the Russian ground troops. At the beginning of the Russian offensive, the German Air Fleet 6 had only forty fighter aircraft ready for action, so that the Russians had almost complete command of the air, and they used it to launch low-flying attacks on the German artillery positions, realizing that because of the numerical weakness of the infantry, the artillery was always the backbone of the German defence. The Russian use of air power also greatly hampered movement on the battlefield, while the presence of Russian fighter planes in such force prevented German air reconnaissance behind the Russian lines. The Russians unleashed a heavy preliminary artillery bombardment which went on for several hours, followed by closely massed infantry attacks supported by armour. When the Russians had broken through the main German defence line they immediately sought to extend the breach in each direction, while behind them other infantry units with accompanying artillery mopped up any remaining pockets of German resistance. During the infantry attack the bigger formations of armour were held back, to be moved forward only after the infantry had torn great gaps in the German front. The Russian armour was brigaded into special mobile units for operational use against distant objectives. In this respect the Russians were greatly favoured by the nature of the terrain, which on both flanks – a broad strip in the north along the Smolensk–Orsha–Minsk motor road, and in the south along the northern edge of the Pripet Marshes – was very suitable for sweeping movements by fast mobile units. On the other hand, the great impassable wooded area on both sides of the Beresina behind the centre of the German front restricted the movements of the defence to a few narrow corridors.

The Destruction of the German Front

The Russian superiority in men and material and the driving force of the Russian offensive tactics were made all the more effective because the German defence – hampered by Hitler's orders – played into its hands by conducting a rigid defence tied down to the front line. This was obvious from the start of the offensive against the 3rd Panzer Army, where the situation became difficult even on June 22nd, and then rapidly developed into a crisis. The 3rd White Russian Front succeeded in making deep penetrations into the lines of VI Army Corps to the southwest of Vitebsk, and the 95th Division was committed to seal them off. To the northwest of the town, the over-extended front of IX Army Corps was ripped open by the 1st Baltic Front on both sides of the River Obol. Apart from a regimental group of the 95th Division, there were no reserves available here. The preliminary attacks mounted against the 4th Army on the same day were repulsed. Opposite the 9th Army the enemy remained inactive.[19]

On June 23rd the offensive was extended to the front of the 4th Army, while preliminary Russian attacks began against the 9th Army. On the front of the 4th Army, the 2nd White Russian Front succeeded in making penetrations into the lines held by XXXIX Panzer Corps to the east of Mogilev, as did the spearhead forces of the 3rd White Russian Front to the north of the motor road. Elements of the 14th Division were committed here, while the mass of the Division was sent from Orsha northwards to the right wing of the 3rd Panzer Army. With this, the two divisions held in reserve on the left wing of the Army Group were now both committed. The proposal of the acting C.-in-C. of the 4th Army, General von Tippelskirch, that the army should be allowed to withdraw into the Dnieper position with a view to forming new reserves was rejected by Field-Marshal Busch: 'Any voluntary abandonment of parts of the main line still intact is out of the question.'[20] The situation of the 3rd Panzer Army on both sides of Vitebsk grew still more critical. The

Russians extended their penetrations of the previous day into a break-through by hurling VI Army Corps to the south over the Luchessa, and IX Army Corps to the west over the Dvina. When parts of the 3rd White Russian Front crossed the Luchessa to the south of Vitebsk, encirclement threatened the four divisions of LIII Army Corps. OKH thereupon gave the Corps permission to withdraw to positions on the edge of the town. One division which thereby became available was sent to keep the line of communications through Ostrovno open by attacking in a southwesterly direction. The other three divisions were instructed to act as the garrison of the 'strongpoint', Vitebsk, and thus were no longer at the disposal of the 3rd Panzer Army.

Early in the morning on June 24th, there was a conference at Army Group HQ in Minsk between Field-Marshal Busch and General Zeitzler, Chief of the Army General Staff. From the development of the situation up to then Busch now concluded that the forces at the disposal of Army Group Centre were not strong enough to allow it to carry out the tasks it had been set, and he pointed out that this applied to 'the Vitebsk area in particular'. Owing to the lack of reserves, it was not possible to restore the situation on the 3rd Panzer Army sector. Busch declared that 'the only possible solution' was for the 3rd Panzer Army to withdraw into the 'Tiger' line, a bolt position to the southwest of Vitebsk, and abandon the strongpoint of Vitebsk. He also asked for further reinforcements, including a Panzer division. General Zeitzler agreed, and promised to put the suggestion favourably to Hitler.

Discussion about counter-measures seems to have been confined to the situation of the 3rd Panzer Army and to the strongpoint of Vitebsk, although that very morning the big attack against the 9th Army positions had started. Busch, in accordance with his previous attitude, obviously saw no reason to discuss the situation of his Army Group as a whole, while the Chief of the General Army Staff was probably thinking with some anxiety of the forth-coming inevitable clash with Hitler, and was glad enough not to have to take back any more such demands.

The previous day, June 23rd, OKH had come to the conclusion that Army Group Centre had insufficient forces to cope with the situation, and that 'to change its battle instructions would be easier than sending reinforcements'. In this connection, the withdrawal of the 4th Army over the Dnieper was mentioned.[21] In retrospect, there can be no doubt that the morning of June 24th, 1944, was perhaps the last chance of saving Army Group Centre by 'changing its battle instructions' and thus warding off the fate that already threatened to engulf it. But even if all the military commands involved had been in agreement, it was by no means certain – as the events of the next few days were to show very clearly – that Hitler would have accepted their judgement and agreed to the necessary orders.

In fact, on June 24th, Zeitzler, on his return from Minsk, did not succeed in persuading Hitler to give his permission for the proposed withdrawal. All that he would agree to was to send the 212nd Division to Lepel and the 5th

Panzer Division to Borisov. He refused to budge where Vitebsk was concerned, and he even sent his personal order direct to General Reinhardt, Commander-in-Chief of the 3rd Panzer Army, that Vitebsk was to remain a strongpoint, and was to be held. And when Busch spoke to him on the telephone that afternoon and again asked to be allowed to abandon Vitebsk, Hitler refused point-blank, saying that 'for political reasons' (the threatened defection of Finland) 'Vitebsk must be held at all costs'. In support of his contention, he pointed to the example of Kovel 'where 4,000 men held up ten divisions for three weeks', and he supplemented his stand by giving instructions that Vitebsk was to be defended with at least a division.[22] That was the end of the matter. On the evening of June 25th, Hitler announced for good measure that 'the 206th Division will hold Vitebsk until it is relieved'!

In the meantime, the situation of the 3rd Panzer Army grew even more difficult, and on June 24th it developed into a crisis. The enemy forces which had crossed the Luchessa were spreading out to the northwest and cutting the rearward communications of LIII Army Corps at Ostrovno, at the same time forcing the inner wings of VI and IX Army Corps still farther back so that a gap of about twenty-five miles had opened between them. LIII Army Corps now received orders to leave the 206th Division in Vitebsk and to fight its own way out towards the southwest. But these orders arrived too late: the tying down of LIII Army Corps to Hitler's 'Fortress Vitebsk' proved – as General Reinhardt said it would, when it was first broached in April 1944 – a curse not only for the troops concerned but for the whole battle operations of the 3rd Panzer Army.

Continuing his attacks against the front of the 4th Army on June 24th, the enemy succeeded in extending the breach in the German lines to the east of Mogilev and in breaking through as far as the Dnieper support line. An assault launched on the same day by the 3rd White Russian Front along the motor road was held, but the left wing of the 4th Army had to be pulled back to the Oreshi Lake line to keep contact with the right wing of the 3rd Panzer Army, VI Army Corps fighting on both sides of Bogushevsk. General von Tippelskirch, now very properly anxious about his left wing, repeated his demand that the elements of the 4th Army which had not been attacked should be allowed to withdraw to the Dnieper line.

After the day's developments, Army Group Centre and OKH now agreed with the proposal, and it was put before Hitler in the evening conference on the situation. But again Hitler refused to budge. Instead, 4th Army Command received orders to remain in its previous positions with XII Army Corps and the north wing of XXXIX Panzer Corps. General von Tippelskirch tried in vain to persuade Army Group HQ to cancel this order, which appeared to him – and not only to him – quite senseless. Field-Marshal Busch regarded it as an order of his 'Führer', and felt that he had to obey it.[23] In this situation von Tippelskirch followed the promptings of his own conscience, and took personal responsibility for ordering a withdrawal to the Dnieper line. 'But this decision also came too late.'[24] This was not only because of the rapidly worsening situation on the north flank of the 4th Army, but also because of the developments which had begun that day farther to the south on the front of the 9th Army.

The big attack launched on June 24th, with the full weight of the 1st White Russian Front against the 9th Army gained its first success on the sector manned by XLI Panzer Corps to the south of the Beresina, where the enemy quickly extended a penetration through Rakovichi towards the Bobruisk–Ratmiroivchi railway line, by promptly throwing in strong armoured forces—which the weak local reserves were quite unable to halt. To the north of Rogachev on the XXXV Army Corps sector, the enemy gained ground on the west bank of the River Drut, but his penetration was sealed off. The 707th Division, which was being held in reserve, was sent forward to deal with a third enemy penetration at the boundary with the 4th Army. It was not until late in the day that a decision was taken about the use of the 20th Panzer Division, which was being held in reserve near Bobruisk. At first, 9th Army Command had judged the greater danger to be to the north of Rogachev, and up to the afternoon it felt that the division should be used on the north wing, and so the appropriate dispositions were set in motion. But by the evening views had changed, and it was decided that the rapid worsening of the situation on XLI Panzer Corps sector called for the despatch of the division southward for a counter-attack near Parichi. But valuable time was lost as the result of this hesitation, and this led to the replacement of the commander of the 9th Army, General Jordan, by General von Vormann. However, the fact remains that even if this one division had been used 'in the theoretically best possible fashion' it could hardly have made much difference to the fate of the 9th Army.[25]

Reports coming in on the morning of June 25th, showed only too clearly that the general situation of the Army Group was worsening very rapidly owing to further enemy successes on both wings. Enemy forces which had broken through the 9th Army lines to the south of the Beresina had already reached the railway line to the south of Bobruisk, and behind them further strong enemy forces were pouring through the breach. The 20th Panzer Division had not yet been committed, but it was being compelled to clear its own deployment area first and could not take up its positions before the afternoon. However, Army Group HQ still insisted on this attack into the flank of the Russian break-through. The situation in the north was still worse: the new defensive front of VI Army Corps had been broken at Bogushevsk by the 3rd White Russian Front, and the German forces thrown back to the motor road to the west of Orsha. With this, the enemy won full freedom of movement to the south and the west.

There was now a growing danger that the mass of the 9th Army and the whole of the 4th Army would be encircled. In a situation report made to OKH on the morning of June 25th, Army Group HQ therefore made the following requests: withdrawal of the 4th Army to the Dnieper line in order to free reserves to strengthen the threatened left wing; the abandonment of Vitebsk; permission for the 206th Division to fight its way out; and the sending of a division each to Slutsk, Minsk and Parafianovo. Army Group HQ realized that even these measures would in all probability not be sufficient to restore the situation, and it therefore urgently requested once more that its general battle instructions should be so modified as to allow further limited withdrawals from the salient while maintaining contact with neighbouring units, as this was the only way to save numerous units from destruction. Given a proper estimate of the situation, the Supreme Command could have decided this on its own as early as June 23rd, and the next morning, June 24th, would probably have been early enough, but now the development of the fighting made these decisions absolutely essential and critically urgent. However, it still proved impossible to convince Hitler of the seriousness of the situation, and all he was prepared to agree to at the midday conference was the withdrawal of those parts of the 4th Army which were to the south of Mogilev into the Dnieper line. He still refused to allow the abandonment of Vitebsk.

The course of the fighting on June 25th only too clearly confirmed the fears expressed in the situation report that morning. On the 9th Army front, the counter-attack launched by the 20th Panzer Division soon came to a halt against strong Russian armoured forces, and was unable to bring the hoped-for relief. In the meantime, the 1st White Russian Front continued to push its southern attacking forces westward and northwestward, with the result that the roads leading to the west from Bobruisk were now threatened. On the north wing the enemy was prevented from extending the breach to the north of Rogachev by committing the last reserves. The situation at the boundary with the 4th Army remained unclear. The 707th Division did not succeed in sealing off the gap. A request made by 9th Army Command that in this situation it should be allowed to withdraw to the enlarged Bobruisk bridgehead was rejected by Busch, who pointed out that his battle instructions had not been changed.

Forces of the 2nd White Russian Front now broke through the Dnieper line to the east of Mogilev held by the 4th Army, and continued to advance towards Mogilev and Shklov. To the north of the motor road, the enemy broke into the Orsha bridgehead at Orekhi. VI Army Corps, which was part of the 4th Army, completely collapsed under the weight of a powerful armoured attack launched by the 3rd White Russian Front, and this enabled the enemy to advance towards the motor road near Smolyany. With this, the 3rd White Russian Front had achieved the first of its operational objectives: possession of the strip of land between the Dvina and the Dnieper; and it now went on to exploit the broad gap torn in the German front to the south of Vitebsk by sending its mobile units forward via Senno to drive into the deep flank of the 4th Army. LIII Army Corps under the 3rd Panzer Army now made an effort to break out to the southwest, but the attempt failed in the face of powerful enemy defences at Ostrovno. The situation was then made even more hopeless by the fact that the right wing of IX Army Corps, which had been holding its position on the Dvina at Beshenkovichi, was now forced back westward to Bocheykovo by the 1st Baltic Front.

In answer to further urgent requests from Field-Marshal Busch to General Zeitzler that Army Group Centre's battle instructions should be modified, Hitler finally decided at the evening conference that only the 4th Army should be allowed to withdraw to the Dnieper line. In actual fact, the withdrawal had already been completed at the orders of von Tippelskirch in the night from June 25th–26th. Hitler also decided that the 12th Panzer Division (of Army Group North) should be sent to the 9th Army at Marina Gorka, but he still refused to change his mind about Vitebsk. 'The 206th Division will hold Vitebsk until it is relieved.'

We have already mentioned this remark of Hitler's, but it is as well to repeat it here in the context to which it belongs. It was passed on as an order in this form to Army Group HQ, and entered word for word into its war diary.[26] The idea that the garrison of Vitebsk could ever be 'relieved' was simply absurd. Hitler's observation has therefore been regarded either as completely cynical or as showing his lack of insight into the operational situation. Today it will be judged in a profounder sense as throwing some light on the psychological attitude of a man who was unwilling to recognize that the die had now been irrevocably cast against him, and who – consciously or unconsciously – obstinately refused to make any decisions which could be interpreted by those around him as an admission of his own mistakes, weaknesses and failure.[27] For Hitler to have given way to the opinions of his military advisers and to the proposals of his Chief of Staff and his Army Group and Field commanders would have meant at this time (and later) that his own will was being forced to subordinate itself to the logic of events. Such a thing he regarded as altogether intolerable, and therefore he continued to postpone the urgently necessary decisions required of him. In the beginning, the lives of tens of thousands of German soldiers were at stake, but before long it was the lives of hundreds of thousands. In the end it was the fate of a whole people.

The situation now developed rapidly, and by June 26th the danger of a double envelopment of Army Group Centre was becoming acute. The danger from the south came from the armoured forces of the 1st White Russian Front, which were now driving forward with nothing to stop them on their way towards Bobruisk and the rearward communications of the 9th Army. From the northeast the danger came from the drive of the 3rd White Russian Front along and across the motor road to the west of Orsha into the long flank of the 4th Army. 9th Army called off the attack of the 20th Panzer Division and sought to meet the danger developing to the west by changing the direction of the division through Bobruisk. On its east front, relentless pressure from vastly superior enemy forces compelled the 9th Army to abandon the Dubissa line. On the north flank, the Russians crossed the Bobruisk–Mogilev road and finally separated the two armies. On the south wing of the 4th Army the German forces were withdrawn across the Dnieper according to plan, but at the same time advance elements of the 2nd White Russian Front captured the right bank of the Dnieper to the north of Mogilev, and heavy attacks were made on Orsha from the east, north and west, though for the time being they were held. Fast mobile elements of the 3rd White Russian Front now pressed forward into the gap and advanced to the west and the southwest on a broad front, cutting the motor road near Tolochin. Further westward, weak German forces tried to cover the detraining of the 5th Panzer Division in Borisov. A battle group of the 3rd Army with IX Army Corps, strengthened by hurriedly collected security forces, had to be withdrawn further west in face of an enemy drive on Bocheykovo and across the Dvina. The Vitebsk strongpoint was now taken by the Russians. LIII Army Corps made a final attempt to break out to the southwest near Ostrovno, but it was caught in enemy counterattacks and broken up.

As, during the course of June 26th, there was no sign that his urgent request, that the Supreme Command should modify his battle orders to suit the changed circumstances, was likely to be granted by Hitler via OKH, Busch decided to take a plan to Berchtesgaden and put the case to Hitler in person. In a discussion of the general situation which took place on the evening of June 26th, Hitler finally agreed to the withdrawal of the 9th Army into the Bobruisk bridgehead, and to a 'stage by stage' withdrawal of the 4th Army to the Beresina line, but he still demanded that the remaining strongpoints of Mogilev and Orsha should be held.

Thus, after two days delay a decision had at last been obtained, but even now it was so narrowed down by restrictions and qualifications that there could be no freedom of decision for Army Group Centre, and Busch still felt himself bound by the instructions given to him by Hitler. The result was further indecision, hesitation and doubts, which prevented the radical steps the situation called for. For example, when Major-General Staedke, Chief of Staff of the 9th Army, appeared at Army Group Centre HQ in Minsk on the morning of June 27th to report his intention of attempting a break out to the northwest with the mass of the 9th Army, because as things stood he was threatened with encirclement, he was expressly forbidden to do so because of the order of the Supreme Command that Bobruisk was to be held as the cornerstone of the Beresina line. Instead, he was instructed to use the 20th Panzer Division to make his rearward communications free. This order forbidding a break out lacked all reference to the actual situation in which the 9th Army found itself. The same was true of the order given at the same time to the 4th Army; it was to hold its positions on the Dnieper and withdraw to the Drut sector 'only if forced'. Even then, it was instructed that it must continue to hold the Mogilev and Orsha strongpoints.

On June 27th the situation of the 9th Army worsened desperately: not only did the enemy now bar the roads to the west and northwest, but strong armoured forces were driving from the northeast along the road to Mogilev towards Bobruisk, seizing the bridges across the river on the way so that the units of XLI Panzer Corps and XXXV Army Corps herded together on the east bank of the Beresina could no longer cross the river. This made it extremely doubtful whether these divisions would be able to fight their way out, as 9th Army Command had intended. Russian mechanized units fanning out to the west of Bobruisk reached Novya Dorogi in the west and Osipovichi in the northwest. The 12th Panzer Division began detraining in Marina Gorka, and the 4th Army was holding the Dnieper line on the south wing as far as Mogilev, but its extended southern flank was now threatened by an enemy drive across the Mogilev–Bobruisk road. On the north wing, the 2nd White Russian Front crossed the Dnieper on a broad front, and the Orsha strong-point fell to heavy attacks from all sides. XXVII Army Corps fought its way through strong enemy forces coming from the north and west, and opened a way southwestward. Fast Russian mechanized units advancing westward along the motor road were temporarily held up by the covering line at Borisov. IX Army Corps of the 3rd Army was too weak to withstand enemy pressure and had to withdraw still farther westward to the Lepel–Ushachi line, pursued by forces of the 1st Baltic Front. It was strengthened on its right wing by the 212th Division, which was detrained in Lepel. The gap to LIII Army Corps had now extended to fifty miles, and on the morning of June 27th the Corps ceased fighting.

In this general situation Army Group Centre issued on the afternoon of June 27th further instructions for the conduct of the fighting. The 2nd Army was instructed to take over the south wing of the 9th Army, which had been forced away from its positions with the rest of the Army, and to secure their connection with the troops fighting in the Oressa sector. The 9th Army itself was instructed to beat a fighting retreat to the Novya Dorogi–Osipovichi line, at the same time leaving a division in the Bobruisk strongpoint. And the 4th Army was instructed to withdraw sector by sector to the Beresina line, while continuing to hold the Mogilev strongpoint. On the same day, Busch made another attempt, through the Chief of the General Staff, to obtain Hitler's permission to abandon the Bobruisk, Mogilev and Orsha strong-points, but once again without success. Operational Order of the Führer No. 8 arrived in the night of June 27th–28th, and merely confirmed the instructions already given to Busch by word of mouth. There were no material changes to the orders already issued by Army Group Centre. Referring to the strong-points, the operational order declared that they must be held at least 'for a few more days in order to facilitate the preparation of a strong defensive front farther back'. But this operational order was based on an estimate of the situation which took it for granted that the German forces enjoyed sufficient freedom of action to be able to limit the successes of the enemy and ultimately bring his advance to a halt before a 'final defence line'. The events of the very next day quickly showed that such instructions were based on wishful thinking.

Not surprisingly, they collapsed in the face of harsh reality. For one thing, the assumption of Germany's Supreme Command that the Russian offensive had now passed its peak was seen to be false – on the contrary, it now entered its second operational phase, driving forward to new and far-reaching objectives.

The Russian Drive in Depth

The commitment of powerful fast mobile units on both wings of the Russian offensive front, in the south towards Slutsk and in the north through Lepel towards Molodechno, on June 28th, indicated that the Russians had no intention of contenting themselves with the capture of Minsk, but were determined to exploit the successes they had already won in order to drive still further westward. And Army Group Centre was well aware that the enemy had not abandoned his plan to complete the encirclement of the 4th Army by a pincers operation against Minsk. The 4th Army was now beating a fighting retreat to the Beresina, and finding itself threatened by pursuing Russian infantry forces which outflanked it. In fact, on June 28th and 29th the Russian High Command issued 'special directives' detailing 'the tasks of the Fronts for the continuation of the offensive'.[28] According to these directives the 1st and 3rd White Russian Fronts were 'to drive on Minsk by means of a double encirclement movement, to take the town and thus completely encircle the German forces withdrawing from the Mogilev area to Minsk'. At the same time, the 2nd White Russian Front was 'to pursue the German forces frontally in order to hamper their systematic withdrawal towards Minsk'. The mechanized forces of the 3rd White Russian Front were given instructions 'to drive towards Vileyka and Molodechno in order to cut off the enemy's retreat from Minsk to Lida and Vilna'. The 1st Baltic Front was given the task of covering the operations of the 3rd White Russian Front, to the north by driving towards Polotsk, and westward towards Glubokoye. 'After the conclusion of the Bobruisk operations, the 1st White Russian Front will continue the pursuit of the enemy towards Baranovichi and Minsk.' At the same time, cavalry and armoured units were sent in the direction of Baranovichi in order to cut the railway line running from Minsk to the southwest.

Reports coming in on the morning of June 28th of the catastrophe which had overtaken the encircled mass of the 9th Army in the Bobruisk area left no room for doubt that, even if there were any possibility of these units breaking out, they were no longer of any fighting value. At the same time, the covering front of the 3rd Army near Lepel was again broken, and communications to Army Group North cut. There was no hope of any relief to the south from the operations of the 3rd Panzer Army, whose fighting strength was now reduced to one weak infantry corps. Although the von Saucken Group, formed of the 5th Panzer Division and security troops (XXXIX Panzer Corps), was temporarily holding up the advance of the enemy on both sides of Borisov and farther northward at the destroyed bridges over the Beresina, the conditions for carrying out Operational Order No. 8 were already non-existent. As Army Group Centre pointed out in a review of the situation, enemy freedom of movement from Bobruisk and Lepel to the west could no longer be prevented. The immediate despatch of powerful new forces to Baranovichi and to the west of Lepel was essential. As the result of telephone conversations with OKH, 'the main task of Army Group in the further course of operations' was now defined as withdrawing the 4th Army safely back to the Minsk area. However, if the few available forces (the 5th Panzer Division at Borisov and the 12th Panzer Division at Marina Gorka) and the new forces brought up (4th Panzer Division and the 28th Division to Baranovichi, and the 170th and 132nd Divisions from Army Group North over Molodechno to Minsk) were to be used to the best strategic effect, mobile fighting tactics were essential. To the south of Minsk, the 12th Panzer Division and, on its arrival, the 4th Panzer Division, and to the northwest of Minsk the 5th Panzer Division, were to hold the way open for the withdrawal of the 4th Army.

On the evening of June 28th, Field-Marshal Model took command of Army Group Centre in place of Field-Marshal Busch. For the time being, Model also retained the command of Army Group Northern Ukraine, in order to help the movement of further reserves from that area.[29] This change of command produced not only a change in the 'style' of the leadership on the spot, but also a change in the relations between Army Group and the Supreme Command. The reputation the new C.-in-C. enjoyed with Hitler immediately made itself felt, and, rather to the amazement of Army Group Operations Staff, Hitler readily agreed to all the measures proposed by Field-Marshal Model.

On June 29th, the enemy continued to push further forces through the great gaps which had been torn in the German lines. In the south, his advanced elements reached Slutsk, and in the north they arrived at the upper Beresina on a broad front between Borisov and to the southwest of Lepel. With cavalry forces it had sent to Slutsk, the 2nd Army was trying to hold this strongpoint. It now received instructions to bring the Russian advance to a standstill here, and to use the forces which were arriving in Baranovichi (4th Panzer Division and the 28th Division) for an attack towards the northeast in order to close the gap between it and the 9th Army south of Minsk. The bolt position set up by the 12th Panzer Division, reinforced by security units, held firm against enemy attacks on both sides of Marina Gorka. Army Group Centre now ordered the 9th Army to re-establish contact with the south wing of the 4th Army, and to use the two divisions that were to be despatched from Army Group North to hold the area to the south of Minsk. However, in view of the tense situation on the south wing of Army Group North, OKH suspended the transfer of one of these divisions, the 132nd. The 4th Army continued to withdraw to the Beresina, increasingly hard pressed by enemy forces on its flanks. On the north wing, the von Saucken battle group still held the Borisov bridgehead. In view of the danger that enemy forces might cross the Beresina farther north and drive into the gap opened up between the 4th Army and the 3rd Panzer Army towards Minsk, elements of the 5th Panzer Division on the west bank of the Beresina were placed in readiness to be sent into action in a northwesterly direction. Under powerful enemy pressure, the weak battle group of the 3rd Panzer Army had to be withdrawn still further westward. Driving through the gap which had opened up between it and Army Group North, advanced elements of the 1st Baltic Front reached the railway line Molodechno–Polotsk.

On June 30th a certain lessening of tension was experienced on both wings of the Army Group; but this was only temporary. Enemy forces attacking the 2nd Army captured Slutsk, but thanks to the obstinate resistance of the weak forces available there they were pinned down and prevented from exploiting their success in the direction of Baranovichi or Minsk, with the result that it was possible to complete the detrainment of the 4th Panzer Division at Baranovichi without interruption. There was no change on the front of the 9th Army at Marina Gorka. German forces breaking their way out of the Bobruisk cauldron to the north got half way to their objective. The fast mobile units of the 3rd White Russian Front attacking the north wing of the 4th Army near Borisov and driving northward continued to meet with obstinate resistance on the Beresina. An enemy group driving forward through Begoml was thrown back by units of the 5th Panzer Division. On the other hand, the situation of the mass of the 4th Army (XII and XXVII Army Corps) still fighting on the east bank of the Beresina was very critical. The main line of retreat Belynichi–Beresino was still being held open, but it did not look as though the crossing from one side of the river to the other at Beresino could be completed before July 3rd.

On July 1st, the situation of Army Group as a whole worsened considerably because of a drive launched by fast mobile units of the 1st White Russian Front from Slutsk towards the railway line Baranovichi–Minsk to the south of Stolbtsy. With this, the wide enveloping movement being carried out by the enemy in the south began to take shape, and a corresponding drive in the north towards Molodechno was obviously to be expected. The 2nd Army now committed the 4th Panzer Division and the 1st Hungarian Cavalry Division to the east of Baranovichi against the south flank of the enemy forces operating towards Stolbtsy. The 28th Division, which arrived late, was to join in this attack. On the 9th Army sector, the 12th Panzer Division gathered the units which had broken out of Bobruisk and sent them back westwards. The situation of the 4th Army now became more and more critical. Enemy forces pressed from the south and the north on the west bank of the Beresina, with the intention of cutting the army's main line of retreat along the Beresino–Minsk road. Enemy forces advancing past Cherven and Chernayavka were held up only with great difficulty. The German divisions to the east of the Beresina, hard pressed in flank and rear, fought their way back to the bridge positions. On the left wing of the army, the Borisov bridgehead was lost after the withdrawal of the 5th Panzer Division into the area east of Minsk. The 3rd Panzer Army withdrew according to plan to the Pronia–Plissa sector.

Army Command Centre now contacted General Heusinger, Chief of Operations, at OKH, where he was representing Chief of General Staff Zeitzler, who was ill, and informed him of the critical turn the situation as a whole was taking as the result of the westward drive of fast Russian mobile forces, and the inevitable consequences for the 9th and 4th Armies operating in the Minsk area. The threat to their rear communications through Stolbtsy and Molodechno made illusory the previous hope that reinforcements could still be sent to them through Minsk. The 170th Division would have to detrain at Molodechno.

On July 2nd, the fast mobile units of the 1st White Russian Front reached the railway line Baranovichi–Minsk at Stolbtsy as expected, while advanced elements of the 3rd White Russian Front reached the railway line Vilna–Minsk at Molodechno and Smorgon. The Russians were obviously trying to close the two narrow corridors to the south and north of the Naliboki forest area to the west of Minsk. If the parts of the 9th and 4th Armies still fighting in the Minsk area were to be brought back, and a new coherent front line established, then it was absolutely essential to hold these routes open. In order to counter the danger, Field-Marshal Model decided to ignore the situation in the Minsk area and to commit the few battleworthy divisions remaining to him in order to throw back the enemy to the southwest and northwest of Minsk, thus opening the corridors again. The 2nd Army was instructed to continue its attack with the 4th Panzer Division on Stolbtsy, and the 9th Army was instructed to withdraw the 12th Panzer Division from the front to the southeast of Minsk and to move it westward against Stolbtsy. The 5th Panzer Division, with the 4th Army, deployed to the north of Minsk and drove northwestward to free the railway line Minsk–Molodechno. But on the same day it was reported to Army High Command that there was now no hope that battleworthy units of the 4th Army would be able to reach the Minsk area. Communications had been cut, and it was no longer possible to affect the battle for Minsk by sending in reinforcements. The report went on to say that in such circumstances there was no justification for continuing to hold Minsk as a strongpoint. It was urgent that reinforcements should be brought up if the operations for keeping open the Baranovichi and Molodechno corridors were to have any hope of success. After hearing the report of the Chief of the Operations Staff, Hitler agreed to Model's proposals and approved the measures he had already taken.

The great battle for White Russia entered its final stage on July 3rd with the recapture of Minsk by the Russians, who broke through the weak lines which were still holding to the southeast of the town, and then entered Minsk almost simultaneously from the east and the south. With this, the 1st and 3rd White Russian Fronts had closed the ring around the mass of the 4th Army, which was still trying to fight its way back across the Beresina. By committing the three Panzer divisions still at the disposal of Army Group Centre, those units of the 9th and 4th Armies still fighting to the south of Minsk were able to retreat over the Neman at Stolbtsy and along the road from Minsk to Molodechno, taking thousands of stragglers with them. A battle group formed of the units of the 9th Army originally trapped in Bobruisk, with units of the 20th Panzer Division as its hard core, managed to reach the western bank of the Neman to the northwest of Stolbtsy. IX Army Corps of the 3rd Panzer Army held a line to the north of Parafianovo against forces of the 1st Baltic Front advancing from Glubokoye. Beyond the south wing of the Army Group North, which was now bent back south of the Dvina to the west of Polotsk, there was a gap through which enemy forces were moving westward. Polotsk was already threatened on three sides by forces of the 1st Baltic Front.

Nevertheless, Hitler still obstinately refused to give permission for the evacuation of the Polotsk strongpoint. He believed that operating from there he could change the fortunes of Army Group Centre, and on July 1st he ordered Army Group North to attack in a southwesterly direction. As there were only two divisions available to carry out this order, it was rejected as impossible by everyone concerned, and Model declared that in his view it would be better if 'such useless experiments' were not attempted.[30] The vigorous resistance put up by Army Group North to this order resulted a little later in the removal of its C.-in-C., General Lindemann, and his replacement by General Friessner. It was only in the night of July 2nd–3rd that Hitler at last allowed General Heusinger to persuade him that his plan was impossible, and he then agreed to the evacuation of Polotsk.

During the next few days, the weak units in the Minsk area still in contact with the enemy, and hard pressed by superior forces on both sides of the Naliboki forest, withdrew towards Baranovichi and Molodechno, where new forces were brought up and committed, with the result that the battle flared up again with renewed fury. Cut-off units of the 4th Army crossed the Beresina and continued their retreat westward, fighting their way free to the south of Minsk. In this 'shifting cauldron', the battle groups of XII and XXVII Army Corps still maintained their tactical cohesion, but all Army Group could do to support the gallant attempt of the remnants of the 4th Army to save themselves was to send in a limited amount of supplies by air. The last batch was flown in on July 5th, at Smilovichi to the southeast of Minsk. But with this, the possibilities of air supply were exhausted, because for one thing the Luftwaffe was now forced to move its airfields back farther westward, and for another there was insufficient fighter cover available for the supply aircraft. On July 8th, 1944, the acting commanding general of XII Army Corps issued the order to lay down arms because an acute shortage of both ammunition and fuel had reduced the effectiveness of his men, among whom were many stragglers, to nil. In the circumstances, and in view of the length of Army Group Centre's front line, further resistance was useless.

Summary

On July 3rd, 1944, the troops of the 1st Baltic and the 1st, 2nd and 3rd White Russian Fronts closed the first phase of the strategic operations with the capture of Minsk, says the official Soviet report.[31] The Russian summer offensive had thus attained its first objective: the liberation of White Russia. At the same time, it had torn a breach in the German front, and Army Group Centre, with 8 scattered divisions, was now fighting on a front over 200 miles long against 116 infantry divisions, 6 cavalry divisions, 16 mechanized infantry brigades and 42 armoured brigades.[32] A few days later the various Russian 'Fronts' advanced again, in accordance with orders issued on July 4th by the Russian High Command to carry the offensive forward across the former Russo-Polish frontier. They now drove forward via Molodechno in the north towards Vilna, and via Baranovichi in the south towards Brest.

If we try to sum up the factors which determined the outcome of the fourteen-day 'Battle for White Russia', then the first is unquestionably the strength of the forces the Russians were able to throw into their offensive. 'In the summer of 1944 the Russians enjoyed such a degree of superiority in numbers, material and equipment – including the air – that they were not in any way limited in their actions or in any way compelled to husband their resources.'[33] The Russians were thus in a position to launch an offensive on a broad front at several points simultaneously, and at the same time to concentrate their forces against those sectors of the German front whose destruction was first necessary if the far-reaching tactical objectives of the offensive were to be attained. On the north wing, their aim was to seize possession of the land bridge between the Dnieper and the Dvina, thus opening the way to Minsk and the Upper Beresina; in the south, their first objective was to prise Bobruisk, the strong cornerstone of the Beresina line, out of the German front, and open the way to the west towards Minsk and Baranovichi. In both cases, the fast mobile units held in readiness for operations in depth were so powerful from the start that the offensive spearheads of the 1st and 3rd White Russian Fronts could let their inner wings continue the advance on Baranovichi and Molo-dechno without weakening the operations against Minsk. The superior speed of their fast mobile units repeatedly allowed the Russians to overtake, cut off, encircle and often destroy retreating German troops, most of whom had to move on foot. Thus the enemy, being in a position to use his forces lavishly, could dictate the course of events to the German commanders, and this was aggravated by the fact that the counter-measures taken were by no means appropriate to the strength, vigour and strategic objectives of the Russian offensive; nor did they keep pace with the rapidly developing situation.

In this connection, we need only recall the difficult conditions in which Army Group Centre had to conduct its operations from the start. First of all, there was the gross disproportion between the over-extended front line and the forces available for its defence, which meant that the line was necessarily very thinly held, and there was no possibility of any defence in depth; then there was the lack of adequate reserves in the neighbourhood of the front (one armoured division and three infantry divisions); then came Hitler's insistence on the establishment of strongpoints, for which six divisions had to be allotted, which were thus not available for mobile fighting; there were no tactical reserves at all; and finally, there was the great weakness of the Luftwaffe, whose operations were still further restricted by the shortage of fuel. Although all this was bad enough, and would in any circumstances have greatly hampered the conduct of the operations, Hitler made things still worse by issuing orders which tied Army Group down to a rigid defence of the main front line; at the same time, he expressly forbade them to prepare rearward positions to retire to in case of necessity, thus making it impossible to wage a mobile battle of defence.

The fact that Germany's Supreme Command underestimated the danger of a Russian offensive, which was launched with greatly superior forces, was part and parcel of its general estimate of the enemy, and stemmed in particular from its unshakable conviction that the Russian summer offensive would be directed against Army Group Northern Ukraine in Galicia, and not against Army Group Centre. Hitler and OKH continued to cling to this idea even when, from the middle of June on, it was clearly not in accordance with the Russian deployment against Army Group Centre. Generally speaking, Army Group Centre was aware of the numerical strength being concentrated against it and also of the focal points of the imminent Russian offensive, but it certainly overestimated its own powers of resistance.

In particular, it awaited the battle in the expectation that once the Russian offensive had begun it would be given a free hand to fight the defensive battle according to its own judgement of the situation. This turned out to be very far from the case. 'The battle was accepted with the objective of holding the forward positions, and so it continued throughout.'[34] But once – against all expectations – the front was broken in the very first few days on both sides of Vitebsk, to the north of Orsha, to the east of Mogilev and on both sides of Bobruisk, the only way to prevent disaster overtaking the whole Army Group was to abandon the so-called strongpoints and fight a mobile defence. This would have meant withdrawing where necessary, and, with the help of strong reinforcements, establishing a new defensive line, perhaps along the Upper Beresina; and, in addition, obtaining help as soon as possible from the other Army Groups, and particularly from Army Group Northern Ukraine, which was particularly well supplied with reserves.

Army Group Centre first put forward these requests on the morning of June 24th, and OKH recognized their reasonableness. However, Hitler refused to give permission for withdrawal from any part of the front which was not attacked, and in particular, he refused to allow the strongpoints to be evacuated. The Commander-in-Chief of Army Group Centre, Field-Marshal Busch, felt that in view of the strict instructions Hitler had given him he was not entitled to change the battle objectives of his forces on his own initiative and thus give his commanders a free hand to conduct a mobile defence. It is probably not possible to spare him the reproach that he submitted to Hitler's orders almost without a protest, and that not once did he bring himself to act independently in the interests of the men for whom he was responsible, and face the Supreme Command with a *fait accompli* – as his successor Field-Marshal Model did.[35] It is true that, on the morning of June 25th, Army Group Centre urgently repeated its request for a modification of its battle instructions, but it was only on the night of June 26th–27th – that is to say after a further delay of thirty-six hours – that Hitler at last gave permission for a step-by-step withdrawal to the Beresina; and even then he still insisted that the strongpoints should be held. But it was then already too late: large parts of the 3rd Panzer Army and of the 9th Army were already destroyed, and the whole of the 4th Army fell victim to the rapid development of the Russian encirclement movement towards Minsk. Looking back now, there can be no doubt that a prompt withdrawal by the 9th and 4th Armies would have freed the reserves necessary to support the threatened flanks, and although this would not have prevented the defeat it would in all probability have prevented the destruction of battleworthy units.

As Hitler's irresponsible procrastination made it impossible to take those radical measures which the situation demanded, the development of the battle right up to the complete collapse of Army Group Centre was inevitable. Thus the catastrophe which overtook the German Army in White Russia – twenty-eight divisions were destroyed and 350,000 men lost – was twice as great as the Stalingrad disaster. The effects on the whole German war situation in the summer of 1944 were even worse: the collapse of Army Group Centre affected the whole Eastern Front, because it allowed the Russians to throw back the centre of the German front as far as the Vistula and the East Prussian frontier, to cut off the German forces in the Baltic provinces, and to threaten the German position in the Balkans both militarily and politically. The collapse of Army Group Centre in White Russia in the summer of 1944 was the beginning of the end for Germany's military efforts on the Eastern Front.

Chronicle XI

September 1944

to

August 1945

Politics		Conduct of the War
Neutrals	Germany and Japan	Germany and Japan
	September 4, 1944: Finland lays down arms.	September 2, 1944: Evacuation of most o German garrisons on the Aegean Isles b September 4 to 15, 1944: Evacuation of Fir September 8, 1944: First V–2 rocket fal London.
	September 25, 1944: Hitler orders the raising of the German 'Volkssturm' (People's Army).	September 16, 1944: First use of V–1 from ai September 16 to 23, 1944: Evacuation of E
		October 3, 1944: Evacuation of Athens.
October 15, 1944: Hungary offers Russia an armistice. Hitler compels Horthy to withdraw armistice offer.		October 11, 1944: First operational plans Ardennes counter-offensive. October 13, 1944: Evacuation of Riga.
	October 14, 1944: Field-Marshal Rommel forced to commit suicide. October 19, 1944: Destruction of Warsaw ordered by Hitler.	October 25, 1944: German troops leave K
		November 2, 1944: End of the evacu Greece.
		November 10, 1944: Wehrmacht High C orders Ardennes counter-offensive. November 10 to 11, 1944: Japanese take bases at Kweilin and Linchow in Chi November 16, 1944: Battle of the Roer b November 23, 1944: Allies capture Stras
		December 16, 1944: Last German offensi in the West. December 18, 1944: German counter- halted. January 1, 1945: Last German air attack airfields in Belgium and northern F January 1945: Japanese operational p for the defence of Formosa, the Islands and Japan.

stern Allies and the Soviet Union	Western Allies and the Soviet Union	Neutrals

nber 3, 1944: Recapture of Brussels. nber 4, 1944: Recapture of Antwerp.		
nber 8, 1944: Recapture of Liège. nber 11, 1944: US 1st Army reaches German ontier to the north of Trier. US armies unite est of Dijon: the 3rd US Army (Normandy) id the 7th US Army (south France).	September 5, 1944: Soviet Union declares war on Bulgaria. September 8, 1944: Bulgaria declares war on Germany. September 12, 1944: Soviet-Rumanian armistice signed in Moscow. September 14, 1944: Strategic bombing forces released from Eisenhower's command.	
nber 15, 1944: Russian break-through at arva. ussians occupy Sofia. S landings on Palau and Morotai. iber 17, 1944: Allied airborne landings at rnhem and Nijmegen.		
er 1944: Heavy Allied air attacks on Duis-irg, Essen and Cologne. er 2, 1944: Polish insurrectionaries in Warsaw pitulate. er 3, 1944: Walcheren dyke destroyed by air tack. er 5, 1944: Russian break-through to the ltic south of Riga. Army Group North circled. er 11, 1944: First Russian drive into East ussia. er 10 to 13, 1944: Formosa air battle between 3 carrier-borne and Japanese land-based craft.	September 19, 1944: Soviet-Finnish armistice signed in Moscow. September 22, 1944: Roosevelt withdraws his signature from the Morgenthau Plan, which he and Churchill had approved on September 15th. October 9 to 20, 1944: Churchill in Moscow for talks with Stalin.	
er 19, 1944: Landing on Leyte. Beginning of acArthur's offensive to recapture the ilippines. 00 bomber RAF daylight raid on Duisburg, d heavy US air raid on Cologne. er 20, 1944: Russian troops and Tito partisans cupy Belgrade. er 21, 1944: US troops occupy Aachen (Aix-Chapelle). er 23, 1944: Russian forces reach East issian frontier. er 23 to 26, 1944: Naval battle of Leyte; shing defeat of the Japanese fleet. Japanese val planes make first *kamikaze* attacks. er 27, 1944: Russian forces reach Kirkenes–eden–Nautsi line. per 1, 1944: Anglo-Canadian forces attack lcheren.	October 18, 1944: General Stillwell recalled as Chiang Kai-shek's Chief of Staff. October 28, 1944: Soviet-Bulgarian armistice signed in Moscow.	
	November 7, 1944: Roosevelt elected President of the United States for the fourth time in succession.	
er 12, 1944: RAF destroys battleship *itz* near Tromso. er 22, 1944: Free French troops take ort and Mulhouse. er 24, 1944: First attack by US 'Super-tresses' against Tokyo from Saipan base. er 3, 1944: West Wall pierced near Saar-ern. er 15, 1944: US Corps lands on Mindoro.	December 10, 1944: Franco-Soviet alliance.	
er 18, 1944: Heavy incendiary bomb attack US air force on Hankow. er 24, 1944: Budapest encircled. ture of Akyab (Burma). 9, 1945: US 6th Army lands on Luzon. vy *kamikaze* attacks. 12, 1945: Russian forces at Baranov gehead start direct attack on Reich.	January 1, 1945: The Communist 'Lublin Committee' declares itself the government of Poland.	

	Politics	Conduct of the War
Neutrals	Germany and Japan	Germany and Japan
		January 17, 1945: Evacuation of Warsaw. January 23 to May 8, 1945: Mass evacua[tion] East Prussia by sea. Over two milli[on] habitants moved. Losses: 1 per cent.
	February 15, 1945: Reich Minister of Justice orders the establishment of exceptional courts martial. February 19, 1945: Himmler approaches Bernadotte of Sweden.	
	February 26, 1945: Himmler issues instructions for the establishment of 'special courts to combat indications of dissolution'. March 5, 1945: Germany calls up 1929 Class.	
	March 19, 1945: Hitler issues 'scorched-earth' order for the destruction of all plant, etc.	March 27, 1945: Last V–2 fired against [London] March 30, 1945: Russians capture Danzig[.] End of March 1945: 'Kettsu', last Japanes[e opera]tional plan for defence of Japan.
		April 9, 1945: Russians capture Königsbe[rg] April 10, 1945: Japanese offensive aga[inst] bases in China.
	April 25, 1945: Himmler's armistice offer reaches London. April 28, 1945: Italian partisans shoot Mussolini. April 30, 1945: Hitler commits suicide in Berlin.	April 21, 1945: Collapse of the German [front in] Italy.
	May 2, 1945: New German Government formed under Grand Admiral Dönitz. Capitulation of Berlin. May 4, 1945: Signing of the capitulation for the northwest theatre.	
	May 7, 1945: German Wehrmacht signs unconditional surrender.	

Conduct of the War	Politics	
estern Allies and the Soviet Union	Western Allies and the Soviet Union	Neutrals
...ary 12 to 22, 1945: US carrier fleet launches ...aids on South China Sea.	January 12, 1945: General Wedemeyer proposes withdrawal of US strategic bomber forces from China. January 15, 1945: Transfer begins of US strategic bomber forces from China, first to India and then to the Marianas.	
...ary 28, 1945: Reopening of the Burma Road. ...ary 1, 1945: Russians occupy Bucharest. ...ary 3, 1945: 1,000 bomber US air raid on ...erlin. ...ary 4, 1945: US forces occupy Manila. ...ary 13, 1945: Capture of Budapest. ...ary 13 to 14, 1945: Terror raid on Dresden.	February 4 to 12, 1945: Yalta Conference.	
...ary 16 to 17, 1945: First big carrier-based ...aid on Tokyo.		
...ary 19, 1945: US landing on volcanic island ...f Iwojima. ...ary 22, 1945: Almost 9,000 Allied aircraft ...ttack German transport targets.	February 20, 1945: Hungarian counter-government formed in Debrecen signs armistice agreement in Moscow.	
...ary 28, 1945: Recapture of Corregidor.	February 27, 1945: Soviet Deputy Commissar for Foreign Affairs, Vyshinsky, forces King of Rumania to appoint Communist Groza government.	
...9, 1945: Capture of Lashio. ...9 to 10, 1945: Heavy US incendiary air ...tack on Tokyo from the Marianas. One-...uarter of the built-up area destroyed. 83,800 ...ead. ...12, 1945: Heavy US air raid on Swine-...ünde.		
	March 27, 1945: Argentine declares war on Germany.	
...1, 1945: US landing on island of Okinawa. ...eavy fighting goes on until June 21st. ...ersistent *kamikaze* attacks. ...ncirclement of Ruhr district completed.	April 3, 1945: Change of command in the Pacific: Admiral Nimitz, sea; General MacArthur, land. April 5, 1945: Soviet Union renounces Non-aggression Pact with Japan.	
...7, 1945: First US bombing raid on Tokyo ...ith fighter protection launched from Iwo-...ma.		
...14, 1945: Capture of Vienna.	April 12, 1945: Death of President Roosevelt. Truman succeeds him.	
...24, 1945: Encirclement of Berlin completed. ...25, 1945: Russian and US troops meet on the ...lbe.		April 25, 1945 to June 26, 1945: San Francisco Conference.
..., 1945: Australian troops land on Borneo. ..., 1945: British land near Rangoon.		
..., 1945: Czech insurrection in Prague.		
...5, 1945: Japanese offensive against Chinkiang ...lted by Chinese land and US air forces. ...3 and 25, 1945: Heavy US incendiary attack ...Tokyo.	May 23, 1945: Churchill forms new cabinet, without the Labour Party.	
...9, 1945: Heavy US incendiary attack on ...okohama.	May 25, 1945: Plans for invasion of Japan agreed.	

Politics		Conduct of the War
Neutrals	Germany and Japan	Germany and Japan
	July 2, 1945: Tokyo evacuated, except for 200,000 people.	
		September 2, 1945: Japan signs unconditional surrender.

Conduct of the War	Politics	
estern Allies and the Soviet Union	Western Allies and the Soviet Union	Neutrals
		June 26, 1945: Foundation of UNO.
16, 1945: First atom bomb tests in Alamogordo New Mexico). Formation of US Army Strategic Air Forces for operations against Japan. 16 to 17, 1945: First coastal bombardment of Japan by British and US warships. 10 to 30, 1945: Repeated US carrier-borne air raids on Japan. st 6 and 9, 1945: Atom bombs dropped on Hiroshima and Nagasaki. 100,000 dead. st 9, 1945: Russian attack in Manchuria. st 10, 1945: Japanese offer of capitulation. st 15, 1945: Armistice in the Far East.	July 17 to August 2, 1945: Potsdam Conference July 26, 1945: Electoral victory of the Labour Party in Britain.	

The Battle of the Ardennes 1944–5

BY HASSO VON MANTEUFFEL

The Preparations

Hitler had been considering an offensive against the Western Allies in the late autumn of 1944 since August of that year. It is, therefore, desirable to give a brief sketch of the military developments on the Western Front from August to the start of the offensive on December 16th, 1944, particularly as the heavy defensive fighting on all sectors of the Western Front during this time must be seen in connection with the preparations for the offensive itself.

Military Developments on the Western Front in the Autumn of 1944

When the enemy broke out of the Cotentin Peninsula in Normandy, Hitler called for a defensive struggle to pin down the enemy far away from the West Wall. This was to gain time, not only to bring up reinforcements and put the neglected West Wall into a more effective state of defence, but also to create the conditions for tactical counter-attacks to the west of the German frontier. However, once the Allied forces had broken through at Avranches on July 31st, and had advanced out of the narrow Normandy peninsula eastwards into open country where there were very few troops to oppose them, they were able for the first time to take full advantage of their greater mobility and their air superiority. The Western Allies had seized the initiative.

As far as the Germans were concerned, there were neither positions nor adequate reserves to enable them to hold up the enemy for any length of time. Forced into a war of manœuvre, the few and barely mobile reserves, some with make-shift transport, did their best to fight a delaying action. They were over-run and left behind by the enemy, whose operations were helped by a good network of roads and by their air supremacy over the whole operational area. New break-throughs and rapid advances forced the Germans to give ground again and again in the hope of improvising a new line of resistance in some new defence zone. As the mass of the armoured forces available to Commander-in-Chief West (von Kluge) had been encircled and almost completely destroyed at Falaise (August 13th to 20th), no further armoured or mechanized divisions were available, and it was impossible to make good the losses in such a short time. The armoured forces which were left were insufficient for counter-attacks on the scale that Hitler had in mind. The few new units which it had proved possible to raise during the summer of 1944 were equipped with horse-drawn artillery and had very little battle experience.

To the south of the German West Front, the withdrawal of the whole of Army Group G under the command of General Blaskowitz (1st and 19th Armies) from southern and southwestern France had been permitted by Hitler only at the very last moment, and thus once again much too late. By this time, the spearhead of the US armoured forces was already on the lower Loire, and threatening the retreat of the two armies. Although in August C.-in-C. West had reported to Hitler that the only thing to do now was to strengthen the West Wall in every possible way and withdraw all the German forces behind it, Hitler rejected the proposal. The advance of enemy forces along the Swiss Jura towards Chalons, Besançon and Beaune now made it necessary to withdraw the German forces into the Gray–Langres line. On September 13th, US forces broke through at Château Salins and reached Lorraine. Local successes obtained by the 5th Panzer Army (von Manteuffel), which had been brought up into the area to the east of Nancy, did succeed in closing the gap between the 1st and the 19th Armies,[1] but this did not decisively alter, as Hitler had hoped, the situation on this sector of the Western Front. There was no weak point to be found on the right (southern) flank of the US attack. On the contrary, the enemy battering ram had become so strong that as far as Army Group G was concerned the task of preventing a break-through over-shadowed all else. The necessity to husband the German forces led to the temporary abandonment of the offensive plans drawn up by Hitler, and Army Group G as a whole was withdrawn to the Vosges. Metz was lost on November 22nd, and Strasbourg the following day. Southern Alsace was now lost.

On the northern sector of the German West Front, held by Army Group B (Field-Marshal Model), British forces took Antwerp on September 4th. The airborne operations of the Allies at Arnhem (September 17th to 30th) put them into possession of important bridges across the Meuse and the Waal, provided them with a favourable springboard for further operations, and tied down considerable German forces; on the whole, however, they were a failure, particularly as the clearing of the Scheldt estuary had to be postponed. The 15th Army (von Zangen) was in a difficult situation and had to content itself with holding the Scheldt estuary, thus preventing the Western Allies from using the port of Antwerp. The objective of the US forces in the sector held by this Army Group was to extend the breach they had already made in the West Wall (near Vossenack to the southwest of Aachen), as the necessary preliminary to an attack across the River Roer to the Rhine, after which they would be in a position to capture the two dams on the Roer and the Urft. This intention was frustrated in weeks of attack and counter-attack.

All of the heavy defensive fighting which took place in this sector from the middle of September to November was largely influenced by the preparations for a new offensive. The writer of the Wehrmacht Operations Staff War Diary was right when he noted: 'If one regards this defensive fighting on the Roer as part of the preparations for an offensive, then it was by far the most difficult part of the operation.' And von Tippelskirch writes: 'The battle on this sector of the front was a notable success for the defence, and its significance extended beyond its local context.' But this fighting had been costly in men and materials for both sides. On the Allied side, this led to a succession of fresh units appearing in or behind the front line with a consequent shrinking of tactical reserves.

In the meantime, the tense military situation on the Eastern Front made it impossible to send any worth-while reinforcements to the Western Front. On the southern front, the Red Army was now directing an all-out attack on the Reich. General Guderian is right when, referring to the fighting in the autumn of 1944 on the Western Front, he writes: 'The rapid loss of the Western fortifications (Atlantic Wall) compelled us to fight a mobile war with almost immobile units, a bombed communications network in our rear, and the enemy in command of the air above us. While our Panzer units still existed, our leaders had chosen to fight a static battle in Normandy. Now that our motorized forces had been squandered and destroyed, they were forced to fight the mobile battle that they had hitherto refused to face. The favourable chances which the boldness of the American Command occasionally offered us we were no longer in a position to exploit.'[2]

However, it was now well into October and the Allied forces had not succeeded, as General Eisenhower had optimistically ordered at the beginning of September, in reaching the Rhine in pursuit of the defeated German armies – and they certainly had not succeeded in establishing bridgeheads on its eastern banks. The overwhelming superiority of the Allied forces on land and in the air would have been sufficient to keep the German front on the run, but for the fact that supply difficulties prevented the full commitment of all the forces that Eisenhower regarded as necessary.[3] It was therefore a matter of great urgency for the Allies that the port of Antwerp should be opened. In fact, the way into the port was cleared on November 3rd, and the first convoy steamed in on November 28th, 1944. But Eisenhower felt that until Antwerp could be used, the only thing to do was to leave the German armies no peace and to give them as little time and opportunity as possible to settle down in the defensive positions they had reached.[4] However, thanks to the steadiness and determination of its troops, the German Command succeeded in holding up the enemy and establishing a bolt position which stood up for weeks to attack after attack launched against it with a quite extraordinary expenditure of material. By dint of great efforts, the Germans finally succeeded in setting up a defensive wall on the western frontiers of the Reich. The past months had shown the enemy that minor attacks planned and launched in a great variety of different ways were unsuccessful everywhere, and completely failed to create the preliminary conditions for a bigger offensive on a tactical scale. In consequence he now relaxed his pressure, brought up his rearward forces, and began to prepare carefully for further operations.

Hitler regarded this noticeable decrease of enemy pressure from the beginning of October on as an opportunity – which he grossly overrated – to turn the tables on the Western Front. He therefore revived the idea of a large-scale offensive on the Western Front with renewed enthusiasm, and he subordinated the whole conduct of the war in the West to it. The new front, which had been built up with great difficulty and which was still far from consolidated, was instructed to carry on as best it could with what forces it had available until November, when the planned offensive was to take place – and it was to do this even, according to Hitler's own words, if it meant the loss of territory, particularly in the south. Hitler attached very high hopes to this offensive: 'nothing less than a decisive turning point on this sector of the front, and perhaps even of the whole war'. He even thought that 'what had proved impossible in front of the West Wall might become possible as a result of an attack from within the West Wall', meaning the defeat of the Western Allies.

The German Plan

The use of the port of Antwerp was still denied to the Allies, and they had failed in their attempt to break through the West Wall swiftly; so Hitler now proceeded to work out detailed plans for the offensive in the West he had always hankered after.[5] First, he quite correctly estimated that the seventy divisions at the disposal of the Allies would not allow them to be equally strong throughout the almost 500 miles of front they were manning; secondly, he counted on the November weather to end the absolute air superiority enjoyed by the enemy, or at least to reduce it very considerably for a time – the time in which the German offensive would be launched. He was, therefore, anxious to get the offensive going before the arrival of winter brought clear days again and restored the enemy's air superiority. Without asking the advice of C.-in-C. West – in fact without even consulting him – Hitler now laid down the fundamental principles of the offensive in conjunction with the Wehrmacht Operations Staff.

As the offensive had to be launched at a point where the forces available could quite certainly achieve a break-through, it was necessary to choose a sector on which the enemy forces were thinner on the ground – not only in the front line but also in reserve. Further, the break-through had to be developed to such an extent as to change the whole situation on the Western Front in Germany's favour. Hitler's idea of launching a large-scale attack from the West Wall position against a weak sector of the enemy front, after a thorough overhaul of the army in the West and very careful preparation, had already advanced so far that the Eifel sector had been selected, with Antwerp as it ultimate objective.

In instructions given on November 3rd to C.-in-C. West, to Army Group B and the 5th Panzer Army, in Field-Marshal Model's HQ, Jodl, acting for Hitler, explained that the offensive must be launched at a point where the forces available could quite definitely achieve a break-through. He then informed them that the Monschau–Echternach sector (Eifel) had been chosen as the most suitable for the attempt because the enemy forces there were relatively weak, having already suffered considerable losses in previous frontal attacks. Moreover, the enemy's reserves on this sector had been brought up into the neighbourhood of the front line, and his supply position was precarious. Because this sector of the front was relatively thinly held by the enemy, and because he would not be expecting a German attack here, if at all, it was possible to count on a quick break-through of the German forces provided surprise was fully attained and the attack launched in weather unfavourable for air activity. The break-through would win freedom of movement for the German armoured forces, which would then drive forward swiftly, establishing bridgeheads over the Meuse between Liège and Namur, and move rapidly westwards towards Antwerp, passing Brussels to the east. It was to be assumed that after crossing the Meuse the German armour would cut the rearward communications of the US 1st Army, which probably ran through the valley of the Meuse. As soon as the armour reached the Brussels–Antwerp area, the rearward communications of the British 21st Army Group would also be threatened, and – if Antwerp were taken – likewise be cut.

The enemy had still not succeeded in fully clearing this highly efficient port, though its use was essential for him. However, it was only a matter of time before he did succeed, and then he would be in a position to crush the German defence by sheer weight of numbers, weapons and supplies brought in through the port of Antwerp.[6] If the immediate objectives of the offensive were attained, then the German forces would be admirably situated for dealing with both the US 1st Army and the British 21st Army Group, both of which would be cut off from their sources of supply. Its success would therefore destroy between twenty-five and thirty enemy divisions, and, in addition, it would lead to the capture or destruction of vast quantities of material and equipment of all kinds which were now being piled up in this area, in readiness for the Allied offensive against the West Wall and their intended drive to the Rhine.

The German break-through on the entire offensive front would be carried out by the ordinary line divisions, and it would have to proceed swiftly and in such a way as to make it possible to commit the armour quickly. Exploiting the shock suffered by the enemy, and the general confusion, the German armour would immediately drive westward. The essential point was that the armoured divisions should not allow themselves to be held up in any way during their advance to the Meuse. They would have to go round strongly defended places and positions which could not be captured quickly, and they must not allow themselves to be deterred by open flanks. All in all, these were the same tactics that had been used with such success in the Eastern campaign in 1941. However, at the express orders of the Führer, Bastogne was to be taken.

In the instructions he gave to the three commanders, Jodl mentioned

November 25th as the day on which the attack was to be launched, adding that this was the most favourable phase of the moon. There would be a new moon then, and the darkness would provide additional cover for the deployment operations, particularly against air reconnaissance. From the beginning, Jodl left no doubt that 'Hitler was determined to stick to the far-reaching objective of the offensive, to the arrangements which had been made, and to the commitment of the available forces'.

Jodl then outlined the tasks of the armies involved, as follows: the 6th SS Panzer Army (SS General Sepp Dietrich) was to make a dash for the crossings of the Meuse on both sides of Liège, and of its tributary the Vesare. It would set up a strong defensive front in the eastward fortifications of Liège, and then make for the Albert Canal between Maastricht and Antwerp, reaching the area to the north of Antwerp later. Nine divisions, including four armoured divisions, would be available for this purpose.

The 5th Panzer Army (General von Manteuffel) was to cross the Meuse between Amay (to the west of Liège) and Namur, and prevent enemy reserves from the west from attacking the flanks and the rear of the 6th Panzer Army along the Antwerp–Brussels–Dinant line. For this purpose, the Army would have seven divisions, including four armoured divisions.

The 7th Army, with approximately seven divisions, including one mobile division (General Brandenberger), was to defend the flank of the battering-ram, represented by the two Panzer armies, against attacks from the south and southwest. Its immediate objective would be to reach the Meuse and its tributary the Semois, and then make contact with the Moselle front in the Luxembourg area. It was also to set up blocks, in order to establish a firm defensive front farther back.

Six or seven divisions, mostly armoured or mechanized, would act as reserves for the offensive.

Jodl also informed the three commanders that in support of the Ardennes offensive the Supreme Command would launch a secondary drive by Army Group H from its bridgehead to the west of the Roer between Sittard and Geilenkirchen, on the sector manned by XII SS Panzer Corps. This attack would start as soon as the enemy began to use any considerable forces against the flank positions to be set up by the 6th SS Panzer Army.

The far-reaching objectives of the proposed offensive caused some surprise and aroused misgiving amongst those who were present when the first instructions were given. The commanders concerned were unanimously of the opinion that the forces earmarked for the task were insufficient – even if they really were provided in the promised strength. They expressed doubts whether their numbers, equipment, arms, mobility and supplies were sufficient to sustain an attack over a front of something like 125 miles under winter conditions, and then to hold the western flank sufficiently long to encompass the destruction of the twenty-five to thirty enemy divisions it was hoped to encircle. Whereas, according to Jodl, the Supreme Command said that the Meuse could be reached on the evening of the second day of the offensive, the three commanders were of the opinion that it would take at least four days because of the very unfavourable nature of the terrain, the difficulty of the roads, and the general condition of the vehicles available. They also feared that in that time the enemy would be in a position to bring up sufficiently strong forces to defend the Meuse successfully. They were, therefore, in favour of limiting the objectives of the offensive to straightening out the indentation in the German defensive positions at Aix-la-Chapelle (Aachen) and closing the one breach which the enemy had so far made in the West Wall. At the very utmost, they felt that it might be possible to push the Allies back from the Roer to the Meuse and perhaps take Liège. Jodl replied that Hitler would certainly not agree with them and would reject all such proposals. 'Such an operation as they suggested,' he said, 'would merely postpone the evil day,' if he had understood Hitler correctly. 'It would not make the Western Allies more inclined to negotiate.'

During the further course of the discussion, in which it became very clear how badly informed the Supreme Command was about the condition, armaments, equipment and training of the available troops,[7] Model put forward his own proposals, which took account of the forces available. This was the so-called 'modified solution'. Following a discussion which took place on November 4th, Hitler was informed in writing that C.-in-C. West had independently arrived at these same conclusions. Having regard to the size of forces earmarked in Hitler's plan, and to the general condition of the troops, and in view of the doubt whether the assurances given by Jodl about their numbers, strength, supplies and mobility could be made good in time, it would be very much better not to attempt to cross the Meuse with the two Panzer armies for the time being. They should be allowed to turn north or northwest after the successful break-through, so that the left wing of the 5th Panzer Army would then be protected by the Meuse. But in the opinion of C.-in-C. West, even this much more modest variant could hope for success only if, after the period of bad weather under cover of which the first break-through was to take place, the Luftwaffe was strong enough to provide temporary air superiority on at least a local scale over the area of operations during the decisive days.

Neither Model nor Manteuffel doubted that the attacking armies would, in fact, succeed in breaking through the US front, but they both stressed that it was essential that the two neighbouring armies (the 15th Army in the north and the 7th Army in the south) should be sufficiently strong to contain and pin down the enemy forces opposite them. If the enemy were in a position to withdraw strong forces from sectors of the front that were not threatened, and commit them against the flanks of the German spearhead, then the impetus of the latter would inevitably be progressively weakened, since as its flanks became longer it would have to detach more and more forces to protect them. The inevitable result would be that after a few days the concentration of strength in the spearhead would become too weak to achieve its objectives.

The two officers therefore demanded that the main drive should be supported by a 15th Army attack from the Sittard–Geilenkirchen sector, so that the two armies could close the pincers, perhaps in the neighbourhood of Tongres to the northwest of Liège. The successful carrying out of this action would encircle the Anglo-American forces between Sittard and Monschau.

If the situation developed favourably for the advancing armies, then, after a quick regrouping of forces, the attack on Antwerp worked out by OKW Operations Staff could still be carried out. A detailed discussion then followed, because to carry out this plan would require a shift of the focal point from the 6th SS Panzer Army to the 5th Panzer Army, and therefore a regrouping of forces – though there was still time to take this into account.

In their talks with Jodl, Field-Marshal Model and the commander of the 5th Panzer Army stressed that in their view the swift capture of Bastogne was essential to the development of Hitler's plan. They assumed that for the first two or three days after the launching of the attack, enemy counter-operations to the east of the Meuse from the north against the two Panzer armies would not, at least at first, be very powerful, and that the 15th Army would be in a position to contain and pin down the enemy forces in its sector. It was assumed that there were no worth-while reserves behind the enemy's line divisions available for immediate commitment, and it was therefore also assumed that after the break-through towards the Meuse the 5th Panzer Army would encounter only weak enemy forces. On the other hand, it was thought that there would soon be strong enemy reactions from the south. This meant that by then the 7th Army should have provided effective protection for the flanks – which would now be greatly extended – of the German forces driving westward after their successful break-through. The enemy must thus be prevented from using his reserves to good purpose against the southern flank of the spearhead. However, the strength to be made available to the 7th Army for this purpose appeared inadequate, as also did its equipment and mobility. Incidentally, the commander of the 7th Army completely shared these views. But at the conclusion of the discussion, Jodl declared sharply that Hitler's plan was fixed and 'unalterable', adding that the promised forces – based on detailed calculations on the part of OKW Operations Staff – would be made available in good time, and that all the arrangements had Hitler's complete approval. However, the first calculations as to the time necessary for the various preparations showed that it would be quite impossible to keep to the date for the launching of the offensive – November 25th. The earliest date the commander of the 5th Panzer Army could suggest was December 10th. Jodl replied that Hitler would 'never, no never' agree to this.

In view of Hitler's obstinacy, it appeared hopeless to attempt to persuade him to alter the terms of the undertaking as he had planned it and as Jodl had explained it to them. The only course now open was to propose an operation whose immediate objectives were much more modest, but one which would, if it were successful, allow itself to be extended in the spirit of Hitler's own ideas. The result of the discussion on November 4th between Model and Manteuffel became known as the 'modified solution', and it was taken as the basis for their counter-proposal. The whole of November passed in discussing and exploring every conceivable way in which Hitler might be persuaded to accept it. Hitler, however, rejected any and every proposal for a change in his plan, except that he no longer insisted on the date which had at first been fixed for launching the offensive. Hitler and his closest military advisers had failed to realize the consequences of the collapse of the German armies in the West, and they were simply ignoring the fact that it was practically impossible in the time available – in about three weeks up to the day originally fixed for the launching of the offensive – to put sufficient units in a condition in which they could have any hope of attaining such far-reaching objectives. In addition, in this short space of time it proved impossible to come to any agreement about the mechanics of the offensive (time, artillery preparation, and so on), as the commander of the 5th Panzer Army had other views on the subject than those laid down in Hitler's plan.

The final attempt to get Hitler to agree to changes in his plan was made on December 2nd, in the Reich Chancellery in Berlin. Field-Marshal Model, the Commanders of the 5th and 6th SS Panzer Armies, and the Chief of Staff, Western Command, General Westphal, were ordered to be present. Field-Marshal Model put his views forward with great frankness and firmness. They were based on his own intimate knowledge of the weakness of the forces available, and on what he knew the German Army could and could not attempt in the sixth year of the war. Hitler was obviously impressed by what both Model and Manteuffel had to say, particularly as they both presented him with indisputable proof that the necessary preliminary conditions for the success of his plans were not available. Despite this, the many hours of discussion did not really sway Hitler. He refused to allow any fundamental changes in the basis of his plan – the objectives, focal points, grouping and commitment of the German forces. The great unsolved problems were just left unsolved.

Once again, Hitler simply refused even to discuss the 'modified solution', which he roundly dismissed as 'half a solution' only. No decision was taken about the proposed subsidiary attack by the northern wing of the 15th Army, and there was no decision to send to the 7th Army those reinforcements that all the field commanders on the offensive front had for many weeks been requesting. It also proved impossible to secure any binding assurance about the forces and supplies which were still lacking, and therefore to feel certain that they would, in fact, be made available in good time for the launching of the offensive. Finally, it proved impossible to obtain any information whether, and if so to what extent, there would be any feint or holding attacks of a tactical nature on other sectors of the Western Front. The day was now fixed for December 10th. On December 7th it was postponed to December 14th, and, finally, on December 12th, it was fixed for December 16th.

The commander of the 5th Panzer Army was not particularly surprised when at the end of the general discussion Hitler kept him for an hour and a half's further discussion. Hitler had not failed to notice that he and Model had been far from satisfied by the results of the discussion in the wider circle. General von Manteuffel was now able to submit some further details to Hitler, who had one of his Wehrmacht adjutants with him. This did not result in any great changes in the dispositions; but at least Hitler did agree to von Manteuffel's proposal that the attack should take place at night without artillery preparation. An order was also issued for the immediate provision of a part of the urgently necessary arms and equipment.

On December 11th and 12th, Hitler called together at his advanced HQ in Ziegenberg near Giessen (Hessen) all the commanders whose troops were to take part in the attack (down to the rank of divisional commander). The great majority of the generals thus assembled were disappointed at the speech the Supreme Commander of the Wehrmacht delivered to them, because he said nothing at all about the thing that interested them most at this stage of the preparations; namely, what was to be done in the few days remaining before the offensive to remedy the deficiencies still outstanding. Even Hitler's own 'preliminary condition' for the successful execution of the operation, 'the provision of only fresh units of full fighting capacity for the offensive' had so far not been complied with; at least, not to the extent promised and urgently necessary, although C.-in-C. West had constantly sought to secure a reinforcement of the units allocated for the operation.

The absence of an adviser independent of all three branches of the Wehrmacht, who could match the personal influence of their commanders-in-chief by reason of his own relationship to Hitler, once again proved a great disadvantage, particularly in these critical weeks.

The one positive thing the commanders took away from the discussions on December 11th and 12th was Hitler's description of the enemy situation as a whole. It was a general judgement from the only quarter which was in a position to see the military position as a whole, and it seemed to suggest that the conditions for successfully carrying out their task were favourable.

Nothing was said about the intention to use paratroops and the Skorzeny unit, Operation '*Greif*', in the area chosen for the attack, and it was only on December 15th that the Commander of the 5th Panzer Army was given a general indication of how these special detachments were to be used. Neither the strength of the paratroops nor the place and time for their use was known to him until the attack had begun.

Hitler's Political Motives

In the first instructions issued on December 3rd, Jodl confined himself largely to discussing the military reasons which had persuaded Hitler to decide on an offensive on such a scale in the West, after which he discussed its military execution with the three C's-in-C. In his discussion with Model and Manteuffel in Berlin on December 2nd, Hitler also confined himself to the requirements of the military sphere. But in the subsequent discussion with the Commander of the 5th Panzer Army on that date, he explained the political reasons for the offensive. At the gatherings of the generals on December 11th and 12th, he explained them again at wearisome length.[8]

He stressed that at the beginning of that autumn it had been necessary to come to a fundamental decision about the further prosecution of the war, and he had had to make up his mind to choose the focal point of the necessary defensive operations. He was in no doubt whatever that Germany must continue to defend herself, and his advisers were in complete agreement with him. Any idea of negotiating with her enemies, or negotiating separately with either the West or the East, had been put right out of the question by the repeated demand for Germany's 'unconditional surrender' put forward by all Germany's enemies in common. In his opinion, and provided the available reserves were used promptly and to good purpose, the shifting of the focal point of the defence to the Western Front offered an opportunity to Germany to deal the Western Allies 'a powerful blow' before their forces reached the Rhine, particularly as he expected a continuation of their great efforts to drive forward to and across the Rhine. 'In the whole of world history,' he went on, 'there has never been a coalition which consisted of such heterogeneous elements with such diametrically opposed objectives as the present hostile coalition against us. Ultra-capitalist states on the one hand, ultra-Marxist states on the other. On the one side a dying world empire, that of Great Britain, and on the other a "colony", the United States, anxious to take over the inheritance. The United States is determined to take Britain's place in the world. The Soviet Union is anxious to lay hands on the Balkans, the Dardanelles, Persia and the Persian Gulf. Britain is anxious to keep her ill-gotten gains and to make herself strong in the Mediterranean. These states are already at loggerheads, and their antagonisms are growing visibly from hour to hour. If Germany can now deal out a few heavy blows, this artificially united front will collapse at any moment with a tremendous thunderclap. In the last resort, wars end when one side or the other realizes that victory is impossible. We must not allow a single moment to pass without showing the enemy that no matter what he may do he will never be able to reckon with our capitulation. Never! Never!' A successful offensive on this tactical scale would in any case thwart the plans of the Allies for a long time to come, and compel the Allies to face problems which would first have to be discussed between their political leaders. Because of this there could again be fateful delays for their military leaders before the requisite counter-measures could be taken.

Hitler did admit, however, that the objective of Antwerp was something of a risk and might seem beyond the capacity of the forces available and their condition. Nevertheless, he had decided to stake everything on one card, because Germany needed a breathing-space. He hoped by means of this offensive – of whose success he had, despite all the objections, no doubt – to obtain the initiative again, and thus gain time for the development and use of new kinds of weapons, and time for the expected split in the Allied camp to take place.

Utterly failing to recognize the strength of the ties which have attached Canada to the British Commonwealth for so long, he even went so far as to declare that she would be the first to withdraw her troops from the European mainland. 'A defensive struggle could only postpone the decision, and not change the general situation.' For this there was only one thing to do: to stake everything that remained on one card, the card of attack. With such an objective in view, he could see better opportunities in the West at the moment than in the East. The distances in the West were shorter, the costs of bringing up the necessary fuel lower, and the important strategic objectives were more within reach of the available forces and means than in the East, where the war had to be waged under altogether different conditions.

Further, he did not regard the British and the Americans as such tough opponents as the Red Army or the Soviet political leaders. The British – he persuaded himself – would soon be at the end of their tether, while the Americans would probably lose courage if events took an unfavourable turn for them. 'If we succeed, then we shall smash up half the enemy front, and then we'll see what happens: I do not believe that in the long run the enemy will be able to stand up to the forty-five German divisions we will have available by that time.' The situation on the Western Front would be temporarily stabilized, and this would allow him to withdraw forces to send to the threatened sectors of the Eastern Front. 'We shall master our fate all right.'

Hitler attached great importance to the psychological effect on the Party leaders, the front and the home front, and also on public opinion in the Allied countries and on their armies. He promised himself 'a permanent psychological weakening of the Western Powers', and he hoped in this way to shake the confidence of his enemies in total victory and thus to persuade them to abandon their demand for Germany's 'unconditional surrender', and make them more inclined to accept a negotiated peace. Hitler concluded his speech by declaring: 'I am determined to carry out this operation even if the greatest risks have to be accepted, and even if the enemy counter-attack on both sides of Metz and the coming drive towards the Ruhr result in considerable losses of territory and position'. This remark is particularly illuminating for the light it sheds on Hitler's obstinacy. He was determined to stand by his preconceived opinions even at the cost of abandoning his usual principle not to surrender one inch of ground. On December 2nd, he also spoke at some length on the subject of the indissoluble bond between his régime and the German people.

The Course of the Offensive

During the first two weeks of November, Army Group B had to cope only with attacks that were local, although extraordinarily persistent and therefore costly to both sides, to the east of Aix-la-Chapelle (Aachen) between Würselen and Stolberg. The expected large-scale attack over the Roer to the Rhine began on November 16th, and in the following weeks it extended to the whole Geilenkirchen–Eschweiler–Stolberg sector.[9] But once again, the Anglo-American forces failed to break through and the German front remained intact. The inequality of the forces and the constant attacks launched by the Anglo-American forces at the various focal points frequently led to critical situations which made it necessary to call on the reserves which were being husbanded for the German offensive. In addition, it delayed the withdrawal of the units which had been allotted to the offensive, and at the same time reduced their fighting strength. To some extent, it even prevented renewal and replacements, even of smaller sections.

However, though the conditions were clearly unfavourable, Hitler still insisted on his plan to launch an offensive in the Ardennes. This last German offensive began on December 16th, 1944. The fighting, which lasted several weeks, can be divided into the following battle phases, which are listed here for the better understanding of the campaign as a whole:

December 16th–17th: First preliminary success of the 5th Panzer Army; this did not, however, entirely justify the expectations in territorial gains, particularly on the right wing. Minor successes in the Monschau–Malmédy area;

December 18th–19th: Intervention of the local Allied reserves begins to make itself felt; in particular against the northern flank of the 6th SS Panzer Army and the south flank of the 7th Army, giving rise to misgivings. Enemy succeeds in holding St Vith;

December 20th: A worsening of the situation of the 6th SS Panzer Army and of the 7th Army becomes clearly visible. Along the whole offensive front, operations lagged considerable behind the schedule;

Up to December 24th: Further progress in the centre of the offensive front (5th Panzer Army), with temporary progress by weak advance elements to about three miles to the east of Dinant. In this phase Bastogne still held out, making it necessary to invest the town with part of the spearhead forces, thus inevitably and, as it turned out, fatally weakening the drive towards the Meuse;

December 21st–22nd: Weather clears up, and strong enemy air activity begins;

December 23rd: Enemy garrison in Bastogne supplied from the air;

December 24th–25th: Situation changes. Roles begin to reverse: the attacker becomes the attacked. The 5th Panzer Army also forced on the defensive;

December 26th: Enemy breaks the circle around Bastogne. With this the operation loses all sense, but Hitler orders a continuation of the attacks on Bastogne – all retreat forbidden;

January 3rd, 1945: Allies launch their counter-attack. In heavy fighting, and with strong support from the air, the enemy pushes in the flanks of the German spearhead. The danger of encirclement begins to develop;

January 10th: Situation of the German forces becomes critical. For them, the Ardennes battle is now a bitter rearguard action involving heavy losses in both men and material, diminishing supplies and an acute shortage of fuel.

The Individual Phases of the Battle

As far as the 5th Panzer Army was concerned, the carefully prepared and determinedly executed attack without artillery preparation was completely successful. In accordance with orders, the centre of the Schnee–Eifel sector was not attacked, but on the right wing the enemy's defensive positions were completely overrun. However, much less progress was made on the left wing of this corps (LXVI Army Corps), so that the speedy encirclement of the Schnee–Eifel position became unlikely, though it was the necessary preliminary to the further advance on St Vith; this, as a junction of many roads, was of similar importance on the right wing as Bastogne on the left. The task here was made more difficult because the left wing of the 6th SS Panzer Army was making very little progress, and the enemy was still in a position to direct heavy fire into the open flank of LXVI Army Corps, and did not neglect the opportunity to do so. The attack of the 6th SS Panzer Army was not entirely successful; and the fact that one armoured unit was able to advance right into the Malmédy area, after breaking through the enemy position at Losheim, made no material difference. In fact, this unit itself was very soon in danger of being cut off, and its swift drive had no effect on the rest of the sector in which the 6th SS Panzer Army was operating.

The attack launched on the north wing and in the centre of this Army met with minor local successes at first, but on December 18th it came to a standstill, and repeated efforts were unable to get it moving again. Further, in complete misunderstanding of its main task the 6th SS Panzer Army allowed strong forces to be tied down in the Elsenborn–Krinkelt area where heavy fighting developed which was pointless in view of the Panzer Army's real objective. This fighting resulted in heavy losses, made it necessary to commit increasing forces, and attained nothing in the end. The Panzer Army was too close here to the strong US front on the Roer, just the place from which speedy help could and did come for the Allied sectors which were under pressure, and which had been pushed back in places. The dropping of a parachute unit (von der Heydte) during the night of December 16th–17th, as ordered by Hitler, had no effect on the general situation in this area or on the position of the neighbouring 5th Panzer Army. The actual dropping area, to the north of Malmédy, was suitable only for a sealing-off operation to the north, whereas Army Group B would have preferred the choice of the Krinkelt area in order to break up the defence there, which was regarded as very strong.

On the whole, it was now already quite clear that the 6th SS Panzer Army, which Hitler had committed on the right wing with a decisive role to play in the offensive, would no longer be able to reach the Meuse rapidly. The right-wing corps of the 5th Panzer Army was also behind schedule. Under pressure from a new attack by forces drawn from LXVI Army Corps, the enemy withdrew from St Vith on the night of December 21st–22nd, and took up positions on the heights to the west of the town.

Both the neighbouring 5th Panzer Army corps, LVIII under General Krüger and XLVII under General von Lüttwitz, together with the corps on the right wing, attacking to the south, had broken through the enemy front after crossing the Our, thus creating the necessary conditions for a drive to the west. In this sector, work began on the morning of December 16th on an improvised bridge at Dasburg, and by 16.00 hours the first tanks were rolling over it across the Our. However, they were able to go forward only very slowly, because the road from Dasburg to Clerf was blocked in depth by tree trunks which the German troops had themselves put there during their retreat in the autumn. Traffic jams on the bridge itself and along the roads leading to it caused further delays.

On December 17th, the 2nd Panzer Division on the left wing of the 5th Panzer Army managed to cross the River Clerf at Clerf railway station. Before long, there was no further resistance worth mentioning. Its neighbour on the left, the 5th Parachute Division of the 7th Army, also fought its way across the river, and thus prepared the ground for a further drive through Wiltz to the west. At the boundary between these two armies there seemed to be a particularly weak spot in the enemy front, and this helped a great deal because the south wing of the 5th Panzer Army also continued to make good progress. Despite preliminary successes, however, it was not until December 18th–19th that the 7th Army, which was short of sappers, managed to throw five improvised bridges over the Our. Army HQ judged accurately that the consequent loss of time at that critical moment when the enemy was to be taken by surprise would rob it of its already slender chance of success. It began to look as though it would no longer be possible to provide extended flank cover for the 5th Panzer Army as it advanced farther and farther westward.

During the course of December 18th, the road blocks and traffic jams mentioned above had their full effect. It was not until 09.00 hours on December 18th that the Panzerlehr Division began to cross the Clerf. It reached Nieder-Wampach by the evening, and in the night it drove forward to Mageret (to the east of Bastogne). The following day it went on towards Bastogne itself. The same day it fought its way into Neffe and Wardin, but, although it was assisted by the 26th Volks Grenadier Division, it was unable to force its way into Bastogne. If the 5th Panzer Army had now committed the total strength of XLVII Panzer Corps in order to take Bastogne this would have meant holding up the advance and, in fact, practically abandoning the idea of an offensive – as early as December 18th – particularly as the right-wing neighbour of this corps, the 116th Panzer Division, was engaged in an attack on Houffalize. The Army therefore ordered the 2nd Panzer Division to take

Noville to the northwest of Bastogne, and then press on westward without delay.

Elements of the Panzerlehr Division were ordered to support the 26th Grenadier Division in its attack on Bastogne, at the same time holding other elements in readiness to advance westward via Sibret to the southwest of Bastogne. However, the position of the Panzerlehr Division now developed unfavourably. The division had been still further delayed by the bad condition of the approach roads. In addition, the attack launched by the 26th Grenadier Division before Bizory to the northeast of Bastogne came to a standstill. The failure at Bastogne was all the more critical because the forces actually available to the Army for both tasks – the drive towards the Meuse and the protection of the long southern flank, while at the same cutting off Bastogne – were not regarded as adequate even before the attack began. What was feared before the opening of the offensive now happened: the defence at Bastogne encouraged the enemy to turn this sector into a springboard for a decisive counter-attack, and more and more enemy forces were sent in.

On December 20th, the 2nd Panzer Division succeeded in reaching the Noville area. At midnight it took Ortheuville (half-way between Bastogne and Marche), and captured the bridge over the Ourthe intact. It left a covering force there and continued its westward advance. On the morning of December 19th, the 116th Panzer Division of the neighbouring corps to the right approached Houffalize, and the reconnaissance battalion of the division reached Bertogne, about four miles west-northwest of Noville, at midday. On December 20th, the attacks on Bastogne made little progress against stiffening enemy resistance; the encircling ring was extended to the northwest, but Army Group insisted that Bastogne should be taken. On December 21st, the weather cleared up a little and here and there the cloud cover opened sufficiently to permit the first enemy fighter-bombers to appear over the battle area of the two Panzer armies, though for the moment there were not many of them. Through lack of fuel, the 2nd Panzer Division made very little progress, and on December 21st it had to content itself with extending the bridgehead over the Ourthe as far as Tenneville (to the north of Ortheuville). In its drive towards the Meuse the Panzerlehr Division reached Morhet. The reconnaissance battalion, reinforced by a sapper battalion, reached Tillet–Gerimont–Amberloup (all half-way to St Hubert) after the 26th Grenadier Division had taken Sibret in heavy fighting. The attacks to the north and east of Bastogne were a failure. Apart from the sector between Champs and Senonchamps to the east of the town, the encirclement of Bastogne was now complete, though with weak forces only. On December 22nd, the tanks of the 2nd Panzer Division were immobilized by lack of fuel. They were not in sufficient force to take the more strongly held heights around Marche. A battle group remained behind in a bolt position, while on the same day (December 22nd) the rest of the division succeeded in occupying Hargimont and On (half-way between Rochefort and Marche). It was on this day that Anglo-American air activity began to increase noticeably. Nevertheless, the Panzerlehr Division continued to move towards St Hubert, which was taken in the night. At the same time, the 7th Army reported that the 5th Parachute Division had been attacked from the south several times during the day.

On December 23rd, an Allied air lift began to keep Bastogne supplied.[10] The ring encircling Bastogne was now to some extent itself forced on the defensive. In the centre of the break-through area – in LVIII Panzer Corps's sector – the 116th Panzer Division was committed to the north of the Ourthe because its right-hand neighbour was still fighting on the Ourthe. However, in the night of December 19th–20th, it was reported that the bridge over the Ourthe about three miles to the northwest of Bertogne had been destroyed, and that with the means at the disposal of the division it would be the evening of December 20th at the earliest before it could be repaired. On orders from Army HQ, therefore, this division was on the same night halted, turned, and sent via Houffalize towards Samree (northwest of Houffalize). Early on December 20th it captured Samree. By evening it had reached Dochamps, but its attacks across the Soy–Hotton road made no progress. As the forward movement of this Panzer corps also had to be got into its swing again, the 116th Panzer Division was instructed to break off contact with the enemy during the course of December 22nd, and move via Laroche along the southern bank of the Ourthe towards the northwest, in order to make contact and co-operate with the 2nd Panzer Division, which had in the meantime driven forward considerably. Cover in the Soy–Hotton sector and to the north of the Ourthe was provided by the 560th Volks Grenadier Division supported by elements of the 2nd SS Panzer Division, which was just coming up, and was committed towards Tailles (north of Houffalize).

When the 2nd Panzer Division broke through the enemy's bolt position between Marche and Rochefort near Hargimont on December 22nd, taking Hassonville and Jamodine the same evening, it began to look as though the preliminary conditions for a successful drive to the Meuse at Dinant had been won after all, though the threat from the north and south was still dangerous. The advance involved some element of risk because it was carried out from the narrow westward spearheads of the 116th Panzer Division and the 2nd Panzer Division, and thus lacked breadth in its operations. By this time, the 6th SS Panzer Army and the 7th Army were already bogged down and on the defensive. Enemy resistance to the 116th Panzer Division to the east of Marche was stiffening, and the pressure on the 7th Army was also growing. However, provided Bastogne were captured and the south flank held, and further battle-worthy units were brought into the break-through area in good time, there was still a possibility that the successes of the armoured divisions of the 5th Panzer Army could be exploited, and that when the Meuse was reached the lagging north wing and the 6th SS Panzer Army could be brought into movement again by wheeling northward.

On December 23rd, the advancing 2nd Panzer Division had to defend itself repeatedly against persistent enemy pressure from the north, as a result of which it was forced to detach units to protect its northern flank; for example, at Hogne and Harvesin to the west of Marche. That day, the reconnaissance battalion of this division reached Foy Notre Dame, to the east of Dinant. The rest of the division, which was following, also made good progress at first, but before long it was having to defend itself against increasing enemy pressure from the north and northwest. In consequence, the advance of the division began to slow down. It was forced to defend itself in two groups, fighting on all sides around Conneux. At the same time its fighting strength was weakened by a lack of fuel, and, later on, by a shortage of ammunition. In the end, it was overwhelmed by superior enemy forces.

At midnight on December 23rd, the Panzerlehr Division captured Rochefort. The reconnaissance battalion sent southwards discovered that Librament was occupied by strong enemy forces. Its left-hand neighbour was now engaged in heavy fighting in the Vaux-les-Rosière area to the southwest of Bastogne.

On December 24th, the reconnaissance battalion of the Panzerlehr Division came to Ciergnon, half-way between Rochefort and Dinant, and in the afternoon Ciergnon was captured. Considerable enemy air activity greatly hampered the bringing up of all kinds of supplies for the spearhead groups fighting far to the west. Enemy pressure from the north continued to increase and the enemy succeeded in throwing back parts of the 2nd Panzer Division operating to the west of Marche. The advance of the 9th Panzer Division was now held up for lack of fuel; so that it was no longer possible to reckon with relief for the 2nd Panzer Division from that quarter.

LVIII Panzer Corps failed in its attempt to break through the US lines from Soy–Hotton–Grandmenil towards the northwest, where the enemy had succeeded in consolidating his positions and was launching a growing number of counter-attacks.

On December 25th, the 5th Panzer Army at Bastogne found itself on the defensive because the forces and material available to it were not sufficient to continue the attack on the town, though the Supreme Command was still demanding it. On December 26th, enemy armour broke into the town from the southwest, and with this the encirclement of Bastogne was broken. The failure at Bastogne now began to make itself felt more and more between Rochefort and the Meuse, because the Panzerlehr Division and the 2nd Panzer Division had taken three days to make their way past the town, and the Führer Escort Brigade, which was originally intended to support the 2nd Panzer Division and the 116th Panzer Division from the rear, had to wheel in on Bastogne to join in the attack on the town. Although by December 24th, an armoured division had actually advanced to a point about three miles to the east of Dinant on the Meuse, nevertheless the general progress of the situation up to December 25th indicated no more than a partial success. With this the hopes of the 5th Panzer Army that it could make further progress, even on this side of the Meuse, disappeared – unless reinforcements could be brought up rapidly, unless the situation in the air could be made more tolerable, and unless something could be done to improve the quite inadequate provision of fuel, which was so bad that even at the start of the offensive a big part of the artillery support had had to be left behind in its deployment positions. The lack of this artillery support made itself painfully felt as soon as the attack on Bastogne began. December 25th found the 2nd Panzer Division in a very difficult position, particularly as lack of fuel hindered considerable elements of the division on their way to front-line battle groups. Only weak forces managed to go forward. The reconnaissance battalion, fighting heroically, was now overwhelmed by superior enemy forces. In the face of increasing enemy pressure, the mass of the 2nd Panzer Division had to be withdrawn from the Rochefort area. With this, XLVII Panzer Corps now found itself on the defensive.

The further clearing up of the weather on December 24th was decisive, since it allowed the enemy to attack from the air in great strength. They carpeted the roads and the railways with bombs, and succeeded in bringing the already inadequate German supply organization almost to a standstill. The mobility of the German forces, and thus the ability of their leaders to manœuvre, now disappeared rapidly. Snow began to fall, and the weather became much colder.

The commander of the 5th Panzer Army tried in vain to obtain clear and definite instructions about the continuance of operations. As the offensive had now obviously lost its momentum, C.-in-C. West tried to persuade Hitler to stop all offensive operations and withdraw the German forces before the Allies were in a position to counter-attack in full force. He pointed out that not even the 'modified solution' was now possible, because neither reinforcements nor supplies could speedily be brought up to the extent required. But Hitler scorned this advice, too; he was determined to reopen the offensive against the Meuse, from the positions the German forces had so far been able to take up, just as soon as he had been able to carry through the next phase of his plans – an attack in Alsace. On the evening of December 25th, typical orders arrived from Hitler instructing the 5th Panzer Army – without any consideration for the situation which had developed in the meantime – to use all available forces to seize the heights around Marche. At the same time, two further divisions were promised – from the command of the 6th SS Panzer Army. It was impossible to guess when these promised reinforcements would arrive, and now that the weather had improved the 9th Panzer Division had only weak elements ready for action. Hitler justified his decision with the argument that 'the offensive in Alsace will compel Patton to withdraw the mass of his forces, which are now seeking to relieve Bastogne, in order to meet the offensive. With this the pressure on the south flank of the Ardennes offensive will relax and we shall have a free hand for a drive northwards again.'

The battle of the 5th Panzer Army for Bastogne now entered its final stage.

During the following weeks it became the epilogue to the unsuccessful offensive, and the centre of very bitter and costly fighting for both sides. Division after division was sent up, arriving successively in the Bastogne area to be committed against the town. For a time Bastogne occupied nine German divisions with two Corps HQ, and it forced the 6th SS Panzer Army to give up some of its strength to the 5th Panzer Army, and with this the offensive intentions of the German command were completely frustrated. Thus, in a very difficult situation, Bastogne was a decisive success for the defensive plans of the Allied command. An enemy counter-attack launched on January 3rd, 1945, finally put an end to the German struggle for the town.

This counter-attack was directed towards the Houffalize area from the north and the south, and aimed at cutting off all German forces to the west. It did not succeed in attaining this objective. Heavy falls of snow made it necessary to confine operations largely to the roads. Thanks to their long years of experience in Russia, the German forces were in a better position to cope with such conditions. The result was that the extremely difficult withdrawal was carried out according to plan under cover of desperately fighting rearguards[11] before the pincers of the enemy offensive closed around Houffalize, which they did on January 16th. However, the destruction or abandonment of large quantities of valuable supplies and equipment was unavoidable, owing to the lack of proper repair and recovery services, and because the available supplies of fuel were not nearly sufficient to provide the fighting troops with what they needed. It was also a heavy psychological blow to the morale of the men when they learned that all SS divisions had been withdrawn from the front in the first few days of the retreat. Although the intention was to rest and re-equip them for use elsewhere (they were actually sent to Hungary), the decision made the worst possible impression on the Army units, which felt that they were being left to carry out the most difficult and costly part of the unsuccessful offensive on their own. This was a big psychological error, and it still further undermined the confidence of the Army in the Supreme Command.

When the German armies got back to the positions from which they had started, which was towards the end of January, they found that no arrangements had been made, despite all their requests, to reinforce their diminished battle strength. There were no adequate supplies of ammunition, there was neither equipment nor material to consolidate their positions, and there were no reinforcement of any kind available.

The additional commitment of the special Skorzeny detachment, which had been specially ordered and supervised by Hitler himself – Operation '*Greif*' – exercised no material influence on the course of the fighting, because it soon became known to the enemy (December 17th) and therefore caused relatively little confusion; it petered out before it managed to get properly under way.[12]

In Retrospect

It is possible to agree with Major-General Fuller that the plan for the offensive was strategically justifiable. However, its results were militarily nil, and – apart from the insufficient strength of the German forces engaged and the inadequacy of their supply organization – the following factors must be regarded as decisive for the failure: the enemy reacted more rapidly to the offensive than the German Supreme Command had expected, quickly adopting vigorous counter-measures; secondly, the enemy had undisputed command of the air, not only over the battle area but deep into Germany itself.

The Allied High Command reacted swiftly and powerfully to the offensive.[13] When the German offensive broke unexpectedly on December 16th, the Allies immediately halted all offensive operations on other sections of the front, and on the very same day two infantry divisions were committed against the 6th SS Panzer Army, and an armoured division against each of the flanks of the 5th Panzer Army. One of these two divisions (the 7th US Armoured Division) quickly sent some of its units into action at St Vith.[14] The other (the 10th US Armoured Division) hampered the advance of the 7th Army and moved some of its units before Bastogne. The 101st US Airborne Division arrived in Bastogne at dawn on December 19th in the nick of time, after parts of Combat Command B of 10th US Armoured Division (CCB) had fought almost to the point of annihilation to hold up the German attack on the town. As the 1st US Army and VIII US Corps had only tactical reserves, they fulfilled their task of conducting a fighting withdrawal until adequate reserves could be brought up to allow them to make a successful stand, and eventually launch counter-measures. This was not a prepared withdrawal, because certain terrain suitable for the purpose was not held; nevertheless, as a holding withdrawal it was successful. It slowed down the German advance, even though resistance petered out again and again. Further, by his success in and around St Vith and his obstinate defence of Bastogne, the enemy succeeded in turning the fighting in these sectors to his own advantage. The enemy tied down more German forces here than had been bargained for, and as a result they were not available elsewhere. Thus this action made a valuable contribution to sealing off the break-through area both to the north and the south.

By its aggressive defence, the garrison of Bastogne succeeded in delaying the westward drive of the Panzerlehr Division and the 2nd Panzer Division for three days, and it tied down other forces which were thus not available for the main objective – the drive to the Meuse. This compelled the 5th Panzer Army to take evasive action (with the 116th Panzer Division) further to the south than had been intended, and the result was further delay.

In deciding to stop at once his attacks on all other sectors of the front, the enemy took a really radical step towards countering the German offensive. The result was that he was then in a position to concentrate an extraordinary mass of strength against the attacking German armies. From December 20th, the defence operations and the subsequent counter-attack were centralized and the whole defence was placed in the hands of Field-Marshal Montgomery. For this purpose the US 1st Army was subordinate to British 21st Army Group, and the difficulties Hitler had expected to arise between the Allied political and military leaders were obviated, even though there were certain differences of opinion between Eisenhower and his generals.[15]

When Montgomery took command he reckoned that the situation for the Western Allies could become really dangerous only if the Germans succeeded in breaking through between Malmédy and Marche, and thus opening the roads leading to the northwest and to Brussels and Antwerp. He therefore extended the defensive front from Stavelot to Marche, and prepared strong forces for a counter-attack.

This decision to centralize the Allied command in the hands of one man was taken not a moment too soon, because the battle was rapidly slipping out of control. Apart from the northern and southern flanks of the break-through area, there was hardly a co-ordinated front in existence any more (in the area of the offensive),[16] and the operations of the US 1st Army had developed into a series of individual holding actions. Montgomery's contribution to restoring the situation was that he turned a series of isolated actions into a coherent battle fought according to a clear and definite plan. It was his refusal to engage in premature and piecemeal counter-attacks which enabled the Americans to gather their reserves and frustrate the German attempts to extend their break-through. But at a time when the C.-in-C. was looking for reserves to extend his western flank, it took the greater part of six US divisions – half the strength of the US 1st Army – to hold this northern sector of the defence flank. However, the counter-attack of the Allied forces launched on January 3rd, 1945, came too soon to destroy the German offensive forces, though this had certainly been a possibility. It achieved only a limited success. The enemy had to fight hard once again to recapture territory for which he had already fought.

As far as developments on the German side were concerned, it was enemy air operations which tipped the scales. When the weather cleared up on December 21st–22nd the Anglo-American air forces completely dominated the German supply lines. Despite the utmost self-sacrifice on the part of the Luftwaffe crews, very little indeed could be done to relieve the burden on the ground troops. The result of these heavy attacks from the air was further fatal delay in bringing up even the most urgently needed ammunition and supplies for the fighting troops; for camouflage reasons, most of the supply depots were on the other side of the Rhine. The supply of fuel suffered particularly in this respect. Thus from the beginning the troops engaged in the offensive lived virtually from hand to mouth.[17] As far as supplies were concerned, the battle area was practically isolated.

Looking back from the German standpoint the following observations can be made. The deployment area and the sector for launching the offensive were both correctly chosen. The time chosen for the attack and the method of the 5th Panzer Army in launching it were both in accordance with the given circumstances, and they were both correct. Enemy intelligence and air reconnaissance failed to recognize the preparations for deployment. The camouflage measures taken proved effective, though it was risky not to inform the troops concerned about the offensive until one day before it was launched. Both strategic and tactical surprise were obtained.

The fact that despite all these favourable factors the offensive itself was not a success must be ascribed to the following mistakes on the part of the German command. The Supreme Command did not shift the focal point of the operations from the 6th SS Panzer Army to the 5th Panzer Army in time to allow the latter's success to be exploited suitably. It also failed to do so later, at a time when it was perhaps still possible to adopt the so-called 'modified solution'. The drive of the 5th Panzer Army was unfavourably affected by the lack of preliminary success attained by the two neighbouring armies. Further, when its failure was obvious, the offensive was not called off soon enough, nor were new decisions taken when its lack of success made them necessary. In addition, the numbers of men and the quantities of material available were not nearly sufficient to allow the offensive to be exploited in depth.

When the attack launched by the 6th SS Panzer Army broke down, while that of the 5th Panzer Army was successful and began to develop into a breakthrough, the focal point of the offensive should have been immediately transferred to the 5th Panzer Army, because the attacking forces were already well behind their schedules. However, all the suggestions of the front-line commanders to this effect were ignored.

According to Hitler's plan, the focal point of the offensive was to lie to the north with the 6th SS Panzer Army, and the reserve armour was positioned with this in view. As early as December 18th, Field-Marshal Model proposed that the reserve divisions, or some of them, should be used to exploit the successes of the 5th Panzer Army. However, for political reasons Hitler was anxious that 'his Waffen SS' should deliver the decisive blow. He therefore insisted that those divisions which were sent forward should remain to the north of the main attack, so that Sepp Dietrich, the SS commander, should have another chance.[18] The 2nd and 12th SS Panzer Divisions, ultimately sent to reinforce the 5th Panzer Army, arrived too late to be of any real use; by that time the 5th Panzer Army itself had already been forced on the defensive. Once again a decision was taken too late.

One cannot help comparing the concentration of forces which took place in a small area around Bastogne in the last days of December with the forces made available to the 5th Panzer Army for the main objective of the drive to the Meuse crossings.

At the very latest on December 24th–25th, the German High Command should have restricted its tactical objectives – particularly because of the critical situation on the Eastern Front.

The paucity of the preliminary successes obtained by the neighbouring armies had a great deal to do with the ultimate failure of the 5th Panzer Army, because as its flanks grew longer so its spearhead was weakened by the detachment of forces to protect the two flanks.

St Vith held out longer than had been expected, and although the attack across the Soy–Hotton–Marche road was prompt enough it lacked strength. The result was that the army was forced back into the southern sector of its offensive front, and its room to manœuvre was cramped. As the 7th Army very soon found itself in difficulties, elements of the 5th Panzer Army had to turn southward in order to strengthen the threatened flank.

Despite the exemplary devotion of both officers and men the German advance was not quick enough to win the decisive race against the enemy reserves which were being rushed up. Before long, too, the offensive began to lack the strength and mobility which are essential conditions of any success. The advancing mobile forces had only between one and two fuel allowances instead of the five which had been promised. One standard allowance is sufficient for 100 kilometres, or rather more than 60 miles.

The forces available for the offensive on December 16th and in the following weeks bore no proper relation to the far-reaching objectives which had been set for it, and in the end even fewer divisions were available than had been calculated.[19] The deployment of some of them had not even been completed when the offensive actually started. Other promises of the Supreme Command were also not kept. Thus, from the beginning the operation lacked the numbers, equipment and material which would have permitted a speedy and vigorous exploitation of the break-through actually achieved. The known inadequacy of the forces available, including numbers, arms, equipment and supplies, should have made the German High Command think again, and come to a new decision even before the offensive began. In the same way, the development of the situation during the actual offensive should have persuaded the Command to go over to the defensive in good time, and withdraw their forces to their original positions.

It was an error to cling to the first plan, with its over-ambitious objectives, its grouping of the forces available and its commitment of them. The decision here was entirely in Hitler's hands. The Allied war correspondent Chester Wilmot was right when he pointed out in this connection that Germany's military strategy was no longer being determined by purely military considerations, and that the ultimate decision did not lie in the hands of von Rundstedt, but with Hitler.[20]

Really effective measures for hoodwinking the enemy and holding down his forces on the neighbouring sectors of the front – as promised in advance by Jodl – were not taken. The enemy was, therefore, in a position to withdraw forces from those parts of the line which were not being attacked, without running the danger of having to abandon valuable territory which he had only just captured and which he needed as the spring-board for further offensive operations. The decision to retire behind the West Wall, i.e. to withdraw to the original positions at the start of the offensive, was taken too late. Hitler allowed this decision to be imposed upon him by the superior strength of the enemy, and he had to pay for this further hesitation and delay with heavy losses both in men and material. Nothing but a little time, which was of no particular value, was to be gained by staying any longer in the captured territory, particularly as the time thus gained stood in no reasonable relationship to the heavy losses it involved.

On two occasions, General Guderian sought to persuade Hitler to abandon the obviously unsuccessful offensive and to send the troops thus released to the Eastern Front. 'On December 28th . . . Hitler . . . admitted that the attack in the Ardennes had "not resulted in the decisive success which might have been expected" . . . Nevertheless "a tremendous easing of the situation has come about. The enemy has had to abandon all his plans for attack. He has been obliged to regroup his forces. He has had to throw in again units which were fatigued. . . . He is severely criticized at home. . . . Already he has had to admit that there is no chance of the war being decided before August, perhaps not before the end of next year. This means a transformation in the situation such as nobody would have believed possible a fortnight ago".'[21]

When General Guderian tried to draw Hitler's attention to the critical situation on the Eastern Front in the situation conference on January 9th, 1945, he was met with an hysterical outburst of anger. As Wilmot points out: 'Hitler refused to heed these facts, for, says Guderian, "he had a special picture of the world, and every fact had to fit into that fancied picture. As he believed, so the world must be; but, in fact, it was a picture of another world".'[22] Reality was soon to prove stronger than fantasy. However, in the meantime Hitler continued to insist that the Western Front must be given priority 'so that we can keep the initiative there'. He also insisted that the Eastern Front should not be reinforced, declaring that from now on he would permit no retreats of any sort. He even declared: 'I get an attack of the horrors whenever I hear that there must be a withdrawal somewhere or other in order to have room to manœuvre. I've heard that sort of thing for the past two years and the results have always been appalling.'[23]

On January 10th, Hitler announced that the 6th SS Panzer Army was to be withdrawn from the Ardennes for rest and replacements, but that nevertheless it would remain at the disposal of C.-in-C. West.

As Jodl had explained on November 3rd, Hitler believed that the forces necessary for the offensive could be chiefly obtained by resting and reinforcing the units in the West, and by raising new units in the Reich itself. Instead of bringing the available divisions up to their normal strength, or dissolving them altogether, Hitler preferred to establish new divisions while leaving the old battle-trained divisions at half their strength or even less. In this way he was able to persuade himself that he could increase his forces in order to deal with the threatening crisis. In fact, such extra forces could be obtained only by a fundamental change in the prosecution of the war as a whole, and this Hitler constantly refused to accept. He simply refused to draw the necessary conclusions for the conduct of the war as a whole, and to give the necessary orders to the fronts affected by the offensive. Thus we can see that under the recent dictatorship the forces available were by no means as organized as they could have been and should have been in order to form a decisive focal point.[24]

Co-ordination of the strategic and tactical camouflage measures had taken the enemy completely by surprise.[25] The storing of supplies of all kinds to the east of the Rhine as part of the preparations to cope with the expected enemy offensive against and across the Rhine led to unexpected and very serious difficulties, because the transport columns of the Speer Organization, which had been personally promised to the commander of the 5th Panzer Army, did not materialize.

Further, the training of the troops was not all it should have been in all units to cope with a rested and well-supplied enemy, superior in both numbers and equipment. Every front-line commander was aware of this, and it was not at all surprising, because no such large-scale offensive operations had been conducted since 1942. The situation could have been considerably improved, and the divisions properly prepared for their forthcoming task, only by withdrawing them from the front line, affording them rest, recuperation and replenishment, and creating the most favourable conditions for such training. Hitler did provide all this for many of his SS divisions, but the army units which were earmarked for the offensive operations were not similarly privileged. The ordinary line divisions, which were to be the first to shoulder the main task of breaking through the enemy's lines, were only able to carry out the systematic training of their replacements to a very limited and inadequate extent, and this was certainly not their own fault. The SS units were far better supplied with both arms and equipment, particularly tanks, than the units of the 5th Panzer Army, and this also represented a heavy psychological burden for the army units entrusted with the offensive.

What they lacked was made up to some extent by the heroism and devotion of the men themselves. Despite many unfavourable influences on the morale of the men at the front, the successful repulse of the airborne landings at Nijmegen and Arnhem, and the successful defence of the Roer against a numerically and materially far superior enemy, had imbued them with the conviction that 'the watch on the Rhine' still stood firm; that by their steadfastness in the West they were protecting the rear of their comrades who were desperately defending the frontiers of the Reich on the Eastern Front; and that, at the same time, they were giving the political leaders of the Reich time in which to come to further decisions.

The willingness of the ordinary soldier to fight on was reinforced by the fact that he accepted the official propaganda, which told him that if the enemy were victorious the German people would be enslaved. The demand for 'unconditional surrender', and the publication of the notorious Morgenthau

Plan, which was now becoming known, threatened the worst for all Germans, and left the man in the field no alternative but to fight on, even without a glimmer of hope.[26] The Morgenthau Plan in particular seemed to show that Goebbels was right after all. The gloomy picture of the fate of the German people under Russian occupation which he and Hitler had been painting for months past, and which was already confirmed in the experience of a large part of the population and many millions of soldiers, was now reinforced by the prospect of falling victim to a terrible revenge on the part of the Western Allies too. The Russians were already at the frontier of East Prussia and the British and Americans at the gates of the Reich in the West, so Hitler's arguments were more than usually convincing. The demand of the Allies for 'unconditional surrender' was thus a gross political error. All it did was to lengthen the war, imposing great sacrifices on both sides which it would otherwise have been possible to avoid. As Chester Wilmot writes: 'Moreover, it was realized by soldiers and civilians alike that any internal revolution at this stage would only precipitate the engulfment of the Reich and its collapse in chaos.'[27] That is quite right, and it only remains to add that because of the millions of foreign workers who had been brought into the Reich for forced labour, the resulting chaos would have been even worse. The man at the front was therefore looking for some chance or other to avoid this.

As far as he was concerned he did not want to lag behind the home front in willingness and self-sacrifice; there old and young, men and women, even boys and girls, struggled on to the detriment of their health and often at the cost of their lives, under the terrible conditions imposed on the German people by the merciless bombing terror of the Allies,[28] holding on daily in a way that aroused the admiration and respect of the man at the front and imposed an obligation on him also to give his utmost. Finally, the deliberately misleading encouragement handed out in official publications about new weapons, about the mass introduction of new and improved aircraft types, and submarines throughout the seas of the world, and about the increased production of German industry, did not fail to have their strengthening effect on the morale of the German people and the German Army. In addition, the confidence of the German soldier in his officers and non-commissioned officers was still unshaken.

Thus certain psychological conditions for continued resistance were still present, though this meant that the reaction when the last offensive was seen to be a failure would be all the greater. With the failure of the Ardennes offensive Germany had exhausted her last reserves, and what strength remained to her was not enough to maintain an effective defence. For a while, the spirit of duty, self-sacrifice, and comradeship made it possible to carry on, but then the will to resist finally collapsed. Helplessly, the man at the front was forced to recognize that the superiority of the enemy on land, in the air and at sea was now so great that there was no longer any chance whatever of putting up a successful resistance.

One of the reasons for this final set-back lay in the fact that Hitler had publicly prophesied that the Wehrmacht would repeat its victories of 1940.[29] His plans were based on an exaggerated idea of Germany's strength, and a gross underestimate of the strength of the Western Allies, and in particular the capacity of the Americans to take set-backs and then recover.

The persisting inequality between the resources which Germany had available at the end of 1944 and those which were available to the three strongest powers in the world could not be abolished 'at one blow' – as Hitler expressed it – and certainly not with the forces he was now in a position to concentrate in the West. Even if the last German offensive had managed to reach its objective and recapture Antwerp, it would have been no more than a temporary set-back for the Allied armies and not in the least their final defeat. At the utmost, it would have postponed the execution of the plans of the Western Allies by a few weeks – and even then this would have been a real gain only if the time thus won were used to obtain military and, in particular, political advantage. But any such thing was excluded from the start, since in the hate-filled atmosphere in which the two sides fought each other there was no possibility of any political agreement, while the military delay was bought at too great a price and was therefore useless. The offensive had not even secured any material weakening of the enemy forces attacking Germany, while the German divisions, which had been strengthened and regrouped for the offensive, lost many men and a great deal of material, and the Army lost its last laboriously gathered reserves, whose absence henceforth made itself painfully felt both on the Western and Eastern Fronts. To have shifted the focal point of resistance in good time from the West to the East would quite certainly have made it possible to hold the line there longer; though, of course, if this solution had been adopted the Western Front would have been left to its own devices, and within a very short space of time it would have collapsed in face of the overwhelming superiority of the Western Allies.[30]

As Hitler was well aware that the Allies would never agree to make a separate peace with him without the Soviet Union, he preferred to attack in the West, though the pulverization of the last German reserves as a result of the failure of this offensive primarily benefited the Russians. On January 12th, 1945, they broke out of the Baranovichi bridgehead in their last great offensive against the Reich. The surprisingly swift success of this offensive undoubtedly had its roots in the German offensive in the Ardennes. The supposed gain of time in the West turned out to be a terrible illusion: the Red Army was the first to storm the Reich's capital, and on April 25th their advance guards made contact with the Americans on the Elbe. It was only under the influence of this manifest enemy success that on May 7th, 1945 – much too late – Germany finally accepted 'unconditional surrender'.

DUNKIRK 1940

1. Hitler's speech of November 23, 1939: *International Military Tribunal (IMT)*, vol. XXVI, doc. PS–789; case XII (Process against W. von Leeb and others), doc. NOKW–482; Memo. of General F. von Bock of November 23, 1939; Memo. of Colonel Hoffmann von Waldau of November 23, 1939. General: H. A. Jacobsen: *Fall Gelb*, Wiesbaden, 1957 (hereafter referred to as Jacobsen). pp. 59 et seq. and 279 et seq.

2. Jacobsen, p. 8 et seq.; also H. Krausnick: *Die Wehrmacht im Dritten Reich, 1933–1939*, in: *Schicksalsfragen der Gegenwart*, Tübingen, 1957. vol. II, p. 282 et seq.; K. Sendtner: *Die deutsche Militäropposition im ersten Kriegsjahr*, in: *Die Vollmacht des Gewissens*, Munich, 1956. p. 381 et seq.

3. Jacobsen, p. 25 et seq.

4. *Documents on German Foreign Policy, 1918–1945*, London, HMSO, 1957. Series D, vol. X, doc. No. 73, p. 79. Cf. also: *Les archives secrètes du Comte Ciano, 1936–1942*, Paris, 1948. Memo. of July 7, 1940, p. 379.

5. Jacobsen, p. 44 et seq. Cf. also G. Ritter: *Carl Goerdeler und die deutsche Widerstandsbewegung*, 2nd ed., Stuttgart, 1956. p. 236 et seq.

6. E. Kosthorst: *Die deutsche Opposition gegen Hitler zwischen Polen- und Frankreichfeldzug*, Bonn, 1954. p. 54 et seq., p. 155 et seq.

7. Ritter, op. cit., p. 232 et seq.

8. Memo. of General von Bock of November 23, 1939. Cf. Halder Diary of November 23, 1939.

9. *Dokumente zur Vorgeschichte des Westfeldzuges 1939–40*, ed. by H. A. Jacobsen, Göttingen, 1956 (hereafter referred to as *Dokumente*). p. 41 et seq. For the strategic planning cf. Jacobsen, p. 12 et seq. (with detailed list of sources and bibliography). Cf. also T. Taylor: *The March of Conquest*, New York, 1958. p. 155 et seq.

10. Memo. of General von Bock of October 25, 1939; Halder Diary and Jodl Diary of October 25, 1939. (Cf. also Jacobsen, p. 39 et seq.).

11. Jacobsen, p. 51 et seq. Cf. also E. von Manstein: *Lost Victories*, London, Methuen, 1958 (hereafter referred to as Manstein). p. 94 et seq. H. Guderian: *Panzer Leader*, London, Michael Joseph, 1956 (hereafter referred to as Guderian.) p. 85 et seq.

12. *Dokumente*, p. 23 et seq.

13. Cf. also Manstein, p. 273 et seq.

14. J. Vanwelkenhuyzen: *L'alerte du 10 janvier 1940*, Brussels, 1954; also Jacobsen, p. 93 et seq. and p. 99 et seq.

15. Manstein, p. 110. Cf. also Jacobsen, p. 69 et seq. Also H. Hoth: 'Mansteins Operationsplan für den Westfeldzug 1940 und die Aufmarschanweisung des OKH vom 24.2.1940', in: *Wehrkunde*, March 1958, p. 127 et seq. And the reply: H. A. Jacobsen: 'Zur Entstehung des Sichelschnittplanes vom 24.2.1940' in: *Wehrkunde*, April 1958, p. 226 et seq. Further: H. Hoth: in: *Wehrkunde*, August 1958, p. 459.

16. Jacobsen, pp. 99 et seq., 107 et seq., 112 et seq. Cf. also A. Goutard: *La guerre des occasions perdues*, Paris, 1956. p. 126 et seq.

17. Jacobsen, pp. 113 et seq., 152 et seq.

18. *Dokumente*, p. 64 et seq. Cf. also: Army Group B War Diary of March 13, 1940. For the commitment of the paratroops cf.: Jacobsen, p. 154 et seq.; W. Melzer: *Albert-Kanal und Eben-Emael*, Heidelberg, 1957.

19. Goutard, op. cit., p. 98 et seq. (cf. also the bibliography quoted there). L. F. Ellis: *The War in France and Flanders, 1939–1940*, London, 1953. J. R. M. Butler: *Grand Strategy*, vol. 5, September 1939–June 1941, London, 1957. There is still no thorough investigation of the plans of the Western Powers 1939–40 drawn up on the basis of the full Allied source material.

20. On the question of Dutch and Belgian neutrality in the winter of 1939–40: P. Marnay (i.e. Vanwelkenhuyzen): 'Une campagne de presse en faveur d'une entente militaire hollando-belge en 1939', in: *L'Armée–La Nation*, May 1958. (cf. also the bibliography quoted there); H. A. Jacobsen: 'War die deutsche Westoffensive 1940 eine Präventivmassnahme?', in: *Wehrwirtschaftliche-Rundschau*, 1957, p. 275 et seq.

21. Goutard, op. cit., p. 139 et seq.

22. Ibid., p. 140 et seq. Ellis, op. cit., p. 22 et seq.

23. For the Belgian and Dutch defensive measures, cf. *L'Armée–La Nation*, Brussels, May 1954, 1955, 1956, 1957 and 1958.

24. Jacobsen, H. A.: 'Motorisierungsprobleme im Winter 1939–40', in: *Wehrw. Rdschau*, 1956, p. 497 et seq.

25. On the 'Rotterdam question' from the Dutch standpoint: *De strijd om Rotterdam Mei 1940*, The Hague, 1952; H. C. Bajetto: 'Het Bombardement van Rotterdam', in: *De militaire spectator*, January 1959, p. 31 et seq. From the German standpoint: H. A. Jacobsen: 'Der deutsche Luftangriff auf Rotterdam (14 Mai 1940)', attempt at an explanation, in: *Wehrw. Rdschau*, 1958, p. 257 et seq. Cf. also Taylor, op. cit., p. 200 et seq.

26. According to the Army Group B War Diary from May 10 to 15, 1940. Cf. also: *Dokumente zum Westfeldzug, 1940*, ed. by H. A. Jacobsen, Göttingen 1960. p. 6 et seq.

27. Halder Diary of May 13, 1940. Situation Reports West Nos. 303 and 304.

28. Cf. the chapter headed 'Die Allierten in Abwehr des deutschen Angriffs' by K. J. Müller in: H. A. Jacobsen: *Dünkirchen*, 1958. pp. 60 et seq., and 214 et seq.

29. Memo. von Bock of May 13, 1940.

30. Müller, op. cit; cf. also Goutard, op. cit., p. 234 et seq.

31. Army Group A War Diary of May 13–15, 1940.

32. Müller, op. cit.; cf. also K. J. Müller: *Das Ende der Entente Cordiale*, Frankfurt/Main, 1956 (with detailed bibliography).

33. Halder Diary of May 16, 1940.

34. Von Bock Diary of May 16, 1940.

35. Jodl and Halder Diaries, Army Group A War Diary of May 17, 1940.

36. Ibid., of May 18, 1940.

37. The sources for the study of the operations of the Luftwaffe are still very poor. The documents so far discovered permit only a general review. *Der Einsatz der Luftwaffe in der ersten Phase des Westfeldzuges 1940*, issued by the Study Group for the History of Air Warfare, Hamburg, 1956.

38. 4th Army, XVI Corps and Army Group A War Diaries of May 20/21, 1940.
39. XVI Corps War Diary of May 21, 1940.
40. 4th Army War Diary of May 21, 1940.
41. Goutard, op. cit., p. 292 et seq.; Ellis, op. cit., p. 87 et seq.
42. Army Group A War Diary and Jodl and Halder Diaries of May 22, 1940; cf. also *Dokumente zum Westfeldzug*, p. 115.
43. C.-in-C. Luftwaffe, Int. Branch, Situation Report of May 23, 1940.
44. This study refrains from dealing with the controversial literature on the subject. A critical discussion of all the points at issue is contained in Jacobsen's *Dünkirchen*, p. 216 et seq. Cf. also *Dokumente zum Westfeldzug*, p. 116 et seq.
45. Army Group B War Diary of May 23, 1940.
46. 4th Army War Diary and the Halder Diary of May 23, 1940.
47. Army Group A and 4th Army War Diaries of May 23, 1940.
48. Ibid., Halder Diary of May 23, 1940. Cf. also *Dokumente zum Westfeldzug*, p. 68 et seq.
49. Jodl Diary of May 20, 1940; Memo. of Lieutenant-General Engel of May 23, 1940 – Army adjutant seconded to the Führer and Reichs Chancellor.
50. Halder Diary of May 24, 1940.
51. Army Group A War Diary; Jodl Diary; Memo. Engel; 4th Army War Diary of May 24, 1940.
52. Appendix to Army Group A War Diary of May 25, 1940. Cf. also *Dokumente zum Westfeldzug*, p. 127.
53. Army Group A War Diary of May 25, 1940.
54. *Dokumente zum Westfeldzug*, p. 121 et seq.: '. . . the next objective is the destruction of the French, British and Belgian forces encircled in Artois and Flanders by a concentric attack. . . .'
55. Jacobsen, *Dünkirchen*, p. 232.
56. Halder Diary of May 25, 1940.
57. Army Groups B and A War Diaries of May 25, 1940; C.-in-C. Luftwaffe, Int. Branch. Situation Report of May 26, 1940.
58. Müller, op. cit., pp. 68, 103 et seq., 111 et seq.; Ellis, op. cit., p. 171 et seq.
59. Halder Diary of May 26, 1940.
60. Ibid., of May 26; Army Group A War Diary of May 26, 1940.
61. *Dokumente zum Westfeldzug*, p. 137.
62. Army Group B and 6th Army War Diaries of May 26, 1940.
63. 4th Army War Diary of May 27, 1940.
64. Details: Jacobsen, p. 123 et seq.
65. Statements contained in Guderian, p. 120, should be corrected.
66. Cf. also Jacobsen, p. 183 et seq. (The German Luftwaffe against 'Dynamo'). The decisive reasons for the failure of the Luftwaffe were: (1) uninterrupted commitments of all kinds from May 10th on; (2) the task was imposed too unexpectedly with the result that not all the available units could be committed quickly enough; (3) difficulties of the strategic units in hitting pinpoint targets; (4) supplies for the tactical units did not proceed smoothly enough; (5) above all, the weather hampered commitment ($2\frac{1}{2}$ days no flying weather); (6) the strategic units were withdrawn too quickly from the Flanders cauldron; (7) strong British resistance; (8) it was possible to inflict heavy material losses on the enemy, but not heavy manpower losses (the effect of bombs dropped on the beaches was slight).

67. Cf. also Wilmot: *The Struggle for Europe*, 1952, and Liddell Hart: *The Other Side of the Hill*, London, Cassell, 1951. p. 219.

68. On the course of the second phase cf. Goutard, op. cit., p. 331 et seq.; Benoist-Méchin, op. cit., p. 244 et seq.; Taylor, op. cit., p. 276 et seq. Also: *Dokumente zum Westfeldzug*, p. 152 et seq. Generally on the point: H. A. Jacobsen: 'Der Westfeldzug 1940', in: *Bücherschau der Weltkriegsbücherei*, Stuttgart, vol. 30, 1958 (with detailed bibliography).

THE BATTLE OF BRITAIN

1. Cf. bibliography. The best summary is given by Theo Weber, who has used the whole of the material on the subject so far published.

2. The most complete collection of material on air warfare, containing excellent source material, is in the archives of the Luftwaffe Study Group under General Paul Deichmann attached to the Führungsakademie of the Bundeswehr in Hamburg-Blankensee. The archives were in the charge of Lieutenant-Colonel Greffrath. The author of the present study is grateful to them both for the assistance they have given him in its writing.

3. In this respect, cf. the two studies published almost simultaneously by Wheatley and Klee, both of which are listed in the bibliography. Cf. also: *Dokumente zum Unternehmen 'Seelöwe', die geplante deutsche Landung im England 1940,* edited by Karl Klee, Göttingen, 1959 (*Studien und Dokumente zur Geschichte des Zweiten Weltkrieges*, 4b).

4. In this study the term 'command of the air' is taken to mean the existence of a situation in which the enemy air force is destroyed, crippled, or, for whatever reason, is no longer in a position to commit its units effectively and systematically. At the same time the term 'air superiority' is taken to mean a situation in which command of the air is won by one side or the other by concentrating its own resources for a limited time in a limited space.

5. For the sources here, and for all further information concerning the preparation and carrying out of the air war against Britain up to the end of the campaign in France, cf. the notes to Klee, *Seelöwe* (text volume), pp. 31 to 50.

6. Ob.d.L. Füst. Ia, No. 5835/40 g.K. (op 1) Chefs., of June 30, 1940.

7. Obd.L. Füst. Ia, No. 5841/40 g.Kdos (op 1) Chefs., of July 11, 1940.

8. Minutes of Luftwaffe Operations Staff meeting of July 21, 1940.

9. Cf. in particular: 'Der Führer und Oberste Befehlshaber der Wehrmacht (i.e. Hitler)', OKW/WFA/L No. 33160/40 g.Kdos. Chefs., of July 16, 1940. Concerning the preparations for the landing in Britain: Nbg (Nuremberg) Doc. PS–442.

10. These figures and all other information in this study concerning strength, commitment, losses, etc., are taken from the comprehensive source material in the archives of the Luftwaffe Study Group attached to the Führungsakademie of the Bundeswehr. Especially important are some studies by the General Staff Dept. 8 of OKL, and also the Gefechtskalender of the air war against Britain from August 1, 1940, to June 30, 1941.

11. General Kommando I.Fl.K., Ia, No. 10260/40 g.Kdos of July 24, 1940, and Gen.Kdo. VIII. Fl.K. (July 1940).

12. Ob.d.L. Füst. Ia, No. 5881/40 g.Kdos. Chefs., of August 2, 1940.

13. War Diary of OKW Op. Staff (Air) of August 8, 1940.

14. Ob.d.L. Füst. Ia, No. 2980/40 sec. (II) of August 19, 1940.

15. Obd.L. Report, September 1, 1940, para. 6.

16. Halder Diary, July 31, 1940.

17. Cf. *Seelöwe* (text volume), pp. 172–177; also Collier, *The Defence of the United Kingdom*, in: *History of the Second World War – U.K. Military Series*, London, H.M.S.O., 1957. p. 221.

18. Cf. the memoranda of Jodl of June 30, 1940, July 12, 1940, and August 13, 1940.

THE BATTLE FOR CRETE 1941

1. Cf. the previous contribution by Karl Klee concerning the air war against Britain, and also the more thorough investigation by Karl Klee: *Das Unternehmen Seelöwe, 1940*, Göttingen 1958, concerning the planned German landing in England.
2. W. Warlimont: 'Die Insel Malta in der Mittelmeer-Strategie des Zweiten Weltkrieges', in: *Wehrwissentschaftliche Rundschau*, No. 8, 1958. pp. 421–436.
3. K. Assmann: *Deutsche Seestrategie in zwei Weltkriegen*, Heidelberg, 1957, in which special reference is made on p. 186 to the reports of Grand Admiral Raeder of September 6, and 26, 1940.
4. The italics are not in the original. The British landed in Crete on October 29, 1940.
5. Operation 'Hannibal'; Ob.d.L. Fü. Stab (Robinson) Ia No. 6294/41 (op. 3) g.Kdos, Chefsache of March 22, 1941, and Gen. Qu. Genst. 4 Abt.(1) No. 222/41 g.Kdos, Chefs. of March 23, 1941.
6. Cf. letter 6294/41, quoted above.
7. Gen. Kdo. XI Fl. K., Ia No. 28/41 g.Kdos of March 25, 1941.
8. Battle Report of XI Fl. K., Abt. Ia, No. 2980/41 g.Kdos Kreta Einsatz, June 11, 1941.
9. OKW/WEST/Abt. L. (I op) No. 4360/41 g.Kdos. March 25, 1941.
10. Luftflottenkommando 4. Bericht 'Kreta'. Führungsabt No. 6340/41 g.Kdos. November 28, 1941.
11. Interview with General Student on March 12, 1955.
12. Directive No. 28 (Operation 'Merkur') of April 25, 1941.
13. Cf. study by W. Warlimont, op. cit., p. 426. General Student reports in *Weltbild*, vol. 6, No. 14, concerning a discussion with Keitel and Jodl in which both were in favour of the urgent seizure of Malta, but Hitler said: 'The seizure of Crete will make a good conclusion to the Balkan campaign.'
14. Battle Report of XI Fl. concerning the preparation of point 2.
15. W. Warlimont, op. cit., p. 428.
16. Lecture notes of General Warlimont, April 28, 1941.
17. Werner Pissin reports in his exhaustive work *Die Eroberung der Insel Kreta durch deutsche Fallschirmjäger und Luftlandetruppen im Jahre 1941*, Karlsruhe, 1957, on p. 139 that Air Fleet 4 was of the opinion that 'a parachute regiment' would be sufficient.
18. Cf. D. M. Davin: *Crete. Official History of New Zealand in the Second World War, 1939–1945*, London, 1953.
19. To Lord Ismay on November 3, 1940.
20. The MNBDO was a naval unit whose job was to establish a naval base, defend it and maintain it anywhere it was needed. In addition to the normal establishment of such a naval base it had a coastal defence group equipped with anti-aircraft and searchlight batteries, and infantry forces with light artillery and machine-guns.

21. D. Richards: *Royal Air Force, 1939–1945*, London, 1953. vol. I, pp. 255–6.

22. ANZAC = Australian and New Zealand Army Corps.

23. Cf. S. W. Roskill: *The War at Sea*, vol. I of *History of the Second World War*, London, 1954, pp. 427–431. I. S. O. Playfair: *The Mediterranean and Middle East*, vol. II of *History of the Second World War*, London, 1956, pp. 61–70. M. A. Bragadin: *The Italian Navy in World War II*, Annapolis, 1957, pp. 81–98.

24. JPS Paper 49 (April 21, 1941).

25. Cf. Playfair, op. cit., vol I, pp. 407–428, vol. II, pp. 303–321.

26. Cf. Playfair, op. cit., vol. II, pp. 177–198.

27. Karl Gundelach: 'Das Kampfgeschwader General Wever 4 im Kriege', unpublished manuscript.

28. Richards, op. cit., p. 321.

29. By May 30th the British were once again masters of the situation.

30. Cf. Roskill, op. cit., vol. I, pp. 431–433; Bragadin, op. cit., pp. 69–72.

31. Davin, op. cit., p. 19.

32. Fulmars, Gladiators and Brewsters.

33. Battle Report of XI Fl. Korps – Einsatz Kreta, June 11, 1941, Anlage II.1.

34. Cf. Playfair, op. cit., vol. II, p. 105.

35. The King went on board a British destroyer on the night of May 22nd–23rd in Ayiarumeli on the south coast.

36. Tobruk had been invested since April 8th and it could be supplied only from the sea.

37. Davin, op. cit., p. 51.

38. Al-Gelani's movement failed because of ineffective co-operation and the insufficient forces with which it was undertaken and with which it was supported by the Germans. Hitler's intentions are best set out in his own directive on the Middle East of May 23, 1941. He intended to support al-Gelani by supplying him with arms and by sending a military mission (Special Staff F under General Felmy, who was also in command of the Syria liaison mission) and despatching numerically limited Luftwaffe forces in order to bolster up the self-confidence of the Iraqis and their will to resist. In fact, the disturbances in Iraq did force the British to divide their forces during a period when decisive happenings were taking place in Crete and North Africa.

39. Cf. Playfair, op. cit., p. 114. Because of the acute shortage of tanks in North Africa the longer forty days' journey round Africa was not used. The convoy took from May 5th to May 12th to sail from Gibraltar to Alexandria, and, according to X Fl. K., this was the first attempt since January. One merchantman carrying 57 tanks and 10 Hurricanes was lost.

40. Operation 'Scorcher' code name for the expected invasion of Crete. On May 13th Churchill proposed to send another twelve tanks to Crete, but Wavell opposed the idea because they would in all probability arrive too late. This is a typical example of interference on the part of political leaders even in minor matters in times of crisis. There was no shortage of this sort of interference on the German side.

41. 'The Battle of Crete', supplement to the *London Gazette*, May 24, 1948, No. 38296.

42. Ibid.

43. Richards, op. cit., p. 324.

44. Davin, op. cit., pp. 44–5 and Appendix IV which contains an exact list of the units concerned. The above figures are those for the beginning of the battle on May 20th.

45. The last airworthy aircraft of the RAF left the island on May 19th.

46. W. Pissin, op. cit., p. 32.

47. Report of XI Fl. Korps, op. cit.

48. We have deliberately refrained from dealing with tactical details here or listing the forces engaged.

49. The division of Centre Group into two waves does not seem to have been a fortunate arrangement, nor that the commander of the group went in with the first wave (and was killed).

50. In view of the known movements of the British Fleet in Cretan waters, XI Fl. K. agreed to postpone the landing of the Maleme squadron to the second day of the attack.

51. The account of the critical moments of the battle for Crete are based, except where otherwise mentioned, on the following sources of information:
    (a) Report of XI Fl. K. of June 11, 1941, op. cit.;
    (b) Report of Air Fleet 4 on November 28, 1941, op. cit.; and
    (c) Werner Pissin, op. cit.

52. Referring to this 'leap into the enemy stronghold', which was to lead to heavy losses, the Battle Report of Air Fleet 4 says: 'It will not be possible to repeat an action in this form. Future use of para- and airborne troops will presumably have to take place in territory free of the enemy. The territory necessary for any subsequent airborne landings must first be seized.'

53. The Battle Report of XI Fl. K. declares that when the glider of General Süssmann was overtaken in the air by a Heinkel 111 'the wings detached themselves' – apparently as the result of air pressure. For other versions of the accident cf. Werner Pissin, op. cit., p. 126.

54. General R. von Heyking: Fallschirmeinsatz des K.G. z.b.V.2 – Kreta, Study No. 639. April 16, 1947.

55. Cf. the evidence of those engaged in this question: Pissin, op. cit., p. 134.

56. In an effort to recoup as much as possible of the lost time, the transport aircraft flew to their dropping zones partly in small formations of three to four aircraft. Writing in *Weltbild*, op. cit., p. 19, General Student declares: 'The attack of the second wave on Heraklion and Retimo failed from the start on the airfields of Attica.' It was, in fact, an indication of inadequate co-operation between the operations staffs concerned.

57. Richards, op. cit., p. 333.

58. Battle Report of Western Group (reinforced Assault Regiment) concerning the Crete mission from May 20/28, 1941, of June 7, 1941.

59. Davin, op. cit., p. 114. In chapter III, pp. 88–121, there is a detailed description of the decisive fighting of the 22nd Battalion.

60. According to the diary of General Freiherr von Richthofen, GOC VIII Fl. K., as edited by Colonel Deichmann, who was his adjutant for many years, he also recognized the relatively favourable position at Maleme airfield, and it is said to have been due to his advice that it was decided to give 'definite preferential support to the parachutists at Maleme'.

61. Report of Air Fleet 4, op. cit., p. 4.

62. The source for information concerning the fate of the two flotillas is War Diary, Flag Officer Southeast, for the period from May 16/31, 1941; 1/SKL No. 14196/41 g.Kdos.

63. Playfair, op. cit., p. 135 et seq.

64. Playfair, op. cit., p. 137, mentions the loss of 800 men. In reality the losses were seen later on to have been considerably smaller. They actually amounted to 297 men. Cf. also Pissin, op. cit., p. 159. Air-sea rescue units played a big role in saving the shipwrecked. For the operations of the Italian torpedo-boats cf. Bragadin, op. cit., pp. 108-9.

65.. Report of Air Fleet, op. cit., pp. 41-2. The primary task of VIII Fl. K. in the concluding battles for Crete is given as supporting the ground forces.

66. Davin, op. cit., p. 486.

67. Cf. also the report of XI Fl. Korps, op. cit.; report of Air Fleet 4, op. cit; and the investigations of Davin and Pissin. In addition, the total loss of 151 Junkers 52's had an unfavourable effect on the transport wings and the training of new pilots.

68. General Kurt von Tippelskirch: 'Der deutsche Balkanfeldzug 1941', in: *Wehrwissenschaftliche Rundschau* (5) 1955, pp. 49–65.

69. With this the taking of Crete proved itself the best form of relief for North Africa.

70. This high estimate of the fighting qualities of the Italian Fleet does not take into account the fact that its operational *élan* was considerably less as a result of the set-back at Cape Matapan. Since then, too, the Supermarina knew that the British were in possession of a very effective system of radar.

71. General Blamey as Wavell's representative to the Australian Government on June 6, 1941.

72. Playfair in particular, op. cit., 149–150.

73. General Student in 'Weltbild', op. cit.

74. Cf. Warlimont, op. cit. A further reason was his doubt as to the fighting qualities of the Italian Army.

75. The extension of Germany's area of military power into the eastern Mediterranean meant, as far as he was concerned, in the first place only the more certain protection of the deep flank of the Eastern Front.

THE BATTLE FOR MOSCOW 1941

1. Cf. OKW/WFSt/Abt L (I) No. 33/408/40 gK Chefsache (cf. also H. Greiner: *Die Oberste Wehrmachtführung 1939–43*, Wiesbaden, 1951. p. 288 et seq.).
2. Cf. de Mendelsohn: *Die Nürnberger Dokumente*, 1947, p. 332 et seq.
3. German Army Groups in the first year of the Eastern Front campaign: Army Group South; C.-in-C. Field-Marshal von Rundstedt. Three armies (11th, 17th, 6th), Panzer Group 1. Dependent on co-operation with Air Fleet 4 (General Löhr);

   Army Group Centre: C.-in-C. Field-Marshal von Bock. Three Armies (2nd, 4th, 9th), Panzer Groups 2 and 3. Dependent for co-operation on Air Fleet 2 (Field-Marshal Kesselring);

   Army Group North: C.-in-C. Field-Marshal von Leeb. Two Armies (16th and 18th), Panzer Group 4. Dependent for co-operation on Air Fleet 1 (General Keller).
4. The directive issued by Hitler to C.-in-C. Army on August 21, 1941, begins with the words: 'The Army's proposal of August 18th for the further conduct of operations on the Eastern Front does not agree with my intentions. I order the following:

   1. The most important objective to be attained before the onset of winter is *not* the capture of Moscow, but the seizure of the Crimea and the Donetz industrial and coal area, and the cutting off of the Russian oil supplies from the Caucasian area; and to the north the investment of Leningrad and a campaign to link up with the Finns'. The subsequent paragraphs set out the instructions which ultimately led to the battle for Kiev. Cf. Halder's Diary on August 22, 1941.
5. The following is an extract from Hitler's Directive No. 35 of September 6, 1941:

   '1. Army Group South is . . . to destroy the enemy in the Kremenchug–Kiev–Konotop triangle. As quickly as possible thereafter those units of the 2nd and 6th Armies and of Panzer Group 2 which become free in consequence are to be regrouped for further operations.

   '2. Army Group Centre is to attack as soon as possible, by the end of September at the latest. Objective: to drive the enemy to the east of Smolensk in a double encircling movement in the direction of Vyazma with strong armoured forces. In order to cover Army Group Centre's southern wing, Army Group South is to move forward its flank units in a northeasterly direction. Army Group North to move forces likewise for the protection of Army Group Centre's northern wing.

   '3. . . .

   '4. Take up positions as soon as possible.'
6. Cf. Halder's Diary on September 13, 1941.
7. Cf. Halder on September 9th: 'We lack 200,000 men on the Eastern Front, and there is no way of replacing them except by wounded men who have recovered.'
8. Cf. von Bock's War Diary of December 1, 1941. Soviet accounts in this respect

which have so far been published are completely worthless. For example, *Die wichtigsten Operationen des Grossen Vaterländischen Krieges 1941–45*, edited by Colonel Zhilin, Berlin, 1958 (German translation of the Russian original, Moscow, 1956), p. 55 et seq.

9. Cf. Halder of August 8th: 'At the beginning of the war we reckoned with about 200 enemy divisions. We can already count 360. Of course, these divisions are not armed and equipped according to our standards, and they are often inadequately led tactically speaking, but the point is – they're there! And when we smash up a dozen of them the Russian just replaces them with another dozen. The Russian gains time because he is near his own sources of manpower, whereas we are moving farther and farther away from ours.'

10. Cf. A. M. Samsonov: *Velikaya Bitva pod Moskvoi 1941–1942*, Moscow, 1958. p. 65.

11. HQ Army Group Centre, Ops. Branch, Order No. 1620/41 g.Kdos. Chefs. of September 26, 1941. In addition the war diaries of Army Group Centre, of the 2nd, 4th and 9th Armies and of Panzer Groups 2, 3 and 4 were also used to document this account of the battle for Moscow.

12. HQ Army Group Centre, Ops. Branch, Order No. 1870 g.Kdos. Chefs. of October 7, 1941.

13. Von Bock's War Diary on October 7, 1941.

14. Ibid., of October 19, 1941.

15. Cf. Tippelskirch: *Geschichte des zweiten Weltkriegs*, Bonn, 1951 (hereafter referred to as Tippelskirch), p. 240; and in particular Samsonov, op. cit., p. 67 et seq.

16. Hitler refuses to accept a capitulation of Moscow. Cf. file 'Barbarossa', vol. III of the Operations Branch of the Army General Staff of October 12, 1941: 'The Führer has once again decided that the capitulation of Moscow shall not be accepted even if the enemy should offer it.' The reason for this decision is then given: it was to be expected that the population of Moscow would flee into the interior, and add to the general chaos in Russia.

17. Von Bock's War Diary on October 14, 1941. It is not possible to say at this stage whether the idea of this non-concentric movement originated with Hitler himself or with OKH.

18. Guderian: *Panzer Leader*, London, Michael Joseph, 1952, p. 242: 'The single road that was available for this purpose, the one from Orel to Tula, was certainly not intended to carry heavy vehicles and tanks, and began to disintegrate after a few days' use. Furthermore, the Russians, experts at demolition, had blown all the bridges along the line of their withdrawal, and had laid extensive minefields on either side of the road in all suitable localities.'

19. File 'Barbarossa', vol. III of the Operations Branch of the Army General Staff, No. 31903, 1609 and 1610 g.Kdos, Chefs. of October 23, 29 and 30, 1941.

20. Von Bock's War Diary, October 27 and 28, 1941.

21. Cf. note 16.

22. Von Bock's diary, November 1, 1941.

23. Ibid., October 31, 1941.

24. Samsonov, op. cit., p. 94.

25. Ibid., p. 72: 'Soon after the outbreak of hostilities, "within four days", eleven new

divisions with a total strength of 106,000 men were raised in the Moscow area alone.'

26. According to Soviet sources (Samsonov, op. cit., p. 97) approximately half a million men were used for this purpose.

27. Figures from the Organization Branch of OKH of November 6, 1941.

28. Kesselring: *Memoirs*, London, Kimber, 1953, p. 97.

29. Cf. Platonov: *Vtoraya mirovaya voina 1939–1945*, Moscow, 1958, p. 208 ff.; see also Sokolovski: *Die sowjetische Kriegskunst in der Schlacht vor Moskau*. German translation from *Voyenno istoricheskii Zhurnal*, 1961, No. 11, p. 15 ff. In: *Wehrwissensch. Rundschau* 13 (1962), p. 75 ff.

30. Guderian, op. cit., p. 255.

31. Von Bock's diary, November 18, 1941; Samsonov, op. cit., p. 65 et seq.; Cf. also *Die wichtigsten Operationen . . .*, p. 131 et seq.

32. Halder's diary, November 27, 1941 .

33. Von Bock's diary of December 1, 1941. The fact that Army High Command (OKH) and Wehrmacht High Command (OKW) were next door to each other, so to speak, and nevertheless 'corresponded' with each other gives some idea of how deep was the chasm that separated them.

34. Ibid., December 1, 1941.

35. Halder's diary, December 4, 1941.

36. Nevertheless, Brauchitsch had reported to Hitler on this matter as early as the summer. Cf. also Blumenritt in: *The Fatal Decisions*, New York, p. 74.

37. Von Bock's diary, November 18, 1941: 'No less than 21 of the 34 new divisions from Siberia were on the front of Army Group Centre!'

38. As early as the middle of November the Russians had brought up strategic reserves from Siberia and Central Asia, and they formed them into three new armies (1st Assault Army, and 10th and 20th Armies) – Samsonov, op. cit., p. 132. Also p. 173 et seq. For long-range air reconnaissance cf. Kesselring, op. cit., p. 96. The unsatisfactory position about Luftwaffe source material makes it impossible to examine this question in any detail.

39. Der Führer und Oberste Befehlshaber der Wehrmacht, No. 442182/a g.K. Chefs. WFSt/Abt.L. (I op) of December 16, 1941; OKH Gen Stab d.H.Op. Abt 1736/41 g.Kdos. Chefs. of December 18, 1941.

40. Halder: *Hitler als Feldherr*, p. 45.

41. For example, the observations of Samsonov (op. cit., p. 170) on the fundamental principles behind the Russian operations, approved by Stalin on November 30th.

42. Cf. also Platonov, op. cit., p. 234: '. . . some of our troops and units did not seek to envelop and encircle enemy positions but attacked them frontally. The War Council of the "Western Front" on December 13th ordered an end to these foolish, bloody and mistaken tactics. . . .'

43. The Panzer Groups 3 and 4 were renamed 'Panzer Armies' on January 1, 1942.

44. Examples of reduced fighting strengths, taken from reports of Army Group to OKH on December 28, 1941:

   (*a*) losses of the 6th Division from December 22nd to 25th: officers, 20; NCO's and men, 586;

   (*b*) battle strength of the 58th Infantry Regiment: 350 men, 15 light machine-guns and no anti-tank weapons;

   (*c*) frostbite cases in 26th Division: 77th Inf. Rgt.: 34 serious; 74 slight cases;

78th Inf. Rgt.: 200 serious cases; 400 slight cases; 26 Recce Bn.: 51 serious cases; 45 slight cases;

(*d*) 58th Inf. Rgt.: the men had hot meals only twice in seven days.

Taken from the War Diary of Panzer Group 4 of December 27, 1941:

(*a*) the battle strength of the 106th Division amounts to 300 men capable of carrying rifles;

(*b*) 80 per cent of those units of XLVI Panzer Corps actually at the front are without rations and must therefore be supplied by air.

45. OKW No. 442277/41 g.Kdos. Chefs. WFSt/Op of December 28, 1941.

46. On January 14, 1942, Halder noted in his diary: 'The Führer does see the necessity for withdrawal, but he can't make up his mind to issue the necessary orders. This sort of leadership will lead to the destruction of the army.'

47. It is significant that even today official Soviet sources declare – probably with some degree of exaggeration – that the Soviet Union had never before faced such a 'deadly threat'. (Cf. Samsonov, op. cit., p. 142).

48. Reinforcements for the two fronts:

Army Group Centre		*December 1941 to February 1942*						
December:	0	30 Divs, 33 Brigs, 6 Panzer Brigs, 3 Cav. Divs.						
January:	4 Divs.	11 „	5 „	5 „	„ 2 „	„		
February:	5 „	10 „	6 „	6 „	„ 0 „	„		

49. Summary of losses and replacements, December 1941 to February 1942. Statistics from the Org. Abt/Genst. d.Heeres:

Month	*Losses*	*Replacements*	*Losses not made good*
December	103,600	40,800	62,800
January	144,900	19,100	125,800
February	108,700	69,700	39,000
Total	357,200	129,600	227,600

50. Tippelskirch, pp. 248–9.

51. Cf. also the severe criticism of General Hoepner, who had set down one or two of his ideas concerning 'the failure of the operations before Moscow' in December 1941. Cf. also Châles de Beaulieu (see Bibliography, *Part II – The Battle for Moscow, 1941*), p. 433 et seq., and p. 439.

THE DECISION IN THE MEDITERRANEAN 1942

1. I. S. O. Playfair: *The Mediterranean and the Middle East*, vol. I of *The History of the Second World War*, London, 1954. p. 23 et seq., p. 81 et seq.

2. H. Greiner: *Die Oberste Wehrmachtführung 1939–43*, Wiesbaden, 1951, p. 203 et seq.; 'Führer Conferences on Matters dealing with the German Navy 1939–1945' (Naval Conferences), vol. II/1940, vol. I/1941. See also K. Gundelach's contribution, 'The Battle for Crete'.

3. Karl Klee: 'Entwurf der OKW-Weisung No. 32 vom 11. Juni, 1941, eine quellen-kritische Untersuchung', in: *Wehrwissenschaftliche Rundschau* (6) 1956, pp. 127–141. For the British view, which agrees with the German, cf. Playfair, op. cit., vol. II, p. 248.

4. Cf. Karl Gundelach's contribution on Crete, op. cit.

5. Drawn up according to Playfair, vol. II, pp. 338–339.

6. Cf. (a) *Naval Conferences*, Vol. 1942; (b) *Ufficio Storico, Stato Maggiore Esercito: Il Esercito Italiano nella Seconda Guerra Mondiale, Seconda Controffensiva Italo-Tedesca in Africa Settentrionale da El Agheila a El Alamein, Gennaio-Settembre 1942* (subsequently referred to as *Controffensiva 1942*) p. 140; (c) G. Ciano: *L'Europa verso la Catastrofe*, Milan, 1948 (hereafter referred to as Ciano, *Catastrofe*).

7. OKW Directive of October 29, 1941.

8. Cf. (a) E. von Rintelen: *Mussolini als Bundesgenosse*, Tübingen, 1951. p. 266 et seq., though to some extent his observations have had to be corrected by (b) *Controffensiva 1942*, pp. 86–88 and 352; and (c) U. Cavallero: *Comando Supremo, Diario 1940–43 del Capo di S.M.G.* (hereafter referred to as 'Cavallero, *Diario*'), pp. 240, 216, 222–3, 231–2, 234, 236, 247; and (d) G. Ciano: *Diario 1939–45*, entries of April 28th, and May 12th and 13th, 1942.

9. W. S. Churchill: *The Second World War*, vol. IV, *The Hinge of Fate*, 2nd ed., London, 1951. pp. 260–272.

10. Cf. Note 8, and also Cavallero, *Diario*, p. 251.

11. Cf. the notes on the War Diary of the Kriegsgesch. Abt. of OKW of May 1942, supplemented by recollections of the author as a participant.

12. Cf. notes on the War Diary of OKW of May 1942, and 'Naval Conferences', vol. 1942; entries of June 17th. In fact, in the middle of June 1942 only 2 badly damaged ships of a convoy of 17 transport vessels actually arrived in Malta, while as the result of German and Italian air activity, U-boats, fast MTB's and and an Italian cruiser squadron, as well as minefields laid in the neighbourhood of Malta, 1 cruiser, 5 destroyers and 6 merchantmen were sunk, and 3 cruisers, 1 AA cruiser, 3 destroyers, 1 minesweeper, 1 corvette and 2 merchantmen were damaged. In August 1942 only 5 ships, and 2 of those badly damaged, actually arrived in Malta out of a total of 14 ships in the convoy. German and Italian submarines, fast MTB's and aircraft sank 1 carrier, 2 cruisers, 1 destroyer and 9 merchantmen, and damaged 1 carrier, 2 cruisers and 2 merchantmen.

Cf. also S. W. Roskill: *The War at Sea*, vol. II of *History of the Second World War*, London, 1956. Pp. 63–68, 301–306.

13. For the fighting in North Africa cf. the following versions: (a) George Howe: *United States Army in World War II, The Mediterranean Theater of Operations, Northwest Africa, Seizing the Initiative in the West*, Office of the Chief of Military History, Department of the Army, Washington D.C., 1957; (b) J. A. I. Agar-Hamilton and L. C. F. Turner: *Crisis in the Desert, May–July 1942*, London, 1952; (c) J. L. Scoullar: *Battle for Egypt, The Summer of 1942*, in *Official History of New Zealand in the Second World War 1939–45*, Wellington, 1955; (d) D. Prasad: *The North African Campaign 1940–43*, in *Official History of the Indian Armed Forces in the Second World War 1939–45*, Combined Inter-Services Historical Section of India and Pakistan, 1956; (e) D. Richards and H. St G. Saunders: *Royal Air Force 1939–45*, vol. II, *The Fight Avails*, London, 1954; (f) J. Herington: *Air War against Germany and Italy 1939–43*, in *Australia in the War of 1939–45*, Canberra, 1954.

14. Cavallero, *Diario*, p. 274; *Controffensiva 1942*, p. 137 et seq., and p. 374.

15. Ciano: *Catastrofe* (Report dated June 23rd).

16. Erwin Rommel: *Krieg ohne Hass*, Heidenheim, 1950. P. 163 et seq., and p. 198. Cf. also *The Rommel Papers*, New York, 1953, and London, Collins, 1953, p. 233.

17. Freiherr von Esebeck: *Afrikanische Schicksalsjahre*, Wiesbaden, 1949. P. 119.

18. Ciano: *Diario*, June 20th.

19. *Controffensiva 1942*, pp. 139–141, 150–51, 382, 385.

20. Cf. Agar-Hamilton, op. cit., pp. 227–316; Scoullar, op. cit., pp. 59–177; Prasad, op. cit., pp. 410–442.

21. Cf. Richards and Saunders, op. cit., pp. 217–231; Herington, op. cit., p. 234.

22. Cf. *Controffensiva 1942*, p. 186 et seq.; Cavallero *Diario*, p. 289; *The Rommel Papers*, p. 257.

23. Cf. *Controffensiva 1942*, pp. 263, 338 and 390; Cavallero: *Diario*, p. 288.

24. Cavallero: *Diario*, p. 285 in connection with p. 277. In addition, Ufficio Storico, Stato Maggiore Esercito: *Il XXX Corpo d'Armata Italiano in Tunisia*, Rome, 1950, p. 48.

25. Cf. also *Controffensiva 1942*, pp. 194 and 215–219; Cavallero: *Diario*, p. 300; Ciano: *Diario*, August 6th.

26. *Controffensiva 1942*, pp. 226 and 409–411; Cavallero: *Diario*, pp. 313–314; concerning the prospects of a renewal of the attack from British sources cf. *The Memoirs of Field Marshal the Viscount Montgomery of Alamein*, London, 1958 (hereafter referred to as 'Montgomery I'), pp. 94, 99 and 102.

27. Such plans were discussed in the staff of the Japanese Combined Fleet during the first months of 1942 but they had to be abandoned in their more far-reaching aspects because at that time it was impossible to secure the necessary German–Italian co-operation (January/February 1942). Cf. M. Fuchida [and] M. Okumiya: *Midway. The Battle that Doomed Japan*, Annapolis, 1956; also J. Rohwer: *Die Seeluftschlacht bei Midway 1942*, in: *Entscheidungsschlachten des zweiten Weltkrieges. Deutsche Ausgabe*. Frankfurt on Main, 1960, pp. 190–194.

28. Cf. Richardson and Saunders, op. cit., p. 222.

29. *Controffensiva 1942*, p. 230; cf. also Ciano: *Diario*, August 31st. For further important changes that General Montgomery introduced to improve the situation of the 8th Army after he took command on August 13th, cf. Mont-

gɔmery I, p. 94 et seq., supplemented by his *El Alamein to the River Sangro,* New York, 1949 (hereafter referred to as 'Montgomery II'), pp. 16–17.

30. *Controffensiva 1942,* pp. 231–233; Cavallero: *Diario,* pp. 315 and 318.
31. Montgomery I, p. 107 et seq.; II, pp. 23–4.
32. *Controffensiva 1942,* p. 242 et seq.; Cavallero: *Diario,* pp. 324–5; Ciano: *Diario,* September 2nd, 3rd and 8th, 1942.
33. For the British viewpoint cf. W. S. Churchill: *The Second World War.* Vol. III, pp. 479–490, 507, 561, 574–578, 582, 703 and 751; vol. IV, pp. 20, 168–175, 289–291, 318, 343, 390–398, 401–404, 475–485; Arthur Bryant: *The Turn of the Tide 1939–1943,* London, Collins, 1957. Pp. 278–280, 287, 296, 374, 421–424, 427–441; for the US viewpoint cf. Maurice Matloff and Edwin M. Snell: *The War Department – Strategic Planning for Coalition Warfare 1941–42,* in *United States Army in World War II,* Washington, 1953. Pp. 111–113, 147, 174–201, 233–243; Samuel E. Morison: *Operations in North African Waters, October 1942–June 1943,* in: *History of the United States Naval Operations in World War II,* Boston, 1947. Pp. 3–18; Wesley Frank Craven and James Lea Cate; *Europe: Torch to Pointblank, August 1942 to December 1943,* in *The Army Air Forces in World War II,* vol. II, Chicago, 1949, pp. 3–66.
34. B. H. Liddell Hart: *Strategy,* Faber & Faber, London, 1954.
35. W. S. Churchill, op. cit., vol. IV, p. 398.
36. Ibid., pp. 398–400.
37. Ibid., pp. 412–424; Montgomery I, pp. 91–106.
38. Cavallero: *Diario,* pp. 325–328.
39. Ibid., p. 293 (July 20th) in connection with p. 250 (April 30th).
40. Cf. 'Naval Conferences', vol. 1942 (August 26th); Notes on War Diary of the W.F.Stab. of September 8th and October 9th.
41. Cavallero: *Diario,* pp. 334–335, 341, 345; cf. also *The Rommel Papers,* pp. 293–4.
42. Cf. note 38.
43. Cavallero: *Diario,* pp. 338, 341, 343, 345, 348–9, 350.
44. Ibid., pp. 346–7.
45. Notes on War Diary of the Wehrmacht Operations Staff of October 20, 1942.
46. Montgomery I, pp. 124–5; Kurt von Tippelskirch: *Geschichte des zweiten Weltkriegs,* Bonn, 1956. Pp. 277–8.
47. Cavallero: *Diario,* p. 349 (October 22nd).
48. Ibid., pp. 359–361.
49. Ibid., pp. 361–365; Rintelen, op. cit., p. 176; Ciano, *Diario,* November 2nd.
50. Esebeck: op. cit., pp. 174–5.
51. Notes on War Diary of the Wehrmacht Operations Staff of November 3, 1942; Rintelen, op. cit., p. 176; Rommel, *Papers,* pp. 257–259; Montgomery I, p. 116 et seq.
52. Rommel, p. 268 et seq.
53. Notes on War Diary of the Wehrmacht Operations Staff of November 5, 1942; cf. also Esebeck, op. cit., p. 176.
54. Montgomery I, p. 33.
55. US Department of the Army: *Seizing the Initiative in the West,* pp. 10–14, 15–31; W. S. Churchill, op. cit., vol. IV, p. 596; Craven and Cate, op. cit., vol. II, pp. 47–50.

56. According to unpublished reports from the archives of the German Armistice Commission.
57. Notes on War Diary of the Wehrmacht Operations Staff of October 15, 1942; 'Naval Conferences', 1942.
58. Ciano: *Catastrofe*.
59. Cavallero: *Diario*, p. 348, supplemented from unpublished reports.
60. Notes on War Diary of the Wehrmacht Operations Staff of October 25, 1942.
61. Only a fragment of the review is still extant and it has never been published.
62. Cavallero: *Diario*, p. 334; Rintelen, op. cit., p. 180; Ciano, *Diario*.
63. Cavallero: *Diario*, p. 348; Ciano, *Catastrofe*.
64. Notes on War Diary of the Wehrmacht Operations Staff of November 2 and 4, 1942; Cavallero: *Diario*, pp. 361, 363, 367, 370; Ciano: *Diario*, November 4, 1942.
65. Notes on War Diary of the Wehrmacht Operations Staff of November 6 and 7, 1942; Cavallero: *Diario*, pp. 371–5, and other unpublished reports.
66. According to the (unpublished) report of a participant.
67. According to the stenographic report of a discussion on the military situation at midday on April 6, 1944, with Hitler.
68. According to unpublished reports.
69. Cavallero: *Diario*, pp. 376 and 378.
70. Cf. Jacques Mordal: 'Die französische Marine und die allierten Landungen in Nordafrika – Ein Beitrag zum Problem des militärischen Gehorsams', in *Wehrwiss. Rdsch.* 7 (1957); Admiral Auphan and Jacques Mordal: *La Marine Française pendant la Seconde Guerre Mondiale*, Paris, 1958. Pp. 263–293.
71. Notes on War Diary of the Wehrmacht Operations Staff of November 8 to 17, 1942; Ciano: *Diario*, November 9, 1942, et seq.; Cavallero, *Diario*, p. 381.
72. Ciano: *Catastrofe*, December 1, 1942; Cavallero, *Diario*, pp. 404–5.
73. Notes on War Diary of the Wehrmacht Operations Staff of March 14, 1943.
74. 'Naval Conferences, 1942', 'Assessment of the Situation of November 19, 1943, and Naval Conferences 1943', 'Experts Report' of April 11th.

1. Halder Diary of November 7, 1941. Cf. also Halder Diary of July 31, 1940, in which is recorded Hitler's reference to his idea that what was really necessary in order to crush 'Russia's vital sources of power' was a 'limited operation' to seize the Baku oilfields. Cf. also Halder of November 19, 1941! Incidentally, on October 24, 1941, the Operations Branch of the Army General Staff had put forward its own preliminary draft for an offensive to the Caucasus. For details cf. 'The German Campaign in Russia', US Dept. of the Army Pamphlet No. 20–261a, 1955. P. 110 et seq.

2. Hans Doerr: *Der Feldzug nach Stalingrad*, Darmstadt, 1955. P. 15 (hereafter referred to as Doerr). Cf. also Halder Diary of November 13, 1941.

3. Cf. also Rudolf Hofmann's contribution *The Battle for Moscow*.

4. Helmuth Greiner: *Die Oberste Wehrmachtsführung 1939–1943*, Wiesbaden, 1951. P. 395 et seq. (hereafter referred to as Greiner).

5. Cf. also Walter Görlitz: *Der Zweite Weltkrieg*, vol. I, p. 350.

6. These ideas have also been put forward, for example, by the British military writer Major-General J. F. C. Fuller: *The Second World War 1939–45*, Eyre and Spottiswoode, London, 1948.

7. In this connection cf. also Karl Klee: 'Entwurf zur Führerweisung No. 32', in *Wehrwiss. Rdschau*. 1956, p. 127 et seq. Cf. also for general details Goebbels' Diary of March 20, 1942. Cf. also the contributions of Rohwer and Warlimont.

8. Doerr, p. 15.

9. For the spring battle of Kharkov cf., inter alios, Adolf Heusinger: *Befehl im Widerstreit*, Tübingen-Stuttgart, 1950. P. 191 et seq; Giovanni Messe: *Der Krieg im Osten*, Zurich, 1948. P. 203 et seq. (hereafter referred to as Messe). Also collection of the author, 'Auszüge aus OKW-Berichten 1939–45'. Cf. also the evidence of Lieutenant-General Arthur Schmidt, former Chief of Staff of the 6th Army, subsequently referred to as 'AS-Protokoll'. It should be borne in mind that Schmidt was in a position to compare his notes with 6th Army War Diary, which is, for the moment, still in the hands of the US Historical Division.

10. Cf. the misfortune which attended the two German Luftwaffe officers near Mechelen (Belgium) on January 10, 1940, which led to the issue of Führer Directive No. 1 (Jacobsen: *Fall Gelb*, Mainz, 1957. P. 93 et seq.)

11. Cf. AS-Protokoll (in the possession of the author).

12. Doerr, p. 18, approves of Hitler's refusal on July 4, 1942, to allow Voronezh to be taken and the Don to be crossed. Doerr is of the opinion that Field-Marshal von Bock was at fault here in a purely tactical judgement.

13. Cf. Doerr, p. 24 (note 11), who expresses the not altogether unfounded suspicion that Hitler deliberately deceived the Army General Staff, and that the plans for the envelopment battle were only a pretext for shifting the main weight of operations in order to seize the Caucasian oilfields.

14. Cf. Doerr, p. 30.

15. Cf. Doerr, p. 28; AS-Protokoll; Siegmar Quilitsch: *Die Ursache für den Sieg*

der Sowjetarmee in der Schlacht von Stalingrad in der Darstellung westdeutscher Historiker – Minutes of the meeting of the Historians of the DDR (East-German Democratic Republic) and of the Soviet Union in Leipzig from November 25 to 30, 1957, vol. II, Akademie-Verlag, Berlin, 1958.

16. Hans Detlef Herhudt von Rohden: *Die Luftwaffe ringt um Stalingrad*. Wiesbaden, 1950. P. 11.

17. Cf. Heinz Schröter: *Stalingrad – bis zur letzten Patrone*, published by the author, Osnabrück, p. 13. *Si non è vero, è ben trovato* (WG).

18. AS-Protokoll.

19. Greiner, p. 401.

20. Cf. Doerr's too severely critical attitude in this matter, p. 43.

21. In this connection cf. Erich von Manstein: *Lost Victories*, London, Methuen, 1958. Pp. 261–262 (hereafter referred to as Manstein). Manstein was well aware that Operation 'Northern Light' was unnecessary and, in any case, highly problematical.

22. Greiner, p. 401.

23. Messe, p. 240 et seq.

24. AS-Protokoll: observations of Field-Marshal Paulus.

25. Greiner, p. 407.

26. AS-Protokoll: observations of Field-Marshal Paulus.

27. Greiner, p. 411 et seq.

28. Quoted by Doerr, p. 53, footnote no. 32.

29. Cf. the latest Soviet study by Telpukhovskii in: *Voprosy istorii*, Moscow, April 1959, pp. 23–45, containing a review of Soviet discussions on Stalingrad. General Zhilin: *Die wichtigsten Operationen* . . . P. 171 et seq.

30. Greiner, p. 146.

31. Manstein, p. 269. Cf. also the discussions given in Heusinger's *Befehl im Widerstreit*, p. 213 et seq.

32. AS-Protokol: observations of Field-Marshal Paulus.

33. Cf. also Doerr, p. 62 et seq.; Greiner, p. 422 et seq., and AS-Protokoll.

34. AS-Protokoll and Herhudt von Rhoden, op. cit., p. 19 et seq. There is as yet no comprehensive analysis of all the problems that bedevilled the air lift.

35. AS-Protokoll.

36. For a description of the personality of General Walther von Seydlitz-Kurzbach cf., inter alios, Hermann Teske: *Die silbernen Spiegel, Generalstabsdienst unter der Lupe*, Heidelberg, 1952. P. 68. The author was operations officer under Seydlitz with the 12th Infantry Division. He praises the simple, uncomplicated thinking of von Seydlitz, and his modesty, but is of the opinion that he lacked contact with the men under him. The author feels that von Seydlitz lacked mental elasticity and that this led him to accept the views of others if they were presented to him with sufficient cogency.

37. Cf. his report, published in: *The Fatal Decisions*. New York, 1956, p. 124 et seq.

38. AS-Protokoll: evidence of Lieutenant-General Schmidt and the observations of Field-Marshal von Paulus.

39. Manstein, p. 303.

40. Greiner, p. 424.

41. Herhudt von Rohden, op. cit., p. 19 et seq.

42. The Diary of the C.-in-C. of Air Fleet 4, General von Richthofen, contains the

following entry for February 10, 1943: 'at 21.30 had a confidential conversation with Reichsmarshal Göring (*in Rominten*). During this discussion the Commander-in-Chief of the Luftwaffe declared . . . that at first he had himself been very optimistic in regard to Stalingrad and had supported the Führer in his decision to hold on there. At first it had seemed as though the envelopment need be no more than temporary. It was only when the Italians gave way that the affair had developed catastrophically. I (*Richthofen*) agreed that this was so, but insisted that we should have seen all the consequences from the start, even before the Italians had broken down. All the decisions that had been taken both before and after that had not been far-sighted, seldom sufficiently determined, and always too late. He (*Göring*) admitted all this, put a good deal of the blame on the army, a good deal on circumstances beyond our control, and a good deal on the fact that although the ideas of the Führer had been correct and prompt the appropriate orders had been too feeble in conception and or execution. . . .'

43. Cf. Manstein, p. 273 et seq., where the Field-Marshal expresses himself in some detail concerning the particular difficulties of commanding an Army Group for the first time in a situation of crisis under the direct influence of the Commander-in-Chief of the Army, i.e. Hitler. On p. 294 et seq., Manstein discusses the development of the situation at Stalingrad.

44. AS-Protokoll.

45. Ibid.

46. Cf. Horst Scheibert: *Nach Stalingrad – 48 Kilometer, Der Entsatzvorstoss der 6. Panzer-Division Dezember 1942*, vol. 10 of *Die Wehrmacht im Kampf*, Heidelberg, 1956. As far as the author is in a position to judge, this is the best description of Operation 'Winter Storm'; Manstein, p. 327 et seq.; Doerr, p. 84 et seq.; Greiner, p. 428 et seq.; AS-Protokoll.

47. AS-Protokoll. Cf. also Manstein, p. 333 et seq., with appendices 10, 11 and 12. Field-Marshal von Manstein takes a very different point of view. According to him Operation 'Winter Storm' logically included the break out and the retreat ('Thunderclap'). Cf. also *Die Welt am Sonntag*, no. 17, April 24, 1960.

48. AS-Protokoll.

49. Ibid.

50. Ibid. Cf. the very severe criticism made by Doerr, p. 118, concerning the attitude of Field-Marshal Paulus during the final phase of the battle for Stalingrad. Major-General Doerr's analysis of the drive for Stalingrad is so far (apart from memoirs such as those of Manstein) the only military historical study of the great battle between the Volga and the Don which is entitled to be taken seriously. Doerr himself writes in his preface: 'The great weakness of my work is that it lacks the evidence of the leading personalities of the 6th Army. Its treatment is also inadequate where the Russian side of the story is concerned because Russian sources could be used only with the greatest caution; they hardly contain any reliable information concerning Russian intentions, instructions and troop movements'. The present investigation was at least in a position to repair the first omission mentioned by Doerr, in that it uses the evidence and the material of the Chief of Staff of the 6th Army. As far as Russian sources are concerned, the situation remains unsatisfactory, though in the meantime the memoirs of Marshal Yeremenko (*Stalingrad Front*) and of Marshal

Zhukov on the 62nd Army have been published. These memoirs were not available to the author at the time of writing. Cf. also note 29.

51. Cf. also V. I. *Chuikov: The Beginning of the Road*, London, MacGibbon & Kee, 1963; and A. M. Samsonov: *Stalingradskaya bitva*, Moscow, 1960.

52. Cf. B. Scheurig: *Freies Deutschland. Das Nationalkommittee und der Bund Deutscher Offiziere in der Sowjetunion 1943–1945*, Munich, 1960.

1. In this connection cf. Erich Raeder: *Struggle for the Sea*, London, Kimber, 1959 (hereafter referred to as Raeder). Pp. 57–69 and 121–134; Karl Dönitz: *Memoirs – Ten Years and Twenty Days*, London, Weidenfeld & Nicolson, 1959 (hereafter referred to as Dönitz). Pp. 9–50; Friedrich Ruge: *Der Seekrieg 1939–45*, Stuttgart, 1955. Pp. 28–40; Kurt Assmann: *Deutsche Seestrategie in zwei Weltkriegen*, Heidelberg, 1957. Pp. 116–129; Rolf Bensel: *Die deutsche Flottenpolitik von 1933–1939, Eine Studie über die Rolle des Flottenbaues in Hitlers Aussenpolitik;* in: Beiheft 3 zur *Marine-Rundschau*, Frankfurt, 1958.
2. Cf. IMT, vol. XXXV, Doc. 855–D. Cf. also Ruge, op. cit., 27–9. For ships' types cf. Erich Gröner: *Die Schiffe der deutschen Kriegsmarine und Luftwaffe 1939–45 und ihr Verbleib*, Munich, 1954. For building dates of ships cf. Bensel, pp. 71–7.
3. Cf. Dönitz, p. 33. The Memorandum of C.-in-C. U-boats of August 28, 1939, is contained in extract in: Brassey's *Naval Annual*, 1948. Pp. 36–7.
4. Main sources: Kriegstagebuch der Seekriegsleitung (Skl), Part A, and KTB des Führers bzw. Befehlshabers der Unterseeboote (F.bzw. B.d.U.) for the period from August 18, 1939, to April 8, 1940. Cf. also: Raeder, pp. 170–198; Dönitz, pp. 51–74. For the Allied side: S. W. Roskill: *The War at Sea*, vol. I, *The Defensive*, in: *History of the Second World War* (hereafter referred to as Roskill I), London, HMSO, 1954. Pp. 41–145.
5. For the development of international law in respect of submarine warfare, cf. Herbert Sohler: *U-Bootkrieg und Völkerrecht*, Beiheft 1 zur *Marine-Rundschau*, Frankfurt, 1956.
6. The figures for losses given here and subsequently have been arrived at by the author in close co-operation with many German and foreign experts. The basis is the British list: 'British and Foreign Merchant Vessels lost or damaged by Enemy Action during the Second World War from September 3, 1939, to September 2, 1945. Naval Staff (Trade Division) Admiralty, October 1, 1945 (BR 1337 Restricted).' The information was checked against German war diaries, the official lists of ships lost published in many other countries, and numerous published and unpublished sources and studies.
7. In this connection cf. Raeder, pp. 173–5; Dönitz, pp. 75–99 and 482–5. A subsequent calculation by the Naval Staff Operations Officer came to the conclusion that if the torpedoes discharged during the Norwegian operation had functioned accurately at least 1 of 4 battleships attacked, 7 of 12 cruisers and 7 of 10 destroyers would have been hit. Similarly, during the five attacks on transport vessels numerous hits would have been recorded.
8. Of the 20 U-boats committed, 2 sank over 40,000 GRT, 5 others sank more than 30,000 GRT, and 6 sank between 20,000 and 30,000 GRT. The most successful of these U-boats was *U.47*, which sank 55,577 GRT.
9. For this period cf. KTB des B.d.U. for the period from July 1940 to March 1941: Dönitz, pp. 100–117; Roskill I, pp. 343–365.

10. In the night of September 21st to 22nd, 5 U-boats (*U.47, U.48, U.99, U.100* and *U.65*) sank 12 vessels sailing in Convoy HX. 72 amounting to a total of 77,863 GRT; from October 17th to 20th, 8 U-boats (*U.46, U.47, U.48, U.99, U.100, U.101, U.38* and *U.123*) sank in two immediately successive battles 31 ships amounting to a total of 152,849 GRT sailing in Convoys SC. 7 and HX. 79; in the night of December 1st to 2nd, 7 U-boats (*U.47, U.52, U.94, U.95, U.99, U.101* and *U.103*) sank 11 ships amounting to a total of 70,352 GRT sailing in Convoy HX. 90. U-boats also recorded successes in individual attacks on convoys, for example the *U.100*, which sank 20,975 GRT in Convoy HX. 65 on August 29th, and 24,601 GRT in Convoy SC. 11 on November 23rd. It is noticeable that it was the same U-boats which were successful again and again.

11. Cf. KTB des B.d.U. from July to December 1940, and in particular the entry for December 5, 1940; Dönitz, pp. 144–150; and also an unpublished study by the author: 'The operations of Italian submarines in the Atlantic 1940–43', which is based on material supplied by the Ufficio Storico della Marina Militare in Rome, and various German war diaries.

12. Cf. in particular the KTB des B.d.U. for January 6, 1941; Dönitz, pp. 127–142; Walter Gaul: *Marinefliegeverbände und operative Luftwaffe in Einsatz über See*, in: *Marine-Rundschau*, No. 50 (1950), pp. 71–6.

13. This was the *U.47* (Prien), which was sunk on March 8, 1941, by the destroyer *Wolverine* while attacking Convoy OB. 293; and the *U.99* (Kretschmer) and the *U.100* (Schepke), which were sunk on March 17, 1941, by the destroyers *Vanoc* and *Walker* while attacking Convoy HX. 112. In the second phase of the Battle of the Atlantic, Kretschmer's U-boat sank 37 ships amounting to a total of 241,523 GRT, Schepke's U-boat sank 28 ships amounting to a total of 141,043 GRT, and Prien's U-boat sank 22 vessels amounting to a total of 134,950 GRT. Cf. the British account of the destruction of these three U-boats, in Donald Macintyre: *U-boat Killer*, Weidenfeld & Nicolson, London, 1956. Pp. 301–344.

14. Cf. in this respect KTB der Skl, Part A for October 1940 to May 1941; KTB des B.d.U. from March to December 1941; Dönitz, pp. 171–182; Roskill I, pp. 451–482.

15. Cf. in addition to many individual descriptions, the summary by Gerhard Hümmelchen: *Handelsstörer. Handelskrieg deutscher Überwasserstreitkräfte im Zweiten Weltkrieg*, Munich, 1960; Roskill I, pp. 381–8 and pp. 541–552; David Woodward: *The Secret Raiders*, London, 1955.

16. Cf. Raeder, pp. 203–216; Kurt Assmann: *Deutsche Schicksalsjahre*, Wiesbaden, 1950. Pp. 231–254.

17. Gerhard Bidlingmaier: *Erfolg und Ende des Schlachtschiffes Bismarck*, in *Wehrwissensch. Rdsch.* No. 9 (1959), pp. 261–281; Roskill I, pp. 393–418.

18. Roskill I, pp. 541–7. The question, of course, arises as to what influence the capture of the *U.110* off Iceland on May 9, 1941, together with secret material found on board (code and cypher books, operational orders, etc.), a success the British kept secret, had on the subsequent *Bismarck* operation, and, in particular, on the mopping up of the German ocean supply organization. In his book *The Secret Capture*, S. W. Roskill gives nothing away on this point – obviously on higher instructions.

19. The most successful was the *U.107* (Hessler) with 86,699 GRT, followed by *U.105* with 74,932 GRT, the *U.103* with 62,834 GRT, the *U.106* with 57,652 GRT (the *U.106* also torpedoed the battleship *Malaya*), the *U.124* with 57,626 GRT and the *U.38* with 46,678 GRT.

20. KTB des B.d.U. from March 26 to 28, 1941. For the British counter-measures to the U-boat campaign cf. Roskill I, pp. 354–365 and pp. 451–467; Richards and Saunders: *Royal Air Force 1939–1945*, vol. I, London, HMSO, 1953. Pp. 343–375.

21. For example, the attack on Convoy OB. 318 from May 7th to 10th with 4 U-boats, including the *U.110*, which sank 57,941 GRT; and the attack on Convoy HX. 126 with 5 U-boats on May 20th and 21st, which sank 54,452 GRT.

22. Attack on Convoy HX. 133 with 7 U-boats from June 24th to 29th during which 57,219 GRT were sunk. Cf. KTB des B.d.U. from June 23 to 30, 1941.

23. Cf. KTB des B.d.U. for July and August 1941. In the attack on Convoy OG. 69, from July 27th to 29th, 5 out of 9 U-boats managed to get into position to attack and 9 ships were sunk totalling 25,288 GRT. In the attack on Convoy SL. 81 from August 1st to 15th, 4 out of 12 U-boats managed to attack, sinking 5 ships totalling 23,190 GRT. In the attack on Convoy HG. 69 between August 10th and 16th all 9 U-boats were driven off. 4 out of 7 U-boats managed to attack Convoy OG. 71 between August 17th and 23rd, and 2 escort vessels and 8 other ships were sunk representing a total of 13,223 GRT. In the attack on Convoy OS. 4, 2 out of 6 U-boats managed to go into action, sinking 5 ships representing a total of 30,705 GRT.

24. The Pan-American Security Zone in the North Atlantic ran from 60° W. Off the coasts of South America it was respected by Germany up to three hundred sea miles from the shore. For the story of its development cf. Jürgen Rohwer: *Das deutsch-amerikanische Verhältnis 1937–1941*, phil., diss., Hamburg, 1953, unpublished MS., pp. 84–114.

25. 2 out of 5 U-boats which attacked Convoy SC. 44 (September 19th to 20th) sank 25,652 GRT; 5 out of 9 U-boats which attacked Convoy SC. 48 between October 15th and 17th sank 47,719 GRT including 2 escort vessels, and not including the torpedoed US destroyer *Kearny*; and 3 out of 12 U-boats which attacked Convoy SC. 52 (November 3rd) in fog sank 20,003 GRT. At the same time operations were continued on the Gibraltar–Freetown route, and the following convoys were attacked and heavy losses inflicted: OG. 74 (8,692 GRT); HG. 73 (25,818 GRT); SL. 81 (33,290 GRT); HG. 74 (8,772 GRT). All the U-boats which tried to attack Convoy OG. 75 were driven off.

26. Cf. Dönitz, pp. 183–194; Samuel E. Morison: *The Battle of the Atlantic, September 1939 to May 1943*, in *History of U.S. Naval Operations in World War II*, vol. I, Boston, 1948 (subsequently referred to as Morison). Pp. 56–114. A summary of breaches of neutrality recorded by the German side is to be found in KTB der Skl, Part C, no. VIII, App. 35.

27. According to 'Cinclant Operation Plan No. 7', of September 1, 1941, this 'Denmark Strait Patrol' consisted of 2 battleships, 2 heavy cruisers and 13 destroyers, and thus it was considerably stronger than the previous British naval forces there. At the beginning of November this force sailed to intercept the *Tirpitz* on its planned break-out into the Atlantic. Cf. Morison, pp. 81–2.

28. This directive was issued in addition to the already existing orders (for example,

'Directive for the Conduct of the War against Merchant Shipping of June 10, 1941, 1.Skl, 1a 10970/41 g.Kdos') on June 21, 1941, after the *U.203* had met the US battleship *Texas* on the verge of the German operational area on June 19th (cf. KTB des B.d.U. from June 19 to 21, 1941). Further teleprints issued by the German Admiralty on July 10th, September 5th, September 9th, and November 21st pointed out that this directive was still in force.

29. KTB des B.d.U. of June 21, 1941.

30. Ibid., from September 3 to 9, 1941; Dönitz, pp. 191–2; Morison, pp. 79–81.

31. KTB des B.d.U. from October 15 to 19, 1941; Morison, pp. 92–3; Jürgen Rohwer: *Der 'Kearny' Zwischenfall*, in: *Marine-Rundschau*, No. 56 (1959). P. 288 et seq.

32. Cf. Führer Conferences, September 17, 1941.

33. KTB des B.d.U. of December 9, 1941.

34. Dönitz, pp. 195–7.

35. For example, in April and May the *U.106* and the *U.105* were withdrawn for seven and two weeks respectively during this particularly successful phase of the campaign against merchant shipping on the Freetown route for escort duties within the Pan-American Security Zone, an area in which they were forbidden to use their armaments in any way. Cf. KTB des B.d.U. of April 7, 1941. At the beginning of November 1941 when 49 U-boats were available for active service, the German Naval Operations Staff claimed the services of 20 of them: 6 to escort blockade runners, 4 to carry out reconnaissance duties for a naval surface operation, 4 for service in the North Sea, and another 6 for the Mediterranean. In consequence planned attacks on convoys in the Atlantic had to be abandoned. Cf. KTB des B.d.U. of November 5, 1941.

36. The successes obtained by the U-boats sent into the Mediterranean, including the sinking of the aircraft carrier *Ark Royal* and of the battleship *Barham*, together with the successful results obtained by Italian charioteers with their small underwater craft, and the laying of minefields, contributed materially to the change in the fortunes of the Axis powers in that theatre of the war. Cf. also the contribution of Walter Warlimont to the present book.

37. Cf. KTB des B.d.U. of April 15 and May 3, 1942; Dönitz, pp. 206–211.

38. Dönitz, p. 196.

39. This device was a pressure-resisting container built into the flooded space between the pressure hull and the upper deck. With Type VII 2 extra torpedoes could be stowed away in this fashion, and with the Type IX U-boats between 9 and 12 extra torpedoes could be carried. However, calm weather was necessary before they could be got into the U-boat itself.

40. Roskill: Vol. II, *The Period of Balance*, London, 1957 (subsequently referred to as Roskill II). Pp. 96–102; Morison, pp. 114–157, 202–310.

41. KTB des B.d.U. of May 23, 1942; Dönitz, pp. 219–221.

42. Cf. Jürgen Rohwer: *Die erfolgreichsten Handelskriegs-Unternehmungen von U-Booten im Zweiten Weltkrieg*, in *Marine-Rundschau*, No. 53 (1956). Pp. 252–3. Out of the 27 U-boats operating in this area from April to June 1942 19 U-boats returned to base having sunk over 30,000 GRT each; 14 having sunk over 40,000 GRT each; and 3 having sunk over 50,000 GRT each. The most successful of all was the *U.158* (Commander Rostin) which sank 65,108

GRT. Of the 5 Italian submarines operating in March and April 3 returned to base having sunk more than 20,000 GRT each.

43. 334,057 GRT sunk by U-boats, 153,603 GRT during raids by surface craft other than auxiliary cruisers, which were responsible for sinking 31,342 GRT.

44. 23 U-boats sank only 37,516 GRT between them; the remainder was sunk by the Luftwaffe and the Italian Air Force, S-boats, air and sea mines and an Italian submarine (3,723 GRT).

45. 24 U-boats sank only 82,690 GRT, and 62,536 GRT represented sinkings of ships already damaged by the Luftwaffe. 141,496 GRT sunk by air attack alone, 10,509 GRT by air mines, 10,600 GRT by destroyer attacks, and 31,191 GRT represented ships sunk by accidentally steaming into British-laid minefields.

46. Cf. in this respect Maurice Matloff and Edwin M. Snell: *Strategic Planning for Coalition Warfare*, in *U.S. Army in World War II*, The War Department, Washington, 1953. Pp. 49, 107–8, 308–312; Richard M. Leighton and Robert W. Coakley: *Global Logistics and Strategy, 1940–1943*, ibid., Washington, 1955; C. B. A. Behrens: *Merchant Shipping and the Demands of War*, in *History of the Second World War*, United Kingdom Civil Series, London, 1955.

47. As in February against Convoy ONS. 63 (3 U-boats: 1 corvette sunk); against Convoy SC. 67 (2 U-boats: 1 corvette and 1 merchantship sunk); against Convoy HX. 175 (4 U-boats: failure); against Convoy ONS. 67 (6 U-boats: 8 merchant ships representing 54,750 GRT sunk); and in March against Convoy ONS. 76 (4 U-boats: failure). Cf. KTB des B.d.U., February 4 to 7, 10 to 12, and 22 to 25, and from March 29 to 30, 1942.

48. Cf. KTB des B.d.U., May 1 to 15, 1942; Dönitz, pp. 222–3.

49. Cf. KTB des B.d.U. of July 19, 1942, with situation summary.

50. Ibid., April 15 and October 2, 1942, situation summaries.

51. Descriptions of the convoy battles in this period from the side of the U-boats concerned, cf. Harald Busch: *U-boats at War*, London, Clowes, 1955; Wolfgang Frank: *Die Wölfe und der Admiral*, 2nd ed., Oldenburg, 1957. Pp. 317–344.

52. Roskill II, pp. 103–111.

53. Dönitz, pp. 241–2.

54. Cf. Morison, pp. 377–380; *A marinha brasileira e a segunda guerra mondial 1939–1945*, Rio de Janeiro, 1953. P. 8 et seq.; KTB des B.d.U., May 15, 16, 24, 29 and 30, and June 16 and 29, 1942; War Diary of the U.507 of August 15 to 19, 1942; further Werner Haupt: 'Brasilien im zweiten Weltkrieg', in: *Marine-Rundschau* No. 54 (1957), pp. 141–145.

55. KTB des B.d.U. August 1 to 15, 1942.

56. On September 12th the *U.156* sank the *Laconia*. For details concerning the *Laconia* incident cf. Dönitz, pp. 255–264; Roskill II, pp. 210–11; A. Vulliez: 'A propos l'Affaire du "Laconia",' in *Revue Maritime*, No. 96 (1954), pp. 499–512; and Jacques Mordal: 'Les Survivants du "Laconia",' in *Revue Maritime*, No. 96 (1954), pp. 177–195. At the beginning of October the Italian submarine *Archimede* sank the *Oronsay*, the *U.172* sank the *Orcades*, and the *U.178* sank the *Duchess of Atholl*. On the basis of various reports, wireless monitoring and sinkings since August 22nd, the British Admiralty reckoned with a U-boat campaign in Cape Town waters. Cf. Turner, Gordon-Cumming, Betzler: *The War in the Southern Oceans 1939–1945*, Cape Town, 1961. Pp. 152–188.

57. Of these 'Eisbär' U-boats, *U.68* sank 61,649 GRT, the *U.172* 59,801 GRT, the *U.159* 55,918 GRT, and the *U.504* 41,638 GRT, while of the following Type IX–D–boats, the *U.181* sank 58,381 GRT, the *U.178* sank 53,445 GRT, and the *U.177* 49,371 GRT.

58. Cf. the contribution of Walter Warlimont to the present book.

59. Cf. KTB des B.d.U. of November 8, 1942.

60. As early as November 7th a U-boat torpedoed the troop transport *Thomas Stone*, and on November 11th the *U.380* and the *U.407* sank the big troop transports *Nieuwe Zeeland* and *Viceroy of India* between them. Off Bougie the Italian submarines *Argo* and *Platino* gave the *coup de grâce* to three transports which had been seriously damaged by the Luftwaffe and abandoned.

61. On November 14th, the *U.413* sank the big troop transport *Warwick Castle*, and the *U.155* sank the escort carrier *Avenger* and the merchant vessel *Ettrick*, and torpedoed a further unnamed vessel sailing in convoy. The *U.515* made a number of determined runs carried out with great persistence and finally sank the depot ship *Hecla*.

62. Cf. KTB des B.d.U. from November 16 to 26, 1942.

63. Ibid., from December 26, 1942, to January 1, 1943; Roskill II, p. 216.

64. Cf. KTB des B.d.U., January 15 and 19, 1943.

65. Ibid., February 12, 1943.

66. Cf. also Dönitz on the point, pp. 299–314.

67. This figure was so much above the results actually achieved because the reports of the Luftwaffe, the Italians and the Japanese concerning their successes often exceeded the actual successes several times over, owing to the inability to judge accurately at the time. The reports of U-boat commanders on their successes, which were very accurate on the whole in the days of individual attacks in the Atlantic, now also became progressively less accurate. This was due to the lack of opportunity for observing the results obtained during the convoy battles; when several U-boats attacked the same target a success was often duplicated in the reports of the various commanders.

68. Cf. the KTB des B.d.U. of February 6 and March 5, 1943. Cf. also the record of the discussion between the German Naval C.-in-C. and the Führer at the Berghof on April 11, 1943: 1/Skl, Ib 1197/43 g.Kdos. Chefs.

69. Cf. for example the KTB des B.d.U. of February 25 and March 5, 1943.

70. Ibid., March 5, 1943.

71. Ibid., February 25 and 26, 1943; also the record of the report made by the German Naval C.-in-C. to the Führer at his HQ on February 26, 1943; 1/Skl, Ib 680/43 g.Kdos. Chefs.

72. Cf. KTB des B.d.U. of February 6, 1943.

73. Winston S. Churchill: *The Second World War*, vol. V, *Closing the Ring*, London, 1952. Pp. 3–10; Roskill II, pp. 88–9.

74. John Herington: *Air War against Germany and Italy 1939–1943*, in *Australia in the War of 1939–1945*, Canberra, 1954. P. 416; John Slessor: *The Central Blue*, London, 1956. Pp. 464–507; cf. also Philip Joubert: *The Third Service*, London, 1955. Pp. 191–205; W. S. Chalmers: *Max Horton and the Western Approaches*, London, 1954. Pp. 173–203.

75. Chalmers, op. cit., pp. 156–160; Roskill II, p. 201; Churchill, op.cit., vol. V, p. 8.

76. From 1941 to 1944 Captain Walker with his escort group sank twenty-four U-boats. Cf. Terence Robertson: *Walker R.N.*, London, 1956.
77. Roskill II, pp. 362–373; Richards and Saunders: *The Fight Avails*, in *The Royal Air Force 1939–1945*, vol. II, London, 1954. P. 278; Herington, op. cit., p. 416; Slessor, op. cit., pp. 523–535.
78. Ernest J. King and Walter M. Whitehill: *Fleet Admiral King, A Naval Record*, New York, 1952 (subsequently referred to as King). Pp. 462–474; Morison, vol. X, pp. 26–31; Wesley Frank Craven and James Lea Cate: *The Army Air Forces in World War II*, vol. II, *Torch to Point-Blank, August 1942 to December 1943*, Chicago, 1949. Pp. 378–411.
79. Cf. King, pp. 414–430; Roskill II, pp. 351–362; Morison, vol. X, p. 16; Craven and Cate, op. cit., pp. 305–308; Richards and Saunders, op. cit., p. 278.
80. These bunkers were built in the ports and harbours of Western France by the Organization Todt at Hitler's suggestion. For some inexplicable reason they were never attacked from the air when they were in course of construction in the years 1941 and 1942. By the time the air attacks began they were already completed, and despite all the attacks, which continued until German forces evacuated the area in 1944, they were never seriously damaged and no single bomb ever penetrated inside them. Cf. Dönitz, pp. 409–410; Roskill II, pp. 348–352, 459; Richards and Saunders, op. cit., pp. 281–3; Arthur Harris: *Bomber Offensive*, London, 1947. Pp. 137–9.
81. Richards and Saunders, op. cit., pp. 114–5.
82. According to Roskill II, p. 353.
83. Slessor, op. cit., p. 497.
84. Roskill II, pp. 361–2; Richards and Saunders, op. cit., pp. 106–7; Slessor, op. cit., pp. 497–8.
85. Roskill II, pp. 358–360; Morison, vol. X, pp. 19–20, 27; King, pp. 461–5; Slessor, op. cit., pp. 497–507; Gilbert N. Tucker: *The Naval Service of Canada*, vol. II, *Activities on Shore during the Second World War*, Ottawa, 1952. Pp. 409–417.
86. The KTB des B.d.U. of March 12 to 21, 1943, and Roskill II, pp. 365–6 and Map no. 38, served as the basis for the subsequent description.
87. This is the conclusion of the 'Admiralty Monthly A/S Report (Red Book)' of December 1943, p. 3 (quoted from Morison, vol. X, p. 344).
88. Roskill II, p. 368.
89. Ibid., p. 367; Chalmers, op. cit., p. 188. The composition of the individual groups could vary from mission to mission, but generally speaking an effort was made to keep together the experienced groups used to working with each other. The official name for them was 'escort group', but here and subsequently they are referred to as 'support group' in order to avoid confusion.
90. Naval slang for HF/DF, the 'High-Frequency Direction Finder', which, from being exclusively land-based, was now fitted into sea-going vessels. Morison, vol. II, p. 20.
91. According to KTB des B.d.U. from March 21 to 30, 1942; Roskill II, p. 366.
92. Cf. KTB des B.d.U. from March 31 to April 20, 1942, and April 6 to 16, 1943.
93. At this time there were 12 'ocean escort groups', 7 under British command (B.1 to B.7) and 5 under Canadian command (C.1 to C.5). The three groups under US command (A.1 to A.3) were withdrawn at the beginning of April.

These groups usually consisted of between 7 and 8 vessels: 2 or 3 destroyers, 1 or 2 frigates, and from 4 to 6 corvettes, including vessels with French, Norwegian or Polish crews.

94. The very reliable statistical calculations of Department 3 of the German Naval Operations Staff gave a quite accurate picture of the development of the situation on the whole, but could exercise no effect on the operational decisions of C.-in-C. U-boats.

95. Roskill II, pp. 362–373; Morison, vol. X, p. 44.

96. Cf. KTB des B.d.U. from April 17 to 25, 1943.

97. Macintyre, op. cit., pp. 104–112. 'Asdic', an underwater echo apparatus for detecting submarines, roughly the equivalent of the German 'S. device', and the US 'Sonar'. 'Bold', pot containing chemicals which produced bubbles after release; these bubbles greatly hampered Asdic-location. 'Torpex', a more efficient explosive for depth-charges. 'Hedgehog', a salvo-mortar, which launched 24 light depth-charges with contact fuses ahead of the ship. They detonated only after hitting a submarine and could be used also by ships running very slowly to enable them to maintain Asdic contact with the attacked submarine.

98. According to KTB des B.d.U. from March 26 to May 6, 1943; Morison, vol. X, pp. 64–76; Roskill II, p. 373.

99. Cf. KTB des B.d.U. of May 6, 1943.

100. Ibid., from May 7 to 14, 1943; Morison, vol. X, pp. 77–8; Macintyre op. cit., pp. 122–136.

101. KTB des B.d.U. from May 15 to 24, 1943; *The Battle of the Atlantic, the Official Account*, London, HMSO, 1945. P. 63; Chalmers, op. cit., pp. 195–7; Roskill II, pp. 375–6; Herington, op. cit., pp. 433–4.

102. Dönitz, German edition, p. 339.

103. For example, Assmann, op. cit., pp. 169–172.

104. For example, Karl Silex, review of Dönitz's book *Zehn Jahre und zwanzig Tage*, in *Tagesspiegel*, November 8, 1958.

105. Record of the discussion between the German Naval C.-in-C. and the Führer at the Berghof on May 31, 1943, 1/Skl, 1614/43 g.Kdos-Chefs., June 5, 1943.

106. Ibid.

107. Ibid.

108. Dönitz, German edition, p. 417.

109. Roskill: 'An Epic Victory', in the *Sunday Times*, February 8, 1959.

1. B. Stjernfelt: *Alarm i Atlantvallen*, Stockholm, 1960. P. 33.
2. For full translation see G. A. Harrison: *Cross-Channel Attack*, Washington, 1951. P. 459.
3. Contrary to S. W. Roskill: *The War at Sea*, vol. II, London, 1956. P. 251.
4. Oberkommando der Kriegsmarine 1/Skl. 1b 1363/42 g.k.Chefs.
5. Morison: *U.S.N. Operations in World War II*, vol. II, Boston, 1948. P. 14; M. Matloff and E. M. Snell: *Strategic Planning for Coalition Warfare 1941–42*, Washington, 1959. P. 186.
6. G. A. Harrison, op. cit., p. 69.
7. Various Orders of Naval Operations Staff and Marinegruppen Kdo. West, starting with 'Preparatory Measures for major Enemy Landings' dated January 26, 1942; Luftwaffe High Command Ob.d.L. Füst Ia No. 03071/43 g.Kdos, dated July 23, 1943; Army: Grundlegende Befehle des Oberbefehlhabers West, No. 20 (Principles of coastal defence), dated December 18, 1942; etc.
8. For full text see G. A. Harrison, op. cit., p. 464.
9. A. Norman: *Operation Overlord*, Harrisburg, 1952. Pp. 124–9.
10. Ibid., pp. 32–3.
11. Evaluation of German Naval Operations Staff, dated August 16, 1943.
12. A. Norman, op. cit., pp. 94–5.
13. G. A. Harrison, op. cit., p. 147.
14. Karl Gundelach: 'Drohende Gefahr West', in: *Wehrwissenschaftliche Rundschau*, June 1959.
15. G. A. Harrison, op. cit., p. 153.
16. Von Sodenstern told the author on May 2, 1944, that he had only then fully grasped Rommel's ideas concerning defence, and that he was annoyed with himself that he had not done so earlier.
17. G. A. Harrison, op. cit., p. 261.
18. Ibid., p. 264.
19. W. Gaul: 'Die deutsche Luftwaffe während der Invasion 1944', in: *Wehrwissenschaftliche Rundschau*, March 1953; K. Gundelach, op. cit.
20. Geyr von Schweppenburg: 'Invasion without Laurels', in: *Cosantoir Irish Defence Journal*, December 1949. P. 577.
21. A. Norman, op. cit., pp. 113–121.
22. K. Gundelach, op. cit., p. 318.
23. A. Norman, op. cit., p. 156.
24. K. Edwards: *Operation Neptune*, London, 1946. Pp. 126–7.
25. H. Speidel: *Invasion 1944*, London, Herbert Jenkins, 1951.
26. G. A. Harrison, op. cit., p. 336.
27. H. Speidel, op. cit.
28. Chester Wilmot: *Struggle for Europe*, London, 1952. P. 387.
29. H. Speidel, op. cit.
30. G. A. Harrison, op. cit., p. 441.

31. Ibid., pp. 378–9.
32. KTB des OKW, 1940–45, vol. IV, Part I, Frankfurt on Main, 1961. P. 324.
G. A. Harrison, op. cit., p. 447.
33. K. Edwards, op. cit., p. 238.
34. J. Rohwer: 'Les sousmarines allemands contre les tentatives alliés en Manche 1944', in *Revue Maritime*, No. 181, 1961. Pp. 1,220–1,233.
35. K. Edwards, op. cit., p. 210.
36. KTB des OKW 1940–45, vol. IV, Part I, Frankfurt on Main, 1961. P. 326.
37. For fuller text, see Speidel, op. cit.
38. Ernst Jünger: *Strahlungen*, Tübingen, 1949.
39. J. F. C. Fuller: *The Second World War*, London, 1948. Pp. 299–300.
40. Chester Wilmot, op. cit., p. 354.
41. *Strand Magazine*, July 1946.
42. Chester Wilmot, op. cit., pp. 193–4.

THE COLLAPSE OF ARMY GROUP CENTRE IN 1944

1. The main source for the following account of the collapse of Army Group Centre is its War Diary, for which the author was responsible during the decisive years 1943/5. In August 1944, immediately after these events, the author drew up a comprehensive memorandum, 'The Collapse of Army Group Centre'. This has since been published under the title 'Dokumentation zum Zusammenbruch der Heeresgruppe Mitte im Sommer 1944' in: *Vierteljahrshefte für Zeitgeschichte*, 1955, vol. 3. P. 317 et seq. (hereinafter referred to as 'Dokumentation'). Cf. also: Kurt von Tippelskirch: *Geschichte des zweiten Weltkrieges*, Bonn, 1956. P. 460 et seq.; Edgar Röhricht: *Probleme der Kesselschlacht*, Karlsruhe, 1958. P. 102 et seq.; Otto Heidkämper: *Witebsk, Kampf und Untergang der 3.Pz-Armee*, Heidelberg, 1954; Helmut Teske: *Die silbernen Spiegel*, Heidelberg, 1952. And from the Russian standpoint: *Die wichtigsten Operationen des Grossen Vaterländischen Krieges 1941–1945*, edited and translated by P. A. Zhilin, Berlin, 1958 (henceforth referred to here as Zhilin). Also an older but fuller account by A. Guillaume: *La guerre germano-soviétique 1941–1945*, Paris, 1949. For general reference also: R. L. Garthoff: *Die Sowjetarmee, Wesen und Lehre*, Cologne, 1955; and B. H. Liddell Hart: *The Soviet Army*, London, Weidenfeld & Nicolson, 1956.
2. War Diary Army Group Centre, April 2, 1944.
3. Röhricht, op. cit., p. 107.
4. War Diary Army Group Centre, April 15, 1944; cf. also Heidkämper, op. cit., p. 124 et seq.
5. War Diary Army Group Centre, May 5, 1944.
6. Ibid., June 4, 1944.
7. Röhricht, op. cit., p. 107.
8. 'Dokumentation', p. 321; according to information given by General Krebs to the author at the time.
9. Röhricht, op. cit., p. 116.
10. Ibid., p. 108.
11. Zhilin, op. cit., p. 413.
12. Teske, op. cit., p. 218.
13. Zhilin, op. cit., p. 410.
14. Ibid., p. 415.
15. The strengths are taken from the sketch in Röhricht's book, op. cit., p. 109, and are obviously based on an Operations Branch Situation Map.
16. The description given by Zhilin, op. cit., provides very little accurate and useful information. One gets the impression that he relies a good deal on Tippelskirch and takes over his views. The contention that the Russian High Command originally intended the envelopment of the 4th Army is undoubtedly *ex eventu*.
17. Soviet sources put the date on which the offensive began as June 23, 1944.
18. Röhricht, op. cit., p. 108 et seq.
19. The description of the battle in White Russia is based on the memorandum of

the author of August 1944 ('Dokumentation') which was drawn up at a time when he was in charge of the War Diary and had all the available material at his disposal and, in addition, verbal information from the Chief of Staff and Operations Officer of Army Group Centre. It has now been revised on the basis of the War Diary, and it has been supplemented in respect of the high-level decisions, which had to be treated with great discretion at the time. This also applies to the observations of Tippelskirch, op. cit., and to a later study on the 'envelopment battles', which is used in Röhricht's book referred to above.

20. War Diary Army Group Centre of June 23, 1944.
21. Ibid., June 23, 1944 (telephone conversation Chief of the Operations Branch – Chief of Staff Army Group Centre).
22. Ibid., June 24, 1944; cf. also Heidkämper, op. cit., p. 153.
23. War Diary Army Group Centre, June 24, 1944. In this connection there was a sharp personal conflict between Tippelskirch and Busch, which was subsequently reflected in the accounts of both Tippelskirch and Röhricht.
24. Tippelskirch, op. cit., p. 462.
25. Ibid., p. 463.
26. 'Dokumentation', p. 326. The text is taken literally from the War Diary of Army Group Centre for June 25, 1944. The author readily recalls the indignation this order issued by Hitler caused in the Operations Staff of Army Group Centre.
27. Cf. also the description of the 'military strategist' Hitler given by E. von Manstein in his book *Lost Victories*, London, Methuen, 1958. P. 285 et seq.
28. Zhilin, op. cit., p. 418.
29. War Diary Army Group Centre of June 28, 1944. The War Diary does not indicate the reasons for the withdrawal nor whose idea it was. As far as the author can remember Busch was astonished at the withdrawal. He felt it as mortifying and he avoided the discussion with Field-Marshal Model suggested by General Zeitzler, by leaving. There was no question of any illness.
30. Ibid., July 1, 1944.
31. Zhilin, op. cit., p. 419.
32. War Diary Army Group Centre, July 3, 1944 (Assessment of Situation).
33. Röhricht, op. cit., p. 114.
34. Ibid., p. 110.
35. This view is in accordance with that of General von Tippelskirch, since deceased, who often discussed this particular question with the author. Cf. note 23. The considerably sharper formulations used by Röhricht, op. cit. (although they also derive fundamentally from the views of von Tippelskirch) go too far in their general judgement of the situation. The attempt to place the whole burden of responsibility for the catastrophe on to the shoulders of HQ Army Group Centre is not in accordance with the real facts of the situation. It is not true that the Army Group Command was 'more accommodating than is usual at such a high level of command' (Röhricht, op. cit., p. 116). Open and vehement opposition was no use where Hitler was concerned and it merely led to the dismissal of the commander-in-chief concerned, as witness the fate of von Manstein, Kleist and Lindemann. By 1944 the chain of command in the Wehrmacht was such that the decision of the dictator, at the same time head of the Wehrmacht, was final. It was impossible even for an Army Group commander to oppose a direct *order* given by Hitler. Field-Marshal Model therefore always did his best

not to let things go so far that Hitler could take up an uncompromising position where he was concerned. Model, who was inwardly independent of Hitler, frequently (though by no means always) managed to gain more than Field-Marshal Busch could, who was tied to his 'Führer'.

THE BATTLE OF THE ARDENNES 1944-5

1. Von Tippelskirch: *Geschichte des zweiten Weltkriegs*, Bonn, Athenäum, 1951 (hereafter referred to as von Tippelskirch). P. 518: 'The order to attack given to the 5th Panzer Army lacked all practical foundation, and it developed into defensive instructions, which were far more in accordance with the real situation, to close the gap which had opened up between the 1st and the 19th Armies as far west as possible. These instructions were successfully carried out in fourteen days' hard fighting, at the end of which, by the beginning of October, a continuous front had been established on both sides of Luneville.'

2. Guderian: *Panzer Leader*, London, Michael Joseph, 1952 (hereafter referred to as Guderian). P. 373. Cf. also von Tippelskirch, p. 504: 'The behaviour of Germany's leaders was already a puzzle to those of the enemy camp. They had the feeling that the Germans were deliberately laying themselves open to destruction. In the same way they were quite unable to understand how the Germans could concentrate armoured divisions in such a confined area without air cover'. P. 598: 'How difficult it is to build up powerful new armoured divisions in a short space of time can be seen from the fact that the eleven German armoured divisions on the Western Front in August were only weak groups each consisting of about ten tanks, and with not more than a hundred tanks all told.'

3. Montgomery: *The Memoirs of Field Marshal the Viscount Montgomery of Alamein*, London, Collins, 1958. P. 274: 'My transport is based on operating 150 miles from my ports and at present I am over 300 miles from Bayeux. . . . It is clear therefore that based as I am at present on Bayeux I cannot capture the Ruhr.' Chester Wilmot: *The Struggle for Europe*, London, Collins, 1952 (hereafter referred to as Wilmot). P. 566: 'The ammunition crisis became so acute that Eisenhower himself broadcast a special appeal to the American people for increased output and more rapid despatch.'

4. The following are a few critical voices concerning the Allied operations in the autumn of 1944: J. F. C. Fuller: *The Second World War 1939-45*, London, Eyre & Spottiswoode, 1948 (hereafter referred to as Fuller). P. 339: 'All the situation called for was a co-ordinated push behind one army. . . . A single army could have been driven into Germany through the military chaos that was the Reichswehr then. . . . And that such an army now, rammed home, could in a fortnight wholly destroy the usefulness of both the West Wall and the Rhine as military obstacles, and, capitalizing further on confusion, had at least an even chance of taking Berlin'; Montgomery (p. 286): 'WE did not advance to the Rhine on a *broad* front; we advanced to the Rhine on several fronts, which were unco-ordinated. And what was the German answer? A single and concentrated punch in the Ardennes, when we had become unbalanced and unduly extended. So we were caught on the hop'; (ibid. p. 286): 'After Normandy our strategy became unstitched. There was no plan; and we moved by disconnected jerks'; (ibid. p. 285): 'I am still firmly convinced that had we adopted a proper opera-

454

tional plan in the middle of August, and given it a sound administrative and logistic backing, we should have secured bridgeheads over the Rhine and seized the Ruhr before the winter set in. The whole affair if properly handled would not only have shortened the war; it would also have held out possibilities of bringing it to an end in Europe with a political balance very much more favourable to an early and stable peace than that which actually emerged.'

5. According to Wilmot, it was on October 8th that Jodl presented to Hitler the draft for an offensive at the end of November through the Ardennes with the objective Amsterdam.

6. Cf. R. E. Merriam: *The Battle of the Ardennes*, London, Souvenir Press, 1958 (hereafter referred to as Merriam). P. 208. The date for the start of the offensive was determined by Hitler's anxiety that the Allies might soon succeed in putting the port of Amsterdam into working order again and thus be in a position to make full use of their superiority in men and materials. It was this anxiety that persuaded Hitler to fix the beginning of the offensive for the middle of November.

7. Cf. von Tippelskirch, p. 597; and Guderian, pp. 216 and 460.

8. The very detailed descriptions given both by Wilmot and by von Tippelskirch are based on the questioning of German generals, and, as a footnote by Wilmot indicates, on the stenographic reports of Führer situation discussions. The author, who sat immediately opposite Hitler, is in a position to confirm Wilmot's statement that Hitler had neither MS. nor other notes to hand.

9. Wilmot, p. 568: 'When it was finally launched on November 16th, 2,500 American and British bombers dropped more than 9,400 tons of high explosives on the enemy's forward positions and reserve areas in the heaviest tactical bombardment ever made. The bombing was accurate and intense, but the Germans were well dug in and, though they were badly shaken, they recovered quickly and came up full of fight.'

10. Samuel L. A., Marshall: *Bastogne – the First Eight Days*, The Infantry Journal Press, Washington, 1946 (hereafter referred to as Marshall). P. 137.

11. Wilmot, p. 607: 'For this bitter winter fighting the Germans, with their long experience in Russia, were better trained and better equipped, and they made the attackers pay dearly for every yard gained.'

12. Ibid, p. 588.

13. The author is in agreement with Merriam, who gives the real credit to the successful teamwork of the Allied leadership under Eisenhower.

14. Cf. 'The Defence of St Vith'. Pamphlet issued by US Armored School Research and Evaluation Division, Belgium, p. 28 et seq.

15. Cf. Wilmot, p. 591: 'This decision was prompted by sheer operational necessity and, when Eisenhower made it, he did not realize how strongly it would be resented by Bradley and his staff, and eventually by the American troops and their people at home'. The following observations in the same place are also illuminating: 'Bradley says that "there was ample justification for the Army Group on the north taking temporary command of all armies on that side of the penetration", but he also says that when Bedell Smith rang him on the evening of the 19th he replied: "Certainly if Monty's were an American command I would agree with you entirely." At Bradley's HQ it was believed that this change of command had been "engineered" by Churchill. . . . Eisenhower makes it quite clear, however, that the Prime Minister knew nothing of the change

until it had been decided.' Referring to this Anglo-American tension, Montgomery (p. 263) writes: 'From that time onwards (July/August 1944) there were
always "feelings" between the British and American forces till the war ended.
Patton's remarks from time to time did not help. When stopped by Bradley at
Argentan, he said: "Let me go on to Falaise and we'll drive the British back into
the sea for another Dunkirk".' And again (Montgomery, p. 263): 'The trouble
which began in this way in Normandy was to grow and develop into storms
which at times threatened to wreck the Allied ship.'

16. Wilmot, p. 585: 'Stragglers from the 28th Division, streaming back from the
Our, brought . . . tragic tales (which) indicated a complete disintegration of
regimental defences'. Cf. also Marshall, op. cit., p. 7.

17. Cf. Fuller, p. 348: 'As General Arnold writes: "The AAF took to the air with
enormously superior strength. We headed, with hundreds of planes, for the
supply lines through which the vital means for Rundstedt to go on, or even to
stay where he was, would have to move. From then on there was no let-up.
We prepared to isolate the battlefield" '; Wilmot, p. 603: 'In four days the
American and British air forces flew 15,000 sorties, striking not only at traffic
in the Ardennes, but also at roads, railways and airfields throughout the Rhineland'; Merriam, p. 201: 'More than 1,700 tons of bombs were dropped on
St Vith . . . and with more than 30,000 sorties by the Tactical Air Forces harassing
the Germans in direct support of ground operations, further damage was
inflicted'.

18. Cf. Wilmot, p. 609: 'This decision, said von Rundstedt later, 'was a fundamental
mistake that unbalanced the whole offensive' (Canadian Army interrogation).

19. The following forces were actually available (the figures following in brackets
give the numbers originally provided for in the plan): the 6th SS Panzer Army:
4 (4) armoured divisions and 4 (5) infantry divisions; the 5th Panzer Army:
3 (4) armoured divisions and 3 (3) infantry divisions; the 7th Army: 0 (1)
mechanized divisions and 4 (7) infantry divisions, including one paratroop
division. In any case, the divisions were not up to full strength.

20. Wilmot, p. 575. Cf. also Fuller, p. 346: 'The plan was Hitler's,' Göring said.
'His alone was the plan and the idea. . . . throughout the battle Hitler conducted
the operations by wireless orders.'

21. Wilmot, pp. 605–6.

22. Ibid., p. 622.

23. Ibid. Fragment 33, January 10th, Führer Conferences. Cf. also Guderian, p. 383,
who describes Hitler's reaction to Guderian's report giving exact details provided
by the Foreign Armies (East) Department of the Army General Staff. Hitler:
'It's the greatest imposture since Ghengis Khan! Who's responsible for producing
all this rubbish?' Guderian, ibid., on Himmler 'who thought his military judgement was every bit as good as Hitler's, and, needless to say, far better than that
of the generals.' Talking to Guderian he declared: 'Do you know, General, I
don't believe the Russians will attack at all. It's all an enormous bluff. The
figures given by your department Foreign Armies East are grossly exaggerated.
You're bothering your head far too much about it all. I am absolutely convinced
there's nothing going on in the East.' And in a discussion (at the end of December
1944, *author*) Guderian notes on p. 387 Hitler's reaction to carefully worked out
figures on the situation of the enemy. He declared roundly that they were

'completely idiotic'. Guderian also reproduces on p. 404 an illuminating discussion with 'the architect of Germany's foreign policy', Ribbentrop.

24. Guderian, p. 381: 'But Hitler in those critical days could think of nothing save his own Western Front. The whole tragedy of our military leadership was revealed once again towards the end of the war in this unsuccessful Ardennes offensive.' In this connection the reader must bear in mind the fact that unlike the Eastern Front the Western Front was one of the theatres of war which was the responsibility of the Operations Staff of the Wehrmacht High Command.

25. Cf. Merriam.

26. Wilmot and Fuller both deal with the significance and the effect of the Allied demand for 'unconditional surrender'. Wilmot describes the propaganda campaign waged by Goebbels when the Morgenthau Plan became known, and quotes (p. 550) from Goebbel's organ *Die Völkischer Beobachter*: 'The Quebec decision will serve only to redouble German resistance', and goes on: 'This was indeed its effect, as captured letters written by front-line troops were soon to show.' Fuller (p. 259): 'Fredborg, writing in the spring of 1943, is illuminating: "They (the Germans) realize, too, that this time things might be sevenfold worse. The German people have begun to feel the heat of hatred that smoulders under the ashes throughout Europe and the threat from all the peoples of Europe – the Europe they wanted to unite with Germany, but which Nazism has united against Germany. They feel, too, the pressure of the Slav advance and the latent danger of the millions of foreign workers among them. They feel that they must play the game through to its finish. Is there any way out except fighting . . .? Actually the situation and Germany's *enemies are whipping the Germans together under the Swastika*. 'Victory or Bolshevism' has become Goebbels's slogan. That is his way of telling the German people that there is no third alternative".'

27. Wilmot, op. cit.

28. Von Tippelskirch (pp. 586–7) quotes Fuller's views *in extenso* on the vandalism of the Allies. Fuller (p. 317): 'And what was the final result of this Mongoloid destructiveness? That whilst the First and Second Fronts were advancing to win the war, the Third Front was engaged upon blowing the bottom out of the peace which was to follow its winning: for cities and not rubble heaps are the foundations of civilization.'

29. Von Tippelskirch (p. 598) also reports that Hitler ignored considerations such as 'the reduced quality of an instrument which in many respects is only a shadow of the well-equipped army of 1940'.

30. Von Tippelskirch on Churchill's 'final attempt' to give military operations a political objective. End of March 1945 (p. 643): 'Churchill was very disappointed that Montgomery had not been instructed to take Berlin at all costs before the Russians got there. Churchill who approached Eisenhower went to the wrong address. Eisenhower rejected any attempt to interfere with his military conduct of the operations, and declared that Berlin was not a particularly important military objective. At the same time he pointed out to Churchill, not without justification, that the political line of demarcation for the subsequent occupation of Germany had already been agreed on with the Russians. . . . The line ran about ninety-five miles to the west of Berlin. . . . Eisenhower was supported in his views by the White House, and he carried out his own plans.' Fuller, p. 346: 'Politically the best course would probably have been to have abandoned the

Western Front altogether and have concentrated everything against the Russians. This would have handed the whole of Germany and Austria over to the Americans and British and have dealt a crushing blow at Russian prestige.' Montgomery agreed with Churchill, and Fuller (p. 360, footnote 46) writes: 'According to Ingersoll, it was General Bradley and not Eisenhower who was responsible for the lack of political insight in not reaching Berlin.'

SELECT BIBLIOGRAPHY

Prepared by the *Bibliothek für Zeitgeschichte*, Stuttgart and Peter Lickfold.

PART I – GENERAL

(a) Bibliographies:

GUNZENHÄUSER, M: 'Die Bibliographien zur Geschichte des Zweiten Weltkrieges', in *Jahresbibliographie. Bibliothek für Zeitgeschichte (Weltkriegsbücherei)* Stuttgart, Jg. 33 (1961). Frankfurt on Main, Bernard & Graefe, 1963. Pp. 511–565.

HERRE, F. and AUERBACH, H: *Bibliographie zur Zeitgeschichte und zum Zweiten Weltkrieg für die Jahre 1945–50*, Munich, Institut für Zeitgeschichte, 1955.

Jahresberichte für Deutsche Geschichte, new series. Published by Institut für Geschichte an der Deutschen Akademie der Wissenschaften, (E) Berlin, 1949–54. Berlin, Akademie-Verlag, 1952 et seq.

VOGELSANG, T: *Bibliographie zur Zeitgeschichte*. Supplement to *Vierteljahrshefte für Zeitgeschichte* (continuation of HERRE above). Stuttgart, Deutsche Verlags-Anstalt, 1953 et seq.

Bücherschau der Weltkriegsbücherei, Stuttgart, Bibliothek für Zeitgeschichte (Weltkriegsbücherei), 1953 et seq. (1960 onwards entitled *Jahresbibliographie*, *Bibliothek für Zeitgeschichte*. Frankfurt on Main, Bernhard & Graefe.)

(b) Chronologies:

Chronology of the Second World War, London, Royal Institute of International Affairs, 1947.

Cronologia della Seconda Guerra Mondiale, Rome, Faro, 1948.

JACOBSEN, H.-A: *1939–1945. Der Zweite Weltkrieg in Chronik und Dokumenten* Darmstadt, Wehr und Wissen, 1959, 5th (enlarged) edition, 1961.

PAYNE, L. G. S: *Air Dates*, New York, Praeger, 1957.

SCHRAMM, P. E. and STANGE, H. O. H: *Geschichte des Zweiten Weltkrieges*, Würzburg, Ploetz, 1956.

TROGOFF, J: *Les grandes Dates de la Guerre sur Mer, 1939–45*, Rennes, Soc. d'Editions 'Ouest-France', 1953.

United States Naval Chronology, World War II. Prepared in the History Division, Office of the Chief of Naval Operations, Navy Dept. Washington, US Government Printing Office, 1953.

(c) Memoirs and Biographies:

ALANBROOKE, Field-Marshal the Viscount – Sir A. Bryant: *Memoirs*, vol. I, *The Turn of the Tide, 1939–43*; vol. II, *Triumph in the West, 1943–46* (based on the diaries and autobiographical notes), London, Collins, 1957 and 1959.

The ALEXANDER Memoirs, 1940–45: ed. John North, London, Cassell, 1962.

ARNOLD, H. H: *Global Mission. By the Chief of the US Navy Air Forces 1938–46*, New York, Harper, 1949.

AUCHINLECK – J. Connell: *A critical biography*. London, Cassell, 1959.

BEDELL SMITH, W: *Eisenhower's Six Great Decisions*. London, Longmans, 1956.

BRADLEY, O. N: *A Soldier's Story*, New York, Holt, 1951.

CAVALLERO, U: *Comando Supremo, Diario 1940–43 del Capo di SMG*, Bologna, Capelli, 1948.

CHALMERS, W. S: *Max Horton and the Western Approaches*, London, Hodder and Stoughton, 1954.

CHUIKOV, V. I: *The Beginning of the Road*, London, MacGibbon & Kee, 1963.

CHURCHILL, W. S: *The Second World War*, 6 vols, London, Cassell, 1948–53.

CLARK, M. W: *Calculated Risk (1940–1947)*, New York, Harper, 1950.

CUNNINGHAM, Viscount A. B: *A Sailor's Odyssey*, London, Hutchinson, 1952.

DÖNITZ, K: *Memoirs – Ten Years and Twenty Days*, translated by R. H. Stevens in collaboration with David Woodward, London, Weidenfeld & Nicolson, 1959.

EISENHOWER, D. D: *Crusade in Europe*, New York, Doubleday, 1948; London, Heinemann, 1948.

GAULLE, C. de: *Mémoires de Guerre 1940–46*, 3 vols, Paris, Plon, 1954–59.

GUDERIAN, H: *Panzer Leader*, London, Michael Joseph, 1956.

HALDER's 'Kriegstagebuch' – edited by H.-A. Jacobsen in collaboration with A. Philippi, 3 vols., Stuttgart, Kohlhammer, 1962–64.

HARRIS, Sir A: *Bomber Offensive*, London, Collins, 1947.

HEUSINGER, A: *Befehl im Widerstreit, Schicksalstunden der deutschen Armee, 1923–45*, Tübingen, Wunderlich, 2nd ed. 1957.

HITLER – A. Bullock: *Hitler. A Study in Tyranny*, London, Odham's Press, 1952. Compl. rev. ed. Pelican Books, 1962.

IACHINO, A: *Tramonto di una grande Marina*, Milan, Mondadori, 1959.

ISMAY, General the Lord: *Memoirs*, London, Heinemann, 1960.

JOUBERT DE LA FERTÉ, Sir P. B: *The Third Service. The Story behind the Royal Air Force*, London, Thames & Hudson, 1955.

KESSELRING, A: *Memoirs*, London, Kimber, 1953. Published also under the title *A Soldier's Record*, New York, 1954.

KING, E. J. and WHITEHILL, W. M: *Fleet Admiral King. A naval record*, New York, Norton, 1952.

LATTRE DE TASSIGNY, J. de: *Histoire de la Première Armée Française*, Paris, Plon, 1949.

LATTRE DE TASSIGNY, Marshal de, A life of – Maj.-Gen. Sir G. Salisbury-Jones: *So Full a Glory*, London, Weidenfeld & Nicolson, 1954.

LEAHY, W. D: *I Was There. The personal story of the Chief of Staff to Presidents Roosevelt and Truman*, New York, McGraw Hill, 1950.

MANSTEIN, E. von: *Lost Victories*, London, Methuen, 1958.

MONTGOMERY, B. L: *The Memoirs of Field Marshal The Viscount Montgomery of Alamein*, London, Collins, 1958.

MORGAN, Sir F: *Overture to Overlord*, New York, Doubleday, 1950; London, Hodder & Stoughton, 1950.

PATTON, G. S: *War as I knew it*, Boston, Mifflin, 1947.

PAULUS, F: *Paulus and Stalingrad*, edited by W. Görlitz and translated by Col. R. H. Stevens, London, Methuen, 1963.

RAEDER, E: *Mein Leben*, 2 vols, Tübingen, Schlichtenmayer, 1956–57; *and* abridged translation: *Struggle for the Sea*, London, Kimber, 1959.

RAMSAY, Admiral Sir B. H: W. S. Chalmers: *Full Cycle, the biography of . . .*, London, Hodder & Stoughton, 1959.

RINTELEN, E. von: *Mussolini als Bundesgenosse. Erinnerungen des deutschen Militärattachés in Rom, 1936–43*, Tübingen, Wunderlich, 1951.

ROMMEL, E. – *Rommel Papers*, edited by B. H. Liddell-Hart, London, Collins, 1953.

ROOSEVELT – R. E. Sherwood: *Roosevelt and Hopkins. An intimate History*, New York, Harpers, 1948.

RUGE, F: *Rommel und die Invasion. Erinnerungen*, Stuttgart, Koehler, 1959.

SLESSOR, Sir J: *The Central Blue. Recollections and Reflections*, London, Cassell, 1956.

SPEIDEL, H: *We Defended Normandy*, London, Herbert Jenkins, 1951.

STALIN, J: *O Velikoi otechestvennoi voiny Sovetskovo Soyuza 1941–45*, Moscow, Ogiz Gospolizdat, 1946.

STIMSON, H. L. and BUNDY, McG: *On Active Service in Peace and War*, New York, Harper, 1947.

(d) Official and Semi-official:

AUSTRALIA:

Australia in the War of 1939–1945. Series 1: Army; 2: Navy; 3: Air; 4: Civil; 5: Medical. Canberra, Australian War Memorial, 1952 et seq.

CANADA:

Official History of the Canadian Army in the Second World War, edited by C. P. Stacey, Ottawa, The Queen's Printer, 1955 et seq.

SCHULL, J: *The Far Distant Ships. An official account of Canadian Naval Operations in the Second World War*, published by the Ministry of National Defence, Ottawa, Cloutier, 1952.

UNITED KINGDOM:

History of the Second World War:
    Military Series: edited by Sir James Butler – *Grand Strategy – Campaigns – Civil Affairs and Military Government*, London, HMSO, 1952 et seq.
    Civil Series: edited by Sir Keith Hancock – *Introductory – General – War Production*, London, HMSO, 1949 et seq.
    Medical Series: edited by Sir Arthur MacNalty – *Clinical Volume – Royal Navy – Army – Royal Air Force – Volumes relating to the Civil Services*, London, HMSO, 1952 et seq.

RICHARDS, D. and SAUNDERS, H. St G: *Royal Air Force 1939–1945*, 3 vols, London, HMSO, 1953–54.

INDIA:

Official History of the Indian Armed Forces in the Second World War 1939–45, edited by B. Prasad, New Delhi, Calcutta, London, Combined Interservice Historical Section (India and Pakistan), Orient-Longmans, 1956 et seq.

ITALY:

L'Esercito Italiano nella Seconda Guerra Mondiale, edited by Ufficio Storico, Stato Maggiore Esercito, Ministero della Difesa, Rome, Istituto Poligrafica dello Stato, 1946 et seq.
La Marina Italiana nella Seconda Guerra Mondiale, edited by Ufficio Storico della Marina Militare, Rome, Istituto Poligrafico dello Stato, 1950 et seq.

NEW ZEALAND:

Official History of New Zealand in the Second World War 1939–45, edited by Sir Howard Kippenberger – *Campaigns*, Wellington, War History Branch, Dept. of Internal Affairs. London, OUP, 1952–63.

SOUTH AFRICA:

AGAR-HAMILTON, J. A. I. and TURNER, L. C. F: *The Sidi Rezeg Battles 1941* (1957) and *Crisis in the Desert, May–July 1942* (1952). Prepared by Union War Histories Section of the Office of the Prime Minister of the Union of South Africa, Cape Town; London, OUP, 1952, 1957.

SOVIET UNION:

Istoriya Velikoi otechestvennoi voiny Sovetskovo Soyuza 1941–45, 6 vols, Moscow, Voenizdat, 1960–63; German edition: *Geschichte des Grossen Vaterländischen Krieges der Sowjetunion*, Berlin, Deutsche Militärverlag, 1962–63 (to date 3 vols).

UNITED STATES OF AMERICA:

The US Army in World War II, edited by K. R. Greenfield. Series: *The War Department – The Army Ground Forces – The Army Service Forces and the Technical Forces – The European Theater of Operations – The War in the Pacific – China–Burma–India Theater – Middle East Theater – Mediterranean Theater – American Theater – Special Duties – Pictorial Record – Civil Affairs – Special Projects*, Washington, Office of the Chief of Military History, Department of the Army, 1948 et seq.
MORISON, S. E: *History of United States Naval Operations in World War II*, 15 vols, Boston, Little Brown & Co, 1948–1962.
History of the US Marine Corps Operations in World War II, edited by C. W. Harrison, prepared by Historical Branch, G–3, HQ, Marine Corps, 5 vols, Washington. US Government Printing Office, 1959 et seq.
The Army Air Force in World War II, edited by W. F. Craven and J. L. Cate, 7 vols, Chicago, The University of Chicago Press, 1950–58.
MORISON, S. E: *The Two-Ocean War. A Short History of the United States Navy in the Second World War*, Boston, Little, Brown, 1963.

(e) **Miscellaneous:**

ASSMANN, K: *Deutsche Seestrategie in zwei Weltkriegen*, Heidelberg, Vowinckel, 1957. (*Die Wehrmacht im Kampf*, vol. 12.)
ASSMANN, K: *Deutsche Schicksalsjahre*, Wiesbaden, Brockhaus, 1950.
BELOT, R. de: *La Guerre aéronavale en Meditérranée 1939–45*, Paris, Payot, 1950; English edition: *The Struggle for the Mediterranean 1939–45*, London, OUP, 1951.

BERNOTTI, R: *La Guerra sui mari nel conflitto mondiale, 1939–45*, 3 vols. Livorno, Soc. ed. Tirrena, 1950–54.

BOWMAN, G: *War in the Air*, London, Evans, 1956.

BRAGADIN, M: *Che ha fatto la Marina?*, Milan, Garzanti, 4th rev. ed. 1959; American edition: *The Italian Navy in World War II*, Annapolis, US Naval Institute, 1957.

BUCHHEIT, G: *Hitler der Feldherr. Die Zerstörung einer Legende*, Rastatt, Grote, 1958.

CIANO DIARIES – edited by M. Muggeridge, London, Heinemann, 1947; American edition, edited by H. Gibson with introduction by Sumner Welles, New York, Doubleday, 1946.

CHURCHILL, Sir W. S: *The Second World War and an Epilogue on the Years 1945–57*. London, Cassell, 1959.

DAHMS, H. G: *Der zweite Weltkrieg*, Tübingen, Wunderlich, 1960.

DEAKIN, F. W: *The Brutal Friendship*, London, Weidenfeld and Nicolson, 1962.

DEBORIN, G. A: *Vtoraya Mirovaya Voina. Voenno-politicheskii ocherk*, Moscow, Voennoe Izdat. Min. oborony SSSR, 1958. German edition: *Der zweite Weltkrieg*, East Berlin, Verlag des Ministeriums für Nationale Verteidigung, 1959.

ERDMANN, K. D: *Die Zeit der Weltkriege*, in B. Gebhardt: *Handbuch der deutschen Geschichte*, vol. 4. Stuttgart, Union Deutsche Verlagsgesellschaft, 8th ed., 1959.

FEUCHTER, G. W: *Geschichte des Luftkrieges*, Bonn, Athenäum, 1954.

FULLER, J. F. C: *The Second World War 1939–45. A Strategical and Tactical History*, London, Eyre & Spottiswoode, 1948; New York, Duell, 1949.

FULLER, J. F. C: *The Decisive Battles of the Western World*, vol. 3, London, Eyre and Spottiswoode, 1956.

GENTILE, R: *Storia delle operazioni aeree nella Seconda Guerra Mondiale*, Firenze, Scuola di Guerra Aerea, 1952.

GÖRLITZ, W: *Der zweite Weltkrieg 1939–45*, 2 vols., Stuttgart, Steingrüben, 1951–52.

GREENFIELD, K. R. (editor): *Command Decisions*, prepared by the Office of the Chief of Military History, New York, Harcourt, Brace, 1959.

GREINER, H: *Die Oberste Wehrmachtführung 1939–43*, Wiesbaden, Limes, 1951.

HERZFELD, H: *Weltmächte und Weltkriege. Die Geschichte unserer Epoche 1890–1945*, in *Die moderne Welt*, part 2, Braunschweig, Westermann, 2nd ed. 1957.

KEMP, P. K: *Victory at Sea 1939–45*, London, Muller, 1957.

KRAUSNICK, H: *Die Wehrmacht im Dritten Reich 1933–39*, in: *Schicksalsfragen der Gegenwart*, Tübingen, Wunderlich, 1957.

LEDERREY, E: *Germany's Defeat in the East. The Soviet Armies at War 1941–45*, London, The War Office, 1955.

LIDDELL-HART, B. H: *Strategy – The Indirect Approach*, London, Faber & Faber, 1954.

LIDDELL-HART, B. H: *The Other Side of the Hill*, London, Cassell, (Revised and enlarged ed.), 1951.

MORISON, S. E: *Strategy and Compromise*, Boston, Little, Brown, 1958.

PHILIPPI, A. and HEIM, F: *Der Feldzug gegen Sowjetrussland, 1941–45*, Stuttgart, Kohlhammer, 1962.

PLATONOV, S. P. (editor): *Vtoraya mirovaya Voina 1939–45. Voenno-istoricheskii ocherk*, Moscow, Voennoe Izdat. Min. oborony SSSR, 1958.

RASGON, I: *Die Sowjet-Union im Grossen Vaterländischen Kriege 1941–45*, in *Enzyklopädie der USSR*, vol 1, East Berlin, Verlag Kultur und Fortschritt, 1950.

RIEKER, K: *Ein Mann verliert einen Weltkrieg. Die entscheidenden Monate des deutsch-russischen Krieges 1942–43*, Frankfurt on Main, Fridericus-Verlag, 1955.

ROSKILL, S. W: *The War at Sea 1939–45*, 3 vols., in *History of the Second World War*, UK Military Series, London, HMSO, 1954–61.

RUGE, F: *Der Seekrieg 1939–45*, Stuttgart, Koehler, 1954.

SANTORO, G: *L'aeronautica italiana nella Seconda Guerra Mondiale*, 2 vols., Milan, Rome, Ed. Esse, 1957.

SCHRAMM, P. E. (editor): *Kriegstagebuch des OKW*, 4 vols. Frankfurt on Main, Bernard & Graefe, 1963, 1961.

SENGER und Etterlin, F. von: *Neither Hope Nor Fear*, London, MacDonald, 1963.

TELPUKHOVSKII, B. S: *Velikaya otechestvennaya Voina Sovetskovo Soyuza 1941–45*, Moscow, Gos. Izdat. Polit. Lit., 1959; German edition: *Die sowjetische Geschichte des Grossen Vaterländischen Krieges 1941–45*. Im Auftr.d. Arbeitskreises für Wehrforschung Stuttgart hrsg.u.erläutert von A. Hillgruber and H.-A. Jacobsen, Frankfurt on Main, Bernard & Graefe, 1961.

TIPPELSKIRCH, K. von: *Geschichte des zweiten Weltkriegs*, Bonn, Athenäum, 1956.

TOYNBEE, A. (editor): *Survey of International Affairs 1939–46*, London, OUP, 1952 et seq.

WARLIMONT, W: *Inside Hitler's Headquarters, 1939–45*, London, Weidenfeld & Nicolson, 1964.

ZHILIN, P. A. (editor): *Vazhneishie operatsii Velikoi Otechestvennoi Voiny 1941–45*, Moscow, Voennoe Izdat, 1956; German (fuller) edition: *Die wichtigsten Operationen des Grossen Vaterländischen Krieges 1941–45*, East Berlin, Verlag des Ministeriums für Nationale Verteidigung, 1958.

Der Weltkrieg 1939–45. Ehrenbuch der deutschen Wehrmacht, Stuttgart, Riegler, 1954.

PART II – THE DECISIVE BATTLES

Dunkirk 1940

BENOIST-MÉCHIN, J: *Soixante jours qui ébranlèrent l'Occident. 10 mai – 10 juillet 1940*, 3 vols., Paris, Michel, 1956.

COLLIER, R: *The Sands of Dunkirk*, New York, Dutton, 1961.

CRAS, H. (Jacques Mordal): *Dunkerque*, Paris, Editions France-Empire, 1960.

ELLIS, L. F: *The War in France and Flanders 1939–40*, in *History of the Second World War*, UK Military Series, London, HMSO, 1953.

DIVINE, D: *The Nine Days of Dunkirk*, London, Faber and Faber, 1959.

GOUTARD, A: *1940. La Guerre des occasions perdues*, Paris, Hachette, 1956.

JACOBSEN, H.-A: *Dünkirchen* (in collaboration with K. J. Müller), Neckargemünd, Vowinckel, 1958 (*Wehrmacht im Kampf*, vol. 19).

LISS, U: *Westfront 1939–40. Erinnerungen des Feindbearbeiters im OKH*, Neckargemünd, Vowinckel, 1959 (*Wehrmacht im Kampf*, vol. 23).

MEIER-WELCKER, H: *Der Entschluss zum Anhalten der deutschen Panzertruppen in Flandern 1940*, in: *Vierteljahrshefte für Zeitgeschichte 2* (1954, pp. 274–290).

MÜLLER, K. J: *Dünkirchen 1940. Ein Beitrag zur Vorgeschichte der britischen und französischen Evakuierung*, in: *Marine-Rundschau*, 1960, pp. 133–168.

SPEARS, Gen. Sir E. L: *Prelude to Dunkirk*, London, Heinemann, 1954.

TAYLOR, T: *The March of Conquest. The German Victories in Western Europe 1940*, New York, Simon & Schuster, 1958.

The Battle of Britain 1940

BISHOP, E: *The Battle of Britain*; German edition: *Die Schlacht um England*, Munich, Lehmann, 1962.

COLLIER, B: *The Defences of the United Kingdom*, in: *History of the Second World War*, UK Military Series, London, HMSO, 1957.

FITZGIBBON, C: *The Blitz*, London, Wingate, 1957.

KLEE, K: *Das Unternehmen 'Seelöwe'. Die geplante deutsche Landung in England 1940*, Göttingen, Musterschmidt, 1958.

KREIPE, W: *The Battle of Britain*, in: *The Fatal Decisions*, London, Michael Joseph, 1956.

McKEE, A: *Strike from the Sky. The Story of the Battle of Britain*, London, Souvenir Press, 1960.

MIDDLETON, D: *The Sky Suspended*, New York, London, Longmans, Green, 1960.

SMITH, N. D: *The Battle of Britain*, London, Faber & Faber, 1962.

WEBER, T: *Die Luftschlacht um England*, Wiesbaden, Flugwelt Verlag, 1956.

WHEATLEY, R: *Operation Sea Lion. German Plans for the Invasion of England 1939–42*, Oxford, Clarendon Press, 1958.

WOOD, D. and DEMPSTER, D: *The Narrow Margin*, London, Hutchinson, 1961.

The Battle for Crete 1941

BUCHNER, A: *Der deutsche Griechenlandfeldzug 1941. Die Operationen der 12. Armee 1941*, Heidelberg, Vowinckel, 1957 (*Wehrmacht im Kampf*, vol. 14).

CLARK, A: *The Fall of Crete*, New York, Morrow, 1962.

DAVIN, D. M: *Crete*, in: *Official History of New Zealand in the Second World War 1939–45*. Wellington, War History Branch, Dept. of Internal Affairs, 1953.

LONG, G: *Greece, Crete and Syria*, in: *Australia in the War of 1939–45*, Series 1, Army, vol. II, Canberra, Australian War Memorial, 1953.

SPENCER, J. H: *Battle for Crete*, London, Heinemann, 1962.

The Battle for Moscow 1941

BELOV, P. A: *Za nami Moskva*, Moscow, Voennoe Izdat. Oborony SSSR, 1963.

BLUMENTRITT, G: *Moscow*, in: *The Fatal Decisions*, London, Michael Joseph, 1956.

BOLTIN, E. A: *Pobeda sovetskoi armii pod Moskvoi 1941*, in *Voprosy Istorii*, 1957, no. 1, pp. 20–32.

CHALES DE BEAULIEU, W: 'Sturm bis vor Moskaus Tore. Der Einsatz der

Panzergruppe 4', in: *Wehrwissenschaftliche Rundschau 6* (1956), pp. 349–365, 423–439.

KORKODINOV, P. D: *Die Zerschlagung der deutsch-faschistischen Truppen bei Moskau*, in Zhilin: *Die wichtigsten Operationen des Grossen Vaterländischen Krieges 1941–45*, East Berlin, Verlag der Ministeriums für Nationale Verteidigung, 1958.

REINHARDT. H: 'Panzer-Gruppe 3 in der Schlacht vor Moskau und ihre Erfahrungen im Rückzug (Okt.–Dez. 1941); in *Wehrkunde 2* (1953), *Heft 9*, pp. 1–11.

SAMSONOV, A. M: *Velikaya bitva pod Moskvoi 1941–42*, Moscow, Izdat. Akad. Nauk SSSR, 1958; German edition: *Die grosse Schlacht vor Moskau 1941–42*, East Berlin, Verlag des Ministeriums für Nationale Verteidigung, 1959.

SOKOLOVSKII, V: 'Die Sowjetische Kriegskunst in der Schlacht vor Moskau', translation from the Russian and commentary by W. Arenz, in *Wehrwissenschaftliche Rundschau*, Jan./Feb. 1963, Frankfurt on Main, Mittler.

UHLIG, H: 'Das Einwirken Hitlers auf Planung und Führung des Ostfeldzuges', in: *Aus Politik und Zeitgeschehen*, supplement to *Das Parlament* of March 16 and 23, 1960.

YEREMENKO, A. I: *Na zapodnom napravlenii. Vospominaniya o boevykh deistviyakh voisk Zapadnovo Brianskovo frontov i 4-j udarnoi armii v pervom periode Velikoi otechestvennoi Voini*, Moscow, Voennoe Izdat. Min. Oborony SSSR, 1959.

The Decision in the Mediterranean 1942

BAYERLEIN, F: *El Alamein*, in *The Fatal Decisions*, London, Michael Joseph, 1956.

BHARUCHA, P. C: *The North African Campaign, 1940–43*, in: *Official History of the Indian Armed Forces in the Second World War 1939–45*, London, Orient-Longmans, Green, 1956.

CARVER, M: *El Alamein*, London, Batsford, 1962.

CORRELLI BARNETT: *The Desert Generals*, London, Kimber, 1960.

ESEBECK, H. G. von: *Afrikanische Schicksalsjahre. Geschichte des Deutschen Afrika-Korps unter Rommel*, Wiesbaden, Limes, 1949.

GAUSE, A: *Der Feldzug in Nordafrika im Jahre 1942*, in *Wehrwissenshaftliche Rundschau*, October/November 1963, Frankfurt on Main, Verlag Mittler.

HOWE, G. F: *Northwest Africa: Seizing the Initiative in the West*, in: *US Army in World War II – The Mediterranean Theater*, Washington, Office of the Chief of Military History, 1957.

KOELTZ, L: *Une compagne que nous avons gagnée: Tunisie 1942–43*, Paris, Hachette 1959.

LIDDELL-HART, B. H: *The Tanks*, 2 vols., London, Cassell, 1959.

LLOYD, Air Marshal Sir H: *Briefed to Attack – Malta's Part in African History*, London, Hodder & Stoughton, 1949.

LUCAS-PHILLIPS, C. E: *Alamein*, London, Heinemann, 1962.

MESSE, G. and SOGNO, V: *Operazioni Italo-Tedesche in Tunisia (11 Nov. 1942–13 Maggio 1943)*, 2 vols., in: *L'Esercito Italiano nella Seconda Guerra Mondiale*, Rome, Istituto Poligrafico dello Stato, 1950, 1952.

PLAYFAIR, I. S. O: *The Mediterranean and Middle East*, 3 vols., in: *History of the, Second World War*, UK Military Series, London, HMSO, 1954–60.

SCOULLAR, J. L: *Battle for Egypt. The Summer 1942*, in: *Official History of New*

Zealand in the Second World War 1939–45, Wellington, War Histories Branch, Dept. of Internal Affairs, 1955.

Seconda Controffensiva Italo-Tedesca in Africa settentrionale da El Agheila a El Alamein (Gennaio–Settembre 1942), in: *L'Esercito Italiano nella Seconda Guerra Mondiale*, Rome, Min. della Difesa, Stato Maggiore Esercito, Ufficio Storico, 1951.

STEVENS, W. G: *Bardia to Enfidaville*, in: *Official History of New Zealand in the Second World War 1939–45*, Wellington, War Histories Branch, Dept. of Internal Affairs, 1962.

TUKER, Lt.-Gen. Sir F: *Approach to Battle*, London, Cassell, 1963.

WARLIMONT, W: *Die Insel Malta in der Mittelmeer-Strategie des zweiten Weltkrieges*, in: *Wehrwissenschaftliche Rundschau*, 8, 1958, pp. 421–436.

WESTPHAL, S: *Der Feldzug in Nordafrika 1941–43*, in: *Schicksal Nordafrika*, Döffingen, Europa Contact Verlag, 1954, pp. 137–265.

The Battle for Stalingrad 1942-3

DEBORIN, G. A: *Stalingrad*, in: *Vtoraya Mirovaya Voina*, Moscow, 1958, pp. 194–224.

DOERR, H: *Der Feldzug nach Stalingrad. Versuch eines operativen Überblicks*, Darmstadt, Mittler, 1955.

Dokumenti o Stalingradskoi bitve, in: *Voyenno-istoricheskii Zhurnal*, Moscow, February, 1959.

HERHUDT von ROHDEN, H. D: *Die Luftwaffe ringt um Stalingrad*, Wiesbaden, Limes, 1950.

JACOBSEN, H.-A: *Zur Schlacht von Stalingrad – 20 Jahre danach*, in: *Allgemeine Schweizerische Militärzeitschrift*, February 1963, pp. 63–70.

KARATYSKIN, A. V. and CHEREMUKHIN, K. A: *Die Schlacht bei Stalingrad*, in: *Die wichtigsten Operationen des Grossen Vaterländischen Krieges 1941–45*, East Berlin, 1958, pp. 171–197.

QUILITZSCH, S: *Die Ursachen für den Sieg der Sowjetarmee in der Schlacht von Stalingrad in der Darstellung westdeutscher Historiker*, in: *Probleme der Geschichte des 2. Weltkrieges*, East Berlin, Akademie-Verlag, 1958, pp. 213–219.

ROONEY, A. A: *Stalingrad*, in ROONEY: *The Fortunes of War. Four great Battles of World War II*, Boston, Little, Brown, 1962.

SAMSONOV, A. M: *Stalingradskaya Bitva*, Moscow, Izd. Akademii Nauk SSSR, 1960; Italian edition: *Stalingrado, fronte russo*, Milan, Garzanti, 1961.

SAMSONOV, A. M: *K. 20-letiyu bitvy na Volge. Postanovleniya Gorodskogo Komiteta Oborony. Okt. 1941 – iyul 1942 gg. Dokumenty*, in: *Istoricheskii Arkhiv*, Vyp. 3, 4, 5, Moscow, Akademiya Nauk SSSR, 1962.

SCHEIBERT, H: *Nach Stalingrad – 48 Kilometer. Der Entsatzvorstoss der 6. Panzer Division*, Heidelberg, Vowinckel, 1956 (*Die Wehrmacht im Kampf*, vol. 10).

SETH, R: *Stalingrad – Point of Return*, London, Gollancz, 1959.

TELPUKHOVSKII, B. S: *Korennoi perelom v knode velikoi otechestvennoi voiny*, in: *Voprosy istorii*, Moscow, April 1959.

VORONOV, N: *Operaciya 'Kol'co'*, in: *Voyenno-istoricheskii Zhurnal*, 1962, no. 5, pp. 71–84; No. 6, pp. 67–76.

WIEDER, J: *Stalingrad und die Verantwortung des Soldaten*, München, Nymphenburger Verlag, 1962.

YEREMENKO, A. I: *Stalingrad. Zapiski komanduyushchego frontom*, Moscow, Voennoe Izd. Minist. Oborony SSSR, 1961.

ZEITZLER, K: *Stalingrad*, in *The Fatal Decisions*, London, Michael Joseph, 1956, pp. 113–171.

The U-Boat War Against the Allied Supply Lines

BEHRENS, C. B. A: *Merchant Shipping and the Demands of War*, in: *History of the Second World War*, UK Civil Series, London, HMSO, 1955.

BUSCH, H: *U–boats at War*, London, Clowes, 1955.

FRANK, W: *Die Wölfe und der Admiral*, Oldenburg, Stalling, 2nd impression, 1957.

GODT, E: *Der U-Bootkrieg*, in: Bilanz des zweiten Weltkrieges, Oldenburg, Stalling, 1954, pp. 133–144.

LEIGHTON, R. M. and COAKLEY, R. W: *Global Logistics and Strategy, 1940–43* in: *US Army in World War II*, The War Department, Washington, Office of the Chief of Military History, 1955.

MACINTYRE, D: *U-Boat Killer*, London, Weidenfeld & Nicolson, 1956.

MORISON, S. E: *The Battle of the Atlantic, September 1939 – May 1943*, and *The Atlantic Battle Won, May, 1943 – May, 1945*, in: *History of US Naval Ooperations in World War II*, vols. 1 and 10, Boston, Little, Brown, vol. 1, 2nd ed. 1955; vol. 10, 1956.

ROSKILL, S. W: *The War at Sea*, vols. 2 and 3, part I, in: *History of the Second, World War*, UK Military Series, London, HMSO, 1956 and 1960.

The Invasion of Normandy 1944

EHRMAN, J: *Grand Strategy*, vol. 5: *August 1943 – September 1944*, in: *History of the Second World War*, UK Military Series, London, HMSO, 1956.

ELLIS, L. F: *Victory in the West*, vol. 1, in *History of the Second World War*, UK Military Series, London, 1962.

HARRISON, G. A: *The Cross Channel Attack*, in: *The US Army in World War II – The European Theater of Operations*, Washington, Office of the Chief of Military History, 1951.

HAYN, F: *Die Invasion. Vom Cotentin bis Falaise (Juni–August 1944)*, Heidelberg, Vowinckel, 1954 (*Die Wehrmacht im Kampf*, vol. 2).

HIGGINS, I: *Winston Churchill and the Second Front 1940–43*, New York, OUP, 1957.

HOWARTH, D: *Dawn of D–Day*, London, Collins, 1959.

MATLOFF, M: *Strategic Planning for Coalition Warfare 1943–44*, Washington, Office of the Chief of Military History, 1959.

NORMAN, A: *Operation Overlord. Design and Reality. The Allied Invasion of Western Europe*, Harrisburg, Military Service Publ. Co., 1952.

POGUE, F. C: *The Supreme Command*, in: *The US Army in World War II – The European Theater of Operations*, Washington, Office of the Chief of Military History, 1954.

RYAN, C: *The Longest Day – June 6, 1944*, New York, Simon & Schuster, 1960; London, Gollancz, 1960.

SPEIDEL, H: *We Defended Normandy*, London, Herbert Jenkins, 1951.

STACEY, C. P: *The Victory Campaign. The Operations in North-West Europe 1944–*

1945, in: *Official History of the Canadian Army in the Second World War*, Ottawa, The Queen's Printer, 1960.

STANFORD, A: *Force Mulberry. The Artificial Harbor of US Normandy Beaches in World War II*, New York, Morrow, 1951.

WILMOT, C: *The Struggle for Europe*, London, Collins, 1952.

ZIMMERMANN, B: *France 1944*, in: *The Fatal Decisions*, London, Michael Joseph, 1956.

The Collapse of Army Group Centre in 1944

BAGRAMJAN, J: *Nastuplenie voysk 1-go Pribaltiiskogo fronta v belorusskoy operacii*, in: *Voyenno-istoricheskii Zhurnal*, 1961, no. 4, pp. 12–27, no. 5, pp. 15–31.

GACKENHOLZ, H. (editor): *Zum Zusammenbruch der Heeresgruppe Mitte im Sommer 1944*, in *Vierteljahrshefte für Zeitgeschichte 3* (1955), pp. 317–333.

HEIDKÄMPER, O: *Witebsk, Kampf und Untergang der 3. Panzerarmee*, Heidelberg, Vowinckel, 1954 (*Der Wehrmacht im Kampf*, vol. 1).

LIDDELL-HART, B. H: *The Soviet Army*, London, Weidenfeld & Nicolson, 1956.

MALANIN, K. A: *Razgrom vraga v Belorussii* (1944 god), Moscow, Voennoe Izdat. Minist. Oborony SSSR, 1961.

MINASSYAN, M. M: *Die belorussische Operation 1944*, in Zhilin: *Die wichtigsten Operationen des Grossen Vaterländischen Krieges 1941–45*, East Berlin, 1958, pp. 410–430.

RÖHRICHT, E: *Probleme der Kesselschlacht*, Karlsruhe, Condor, 1958, pp. 102 et seq.

TIPPELSKIRCH, K. von: *Die Zertrümmerung der deutschen Ostfront im Sommer 1944*, in *Geschichte des zweiten Weltkrieges*, Bonn, Athenäum, 1956, pp. 527–577.

VOZNENKO, V: *Strategicheskoe nastuplenie sovetskich vooruzhennych sil na central nom uchaske sovetsko-germanskogo fronta v iyune – avguste 1944 goda*, in: *Voyenno-istoricheskii Zhurnal*, 1960, no. 10, pp. 3–13.

The Battle of the Ardennes 1944–45

COLE, H. M: *The Ardennes Campaign*, in: *The US Army in World War II – The European Theater of Operations*, Washington, Office of the Chief of Military History (to be published shortly).

ELLIS, L. F: *Victory in the West*, vol. 2, in: *History of the Second World War*, UK Military Series (in preparation).

MANTEUFFEL, H. von: *The Ardennes*, in: *The Fatal Decisions*, London, Michael Joseph, 1956.

MARSHALL, S. L. A: *Bastogne – The First Eight Days*, Washington, The Infantry Journal Press, 1946.

MERRIAM, R. B: *The Battle of the Ardennes*, London, Souvenir Press, 1958.

NOBECOURT, J: *Le dernier coup de dés de Hitler. La bataille des Ardennes* (*Décembre 1944*), Paris, Laffont, 1962.

ROONEY, A. A: *The Bulge*, in ROONEY: *The Fortunes of War. Four great Battles of World War II*, Boston, Little, Brown, 1962, pp. 192–236.

TOLAND, J: *Battle: The Story of the Bulge*, New York, Random House, 1959; English editions: Muller, 1960 and Corgi, 1961.

WAGENER, C: *Strittige Fragen zur Ardennenoffensive*, in *Wehrwissenschalftliche Rundschau*, 11, pp. 26–54, January 1961, Frankfurt on Main, Mittler.

THE AUTHORS

GACKENHOLZ, Hermann:
Professor D Phil. Born Lüneburg 1908; studied history 1927–32; scientific adviser to the *Gesellschaft für Wehrwissenschaften* under General von Cochenhausen. Attached to the War Historical Department of the Army since 1936. Called up at the beginning of the war in 1939. After alternating active and departmental duties became responsible for the War Diary at HQ Army Group Centre in the spring of 1943, and held the post until the end of the war. Lieutenant of the Reserve. Prisoner of war until May 1946. Taught history at the Lüneburg Academy. 1950, appointed professor of history there. Member of the Presidium of the Arbeitskreis für Wehrforschung (Association for Military Research).

GÖRLITZ, Walter:
Journalist ('Die Welt') and historical writer. Born in 1913 in Hamburg. Military service 1939 and 1943–45. Author of numerous historical publications.

GUNDELACH, Karl:
D Phil., Staff Lt.-Col. (Air Force). Born in 1914 in Hamburg. 1933, studied in Göttingen and Bonn. 1935 called up for the Luftwaffe. January 1938, Lieutenant of the Reserve. Autumn 1938, continuation of studies in Berlin. Took degree 1940. Active service with the Luftwaffe on the Eastern Front. Prisoner of war in Russian hands from May 1945 to January 1948. With the Bundeswehr since 1956; first of all attached to the Study Group for Air Warfare, in Karlsruhe. Since 1958, lecturer on the history of air warfare at the Military Academy of the Bundeswehr.

HOFMANN, Rudolf:
General of the infantry (retd.). Born in Reit im Winkl in 1895. Lieutenant in 1915. General Staff training 1923 to 1928. Promoted Captain. Four years with the Reichswehr Ministry (Organization Department). Company commander, then uninterruptedly in General Staff appointments. Chief of Staff XII Army Corps in the West and on the Eastern Front. From November 1, 1941, Chief of Staff of the 9th Army; from May 1942, Chief of Staff of the 15th Army. October 1944, Chief of Staff Army Group H. Finally, Chief of Staff to C.-in-C. 'North'. Employed by the Historical Division of the US Army from 1952 to 1957.

JACOBSEN, Hans-Adolf:
D Phil., born in Coblenz-Pfaffendorf in 1925. Training officer at a Cadet Academy at the end of the war. Prisoner of war in Russian hands from 1945 to 1949. Studied at the Universities of Heidelberg and Göttingen, 1950–55. 1956 at the Institute for European History (Mainz) and the Institute for European Politics and Economics (Frankfurt on Main). 1956 to 1960, lecturer on contemporary history at the Training School for Education of the Bundeswehr. 1960, Director of the Research Institute of the German Association for Foreign Policy, Bonn.

KLEE, Karl:

D Phil., Staff Lt.-Col. (Air Force). Born at Frankfurt on Main 1921. Regular officer, 1939–45. Front-line and staff duties. Prisoner of war in Russia, 1945–1950. Merchant in Hamburg 1950. 1951–1955, studied history, philosophy and economics at Hamburg University. 1956, joined the Bundeswehr with the rank of captain. 1957, took degree at Hamburg University. General Staff training, 1958–59. 1956–58 and 1959–62, attached to the Operations Staff of the Air Force. 1961–2, Battalion Commander. 1962–1964 Lecturer at the Military Academy of the Bundeswehr. Since 1965 Adjutant to the Inspector of the Air Force.

VON MANTEUFFEL, Hasso:

General (retd.) Born in Neuss on Rhine in 1897. Cadet Corps, 1907–1916. Served in the cavalry from 1916 to 1918. 1939, Senior Training Officer at Tank Corps School. Second World War: Commander of a Panzer-Grenadier Regiment; Commander of a Panzer-Grenadier Brigade; Commander of the 7th Panzer Division; Commander of the Gross-Deutschland Division. C.-in-C. of the 5th Panzer Army during the Ardennes Offensive. At the end of the war C.-in-C. of the 3rd Panzer Army. Commercial activity after the war. Member of the Bundestag, 1953–57.

ROHWER, Jürgen:

D Phil. Born in Friedrichroda, Thuringia, in 1924. Naval service 1942–45: service with destroyers, U-boats, and minesweepers. Ended the war with the rank of Lieutenant. Studied at Hamburg University (history, international law and geography) 1948–54. Secretary of the Arbeitskreis für Wehrforschung, 1954–59. From 1959 Director of the Library for Contemporary History (Bibliothek für Zeitgeschichte Weltkriegsbücherei) in Stuttgart.

RUGE, Friedrich:

Vice-Admiral (retd). Born in 1894, entered the Imperial Navy in March, 1914. Took part in operations in the Baltic and destroyer raids on the English coast. Began specializing in mine warfare in 1920, and soon after started writing. Went to a technical college, was captain of a minesweeper twice, then senior officer of a minesweeping flotilla. Worked on mine-development. 1937, Senior Officer Minesweepers. Took part in the Polish campaign; from 1940 to 1943 in charge of minesweeping along the Dutch, Belgian, and French coasts; from 1941, also in charge of escorts, patrols and subchasers. Promoted Rear-Admiral in 1942, Vice-Admiral in 1943. In that year, six months in Italy. Then from November 1943 to August 1944, naval adviser to Field-Marshal Rommel before and during the Invasion of Normandy. Then to the end of the war Director of naval construction. After return from captivity wrote books (*Entscheidung in Pazifik*, *Der Seekrieg 1939–1945* and *Rommel und die Invasion*) and articles. Town Councillor at Cuxhaven. From 1956 to 1961 *Inspekteur der Bundesmarine*. September 1961, retired to Tübingen where he lectures on 'Politics, the Armed Forces, and NATO'. In addition, chairman of Arbeirskreis für Wehrforschung, president of League of the Veterans of the Bundeswehr.

WARLIMONT, Walter:

General of the Artillery (retd.). Born in Rottach-Egern in 1894. Regular artillery officer from June 1914 on. Front-line service during the First World War on the Western and the Italian Fronts. After three years special training, various appointments with the Army General Staff and with Wehrmacht High Command, from 1926. Various appointments abroad, for example 1929–30 in the USA; 1936, representative of the Reich War Ministry and of the Supreme Commander of the Wehrmacht with General Franco. Ordinary military duties as Troop Commander (Allenstein), Battery Commander (Trier) and Regimental Commander (Düsseldorf). From 1938 Head of a branch of the Operations Staff of OKW; later Deputy Chief of the Wehrmacht Operations Staff. Injured during the bomb attempt on Hitler's life on July 20th and transferred to OKH reserve. No further active service. Prisoner of war from 1945 to 1954. Imprisoned in Nuremberg and Landsberg.

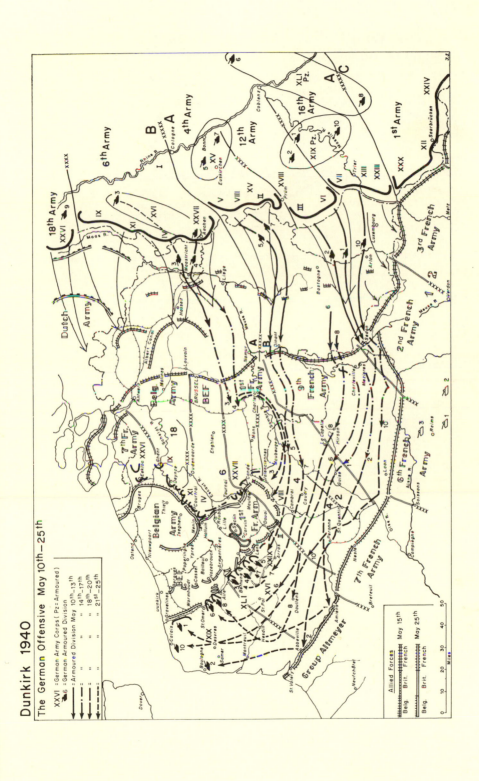

Dunkirk 1940

The German Offensive May 10th–25th

XXVI = German Army Corps (Pz.= Armoured)

6 = German Armoured Division

Armoured Division May 10th–13th

" " " 14th–17th

" " " 18th–20th

" " " 21st–25th

Allied Forces

Belg. Brit. French   May 15th

Belg. Brit. French   May 25th

Miles

0   10   20   30   40   50

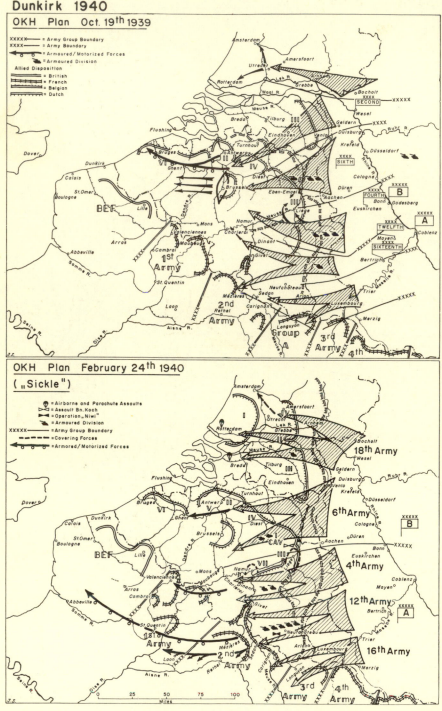

Dunkirk 1940

OKH Plan Oct. 19th 1939

XXXXX = Army Group Boundary
XXXX = Army Boundary
⬛⬅ = Armoured/Motorized Forces
⬅ = Armoured Division

Allied Disposition
= British
= French
= Belgian
= Dutch

OKH Plan February 24th 1940
("Sickle")

= Airborne and Parachute Assaults
= Assault Bn. Koch
= Operation „Niwi"
= Armoured Division
XXXXX = Army Group Boundary
= Covering Forces
⬅ = Armored/Motorized Forces

Miles
0   25   50   75   100

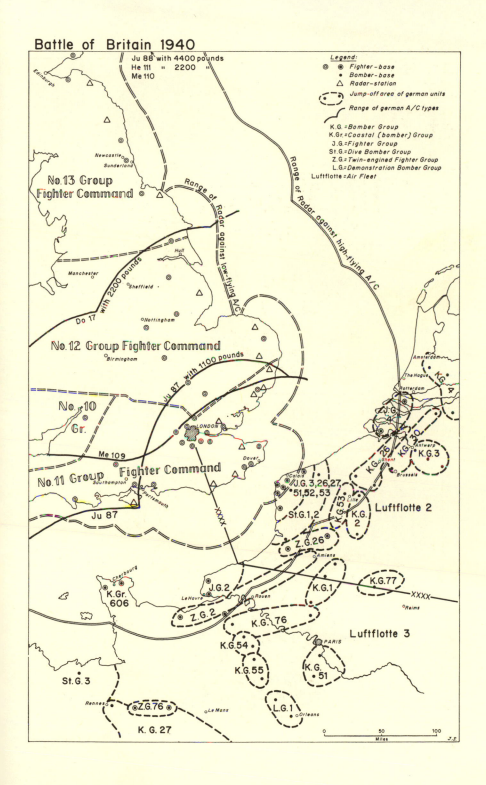

Battle of Britain 1940

Ju 88 with 4400 pounds
He 111 " 2200 "
Me 110

Legend:

◎ Fighter-base
• Bomber-base
△ Radar-station
⊂⊃ Jump-off area of german units

Range of german A/C types

K.G. = Bomber Group
K.Gr. = Coastal (bomber) Group
J.G. = Fighter Group
St.G. = Dive Bomber Group
Z.G. = Twin-engined Fighter Group
L.G. = Demonstration Bomber Group
Luftflotte = Air Fleet

Edinburgh

Newcastle
Sunderland

No.13 Group
Fighter Command

Range of Radar against high-flying A/C

Range of Radar against low-flying A/C

Hull

Manchester
Sheffield

Do 17 with 2200 pounds

Nottingham

No.12 Group Fighter Command

Birmingham

Ju 87 with 1100 pounds

Amsterdam
The Hague
Rotterdam

K.G. 4

Z.G. 4

No. 10 Gr.

Me 109

LONDON

Dover

K.G. 30

Antwerp
K.G. 3

K.G. 26
Ghent

Brussels

No. 11 Group Fighter Command

Southampton
Portsmouth

Ju 87

Calais
J.G. 3,26,27
51,52,53
J.G. 53
St.G.1,2
K.G. 2

Lille

Luftflotte 2

Z.G. 26

XXXX

Amiens

Cherbourg
K.Gr. 606

J.G. 2

Le Havre
Rouen

K.G.1

K.G.77

Reims

XXXX

Z.G. 2

K.G. 76

PARIS

Luftflotte 3

K.G.54

K.G.55

K.G. 51

St.G. 3

Rennes

Z.G.76

Le Mans

L.G. 1

Orleans

K. G. 27

0   50   100
Miles

J.S.

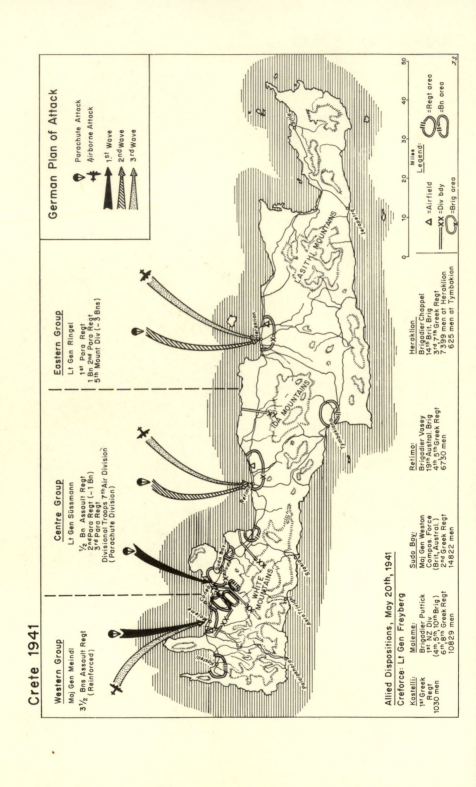

Crete 1941

German Plan of Attack

Western Group
Maj Gen Meindl

3½ Bns Assault Regt
(Reinforced)

Centre Group
Lt Gen Süssmann

½ Bn Assault Regt
2nd Para Regt (−1 Bn)
3rd Para Regt
Divisional Troops 7th Air Division
(Parachute Division)

Eastern Group
Lt Gen Ringel

1st Para Regt
1 Bn 2nd Para Regt
5th Mount Div (−3 Bns)

Parachute Attack
Airborne Attack

1st Wave
2nd Wave
3rd Wave

Legend:
Miles
0   10   20   30   40   50

△ =Airfield
XX =Div bdy
X =Brig area
III =Regt area
II =Bn area

Allied Dispositions, May 20th, 1941

Creforce: Lt Gen Freyberg

Kastelli:
1st Greek
Regt
1030 men

Maleme:
Brigadier Puttick
1st NZ Div
(4th, 5th, 10th Brig)
6th, 8th Greek Regt
10829 men

Suda Bay:
Maj Gen Weston
Compos. Force
(Brit, Austral.)
2nd Greek Regt
14822 men

Retimo:
Brigadier Vasey
19th Austral. Brig
4th 5th Greek Regt
6750 men

Heraklion:
Brigadier Chappel
14th Brit. Brig
3rd 7th Greek Regt
7399 men at Heraklion
625 men at Tymbakion

WHITE MOUNTAINS
IDA MOUNTAINS
LASITHI MOUNTAINS

Kastelli
Maleme
Canea
Suda Bay
Retimo
Heraklion
Tymbakion

Moscow 1941

The German Offensive Sept. 30th – Dec. 5th 1941

Legend:
- Frontline Sept. 30th
- German thrusts Sept. 30th – Oct. 10th
- Pursuit to Oct. 30th
- Frontline Oct. 30th – Nov. 15th
- Offensive Nov. 15th – Dec 5th
- XXIII German Corps (Pz) Panzer (Armoured)
- 49 Soviet Army

16th Army

9th Army

3rd Panzer Group

4th Army

2nd Panzer Group (Army)

WESTERN

RESERVE

BRYANSK

6th Army

0 25 50 75
Miles

Velikiye Luki · Velizh · Demidov · Smolensk · Roslavl · Kirov · Bryansk · Lgov · Kursk · Ostashkov · Belyye · Sychevka · Rzhev · Starifsa · Vyazma · Yelnya · Yuzhnov · Sukhinichi · Kozelsk · Belev · Bolkhovo · Orel · Mtsensk · Gr. Jermakov · Torjok · Kalinin · Volokolamsk · Klin · Moskva R. · MOSCOW · Medyn · Maloyaroslavets · Serpukhovo · Tarusa · Kaluga · Alexin · Tula · Venev · Mikhaylov · Kashira · Kolomna · Yefremov · Yelets · Voronezh · Barlova

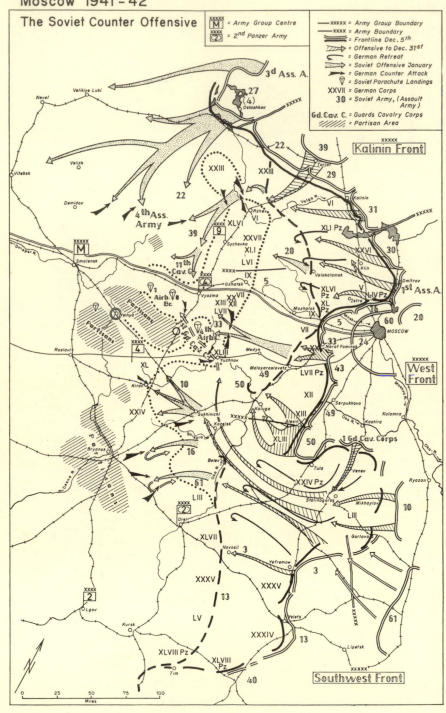

Moscow 1941-42

The Soviet Counter Offensive

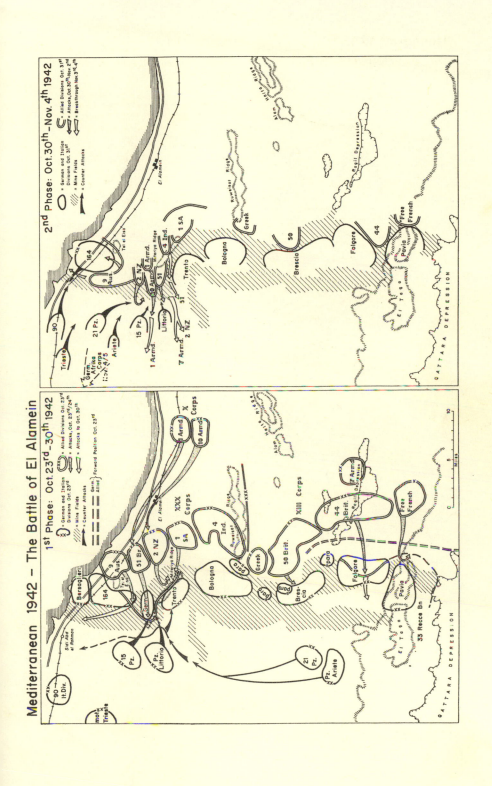

Mediterranean 1942 – The Battle of El Alamein

1st Phase: Oct. 23rd–30th 1942

XXX = German and Italian Divisions Oct. 23rd
⊐⊐ = Allied Divisions Oct. 23rd
⇨ = Attacks, Oct. 23rd/24th
⇨ = Attacks to Oct. 30th
▨ = Mine Fields
▶ = Counter Attacks
––– Germ.
- - - Allied } Forward Position Oct. 23rd

2nd Phase: Oct. 30th–Nov. 4th 1942

⊐⊐ = German and Italian Divisions Oct. 31st
⊃ = Allied Divisions Oct. 31st
⇨ = Attacks, Oct. 30th–Nov. 2nd
⇨ = Breakthrough Nov. 3rd/4th
▨ = Mine Fields
▶ = Counter Attacks

Stalingrad 1942

Bryansk
CENTRE
Orel
BRYANSK Fr.
Gr. Weichs
2
4 Pz.
Kursk
2 Hung.
Sumy
Belgorod
6
Kharkov
Krasnograd
Dnepropetrovsk
1. Pz.
Zaporozhye
Staline
Gr. Ruoff
17
Mariupol
Melitopol
Tagonrog

WORONEZH Front
Livny
5 Tk
Voronezh
60
40
Svoboda
SOUTH WEST Front
Valuyki
28
Rossosh
8 Ital.
63
3 Rum.
Don R.
Millerovo
STALINGRAD Front from Sept. 28
DON Front
Serafimovich
21
4 Tk
66
Volga R.
Kalach
STALINGRAD
62
SOUTHEAST Fr. from Sept. 28
STALINGRAD Front
51
Morozovsk
64
Tsymlyanskaya
Kotelnikovsk
Don R.
4 Pz.
4 Rum.
Elista
16 mot. Div.
28

Izyum
57
9
Voroshilovgrad
Kamensk-Shakhtinski
SOUTH Fr.
Rostov
SEA OF AZOV
Gr. Ruoff
Tikhoretsk
Manych R.
Sal R.
1 Pz.
LII
Kuma R.
Kerch
11
Tamen
Krasnodar
Kuban R.
Armavir
Maykop
Pyatigorsk
Mozdok
44
Terek R.
Grozny
Novorossiysk
Black Sea Gr.
Tuapse
SUPPLY-ROUTE BLACK SEA FLEET
Mt. Elbrus
Orjonikidze
CAUCASUS MTS.
TRANSCAUCASIAN Front

BLACK SEA
Poti
Tiflis
Batum

0 50 100 150 200
Miles

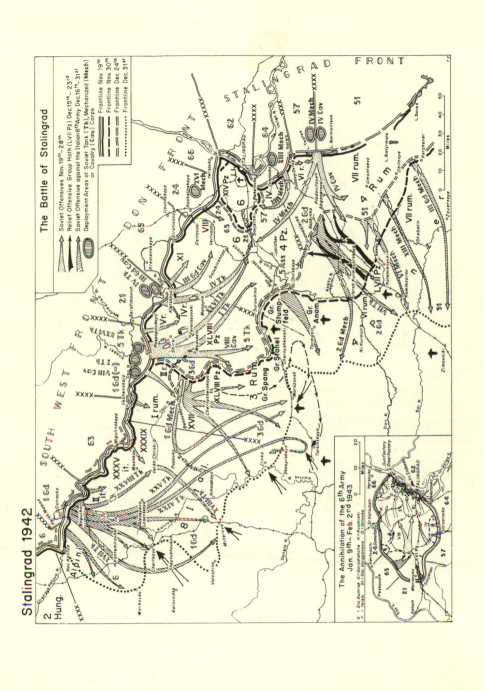

Stalingrad 1942

The Battle of Stalingrad

Soviet Offensives Nov.19th–28th
Relief Offensive Group Hoth (LVII Pz) Dec.15th–23rd
Soviet Offensive against the Italian 8th Army Dec.16th–31st
Deployment Areas of Soviet Tank (Tk), Mechanized (Mech)
or Cavalry (Cav) Corps

Frontline Nov.19th
Frontline Nov.30th
Frontline Dec.24th
Frontline Dec.31st

The Annihilation of the 6th Army
Jan. 9th – Feb. 2nd 1943

Battle of the Atlantic 1943

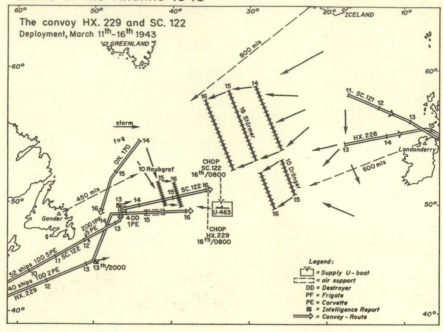

The convoy HX. 229 and SC. 122
Deployment, March 11th-16th 1943

GREENLAND

ICELAND

800 mls

storm

fog

ON. 170

14

15

10 Raubgraf

15 16

15 16

SC.122 16

CHOP
SC.122
16th/0800

U-463

CHOP
HX.229
16th/0800

18 Stürmer

16 15 14

10 Dränger

15

16

11. SC.121 12

13

15°

HX. 228 14

13 14

Londonderry

600 mls

13

Gander

16

13 14

4DD
1PE

15 16

2DD1PF14
5PE
13

52 ships 1DD 5PE
SC. 122
11
10
12

1DD 2PE

40 ships

HX. 229 12

13 13th/2000

450 mls

Legend:
= Supply U-boat
= air support
DD = Destroyer
PF = Frigate
PE = Corvette
= Intelligence Report
= Convoy - Route

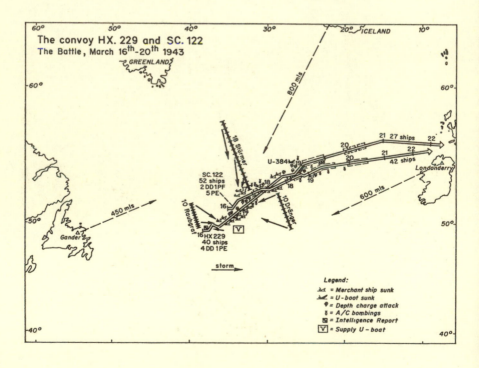

The convoy HX. 229 and SC. 122
The Battle, March 16th-20th 1943

GREENLAND

ICELAND

800 mls

18 Stürmer

U-384

20

21 27 ships 22

20

21 22

42 ships

Londonderry

SC.122
52 ships
2 DD 1PF
5 PE

19

18

18

19

10 Dränger

600 mls

16

10 Raubgraf

V

16 HX 229
40 ships
4 DD 1PE

450 mls

Gander

storm

Legend:
= Merchant ship sunk
= U-boot sunk
= Depth charge attack
= A/C bombings
= Intelligence Report
= Supply U-boat

Battle of the Atlantic 1943

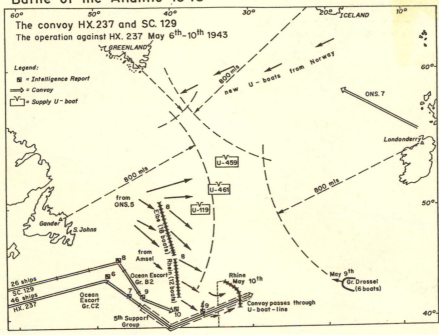

The convoy HX. 237 and SC. 129
The operation against HX. 237 May 6th–10th 1943

Legend:
- ⊡ = Intelligence Report
- ⇒ = Convoy
- ⊔ = Supply U–boat

ICELAND
GREENLAND
new U – boats from Norway
800 mls
ONS. 7
Londonderry
U–459
U–461
U–119
800 mls
from ONS.5
Elbe (18 boats)
8
from Amsel
8
Ocean Escort Gr. B2
Rhein (12 boats)
7 9
Rhine May 10th
May 9th
Gr. Drossel (6 boats)
Gander
S. Johns
26 ships
SC. 129
46 ships
HX. 237
Ocean Escort Gr. C2
9
4 9
10
Convoy passes through U–boat–line
5th Support Group

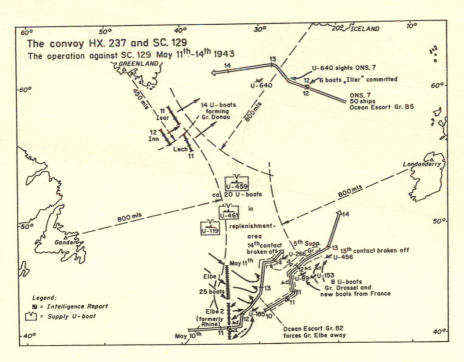

The convoy HX. 237 and SC. 129
The operation against SC. 129 May 11th–14th 1943

Legend:
- ⊡ = Intelligence Report
- ⊔ = Supply U–boat

ICELAND
GREENLAND
14
13
U–640 sights ONS. 7
U–640
12 6 boats „Iller" committed
12
ONS. 7
50 ships
Ocean Escort Gr. B5
450 mls
11
Isar
14 U–boats forming Gr. Donau
12
Inn
800 mls
Lech
11
Londonderry
U–459
ca. 20 U–boats
U–461
in
U–119
replenishment- area
800 mls
800 mls
14th contact broken off
5th Supp.
U–266 Gr.
13 13th contact broken off
U–456
U–89 U–153
8 U–boats Gr. Drossel and new boats from France
May 11th
14
13
Elbe
25 boats
13
11
11
Gander
Elbe 2 (formerly Rhine)
U–185 10
12
May 10th 11
Ocean Escort Gr. B2 forces Gr. Elbe away

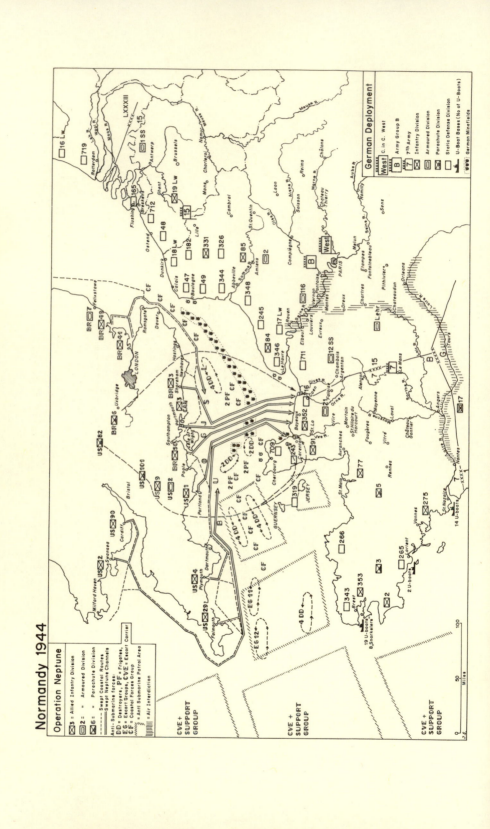

Normandy 1944

Operation Neptune

- ☒ 3 = Allied Infantry Division
- ☒ 2 = " Armoured Division
- ☒ 6 = " Parachute Division
- – – – – Swept Coastal Routes
- ——— Swept Neptune Channels

Anti-Submarine Forces:
- DD = Destroyers, PF = Frigates,
- EG = Escort Groups, CVE = Escort Carrier
- CF = Coastal Forces Group
- ▥ = Anti Submarine Patrol Area
- ▨ = Air Interdiction

German Deployment

- ⊠ West = C. in C. West
- ☒ B = Army Group B
- ☒ 7 = 7th Army
- ☒ = Infantry Division
- ☒ = Armoured Division
- ☒ = Parachute Division
- ☐ = Static Defense Division
- ∨∨∨ = German Minefields
- ≁ = U-Boat Bases (No of U-Boats)

Normandy 1944

Operation „Neptune"
June 6th-12th 1944

Legend:
- Positions June 6th/12 p.m.
- German Counterattacks June 6th
- Allied Drives June 6th-12th
- German Reinforcements
- Positions June 12th

21st Army Group

Western Task Force
1st US Army

Eastern Task Force
2nd Brit. Army

VII US Corps

V US Corps

I Brit. Corps

Sta. = Ste.Mere Eglise
V. = Vierville
S. = St.Laurent
C. = Colleville sur Mer
P. = Port en Bessin
Ar. = Arromanches
L. = Lion sur Mer

Miles 0   5   15   20

White Russia 1944

Deployment and Breakthrough, June 22nd–28th

XXXX

1st BALTIC FRONT

Dvinsk

Dvina R. Drissa

16th Army

290

4 Ass.

I Mech.

6 Gd

Polotsk

43

24

IX

LIII

39

Vitebsk

Dvina R.

3rd WHITE RUSSIAN FR.

III Cav. Mech. Gr.

5

5 Gd Tk Army

11 Gd

II Gd Tk

Smolensk

Beshenkovichi

Lepel

Senno

VI

Dnieper R.

31

Paratjanow

3rd Panzer Army

ARMY GROUP

CENTRE

Molodechno

Borisov

XXX

Orsha

XXVII

33

Shklov

49

Rasno

Minsk

Berezino

4th Army

Dnepr R.

Mogilev

XXXIX Pz

Maryina Gorka

Berezina R.

XXXX

Bykhov

XII

50

Stolbtsy

Osipovichi

707

3

IX Tk

Slutsk

Bobruysk

Rogachev

2nd Army

9th Army

Zhlobin

48

2 Pz

XXXV

Parichi

XXXX

I Gd Tk

Luninec

65

Cav Mech Gr Plieve

LV

28

Kalinkovichi

Pripet R.

XXIII

Dnieper R.

61

1st WHITE RUSSIAN FRONT

0   50   100
Miles

J.S.

Legend

	Soviet Mechanized Forces
	Thrust of Mechanized Forces
	Other Forces
39	Soviet Army (Gd = Guards)
Cav. Mech. Gr.	Cavalry Mechanized Group
Tk	Armoured Corps
Mech.	Mechanized Corps
XXVII	German Corps

White Russia 1944

Annihilation of the Army Group Center
June 29th–July 4th 1944

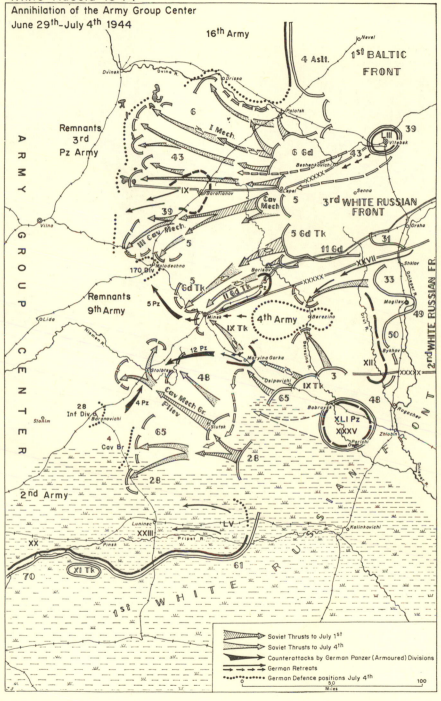

Legend:

- Soviet Thrusts to July 1st
- Soviet Thrusts to July 4th
- Counterattacks by German Panzer (Armoured) Divisions
- German Retreats
- German Defence positions July 4th

0   50   100
Miles

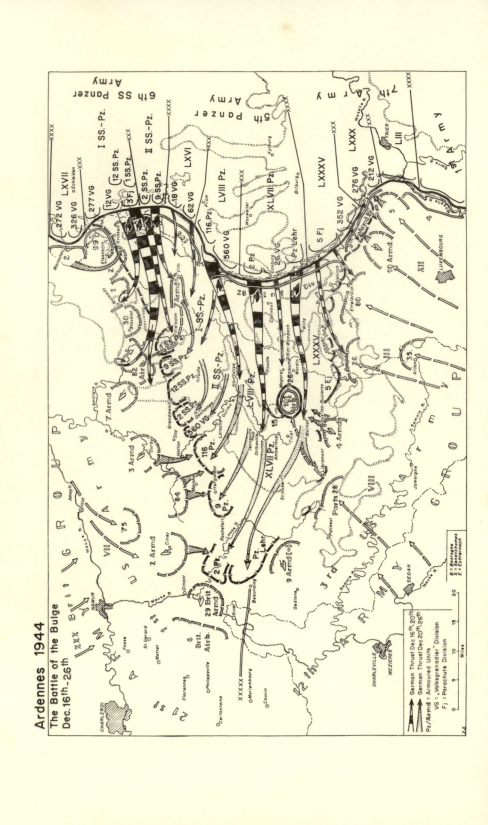

Ardennes 1944
The Battle of the Bulge
Dec. 16th – 26th

INDEX